Copyright©2018 All Rights Reserved

ISBN: 978-0692061961

Publication rights Sefer Press Publishing House
Questions Comments; SeferPress@Israelmail.com

Publisher grants permission to reference short quotations (less than 400 words) in reviews, magazines, newspapers, Websites, or other publications in accordance with the citation standards at Sefer Press. Request permission to reproduce more than 400 words to SeferPress@Israelmail.com

Cover by Sefer Press 2018

Book Format by Sefer Press 2018

Hebrew:Modern Hebrew Text Form
Greek:Majority Text (Byzantine) Text Form

Commentary Editing by Al Garza PhD

For Questions Contact DrAlGarza@email.com At
DrAlGarza@email.com

Printed in the United States of America© 2018

Epistles

A RABBINIC JEWISH SOURCE

COMMENTARY

AND LANGUAGE STUDY BIBLE

Volume 7: Hebrews-Jude

KJV-GREEK-HEBREW

WITH *TRANSLITERATION*

Greek Majority Text And Modern Hebrew

PUBLISHED BY SEFER PRESS PUBLISHING HOUSE©2018

TABLE OF CONTENTS

Hebrews...pg.5
   Chapter 2..pg.19
   Chapter 3..pg.29
   Chapter 4..pg.39
   Chapter 5..pg.49
   Chapter 6..pg.56
   Chapter 7..pg.67
   Chapter 8..pg.84
   Chapter 9..pg.95
   Chapter 10..pg.119
   Chapter 11..pg.138
   Chapter 12..pg.165
   Chapter 13..pg.182

James..pg.196
   Chapter 2..pg.209
   Chapter 3..pg.222
   Chapter 4..pg.232
   Chapter 5..pg.240

1Peter...pg.252
   Chapter 2..pg.268
   Chapter 3..pg.282
   Chatper 4..pg.295
   Chapter 5..pg.305

2Peter...pg.314
   Chapter 2..pg.324
   Chapter 3..pg.340

1John..pg.353
   Chapter 2..pg.361
   Chapter 3..pg.377
   Chapter 4..pg.389
   Chapter 5..pg.399

2John..pg.412

3John..pg.419

Jude...pg.425

Bibliography..**pg.441**

THE EPISTLE OF PAUL THE APOSTLE TO THE HEBREWS

Hebrews, Chapter 1

1. God, who at sundry times and in divers manners spake in time past unto the fathers by the prophets,

1. Πολυμερῶς καὶ πολυτρόπως πάλαι ὁ θεὸς λαλήσας τοῖς πατράσιν ἐν τοῖς προφήταις, ἐπ᾽ ἐσχάτου τῶν ἡμερῶν τούτων ἐλάλησεν ἡμῖν ἐν υἱῷ,

1. Polumeros kai polutropos palai 'o theos laleisas tois patrasin en tois propheitais, ep eschatou ton 'eimeron touton elaleisen 'eimin en 'wio,

א: הָאֱלֹהִים אֲשֶׁר-דִּבֶּר מִקֶּדֶם אֶל-אֲבוֹתֵינוּ פְּעָמִים רַבּוֹת וּבְפָנִים שׁוֹנִים עַל-יְדֵי הַנְּבִיאִים

1. Ha•Elohim asher - di•ber mi•ke•dem el - avo•tey•noo pe•a•mim ra•bot oov•fa•nim sho•nim al - ye•dey ha•n`vi•eem.

Rabbinic Jewish Commentary
spake in time past unto the fathers by the prophets; by Moses, and other succeeding prophets, as David, Isaiah, Jeremiah, Micah, Zechariah, Malachi, and others; who were sent to the Jewish fathers, the ancestors of the people of the Jews, to whom they prophesied and declared the will of God, as they were moved and inspired by the Holy Spirit: and the apostle suggests, by this way of speaking, that it was a long time since God spake to this people; for prophecy had ceased ever since the times of Malachi, for the space of three hundred years; and this time past includes the whole Old Testament dispensation, from the beginning to the end of it, or of prophecy in it.

---

2. Hath in these last days spoken unto us by his Son, whom he hath appointed heir of all things, by whom also he made the worlds;

2. ὃν ἔθηκεν κληρονόμον πάντων, δι᾽ οὗ καὶ τοὺς αἰῶνας ἐποίησεν,

2. 'on etheiken kleironomon panton, di 'ou kai tous aionas epoieisen,

ב. דִּבֶּר אֵלֵינוּ לְקֵץ הַיָּמִין הָאֵלֶּה עַל-פִּי הַבֵּן אֲשֶׁר שָׂמָהוּ לְבַעַל נַחֲלָה בַּכֹּל וַאֲשֶׁר בּוֹ עָשָׂה גַּם-שָׁמַיִם וָאָרֶץ:

2. Di•ber e•ley•noo le•ketz ha•ya•min ha•e•le al - pi ha•Ben asher sa•ma•hoo le•va•al na•cha•la va•kol va•a•sher bo asa gam - sha•ma•yim va•a•retz.

Rabbinic Jewish Commentary

"in these last days"; the Alexandrian copy, the Complutensian edition, and several other copies, read, "in the last of these days": perfectly agreeable to the phrase באחרית הימים, used in Gen_49:1 to which the apostle refers, and in which places the days of the Messiah are intended; and it is a rule with the Jews (m), that wherever the phrase, "the last days", is mentioned, the days of the Messiah are designed: and they are to be understood not of the last days of the natural world, but of, the Jewish world and state; indeed the times of the Messiah, or Gospel dispensation, may be called the last days of the natural world, according to the tradition of the house of Elias; which teaches, that the duration of the world will be six thousand years, and divides it into three parts, the last of which is assigned to the Messiah, thus; two thousand years void, (or without the law,) two thousand years the law, and two thousand years the days of the Messiah (n):

By whom also he made the worlds; this is said in agreement with the notions of the Jews, and their way of speaking, who make mention of three worlds, which they call, the upper world (the habitation of God), the middle world (the air), and the lower world (o) (the earth); and sometimes they call them the world of angels (where they dwell), the world of orbs (where the sun, moon, and stars are), and the world below (p) (on which we live); and it is frequent in their writings, and prayer books (q), to call God רבון כל העולמים, "Lord of all worlds"; Heb_11:3, these God made by his Son, not as an instrument, but as an efficient cause with him; for by him were all things made, whether visible or invisible; and the preposition "by" does not always denote instrumentality, but sometimes efficiency; and is used of God the Father himself, and in this epistle, Heb_2:10.

(m) Kimchi & Aben Ezra in Isa. ii. 2. (n) T. Bab. Sanhedrin, fol. 97. 1. (o) Tzeror Hammor, fol. 1. 4. & 3. 2, 3. Caphtor, fol. 79. 1. (p) Tzeror Hammor, fol. 83. 2. Caphtor, fol. 90. 1. (q) Seder Tephillot, fol. 5. 2. & 40. 2. Ed. Amstelod.

---

3. Who being the brightness of his glory, and the express image of his person, and upholding all things by the word of his power, when he had by himself purged our sins, sat down on the right hand of the Majesty on high;

3. ὃς ὢν ἀπαύγασμα τῆς δόξης καὶ χαρακτὴρ τῆς ὑποστάσεως αὐτοῦ, φέρων τε τὰ πάντα τῷ ῥήματι τῆς δυνάμεως αὐτοῦ, δι' ἑαυτοῦ καθαρισμὸν ποιησάμενος τῶν ἁμαρτιῶν ἡμῶν, ἐκάθισεν ἐν δεξιᾷ τῆς μεγαλωσύνης ἐν ὑψηλοῖς,

3. 'os on apaugasma teis doxeis kai charakteir teis 'upostaseos autou, pheron te ta panta to 'reimati teis dunameos autou, di 'eautou katharismon poieisamenos ton 'amartion 'eimon, ekathisen en dexya teis megalosuneis en 'upseilois,

ג. וְהוּא זֹהַר כְּבוֹדוֹ וְצֶלֶם פָּנָיו וְנֹשֵׂא-כֹל בְּכֹחַ דְּבָרוֹ וְאַחֲרֵי אֲשֶׁר טִהַר אֹתָנוּ בְּנַפְשׁוֹ מֵחַטֹּאתֵינוּ יָשַׁב מִיָּמִין אֲשֶׁר לוֹ הַגְּדֻלָּה בַּמָּרוֹם:

3. Ve•hoo zo•har k`vo•do ve•tze•lem pa•nav ve•no•se - chol be•cho•ach de•va•ro ve•a•cha•rey asher ti•her o•ta•noo be•naf•sho me•cha•to•tey•noo ya•shav miy•min asher lo ha•g`doo•la ba•ma•rom.

Rabbinic Jewish Commentary

The phrase זיו יקריה, "the brightness of his glory", is used of the divine Being, in the Chaldee paraphrases (r); see the Apocrypha.

"For she is the brightness of the everlasting light, the unspotted mirror of the power of God, and the image of his goodness." (Wisdom 7:26)

(r) Targum in 2 Sam xxii. 13. & in Cant. v. 10.

brightness of his glory — *Greek,* the *effulgence* of His glory. "Light of (from) light" [*Nicene Creed*]. "Who is so senseless as to doubt concerning the eternal being of the Son? For when has one seen light without effulgence?" [Athanasius, *Against Arius, Orations,* 2]. "The sun is never seen without effulgence, nor the Father without the Son" [Theophylact]. It is *because* He is the brightness, etc., and *because* He upholds, etc., that He *sat down on the right hand,* etc. It was a return to His divine glory (Joh_6:62; Joh_17:5; compare Wisdom of Solomon 7:25, 26, where similar things are said of wisdom).

express image — "impress." But veiled in the flesh.
The Sun of God in glory beams
Too bright for us to scan;
But we can face the light that streams
For the mild Son of man.
(2Cor. 3:18 reference.)

of his person — *Greek,* "of His substantial essence"; "hypostasis."
(JFB Commentary)

God ***created the universe through*** him, as taught also at Joh.1:3, Col.1:16. That the universe was created through an intermediary-the Word (Joh.1:1-3), the *Sh'khinah*. Wisdom, the *Torah*-is not an idea alien to Judaism, as shown by this quotation from Rabbi Akiva in the Mishna:

"He used to say, '... God loves Israel, because he gave them a precious instrument [Hebrew *kli*, "instrument, vessel"]. But he enhanced that love by letting them know that the precious instrument they had been given was the very one through which the universe was created-as it is said, "For I give you good doctrine; do not forsake my *Torah*" (Pro_4:2).' "
(Avot 3:14)

This Son is the radiance of, literally, "the glory," best rendered Jewishly as the *Sh'khinah*, which the *Encyclopedia Judaica* article on it (Volume 14, pp. 1349-1351) defines as

"The Divine Presence, the numinous immanence of God in the world,... a revelation of the holy in the midst of the profane ...."
The article continues:

"One of the more prominent images associated with the *Shekhinah* is that of light. Thus on the verse, '... the earth did shine with His glory' (Eze_43:2), the rabbis remark, 'This is the face of the *Shekhinah*' (*Avot diRabbi Natan* [18b-19a]; see also Chullin 59b-60a). Both the angels in heaven and the righteous in *olam ha-ba* ('the world to come') are sustained by the radiance of the *Shekhinah* (Exodus Rabbah 32:4, B'rakhot 17a; cf. Exo.34:29-35)....

"According to Saadiah Gaon [882-942 C.E.], the *Shekhinah* is identical with *kevod ha-Shem* ('the glory of God'), which served as an intermediary between God and man during the prophetic experience. He suggests that the 'glory of God' is the biblical term, and *Shekhinah* the talmudic term for the created splendor of light which acts as an intermediary between God and man, and which sometimes takes on human form. Thus when Moses asked to see the glory of God, he was shown the *Shekhinah*, and when the prophets in their visions saw God in human likeness, what they actually saw was not God Himself but the *Shekhinah*
(see Saadiah's interpretation of Eze_1:26, 1Ki_22:19, and Dan_7:9 in *Book of Beliefs and Opinions* 2:10)."

The Greek word "*charactêr*" ("very expression"), used only here in the New Testament, delineates even more clearly than "*eikon*" ("image," 2Co_4:4, Col_1:15) that **God's essence** is manifested in the Messiah (Joh_14:9). Compare Num_12:8 : Moses, unlike Miriam and Aaron, saw the *t'munah* ("likeness, representation"; in modern Hebrew, "picture") of *Adonai*.

Raphael Patai brings the following extraordinary paragraph from the works of the Alexandrian Jew Philo (20 B.C.E.-50 C.E.), noting that he "does not mention the Messiah by this name, but speaks of the 'Shoot' (rather infelicitously rendered in the Loeb Classical Library edition as the 'rising'),... who-remarkable words in the mouth of a Jewish thinker-'differs not a whit from the divine image,' and is the Divine Father's 'eldest son' ...."
(Jewish New Testament Commetary)

The phrase "radiance of His glory" in Hebrew is "zohar kvodo." Interestingly, there was an Ashkenazi commentary on the names of Metatron,

"*Ruach pisqonit* [=930] is the numerical equivalent of [the expression] Yah Yah Demut Demut [=930], for he [**Metatron**] had two images [demuyot], at first the image of a man and in the end the image of an angel. Ruach pisqonit is equal numerically to [the expression] *ke-rl'w elev ribbo parsa* [=930], for this is the measure of the stature (*shi'ur haqomah*). This is to inform you that the Holy One, blessed be He, has no measurement, and He has no boundary or set limit…and no eye has ever seen Him. Thus, when He selects a prophet to worship Him, he sees the splendor of His glory (zohar kevodo) on the throne in this measure."

(MSS Cambridge Heb. Add. 405, fol 302b; Oxford-Bodeleian 2286, fol. 156a; Moscoq Guenzberg 90, fol 127a; New York – JTSA Mic 2206, fol 11a, cited in Through a Speculum that Shines, Elliot R. Wolfson, Princeton University Press, pg. 223)

---

4. Being made so much better than the angels, as he hath by inheritance obtained a more excellent name than they.

4. τοσούτῳ κρείττων γενόμενος τῶν ἀγγέλων, ὅσῳ διαφορώτερον παρ' αὐτοὺς κεκληρονόμηκεν ὄνομα.

4. tosouto kreitton genomenos ton angelon, 'oso dyaphoroteron par autous kekleironomeiken onoma.

ד: וַיִּגְבַּהּ לְמַעְלָה מִן-הַמַּלְאָכִים כַּאֲשֶׁר קָנָה לוֹ שֵׁם רָם וְנִשָּׂא מֵהֶם.

4. Va•yig•ba le•ma•a•la min - ha•mal•a•chim ka•a•sher ka•na lo shem ram ve•ni•sa me•hem.

Rabbinic Jewish Commentary

The phrase, "being made", signifies no more than that "he was"; and so the Syriac version renders it, "and he was so much better than the angels"; and so the Ethiopic version, "he is so much better": and this is observed, to prove him to be more excellent than any creature, since he is preferred to the most excellent of creatures; and to show, that the Gospel dispensation is superior to the legal dispensation, which was introduced by the ministration of angels; and to take off the Jews from the worship of angels, (a Greek concept) to which they were prone: and this doctrine of his could not be well denied by them, since it was the faith of the Jewish church, that the Messiah should be preferred to the angels: for in their ancient writings they say of him, he shall be exalted above Abraham, he shall be lifted up above Moses, and be higher than the ministering angels (s);

(s) Tanchuma spud Huls. p. 321.

In one *midrash* the rabbis portray righteous people as better than angels (Genesis Rabbah 78:1), and this picture fits Yeshua well because "he did not sin" (Heb_4:15). But in another *midrash* the Messiah himself is so described-and, incidentally, it is also an instance of a Jewish application of Isa. 52:13-Isa. 53:12 to the Messiah:

" 'Behold, my servant shall (deal wisely) prosper.' This is King Messiah. 'He shall be exalted and extolled and be very high.' He shall be exalted beyond Avraham, and extolled beyond Moses, and raised high above the ministering angels."
(*Yalkut Shim'oni* 2:53:3, on Isa_52:13; quoted in B. F. Westcott, *The Epistle to the Hebrews*, p. 16)

Yalkut Shim'oni itself is a collection of some 10,000 stories and comments from the Talmud and *midrashim*, arranged in biblical order in the 13th century by Rabbi Shim'on HaDarshan (Simon the Expositor, or Simon the Preacher). (Jewish New Testament Commentary)

5. For unto which of the angels said he at any time, Thou art my Son, this day have I begotten thee? And again, I will be to him a Father, and he shall be to me a Son?

5. Τίνι γὰρ εἶπέν ποτε τῶν ἀγγέλων, Υἱός μου εἶ σύ, ἐγὼ σήμερον γεγέννηκά σε; Καὶ πάλιν, Ἐγὼ ἔσομαι αὐτῷ εἰς πατέρα, καὶ αὐτὸς ἔσται μοι εἰς υἱόν;

5. Tini gar eipen pote ton angelon, 'Wios mou ei su, ego seimeron gegenneika se? Kai palin, Ego esomai auto eis patera, kai autos estai moi eis 'wion?

ה. כִּי לְמִי מִן-הַמַּלְאָכִים אָמַר מֵעוֹלָם בְּנִי אַתָּה אֲנִי הַיּוֹם יְלִדְתִּיךָ וְכֵן עוֹד אֲנִי אֶהְיֶה-לּוֹ לְאָב וְהוּא יִהְיֶה-לִי לְבֵן:

5. Ki le•mi min - ha•mal•a•chim amar me•o•lam B`ni ata ani ha•yom ye•lid•ti•cha ve•chen od ani e•he•ye - lo le•Av ve•hoo yi•hee•ye - li le•Ven?

Rabbinic Jewish Commentary

In Judaism Psalm 2, quoted here, has been variously held to refer to Aaron, David, the people of Israel in Messianic times, *Mashiach Ben-David* and *Mashiach Ben-Yosef*. But the oldest reference, Psalms of Solomon 17:21-27, from the middle of the 1st century B.C.E., applies it to *Mashiach Ben-David*, as does the Talmud at Sukkah 52a.
(Jewish New Testament Commentary)

---

6. And again, when he bringeth in the firstbegotten into the world, he saith, And let all the angels of God worship him.

6. Ὅταν δὲ πάλιν εἰσαγάγῃ τὸν πρωτότοκον εἰς τὴν οἰκουμένην λέγει, Καὶ προσκυνησάτωσαν αὐτῷ πάντες ἄγγελοι θεοῦ.

6. 'Otan de palin eisagagei ton prototokon eis tein oikoumenein legei, Kai proskuneisatosan auto pantes angeloi theou.

ו. וְכֵן בְּתִתּוֹ אֶת-בְּכוֹרוֹ לָשׁוּב לְתֵבֵל אַרְצָה הוּא אֹמֵר הִשְׁתַּחֲווּ לוֹ כָּל-מַלְאֲכֵי אֱלֹהִים:

6. Ve•chen be•ti•to et - be•cho•ro la•shoov le•te•vel ar•tza hoo o•mer hish•ta•cha•voo lo kol - mal•a•chey Elohim.

Rabbinic Jewish Commentary

This is a name given him in the Old Testament, and is what the Hebrews were acquainted with, and therefore the apostle uses it; it is in Psa_89:27 from whence it seems to be taken here, and which the ancient Jews (u) acknowledge is to be understood of the Messiah.

Philo the Jew (w) often calls the Logos, or Word of God, his first begotten.

(u) Shemot Rabba, sect. 19. fol. 104. 4. (w) De Agricultura, p. 195. De Confus. Ling. p. 329, 341. Somniis, p. 597.

The Hebrew text of Psa_97:7 says, "*Worship him, all gods (elohim)*." Since Judaism allows that *elohim* sometimes means "angels," the Septuagint's rendering, "*Let all God's angels worship him,*" is not surprising. What is surprising is that whereas in the original, the object of worship is *Adonai*, here it is the Son. (Jewish New Testament Commentary)

---

7. And of the angels he saith, Who maketh his angels spirits, and his ministers a flame of fire.

7. Καὶ πρὸς μὲν τοὺς ἀγγέλους λέγει, Ὁ ποιῶν τοὺς ἀγγέλους αὐτοῦ πνεύματα, καὶ τοὺς λειτουργοὺς αὐτοῦ πυρὸς φλόγα·

7. Kai pros men tous angelous legei, 'O poion tous angelous autou pneumata, kai tous leitourgous autou puros phloga.

ז. וְעַל-הַמַּלְאָכִים הוּא אֹמֵר עֹשֶׂה מַלְאָכָיו רוּחוֹת מְשָׁרְתָיו אֵשׁ לֹהֵט:

7. Ve•al - ha•mal•a•chim hoo o•mer o•se mal•a•chav roo•chot me•shar•tav esh lo•het.

Rabbinic Jewish Commentary

Psa 104:4 "He makes the winds His messengers, Flaming fire His ministers." The Jews (x) say of the angels,"all the angels, their horses are horses of fire, and their chariots fire, and their bows fire, and their spears fire, and all their instruments of war fire." And they have a notion, that an angel is half water, and half fire (y). (x) Sepher Jetzirah, p. 16. Ed. Rittangel. (y) T. Hieros. Roshhashana, fol. 58. 1.

8. But unto the Son he saith, Thy throne, O God, is for ever and ever: a sceptre of righteousness is the sceptre of thy kingdom.

8. πρὸς δὲ τὸν υἱόν, Ὁ θρόνος σου, ὁ θεός, εἰς τὸν αἰῶνα τοῦ αἰῶνος· ῥάβδος εὐθύτητος ἡ ῥάβδος τῆς βασιλείας σου.

8. pros de ton 'wion, 'O thronos sou, 'o theos, eis ton aiona tou aionos. 'rabdos euthuteitos 'ei 'rabdos teis basileias sou.

ח. אַךְ עַל־הַבֵּן אֹמֵר כִּסְאֲךָ אֱלֹהִים עוֹלָם וָעֶד שֵׁבֶט מִישֹׁר שֵׁבֶט מַלְכוּתֶךָ:

8. Ach al - ha•Ben o•mer kis•acha Elohim o•lam va•ed she•vet mi•shor she•vet mal•choo•te•cha.

Rabbinic Jewish Commentary

The Targum applies it to the Messiah, and mentions him by name in Heb.1:2 and some of their modern writers (z) affirm it is said of the Messiah; though Aben Ezra seems doubtful about it, saying, it is spoken concerning David, or Messiah his Son.

(z) Kimchi & R. Sol. ben Melech in loc. & R. Abraham Seba, Tzeror Hammor, fol. 49. 2.

Psalm 45 is a wedding poem for David, Solomon or some other Israelite king. A Jewish commentator writes: "This Psalm came to be understood as referring to King Messiah (so the Targum), and his marriage as an allusion to his redemption of Israel" (A. Cohen's note to Psalm 45 in the Soncino Hebrew-and-English edition of the Hebrew Bible, *Psalms*, p. 140).

Cohen suggests instead, "Thy throne, given of God," and comments: "The Hebrew is difficult. A.V. and R.V., 'Thy throne, O God,' appears to be the obvious translation but does not suit the context."
Clearly the reason he thinks it "does not suit the context" is that even though he refers Psalm 45 to the Messiah, he is unwilling to allow that the psalmist may be prophesying the Messiah's divine character.
(Jewish News Testament)

The words here quoted are taken from Psa_45:6, Psa_45:7, which the ancient Chaldee paraphrast, and the most intelligent rabbins, refer to the Messiah. On the third verse of this Psalm, Thou art fairer than the children of men, the Targum says: "Thy beauty, מלכא משיחא malca Meshicha, O King Messiah, is greater than the children of men." Aben Ezra says: "This Psalm speaks of David, or rather of his son, the Messiah, for this is his name," Eze_34:24 : And David my servant shall be a Prince over them for ever. Other Rabbis confirm this opinion.

A scepter of righteousness - The scepter, which was a sort of staff or instrument of various forms, was the ensign of government, and is here used for government itself. This the ancient Jewish writers understand also of the Messiah.

Hebrews 1

9. Thou hast loved righteousness, and hated iniquity; therefore God, even thy God, hath anointed thee with the oil of gladness above thy fellows.

9. Ἠγάπησας δικαιοσύνην, καὶ ἐμίσησας ἀνομίαν· διὰ τοῦτο ἔχρισέν σε ὁ θεός, ὁ θεός σου, ἔλαιον ἀγαλλιάσεως παρὰ τοὺς μετόχους σου.

9. Eigapeisas dikaiosunein, kai emiseisas anomian. dya touto echrisen se 'o theos, 'o theos sou, elaion agallyaseos para tous metochous sou.

ט. אָהַבְתָּ צֶּדֶק וַתִּשְׂנָא רֶשַׁע עַל־כֵּן מְשָׁחֲךָ אֱלֹהִים אֱלֹהֶיךָ שֶׁמֶן שָׂשׂוֹן מֵחֲבֵרֶךָ:

9. Ahav•ta tze•dek va•tis•na re•sha al - ken me•sha•cha•cha Elohim Elohe•cha she•men sa•son me•cha•ve•re•cha.

Rabbinic Jewish Commentary
Jerome, Augustine, and others translate Psa_45:7, "O God, Thy God, hath anointed thee," whereby Christ is addressed as God. This is probably the true translation of the *Hebrew* there, and also of the *Greek* of Hebrews here; for it is likely the Son is addressed, "O God," as in Heb_1:8.

---

10. And, Thou, Lord, in the beginning hast laid the foundation of the earth; and the heavens are the works of thine hands:

10. Καί, Σὺ κατ' ἀρχάς, κύριε, τὴν γῆν ἐθεμελίωσας, καὶ ἔργα τῶν χειρῶν σού εἰσιν οἱ οὐρανοί·

10. Kai, Su kat archas, kurie, tein gein ethemeliosas, kai erga ton cheiron sou eisin 'oi ouranoi.

י. וְכֵן עוֹד אַתָּה אֲדֹנָי לְפָנִים הָאָרֶץ יָסַדְתָּ וּמַעֲשֵׂי יָדֶיךָ שָׁמָיִם:

10. Ve•chen od ata Adonai le•fa•nim ha•a•retz ya•sa•de•ta oo•ma•a•sey ya•de•cha sha•ma•yim.

Rabbinic Jewish Commentary

For the words are a continuation of the speech to Yeshua, though they are taken from another psalm, from Psa_102:25. The phrase, "thou, YHVH" is taken from Psa_102:12 and is the same with, "O my God", Psa_102:24 and whereas it is there said, "of old", and here, in the beginning, the sense is the same; and agreeably to the Septuagint, and the apostle, Jarchi interprets it by מתחילה, "at", or "from the beginning"; and so the Targum paraphrases it, מן שרויז, "from the beginning", that the creatures were created.

---

11. They shall perish; but thou remainest; and they all shall wax old as doth a garment;

11. αὐτοὶ ἀπολοῦνται, σὺ δὲ διαμένεις· καὶ πάντες ὡς ἱμάτιον παλαιωθήσονται,

11. autoi apolountai, su de dyameneis. kai pantes 'os 'imation palaiotheisontai,

:יא. הֵמָּה יֹאבֵדוּ וְאַתָּה תַעֲמֹד וְכֻלָּם כַּבֶּגֶד יִבְלוּ

11. He•ma yo•ve•doo ve•a•ta ta•a•mod ve•choo•lam ka•be•ged yiv•loo.

---

12. And as a vesture shalt thou fold them up, and they shall be changed: but thou art the same, and thy years shall not fail.

12. καὶ ὡσεὶ περιβόλαιον ἑλίξεις αὐτούς, καὶ ἀλλαγήσονται· σὺ δὲ ὁ αὐτὸς εἶ, καὶ τὰ ἔτη σου οὐκ ἐκλείψουσιν.

12. kai 'osei peribolaion 'elixeis autous, kai allageisontai. su de 'o autos ei, kai ta etei sou ouk ekleipsousin.

:יב. כַּלְּבוּשׁ תַּחֲלִיפֵם וְיַחֲלֹפוּ וְאַתָּה הוּא וּשְׁנוֹתֶיךָ לֹא יִתָּמּוּ

12. Kal•voosh ta•cha•li•fem ve•yach•lo•foo ve•a•ta hoo oosh•no•te•cha lo yi•ta•moo.

Rabbinic Jewish Commentary

In the Hebrew text it is, "as a vesture shalt thou change them"; but the sense is the same, for a garment is changed by folding it, or turning it; agreeably to which Jarchi interprets the Hebrew phrase thus, "as a man turns his garment to put it off;"

The Vulgate Latin version reads as the Hebrew does, and one of the manuscripts of New College, Oxford.

Hebrews 1

13. But to which of the angels said he at any time, Sit on my right hand, until I make thine enemies thy footstool?

13. Πρὸς τίνα δὲ τῶν ἀγγέλων εἴρηκέν ποτε, Κάθου ἐκ δεξιῶν μου, ἕως ἂν θῶ τοὺς ἐχθρούς σου ὑποπόδιον τῶν ποδῶν σου;

13. Pros tina de ton angelon eireiken pote, Kathou ek dexion mou, 'eos an tho tous echthrous sou 'upopodion ton podon sou?

:יג. וּלְמִי אֵיפוֹא מִן-הַמַּלְאָכִים אָמַר מֵעוֹלָם שֵׁב לִימִינִי עַד-אָשִׁית אֹיְבֶיךָ הֲדֹם לְרַגְלֶיךָ

13. Ool•mi ey•fo min - ha•mal•a•chim amar me•o•lam shev li•y`mi•ni ad – asheet oy•ve•cha ha•dom le•rag•le•cha.

Rabbinic Jewish Commentary

"YHVH says to my Lord, 'Sit at my right hand, until I make your enemies your footstool for your feet." The Targum is, "YHVH said to his Word." Galatinus (q) says the true Targum of Jonathan has it, "YHVH said to his Word;"

(q) De Cathol. Arean. Ver. l. 3. c. 5. & l. 8. c. 24.

Some interpret this passage as referring to Abraham, R. Hana b. Liwai said: Shem, [Noah's] eldest son, said to Eliezer [Abraham's servant], 'When the kings of the east and west attacked you, what did you do?' – He replied, 'The Holy One, blessed be He, took Abraham and placed him at His right hand, and they [God and Abraham] threw dust which turned to swords and chaff which turned to arrows, as it is written, "A Psalm of David. The Lord said unto my master, Sit thou at my right hand, until I make thine enemies thy footstool."
(Sanhedrin 108b, Soncino Press Edition)

The Midrash Rabbah says,

R. Ishmael and R. Akiba [reasoned as follows]. R. Ishmael said: Abraham was a High Priest, as it says, "The Lord hath sworn, and will not repent: Thou art a priest for ever after the manner of Melchizedek" (Ps. CX, 4). (Genesis Rabbah 46:5, Soncino Press Editon, Cf. Gen. Rabbah 55:6, 55:7, Lev. Rabbah 25:6, Deut. Rabbah 2:7)

One thing we know for sure, is that whoever the speaker is in this psalm, the second "Lord" is greater than the speaker. While the above passages speak of Abraham as the one at God's Right hand, the Midrash on Psalms places the Messiah there, R. Yudan said in the name of R. Hama: In the time-to-come, when the Holy One, blessed be He, seats the lord Messiah at His right hand, as is said The Lord saith unto my lord: "Sit thou at My right hand" (Ps. 110:1), and seats Abraham at His left, Abraham's face will pale, and he will say to the Lord: "My son's son sits at the right, and I at the left!" Thereupon the Holy One, blessed be He, will comfort Abraham, saying: "Thy son's son is at My right, but I, in a manner of speaking, am at thy right": The Lord [is] at thy right hand (Ps. 110:5).
(Midrash Tehillim 18.29, translated by William G. Braude, Yale University Press Edition, pg. 261)

Another Midrash,
[God says:] "Ephraim, My firstborn, you sit on My right until I subdue the army of the hosts of God and Magog, your enemies, under your footstool .
(Mid. Alpha Betot, 2:438-42)

The Rashbi is attributed as saying
" . . .the Holy One, blessed be He, will fight for Israel and will say to the Messiah : "Sit at my right." And the Messiah will say to Israel:"Gather together and stand and see the salvation of the Lord." And instantly the Holy One, blessed be He, will go forth and fight against them . . .May that time and that period be near!
(T'fillat R' Shimon ben Yochai, BhM 4:124-26)

The incredibly fascinating book by R' Hillel Shklover, the disciple of the Vilna Gaon, entitled Kol HaTor (The Voice of the Turtledove), makes this amazing statement, יָדִין בַּגּוֹיִם מָלֵא גְוִיּוֹת *"He will judge the nations filled with corpses* (Psalm 110:6) – The entire Psalm, beginning with "Sit on my right" was said about *Mashiach ben Yosef*, whose name is hinted at in the initial letters יָדִין בַּגּוֹיִם מָלֵא גְוִיּוֹת going from left to right. . ."

(Kol HaTor 2.61, translated by Rabbi Yechiel Bar Lev and K. Skaist, YedidNefesh.com)

Indeed, the Pharisees did have a great depth of knowledge about the Tanakh: *"These are the two anointed ones, that stand by the Lord of the whole earth* (Zech. 4:14). This is a reference to Aaron and the Messiah, but I cannot tell which is the more beloved. However, from the verse, *The Lord hath sworn and will not repent: Thou art a priest for ever after the manner of Mechizedek* (Psalm 110:4), one can tell that the Messianic King is more beloved that the righteous priest."
(The Fathers According to Rabbi Nathan, Translated by Judah Goldin, Chapter 34, Yale University Press, pg. 137-138.)

---

14. Are they not all ministering spirits, sent forth to minister for them who shall be heirs ofsalvation?

14. Οὐχὶ πάντες εἰσὶν λειτουργικὰ πνεύματα, εἰς διακονίαν ἀποστελλόμενα διὰ τοὺςμέλλοντας κληρονομεῖν σωτηρίαν;

14. Ouchi pantes eisin leitourgika pneumata, eis dyakonian apostellomena dya tous mellontaskleironomein soteirian?

:יד. הֲלֹא כֻלָּם מַלְאֲכֵי הַשָּׁרֵת הֵם הַשְּׁלוּחִים לְשָׁרֵת לִפְנֵי הַבָּאִים לִנְחֹל יֵשַׁע נַחֲלָתָם

14. Ha•lo choo•lam mal•a•chey ha•sha•ret hem ha•sh`loo•chim le•sha•ret lif•neyha•ba•eem lin•chol ye•sha na•cha•la•tam.

Rabbinic Jewish Commentary
The phrase is Rabbinical; frequent mention is made in Jewish writings (a) of מלאכי השרת, "the messengers of ministry", or "the ministering messengers"; this is their common appellation with the Jews.

(a) T. Bab. Chagiga, fol. 12. 2. & 14. 1, 2. & 16. 1. Taanith, fol. 11. 1. & Megilia, fol. 15. 2. & in Zohar passim.

(Hebrews Chapter 1 End)

Hebrews, Chapter 2

1. Therefore we ought to give the more earnest heed to the things which we have heard, lest at any time we should let them slip.

1. Διὰ τοῦτο δεῖ περισσοτέρως ἡμᾶς προσέχειν τοῖς ἀκουσθεῖσιν, μήποτε παραρρυῶμεν.

1. Dya touto dei perissoteros 'eimas prosechein tois akoustheisin, meipote pararruomen.

א: עַל־כֵּן הַמִּצְוָה אֵלֵינוּ לְהִזָּהֵר עַד־מְאֹד בַּדְּבָרִים אֲשֶׁר שָׁמָעְנוּ פֶּן־יָלוֹזוּ מֵעֵינֵינוּ

1. Al - ken ha•mitz•va e•ley•noo le•hi•za•her ad - me•od bad•va•rim asher sha•ma•a•noo pen - ya•loo•zoo me•ey•ney•noo.

---

2. For if the word spoken by angels was stedfast, and every transgression and disobedience received a just recompence of reward;

2. Εἰ γὰρ ὁ δι' ἀγγέλων λαληθεὶς λόγος ἐγένετο βέβαιος, καὶ πᾶσα παράβασις καὶ παρακοὴ ἔλαβεν ἔνδικον μισθαποδοσίαν,

2. Ei gar 'o di angelon laleitheis logos egeneto bebaios, kai pasa parabasis kai parakoei elaben endikon misthapodosian,

ב: כִּי אִם־הַדָּבָר דָּבֶר עַל־פִּי מַלְאָכִים עָמַד בְּתָקְפּוֹ וְכָל־עָוֹן וָפֶשַׁע נִפְקַד בְּשֵׁבֶט מִשְׁפָּט

2. Ki eem - ha•da•var da•voor al - pi mal•a•chim amad be•tok•fo ve•chol - a•von va•fe•sha nif•kad be•she•vet mish•pat.

---

3. How shall we escape, if we neglect so great salvation; which at the first began to be spoken by the Lord, and was confirmed unto us by them that heard him;

3. πῶς ἡμεῖς ἐκφευξόμεθα τηλικαύτης ἀμελήσαντες σωτηρίας; Ἥτις, ἀρχὴν λαβοῦσα λαλεῖσθαι διὰ τοῦ κυρίου, ὑπὸ τῶν ἀκουσάντων εἰς ἡμᾶς ἐβεβαιώθη,

3. pos 'eimeis ekpheuxometha teilikauteis ameleisantes soteirias? 'Eitis, archein labousa laleisthai dya tou kuriou, 'upo ton akousanton eis 'eimas ebebaiothei,

ג. אֵיךְ נִמָּלֵט אֲנַחְנוּ אִם-לֹא נָשִׁית לֵב לִישׁוּעָה רַב כָּמוֹהוּ אֲשֶׁר בִּשֵּׂר הָאָדוֹן מֵרֹאשׁ וַיֵּאָמֵן דְּבָרוֹ לָנוּ מִפִּי שֹׁמְעָיו:

3. Eych ni•ma•let a•nach•noo eem - lo na•sheet lev le•ye•sha rav ka•mo•hoo asher bi•sar ha•Adon me•rosh va•ye•a•men de•va•ro la•noo mi•pi shom•av.

---

4. God also bearing them witness, both with signs and wonders, and with divers miracles, and gifts of the Holy Ghost, according to his own will?

4. συνεπιμαρτυροῦντος τοῦ θεοῦ σημείοις τε καὶ τέρασιν, καὶ ποικίλαις δυνάμεσιν, καὶ πνεύματος ἁγίου μερισμοῖς, κατὰ τὴν αὐτοῦ θέλησιν.

4. sunepimarturountos tou theou seimeiois te kai terasin, kai poikilais dunamesin, kai pneumatos 'agiou merismois, kata tein autou theleisin.

ד. וְגַם-אֱלֹהִים נָתַן עֵדוּת עַל-זֹאת בְּאֹתוֹת וּבְמוֹפְתִים וְנִפְלָאוֹת וּבְמַתְּנוֹת רוּחַ קָדְשׁוֹ אֲשֶׁר חִלֵּק כִּרְצוֹנוֹ:

4. Ve•gam - Elohim na•tan e•doot al - zot be•o•tot oov•mof•tim ve•nif•la•ot oov•mat•not Roo•ach Kod•sho asher chi•lek kir•tzo•no.

Hebrews 2

5. For unto the angels hath he not put in subjection the world to come, whereof we speak.

5. Οὐ γὰρ ἀγγέλοις ὑπέταξεν τὴν οἰκουμένην τὴν μέλλουσαν, περὶ ἧς λαλοῦμεν.

5. Ou gar angelois 'upetaxen tein oikoumenein tein mellousan, peri 'eis laloumen.

ה. כִּי לֹא תַחַת יְדֵי-הַמַּלְאָכִים שָׁת אֶת-הָעוֹלָם הֶעָתִיד לָבֹא אֲשֶׁר עָלָיו אֲנַחְנוּ מְדַבְּרִים:

5. Ki lo ta•chat ye•dey - ha•mal•a•chim shat et - ha•o•lam he•a•tid la•vo asher alav a•nach•noo me•dab•rim.

Rabbinic Jewish Commentary
Here called "the world to come", as the times of the Messiah are frequently called by the Jews עולם הבא, "the world to come." And hence mention is made in the Jewish writings of עלמא דאתי דמשיחא, "the world to come of the Messiah" (d).

(d) Targum in 1 Kings iv. 33.

---

6. But one in a certain place testified, saying, What is man, that thou art mindful of him? Or the son of man, that thou visitest him?

6. Διεμαρτύρατο δέ πού τις λέγων, Τί ἐστιν ἄνθρωπος, ὅτι μιμνῄσκῃ αὐτοῦ; Ἢ υἱὸς ἀνθρώπου, ὅτι ἐπισκέπτῃ αὐτόν;

6. Diemarturato de pou tis legon, Ti estin anthropos, 'oti mimneiskei autou? Ei 'wios anthropou, 'oti episkeptei auton?

ו. כִּי אִם-כְּעֵדוּת הַכָּתוּב הָאוֹמֵר שָׁם מָה-אֱנוֹשׁ כִּי-תִזְכְּרֶנּוּ וּבֶן-אָדָם כִּי תִפְקְדֶנּוּ:

6. Ki eem - ke•e•doot ha•ka•toov ha•o•mer sham ma - enosh ki - tiz•ke•re•noo oo•ven - adam ki tif•ke•de•noo.

Rabbinic Jewish Commentary
It is common with them to say, התורה העידה, "the Torah testified" (e), as it is said in such or such a place.

(e) T. Bab. Sanhedrin, fol. 37. 1. Maimon. Hilchot Yesode Hattorsh, 3. 7. sect. 6. & Melachim, c. 11. sect. 1. Vid. Aben Ezra in Lev. xvi. 8.

What is man - This quotation is verbatim from the Septuagint; and, as the Greek is not as emphatic as the Hebrew, I will quote the original: מה אנוש כי תזכרנו ובן אדם כי תפקדנו; "What is miserable man, that thou rememberest him? and the son of Adam, that thou visitest him?" The variation of the terms in the original is very emphatic.

---

7. Thou madest him a little lower than the angels; thou crownedst him with glory and honour, and didst set him over the works of thy hands:

7. Ἡλάττωσας αὐτὸν βραχύ τι παρ' ἀγγέλους· δόξῃ καὶ τιμῇ ἐστεφάνωσας αὐτόν·

7. Eilattosas auton brachu ti par angelous. doxei kai timei estephanosas auton.

ז. וַתְּחַסְּרֵהוּ מְּעַט מֵאֱלֹהִים וְכָבוֹד וְהָדָר תְּעַטְּרֵהוּ תַּמְשִׁילֵהוּ בְּמַעֲשֵׂי יָדֶיךָ:

7. Vat•chas•re•hoo me•at me•Elohim ve•cha•vod ve•ha•dar te•at•re•hoo tam•shi•le•hoo be•ma•a•sey ya•de•cha.

Rabbinic Jewish Commentary

Thou madest him a little lower than the angels - We must again have recourse to the original from which this quotation is made: ותחסרהו מעט מאלהים. In the Hebrew text it is, "than Elohim", which some render, "than God." If this be spoken of man as he came out of the hands of his Maker, it places him at the head of all God's works; for literally translated it is: Thou hast made him less than God. And this is proved by his being made in the image and likeness of God, which is spoken of no other creature either in heaven or earth; and it is very likely that in his original creation he stood at the head of all the works of God, and the next to his Maker.

The Targum, Jarchi, Aben Ezra, Kimchi, and Ben Melech, interpret it "than the angels." But Why? The Jews had adopted much of the pagan and Greek thought during and after the Babylonian exile regarding dualism and "angels" who, they believed, are also called god or elohim in the Hebrew Bible. This made it easier to explain away verses where God appeared to men as just angels who appeared who were also called elohim.

---

8. Thou hast put all things in subjection under his feet. For in that he put all in subjection under him, he left nothing that is not put under him. But now we see not yet all things put under him.

8. πάντα ὑπέταξας ὑποκάτω τῶν ποδῶν αὐτοῦ. Ἐν γὰρ τῷ ὑποτάξαι αὐτῷ τὰ πάντα, οὐδὲν ἀφῆκεν αὐτῷ ἀνυπότακτον. Νῦν δὲ οὔπω ὁρῶμεν αὐτῷ τὰ πάντα ὑποτεταγμένα.

8. panta 'upetaxas 'upokato ton podon autou. En gar to 'upotaxai auto ta panta, ouden apheiken auto anupotakton. Nun de oupo 'oromen auto ta panta 'upotetagmena.

ח. כֹּל שַׁתָּה תַחַת-רַגְלָיו אַךְ בַּאֲשֶׁר שָׁת כֹּל תַּחְתָּיו לֹא הוֹתִיר דָּבָר אֲשֶׁר לֹא הוּשַׁת תַּחְתָּיו וְעַתָּה לֹא רָאִינוּ עוֹד:כַּיּוֹם כִּי הַכֹּל הוּשַׁת תַּחְתָּיו

8. Kol sha•ta ta•chat - rag•lav ach ba•a•sher shat kol tach•tav lo ho•tir da•var asher lo hoo•shat tach•tav ve•a•ta lo ra•ee•noo od cha•yom ki ha•kol hoo•shat tach•tav.

Hebrews 2

9. But we see Jesus, who was made a little lower than the angels for the suffering of death, crowned with glory and honour; that he by the grace of God should taste death for every man.

9. Τὸν δὲ βραχύ τι παρ᾽ ἀγγέλους ἠλαττωμένον βλέπομεν Ἰησοῦν, διὰ τὸ πάθημα τοῦ θανάτου δόξῃ καὶ τιμῇ ἐστεφανωμένον, ὅπως χάριτι θεοῦ ὑπὲρ παντὸς γεύσηται θανάτου.

9. Ton de brachu ti par angelous eilattomenon blepomen Yeisoun, dya to patheima tou thanatou doxei kai timei estephanomenon, 'opos chariti theou 'uper pantos geuseitai thanatou.

ט. אֲבָל רֹאִים אֲנַחְנוּ אֶת-יֵשׁוּעַ הַהוּא אֲשֶׁר חִסְּרוֹ מְעַט מֵאֱלֹהִים וַיְעַטְּרֵהוּ כָּבוֹד וְהָדָר עֵקֶב חֶבְלֵי הַמָּוֶת אֲשֶׁר אֲפָפוּהוּ כִּי בְחֶסֶד-אֵל טָעַם טַעַם הַמָּוֶת בְּעַד כֻּלָּם

9. Aval ro•eem a•nach•noo et - Yeshua ha•hoo asher chis•ro me•at me•Elohim vay•at•re•hoo cha•vod ve•ha•dar e•kev chev•ley ha•ma•vet asher afa•foo•hoo ki ve•che•sed - El ta•am ta•am ha•ma•vet be•ad koo•lam.

Rabbinic Jewish Commentary
(See Hebrews 2:7 for commentary)

---

10. For it became him, for whom are all things, and by whom are all things, in bringing many sons unto glory, to make the captain of their salvation perfect through sufferings.

10. Ἔπρεπεν γὰρ αὐτῷ, δι᾽ ὃν τὰ πάντα, καὶ δι᾽ οὗ τὰ πάντα, πολλοὺς υἱοὺς εἰς δόξαν ἀγαγόντα, τὸν ἀρχηγὸν τῆς σωτηρίας αὐτῶν διὰ παθημάτων τελειῶσαι.

10. Eprepen gar auto, di 'on ta panta, kai di 'ou ta panta, pollous 'wious eis doxan agagonta, ton archeigon teis soteirias auton dya patheimaton teleiosai.

י. כִּי הוּא אֲשֶׁר הַכֹּל לְמַעֲנֵהוּ וּמִיָּדוֹ הַכֹּל הָדָר הוּא לוֹ לְהַנְחוֹת בָּנִים רַבִּים לִגְאוֹן עֻזָּם וּלְהַשְׁלִים אֶת־שַׂר־יְשׁוּעָתָם בְּכוּר עֳנִי.

10. Ki hoo asher ha•kol le•ma•a•ne•hoo oo•mi•ya•do ha•kol ha•dar hoo lo le•han•chot ba•nim ra•bim lig•on oo•zam ool•hash•lim et - sar ye•shoo•a•tam be•choor o•ni.

---

11. For both he that sanctifieth and they who are sanctified are all of one: for which cause he is not ashamed to call them brethren,

11. Ὅ τε γὰρ ἁγιάζων καὶ οἱ ἁγιαζόμενοι, ἐξ ἑνὸς πάντες· δι' ἣν αἰτίαν οὐκ ἐπαισχύνεται ἀδελφοὺς αὐτοὺς καλεῖν,

11. 'O te gar 'agyazon kai 'oi 'agyazomenoi, ex 'enos pantes. di 'ein aitian ouk epaischunetai adelphous autous kalein,

יא. כִּי הַמְכַפֵּר וְהֵם אֲשֶׁר עֲלֵיהֶם יְכַפֵּר מֵאָב אֶחָד הֵם כֻּלָּם עַל־כֵּן לֹא בוֹשׁ מִקְרֹא לָהֶם אַחִים:

11. Ki ham•cha•per ve•hem asher aley•hem ye•cha•per me•av e•chad hem koo•lam al - ken lo vosh mik•ro la•hem a•chim.

Rabbinic Jewish Commentary

for which cause he is not ashamed to call them brethren: The Targumist on Song.8:1 paraphrases the words thus;
"When the King Messiah shall be revealed to the congregation of Israel, the children of Israel shall say unto him, Come, be thou with us, לאח, for "a brother", or "be thou our brother"." The Israelites, they say (f), are called, אחים להקבה "the brethren of the holy blessed God"; in proof of which they often produce Psa_122:8 as being the words of God to them; and again, interpreting those words in Lev_25:48 "one of his brethren may redeem him", this, say (g) they, is the holy blessed God.

(f) Zohar in Exod. fol. 23. 3. & in Lev. fol. 3. 3. & 9. 3. & 32. 2. (g) Tzeror Hammor, fol. 106. 3.

12. Saying, I will declare thy name unto my brethren, in the midst of the church will I sing praise unto thee.

12. λέγων, Ἀπαγγελῶ τὸ ὄνομά σου τοῖς ἀδελφοῖς μου, ἐν μέσῳ ἐκκλησίας ὑμνήσω σε.

12. legon, Apangelo to onoma sou tois adelphois mou, en meso ekkleisias 'umneiso se.

:יב. בְּאָמְרוֹ אֲסַפְּרָה שִׁמְךָ לְאֶחָי בְּתוֹךְ קָהָל אֲהַלְלֶךָּ

12. Be•om•ro a•sap•ra shim•cha le•e•chai be•toch ka•hal aha•la•le•cha.

Rabbinic Jewish Commentary
With the Jews (h), ten men made a congregation.

(h) Misn. Sanhedrin, c. 1. sect. 6.

Hebrews 2

13. And again, I will put my trust in him. And again, Behold I and the children which God hath given me.

13. Καὶ πάλιν, Ἐγὼ ἔσομαι πεποιθὼς ἐπ' αὐτῷ. Καὶ πάλιν, Ἰδοὺ ἐγὼ καὶ τὰ παιδία ἅ μοι ἔδωκεν ὁ θεός.

13. Kai palin, Ego esomai pepoithos ep auto. Kai palin, Ydou ego kai ta paidia 'a moi edoken 'o theos.

:יג. וְעוֹד יֵאָמֵר וְקִוֵּיתִי לוֹ וְעוֹד יוֹסִיף הִנֵּה אָנֹכִי וְהַיְלָדִים אֲשֶׁר נָתַן-לִי יְהוָה

13. Ve•od ye•a•mer ve•ki•vei•ti lo ve•od yo•sif hee•ne ano•chi ve•hay•la•dim asher na•tan - li Adonai.

Rabbinic Jewish Commentary
The Targum upon it makes mention of the Messiah in Psa_18:32 and he is manifestly spoken of under the name of David, in Psa_18:50 and which verse is applied to the Messiah, by the Jews, both ancient and modern (i)

(i) Echa Rabbati, fol. 50. 2. Tzeror Hammor, fol. 47. 3.

14. Forasmuch then as the children are partakers of flesh and blood, he also himself likewise took part of the same; that through death he might destroy him that had the power of death, that is, the devil;

14. Ἐπεὶ οὖν τὰ παιδία κεκοινώνηκεν σαρκὸς καὶ αἵματος, καὶ αὐτὸς παραπλησίως μετέσχεν τῶν αὐτῶν, ἵνα διὰ τοῦ θανάτου καταργήσῃ τὸν τὸ κράτος ἔχοντα τοῦ θανάτου, τοῦτ᾽ ἔστιν τὸν διάβολον,

14. Epei oun ta paidia kekoinoneiken sarkos kai 'aimatos, kai autos parapleisios meteschen ton auton, 'ina dya tou thanatou katargeisei ton to kratos echonta tou thanatou, tout estin ton dyabolon,

יד. וְיַעַן כִּי הַיְלָדִים בָּשָׂר וָדָם מְנָת חֶלְקָם כֵּן גַּם-הוּא לָבַשׁ בָּשָׂר וָדָם כְּמוֹהֶם לְמַעַן יְבַלַּע בְּמוֹתוֹ אֶת-מַלְאַךְ־הַמָּוֶת הוּא הַשָּׂטָן

14. Ve•ya•an ki ha•y`la•dim ba•sar va•dam m`nat chel•kam ken gam - hoo la•vash ba•sar va•dam ke•mo•hem le•ma•an ye•va•la be•mo•to et - mal•ach ha•ma•vet hoo ha•Satan.

Rabbinic Jewish Commentary
...him that had the power of death, that is, the devil;

The apostle here speaks in the language of the Jews, who often call Samael, or Satan, מלאך המות, "the angel of death", in their Targums (k), Talmud (l), and other writings (m); and say, he was the cause of death to all the world; and ascribe much the same things to him, for which the apostle here so styles him: and they moreover say (n), that he will cease in the time to come; that is, in the days of the Messiah: and who being come, has destroyed him, not as to his being, but as to his power; he has bruised his head, destroyed his works, disarmed his principalities and powers, and took the captives out of his hands, and saved those he would have devoured: and this he has done by death; "by his own death", as the Syriac and Arabic versions read; whereby he has abolished death itself, and sin the cause of it, and so Satan, whose empire is supported by it.

(k) Targum Jon. in Gen. iii. 6. & in Hab. iii. 5. (l) T. Bab. Succa, fol. 53. 1. & Avoda Zara, fol. 5. 1. & 20. 2. (m) Zohar in Gen. fol. 27. 1, 2. Tzeror Hammor, fol. 6. 2. & 22. 4. Caphtor, fol 26. 2. & alibi. (n) Baal Hatturim in Numb. iv. 19.

---

15. And deliver them who through fear of death were all their lifetime subject to bondage.

15. καὶ ἀπαλλάξῃ τούτους, ὅσοι φόβῳ θανάτου διὰ παντὸς τοῦ ζῆν ἔνοχοι ἦσαν δουλείας.

15. kai apallaxei toutous, 'osoi phobo thanatou dya pantos tou zein enochoi eisan douleias.

טו. וְשִׁלַּח לַחָפְשִׁי אֶת-אֵלֶּה אֲשֶׁר מֵאֵימַת מָוֶת הָיוּ נִכְבָּשִׁים כָּל-יְמֵי חַיֵּיהֶם כַּעֲבָדִים:

15. Ve•shi•lach la•chof•shi et - ele asher me•ey•mat ma•vet ha•yoo nich•ba•shim kol - ye•mey cha•ye•hem ka•a•va•dim.

Rabbinic Jewish Commentary
The Jews especially were in fear of, from their frequent violations of the precepts, both of the moral, and of the ceremonial law, which threatened with death; and this they lived in a continual fear of, because they were daily transgressing, which brought on them a spirit of bondage unto fear: and, as Philo the Jew (o) observes, nothing more brings the mind into bondage than the fear of death.

(o) Quod omnis Probus Liber, p. 868.

Hebrews 2

16. For verily he took not on him the nature of angels; but he took on him the seed of Abraham.

16. Οὐ γὰρ δήπου ἀγγέλων ἐπιλαμβάνεται, ἀλλὰ σπέρματος Ἀβραὰμ ἐπιλαμβάνεται.

16. Ou gar deipou angelon epilambanetai, alla spermatos Abra'am epilambanetai.

טז. כִּי לֹא לַמַּלְאָכִים נָטָה יָדוֹ לְהוֹשִׁיעָם כִּי אִם-לְזֶרַע אַבְרָהָם הוּא לְמוֹשִׁיעַ:

16. Ki lo la•mal•a•chim na•ta ya•do le•ho•shi•am ki eem - le•ze•ra Avraham hoo le•mo•shia.

17. Wherefore in all things it behoved him to be made like unto his brethren, that he might be a merciful and faithful high priest in things pertaining to God, to make reconciliation for the sins of the people.

17. Ὅθεν ὤφειλεν κατὰ πάντα τοῖς ἀδελφοῖς ὁμοιωθῆναι, ἵνα ἐλεήμων γένηται καὶ πιστὸς ἀρχιερεὺς τὰ πρὸς τὸν θεόν, εἰς τὸ ἱλάσκεσθαι τὰς ἁμαρτίας τοῦ λαοῦ.

17. 'Othen opheilen kata panta tois adelphois 'omoiotheinai, 'ina eleeimon geneitai kai pistos archiereus ta pros ton theon, eis to 'ilaskesthai tas 'amartias tou laou.

יז. וְעַל־כֵּן נִמְשַׁל נִדְמָה לְאֶחָיו בַּכֹּל לְמַעַן יְהִי כֹהֵן גָּדוֹל בְּרַחֲמָיו וּבֶאֱמוּנָתוֹ לִפְנֵי אֱלֹהִים לְכַפֵּר עַל־חַטֹּאת־הָעָם:

17. Ve•al - ken nim•shal nid•ma le•e•chav ba•kol le•ma•an ye•hee cho•hen ga•dol be•ra•cha•mav oo•ve•e•moo•na•to lif•ney Elohim le•cha•per al - cha•tot ha•am.

Rabbinic Jewish Commentary

to make reconciliation for the sins of the people; The allusion seems to be to the two goats on the day of atonement, one of which was to be slain, and the other let go; which were to be, as the Jews say (p), שוין, "alike", in colour, in stature, and in price; and so were the birds to be alike in the same things, that were used at the cleansing of the leper (q): and the Jews tell us (r), that the high priest was to be greater than his brethren, in beauty, in strength, in wisdom, and in riches; all which is true of the Messiah.

(p) Misna Yoma, c. 6. sect. 1. (q) Misna Negaim, c. 14. sect. 5. (r) T. Bab. Horayot, fol. 9. 1. Maimon. Cele Hamikdash, c. 5. sect. 1.

---

18. For in that he himself hath suffered being tempted, he is able to succour them that are tempted.

18. Ἐν ᾧ γὰρ πέπονθεν αὐτὸς πειρασθείς, δύναται τοῖς πειραζομένοις βοηθῆσαι.

18. En 'o gar peponthen autos peiratheis, dunatai tois peirazomenois boeitheisai.

יח. כִּי כַּאֲשֶׁר הָיָה אִישׁ מַכְאֹבוֹת וִידוּעַ מַסָּה בְּנַפְשׁוֹ כֵּן יוּכַל לְהוֹשִׁיעַ בְּחוּנֵי מַסָּה:

18. Ki cha•a•sher ha•ya eesh mach•o•vot viy•doo•a ma•sa be•naf•sho ken yoo•chal le•ho•shi•a be•choo•ney ma•sa.

(Hebrews Chaper 2 End)

Hebrews, Chapter 3

1. Wherefore, holy brethren, partakers of the heavenly calling, consider the Apostle and High Priest of our profession, Christ Jesus;

1. Ὅθεν, ἀδελφοὶ ἅγιοι, κλήσεως ἐπουρανίου μέτοχοι, κατανοήσατε τὸν ἀπόστολον καὶ ἀρχιερέα τῆς ὁμολογίας ἡμῶν Ἰησοῦν χριστόν,

1. 'Othen, adelphoi 'agioi, kleiseos epouraniou metochoi, katanoeisate ton apostolon kai archierea teis 'omologias 'eimon Yeisoun christon,

א. עַל־כֵּן אַחַי אַנְשֵׁי קֹדֶשׁ חֲבֵרִים מַקְשִׁיבִים לִקְרִיאַת מָרוֹם הַבִּיטוּ פְנֵי מַלְאָכוֹ הַכֹּהֵן הַגָּדוֹל אֲשֶׁר לוֹ תִשָּׁבַע:לְשׁוֹנֵנוּ הוּא הַמָּשִׁיחַ יֵשׁוּעַ

1. Al - ken a•chai an•shey ko•desh cha•ve•rim mak•shi•vim lik•ri•at ma•rom ha•bi•too f ney Mal•a•cho ha•Ko•hen ha•Ga•dol asher lo ti•sha•va le•sho•ne•noo hoo ha•Ma•shi•ach Yeshua.

Rabbinic Jewish Commentary
The high priest among the Jews was, on the day of atonement, considered as שליח, "an apostle", or "messenger" (s); for so the elders of the Sanhedrim address him on that day, saying,"Lord high priest, we are the messengers of the Sanhedrim, and thou art שלוחינו, "our apostle", or "messenger", and the messenger of the Sanhedrim."

(s) Misn. Yoma, c. 1. sect. 5.

---

2. Who was faithful to him that appointed him, as also Moses was faithful in all his house.

2. πιστὸν ὄντα τῷ ποιήσαντι αὐτόν, ὡς καὶ Μωϋσῆς ἐν ὅλῳ τῷ οἴκῳ αὐτοῦ.

2. piston onta to poieisanti auton, 'os kai Mouseis en 'olo to oiko autou.

ב. אֲשֶׁר נֶאֱמָן הוּא לְעֹשֵׂהוּ בְּכָל־בֵּיתוֹ כְּמֹשֶׁה:

2. Asher ne•e•man hoo le•o•se•hoo be•chol - bei•to ke•Moshe.

Rabbinic Jewish Commentary
The Torah says of Moses, "He is faithful in all my house."
(Numbers 12:7)

This verse is applied to Messiah,
"The soul of Messiah preceded the world. . . All the acts of devotion of all the world, all the incarnations, refinements and tests, and the revelation of faith – all are through him, as it is written: "He is faithful in all My house" (The Seven Pillars of Faith, R' Yitzhak Breiter, Breslov.org)

The Hebrew word נאמן, in Misnic writings (t), signifies, as it does, one that is trusted, or is fit to be trusted, as Messiah and Moses were; though the former is much more worthy than the latter, as follows.

(t) Misn. Sanhedrin, c. 3. sect. 2.

---

3. For this man was counted worthy of more glory than Moses, inasmuch as he who hath builded the house hath more honour than the house.

3. Πλείονος γὰρ δόξης οὗτος παρὰ Μωϋσῆν ἠξίωται, καθ᾽ ὅσον πλείονα τιμὴν ἔχει τοῦ οἴκου ὁ κατασκευάσας αὐτόν.

3. Pleionos gar doxeis 'outos para Mousein eixiotai, kath 'oson pleiona timein echei tou oikou 'o kataskeuasas auton.

ג. כִּי־יָאֲתָה לוֹ יֶתֶר שְׂאֵת עַל־מֹשֶׁה כַּאֲשֶׁר בֹּנֶה בַיִת רַב כְּבוֹדוֹ מִן־הַבָּיִת:

3. Ki - ya•a•ta lo ye•ter s`et al - Moshe ka•a•sher bo•ne va•yit rav k`vo•do min - ha•ba•yit.

Rabbinic Jewish Commentary
The Midrash Tanchuma says,
"What does it mean, *Who are you O great mountain*? This is King Messiah. And why does he call him *great mountain*? Because he is greater than the Fathers…loftier than Abraham…more elevated than Moses…and higher than the ministering angels…and from whom will he issue? From Zerubbabel…"
(Midrash Tanchuma, Toledot 14, ed. Buber 1:139, cited in the Messiah Texts by Raphael Patai, pg. 41)

The Jews give very great commendations of Moses; they call him a father in the Torah, a father in wisdom, and a father in prophecy (u); and say, that he is the father, master, head, and prince of all the prophets (w); yea, the great prophet expected in the last days, they say, will be but next to Moses, their master (x): they observe, that there were more miracles wrought by, and for him, than were wrought by, and for all the prophets that have been since the world began. (y) The Messiah will be the only prophet greater than Moses who will appear in the last day at the resurrection.

(u) T. Bab. Megilia, fol. 12. 1. (w) Shemot Rabba, sect. 21. fol. 106. 3. Maimon. Yesode Hattorah, c. 7. sect. 6. Obede Cochabim, c. 1. sect. 3. & in Misn Sanhedrin, c. 11. sect. 1. Tzeror Hammor, fol. 18. 3. (x) Maimon. Teshubah, c. 9. sect. 2. (y) Menasseh ben Israel, Conciliat. in Deut. qu. 11.

---

4. For every house is builded by some man; but he that built all things is God.

4. Πᾶς γὰρ οἶκος κατασκευάζεται ὑπό τινος· ὁ δὲ τὰ πάντα κατασκευάσας Θεός.

4. Pas gar oikos kataskeuazetai 'upo tinos. 'o de ta panta kataskeuasas theos.

:ד. כִּי כָל־בַּיִת בָּנוּי בִּידֵי בֹנֶה וּבֹנֶה־כֹל הוּא אֱלֹהִים

4. Ki chol - ba•yit ba•nooi biy•dey vo•ne oo•vo•ne - chol hoo Elohim.

Hebrews 3

5. And Moses verily was faithful in all his house, as a servant, for a testimony of those things which were to be spoken after;

5. Καὶ Μωϋσῆς μὲν πιστὸς ἐν ὅλῳ τῷ οἴκῳ αὐτοῦ ὡς θεράπων, εἰς μαρτύριον τῶν λαληθησομένων·

5. Kai Mouseis men pistos en 'olo to oiko autou 'os therapon, eis marturion ton laleitheisomenon.

:ה. אָמְנָם מֹשֶׁה כְּעֶבֶד נֶאֱמָן הָיָה בְּכָל־בֵּיתוֹ לְעֵדוּת עַל־אֲמָרָיו אֲשֶׁר יֵאָמְרוּן

5. Om•nam Moshe ke•e•ved ne•e•man ha•ya ve•chol - bei•to le•e•doot al - ama•rav asher ye•a•me•roon.

6. But Christ as a son over his own house; whose house are we, if we hold fast the confidence and the rejoicing of the hope firm unto the end.

6. χριστὸς δὲ ὡς υἱὸς ἐπὶ τὸν οἶκον αὐτοῦ· οὗ οἶκός ἐσμεν ἡμεῖς, ἐάνπερ τὴν παρρησίαν καὶ τὸ καύχημα τῆς ἐλπίδος μέχρι τέλους βεβαίαν κατάσχωμεν.

6. christos de 'os 'wios epi ton oikon autou. 'ou oikos esmen 'eimeis, eanper tein parreisian kai to kaucheima teis elpidos mechri telous bebaian kataschomen.

ו. אַךְ הַמָּשִׁיחַ נֶאֱמָן כְּבֵן בְּבֵיתוֹ וּבֵיתוֹ אֲנַחְנוּ אִם רַק נֹאחֵז בְּמִבְטָחֵנוּ וְעֹז תִּקְוָתוֹ עַד-הַקֵּץ:

6. Ach ha•Ma•shi•ach ne•e•man ke•ven be•vey•to oo•vey•to a•nach•noo eem rak no•chez be•miv•ta•che•noo ve•oz tik•va•to ad - ha•ketz.

Rabbinic Jewish Commentary
But Christ as a Son over his own house,.... As Moses was not, though the Jews say that he was מאריה דבית (a) and בעל הבית (b), "lord and master of the house"; yea, and בן בית, "the Son of the house" (c); but this he was not.

(a) Zohar in Lev. fol. 2. 2. (b) Tzeror Hammor, fol. 35. 2. (c) Lexic. Cabalist. p. 203.

---

7. Wherefore (as the Holy Ghost saith, Today if ye will hear his voice,

7. Διό, καθὼς λέγει τὸ πνεῦμα τὸ ἅγιον, Σήμερον ἐὰν τῆς φωνῆς αὐτοῦ ἀκούσητε,

7. Dio, kathos legei to pneuma to 'agion, Seimeron ean teis phoneis autou akouseite,

ז. עַל-כֵּן כְּמוֹ שֶׁנֶּאֱמַר עַל-פִּי רוּחַ הַקֹּדֶשׁ הַיּוֹם אִם-בְּקֹלוֹ תִשְׁמָעוּ:

7. Al - ken k`mo she•ne•e•mar al - pi Roo•ach ha•Ko•desh ha•yom eem - be•ko•lo tish•ma•oo.

Rabbinic Jewish Commentary
These very words are often made use of by the Jews, and applied to the Messiah, showing that if the Jews would repent but one day, or keep the sabbath but one day, the son of David, the Messiah, would come; since it is

said, "*Today if you will hear his voice*" (d); which the Chaldee paraphrase renders מימריה, "his Word", his essential Word, the Lord Yeshua Messiah.

(d) T. Bab. Sanhedrin, fol. 98. 1. Shemot Rabba, sect. 25. fol. 109. 3. & Shirhashirim Rabba, fol. 19. 3.

The Talmud says,

"R' Yehoshua ben Levi met Elijah standing by the entrance of R. Shimon bar Yochai's tomb...and he asked him,"When will the Messiah come?" "Go and ask him himself," Elijah replied. "Where is he sitting?" "At the entrance." (Vilna Gaon: at the gate of Rome) "And by what sign may I recognize him?" "He is sitting among the poor lepers..."
R' Joshua ben Levi found the Messiah, and asked him, "When will you come Master?" "Today," answered the Messiah.
On his returning to Elijah, he asked, "What did he say to you?' "He lied to me", R' Yehoshua said, "he said that he would come today, but he has not." Elijah answered him, "This is what he said to you,
'Today, if you will hear his voice."
(Sanhedrin 98a, Soncino Press Edition)

---

8. Harden not your hearts, as in the provocation, in the day of temptation in the wilderness:

8. μὴ σκληρύνητε τὰς καρδίας ὑμῶν, ὡς ἐν τῷ παραπικρασμῷ, κατὰ τὴν ἡμέραν τοῦ πειρασμοῦ ἐν τῇ ἐρήμῳ,

8. mei skleiruneite tas kardias 'umon, 'os en to parapikrasmo, kata tein 'eimeran tou peirasmou en tei ereimo,

ח. אַל-תַּקְשׁוּ לְבַבְכֶם כִּמְרִיבָה כְּיוֹם מַסָּה בַּמִּדְבָּר:

8. Al - tak•shoo le•vav•chem kim•ri•va ke•yom ma•sa ba•mid•bar.

---

9. When your fathers tempted me, proved me, and saw my works forty years.

9. οὗ ἐπείρασάν με οἱ πατέρες ὑμῶν, ἐδοκίμασάν με, καὶ εἶδον τὰ ἔργα μου τεσσαράκοντα ἔτη.

9. 'ou epeirasan me 'oi pateres 'umon, edokimasan me, kai eidon ta erga mou tessarakonta etei.

ט. אֲשֶׁר נִסּוּנִי אֲבוֹתֵיכֶם בְּחָנוּנִי גַם־רָאוּ פָעֳלִי אַרְבָּעִים שָׁנָה:

9. Asher ni•soo•ni avo•tei•chem be•cha•noo•ni gam - ra•oo fa•a•lai ar•ba•eem sha•na.

Hebrews 3

10. Wherefore I was grieved with that generation, and said, They do always err in their heart; and they have not known my ways.

10. Διὸ προσώχθισα τῇ γενεᾷ ἐκείνῃ, καὶ εἶπον, Ἀεὶ πλανῶνται τῇ καρδίᾳ· αὐτοὶ δὲ οὐκ ἔγνωσαν τὰς ὁδούς μου·

10. Dio prosochthisa tei genea ekeinei, kai eipon, Aei planontai tei kardia. autoi de ouk egnosan tas 'odous mou.

י. לָכֵן אָקוּט בַּדּוֹר הַהוּא וָאֹמַר תָּמִיד תֹּעֵי לֵבָב הֵם וְהֵם לֹא־יָדְעוּ דְרָכָי:

10. La•chen a•koot ba•dor ha•hoo va•o•mar ta•mid to•ey le•vav hem ve•hem lo - yad•oo d`ra•chai.

Rabbinic Jewish Commentary
Wherefore I was grieved with that generation,..... דור המדבר, "the generation of the wilderness", as the Jews often call them; and which they say was more beloved than any generation (e); and yet they will not allow them a part in the world to come;

(e) T. Hieros. Avoda Zara, fol. 39. 2.

---

11. So I sware in my wrath, They shall not enter into my rest.)

11. ὡς ὤμοσα ἐν τῇ ὀργῇ μου, Εἰ εἰσελεύσονται εἰς τὴν κατάπαυσίν μου.

11. 'os omosa en tei orgei mou, Ei eiseleusontai eis tein katapausin mou.

:יא. אֲשֶׁר־נִשְׁבַּעְתִּי בְאַפִּי אִם־יְבֹאוּן אֶל־מְנוּחָתִי

11. Asher - nish•ba•a•ti ve•a•pi eem - ye•vo•oon el - me•noo•cha•ti.

Rabbinic Jewish Commentary
The Jews say (f),
"The generation of the wilderness have no part in the world to come:" but this seems too harsh, for doubtless there were many who died in the wilderness, that went safe to paradise, notwithstanding all their sins and provocations.

(f) Tzeror Hammor, fol. 118. 1.

---

12. Take heed, brethren, lest there be in any of you an evil heart of unbelief, in departing from the living God.

12. Βλέπετε, ἀδελφοί, μήποτε ἔσται ἔν τινι ὑμῶν καρδία πονηρὰ ἀπιστίας ἐν τῷ ἀποστῆναι ἀπὸ θεοῦ ζῶντος·

12. Blepete, adelphoi, meipote estai en tini 'umon kardia poneira apistias en to aposteinai apo theou zontos.

:יב. רְאוּ־נָא אַחַי גַּם־אַתֶּם פֶּן־יֵשׁ בָּכֶם לֵב רַע חֲסַר אֱמוּנָה לָסוּר מֵאַחֲרֵי אֱלֹהִים חַיִּים

12. R`oo - na a•chai gam - atem pen - yesh ba•chem lev ra cha•sar e•moo•na la•soor me•a•cha•rey Elohim cha•yim.

---

13. But exhort one another daily, while it is called To day; lest any of you be hardened through the deceitfulness of sin.

13. ἀλλὰ παρακαλεῖτε ἑαυτοὺς καθ᾽ ἑκάστην ἡμέραν, ἄχρι οὗ τὸ σήμερον καλεῖται, ἵνα μὴ σκληρυνθῇ ἐξ ὑμῶν τις ἀπάτῃ τῆς ἁμαρτίας·

13. alla parakaleite 'eautous kath 'ekastein 'eimeran, achri 'ou to seimeron kaleitai, 'ina mei skleirunthei ex 'umon tis apatei teis 'amartias.

יג. אַךְ הוֹכִיחוּ אִישׁ אֶת־רֵעֵהוּ יוֹם בְּיוֹם כָּל־עוֹד אֲשֶׁר יִקָּרֵא הַיּוֹם לְבִלְתִּי יִקְשֶׁה לֵב אִישׁ מִכֶּם בְּנִכְלֵי חַטָּאתוֹ:

13. Ach ho•chi•choo eesh et - re•e•hoo yom be•yom kol - od asher yi•ka•re Ha•yom le•vil•ti yi•kesh lev eesh mi•kem be•nich•ley cha•ta•to.

Rabbinic Jewish Commentary
Every day, as long as it is called Today (as in Psalm 95). Between 1891 and 1904 the Institutum Delitzschianum in Leipzig, Germany, published a commentary on the New Testament by Yechiel Lichtenstein. So far as I know it is the only commentary on the entire New Testament by a Messianic Jew, apart from this one. It was written in Hebrew, with the Scripture text printed in block letters and the comments in Rashi script, like any rabbinic commentary. In it he points out that the urgency Sha'ul communicates in this verse is echoed by a well-known exhortation found in the Talmud:
"Rabbi 'Eli'ezer said, 'Repent one day before you die.' His *talmidim* objected, 'Does one know in advance the day of one's death?' He replied, 'All the more reason to repent today, lest you die tomorrow! In this way, your entire life will be one of repentance.' " (Shabbat 153a)
(Jewish New Testament Commentary)

Hebrews 3

14. For we are made partakers of Christ, if we hold the beginning of our confidence stedfast unto the end;

14. μέτοχοι γὰρ γεγόναμεν τοῦ χριστοῦ, ἐάνπερ τὴν ἀρχὴν τῆς ὑποστάσεως μέχρι τέλους βεβαίαν κατάσχωμεν·

14. metochoi gar gegonamen tou christou, eanper tein archein teis 'upostaseos mechri telous bebaian kataschomen.

יד. כִּי חֲבֵרִים אֲנַחְנוּ לַמָּשִׁיחַ אִם רַק נֹאחֵז בְּמִבְטָחֵנוּ מֵהָחֵל וְעַד־כַּלֵּה:

14. Ki cha•ve•rim a•nach•noo la•Ma•shich eem rak no•chez be•miv•ta•che•noo me•ha•chel ve•ad - ka•le.

15. While it is said, To day if ye will hear his voice, harden not your hearts, as in the provocation.

15. ἐν τῷ λέγεσθαι, Σήμερον ἐὰν τῆς φωνῆς αὐτοῦ ἀκούσητε, μὴ σκληρύνητε τὰς καρδίας ὑμῶν, ὡς ἐν τῷ παραπικρασμῷ.

15. en to legesthai, Seimeron ean teis phoneis autou akouseite, mei skleiruneite tas kardias 'umon, 'os en to parapikrasmo.

טו: וְכַאֲשֶׁר נֶאֱמַר הַיּוֹם אִם-בְּקֹלוֹ תִשְׁמָעוּ אַל-תַּקְשׁוּ לְבַבְכֶם כִּמְרִיבָה

15. Ve•cha•a•sher ne•e•mar ha•yom eem - be•ko•lo tish•ma•oo al - tak•shoo le•vav•chem kim•ri•va.

Rabbinic Jewish Commentary
(See Hebrews 3:7 for commentary)

---

16. For some, when they had heard, did provoke: howbeit not all that came out of Egypt by Moses.

16. Τινὲς γὰρ ἀκούσαντες παρεπίκραναν, ἀλλ᾽ οὐ πάντες οἱ ἐξελθόντες ἐξ Αἰγύπτου διὰ Μωϋσέως.

16. Tines gar akousantes parepikranan, all ou pantes 'oi exelthontes ex Aiguptou dya Mouseos.

טז: וּמִי הָיוּ הַשֹּׁמְעִים בַּעֲלֵי הַמְּרִיבָה הֲלֹא כָל-הַיֹּצְאִים מִמִּצְרַיִם בְּיַד-מֹשֶׁה

16. Oo•mi ha•yoo ha•shom•eem ba•a•ley ha•me•ri•va ha•lo chol - ha•yotz•eem mi•Mitz•ra•yim be•yad - Moshe.

---

17. But with whom was he grieved forty years? was it not with them that had sinned, whose carcases fell in the wilderness?

17. Τίσιν δὲ προσώχθισεν τεσσαράκοντα ἔτη; Οὐχὶ τοῖς ἁμαρτήσασιν, ὧν τὰ κῶλα ἔπεσεν ἐν τῇ ἐρήμῳ;

17. Tisin de prosochthisen tessarakonta etei? Ouchi tois 'amarteisasin, 'on ta kola epesen en tei ereimo?

יז: וּבְמִי הִתְקוֹטֵט אַרְבָּעִים שָׁנָה הֲלֹא בַחַטָּאִים אֲשֶׁר פִּגְרֵיהֶם נָפְלוּ בַמִּדְבָּר

17. Oov•mi hit•ko•tet ar•ba•eem sha•na ha•lo va•cha•ta•eem asher pig•rey•hem naf•loo va•mid•bar.

Hebrews 3

18. And to whom sware he that they should not enter into his rest, but to them that believed not?

18. Τίσιν δὲ ὤμοσεν μὴ εἰσελεύσεσθαι εἰς τὴν κατάπαυσιν αὐτοῦ, εἰ μὴ τοῖς ἀπειθήσασιν;

18. Tisin de omosen mei eiseleusesthai eis tein katapausin autou, ei mei tois apeitheisasin?

יח. וְעַל־מִי נִשְׁבַּע אִם־יְבֹאוּן אֶל־מְנוּחָתוֹ הֲלֹא עַל־אֵלֶּה אֲשֶׁר לֹא הֶאֱמִינוּ:

18. Ve•al - mee nish•ba eem - ye•vo•oon el - me•noo•cha•to ha•lo al - ele asher lo he•e•mi•noo.

---

19. So we see that they could not enter in because of unbelief.

19. Καὶ βλέπομεν ὅτι οὐκ ἠδυνήθησαν εἰσελθεῖν δι᾽ ἀπιστίαν.

19. Kai blepomen 'oti ouk eiduneitheisan eiselthein di apistian.

יט. וַאֲנַחְנוּ רֹאִים כִּי לֹא יָכְלוּ לָבֹא מִפְּנֵי חֹסֶר אֱמוּנָתָם:

19. Va•a•nach•noo ro•eem ki lo yach•loo la•vo mip•ney cho•ser emoo•na•tam.

(Hebrews Chapter 3 End)

Hebrews, Chapter 4

1. Let us therefore fear, lest, a promise being left us of entering into his rest, any of you should seem to come short of it.

1. Φοβηθῶμεν οὖν μήποτε καταλειπομένης ἐπαγγελίας εἰσελθεῖν εἰς τὴν κατάπαυσιν αὐτοῦ, δοκῇ τις ἐξ ὑμῶν ὑστερηκέναι.

1. Phobeithomen oun meipote kataleipomeneis epangelias eiselthein eis tein katapausin autou, dokei tis ex 'umon 'ustereikenai.

א. עַל-כֵּן בְּהִוָּתֵר לָנוּ הַהַבְטָחָה לָבֹא אֶל-מְנוּחָתוֹ נִדְאַג לְנַפְשֵׁנוּ פֶּן-יֵחָשֵׁב אִישׁ מִכֶּם כִּמְאַחֵר לָבֹא שָׁמָּה:

1. Al - ken be•hi•va•ter la•noo ha•hav•ta•cha la•vo el - me•noo•cha•to nid•ag le•naf•she•noo pen - ye•cha•shev eesh mi•kem kim•a•cher la•vo sha•ma.

---

2. For unto us was the gospel preached, as well as unto them: but the word preached did not profit them, not being mixed with faith in them that heard it.

2. Καὶ γάρ ἐσμεν εὐηγγελισμένοι, καθάπερ κἀκεῖνοι· ἀλλ᾽ οὐκ ὠφέλησεν ὁ λόγος τῆς ἀκοῆς ἐκείνους, μὴ συγκεκραμένους τῇ πίστει τοῖς ἀκούσασιν.

2. Kai gar esmen eueingelismenoi, kathaper kakeinoi. all ouk opheleisen 'o logos teis akoeis ekeinous, mei sugkekramenous tei pistei tois akousasin.

ב. כִּי בְשׂוֹרָה טוֹבָה בָּאָה גַם-אֵלֵינוּ גַם-אֲלֵיהֶם אַךְ הַדָּבָר אֲשֶׁר שָׁמְעוּ הֵם לֹא-הוֹעִיל לָהֶם כִּי לֹא הִתְעָרַב:בֶּאֱמוּנַת לִבָּם

2. Ki ve•so•ra to•va ba•ah gam - e•ley•noo gam - aley•hem ach ha•da•var asher sham•oo hem lo - ho•eel la•hem ki lo hit•a•rav be•e•moo•nat li•bam.

---

3. For we which have believed do enter into rest, as he said, As I have sworn in my wrath, if they shall enter into my rest: although the works were finished from the foundation of the world.

39

3. Εἰσερχόμεθα γὰρ εἰς τὴν κατάπαυσιν οἱ πιστεύσαντες, καθὼς εἴρηκεν, Ὡς ὤμοσα ἐν τῇ ὀργῇ μου, Εἰ εἰσελεύσονται εἰς τὴν κατάπαυσίν μου· καίτοι τῶν ἔργων ἀπὸ καταβολῆς κόσμου γενηθέντων.

3. Eiserchometha gar eis tein katapausin 'oi pisteusantes, kathos eireiken, 'Os omosa en tei orgei mou, Ei eiseleusontai eis tein katapausin mou. kaitoi ton ergon apo kataboleis kosmou geneithenton.

ג. כִּי אֲנַחְנוּ הַמַּאֲמִינִים בָּאִים אֶל-מְנוּחָתוֹ כַּאֲשֶׁר אָמַר אֲשֶׁר-נִשְׁבַּעְתִּי בְאַפִּי אִם-יְבֹאוּן אֶל-מְנוּחָתִי וּמְנוּחָה זוּ:הִיא מִן-הַמְּלָאכָה אֲשֶׁר נֶעֶשְׂתָה בְּהִוָּסֵד אֶרֶץ וְשָׁמָיִם

3. Ki a•nach•noo ha•ma•a•mi•nim ba•eem el - me•noo•cha•to ka•a•sher amar asher - nish•ba•a•ti ve•a•pi eem - ye•vo•oon el - me•noo•cha•ti oom•noo•cha zoo hee min - ha•m`la•cha asher ne•es•ta be•hi•va•sed e•retz ve•sha•ma•yim.

Hebrews 4

4. For he spake in a certain place of the seventh day on this wise, And God did rest the seventh day from all his works.

4. Εἴρηκεν γάρ που περὶ τῆς ἑβδόμης οὕτως, Καὶ κατέπαυσεν ὁ θεὸς ἐν τῇ ἡμέρᾳ τῇ ἑβδόμῃ ἀπὸ πάντων τῶν ἔργων αὐτοῦ·

4. Eireiken gar pou peri teis 'ebdomeis 'outos, Kai katepausen 'o theos en tei 'eimera tei 'ebdomei apo panton ton ergon autou.

ד. כִּי עַל-יוֹם הַשְּׁבִיעִי אֹמֵר בְּמָקוֹם אַחֵר וַיִּשְׁבֹּת אֱלֹהִים בַּיּוֹם הַשְּׁבִיעִי מִכָּל-מְלַאכְתּוֹ:

4. Ki al - yom ha•sh`vi•ee o•mer be•ma•kom a•cher va•yish•bot Elohim ba•yom ha•sh`vi•ee mi•kol - me•lach•to.

Rabbinic Jewish Commentary
"The heavens and the earth were finished, and all their vast array. On the seventh day God finished his work which he had made; and he rested on the seventh day from all his work which he had made. God blessed the seventh day, and made it holy, because he rested in it from all his work which he had created and made."
(Genesis 2:1-3)

5. And in this place again, If they shall enter into my rest.

5. καὶ ἐν τούτῳ πάλιν, Εἰ εἰσελεύσονται εἰς τὴν κατάπαυσίν μου.

5. kai en touto palin, Ei eiseleusontai eis tein katapausin mou.

ה. וּבַמָּקוֹם הַזֶּה יֹאמַר עוֹד אִם-יְבֹאוּן אֶל-מְנוּחָתִי:

5. Oo•va•ma•kom ha•ze yo•mar od eem - ye•vo•oon el - me•noo•cha•ti.

Rabbinic Jewish Commentary
"Oh come, let us worship and bow down. Lets kneel before HaShem, our Maker, for he is our God. We are the people of his pasture, and the sheep in his care. Today, oh that you would hear his voice! Do not harden your heart, as at Meribah, as in the day of Massah in the wilderness, when your fathers tempted me, tested me, and saw my work. Forty long years I was grieved with that generation, and said, It is a people that errs in their heart. They have not known my ways. Therefore I swore in my wrath, They wont enter into my rest."
(Psalms 95:6-11)

---

6. Seeing therefore it remaineth that some must enter therein, and they to whom it was first preached entered not in because of unbelief:

6. Ἐπεὶ οὖν ἀπολείπεται τινὰς εἰσελθεῖν εἰς αὐτήν, καὶ οἱ πρότερον εὐαγγελισθέντες οὐκ εἰσῆλθον δι᾽ ἀπείθειαν,

6. Epei oun apoleipetai tinas eiselthein eis autein, kai 'oi proteron euangelisthentes ouk eiseilthon di apeitheyan,

ו. הַיֹּצֵא לָנוּ מִכָּל-זֶה כִּי יֵשׁ בָּאִים אֶל-הַמְּנוּחָה וְהַשֹּׁמְעִים אֶת-בְּשׂוֹרָה טוֹבָה מֵרֹאשׁ לֹא-בָאוּ מִפְּנֵי חֹסֶר:אֱמוּנָתָם

6. Ha•yo•tze la•noo mi•kol - ze ki yesh ba•eem el - ham•noo•cha ve•ha•shom•eem et - be•so•ra to•va me•rosh lo - va•oo mip•ney cho•ser emoo•na•tam.

---

7. Again, he limiteth a certain day, saying in David, Today, after so long a time; as it is said, Today if ye will hear his voice, harden not your hearts.

41

7. πάλιν τινὰ ὁρίζει ἡμέραν, Σήμερον, ἐν Δαυὶδ λέγων, μετὰ τοσοῦτον χρόνον, καθὼς εἴρηται, Σήμερον ἐὰν τῆς φωνῆς αὐτοῦ ἀκούσητε, μὴ σκληρύνητε τὰς καρδίας ὑμῶν.

7. palin tina 'orizei 'eimeran, Seimeron, en Dauid legon, meta tosouton chronon, kathos eireitai, Seimeron ean teis phoneis autou akouseite, mei skleiruneite tas kardias 'umon.

ז. וּלְקֵץ יָמִים רַבִּים הוֹסִיף וַיָּעַד יוֹם אַחֵר בְּאָמְרוֹ עַל-פִּי דָוִד הַיּוֹם כְּמוֹ שֶׁנֶּאֱמַר הַיּוֹם אִם- בְּקֹלוֹ תִשְׁמָעוּ אַל:תַּקְשׁוּ לְבַבְכֶם -

7. Ool•ketz ya•mim ra•bim ho•sif ve•ya•ad yom a•cher be•om•ro al - pi David ha•yom k`mo she•ne•e•mar ha•yom eem - be•ko•lo tish•ma•oo al - tak•shoo le•vav•chem.

Rabbinic Jewish Commentary
saying in David; or by David, who was the penman of the 95th psalm, as may be learned from hence; and this is agreeably to, and confirms a rule which the Jews give, that those psalms which are without a title were written by David (g); the Spirit of God spake in him and by him, and plainly pointed out another day of rest from the above mentioned

(g) Aben Ezra & Kimchi Praefat. in Tillim.

Hebrews 4

8. For if Jesus had given them rest, then would he not afterward have spoken of another day.

8. Εἰ γὰρ αὐτοὺς Ἰησοῦς κατέπαυσεν, οὐκ ἂν περὶ ἄλλης ἐλάλει μετὰ ταῦτα ἡμέρας.

8. Ei gar autous Yeisous katepausen, ouk an peri alleis elalei meta tauta 'eimeras.

ח. כִּי אִלּוּ הֱבִיאָם יְהוֹשֻׁעַ אֶל-הַמְּנוּחָה הַנְּכוֹנָה לֹא הָיָה מְדַבֵּר אַחֲרֵי-כֵן עַל-יוֹם אַחֵר:

8. Ki ee•loo he•vi•am Yeho•shooa el - ham•noo•cha han•cho•na lo ha•ya me•da•ber a•cha•rey - chen al - yom a•cher.

Rabbinic Jewish Commentary
For if Jesus had given them rest,.... That is, Joshua; for Hosheah, Joshua, and Jesus, are one and the same name; or Jesus himself, as two of

Stephens's copies read; and so Joshua is called Jesus by the Septuagint interpreters on Exo.17:10 and other places where he is mentioned; and also, by Josephus (h), and Philo (i) the Jew. The Syriac version, lest any should mistake this for Jesus Christ, adds, "the son of Nun."

(h) Antiqu. Jud. l. 4. c. 7. sect. 2. c. 8. sect. 46, 47, 48. & l. 5. c. 1. sect. 1. & passim. (i) De Charitate, p. 698, 699, 700.

---

9. There remaineth therefore a rest to the people of God.

9. Ἄρα ἀπολείπεται σαββατισμὸς τῷ λαῷ τοῦ θεοῦ.

9. Ara apoleipetai sabbatismos to lao tou theou.

ט. וְלָכֵן עוֹד נִשְׁאַר יוֹם שַׁבָּתוֹן לְעַם אֱלֹהִים:

9. Ve•la•chen od nish•ar yom sha•ba•ton le•am Elohim.

Rabbinic Jewish Commentary

Shabbat-keeping, Greek *sabbatismos*, used only here in the New Testament. In the Septuagint, the related Greek word "*sabbatizein*" was coined to translate the Hebrew verb *shabat* when it means "to observe *Shabbat*." (Jewish New Testament Commentary)

---

10. For he that is entered into his rest, he also hath ceased from his own works, as God did from his.

10. Ὁ γὰρ εἰσελθὼν εἰς τὴν κατάπαυσιν αὐτοῦ καὶ αὐτὸς κατέπαυσεν ἀπὸ τῶν ἔργων αὐτοῦ, ὥσπερ ἀπὸ τῶν ἰδίων ὁ θεός.

10. 'O gar eiselthon eis tein katapausin autou kai autos katepausen apo ton ergon autou, 'osper apo ton idion 'o theos.

י. כִּי הַבָּא אֶל־מְנוּחָתוֹ יִשְׁבֹּת מִמְּלַאכְתּוֹ כַּאֲשֶׁר גַּם־שָׁבַת אֱלֹהִים מִמְּלַאכְתּוֹ שֶׁלּוֹ:

10. Ki ha•ba el - me•noo•cha•to yish•bot mim•lach•to ka•a•sher gam - sha•vat Elohim mim•lach•to she•lo.

11. Let us labour therefore to enter into that rest, lest any man fall after the same example of unbelief.

11. Σπουδάσωμεν οὖν εἰσελθεῖν εἰς ἐκείνην τὴν κατάπαυσιν, ἵνα μὴ ἐν τῷ αὐτῷ τις ὑποδείγματι πέσῃ τῆς ἀπειθείας.

11. Spoudasomen oun eiselthein eis ekeinein tein katapausin, 'ina mei en to auto tis 'upodeigmati pesei teis apeitheias.

יא. לָכֵן נִתְאַמְּצָה לָבֹא אֶל-הַמְּנוּחָה הַהִיא פֶּן-יִכָּשֵׁל אִישׁ בְּלֶכְתּוֹ בְּעִקְּבוֹת הַמַּמְרִים:

11. La•chen nit•am•tza la•vo el - ham•noo•cha ha•hee pen - yi•ka•shel eesh be•lech•to be•eek•vot ha•mam•rim.

Hebrews 4

12. For the word of God is quick, and powerful, and sharper than any twoedged sword, piercing even to the dividing asunder of soul and spirit, and of the joints and marrow, and is a discerner of the thoughts and intents of the heart.

12. Ζῶν γὰρ ὁ λόγος τοῦ θεοῦ, καὶ ἐνεργής, καὶ τομώτερος ὑπὲρ πᾶσαν μάχαιραν δίστομον, καὶ διϊκνούμενος ἄχρι μερισμοῦ ψυχῆς τε καὶ πνεύματος, ἁρμῶν τε καὶ μυελῶν, καὶ κριτικὸς ἐνθυμήσεων καὶ ἐννοιῶν καρδίας.

12. Zon gar 'o logos tou theou, kai energeis, kai tomoteros 'uper pasan machairan distomon, kai di'iknoumenos achri merismou pucheis te kai pneumatos, 'armon te kai muelon, kai kritikos enthumeiseon kai ennoion kardias.

יב. כִּי-חַי דְּבַר אֱלֹהִים חָזָק וְחַד מִכָּל-חֶרֶב פִּיפִיּוֹת חֹצֵב וּבֹקֵעַ נֶפֶשׁ וָרוּחַ גַּם-מֹחַ וַעֲצָמוֹת וּבֹחֵן מַחְשְׁבוֹת לֵב וְיִצְרוֹ:

12. Ki - chai de•var Elohim cha•zak ve•chad mi•kol - che•rev pi•fi•yot cho•tzev oo•vo•ke•a ne•fesh va•roo•ach gam - mo•ach va•a•tza•mot oo•vo•chen mach•she•vot lev ve•yitz•ro.

Rabbinic Jewish Commentary
Yehovah is called a twoedged sword with the Jews (m); and Philo the Jew speaks of the flaming sword of the Logos (n).

The like property Philo the Jew ascribes to the "Logos", or Word; he calls him τομευς, "a cutter", and says he cuts and divides all things, even all sensible things, yea, atoms, and things indivisible (o); the apostle seems here to have respect to the several names with which the soul of man is called by the Jews, נקש רוח ונשמה, "soul, spirit, and breath" (p); the latter of these, they say, dwells between the other two.

(m) Zohar in Cab. Lex. p. 364. (n) De Cherubim, p. 112. (o) Onis rerum divin. Haeres, p. 499, 500, 510, 511, 513. (p) Zohar in Gen. fol. 55. 2. & 113. 1, 2. & is Exod. fol. 58. 3, 4. & in Lev. fol. 29. 2. T. Hieros. Celaim, fol. 31. 3. Tzeror Hammor, fol. 2. 1.

"And the flaming sword…" (Genesis 3:24)" Rabbis said: 'Sword' refers to the Torah, as it is written, *And a two-edged sword in their hand* (Ps. 149:6). (Genesis Rabbah 21:9, Soncino Press Edition)

13. Neither is there any creature that is not manifest in his sight: but all things are naked and opened unto the eyes of him with whom we have to do.

13. Καὶ οὐκ ἔστιν κτίσις ἀφανὴς ἐνώπιον αὐτοῦ· πάντα δὲ γυμνὰ καὶ τετραχηλισμένα τοῖς ὀφθαλμοῖς αὐτοῦ πρὸς ὃν ἡμῖν ὁ λόγος.

13. Kai ouk estin ktisis aphaneis enopion autou. panta de gumna kai tetracheilismena tois ophthalmois autou pros 'on 'eimin 'o logos.

:יג. וְאֵין יְצוּר נֶעְלָם מִלְּפָנָיו אַךְ הַכֹּל חָשׂוּף וְגָלוּי לְעֵינֵי הַהוּא אֲשֶׁר עָלֵינוּ לָתֵת דִּין לְפָנָיו

13. Ve•eyn ye•tzoor ne•e•lam mil•fa•nav ach ha•kol cha•soof ve•ga•looy le•ei•ney ha•hoo asher aley•noo la•tet din le•fa•nav.

Rabbinic Jewish Commentary
So Philo the Jew says (q) the divine Word reaches to, and comprehends all things, nothing escapes him: and this phrase is very commonly used of the divine Being by the Jews, הכל גלוי לפניו, "all things are manifest before him" (r); and this being used of Messiah , is considerable proof of his proper deity.

(q) De Sacrif. Abel, p. 140. (r) Tzeror Hammor, fol. 122. 2. Vid. Seder Tephillot, fol. 281. 1. Ed. Basil.

14. Seeing then that we have a great high priest, that is passed into the heavens, Jesus the Son of God, let us hold fast our profession.

14. Ἔχοντες οὖν ἀρχιερέα μέγαν, διεληλυθότα τοὺς οὐρανούς, Ἰησοῦν τὸν υἱὸν τοῦ θεοῦ, κρατῶμεν τῆς ὁμολογίας.

14. Echontes oun archierea megan, dieleiluthota tous ouranous, Yeisoun ton 'wion tou theou, kratomen teis 'omologias.

יד. וְעַתָּה בִּהְיוֹת-לָנוּ כֹהֵן גָּדוֹל נַעֲלָה עַד-מְאֹד אֲשֶׁר צָלַח אֶת-הַשָּׁמַיִם יֵשׁוּעַ בֶּן-אֱלֹהִים נִשְׁמְרָה אֶת-הַשְּׁבוּעָה:אֲשֶׁר נִשְׁבַּעְנוּ לוֹ

14. Ve•a•ta bi•hee•yot - la•noo cho•hen ga•dol na•a•le ad - me•od asher tza•lach et - ha•sha•ma•yim Yeshua Ben - Elohim nish•me•ra et - hash•voo•ah asher nish•ba•a•noo lo.

Rabbinic Jewish Commentary
The divine Logos, or Word, is often called a priest, and an high priest, by Philo the Jew (t).

(t) Alleg. 1. 2. p. 76. De Profugis, p. 466. & de Somniis, p. 597.

Avraham Abulafia made the statement,
"The more noble man in his species is Israel…and the most noble of Israel is Levi, and the most noble of Levi is the priest, and the most noble of the priest is the Messiah, who is the high priest, who is the greatest among his breathren, and knows the [divine] name and blesses the people of Israel by dint of the Explicit Name in the Temple…"
(Avraham Abulafia, Sefer Chayyei Olam Haba 13a, Ms. Oxford 1582, cited in Messianic Mystics, Moshe Idel, Yale University Press, pg. 95)

Perhaps this may reveal the seeming convergence of the King in Priest in Zechariah,
"Thus says YHVH of Hosts, Behold, the man whose name is the Branch (A name for the Messiah): and he shall grow up out of his place; and he shall build the temple of YHVH; even he shall build the temple of YHVH; and he shall bear the glory, and shall sit and rule on his throne; and he shall be a priest on his throne; and the counsel of peace shall be between them both. (Zechariah 6:12-13)

15. For we have not an high priest which cannot be touched with the feeling of our infirmities; but was in all points tempted like as we are, yet without sin.

15. Οὐ γὰρ ἔχομεν ἀρχιερέα μὴ δυνάμενον συμπαθῆσαι ταῖς ἀσθενείαις ἡμῶν, πεπειραμένον δὲ κατὰ πάντα καθ᾽ ὁμοιότητα, χωρὶς ἁμαρτίας.

15. Ou gar echomen archierea mei dunamenon sumpatheisai tais astheneiais 'eimon, pepeiramenon de kata panta kath 'omoioteita, choris 'amartias.

טו. כִּי אֵין לָנוּ כֹּהֵן גָּדוֹל אֲשֶׁר לֹא-יוּכַל לָחוּשׁ לְשִׁבְרֵנוּ אַחֲרֵי אֲשֶׁר גַּם-הוּא נִבְחַן בְּמַסּוֹת כָּמוֹנוּ וְחֵטְא לֹא נִמְצָא-בוֹ:

15. Ki eyn la•noo cho•hen ga•dol asher lo - yoo•chal la•choosh le•shiv•re•noo a•cha•rey asher gam - hoo niv•chan be•ma•sot ka•mo•noo ve•chet lo nim•tza - vo.

Hebrews 4

16. Let us therefore come boldly unto the throne of grace, that we may obtain mercy, and find grace to help in time of need.

16. Προσερχώμεθα οὖν μετὰ παρρησίας τῷ θρόνῳ τῆς χάριτος, ἵνα λάβωμεν ἔλεον, καὶ χάριν εὕρωμεν εἰς εὔκαιρον βοήθειαν.

16. Proserchometha oun meta parreisias to throno teis charitos, 'ina labomen eleon, kai charin 'euromen eis eukairon boeitheyan.

טז. עַל-כֵּן נִגְּשָׁה בְפֶה מָלֵא אֶל-כִּסֵּא הָרַחֲמִים לָקַחַת חֶסֶד וְלִמְצֹא חֲנִינָה לַעֲזָר-לָנוּ לְעִתּוֹת בַּצָּרָה:

16. Al - ken nig•sha be•fe ma•le el - ki•se ha•ra•cha•mim la•ka•chat che•sed ve•lim•tzo cha•ni•na la•a•zor - la•noo le•ee•tot ba•tza•ra.

Rabbinic Jewish Commentary

The Jews often speak of כסא הדין, "a throne of judgment", and כסא רחמים, "a throne of mercy" (u); and represent God as sitting upon one or other of these, when he is dispensing justice or mercy (w); and the latter they sometimes call, as here, כסא חסד ורחמים, "a throne of grace and mercy" (x): and so they make the first man Adam to pray to God after this manner (y); "let my prayer come before the throne of thy glory, and let my cry come before כסא רחמיך, "the throne of thy mercy"."

(u) Targum in Psal. xxix. 10. T. Bab. Avoda Zara, fol. 3. 2. Zohar in Gen. fol. 38. 3. & in Numb. fol. 91. 2. & 93. 2. (w) Megillat Esther, fol. 95. 1. (x) Raziel, fol. 32. 1. (y) Ibid. fol. 3. 1.

(Hebrews Chapter 4 End)

Hebrews, Chapter 5

1. For every high priest taken from among men is ordained for men in things pertaining to God, that he may offer both gifts and sacrifices for sins:

1. Πᾶς γὰρ ἀρχιερεύς, ἐξ ἀνθρώπων λαμβανόμενος, ὑπὲρ ἀνθρώπων καθίσταται τὰ πρὸς τὸν θεόν, ἵνα προσφέρῃ δῶρά τε καὶ θυσίας ὑπὲρ ἁμαρτιῶν·

1. Pas gar archiereus, ex anthropon lambanomenos, 'uper anthropon kathistatai ta pros ton theon, 'ina prospherei dora te kai thusias 'uper 'amartion.

א. כִּי כָל-כֹּהֵן גָּדוֹל הַמּוּרָם מִבְּנֵי אָדָם נוֹעַד לַעֲמֹד לִפְנֵי אֱלֹהִים בְּעַד בְּנֵי אָדָם לְהַקְרִיב - מִנְחָה וָזֶבַח עַל:חַטֹּאתָם

1. Ki chol - co•hen ga•dol ha•moo•ram mi•b`ney adam no•ad la•a•mod lif•ney Elohim be•ad b`ney adam le•hak•riv min•cha va•ze•vach al - cha•to•tam.

---

2. Who can have compassion on the ignorant, and on them that are out of the way; for that he himself also is compassed with infirmity.

2. μετριοπαθεῖν δυνάμενος τοῖς ἀγνοοῦσιν καὶ πλανωμένοις, ἐπεὶ καὶ αὐτὸς περίκειται ἀσθένειαν·

2. metriopathein dunamenos tois agnoousin kai planomenois, epei kai autos perikeitai astheneyan.

ב. וְהוּא מוּכָן לְהַרְגִּיעַ רִגְשַׁת נַפְשׁוֹ לְשֹׁגְגִים וּלְתֹעִים כִּי גַם-הוּא אֵין מְתֹם בִּבְשָׂרוֹ מִכַּף-רֶגֶל וְעַד-רֹאשׁ:

2. Ve•hoo moo•chan le•har•gi•a rig•shat naf•sho le•sho•ge•gim ool•to•eem ki gam – hoo eyn me•tom biv•sa•ro mi•kaf - re•gel ve•ad - rosh.

---

3. And by reason hereof he ought, as for the people, so also for himself, to offer for sins.

3. καὶ διὰ ταύτην ὀφείλει, καθὼς περὶ τοῦ λαοῦ, οὕτως καὶ περὶ ἑαυτοῦ, προσφέρειν ὑπὲρ ἁμαρτιῶν.

3. kai dya tautein opheilei, kathos peri tou laou, 'outos kai peri 'eautou, prospherein 'uper 'amartion.

ג. בַּעֲבוּר זֹאת הָיָה עָלָיו לְהַקְרִיב בְּעַד חַטַּאת נַפְשׁוֹ כְּמוֹ בְעַד הָעָם:

3. Ba•a•voor zot ha•ya alav le•hak•riv be•ad cha•tat naf•sho k`mo ve•ad ha•am.

Rabbinic Jewish Commentary
he ought, as for the people, so also for himself to offer for sins; as he offered sacrifice for the sins of the people, so he was obliged to offer for his own sins; in this the Messiah differed from the high priest, for he had no sin of his own to offer for, Heb_7:27 but the high priest had, and therefore offered for them, Lev_16:11 and made a confession of them: the form of which, as used on the day of atonement, was this;

"He put both his hands upon the bullock, and confessed, and thus he said: I beseech thee, O Lord, I have done wickedly, I have transgressed, I have sinned before thee, I and my house; I beseech thee, O Lord, pardon the iniquities, transgressions, and sins, which I have done wickedly, transgressed, and sinned before thee, I and my house."

And this he did a second time on that day (z).

(z) Misna Yoma, c. 3. sect. 8. & c. 4. sect. 2.

---

4. And no man taketh this honour unto himself, but he that is called of God, as was Aaron.

4. Καὶ οὐχ ἑαυτῷ τις λαμβάνει τὴν τιμήν, ἀλλὰ καλούμενος ὑπὸ τοῦ θεοῦ, καθάπερ καὶ Ἀαρών.

4. Kai ouch 'eauto tis lambanei tein timein, alla kaloumenos 'upo tou theou, kathaper kai A'aron.

ד. וְלֹא יִקַּח אִישׁ אֶת-הַכָּבוֹד הַזֶּה לְנַפְשׁוֹ כִּי אִם-אֶת-אֲשֶׁר יִבְחַר-בּוֹ הָאֱלֹהִים כְּאַהֲרֹן:

4. Ve•lo yi•kach eesh et - ha•ka•vod ha•ze le•naf•sho ki eem - et - asher yiv•char – bo ha•Elohim ke•A•haron

Hebrews 5

5. So also Christ glorified not himself to be made an high priest; but he that said unto him, Thou art my Son, to day have I begotten thee.

5. Οὕτως καὶ ὁ χριστὸς οὐχ ἑαυτὸν ἐδόξασεν γενηθῆναι ἀρχιερέα, ἀλλ' ὁ λαλήσας πρὸς αὐτόν, Υἱός μου εἶ σύ, ἐγὼ σήμερον γεγέννηκά σε.

5. 'Outos kai 'o christos ouch 'eauton edoxasen geneitheinai archierea, all 'o laleisas pros auton, 'Wios mou ei su, ego seimeron gegenneika se.

ה. כֵּן גַּם-הַמָּשִׁיחַ לֹא הִתְנַשֵּׂא מִנַּפְשׁוֹ לִהְיוֹת כֹּהֵן גָּדוֹל כִּי אִם-עַל-פִּי הָאֹמֵר אֵלָיו בְּנִי אַתָּה אֲנִי הַיּוֹם יְלִדְתִּיךָ:

5. Ken gam - ha•Ma•shi•ach lo hit•na•se mi•naf•sho li•hee•yot co•hen ga•dol ki eem - al - pi ha•o•mer elav B`ni ata ani ha•yom ye•lid•ti•cha.

Rabbinic Jewish Commentary
(See Hebrew 1:5 for commentary)

---

6. As he saith also in another place, Thou art a priest for ever after the order of Melchisedec.

6. Καθὼς καὶ ἐν ἑτέρῳ λέγει, Σὺ ἱερεὺς εἰς τὸν αἰῶνα κατὰ τὴν τάξιν Μελχισεδέκ.

6. Kathos kai en 'etero legei, Su 'iereus eis ton aiona kata tein taxin Melchisedek.

ו. וְכַאֲשֶׁר אָמַר גַּם-בְּמָקוֹם אַחֵר אַתָּה-כֹהֵן לְעוֹלָם עַל-דִּבְרָתִי מַלְכִּי-צֶדֶק:

6. Ve•cha•a•sher amar gam - be•ma•kom a•cher ata - cho•hen le•o•lam al - div•ra•ti Mal•ki - tze•dek.

Rabbinic Jewish Commentary
thou art a priest for ever, after the order of Melchisedec; that the psalm, from whence these words are taken, belongs to the Messiah; and this very passage is applied unto him by the Jewish writers (c)

(c) Moses Hadarsan apud Galatin. l. 10. c. 6. Abot R. Nathan, c. 34.

Malki-Tzedek (Melchizedek; the Hebrew name means "my king is righteousness") appears first at Gen_14:18 as both priest of *El Elyon* ("Most High God") and king of Shalem, identified with Jerusalem (see Heb_7:1-4 below). But in Judaism, kingship and priesthood were separated. Saul, the son of Kish, was the first king; after him came David, and all kings of Judah since then have been from the House of David (including Yeshua). On the other hand, the priestly line ran from Moses' brother Aaron. Thus at Zec_6:13 there is a reference to two persons; by context these must be King Zerubabbel (of the House of David) and Joshua the *cohen hagadol* (a descendant of Aaron). Yeshua is to be compared with Malki-Tzedek because in Yeshua, Jewish priest and Jewish king are united in one person. So far as is known, the author makes a *chiddush* ("innovation") in presenting the idea of king and priest combined in one person.

Joseph Shulam has shown that among the Dead Sea Scrolls the one-page document known as 1Q Melch is unique in early Jewish literature in presenting a picture of Malki-Tzedek very similar to that of the author of the New Testament book of Messianic Jews (Hebrews). This fact strengthens the contention made by some scholars that the author of Messianic Jews, whoever he was (see Heb_1:1), was familiar with the Qumran Community and its ideas.

(Jewish New Testament Commentary)

---

7. Who in the days of his flesh, when he had offered up prayers and supplications with strong crying and tears unto him that was able to save him from death, and was heard in that he feared;

7. Ὅς ἐν ταῖς ἡμέραις τῆς σαρκὸς αὐτοῦ, δεήσεις τε καὶ ἱκετηρίας πρὸς τὸν δυνάμενον σῴζειν αὐτὸν ἐκ θανάτου μετὰ κραυγῆς ἰσχυρᾶς καὶ δακρύων προσενέγκας, καὶ εἰσακουσθεὶς ἀπὸ τῆς εὐλαβείας,

7. 'Os en tais 'eimerais teis sarkos autou, deeiseis te kai 'iketeirias pros ton dunamenon sozein auton ek thanatou meta kraugeis ischuras kai dakruon prosenegkas, kai eisakoustheis apo teis eulabeias,

ז. אֲשֶׁר בִּימֵי מְגוּרָיו בִּבְשָׂרוֹ הִקְרִיב תְּפִלּוֹת וְתַחֲנוּנִים בְּקוֹל שַׁוְעָתוֹ וְדִמְעָתוֹ לִפְנֵי שַׂגִּיא כֹחַ יְחַלְּצֶנּוּ מִמָּוֶת:וַיֵּעָתֶר-לוֹ עֵקֶב יִרְאָתוֹ

7. Asher bi•mey me•goo•rav biv•sa•ro hik•riv te•fi•lot ve•ta•cha•noo•nim be•kol shav•a•to ve•dim•a•to lif•ney sa•gi cho•ach ye•chal•tze•noo mi•ma•vet va•ye•a•ter – lo e•kev yir•a•to.

Rabbinic Jewish Commentary

The word for "supplications" signifies branches of olive trees, covered with wool (d); which such as sued for peace carried in their hands, and so came to signify supplications for peace. The manner in which these were offered up by the Messiah.

It may be observed to our comfort, that as Messiah's crying and tears were confined to the days of his flesh, or to the time of his life here on earth, so shall ours be also. Mention is made of תפלות חזקות, "strong prayers" (e), in Jewish writings.

(d) Harpocration. Lex. p. 152. Alex. ab Alex. Genial. Dier. sect. 5. c. 3. (e) Tzeror Hammor, fol. 37. 4.

---

8. Though he were a Son, yet learned he obedience by the things which he suffered;

8. καίπερ ὢν υἱός, ἔμαθεν ἀφ᾽ ὧν ἔπαθεν τὴν ὑπακοήν,

8. kaiper on 'wios, emathen aph 'on epathen tein 'upakoein,

ח. וְאַף בִּהְיוֹתוֹ בֵן לָמַד בְּסִבְלוֹתָיו לִשְׁמֹעַ בְּקוֹל מְצַוֶּה:

8. Ve•af bi•hee•yo•to ven loo•mad be•siv•lo•tav lish•mo•a be•kol me•tza•ve.

Hebrews 5

9. And being made perfect, he became the author of eternal salvation unto all them that obey him;

9. καὶ τελειωθεὶς ἐγένετο τοῖς ὑπακούουσιν αὐτῷ πᾶσιν αἴτιος σωτηρίας αἰωνίου·

9. kai teleiotheis egeneto tois 'upakouousin auto pasin aitios soteirias aioniou.

ט. וּבְהִמָּצְאוֹ שָׁלֵם הָיָה לְכָל-שֹׁמְעָיו לִמְקוֹר תְּשׁוּעַת עוֹלָמִים:

9. Oov•hi•matz•oh sha•lem ha•ya le•chol - shom•av lim•kor te•shoo•at o•la•mim.

10. Called of God an high priest after the order of Melchisedec.

10. προσαγορευθεὶς ὑπὸ τοῦ θεοῦ ἀρχιερεὺς κατὰ τὴν τάξιν Μελχισεδέκ.

10. prosagoreutheis 'upo tou theou archiereus kata tein taxin Melchisedek.

י. וּפִי אֱלֹהִים יְקָבְנוּ כֹּהֵן גָּדוֹל עַל־דִּבְרָתִי מַלְכִּי־צֶדֶק:

10. Oo•fee Elohim yi•ko•ve•noo co•hen ga•dol al - div•ra•ti Mal•ki - tze•dek.

---

11. Of whom we have many things to say, and hard to be uttered, seeing ye are dull of hearing.

11. Περὶ οὗ πολὺς ἡμῖν ὁ λόγος καὶ δυσερμήνευτος λέγειν, ἐπεὶ νωθροὶ γεγόνατε ταῖς ἀκοαῖς.

11. Peri 'ou polus 'eimin 'o logos kai dusermeineutos legein, epei nothroi gegonate tais akoais.

יא. עַל־זֶה יֶשׁ־לָנוּ הַרְבֵּה לְדַבֵּר וְדַי־בְאֵר כָּבֵד מִמֶּנּוּ בִּהְיוֹתְכֶם עַרְלֵי־אֹזֶן:

11. Al - ze yesh - la•noo har•be le•da•ber ve•dey - va•er ka•ved mi•me•noo bi•hi•yot•chem ar•ley - o•zen.

---

12. For when for the time ye ought to be teachers, ye have need that one teach you again which be the first principles of the oracles of God; and are become such as have need of milk, and not of strong meat.

12. Καὶ γὰρ ὀφείλοντες εἶναι διδάσκαλοι διὰ τὸν χρόνον, πάλιν χρείαν ἔχετε τοῦ διδάσκειν ὑμᾶς, τίνα τὰ στοιχεῖα τῆς ἀρχῆς τῶν λογίων τοῦ θεοῦ· καὶ γεγόνατε χρείαν ἔχοντες γάλακτος, καὶ οὐ στερεᾶς τροφῆς.

12. Kai gar opheilontes einai didaskaloi dya ton chronon, palin chreian echete tou didaskein 'umas, tina ta stoicheia teis archeis ton logion tou theou. kai gegonate chreian echontes galaktos, kai ou stereas tropheis.

יב. כִּי תַחַת אֲשֶׁר הָיָה עֲלֵיכֶם לִהְיוֹת מוֹרִים בְּרֹב הַיָּמִים נָחוּץ הַדָּבָר עַתָּה לָשׁוּב לְחַוּׂת דַּעַת לָכֶם מָה הֵמָּה: אַבְנֵי פִנָּה בְּתוֹרַת אֱלֹהִים וּנְכֹנִים אַתֶּם לְחָלָב וְלֹא לְלֶחֶם שָׁמֵן

12. Ki ta•chat asher ha•ya aley•chem li•hee•yot mo•rim be•rov ha•ya•mim na•chootz ha•da•var ata la•shoov le•cha•vot da•at la•chem ma he•ma av•ney fi•na be•to•rat Elohim oo•n`cho•nim atem le•cha•lav ve•lo le•le•chem sha•men.

---

13. For every one that useth milk is unskillful in the word of righteousness: for he is a babe.

13. Πᾶς γὰρ ὁ μετέχων γάλακτος ἄπειρος λόγου δικαιοσύνης· νήπιος γάρ ἐστιν.

13. Pas gar 'o metechon galaktos apeiros logou dikaiosuneis. neipios gar estin.

:יג. כִּי כָל־מִי אֲשֶׁר חָלָב מְזוֹנוֹ אֵין לוֹ דֵעָה בְּדִבְרֵי צֶדֶק כִּי עוֹלֵל הוּא

13. Ki chol - mee asher cha•lav me•zo•no eyn lo de•ah ve•div•rey tze•dek ki o•lel hoo.

Hebrews 5

14. But strong meat belongeth to them that are of full age, even those who by reason of use have their senses exercised to discern both good and evil.

14. Τελείων δέ ἐστιν ἡ στερεὰ τροφή, τῶν διὰ τὴν ἕξιν τὰ αἰσθητήρια γεγυμνασμένα ἐχόντων πρὸς διάκρισιν καλοῦ τε καὶ κακοῦ.

14. Teleion de estin 'ei sterea trophei, ton dya tein 'exin ta aistheiteirya gegumnasmena echonton pros dyakrisin kalou te kai kakou.

:יד. וְלֶחֶם שָׁמֵן לִשְׁלֵמִים אֲשֶׁר הַסְכֵּן הִסְכִּינוּ בִּבְחִינַת לִבּוֹתָם לְהַבְדִּיל בֵּין־טוֹב לָרָע

14. Ve•le•chem sha•men lish•le•mim asher has•ken his•ki•noo biv•chi•nat li•bo•tam le•hav•dil bein - tov la•ra.

(Hebrews Chapter 5 End)

Hebrews, Chapter 6

1. Therefore leaving the principles of the doctrine of Christ, let us go on unto perfection; not laying again the foundation of repentance from dead works, and of faith toward God,

1. Διό, ἀφέντες τὸν τῆς ἀρχῆς τοῦ χριστοῦ λόγον, ἐπὶ τὴν τελειότητα φερώμεθα, μὴ πάλιν θεμέλιον καταβαλλόμενοι μετανοίας ἀπὸ νεκρῶν ἔργων, καὶ πίστεως ἐπὶ θεόν,

1. Dio, aphentes ton teis archeis tou christou logon, epi tein teleioteita pherometha, mei palin themelion kataballomenoi metanoias apo nekron ergon, kai pisteos epi theon,

א. עַל-כֵּן נֶרֶף כָּעֵת מֵאַבְנֵי פִנָּה בְּתוֹרַת הַמָּשִׁיחַ וְנַעֲלֶה עַד-תַּכְלִיתָהּ וְלֹא נָשׁוּב לִירוֹת אֶת-הַיְסוֹד לִתְשׁוּבָה:מִן-מַעֲשִׂים אֲשֶׁר מָוֶת בָּם אוֹ אֱמוּנַת אֱלֹהִים

1. Al - ken ne•ref ka•et me•av•ney fi•na be•to•rat ha•Ma•shi•ach ve•na•a•le ad - tach•li•ta ve•lo na•shoov li•rot et - ha•y`sod lit•shoo•va min - ma•a•sim asher ma•vet bam oh emoo•nat Elohim.

Rabbinic Jewish Commentary

The Jews were taught the doctrine of repentance, as well as remission of sin; and in and over them did they confess their iniquities; yea, every beast that was slain for sacrifice carried in it a conviction of sin, an acknowledgment of guilt; and it was tacitly owning, that they, for whom the creature was slain, deserved to be treated as that was, and die as that did. So the Jews (f) say,

"When a man sacrifices a beast, he thinks in his own heart, I am rather a beast than this; for I am he that hath sinned, and for the sin which I have committed I bring this; and it is more fitting that the man should be sacrificed rather than the beast; and so it appears that, על ידי קרבנו הוא יחרט, "by the means of his offering he repents"."

(f) Nizzachon Vet. p. 11. Ed. Wagenseil.

---

2. Of the doctrine of baptisms, and of laying on of hands, and of resurrection of the dead, and of eternal judgment.

2. βαπτισμῶν διδαχῆς, ἐπιθέσεώς τε χειρῶν, ἀναστάσεώς τε νεκρῶν, καὶ κρίματος αἰωνίου.

2. baptismon didacheis, epitheseos te cheiron, anastaseos te nekron, kai krimatos aioniou.

ב. אוֹ דִין הַטְבִילוֹת וּסְמִיכַת יָדַיִם וּתְקוּמַת הַמֵּתִים וּמִשְׁפַּט עוֹלָם:

2. Oh din hat•vi•lot oos•mi•chat ya•da•yim oot•koo•mat ha•me•tim oo•mish•pat o•lam.

Rabbinic Jewish Commentary

It was usual with the Jews (g) to call the imposition of hands upon the sacrifice, simply, סמיכה, "laying on of hands"; and they understood by it the transferring of sin from the persons that laid on hands, to the sacrifice, on which they were laid; and that hereby, as they express it, sins were separated from them, and, as it were, put upon the sacrifice (h)

(g) Misn. Kiddushin, c. 2. sect. 8. & Bartenora in ib. (h) R. Levi ben Gersom in Exod. fol. 109. 1. & in Lev. fol. 117. 2.

These were the 4 major teachings of the religious Jews, namely baptism, laying on hands, referring to sacrifice and offering, the resurrection of the dead and eternal judgment that follows.

---

3. And this will we do, if God permit.

3. Καὶ τοῦτο ποιήσωμεν, ἐάνπερ ἐπιτρέπῃ ὁ θεός.

3. Kai touto poieisomen, eanper epitrepei 'o theos.

ג. וַאֲנַחְנוּ נַעֲשֶׂה זֹאת בִּרְצוֹת הָאֵל:

3. Va•a•nach•noo na•a•se zot bir•tzot ha•El.

---

4. For it is impossible for those who were once enlightened, and have tasted of the heavenly gift, and were made partakers of the Holy Ghost,

4. Ἀδύνατον γὰρ τοὺς ἅπαξ φωτισθέντας, γευσαμένους τε τῆς δωρεᾶς τῆς ἐπουρανίου, καὶ μετόχους γενηθέντας πνεύματος ἁγίου,

4. Adunaton gar tous 'apax photisthentas, geusamenous te teis doreas teis epouraniou, kai metochous geneithentas pneumatos 'agiou,

ד. כִּי אֵלֶּה אֲשֶׁר כְּבָר אֹרוּ עֵינֵיהֶם וַיִּטְעֲמוּ אֶת־מַתַּת שָׁמַיִם וְרוּחַ הַקֹּדֶשׁ הָיְתָה לִמְנָת חֶלְקָם:

4. Ki ele asher k`var o•roo ey•ne•hem va•yit•a•moo et - ma•tat sha•ma•yim ve•Roo•ach ha•Ko•desh hai•ta lim•nat chel•kam.

Rabbinic Jewish commentary
For it is impossible for those who were once enlightened,.... The Syriac and Ethiopic versions render it, "baptized"; and the word is thought to be so used in Heb_10:32. And indeed baptism was called very early "illumination" by the ancients, as by Justin Martyr (i), and Clemens Alexandrinus (k), because only enlightened persons were the proper subjects of it;

(i) Apolog. 2. p. 94. (k) Paedagog. l. 1. c. 6. p. 93.

---

5. And have tasted the good word of God, and the powers of the world to come,

5. καὶ καλὸν γευσαμένους θεοῦ ῥῆμα, δυνάμεις τε μέλλοντος αἰῶνος,

5. kai kalon geusamenous theou 'reima, dunameis te mellontos aionos,

ה. וַיִּטְעֲמוּ אֶת־דְּבַר אֱלֹהִים הַטּוֹב וְאֶת־נִפְלְאוֹת הָעוֹלָם הֶעָתִיד:

5. Va•yit•a•moo et - de•var Elohim ha•tov ve•et - nif•le•ot ha•o•lam he•a•tid.

Hebrews 6

6. If they shall fall away, to renew them again unto repentance; seeing they crucify to themselves the Son of God afresh, and put him to an open shame.

6. καὶ παραπεσόντας, πάλιν ἀνακαινίζειν εἰς μετάνοιαν, ἀνασταυροῦντας ἑαυτοῖς τὸν υἱὸν τοῦ θεοῦ καὶ παραδειγματίζοντας.

6. kai parapesontas, palin anakainizein eis metanoyan, anastaurountas 'eautois ton 'wion tou theou kai paradeigmatizontas.

ו. וְאַחֲרֵי-כֵן סָרְרוּ לֹא יִתָּכֵן לָהֶם עוֹד לְהִתְחַדֵּשׁ וְלָשׁוּב כִּי הִצְלִיבוּ לָהֶם מֵחָדָשׁ אֶת-בֶּן-הָאֱלֹהִים וַיְשִׂימוּ אוֹתוֹ:לְחֶרְפָּה

6. Ve•a•cha•rey - chen so•ra•roo lo yi•ta•chen la•hem od le•hit•cha•desh ve•la•shoov ki hitz•li•voo la•hem me•cha•dash et - Ben - ha•Elohim va•ya•si•moo o•to le•cher•pa.

Rabbinic Jewish Commentary

The Jews (l) speak of repentance being withheld by God from Pharaoh, and, from the people of Israel; of which they understand Exo_9:16 and say, that when the holy blessed God withholds repentance from a sinner, אינו יכול לשוב, "he cannot repent"; but must die in his wickedness which he first committed of his own will; and they further observe (m), that he that profanes the name of God has it not in his power to depend on repentance, nor can his iniquity be expiated on the day of atonement, or be removed by chastisement.

The Syriac version connects this clause with the word "impossible", as well as a foregoing one, rendering it, "it is impossible to crucify the Son of God again, and to put him to shame"; and so the Arabic version.

(l) Maimon. Hilchot. Teshuba, c. 6. sect. 3. (m) Vid. R. David Kimchi in Isa. xxii. 14.

---

7. For the earth which drinketh in the rain that cometh oft upon it, and bringeth forth herbs meet for them by whom it is dressed, receiveth blessing from God:

7. Γῆ γὰρ ἡ πιοῦσα τὸν ἐπ᾽ αὐτῆς πολλάκις ἐρχόμενον ὑετόν, καὶ τίκτουσα βοτάνην εὔθετον ἐκείνοις δι᾽ οὓς καὶ γεωργεῖται, μεταλαμβάνει εὐλογίας ἀπὸ τοῦ θεοῦ·

7. Gei gar 'ei piousa ton ep auteis pollakis erchomenon 'ueton, kai tiktousa botanein eutheton ekeinois di 'ous kai georgeitai, metalambanei eulogias apo tou theou.

ז. כִּי הָאָרֶץ הַשֹׁתָה אֶת-הַגֶּשֶׁם אֲשֶׁר הִרְוָה אֹתָהּ כְּפַעַם בְּפַעַם וְתֵלֵד זֶרַע טוֹב לַזֹּרֵעַ תִּשָּׂא בְּרָכָה מֵאֵת:הָאֱלֹהִים

7. Ki ha•a•retz ha•sho•ta et - ha•ge•shem asher hir•va o•ta ke•fa•am be•fa•am ve•te•led ze•ra tov la•zo•rea ti•sa v`ra•cha me•et ha•Elohim.

---

8. But that which beareth thorns and briers is rejected, and is nigh unto cursing; whose end is to be burned.

8. ἐκφέρουσα δὲ ἀκάνθας καὶ τριβόλους, ἀδόκιμος καὶ κατάρας ἐγγύς, ἧς τὸ τέλος εἰς καῦσιν.

8. ekpherousa de akanthas kai tribolous, adokimos kai kataras engus, 'eis to telos eis kausin.

ח. וְכִי-תַצְמִיחַ קוֹץ וְדַרְדַּר אֵין חֵפֶץ בָּהּ צְפוּיָה הִיא אֱלֵי-מְאֵרָה וְאַחֲרִיתָהּ לְבָעֵר:

8. Ve•chi - tatz•mi•ach kotz ve•dar•dar eyn che•fetz ba tze•foo•ya hee eley - me•e•ra ve•a•cha•ri•ta le•va•er.

---

9. But, beloved, we are persuaded better things of you, and things that accompany salvation, though we thus speak.

9. Πεπείσμεθα δὲ περὶ ὑμῶν, ἀγαπητοί, τὰ κρείσσονα καὶ ἐχόμενα σωτηρίας, εἰ καὶ οὕτως λαλοῦμεν·

9. Pepeismetha de peri 'umon, agapeitoi, ta kreissona kai echomena soteirias, ei kai 'outos laloumen.

ט. אָמֵן הוֹחַלְנוּ יְדִידִים כִּי דְבָרִים טוֹבִים מֵאֵלֶּה נִמְצָאִים בָּכֶם דְּבָרִים צְפוּיִם אֱלֵי-יְשׁוּעָה אַף כִּי-כָזֹאת דִּבַּרְנוּ:

9. Amen ho•chal•noo ye•di•dim ki d`va•rim to•vim me•e•le nim•tza•eem ba•chem d`va•rim tze•foo•yim eley - ye•shoo•ah af ki - cha•zot di•bar•noo.

Hebrews 6

10. For God is not unrighteous to forget your work and labour of love, which ye have shewed toward his name, in that ye have ministered to the saints, and do minister.

10. οὐ γὰρ ἄδικος ὁ θεὸς ἐπιλαθέσθαι τοῦ ἔργου ὑμῶν, καὶ τοῦ κόπου τῆς ἀγάπης ἧς ἐνεδείξασθε εἰς τὸ ὄνομα αὐτοῦ, διακονήσαντες τοῖς ἁγίοις καὶ διακονοῦντες.

10. ou gar adikos 'o theos epilathesthai tou ergou 'umon, kai tou kopou teis agapeis 'eis enedeixasthe eis to onoma autou, dyakoneisantes tois 'agiois kai dyakonountes.

י. כִּי לֹא יְעַוֵּל הָאֱלֹהִים וְלֹא יִשְׁכַּח אֶת־מַעֲשֵׂיכֶם וְאֶת־הָאַהֲבָה אֲשֶׁר הֶרְאֵיתֶם לִשְׁמוֹ סֹמְכִים הֱיִיתֶם לִקְדֹשָׁיו:וְעוֹדְכֶם כֵּן גַּם־הַיּוֹם

10. Ki lo ye•a•vel ha•Elohim ve•lo yish•kach et - ma•a•sey•chem ve•et - ha•a•ha•va asher her•ey•tem lish•mo som•chim he•yi•tem lik•do•shav ve•od•chem ken gam - ha•yom.

---

11. And we desire that every one of you do shew the same diligence to the full assurance of hope unto the end:

11. Ἐπιθυμοῦμεν δὲ ἕκαστον ὑμῶν τὴν αὐτὴν ἐνδείκνυσθαι σπουδὴν πρὸς τὴν πληροφορίαν τῆς ἐλπίδος ἄχρι τέλους·

11. Epithumoumen de 'ekaston 'umon tein autein endeiknusthai spoudein pros tein pleirophorian teis elpidos achri telous.

יא. וְחֶפְצֵנוּ כִּי אִישׁ אִישׁ מִכֶּם יוֹדַע מִמְּגַמַּת עֲמָלוֹ כִּי תִקְוָתוֹ נֶאֱמָנָה עַד־הַקֵּץ:

11. Ve•chef•tze•noo ki eesh eesh mi•kem yi•va•da mim•ga•mat ama•lo ki tik•va•to ne•e•ma•na ad - ha•ketz.

---

12. That ye be not slothful, but followers of them who through faith and patience inherit the promises.

12. ἵνα μὴ νωθροὶ γένησθε, μιμηταὶ δὲ τῶν διὰ πίστεως καὶ μακροθυμίας κληρονομούντων τὰς ἐπαγγελίας.

12. 'ina mei nothroi geneisthe, mimeitai de ton dya pisteos kai makrothumias kleironomounton tas epangelias.

יב. וְלֹא תִהְיוּ עֲצֵלִים כִּי אִם־תֵּלְכוּן בְּעִקְבוֹת אֵלֶּה אֲשֶׁר בֶּאֱמוּנָתָם וְאֶרֶךְ רוּחָם יָרְשׁוּ אֶת־הַהַבְטָחוֹת:

12. Ve•lo ti•hi•yoo a•tze•lim ki eem - tel•choon be•eek•vot ele asher be•e•moo•na•tam ve•o•rech roo•cham yar•shoo et - ha•hav•ta•chot.

---

13. For when God made promise to Abraham, because he could swear by no greater, he sware by himself,

13. Τῷ γὰρ Ἀβραὰμ ἐπαγγειλάμενος ὁ θεός, ἐπεὶ κατ᾽ οὐδενὸς εἶχεν μείζονος ὀμόσαι, ὤμοσεν καθ᾽ ἑαυτοῦ,

13. To gar Abra'am epangeilamenos 'o theos, epei kat oudenos eichen meizonos omosai, omosen kath 'eautou,

יג. כִּי כַּאֲשֶׁר הִבְטִיחַ אֱלֹהִים אֶת-אַבְרָהָם וְאֵין גָּדוֹל מִמֶּנּוּ לְהִשָּׁבַע בּוֹ נִשְׁבַּע בְּנַפְשׁוֹ:

13. Ki cha•a•sher hiv•ti•ach Elohim et - Avraham ve•eyn ga•dol mi•me•noo le•hi•sha•va bo nish•ba be•naf•sho.

Rabbinic Jewish Commentary

The note of Philo the Jew (n) on the passage in Gen.22:16 from whence the following words are cited, is worthy of observation, being very near the apostle's words;

"Well does he (God) confirm the promise with an oath, and with an oath that becomes God; for you see that God does not swear by another, for nothing is better than himself, but by himself, who is the best of all; but some have suggested as if it was inconvenient to swear, for an oath is taken for the sake of faith; but God alone is faithful."

(n) Leg. Allegor. l. 2. p. 98.

Hebrews 6

14. Saying, Surely blessing I will bless thee, and multiplying I will multiply thee.

14. λέγων, Ἦ μὴν εὐλογῶν εὐλογήσω σε, καὶ πληθύνων πληθυνῶ σε.

14. legon, Ei mein eulogon eulogeiso se, kai pleithunon pleithuno se.

יד. וַיֹּאמֶר כִּי-בָרֵךְ אֲבָרֶכְךָ וְהַרְבָּה אַרְבֶּה אוֹתָךְ:

14. Va•yo•mar ki - va•rech ava•rech•cha ve•har•ba ar•be o•tach.

---

15. And so, after he had patiently endured, he obtained the promise.

15. Καὶ οὕτως μακροθυμήσας ἐπέτυχεν τῆς ἐπαγγελίας.

15. Kai 'outos makrothumeisas epetuchen teis epangelias.

טו. וּבְכֵן הוֹחִיל בְּאֹרֶךְ רוּחוֹ וַיִּנְחַל אֶת-הַהַבְטָחָה:

15. Oov•chen ho•chil be•o•rech roo•cho va•yin•chal et - ha•hav•ta•cha.

---

16. For men verily swear by the greater: and an oath for confirmation is to them an end of all strife.

16. Ἄνθρωποι μὲν γὰρ κατὰ τοῦ μείζονος ὀμνύουσιν, καὶ πάσης αὐτοῖς ἀντιλογίας πέρας εἰς βεβαίωσιν ὁ ὅρκος.

16. Anthropoi men gar kata tou meizonos omnuousin, kai paseis autois antilogias peras eis bebaiosin 'o 'orkos.

טז. כִּי אָמְנָם אֲנָשִׁים נִשְׁבָּעִים בְּגָדוֹל מֵהֶם וְתֹקֶף הַשְּׁבוּעָה יָבִיא קֵץ לְכָל-רִיב בֵּינֵיהֶם:

16. Ki om•nam a•na•shim nish•ba•eem be•ga•dol me•hem ve•to•kef hash•voo•ah ya•vi ketz le•chol - riv bey•ne•hem.

Rabbinic Jewish Commentary
and an oath for confirmation is to them an end of all strife; it is used to confirm things that are doubtful, and in dispute; and to put an end to strife and contention; so Philo (o) the Jew says,
"By an oath things doubtful are determined, and things uncertain are confirmed, and what were not believed receive credit."

The manner in which an oath was taken among the Jews, to which, the apostle writing to such, must be thought to have respect, was this; "he that swore took the book of the law in his hand, and he stood and swore by the name (of God), or by his surnames; and the judges did not suffer anyone to swear but in the holy tongue; and thus he said, behold I swear by the God of Israel, by him whose name is merciful and gracious, that I do not owe this man anything (p)."

The Hebrew word שבעה, used for an oath, is of the root שבע, which signifies to "fill, satiate, satisfy": for an oath being taken about matters in controversy, not clear but doubtful give content unto and satisfy the minds of men; and the same word also signifies "seven", a number of fulness and perfection; an oath being for the perfecting and finishing an affair in debate; agreeably, when covenants were made by oaths, seven witnesses were used, Gen_21:28 and Herodotus says (q) as Cocceius (r) observes, that the Arabians, when they swore at making covenants, anointed the stones with blood.

(o) De Somniis, p. 567. (p) Moses Kotsensis Mitzvot Torah, pr. Affirm. 123. (q) Thalia, l. 3. c. 8. (r) Lexic. Rad. שבע col. 848.

---

17. Wherein God, willing more abundantly to shew unto the heirs of promise the immutability of his counsel, confirmed it by an oath:

17. Ἐν ᾧ περισσότερον βουλόμενος ὁ Θεὸς ἐπιδεῖξαι τοῖς κληρονόμοις τῆς ἐπαγγελίας τὸ ἀμετάθετον τῆς βουλῆς αὐτοῦ, ἐμεσίτευσεν ὅρκῳ,

17. En 'o perissoteron boulomenos 'o theos epideixai tois kleironomois teis epangelias to ametatheton teis bouleis autou, emesiteusen 'orko,

יז. וְכֵן כַּאֲשֶׁר חָפֵץ הָאֱלֹהִים בְּכָל-תֹּקֶף לְהַרְאוֹת אֶת-יוֹרְשֵׁי הַהַבְטָחָה כִּי עֲצָתוֹ אֵין לְהָשִׁיב עָרַב לִפְנֵיהֶם בִּשְׁבוּעָתוֹ:

17. Ve•chen ka•a•sher cha•fetz ha•Elohim be•chol - to•kef le•har•ot et - yor•shey ha•hav•ta•cha ki a•tza•to eyn le•ha•shiv arav lif•ney•hem bish•voo•a•to.

---

18. That by two immutable things, in which it was impossible for God to lie, we might have a strong consolation, who have fled for refuge to lay hold upon the hope set before us:

18. ἵνα διὰ δύο πραγμάτων ἀμεταθέτων, ἐν οἷς ἀδύνατον ψεύσασθαι Θεόν, ἰσχυρὰν παράκλησιν ἔχωμεν οἱ καταφυγόντες κρατῆσαι τῆς προκειμένης ἐλπίδος·

18. 'ina dya duo pragmaton ametatheton, en 'ois adunaton pseusasthai theon, ischuran parakleisin echomen 'oi kataphugontes krateisai teis prokeimeneis elpidos.

יח. וּבִשְׁתֵּי אֲמָרוֹת אֵלֶּה אֲשֶׁר אֵין חֲלִיפוֹת לָהֶן מִבִּלְתִּי יְכֹלֶת הָאֱלֹהִים לְכַזֵּב נִמְצָא לָנוּ נֹחַם-עֹז הַמְמַלְּטִים:אֶת-נַפְשֵׁנוּ לְהַחֲזִיק בַּתִּקְוָה הָעֲרוּכָה לְפָנֵינוּ

18. Oo•vish•tey ama•rot ele asher eyn cha•li•fot la•hen mi•bil•ti ye•cho•let ha•Elohim le•cha•zev nim•tza la•noo no•cham - oz ha•me•mal•tim et - naf•she•noo le•ha•cha•zik ba•tik•va ha•a•roo•cha le•fa•ney•noo.

Rabbinic Jewish Commentary
Philo the Jew (u) makes the divine Word, or Logos, to be the chief and most profitable refuge to fly unto, of all the six which he takes notice of; and the Jews have a notion that in the time to come, in the days of the Messiah, three other cities of refuge will be added (w).

(u) De profugis, p. 464. (w) T. Hieros. Maccot, fol. 32. 1. Maimon. ut supra, (Hilchot Rotzeach, c. 8.) sect. 4.

Hebrews 6

19. Which hope we have as an anchor of the soul, both sure and stedfast, and which entereth into that within the veil;

19. ἣν ὡς ἄγκυραν ἔχομεν τῆς ψυχῆς ἀσφαλῆ τε καὶ βεβαίαν, καὶ εἰσερχομένην εἰς τὸ ἐσώτερον τοῦ καταπετάσματος·

19. 'ein 'os agkuran echomen teis psucheis asphalei te kai bebaian, kai eiserchomenein eis to esoteron tou katapetasmatos.

יט: אֲשֶׁר-הָיְתָה לָּנוּ עוֹגִין לְנֶפֶשׁ נֶאֱמָן וְחָזָק וּמַגִּיעַ אֶל-מִבֵּית לַפָּרֹכֶת

19. Asher - hai•ta la•noo o•gin le•ne•fesh ne•e•man ve•cha•zak oo•ma•gi•a el - mi•beit la•pa•ro•chet.

---

20. Whither the forerunner is for us entered, even Jesus, made an high priest for ever after the order of Melchisedec.

20. ὅπου πρόδρομος ὑπὲρ ἡμῶν εἰσῆλθεν Ἰησοῦς, κατὰ τὴν τάξιν Μελχισεδὲκ ἀρχιερεὺς γενόμενος εἰς τὸν αἰῶνα.

20. 'opou prodromos 'uper 'eimon eiseilthen Yeisous, kata tein taxin Melchisedek archiereus genomenos eis ton aiona.

כ. אֲשֶׁר-שָׁם בָּא יֵשׁוּעַ הָרָץ לְפָנֵינוּ אֲשֶׁר-הָיָה לְכֹהֵן גָּדוֹל לְעוֹלָם עַל-דִּבְרָתִי מַלְכִּי-צֶדֶק:

20. Asher - sham ba Yeshua ha•ratz le•fa•ney•noo asher - ha•ya le•cho•hen ga•dol le•o•lam al - div•ra•ti Mal•ki - tze•dek.

(Hebrews Chapter 6 End)

Hebrews, Chapter 7

1. For this Melchisedec, king of Salem, priest of the most high God, who met Abraham returning from the slaughter of the kings, and blessed him;

1. Οὗτος γὰρ ὁ Μελχισεδέκ, βασιλεὺς Σαλήμ, ἱερεὺς τοῦ Θεοῦ τοῦ ὑψίστου, ὁ συναντήσας Ἀβραὰμ ὑποστρέφοντι ἀπὸ τῆς κοπῆς τῶν βασιλέων καὶ εὐλογήσας αὐτόν,

1. 'Outos gar 'o Melchisedek, basileus Saleim, 'iereus tou theou tou 'upsistou, 'o sunanteisas Abra'am 'upostrephonti apo teis kopeis ton basileon kai eulogeisas auton,

א. כִּי זֶה מַלְכִּי-צֶדֶק מֶלֶךְ שָׁלֵם כֹּהֵן לְאֵל עֶלְיוֹן אֲשֶׁר יָצָא לִקְרַאת אַבְרָהָם אַחֲרֵי שׁוּבוֹ מֵהַכּוֹת אֶת-הַמְּלָכִים וַיְבָרְכֵהוּ:

1. Ki ze Mal•ki - tze•dek Me•lech Sha•lem co•hen le•El El•yon asher ya•tza lik•rat Avraham a•cha•rey shoo•voo me•ha•kot et - ha•m`la•chim vay•var•che•hoo.

Rabbinic Jewish Commentary

There is nothing said of Melchizedek which proves him to be more than a man: accordingly others take him to have been a mere man; but these are divided; some say that he was Shem, the son of Noah, which is the constant opinion of the Jewish writers (z). Aben Ezra says, his name signifies what he was, the king of a righteous place: Salem, of which he was king, was not Shalem, a city of Shechem, in the land of Canaan, Gen_33:18 afterwards called Salim, near to which John was baptizing. The interpretation of this word is given in the next verse; some of the Jewish writers referred to say, that it was usual for the kings of Jerusalem to be called Melchizedek and Adonizedek, as in Jos.10:3 just as the kings of Egypt were called Pharaoh.

(z) Targum in Jon. & Jerus. Jarchi, Baal Hatturim, Levi ben Gersom & Abendana in Gen. xiv. 18. Bemidbar Rabba, sect. 4. fol. 182. 4. Pirke Eliezer, c. 8. Juchasin, fol. 135. 2. Tzeror Hammor, fol. 16. 2. Shalshelet Hakabala, fol. 1. 2. Peritzol. Itinera Mundi, p. 17.

---

2. To whom also Abraham gave a tenth part of all; first being by interpretation King of righteousness, and after that also King of Salem, which is, King of peace;

2. ᾧ καὶ δεκάτην ἀπὸ πάντων ἐμέρισεν Ἀβραάμ- πρῶτον μὲν ἑρμηνευόμενος βασιλεὺς δικαιοσύνης, ἔπειτα δὲ καὶ βασιλεὺς Σαλήμ, ὅ ἐστιν βασιλεὺς εἰρήνης·

2. 'o kai dekatein apo panton emerisen Abra'am- proton men 'ermeineuomenos basileus dikaiosuneis, epeita de kai basileus Saleim, 'o estin basileus eireineis.

ב. וַאֲשֶׁר חָלַק-לוֹ אַבְרָהָם מַעֲשֵׂר מִכֹּל וּפֵשֶׁר שְׁמוֹ בְּרֹאשׁ מֶלֶךְ צֶדֶק וְגַם-כֵּן מֶלֶךְ שָׁלֵם הוּא מֶלֶךְ הַשָּׁלוֹם:

2. Va•a•sher cha•lak - lo Avraham ma•a•ser mi•kol oo•fe•sher sh`mo be•rosh Me•lech tze•dek ve•gam - ken Me•lech Sha•lem hoo Me•lech ha•sha•lom.

Rabbinic Jewish Commentary

Or tithes, as in Gen.14:20. Philo the Jew (b) renders the Hebrew phrase, מעשר מכל, just as the apostle does δεκατην απο παντων, "a tenth part of all", or "out of all"; not of all that he brought back, as Lot's goods, or the king of Sodom's, or any others.

...which is king of peace; Philo the Jew (c) interprets this name, "king of peace", just as the apostle does.

(b) De Congressu, p. 438. (c) Leg. Alleg. l. 2. p. 75.

---

3. Without father, without mother, without descent, having neither beginning of days, nor end of life; but made like unto the Son of God; abideth a priest continually.

3. ἀπάτωρ, ἀμήτωρ, ἀγενεαλόγητος, μήτε ἀρχὴν ἡμερῶν μήτε ζωῆς τέλος ἔχων, ἀφωμοιωμένος δὲ τῷ υἱῷ τοῦ θεοῦ- μένει ἱερεὺς εἰς τὸ διηνεκές.

3. apator, ameitor, agenealogeitos, meite archein 'eimeron meite zoeis telos echon, aphomoiomenos de to 'wio tou theou- menei 'iereus eis to dieinekes.

ג. בְּלֹא-אָב בְּלֹא-אֵם בְּלֹא יַחַשׂ וְאֵין לוֹ תְּחִלַּת הַיָּמִים וְאַף לֹא קֵץ הַחַיִּים וְדוֹמֶה לְבֶן-הָאֱלֹהִים הוּא עֹמֵד כֹּהֵן:לְעוֹלָם

3. Be•lo - av be•lo - em be•lo ya•chas ve•eyn lo te•chi•lat ha•ya•mim ve•af lo ketz ha•cha•yim ve•do•me le•Ven - ha•Elohim hoo o•med co•hen le•o•lam.

Rabbinic Jewish Commentary

The Syriac version renders it; "Whose father and mother are not written in the genealogies"; or there is no genealogical account of them. The Arabic writers tell us who his father and his mother were; some of them say that Peleg was his father: so Elmacinus (d), his words are these; Peleg lived after he begat Rehu two hundred and nine years; afterwards he begat Melchizedek, the priest whom we have now made mention of. Patricides (e), another of their writers, expresses himself after this manner "They who say Melchizedek had neither beginning of days, nor end of life, and argue from the words of the Apostle Paul, asserting the same, do not rightly understand the saying of the Apostle Paul; for Shem, the son of Noah, after he had taken Melchizedek, and withdrew him from his parents, did not set down in writing how old he was, when he went into the east, nor what was his age when he died; but Melchizedek was the son of Peleg, the son of Eber, the son of Salah, the son of Cainan, the son of Arphaxad, the son of Shem, the son of Noah; and yet none of those patriarchs is called his father. This only the Apostle Paul means, that none of his family served in the temple, nor were children and tribes assigned to him. Matthew and Luke the evangelists only relate the heads of tribes: hence the Apostle Paul does not write the name of his father, nor the name of his mother."

And with these writers Sahid Aben Batric (f) agrees, who expressly affirms that Melchizedek was אבן פאלג, "The son of Peleg": though others of them make him to be the son of Peleg's son, whose name was Heraclim. The Arabic Catena (g) on Gen.10:25, "The name of one was Peleg", has this note in the margin;

"And this (Peleg) was the father of Heraclim, the father of Melchizedek;" and in a preceding chapter, his pedigree is more particularly set forth: "Melchizedek was the son of Heraclim, the son of Peleg, the son of Eber; and his mother's name was Salathiel, the daughter of Gomer, the son of Japheth, the son of Noah; and Heraclim, the son of Eber, married his wife Salathiel, and she was with child, and brought forth a son, and called his name Melchizedek, called also king of Salem: after this the genealogy is set down at length. Melchizedek, son of Heraclim, which was the son of Peleg, which was the son of Eber, which was the son of Arphaxad, &c. till you come to, which was the son of Adam, on whom be peace."

It is very probable Epiphanius has regard to this tradition, when he observes (h), that some say that the father of Melchizedek was called

Eracla, and his mother Astaroth, the same with Asteria. Some Greek (i) writers say he was of the lineage of Sidus, the son of Aegyptus, a king of Lybia, from whence the Egyptians are called: this Sidus, they say, came out of Egypt into the country of the Canaanitish nations, now called Palestine, and subdued it, and dwelled in it, and built a city, which he called Sidon, after his own name.

Some of the Jewish writers themselves say, that the Redeemer, whom God will raise up, shall be without father (j). And he is without mother, though not in a spiritual sense, every believer being so to him as such; nor in a natural sense, as man, for the Virgin Mary was his mother; but in a divine sense, as God: and he is "Without descent or genealogy"

(d) In Hottinger. Smegma Orientale, l. 1. c. 8. p. 269, 254. (e) In ib. p. 305, 306, 254. (f) In Mr. Gregory's Preface to his Works. (g) In ib. (h) Contra Haeres. Haeres. 55. (i) Suidas in voce Melchisedec, Malala, l. 3. Glycas, Cedrenus, & alii. (j) R. Moses Hadarsan apud Galatin. l. 3. c. 17. & l. 8. c. 2.

Hebrews 7

4. Now consider how great this man was, unto whom even the patriarch Abraham gave the tenth of the spoils.

4. Θεωρεῖτε δὲ πηλίκος οὗτος, ᾧ καὶ δεκάτην Ἀβραὰμ ἔδωκεν ἐκ τῶν ἀκροθινίων ὁ πατριάρχης.

4. Theoreite de peilikos 'outos, 'o kai dekatein Abra'am edoken ek ton akrothinion 'o patryarcheis.

ד. וּרְאוּ-נָא מַה-נִּכְבָּד הוּא אֲשֶׁר אַבְרָהָם רֹאשׁ הָאָבוֹת נָתַן-לוֹ מַעֲשֵׂר מֵרֵאשִׁית הַשָּׁלָל:
4. Oor•oo - na ma - nich•bad hoo asher Avraham rosh ha•a•vot na•tan - lo ma•a•ser me•re•sheet ha•sha•lal.

---

5. And verily they that are of the sons of Levi, who receive the office of the priesthood, have a commandment to take tithes of the people according to the law, that is, of their brethren, though they come out of the loins of Abraham:

5. Καὶ οἱ μὲν ἐκ τῶν υἱῶν Λευῒ τὴν ἱερατείαν λαμβάνοντες ἐντολὴν ἔχουσιν ἀποδεκατοῦν τὸν λαὸν κατὰ τὸν νόμον, τοῦτ᾽ ἔστιν τοὺς ἀδελφοὺς αὐτῶν, καίπερ ἐξεληλυθότας ἐκ τῆς ὀσφύος Ἀβραάμ·

5. Kai 'oi men ek ton 'wion Leui tein 'ierateian lambanontes entolein echousin apodekatoun ton laon kata ton nomon, tout estin tous adelphous auton, kaiper exeileiluthotas ek teis osphuos Abra'am.

ה. וְאָמֵן יוֹרְשֵׁי הַכְּהֻנָּה מִבְּנֵי לֵוִי לָהֶם הַמִּשְׁפָּט לָקַחַת מַעֲשֵׂר עַל-פִּי הַתּוֹרָה מֵאֵת הָעָם - מֵאֵת אֲחֵיהֶם אַף כִּי-יֹצְאֵי יֶרֶךְ אַבְרָהָם הֵם

5. Ve•a•men yor•shey ha•k`hoo•na mi•b`ney Levi la•hem ha•mish•pat la•ka•chat ma•a•ser al - pi ha•Torah me•et ha•am me•et a•chey•hem af ki - yotz•ey ye•rech Avraham hem.

Rabbinic Jewish Commentary

who receive the office of the priesthood; As some of them were priests, though not all; and the Levites therefore are sometimes called priests. R. Joshua ben Levi says, that in twenty four places the priests are called Levites; and this is one of them, Eze.44:15 "and the priests and Levites"(k).

Ezra in his time ordered, that the first tithe should not be given to the Levites, but to the priests, because they would not go up with him to Jerusalem (l).

(k) T. Bab. Yebamot, fol. 86. 2. & Becorot, fol. 4. 1. (l) Maimon. Hilchot Maaser, c. 1. sect. 4.

Hebrews 7

6. But he whose descent is not counted from them received tithes of Abraham, and blessed him that had the promises.

6. ὁ δὲ μὴ γενεαλογούμενος ἐξ αὐτῶν δεδεκάτωκεν τὸν Ἀβραάμ, καὶ τὸν ἔχοντα τὰς ἐπαγγελίας εὐλόγηκεν.

6. 'o de mei genealogoumenos ex auton dedekatoken ton Abra'am, kai ton echonta tas epangelias eulogeiken.

ו. וְזֶה אֲשֶׁר לֹא הִתְיַחֵשׂ לְמִשְׁפְּחֹתָם לָקַח מַעֲשֵׂר מֵאַבְרָהָם וְגַם-בֵּרַךְ אֹתוֹ אֲשֶׁר הַהַבְטָחָה נְתוּנָה לוֹ מֵאָז:

6. Ve•ze asher lo hit•ya•ches le•mish•pe•cho•tam la•kach ma•a•ser me•Avraham ve•gam - be•rach o•to asher ha•hav•ta•cha n`too•na lo me•az.

---

7. And without all contradiction the less is blessed of the better.

7. Χωρὶς δὲ πάσης ἀντιλογίας, τὸ ἔλαττον ὑπὸ τοῦ κρείττονος εὐλογεῖται.

7. Choris de paseis antilogias, to elatton 'upo tou kreittonos eulogeitai.

:ז. וְדָבָר יָדוּעַ הוּא מֵאֵין פֹּצֶה פֶה כִּי הַקָּטֹן יְבֹרַךְ מִן-הַגָּדוֹל

7. Ve•da•var ya•dooa hoo me•eyn po•tze fe ki ha•ka•ton ye•vo•rach min - ha•ga•dol.

---

8. And here men that die receive tithes; but there he receiveth them, of whom it is witnessed that he liveth.

8. Καὶ ὧδε μὲν δεκάτας ἀποθνῄσκοντες ἄνθρωποι λαμβάνουσιν· ἐκεῖ δέ, μαρτυρούμενος ὅτι ζῇ.

8. Kai 'ode men dekatas apothneiskontes anthropoi lambanousin. ekei de, marturoumenos 'oti zei.

:ח. וּפֹה לֹקְחִים מַעֲשֵׂר אֲנָשִׁים בְּנֵי תְמוּתָה וְשָׁם זֶה הוּא אֲשֶׁר עֵדוּת לוֹ כִּי הוּא חָי

8. Oo•fo lok•chim ma•a•ser a•na•shim b`ney t`moo•ta ve•sham ze hoo asher e•doot lo ki hoo chai.

Hebrews 7

9. And as I may so say, Levi also, who receiveth tithes, payed tithes in Abraham.

9. Καί, ὡς ἔπος εἰπεῖν, διὰ Ἀβραὰμ καὶ Λευΐ ὁ δεκάτας λαμβάνων δεδεκάτωται·

9. Kai, 'os epos eipein, dya Abra'am kai Leui 'o dekatas lambanon dedekatotai.

ט: וְאִם תִּשְׂאוּ נִיב שְׂפָתַי גַּם-לֵוִי הַלֹּקֵחַ מַעֲשֵׂר נָתַן מַעֲשֵׂר בְּתוֹךְ אַבְרָהָם

9. Ve•eem tis•oo niv s`fa•tai gam - Levi ha•lo•ke•ach ma•a•ser na•tan ma•a•ser be•toch Avraham.

---

10. For he was yet in the loins of his father, when Melchisedec met him.

10. ἔτι γὰρ ἐν τῇ ὀσφύϊ τοῦ πατρὸς ἦν, ὅτε συνήντησεν αὐτῷ ὁ Μελχισεδέκ.

10. eti gar en tei osphui tou patros ein, 'ote suneinteisen auto 'o Melchisedek.

י: כִּי בְיֶרֶךְ אָבִיו הָיָה בְּצֵאת מַלְכִּי-צֶדֶק לִקְרָאתוֹ

10. Ki be•ye•rech aviv ha•ya be•tzet mal•ki - tze•dek lik•ra•to.

---

11. If therefore perfection were by the Levitical priesthood, (for under it the people received the law,) what further need was there that another priest should rise after the order of Melchisedec, and not be called after the order of Aaron?

11. Εἰ μὲν οὖν τελείωσις διὰ τῆς Λευϊτικῆς ἱερωσύνης ἦν- ὁ λαὸς γὰρ ἐπ᾽ αὐτῇ νενομοθέτητο- τίς ἔτι χρεία, κατὰ τὴν τάξιν Μελχισεδὲκ ἕτερον ἀνίστασθαι ἱερέα, καὶ οὐ κατὰ τὴν τάξιν Ἀαρὼν λέγεσθαι;

11. Ei men oun teleiosis dya teis Leuitikeis 'ierosuneis ein- 'o laos gar ep autei nenomotheteito- tis eti chreia, kata tein taxin Melchisedek 'eteron anistasthai 'ierea, kai ou kata tein taxin A'aron legesthai?

יא. וְאִם תַּכְלִית כָּל-חֵפֶץ נִמְצְאָה בִּכְהֻנַּת בְּנֵי לֵוִי אֲשֶׁר בְּיָמֶיהָ נִתְּנָה הַתּוֹרָה לָעָם מַה-לָּכֵן אַחַר כִּי יָקוּם: עַל-דִּבְרָתִי מַלְכִּי-צֶדֶק וְלֹא יִקָּרֵא עַל-דִּבְרָתִי אַהֲרֹן

11. Ve•eem tach•lit kol - che•fetz nim•tze•ah bich•hoo•nat b`ney Levi asher be•ya•me•ha nit•na ha•Torah la•am ma - le•cho•hen a•cher ki ya•koom al - div•ra•ti mal•ki - tze•dek ve•lo yi•ka•re al - div•ra•ti Aharon.

Hebrews 7

12. For the priesthood being changed, there is made of necessity a change also of the law.

12. Μετατιθεμένης γὰρ τῆς ἱερωσύνης, ἐξ ἀνάγκης καὶ νόμου μετάθεσις γίνεται.

12. Metatithemeneis gar teis 'ierosuneis, ex anagkeis kai nomou metathesis ginetai.

יב. כִּי בְהִשְׁתַּנּוֹת הַכְּהֻנָּה גַּם-חֲלִיפַת הַתּוֹרָה בֹּא תָבוֹא אֶל-נָכוֹן:

12. Ki ve•hish•ta•not ha•k`hoo•na gam - cha•li•fat ha•Torah bo ta•vo el - na•chon.

Rabbinic Jewish Commentary

The Jews themselves own, that the high priesthood was to cease in time to come (m), and which they say Azariah the son of Oded prophesied of in 2Ch.15:3.

There is made of necessity a change also of the law;This the Jews most strongly deny; God, they (n) say, will not change nor alter the Torah of Moses for ever. The nineth article of their creed, as drawn up by Maimonides, runs thus (o);

"I believe with a perfect faith that this Torah לא תהא מוחלפת "shall not be changed", nor shall there be another Torah from the Creator, blessed be his name." But the reasoning of the apostle is strong and unanswerable.

(m) Vajikra Rabba, sect. 19. fol. 160. 4. (n) Seder Tephillot, Ed. Amsterd. fol. 2. 1. (o) Apud Seder Tephillot, Ed. Basil. fol. 86. 2.

---

13. For he of whom these things are spoken pertaineth to another tribe, of which no man gave attendance at the altar.

13. Ἐφ᾽ ὃν γὰρ λέγεται ταῦτα, φυλῆς ἑτέρας μετέσχηκεν, ἀφ᾽ ἧς οὐδεὶς προσέσχηκεν τῷ θυσιαστηρίῳ.

13. Eph 'on gar legetai tauta, phuleis 'eteras metescheiken, aph 'eis oudeis prosescheiken to thusyasteirio.

יג. וְהִנֵּה-זֶה אֲשֶׁר-יְדֻבַּר בּוֹ כָזֹאת בֶּן-שֵׁבֶט אַחֵר הוּא אֲשֶׁר אֵין אִישׁ מִמֶּנּוּ קָרֵב אֶל-הַמִּזְבֵּחַ:

13. Ve•hee•ne - ze asher - ye•doo•bar bo cha•zot ben - she•vet a•cher hoo asher eyn eesh mi•me•noo ka•rev el - ha•miz•be•ach.

Hebrews 7

14. For it is evident that our Lord sprang out of Juda; of which tribe Moses spake nothing concerning priesthood.

14. Πρόδηλον γὰρ ὅτι ἐξ Ἰούδα ἀνατέταλκεν ὁ κύριος ἡμῶν, εἰς ἣν φυλὴν οὐδὲν περὶ ἱερωσύνης Μωϋσῆς ἐλάλησεν.

14. Prodeilon gar 'oti ex Youda anatetalken 'o kurios 'eimon, eis 'ein phulein ouden peri 'ierosuneis Mouseis elaleisen.

יד. כִּי מוּדַעַת זֹאת כִּי מִיהוּדָה צָמַח אֲדֹנֵינוּ וְעַל-שֵׁבֶט זֶה לֹא-דִבֶּר מֹשֶׁה מְאוּמָה עַל-אֹדוֹת הַכְּהֻנָּה:

14. Ki moo•da•at zot ki mi•Y`hoo•da tza•mach Ado•ney•noo ve•al - she•vet ze lo - di•ber Moshe me•oo•ma al - o•dot ha•k`hoo•na.

Rabbinic Jewish Commentary

The Jews expect that the Messiah will come from the tribe of Judah, and not from any other (p). This was known to the Jews, and it is owned by them that Yeshua was near to the kingdom (q), which he could not be if he was not of that tribe; and hence he is called the lion of the tribe of Judah.

The Alexandrian copy, the Claromontane manuscript, and the Vulgate Latin version, read, "Concerning the priests"; whence it follows that there is a change of the priesthood, and that the Messiah, as he was not to be, so he is not a priest of Aaron's order, not being of the same tribe.

(p) Raya Mehimna in Zohar in Exod. fol. 49. 3. Tzeror Hammor, fol. 62. 2. (q) T. Bab. Sanhedrin, fol. 43. 1.

15. And it is yet far more evident: for that after the similitude of Melchisedec there ariseth another priest,

15. Καὶ περισσότερον ἔτι κατάδηλόν ἐστιν, εἰ κατὰ τὴν ὁμοιότητα Μελχισεδὲκ ἀνίσταται ἱερεὺς ἕτερος,

15. Kai perissoteron eti katadeilon estin, ei kata tein 'omoioteita Melchisedek anistatai 'iereus 'eteros,

:טו. וְגַם-זֹאת מוּדַעַת בְּיֶתֶר מִדָּה כִּי יָקוּם כֹּהֵן אַחֵר בִּדְמוּת מַלְכִּי-צֶדֶק

15. Ve•gam - zot moo•da•at be•ye•ter mi•da ki ya•koom co•hen a•cher bid•moot mal•ki - tze•dek.

Hebrews 7

16. Who is made, not after the law of a carnal commandment, but after the power of an endless life.

16. ὃς οὐ κατὰ νόμον ἐντολῆς σαρκικῆς γέγονεν, ἀλλὰ κατὰ δύναμιν ζωῆς ἀκαταλύτου·

16. 'os ou kata nomon entoleis sarkikeis gegonen, alla kata dunamin zoeis akatalutou.

:טז. אֲשֶׁר אֵינֶנּוּ לְפִי מִצְוַת הַתּוֹרָה לְחַיֵּי בְשָׂרִים כִּי אִם-לְפִי הַגְּבוּרָה לְחַיֵּי אֵין-סוֹף

16. Asher ey•ne•noo le•fi mitz•vat ha•Torah le•cha•yey ve•sa•rim ki eem - le•fi ha•g`voo•ra le•cha•yey eyn - sof.

---

17. For he testifieth, Thou art a priest for ever after the order of Melchisedec.

17. μαρτυρεῖ γὰρ ὅτι Σὺ ἱερεὺς εἰς τὸν αἰῶνα κατὰ τὴν τάξιν Μελχισεδέκ.

17. marturei gar 'oti Su 'iereus eis ton aiona kata tein taxin Melchisedek.

:יז. כִּי-הֵעִיד לֵאמֹר אַתָּה כֹהֵן לְעוֹלָם עַל-דִּבְרָתִי מַלְכִּי-צֶדֶק

17. Ki - he•eed le•mor ata cho•hen le•o•lam al - div•ra•ti mal•ki - tze•dek.

Hebrews 7

18. For there is verily a disannulling of the commandment going before for the weakness and unprofitableness thereof.

18. Ἀθέτησις μὲν γὰρ γίνεται προαγούσης ἐντολῆς, διὰ τὸ αὐτῆς ἀσθενὲς καὶ ἀνωφελές·

18. Atheteisis men gar ginetai proagouseis entoleis, dya to auteis asthenes kai anopheles.

יח. כִּי אָמְנָם יֵשׁ תְּנוּאָה לְדַת הַנְּתוּנָה מִקֶּדֶם אֲשֶׁר הָיְתָה מִבְּלִי-כֹחַ וְלִבְלִי הוֹעִיל:

18. Ki om•nam yesh t`noo•ah la•dat ha•ne•too•na mi•ke•dem asher hai•ta mi•b`li - cho•ach ve•liv•li ho•eel.

Rabbinic Jewish Commentary
The Jews, though they are strenuous assertors of the unalterableness of the law of Moses, yet sometimes are obliged to acknowledge the abrogation of the ceremonial law in the times of the Messiah; the commandment, they say (r), meaning this, shall cease in the time to come; and again,

"All sacrifices shall cease in the future state, or time to come, (i.e. the times of the Messiah,) but the sacrifice of praise (s)."

(r) T. Bab. Nidda, fol. 61. 2. (s) Vajikra Rabba, scct. 9. fol. 153. 1. & sect. 27. fol. 168. 4.

---

19. For the law made nothing perfect, but the bringing in of a better hope did; by the which we draw nigh unto God.

19. οὐδὲν γὰρ ἐτελείωσεν ὁ νόμος, ἐπεισαγωγὴ δὲ κρείττονος ἐλπίδος, δι' ἧς ἐγγίζομεν τῷ θεῷ.

19. ouden gar eteleiosen 'o nomos, epeisagogei de kreittonos elpidos, di 'eis engizomen to theo.

יט. כִּי הַתּוֹרָה לֹא בִצְּעָה דָבָר לְתַכְלִיתוֹ כִּי אִם-אֶת אֲשֶׁר עַל-יָדָהּ בָּאָה תִקְוָה טוֹבָה מִמֶּנָּה אֲשֶׁר בָּהּ נִקְרַב:אֶל-הָאֱלֹהִים

19. Ki ha•Torah lo vitz•ah da•var le•tach•li•to ki eem - et asher al - ya•da ba•ah tik•va to•va mi•me•na asher ba nik•rav el - ha•Elohim.

Hebrews 7

20. And inasmuch as not without an oath he was made priest:

20. Καὶ καθ᾽ ὅσον οὐ χωρὶς ὁρκωμοσίας- οἱ μὲν γὰρ χωρὶς ὁρκωμοσίας εἰσὶν ἱερεῖς γεγονότες,

20. Kai kath 'oson ou choris 'orkomosias- 'oi men gar choris 'orkomosias eisin 'iereis gegonotes,

כ. וּבַאֲשֶׁר יֵשׁוּעַ לֹא הָיָה לְכֹהֵן מִבְּלִי שְׁבוּעָה:

20. Oo•va•a•sher Yeshua lo ha•ya le•cho•hen mi•b`li sh`voo•ah.

---

21. (For those priests were made without an oath; but this with an oath by him that said unto him, The Lord sware and will not repent, Thou art a priest for ever after the order of Melchisedec:)

21. ὁ δὲ μετὰ ὁρκωμοσίας, διὰ τοῦ λέγοντος πρὸς αὐτόν, Ὤμοσεν κύριος καὶ οὐ μεταμεληθήσεται, Σὺ ἱερεὺς εἰς τὸν αἰῶνα κατὰ τὴν τάξιν Μελχισεδέκ-

21. 'o de meta 'orkomosias, dya tou legontos pros auton, Omosen kurios kai ou metameleitheisetai, Su 'iereus eis ton aiona kata tein taxin Melchisedek-

כא. כִּי הֵמָּה הָיוּ לְכֹהֲנִים מִבְּלִי שְׁבוּעָה וְזֶה בִּשְׁבוּעָה עַל-פִּי הָאֹמֵר אֵלָיו נִשְׁבַּע יְהֹוָה וְלֹא יִנָּחֵם אַתָּה-כֹהֵן:לְעוֹלָם עַל-דִּבְרָתִי מַלְכִּי-צֶדֶק

21. Ki he•ma ha•yoo le•cho•ha•nim mi•b`li sh`voo•ah ve•ze bish•voo•ah al – pi ha•o•mer elav nish•ba Adonai ve•lo yi•na•chem ata - cho•hen le•o•lam al - div•ra•ti Mal•ki - tze•dek.

Rabbinic Jewish Commentary
For these priests were made without an oath,.... It is true indeed that after the sect of the Sadducees arose, the high priest on the day of atonement, was obliged to take an oath that he would not change any of the customs of the day (t); but then this regarded not his investiture, but the execution of his office; and was an oath of his and not of the LORD's, which is here designed.

(t) Misn. Yoma, c. 1. sect. 5.

---

22. By so much was Jesus made a surety of a better testament.

22. κατὰ τοσοῦτον κρείττονος διαθήκης γέγονεν ἔγγυος Ἰησοῦς.

22. kata tosouton kreittonos dyatheikeis gegonen enguos Yeisous.

:כב. אֲשֶׁר לָזֹאת יֵשׁוּעַ הוּא הָעֵרָבוֹן לַבְּרִית הַטּוֹבָה מִן-הָרִאשֹׁנָה

22. Asher la•zot Yeshua hoo ha•e•ra•von la•b`rit ha•to•va min - ha•ri•sho•na.

Hebrews 7

23. And they truly were many priests, because they were not suffered to continue by reason of death:

23. Καὶ οἱ μὲν πλείονές εἰσιν γεγονότες ἱερεῖς, διὰ τὸ θανάτῳ κωλύεσθαι παραμένειν·

23. Kai 'oi men pleiones eisin gegonotes 'iereis, dya to thanato koluesthai paramenein.

:כג. וְרַבִּים הָיוּ כֹהֲנֶיהָ הָהֵם כִּי לֹא יָכְלוּ לָשֶׁבֶת לָעַד מִפְּנֵי הַמָּוֶת

23. Ve•ra•bim ha•yoo cho•ha•ne•ha ha•hem ki lo yach•loo la•she•vet la•ad mip•ney ha•ma•vet.

Rabbinic Jewish Commentary
There were many common priests at a time; and though there was but one high priest at a time, yet there were many of them in a line of succession from Aaron down to the apostle's time. The Jews say (u), that under the

first temple eighteen high priests ministered, and under the second temple more than three hundred: this shows the imperfection of this priesthood, since it was in many hands; no one continuing and being sufficient to execute it. There was another reason besides this which the apostle gives, why the high priests were so many, and especially about this time; and that is, the office was bought for money, and men that would give most were put into it: hence there were frequent changes; the Jews themselves say, they changed every twelve months (w).

(u) T. Bab. Yoma, fol. 9. 1. Piske Tosephot Zebachim, Art. 72. (w) T. Bab. Yoma, fol. 8. 2.

Hebrews 7

24. But this man, because he continueth ever, hath an unchangeable priesthood.

24. ὁ δέ, διὰ τὸ μένειν αὐτὸν εἰς τὸν αἰῶνα, ἀπαράβατον ἔχει τὴν ἱερωσύνην.

24. 'o de, dya to menein auton eis ton aiona, aparabaton echei tein 'ierosunein.

:כד. וְזֶה יַעַן כִּי יֵשֵׁב לְעוֹלָם גַּם-כְּהֻנָּתוֹ לֹא תַעֲבֹר מִמֶּנּוּ

24. Ve•ze ya•an ki ye•shev le•o•lam gam - ke•hoo•na•to lo ta•a•vor mi•me•noo.

25. Wherefore he is able also to save them to the uttermost that come unto God by him, seeing he ever liveth to make intercession for them.

25. Ὅθεν καὶ σῴζειν εἰς τὸ παντελὲς δύναται τοὺς προσερχομένους δι' αὐτοῦ τῷ θεῷ, πάντοτε ζῶν εἰς τὸ ἐντυγχάνειν ὑπὲρ αὐτῶν.

25. 'Othen kai sozein eis to panteles dunatai tous proserchomenous di autou to theo, pantote zon eis to entugchanein 'uper auton.

כה. וּבַעֲבוּר זֹאת רַב הוּא לְהוֹשִׁיעַ תְּשׁוּעַת נֶצַח לְכָל-הַבָּאִים עַל-יָדוֹ לֵאלֹהִים כִּי הוּא חַי לָנֶצַח לְהַפְגִּיעַ:בַּעֲדָם

25. Oo•va•a•voor zot rav hoo le•ho•shi•a te•shoo•at ne•tzach le•chol - ha•ba•eem al - ya•do le•Elohim ki hoo chai la•ne•tzach le•haf•gia ba•a•dam.

---

26. For such an high priest became us, who is holy, harmless, undefiled, separate from sinners, and made higher than the heavens;

26. Τοιοῦτος γὰρ ἡμῖν ἔπρεπεν ἀρχιερεύς, ὅσιος, ἄκακος, ἀμίαντος, κεχωρισμένος ἀπὸ τῶν ἁμαρτωλῶν, καὶ ὑψηλότερος τῶν οὐρανῶν γενόμενος·

26. Toioutos gar 'eimin eprepen archiereus, 'osios, akakos, amiantos, kechorismenos apo ton 'amartolon, kai 'upseiloteros ton ouranon genomenos.

כו. כִּי טוֹב לָנוּ כֹהֵן גָּדוֹל קָדוֹשׁ כָּמוֹהוּ נְקִי כַפַּיִם וּבַר לֵבָב נִבְדָּל מֵחַטָּאִים וְנִשָּׂא מֵעַל הַשָּׁמָיִם:

26. Ki tov la•noo cho•hen ga•dol ka•dosh ka•mo•hoo n`kee cha•pa•yim oo•var le•vav niv•dal me•cha•ta•eem ve•ni•sa me•al ha•sha•ma•yim.

Rabbinic Jewish Commentary
Philo the Jew speaks of the true priest as being not man, but the divine Word, and as free from all sin voluntary and involuntary (x).

The high priests under the law, according to the Jews (y), were to excel their brethren in knowledge, beauty, and riches; but the distinguishing character of our high priest is purity and holiness.

The Syriac and Ethiopic versions read, "separate from sins"; the allusion seems to be, to the separating of the high priest from his own house to one of the courts of the temple seven days before the day of atonement (z), and so before the burning of the heifers (a).

and made higher than the heavens; The allusion may be to the carrying of the high priest on the day of atonement to an upper chamber in the temple, called the chamber of Abtines (b).

(x) De Profugis, p. 466, 467. & de Victimis, p. 843. (y) Maimon, & Bartenora in Misn, Yoma, c, 1. sect. 3. (z) Misn. Yoma, c. 1. sect. 1. (a) Misn. Parah, c. 3. sect. 1. (b) Misn. Yoma, c. 1. sect. 5.

Hebrews 7

27. Who needeth not daily, as those high priests, to offer up sacrifice, first for his own sins, and then for the people's: for this he did once, when he offered up himself.

27. ὃς οὐκ ἔχει καθ' ἡμέραν ἀνάγκην, ὥσπερ οἱ ἀρχιερεῖς, πρότερον ὑπὲρ τῶν ἰδίων ἁμαρτιῶν θυσίας ἀναφέρειν, ἔπειτα τῶν τοῦ λαοῦ· τοῦτο γὰρ ἐποίησεν ἐφάπαξ, ἑαυτὸν ἀνενέγκας.

27. 'os ouk echei kath 'eimeran anagkein, 'osper 'oi archiereis, proteron 'uper ton idion 'amartion thusias anapherein, epeita ton tou laou. touto gar epoieisen ephapax, 'eauton anenegkas.

כז. אֲשֶׁר אֵין-לוֹ חֹק יוֹם יוֹם כַּכֹּהֲנִים הַגְּדוֹלִים לְהַקְרִיב קׇרְבָּן בַּתְּחִלָּה עַל-חַטַּאת נַפְשׁוֹ וְאַחֲרֵי-כֵן בְּעַד הָעָם:כִּי הִשְׁלִים אֶת-זֹאת בְּפַעַם אַחַת בְּהַקְרִיב אֶת-נַפְשׁוֹ

27. Asher eyn - lo chok yom yom ka•ko•ha•nim hag•do•lim le•hak•riv kor•ban bat•chi•la al - cha•tat naf•sho ve•a•cha•rey - chen be•ad ha•am ki hish•lim et - zot be•fa•am a•chat be•hak•riv et - naf•sho.

Rabbinic Jewish Commentary
to offer up sacrifice first for his own sins and then for the people's; As they did on the day of atonement; see Lev.16:6 upon which place the Jews (c) make the same remark the apostle does here;

"He (the high priest, they say) offers sacrifices for the sins of the people, for his own בקדמיתא, "first", ולבתר, "and afterwards for the sins of the people"

(c) Zohar in Lev. fol. 26. 4.

---

28. For the law maketh men high priests which have infirmity; but the word of the oath, which was since the law, maketh the Son, who is consecrated for evermore.

28. Ὁ νόμος γὰρ ἀνθρώπους καθίστησιν ἀρχιερεῖς, ἔχοντας ἀσθένειαν· ὁ λόγος δὲ τῆς ὀρκωμοσίας τῆς μετὰ τὸν νόμον, υἱὸν εἰς τὸν αἰῶνα τετελειωμένον.

28. 'O nomos gar anthropous kathisteisin archiereis, echontas astheneyan. 'o logos de teis 'orkomosias teis meta ton nomon, 'wion eis ton aiona teteleiomenon.

כח. כִּי הַתּוֹרָה הֵקִימָה אֲנָשִׁים לְכֹהֲנִים גְּדוֹלִים אֲשֶׁר רִפְיוֹנָם בָּם אַךְ דְּבַר-הַשְּׁבוּעָה אַחֲרֵי הַתּוֹרָה הֵקִים אֶת:הַבֵּן אֲשֶׁר נַעֲלֶה הוּא בִּשְׁלֵמוּת נֶצַח -

28. Ki ha•Torah he•ki•ma a•na•shim le•cho•ha•nim ge•do•lim asher rif•yo•nam bam ach de•var - hash•voo•ah a•cha•rey ha•Torah he•kim et - ha•Ben asher na•a•le hoo bish•le•moot ne•tzach.

(Hebrews Chapter 7 End)

Hebrews, Chapter 8

1. Now of the things which we have spoken this is the sum: We have such an high priest, who is set on the right hand of the throne of the Majesty in the heavens;

1. Κεφάλαιον δὲ ἐπὶ τοῖς λεγομένοις· τοιοῦτον ἔχομεν ἀρχιερέα, ὃς ἐκάθισεν ἐν δεξιᾷ τοῦ θρόνου τῆς μεγαλωσύνης ἐν τοῖς οὐρανοῖς,

1. Kephalaion de epi tois legomenois. toiouton echomen archierea, 'os ekathisen en dexya tou thronou teis megalosuneis en tois ouranois,

א. סוֹף דָּבָר הַכֹּל נִשְׁמָע יֶשׁ-לָנוּ כֹּהֵן גָּדוֹל הַיּוֹשֵׁב לִימִין כִּסֵּא הַכָּבוֹד בַּשָּׁמָיִם:

1. Sof da•var ha•kol nish•ma yesh - la•noo cho•hen ga•dol ha•yo•shev li•y`min ki•se ha•ka•vod ba•sha•ma•yim.

Rabbinic Jewish Commentary
who is set on the right hand of the throne of the Majesty in the heavens;
He is "set", whereas the Levitical priests stood; which shows that he has done his work, and that with acceptance; and is in a state of ease and rest; and is possessed of honour, glory, majesty, and authority, and which continue: the place where he is set is, "on the right hand of the throne of the Majesty"; the same with the right hand of God; for by the throne of the Majesty is meant God the Father, in his royal glory and dignity; so Tiphereth, one of the ten numbers in the Jews' Cabalistic tree, whose name is Yehovah, is called כסא הכבוד, "the throne of glory" (c); So angels are called thrones, Col.1:16 but God is a throne of majesty superior to them; and at his right hand sits Christ the great high priest; which is expressive of his high honour, glory, and power, and even of his equality with God: the phrase, "in the heavens", may refer both to God the throne of majesty, who is there, and to Christ the high priest, who is passed into them, and received by them, and sits there.

(c) Lex. Cabal. p. 483.

Note: Notice that Hebrews here employs a circumlocution instead of the Divine Name.

---

2. A minister of the sanctuary, and of the true tabernacle, which the Lord pitched, and not man.

2. τῶν ἁγίων λειτουργός, καὶ τῆς σκηνῆς τῆς ἀληθινῆς, ἣν ἔπηξεν ὁ κύριος, καὶ οὐκ ἄνθρωπος·

2. ton 'agion leitourgos, kai teis skeineis teis aleithineis, 'ein epeixen 'o kurios, kai ouk anthropos.

ב: מְשָׁרֵת בַּקֹּדֶשׁ וּבַמִּשְׁכָּן אֱמֶת אֲשֶׁר הֶאֱהִיל יְהֹוָה וְלֹא אָדָם

2. Me•sha•ret ba•ko•desh oov•mish•kan emet asher he•e•hil Adonai ve•lo adam.

Rabbinic Jewish Commentary

The Zohar says,
"R. Jose said: 'How are we to understand the words, "and they saw the G-d of Israel" (Ex. XXIV, 10)? Who can see the Holy One? Is it not written: "No man can see Me and live"? It means that a rainbow appeared above them in radiant colours resplendent with the beauty of His grace. Therefore the saying that he who gazes at a rainbow gazes, as it were, at the Shekinah.... R. Jose further said: "They saw the light of the Shekinah, namely him who is called "the Youth" (Metatron-Henoch), and who ministers to the Shekinah in the heavenly Sanctuary."
(Zohar, Volume III, Beshalah 66b. Soncino Press Edition, pg. 208)

R' Yehudah Chayoun cites a Midrash describing the vision of the Heavenly Temple that Moses experienced before he died,
"Our rabbis said: On the day Moshe Rabbeinu's death approached, God brought him up to the heavens and showed him his Divine reward and what the future held...[he] saw God building the Temple with precious stones and pearls. Between each stone was the glow of the Shechinah, more radiant than pearls. Moshach ben David stood in [the Temple] and Aharon, [Moshe's] brother, stood on his feet, his cloak upon him. . . Moshe fell on his face before God and said to Him, "Master of the world, give me permission to speak with your anointed one before I die." Moshe [then] asked Moshiach ben David, "God spoke to me, [saying] He would build the Temple in the land...and behold, I have seen Him build His Temple by hand in the heavens!" Moshiach said to Moshe, "Moshe! Yaakov you forefather saw the house that will be built on earth...'When Moshe Rabbeinu, peace be upon him, heard these words from Moshiach ben David, he felt great happiness...[Then] he gave his soul to God wholeheartedly."
(Midrash Arakim, Midrash "HaShem BeChochmah Yasad Aretz," cited in Otzros HaAcharis HaYamim, When Moshiach Comes, R' Yehudah Chayoun, pg. 201-202)

Hebrews 8

3. For every high priest is ordained to offer gifts and sacrifices: wherefore it is of necessity that this man have somewhat also to offer.

3. πᾶς γὰρ ἀρχιερεὺς εἰς τὸ προσφέρειν δῶρά τε καὶ θυσίας καθίσταται· ὅθεν ἀναγκαῖον ἔχειν τι καὶ τοῦτον ὃ προσενέγκῃ.

3. pas gar archiereus eis to prospherein dora te kai thusias kathistatai. 'othen anagkaion echein ti kai touton 'o prosenegkei.

ג. וְכָל־כֹּהֵן גָּדוֹל יַעֲמַד לְהַקְרִיב מִנְחָה וָזֶבַח וְעַל־כֵּן נָכוֹן לִהְיוֹת גַּם־לוֹ קָרְבָּן אֲשֶׁר יַקְרִיב:

3. Ve•chol - co•hen ga•dol ya•o•mad le•hak•riv min•cha va•za•vach ve•al - ken na•chon li•hee•yot gam - lo kor•ban asher yak•riv.

Rabbinic Jewish Commentary

"Another explanation of the text, SETTING UP THE TABERNACLE. R. Simon expounded: When the Holy One, blessed be He, told Israel to set up the Tabernacle He intimated to the ministering angels that they also should make a Tabernacle, and when the one below was erected the other was erected on high. The latter was the tabernacle of the youth whose name was Metatron, and therein he offers up the souls of the righteous to atone for Israel in the days of their exile."
(Numbers Rabbah, XII:12, Soncino Press Edition)

---

4. For if he were on earth, he should not be a priest, seeing that there are priests that offer gifts according to the law:

4. Εἰ μὲν γὰρ ἦν ἐπὶ γῆς, οὐδ᾽ ἂν ἦν ἱερεύς, ὄντων τῶν ἱερέων τῶν προσφερόντων κατὰ τὸν νόμον τὰ δῶρα,

4. Ei men gar ein epi geis, oud an ein 'iereus, onton ton 'iereon ton prospheronton kata ton nomon ta dora,

ד. וְאִלּוּ הָיָה בָאָרֶץ לֹא הָיָה כֹהֵן מִפְּנֵי הַכֹּהֲנִים הַמַּקְרִיבִים כָּל־קָרְבָּן כַּתּוֹרָה:

4. Ve•ee•loo ha•ya va•a•retz lo ha•ya cho•hen mip•ney ha•ko•ha•nim ha•mak•ri•vim kol - kor•ban ka•To•rah.

5. Who serve unto the example and shadow of heavenly things, as Moses was admonished of God when he was about to make the tabernacle: for, See, saith he, that thou make all things according to the pattern shewed to thee in the mount.

5. οἵτινες ὑποδείγματι καὶ σκιᾷ λατρεύουσιν τῶν ἐπουρανίων, καθὼς κεχρημάτισται Μωϋσῆς μέλλων ἐπιτελεῖν τὴν σκηνήν, Ὅρα, γάρ φησιν, ποιήσεις πάντα κατὰ τὸν τύπον τὸν δειχθέντα σοι ἐν τῷ ὄρει.

5. 'oitines 'upodeigmati kai skya latreuousin ton epouranion, kathos kechreimatistai Mouseis mellon epitelein tein skeinein, 'Ora, gar pheisin, poieiseis panta kata ton tupon ton deichthenta soi en to orei.

ה. הַמְכַהֲנִים בַּמִקְדָשׁ אֲשֶׁר הוּא דְמוּת וְצֵל לַאֲשֶׁר בַּמָרוֹם כַּאֲשֶׁר צֻוָּה מֹשֶׁה מִפִּי אֱלֹהִים בַּעֲשׂתוֹ וְאֶת-הַמִּשְׁכָּן:כִּי אָמַר רְאֵה וַעֲשֵׂה כֹל כַּתַבְנִית אֲשֶׁר אַתָּה מָרְאֶה בָּהָר

5. Ha•m`cha•ha•nim ba•mik•dash asher hoo d`moot ve•tzel la•a•sher ba•ma•rom ka•a•sher tzoo•va Moshe mi•pi Elohim ba•a•shto ve•et - ha•mish•kan ki amar r`•eh va•a•se chol ka•tav•nit asher ata mar•eh ba•har.

Rabbinic Jewish Commentary

The Jews think this pattern was given him by the ministry of angels; Gabriel, they say (f), girt himself with a girdle, and showed to Moses the work of the candlestick; and they further say, that an ark of fire, and a table of fire; and a candlestick of fire, descended from heaven, and Moses saw them, and made according to them: from whence it may be observed that the tabernacle, and tabernacle worship, were of divine institution

(f) T. Bab. Menachot, fol. 29. 1.

To prove the existence of the Heavenly Tabernacle, the Zohar quotes the exact same passage as the book of Hebrews,

"And again it is written: And you shalt rear up the Tabernacle according to the fashion thereof which was shewed thee in the mount (Ex. 35:30). R. Jose said: From this we see that the Holy One, blessed be He, actually gave Moses all the arrangements and all the shapes of the Tabernacle, each in its appropriate manner, and that he saw Metatron ministering to the High Priest within it. It may be said that, as the Tabernacle above was not erected until the Tabernacle below had been completed, that youth (Metatron) could not have served above before Divine worship had taken place in the earthly Tabernacle. It is true that the Tabernacle above was not

actually erected before the one below; yet Moses saw a mirroring of the whole beforehand, and also Metatron, as he would be later when all was complete. The Holy One said to him: Behold now, the Tabernacle and the Youth; all is held in suspense until the Tabernacle below shall have been built. It should not be thought, however, that Metatron himself ministers; the fact is, that the Tabernacle belongs to him, and Michael, the High Priest, it is that serves there, within the Metatron's Tabernacle, mirroring the function of the Supernal High Priest above, serving within that other Tabernacle, that hidden one which never is revealed, which is connected with the mystery of the world to come. There are two celestial Tabernacles: the one, the supernal concealed Tabernacle, and the other, the Tabernacle of the Metatron. And there are also two priests: the one is the primeval Light, and the other Michael, the High Priest below."
(Zohar, Shemoth, Section 2, Page 159a, Soncino Press Edition)

Hebrews 8

6. But now hath he obtained a more excellent ministry, by how much also he is the mediator of a better covenant, which was established upon better promises.

6. Νυνὶ δὲ διαφορωτέρας τέτυχεν λειτουργίας, ὅσῳ καὶ κρείττονός ἐστιν διαθήκης μεσίτης, ἥτις ἐπὶ κρείττοσιν ἐπαγγελίαις νενομοθέτηται.

6. Nuni de dyaphoroteras tetuchen leitourgias, 'oso kai kreittonos estin dyatheikeis mesiteis, 'eitis epi kreittosin epangeliais nenomotheteitai.

ו. וְעַתָּה הוּא לָקַח-לוֹ כְּהֻנָּה נִשְׂגָּבָה מִזֹּאת כַּאֲשֶׁר גַּם-הַבְּרִית אֲשֶׁר הוּא לְמֵלִיץ לָהּ נִשְׂגָּבָה מִן-הָרִאשׁנָה:וּנְתוּנָה עֲלֵי-הַבְטָחוֹת טוֹבוֹת מִן-הָרִאשֹׁנוֹת

6. Ve•a•ta hoo la•kach - lo che•hoo•na nis•ga•va mi•zot ka•a•sher gam - ha•b`rit asher hoo le•me•litz la nis•ga•va min - ha•ri•sho•na oon•too•na aley - hav•ta•chot to•vot min - ha•ri•sho•not.

7. For if that first covenant had been faultless, then should no place have been sought for the second.

7. Εἰ γὰρ ἡ πρώτη ἐκείνη ἦν ἄμεμπτος, οὐκ ἂν δευτέρας ἐζητεῖτο τόπος.

7. Ei gar 'ei protei ekeinei ein amemptos, ouk an deuteras ezeiteito topos.

ז. כִּי לוּ הָיְתָה הַבְּרִית הָרִאשֹׁנָה בְּלִי חֶסְרוֹן הֲלֹא לֹא-יְבֻקַּשׁ מָקוֹם לִשְׁנִיָּה:

7. Ki loo hai•ta ha•b`rit ha•ri•sho•na v•li ches•ron ha•lo lo - ye•voo•kash ma•kom lish•ni•ya.

---

8. For finding fault with them, he saith, Behold, the days come, saith the Lord, when I will make a new covenant with the house of Israel and with the house of Judah:

8. Μεμφόμενος γὰρ αὐτοῖς λέγει, Ἰδού, ἡμέραι ἔρχονται, λέγει κύριος, καὶ συντελέσω ἐπὶ τὸν οἶκον Ἰσραὴλ καὶ ἐπὶ τὸν οἶκον Ἰούδα διαθήκην καινήν·

8. Memphomenos gar autois legei, Ydou, 'eimerai erchontai, legei kurios, kai sunteleso epi ton oikon Ysraeil kai epi ton oikon Youda dyatheikein kainein.

ח. אַךְ בִּמְצֹא חֶסְרוֹן אָמַר אֲלֵיהֶם הִנֵּה יָמִים בָּאִים נְאֻם-יְהֹוָה וְכָרַתִּי אֶת-בֵּית יִשְׂרָאֵל וְאֶת-בֵּית יְהוּדָה בְּרִית חֲדָשָׁה:

8. Ach bim•tzo ches•ron amar aley•hem hee•ne ya•mim ba•eem n`oom – Adonai ve•cha•ra•ti et - beit Israel ve•et - beit Yehooda b`rit cha•da•sha.

Hebrews 8

9. Not according to the covenant that I made with their fathers in the day when I took them by the hand to lead them out of the land of Egypt; because they continued not in my covenant, and I regarded them not, saith the Lord.

9. οὐ κατὰ τὴν διαθήκην ἣν ἐποίησα τοῖς πατράσιν αὐτῶν ἐν ἡμέρᾳ ἐπιλαβομένου μου τῆς χειρὸς αὐτῶν ἐξαγαγεῖν αὐτοὺς ἐκ γῆς Αἰγύπτου· ὅτι αὐτοὶ οὐκ ἐνέμειναν ἐν τῇ διαθήκῃ μου, κἀγὼ ἠμέλησα αὐτῶν, λέγει κύριος.

9. ou kata tein dyatheikein 'ein epoieisa tois patrasin auton en 'eimera epilabomenou mou teis cheiros auton exagagein autous ek geis Aiguptou. 'oti autoi ouk enemeinan en tei dyatheikei mou, kago eimeleisa auton, legei kurios.

ט. לֹא כַבְּרִית אֲשֶׁר כָּרַתִּי אֶת-אֲבוֹתָם בְּיוֹם הֶחֱזִיקִי בְיָדָם לְהוֹצִיאָם מֵאֶרֶץ מִצְרָיִם אֲשֶׁר-הֵמָּה הֵפֵרוּ אֶת-בְּרִיתִי וְאָנֹכִי בָּחַלְתִּי בָם נְאֻם-יְהֹוָה

9. Lo cha•b`rit asher ka•ra•ti et - avo•tam be•yom he•che•zi•ki ve•ya•dam le•ho•tzi•am me•e•retz Mitz•ra•yim asher - he•ma he•fe•roo et - b`ri•ti ve•a•no•chi ba•chal•ti vam n`oom - Adonai.

Rabbinic Jewish Commentary
and I regarded them not, saith the Lord; The Chaldee paraphrase is just the reverse of the apostle's translation, "and I was well pleased with them": some render them, "I ruled over them", as a lord over his servants, in a very severe manner. Others, observing the great difference there is between the Hebrew text, and the apostle's version, have supposed a different Hebrew copy from the present, used by the Septuagint, or the apostle, in which, instead of בעלתי, it was read either בחלתי, or געלתי; but there is no need of such a supposition(g), that בעל, in the Arabic language, signifies to loath and abhor, and so to disregard; and Kimchi (h) relates it as a rule laid down by his father, that wherever this word is used in construction with ב, it is to be taken in an ill part, and signifies the same as בחלתי, "I have loathed"; in which sense that word is used in Zec.11:8 and so here, I have loathed them, I abhorred them, I rejected them, I took no care of them, disregarded them, left their house desolate, and suffered wrath to come upon them to the uttermost.

(g) Not. Miscell. in Port. Mesis, p. 9. (h) In Jer. xxxi. 32. & Sepher Shorashim, rad. בעל.

---

10. For this is the covenant that I will make with the house of Israel after those days, saith the Lord; I will put my laws into their mind, and write them in their hearts: and I will be to them a God, and they shall be to me a people:

10. Ὅτι αὕτη ἡ διαθήκη ἣν διαθήσομαι τῷ οἴκῳ Ἰσραὴλ μετὰ τὰς ἡμέρας ἐκείνας, λέγει κύριος, διδοὺς νόμους μου εἰς τὴν διάνοιαν αὐτῶν, καὶ ἐπὶ καρδίας αὐτῶν ἐπιγράψω αὐτούς· καὶ ἔσομαι αὐτοῖς εἰς θεόν, καὶ αὐτοὶ ἔσονταί μοι εἰς λαόν.

10. 'Oti 'autei 'ei dyatheikei 'ein dyatheisomai to oiko Ysraeil meta tas 'eimeras ekeinas, legei kurios, didous nomous mou eis tein dyanoyan auton, kai epi kardias auton epigrapso autous. Kai esomai autois eis theon, kai autoi esontai moi eis laon.

י. כִּי זֹאת הַבְּרִית אֲשֶׁר אֶכְרֹת אֶת־בֵּית יִשְׂרָאֵל אַחֲרֵי הַיָּמִים הָהֵם נְאֻם־יְהוָה נָתַתִּי אֶת־תּוֹרָתִי בְּקִרְבָּם וְעַל־לִבָּם אֶכְתֲּבֶנָּה וְהָיִיתִי לָהֶם לֵאלֹהִים וְהֵמָּה יִהְיוּ־לִי לְעָם

10. Ki zot ha•b`rit asher ech•rot et - beit Israel a•cha•rey ha•ya•mim ha•hem n`oom - Adonai na•ta•ti et - To•ra•ti be•kir•bam ve•al - li•bam ech•to•ve•na ve•ha•yi•ti la•hem le•Elohim ve•he•ma yi•hee•yoo - li le•am.

Rabbinic Jewish Commentary
after those days, saith the Lord; after the times of the Old Testament, when the Messiah shall be come, and the Gospel day shall take place. So the Jews (i) apply these days, when they represent the Israelites saying to Moses, O that he (God) would reveal (himself or will) to us a second time! O that he would kiss us with the kisses of his mouth, and that the doctrine of the law was fixed in our hearts; when he (Moses) said to them, this is not to be done now, but לעתיד לבא, in the time to come, (i.e. in the times of the Messiah,) as it is said, Jer.31:33.

I will put my law; and so (k) they are elsewhere applied to the same times. And the first article in it is,

(i) Shirhashirim Rabba, fol. 3. 2. (k) Midrash Kohelet, fol. 64. 3.

---

11. And they shall not teach every man his neighbour, and every man his brother, saying, Know the Lord: for all shall know me, from the least to the greatest.

11. Καὶ οὐ μὴ διδάξωσιν ἕκαστος τὸν πολίτην αὐτοῦ, καὶ ἕκαστος τὸν ἀδελφὸν αὐτοῦ, λέγων, Γνῶθι τὸν κύριον· ὅτι πάντες εἰδήσουσίν με, ἀπὸ μικροῦ αὐτῶν ἕως μεγάλου αὐτῶν.

11. Kai ou mei didaxosin 'ekastos ton politein autou, kai 'ekastos ton adelphon autou, legon, Gnothi ton kurion. 'oti pantes eideisousin me, apo mikrou auton 'eos megalou auton.

יא. וְלֹא יְלַמְּדוּ עוֹד אִישׁ אֶת־רֵעֵהוּ וְאִישׁ אֶת־אָחִיו לֵאמֹר דְּעוּ אֶת־יְהוָה כִּי כוּלָּם יֵדְעוּ אֹתִי לְמִקְּטַנָּם וְעַד־גְּדוֹלָם

11. Ve•lo ye•lam•doo od eesh et - re•e•hoo ve•eesh et - a•chiv le•mor de•oo et - Adonai ki choo•lam yed•oo o•ti le•mik•ta•nam ve•ad - g`do•lam.

Hebrews 8

12. For I will be merciful to their unrighteousness, and their sins and their iniquities will I remember no more.

12. Ὅτι ἵλεως ἔσομαι ταῖς ἀδικίαις αὐτῶν, καὶ τῶν ἁμαρτιῶν αὐτῶν καὶ τῶν ἀνομιῶν αὐτῶν οὐ μὴ μνησθῶ ἔτι.

12. 'Oti 'ileos esomai tais adikiais auton, kai ton 'amartion auton kai ton anomion auton ou mei mneistho eti.

:יב. כִּי אֶסְלַח לַעֲוֹנָם וּלְחַטָּאתָם וּלְפִשְׁעֵיהֶם לֹא אֶזְכָּר-עוֹד

12. Ki es•lach la•a•vo•nam ool•cha•ta•tam ool•fish•ey•hem lo ez•kor - od.

---

13. In that he saith, A new covenant, he hath made the first old. Now that which decayeth and waxeth old is ready to vanish away.

13. Ἐν τῷ λέγειν, Καινήν, πεπαλαίωκεν τὴν πρώτην. Τὸ δὲ παλαιούμενον καὶ γηράσκον, ἐγγὺς ἀφανισμοῦ.

13. En to legein, Kainein, pepalaioken tein protein. To de palaioumenon kai geiraskon, engus aphanismou.

:יג. בְּאָמְרוֹ בְּרִית חֲדָשָׁה בִּלָּה אֶת-הָרִאשֹׁנָה וְהַבָּלָה וְהַנּוֹשֶׁנֶת קָרוֹב קִצָּה

13. Be•om•ro b`rit cha•da•sha bi•la et - ha•ri•sho•na ve•ha•ba•la ve•ha•no•she•net ka•rov ki•tza.

Rabbinic Jewish Commentary

Notice that the author of Hebrews does not say that the Old Covenant has passed away, but that "it is near to vanishing away." Notice that the older covenant is in the process of passing away. It is still here until heaven and earth pass away. The Torah will undergo a transformation when the Olam Hazeh passes away. When YHVH created the world through the Primordial Torah, it was absolutely perfect. There was no death, suffering, sadness or pain. However, when Adam sinned, the letters of the Primordial Torah re-arranged, to apply to a fallen world. The Torah remained perfect, but it now applied to a world that was no longer perfect, as Numbers 19 says,

זֹאת הַתּוֹרָה אָדָם כִּי־יָמוּת בְּאֹהֶל
"This is the Torah when a man dies in a tent…"
(Numbers 19:14)

The Torah's letters re-arranged to apply to situations like death, sickness, divorce, sin, suffering and war. In the New Torah the word 'death' will never be mentioned. Even the Midrash on Psalms hints that the Torah of this world is not in its proper order,

"Man knoweth not the order thereof" (Job 28:13). R. Eleazar taught: The sections of Scripture are not arranged in their proper order, and any man so read them, he would be able to resurrect the dead and perform other miracles. For this reason the proper order of the sections of Scripture is hidden from mortals and is known only to the Holy One, blessed be He, who said: "Who, as I, can read and declare it, and set it in order."
(Isaiah 44:7)
(Midrash Tehillim, translated by William G. Braude, Yale University Press, pg. 48)

Yet the Midrash Talpiyot comments that the letters of the Torah will re-configure itself back to its primordial state,

"The Holy One, blessed is He, will sit and expound the New Torah which He will give through the Messiah. "New Torah" means the secrets and the mysteries of the Torah which have remained hidden until now. It does not refer to another Torah, heaven forbid, for surely the Torah which He gave us through Moshe rabbeinu, peace be upon him, is the eternal Torah, but the revelation of her hidden secrets is called the "New Torah". . . when Adam the first man sinned, God arranged the letters into words, such as, When a man dies in his dent (Num 19:14). For had Adam not sinned, the letters would have arranged themselves into other words. Therefore, in the Olam Haba, the words will return to their primordial state."
(Midrash Talpiyot 58a, cited in the Messiah Texts, Raphael Patai, pg. 256)

It is important to note that the New Torah is the same Torah of Moshe, but with its hidden soul revealed. Yeshua teaches that 'not one jot or tittle shall ever pass from the Torah,

"Do not think that I came to destroy the Torah or the Prophets. I did not come to destroy, but to fulfill. For most certainly, I tell you, until heaven and earth pass away, not even one smallest letter or one tiny pen stroke shall in any way pass away from the Torah, until all things are accomplished." (Yeshua-Matthew 5:17-18)

When 'heaven and earth pass away' is when the Olam Haba, the World to Come arrives. Then the New Torah will be revealed in its fullest measure. HaShem will use the New Torah in order to re-create the Heavens and the Earth.

(Hebrews Chapter 8 End)

Hebrews, Chapter 9

1. Then verily the first covenant had also ordinances of divine service, and a worldly sanctuary.

1. Εἶχεν μὲν οὖν καὶ ἡ πρώτη δικαιώματα λατρείας, τό τε ἅγιον κοσμικόν.

1. Eichen men oun kai 'ei protei dikaiomata latreias, to te 'agion kosmikon.

א. אוּלָם גַּם-הַבְּרִית הָרִאשֹׁנָה הָיוּ לָהּ חֻקֵּי עֲבוֹדַת-אֵל וּמִקְדָּשׁ מַטָּה בָּאָרֶץ:

1. Oo•lam gam - ha•b`rit ha•ri•sho•na ha•yoo la choo•key avo•dat - El oo•mik•dash ma•ta ba•a•retz.

Rabbinic Jewish Commentary

And a worldly sanctuary. Philo the Jew says (l), it was a type of the world, and of the various things in it; though it was rather either a type of the church, or of heaven, or of Messiah's human nature: the better reason of its being so called is, because it consisted of earthly matter, and worldly things; it was in the world, and only had its use in the world, and so is opposed to the heavenly sanctuary; for the Jews often speak of מקדש שלמעלה, "a sanctuary above", and מקדש שלמטה, "a sanctuary below" (m), and of משכנא דלעילא, "a tabernacle above", and משכנא דלתתא, "a tabernacle below" (n); which answered to one another: the words may be rendered "a beautiful sanctuary", a well adorned one; and such especially was the temple, or sanctuary built by Solomon, rebuilt by Zerubbabel, and repaired and adorned by Herod, Luk.21:5. And the Jews say, that he that never saw Herod's building, meaning the temple, never saw a beautiful building.

(l) De Vita Mosis, p. 667. (m) Jarchi in Gen. xxviii. 17. (n) Zohar in Exod. fol. 65. 4. & 94. 4. & 96. 2. & in Lev. fol. 1. 3.

---

2. For there was a tabernacle made; the first, wherein was the candlestick, and the table, and the shewbread; which is called the sanctuary.

2. Σκηνὴ γὰρ κατεσκευάσθη ἡ πρώτη, ἐν ᾗ ἥ τε λυχνία καὶ ἡ τράπεζα καὶ ἡ πρόθεσις τῶν ἄρτων, ἥτις λέγεται ἅγια.

2. Skeinei gar kateskeuasthei 'ei protei, en 'ei te luchnia kai 'ei trapeza kai 'ei prothesis ton arton, 'eitis legetai 'agya.

ב: כִּי נַעֲשָׂה הַמִּשְׁכָּן הַחִיצוֹן אֲשֶׁר שָׁם הַמְּנוֹרָה וְהַשֻּׁלְחָן וְלֶחֶם הַפָּנִים וְהוּא נִקְרָא קֹדֶשׁ

2. Ki na•a•sa ha•mish•kan ha•chi•tzon asher sham ha•m`no•ra ve•ha•shool•chan ve•le•chem ha•pa•nim ve•hoo nik•ra ko•desh.

Rabbinic Jewish Commentary

Which is called the sanctuary; or "holy"; this refers either to the first part of the tabernacle, which was called the holy place, in which the priests in common ministered; or else to the things which were in it, now mentioned, the candlestick table, and shewbread; to which the Ethiopic version adds, and the golden censer, which it leaves out in the fourth verse; which version renders these words, "and these they call holy"; and so the Arabic version, "which are called holy things", as they were, as well as the place in which they were; so the candlestick is called the holy candlestick in the Apocrypha,

"As the clear light is upon the holy candlestick; so is the beauty of the face in ripe age." (Sirach 26:17)

And the ark, candlestick, table, censer, and altar, are called σκευη ιερα, "holy vessels", by Philo the Jew (q); but the former sense seems best, when compared with the following verse.

(q) De Vita Mosis, l. 3. p. 668.

---

3. And after the second veil, the tabernacle which is called the Holiest of all;

3. Μετὰ δὲ τὸ δεύτερον καταπέτασμα σκηνὴ ἡ λεγομένη ἅγια ἁγίων,

3. Meta de to deuteron katapetasma skeinei 'ei legomenei 'agya 'agion,

ג: וּמִבֵּית לַפָּרֹכֶת מִשְׁכָּן הַנִּקְרָא קֹדֶשׁ הַקֳּדָשִׁים

3. Oo•mi•beit la•pa•ro•chet mish•kan ha•nik•ra Ko•desh ha•Ko•da•shim.

Rabbinic Jewish Commentary

Were there more vails than one? the Scripture speaks but of one, Exo. 26:31 there was indeed an hanging for the door of the tent, but that is not called a vail; nor was there more than one vail in the tabernacle, nor in the temple of Solomon; but in the second temple, under which the apostle lived, there were two vails, which divided between the holy place, and the holy of holies; and the innermost of these the apostle means: and so the Jewish writers (r) constantly affirm, that there were two vails between the said places, and that two new ones were made every year (s). So on the day of atonement, when the high priest went into the most holy place, with the incense, it is said (t), that

"He walked in the temple till he came between שתי הפרוכות, "the two vails", which divide between the holy, and holy of holies, and there was the space of a cubit between them."

The reason of these two vails may be seen in the account Maimonides gives of this matter (u):

"In the first temple there was a wall which divided between the holy, and holy of holies, the thickness of a cubit; but when they built the second temple, it was doubted by them, whether the thickness of the wall was of the measure of the holy place, or of the measure of the holy of holies; wherefore they made the holy of holies twenty cubits complete, and the holy place forty cubits complete, and they left the space of a cubit between the holy, and the holy of holies; and they did not build a wall in the second temple, but they made שתי פרוכות, "two vails", one on the side of the holy of holies, and the other on the side of the holy place, and between them a cubit answerable to the thickness of the wall, which was in the first temple; but in the first temple there was but one vail only, as it is said, Exo.26:33 and the vail shall divide unto you."

And to this account other Jewish writers (w) agree; and the space between the two vails is called by them טרקסין (x), ταραξις, from the trouble and perplexity this affair gave them. This vail, or vails, might represent the sin of man, which separates between God and men, excludes from heaven; but is removed by the death of Messiah, when the vail was rent in twain; so that now there is an open way to heaven; Messiah has entered into it by his own blood; and saints have boldness to enter there by faith and hope now, and shall hereafter personally enter into it: or else this vail may signify the ceremonial Torah, which separated between Jew and Gentile, and is abolished by the death of Messiah: or rather it was typical of the flesh, or human nature of Messiah, called the vail of his flesh, Heb.10:20.

(r) T. Bab. Yoma, fol. 54. 1. & Cetubot, fol. 106. 1. Vid. Philo de Vita Mosis, l. 3. p. 667. (s) Misn. Shekalim, c. 8. sect. 5. Maimon. Cele Hamikdash, c. 7. sect. 16. (t) Misna Yoma, c. 5. sect. 1. Vid. Bereshit Rabba, sect. 10. fol. 8. 3. (u) Hilchot Beth Habbechira, c. 4. sect. 2. (w) Gloss. & Tosephot in T. Bab. Yoma, fol. 51. 2. & Bartenora in Misn. Yoma, c. 5. sect. 1. & in Middot, c. 4. sect. 7. (x) Misn. Middot ib. & T. Bab. Yoma ib. & Gloss. in T. Bab. Cetubot, fol. 106. 1.

Hebrews 9

4. Which had the golden censer, and the ark of the covenant overlaid round about with gold, wherein was the golden pot that had manna, and Aaron's rod that budded, and the tables of the covenant;

4. χρυσοῦν ἔχουσα θυμιατήριον, καὶ τὴν κιβωτὸν τῆς διαθήκης περικεκαλυμμένην πάντοθεν χρυσίῳ, ἐν ᾗ στάμνος χρυσῆ ἔχουσα τὸ μάννα, καὶ ἡ ῥάβδος Ἀαρὼν ἡ βλαστήσασα, καὶ αἱ πλάκες τῆς διαθήκης·

4. chrusoun echousa thumyateirion, kai tein kiboton teis dyatheikeis perikekalummenein pantothen chrusio, en stamnos chrusei echousa to manna, kai 'ei 'rabdos A'aron 'ei blasteisasa, kai 'ai plakes teis dyatheikeis.

ד. שָׁם מַחְתַּת הַזָּהָב וַאֲרוֹן הַבְּרִית מְצֻפֶּה זָהָב סָבִיב וְצִנְצֶנֶת זָהָב אֲשֶׁר הַמָּן בְּתוֹכָהּ וּמַטֵּה אַהֲרֹן אֲשֶׁר פָּרַח׃וְלוּחֹת הַבְּרִית

4. Sham mach•tat ha•za•hav va•a•ron ha•b`rit me•tzoo•pe za•hav sa•viv ve•tzin•tze•net za•hav asher ha•man be•to•cha oo•ma•te Aharon asher pa•rach ve•loo•chot ha•b`rit.

Rabbinic Jewish Commentary

There were various censers used by the priests in the daily service, but this was a peculiar one, which was used by the high priest on the day of atonement; on other days he used a silver censer, but on that day a golden one, and with it he entered into the holy of holies (y); and though Moses does not call it a golden one, Lev.16:12 yet Josephus does (z); and so do the Jewish Rabbis in the place referred to, with whom the apostle agrees.

And the ark of the covenant overlaid round about with gold; this is called the ark of the covenant, because the tables of the covenant, afterwards mentioned, were put into it; and that it was overlaid with gold round about, is certain from Exo.25:11 where it is said to be overlaid with pure gold, within and without; and that the ark was within the vail, and in the most holy place, is manifest from Exo.40:21 that this was wanting in the second temple, is generally agreed (b); but who took it away, where it was put, or what became of it various are the sentiments of the Jewish writers: some say (c), it was carried away by Nebuchadnezzar into Babylon, and is meant by the goodly vessels of the house of the Lord, 2Ch.36:10 others say (d), that Jeremiah the prophet took it, and hid it in a cave on Mount Nebo; but the more generally received opinion is, that it was hid by King Josiah in some hidden and deep place, which Solomon had built for that purpose under ground, knowing, that the temple would be destroyed (e); and it is often said, that it was hid under the pavement of a room in the temple, called לשכת דיר העצים, "the wood room" (f).

Wherein was the golden pot that had manna; This pot held an omer, which was more than three pints and a half; some say six pints: and though Moses does not call it a golden pot, yet it is so called, not only by the Septuagint in Exo.16:33 but also by Philo the Jew (g); nor is it reasonable to think, with some Jewish writers (h), that it should be made of earth, which was to continue for ages to come: this also was wanting in the second temple (i); and this, with Aaron's rod, after mentioned, and other things, is said to be hid when the ark was, and along with it (k). And certain it is from the above account from Scripture, that they were near it; and so, by the Jewish writers, they are always mentioned along with it: when that was carried away, and hid, they were hid with it; but what a certain Jewish commentator (l) observes on 1Ki.8:9 is so express, as if it was designed to vindicate our apostle: his remark is this:

"The intention of this is not to deny that there were not the things mentioned in the law, for they were מונחים בו, "left in it", as Aaron's "rod", and "the pot of manna", only to deny, hereby, that there was not anything of the law, save the decalogue."

And Aaron's rod that budded; it is affirmed by the Jews, that in the days of the Messiah, the priesthood shall return, and the rod of Aaron shall flourish (n); it was, very probably, as some have thought (o), an almond tree stick, as that in Jer.1:11. The almond tree has its name, in Hebrew, from a word which signifies haste and vigilance; it being, as Pliny says (p), the first of trees that buds and blossoms, and is very hasty in putting them forth. Philo the Jew says (q) the first of trees that buds and blossoms in the spring, and the last that casts its leaves, it may be, as he observes, a symbol of the priestly tribe; and it may be a figure of the perpetuity of Messiah, and his priesthood.

and the tables of the covenant; About this there is no controversy; though it is a matter of dispute with the Jews, whether the book of the Torah was in the ark or not: some say it was in the side of it, and others within it (r); but Maimonides (s) says, that Moses wrote the whole Torah with his own hand before he died, and gave a book (or copy) to every tribe, and one copy he put בארון, "in the ark": so Jarchi says (t), that the book of the Torah of Moses was put into the midst of the ark, and the ark was glorious and beautiful by that which was בתוכו, "within it".

y) Misn. Yoma, c. 4. sect. 4. Maimon. Yom Hacippurim, c. 2. sect. 5. (z) Antiqu. l. 3. c. 8. sect. 3. (b) T. Bab. Menachot, fol. 27. 2. & Yoma, fol. 21. 2. Menasseh ben Israel Concil. in Gen. qu. 41. Kimchi in Hagg. i. 8. (c) T. Bab. Yoma, fol. 53. 2. Seder Olam Rabba, c. 25. T. Hieros. Shekalim, fol. 49. 3. (d) Joseph ben Gorion, l. 1. c. 17. 2 Maccab. ii. 4, 5. (e) T. Hieros. Sota, fol. 22. 3. T. Bab. Ceritot, fol. 5. 2. Maimon. Beth Habbechira, c. 4. sect. 1. (f) Misn. Shekalim, c. 6. sect. 1, 2. T. Hieros. Shekalim, fol. 49. 3. T. Bab. Yoma, fol. 54. 1. (g) De Cong. Quaer. Erud. Gratia, p. 438. (h) Mechilta, fol. 20. 1. & Tanchuma, fol. 29. 4. (i) Menasseh ben Israel Conciliat. in Gen. qu. 41. (k) T. Hieros. Shekalim, fol. 49. 3. & Sota, fol. 22. 3. T. Bab. Ceritot, fol. 5. 2. & Horayot, fol. 12. 1. Maimon. Beth Habbechira, c. 4. sect. 1. (l) R. Levi ben Gersom in 1 Kings viii. 9. so others in Laniado Celi, Yekar in loc. (n) Baal Hatturim in Numb. xvii. 5. (o) Joseph. Antiqu. l. 4. c. 4. sect. 2. Aben Ezra in Numb. xvii. 8. (p) Nat. Hist. l. 16. c. 25. (q) De Vita Mosis, l. 3. p. 681. (r) T. Bab. Bava Bathra, fol. 14. 1, 2. Jarchi in Deut. xxxi. 26. (s) Praefat. in Yad Chazaka in principio. (t) Gloss. on T. Bab. Avoda Zara, fol. 24. 2.

---

5. And over it the cherubims of glory shadowing the mercyseat; of which we cannot now speak particularly.

5. ὑπεράνω δὲ αὐτῆς Χερουβὶμ δόξης κατασκιάζοντα τὸ ἱλαστήριον· περὶ ὧν οὐκ ἔστιν νῦν λέγειν κατὰ μέρος.

5. 'uperano de auteis Cheroubim doxeis kataskyazonta to 'ilasteirion. peri 'on ouk estin nun legein kata meros.

ה. וּמִלְמַעְלָה כְּרוּבֵי הַכָּבוֹד סֹכְכִים עַל-הַכַּפֹּרֶת וְאֵין לָנוּ עַתָּה לְדַבֵּר עַל-כָּל-חֵלֶק וְחֵלֶק לְבַדּוֹ:

5. Oo•mil•ma•a•la ke•roo•vey ha•ka•vod soche•chim al - ha•ka•po•ret ve•eyn la•noo ata le•da•ber al - kol - che•lek ve•che•lek le•va•do.

Rabbinic Jewish Commentary

And over it the cherubim of glory,.... Or "glorious cherubim", where the Shechinah, or divine glory, dwelt, Psa.80:1. These were over the ark, and were in number two, as were the cherubim which God placed at the garden of Eden, Gen.3:24 according to the opinion of the ancient Jews (u); and very likely these were made after the form of them. Some have thought them to be birds of a very terrible aspect, which were set there to deter Adam and Eve from coming to the tree of life; and both Philo (w) and Josephus (x) say, they were winged fowls; but the generality of the Jewish writers take them for angels (y); and some of them say they were destroying angels, or noxious spirits (z), which is not probable; but why angels should be so called, and what was their appearance, there are different opinions. Jerom says (a) the word signifies a multitude of knowledge; and indeed Philo the Jew (b) observes, that the Greeks would interpret the Hebrew word, much knowledge and understanding; and another Jewish writer (c) affirms, that the word "cherubim" is a name for separate intelligences, as if angels were so called from their great knowledge, and that the word is the same as "cerabbim", as "Rabbis", or teachers; but for the most part they interpret it, "as young men" (d), because that angels have appeared in the form of young men. So in the Talmud (e) it is asked,

"What does cherub signify?" says R. Abhu, כרביא, "as a young man", for so in Babylon they call a young man רביא."

Some think that the word "cherub" is the same with רכוב, "Recub", the letters transposed, which signifies "a chariot", because God is said to ride upon a "cherub" and the angels are called the chariots of the Lord, Psa.18:10 to which may be added, that Ezekiel's vision of the "cherubim" is frequently, by the Jews (f), called מרכבה, "Mercabah", or "the chariot"; and mention is made of the chariot of the cherubim, in 1Ch.28:18 to which reference may be had in Hab.3:8 though I rather think, with others, that the word is derived from כרב, "Carab", which in the Syriac and Arabic languages signifies "to plough", and so in the Talmud (g). Some of late have fancied, that they were an hieroglyphic of the trinity of persons in the Godhead, signified by the ox, the lion, and eagle; and of the incarnation of the Son of God, the face of a man being added to them; to support which notion it is further observed, that the word כרובים should be pronounced "ce-rubbim", and interpreted, "as the mighty ones".

Philo the Jew makes the "cherubim" to signify the two powers of God, his creative and governing powers (h); and the Jews frequently speak of רזא דכרובים, "The mystery of the cherubim" (i).

(u) Targum Jon. &. Hieros. in Gen. iii. 24. (w) De Vita Mosis, l. 3. p. 668. (x) Antiqu. l. 3. c. 6. sect. 5. (y) Bereshit Rabba, sect. 21. fol. 19. 1. & Mattanot Cehunah in ib. Aben Ezra in Gen iii. 24. (z) Jarchi & Baal Hatturim in loc. (a) Ep. Paulino, Tom. III. fol. 3. F. (b) Ut supra. (De Vita Mosis, l. 3. p. 668.) (c) R. Samuel Tzartzah, Sepher Meker Chayim, fol. 8. 3. (d) Zohar in Gen. fol. 122. 3. & Imre Binah in ib. Aben Ezra in Gen. iii. 24. Kimchi Sepher Shorash. in rad. ברוב, & R. Sol. Urbin. Ohel Moed, fol. 58. 2. (e) T. Bab. Chagiga, fol. 13. 2. & Succa, fol. 5. 2. (f) T. Bab. Chagiga, fol. 14. 2. (g) T. Bab. Sabbat, fol. 32. 2. Bava Kama, fol. 96. 2. (h) De Cherubim, p. 112. de Profugis, p. 465. & de Vita Mosis, l. 3. p. 669. (i) Zohar in Gen. fol. 99. 1. & 122. 4.

Hebrews 9

6. Now when these things were thus ordained, the priests went always into the first tabernacle, accomplishing the service of God.

6. Τούτων δὲ οὕτως κατεσκευασμένων, εἰς μὲν τὴν πρώτην σκηνὴν διὰ παντὸς εἰσίασιν οἱ ἱερεῖς, τὰς λατρείας ἐπιτελοῦντες·

6. Touton de 'outos kateskeuasmenon, eis men tein protein skeinein dya pantos eisiasin 'oi 'iereis, tas latreias epitelountes.

‎ו. וְכַאֲשֶׁר נַעֲשׂוּ אֵלֶּה בָּאוּ תָמִיד הַכֹּהֲנִים עֹבְדֵי עֲבֹדָה אֶל-הַמִּשְׁכָּן הַחִיצוֹן:

6. Ve•cha•a•sher na•a•soo ele ba•oo ta•mid ha•ko•ha•nim ov•dey avo•da el - ha•mish•kan ha•chi•tzon.

Rabbinic Jewish Commentary

accomplishing the service of God; by offering sacrifices, burning incense, and trimming the lamps, which they did every day: the priests entered into the holy place every day for service; but they might not go in at any other time but the time of service (l) the phrase, "of God", is not in the text, but is a supplement; and it was usual with the Jews to call the worship of the temple, and especially that part of it which lay in sacrifices, עבודה, "the service": Simeon the just used to say, the world stands upon three things; upon the law, ועל העבודה, "and upon the service", and upon beneficence (m); by "the service", the commentators (n) on the passage understand sacrifices; and again it is said (o), no man enters into the court לעבודה, "for service", though he is clean, until he has dipped himself: the word here used in the Greek text is in the plural number, and may be rendered the services, because there were several sorts of services performed every day, as before observed, and several sacrifices offered; and the Vulgate Latin version renders it, "the offices of sacrifices"; and the Ethiopic version, "their offerings"; and the Arabic version, "offices": and the service which the high priest performed in the holiest of all once a year, was divers, which is mentioned in the following verses, and is called "service", Heb.9:8 it is said, that on the day of atonement there were five עבודות, "services" of the morning daily sacrifice (p), in which the high priest ministered in his golden garments: but here the service of the common priests is meant, which was every day; and it becomes such who are employed in sacred service; both to be constant in it, and to do it fully and completely.

(l) Maimon. Biath Hamikdash, c. 2. sect. 1, 2. (m) Pirke Abot, c. 1. sect. 2. (n) Maimon & Bartenora in ib. (o) Misn. Yoma, c. 3. sect. 3. (p) T. Bab. Yoma, fol. 32. 1.

Hebrews 9

7. But into the second went the high priest alone once every year, not without blood, which he offered for himself, and for the errors of the people:

7. εἰς δὲ τὴν δευτέραν ἅπαξ τοῦ ἐνιαυτοῦ μόνος ὁ ἀρχιερεύς, οὐ χωρὶς αἵματος, ὃ προσφέρει ὑπὲρ ἑαυτοῦ καὶ τῶν τοῦ λαοῦ ἀγνοημάτων·

7. eis de tein deuteran 'apax tou enyautou monos 'o archiereus, ou choris 'aimatos, 'o prospherei 'uper 'eautou kai ton tou laou agnoeimaton.

ז. וְאֶל-הַפְּנִימִי בָּא הַכֹּהֵן הַגָּדוֹל לְבַדּוֹ פַּעַם אַחַת בַּשָּׁנָה לֹא בִּבְלִי-דָם אֲשֶׁר הִזָּה לְכַפֵּר בַּעֲדוֹ וּבְעַד שִׁגְגוֹת:הָעָם

7. Ve•el - ha•p`ni•mi ba ha•ko•hen ha•ga•dol le•va•do pa•am a•chat ba•sha•na lo biv•li - dam asher hi•za le•cha•per ba•a•do oov•ad shi•ge•got ha•am.

Rabbinic Jewish Commentary

Though this is not expressed in so many words in Lev.16:2 only it is said that "Aaron came not at all times into the holy place within the vail"; yet it is the constant and generally received sense of the Jewish writers, in agreement with the apostle here, that the high priest went into the holy of holies but once a year (q), on the day of atonement, which was on the tenth of the month Tisri, and answers to part of September; not but that he went in more than once on that day, for he went in no less than four times (r);

the first time he went in to offer incense; the second time with the blood of the bullock, to sprinkle it; the third time with the blood of the goat; and the fourth time to bring out the censer (s); and if he entered a fifth time, they say he was worthy of death; wherefore Philo the Jew (t) seems to be mistaken when he affirms that, if he went in three or four times on the same day, he suffered death, nor was there any pardon for him; and as it was but one day in a year he might enter, so when he did, no other man, either Israelite or priest, might go in along with him; he went in alone without any attendance: the Jews say (u), that a cord or thong was bound to the feet of the high priest when he went into the holy of holies, that if he died there, the rest might be able to draw him out; for it was not lawful for another priest to go in, no, not an high priest, none besides him on the day of atonement. Pausanias (w) makes mention of a temple of Minerva into which the priests entered once every year; which very likely was observed in imitation of this custom of the Jewish high priest; who in it was a type of Messiah, and of his entrance into heaven, and of his constant and continued intercession there.

(q) T. Hieros. Yoma, fol. 42. 4. & 43. 1. Bab. Pesachim, fol. 86. 1. (r) Bemidbar Rabba, sect 7. fol. 188. 4. Maimon. Biath Hamikdash, c. 2. sect. 3. Moses Kotsensis Mitzvot Tora, pr. neg. 303. (s) Maimon. & Bartenora in Misna Celim, c. 1. sect. 9. (t) De Legatione ad Caium, p. 1035. (u) Zohar in Lev. fol. 43. 3. & Imre Binah in ib. (w) Arcadica, sive l. 8. p. 531.

Hebrews 9

8. The Holy Ghost this signifying, that the way into the holiest of all was not yet made manifest, while as the first tabernacle was yet standing:

8. τοῦτο δηλοῦντος τοῦ πνεύματος τοῦ ἁγίου, μήπω πεφανερῶσθαι τὴν τῶν ἁγίων ὁδόν, ἔτι τῆς πρώτης σκηνῆς ἐχούσης στάσιν·

8. touto deilountos tou pneumatos tou 'agiou, meipo pephanerosthai tein ton 'agion 'odon, eti teis proteis skeineis echouseis stasin.

ח. בְּזֹאת הוֹדִיעַ רוּחַ הַקֹּדֶשׁ כִּי עוֹד לֹא נִפְתַּח הַדֶּרֶךְ לְקֹדֶשׁ הַקֳּדָשִׁים כָּל-עוֹד הַמִּשְׁכָּן הָרִאשׁוֹן עֹמֵד עַל-מְכוֹנוֹ:

8. Be•zot ho•di•a Roo•ach ha•Ko•desh ki od lo nif•tach ha•de•rech le•ko•desh ha•ko•da•shim kol - od ha•mish•kan ha•ri•shon o•med al - me•cho•no.

104

Rabbinic Jewish Commentary

The Vulgate Latin and all the Oriental versions render it, "the way of the saints"; of the priests who ministered in holy things, and were holy to the Lord, and of all the saints that lived before Messiah.

Hebrews 9

9. Which was a figure for the time then present, in which were offered both gifts and sacrifices, that could not make him that did the service perfect, as pertaining to the conscience;

9. ἥτις παραβολὴ εἰς τὸν καιρὸν τὸν ἐνεστηκότα, καθ᾽ ὃν δῶρά τε καὶ θυσίαι προσφέρονται, μὴ δυνάμεναι κατὰ συνείδησιν τελειῶσαι τὸν λατρεύοντα,

9. 'eitis parabolei eis ton kairon ton enesteikota, kath 'on dora te kai thusiai prospherontai, mei dunamenai kata suneideisin teleiosai ton latreuonta,

ט. וְזֶה הוּא לְמָשָׁל לַזְּמָן הַזֶּה בְּהַקְרִיבָם מִנְחָה וָזֶבַח אֲשֶׁר אֵין בָּם לְהָכִין לֵבָב שָׁלֵם אֶל־הָעֹבְדִים:

9. Ve•ze hoo le•mo•shal laz•man ha•ze be•hak•ri•vam min•cha va•ze•vach asher eyn bam le•ha•chin le•vav sha•lem el - ha•ov•dim.

Rabbinic Jewish Commentary

The Vulgate Latin version renders it, it was a "figure of the present time"; it was a shadow of good things to come under that; it prefigured what is now accomplished; or rather it was a "figure unto, or until the present time"; till Messiah came, when all figures, types, and shadows fled away, and were of no more real use and service.

in which were offered both gifts and sacrifices; that is, in which tabernacle, or at which then present time, or καθ' ην, "according to which figure or parable", as the Alexandrian copy and Vulgate Latin version read, gifts and sacrifices were offered by the priests.

---

10. Which stood only in meats and drinks, and divers washings, and carnal ordinances, imposed on them until the time of reformation.

10. μόνον ἐπὶ βρώμασιν καὶ πόμασιν καὶ διαφόροις βαπτισμοῖς καὶ δικαιώμασιν σαρκός, μέχρι καιροῦ διορθώσεως ἐπικείμενα.

10. monon epi bromasin kai pomasin kai dyaphorois baptismois kai dikaiomasin sarkos, mechri kairou diorthoseos epikeimena.

י. כִּי חֻקּוֹת הַגּוּף הֵם עִם־מַאֲכָל וּמִשְׁתֶּה וּטְבִילוֹת שֹׁנוֹת אֲשֶׁר נִתְּנוּ עַד־עֵת הַתִּקּוּן:

10. Ki choo•kot ha•goof hem eem - ma•a•chal oo•mish•te oot•vi•lot sho•not asher nit•noo ad - et ha•ti•koon.

Rabbinic Jewish Commentary

Judaism has never supposed that the mechanical performance of ritual acts causes God to forgive sin. Rather, since the destruction of the Temple, Judaism has taken a different tack, teaching that neither sacrifice nor priesthood is necessary for God to forgive sin. The author Paul expresses the view that sacrifice and priesthood are indeed necessary, that the Mosaic system was *imposed until the time for God to reshape the whole structure*, literally, "until a time of re-formation," and thus prefigured the system established by Yeshua the Messiah.

Hebrews 9

11. But Christ being come an high priest of good things to come, by a greater and more perfect tabernacle, not made with hands, that is to say, not of this building;

11. Χριστὸς δὲ παραγενόμενος ἀρχιερεὺς τῶν μελλόντων ἀγαθῶν, διὰ τῆς μείζονος καὶ τελειοτέρας σκηνῆς, οὐ χειροποιήτου, τοῦτ᾽ ἔστιν, οὐ ταύτης τῆς κτίσεως,

11. Christos de paragenomenos archiereus ton mellonton agathon, dya teis meizonos kai teleioteras skeineis, ou cheiropoieitou, tout estin, ou tauteis teis ktiseos,

יא. אֲבָל בְּבֹא הַמָּשִׁיחַ לִהְיוֹת לְכֹהֵן גָּדוֹל עַל־הַטֹּבוֹת הָעֲתִידוֹת בַּמִּשְׁכָּן הַגָּדוֹל וְהַשָּׁלֵם אֲשֶׁר אֵינֶנּוּ מַעֲשֵׂה יָדַיִם: וְאֵינֶנּוּ מֵהַבְּרִיאָה הַלֵּזוּ

11. Aval be•vo ha•Ma•shi•ach li•hee•yot le•cho•hen ga•dol al - ha•to•vot ha•a•ti•dot ba•mish•kan ha•ga•dol ve•ha•sha•lem asher ey•ne•noo ma•a•se ya•da•yim ve•ey•ne•noo me•hab•ri•ah ha•le•zoo.

12. Neither by the blood of goats and calves, but by his own blood he entered in once into the holy place, having obtained eternal redemption for us.

12. οὐδὲ δι' αἵματος τράγων καὶ μόσχων, διὰ δὲ τοῦ ἰδίου αἵματος εἰσῆλθεν ἐφάπαξ εἰς τὰ ἅγια, αἰωνίαν λύτρωσιν εὑράμενος.

12. oude di 'aimatos tragon kai moschon, dya de tou idiou 'aimatos eiseilthen ephapax eis ta 'agya, aionian lutrosin 'euramenos.

יב. הוּא בָא פַעַם אַחַת אֶל-הַקֹּדֶשׁ לֹא בְדַם שְׂעִירִים וַעֲגָלִים כִּי אִם-בְּדַם נַפְשׁוֹ וַיִּמְצָא פְּדוּת עוֹלָם:

12. Hoo va fa•am a•chat el - ha•ko•desh lo ve•dam s`ee•rim va•a•ga•lim ki eem - be•dam naf•sho va•yim•tza pe•doot o•lam.

Rabbinic Jewish Commentary

Remarkable is the paraphrase of the Tagum by Jonathan ben Uzziel on Gen.49:18.

"Jacob said, when he saw Gideon the son of Joash, and Samson the son of Manoah, who should be redeemers; not for the redemption of Gideon am I waiting, nor for the redemption of Samson am I looking, for their redemption is a temporal redemption; but for thy redemption am I waiting and looking, O Lord, because thy redemption is פורקן עלמין, "an everlasting redemption."

Another copy reads, for the redemption of Messiah the son of David; and to the same purpose is the Jerusalem paraphrase on the place; in Talmudic language it would be called פדייה עולמית (x).

(x) T. Shebuot, fol. 11. 2.

Hebrews 9

13. For if the blood of bulls and of goats, and the ashes of an heifer sprinkling the unclean, sanctifieth to the purifying of the flesh:

13. Εἰ γὰρ τὸ αἷμα ταύρων καὶ τράγων, καὶ σποδὸς δαμάλεως ῥαντίζουσα τοὺς κεκοινωμένους, ἁγιάζει πρὸς τὴν τῆς σαρκὸς καθαρότητα,

13. Ei gar to 'aima tauron kai tragon, kai spodos damaleos 'rantizousa tous kekoinomenous, 'agyazei pros tein teis sarkos katharoteita,

יג. וְאִם דַּם שְׂעִירִים וּפָרִים וְאֵפֶר הַפָּרָה זֹרַק עַל-הַטָּמֵא יְטַהֵר אֶת-בְּשָׂרוֹ וַיְקַדְּשֵׁהוּ:

13. Ve•eem dam s`ee•rim oo•fa•rim ve•e•fer ha•pa•ra zo•rak al - ha•ta•me ye•ta•her et - be•sa•ro vai•kad•she•hoo.

Rabbinic Jewish Commentary

For if the blood of bulls and of goats,.... Shed either on the day of atonement, or at any other time: the former of thee, Pausanias (y) relates, was drank by certain priestesses among the Grecians, whereby they were tried, whether they spoke truth or no if not, they were immediately punished; and the latter, he says (z), will dissolve an adamant stone; but neither of them can purge from sin.

and the ashes of an heifer sprinkling the unclean; the apostle refers to the red heifer, Num.19:1 which being burnt, its ashes were gathered up and put into a vessel, and water poured upon them, which was sprinkled with a bunch of hyssop on unclean persons; the ashes and the water mixed together made the water of separation, or of sprinkling; for so it is called by the Septuagint, υδωρ ραντισμου, "the water of sprinkling", and in the Targum in a following citation: this was the purification for sin, though it only

sanctifieth to the purifying of the flesh; the body, or only in an external and typical way, but did not really sanctify the heart, or purify and cleanse the soul from sin. The Jews say, that the waters of purification for sin were not waters of purification for sin, without the ashes (a); and to this the Targumist, on Eze.36:25 and on Zec.13:1 refers, paraphrasing both texts thus;

"I will forgive their sins as they are cleansed with the water of sprinkling, and with the ashes of the heifer, which is a purification for sin."

(y) Achaica, sive l. 7. p. 450. (z) Arcadica, sive l. 8. p. 485. (a) Misn. Temura, c. 1. sect. 5. Maimon. & Bartenora in ib.

---

14. How much more shall the blood of Christ, who through the eternal Spirit offered himself without spot to God, purge your conscience from dead works to serve the living God?

14. πόσῳ μᾶλλον τὸ αἷμα τοῦ χριστοῦ, ὃς διὰ πνεύματος αἰωνίου ἑαυτὸν προσήνεγκεν ἄμωμον τῷ θεῷ, καθαριεῖ τὴν συνείδησιν ὑμῶν ἀπὸ νεκρῶν ἔργων, εἰς τὸ λατρεύειν θεῷ ζῶντι;

14. poso mallon to 'aima tou christou, 'os dya pneumatos aioniou 'eauton proseinegken amomon to theo, kathariei tein suneideisin 'umon apo nekron ergon, eis to latreuein theo zonti?

יד. אַף כִּי-דַם הַמָּשִׁיחַ אֲשֶׁר בְּרוּחַ עוֹלָם הִקְרִיב אֶת-נַפְשׁוֹ בִּבְלִי-מוּם לֵאלֹהִים יְטַהֵר אֶת-לִבְּכֶם מִן-מַעֲשִׂים: אֲשֶׁר מָוֶת בָּם לַעֲבֹד אֶת-אֱלֹהִים חַיִּים

14. Af ki - dam ha•Ma•shi•ach asher be•Roo•ach o•lam hik•riv et - naf•sho biv•li – moom le•Elohim ye•ta•her et - lib•chem min - ma•a•sim asher ma•vet bam la•a•vod et – Elohim cha•yim.

Hebrews 9

15. And for this cause he is the mediator of the new testament, that by means of death, for the redemption of the transgressions that were under the first testament, they which are called might receive the promise of eternal inheritance.

15. Καὶ διὰ τοῦτο διαθήκης καινῆς μεσίτης ἐστίν, ὅπως, θανάτου γενομένου εἰς ἀπολύτρωσιν τῶν ἐπὶ τῇ πρώτῃ διαθήκῃ παραβάσεων, τὴν ἐπαγγελίαν λάβωσιν οἱ κεκλημένοι τῆς αἰωνίου κληρονομίας.

15. Kai dya touto dyatheikeis kaineis mesiteis estin, 'opos, thanatou genomenou eis apolutrosin ton epi tei protei dyatheikei parabaseon, tein epangelian labosin 'oi kekleimenoi teis aioniou kleironomias.

טו. בַּעֲבוּר זֹאת מַלְאַךְ מֵלִיץ הוּא לַבְּרִית הַחֲדָשָׁה וּמוֹתוֹ נִמְצָא לְכַפָּרַת הַפֹּשְׁעִים תַּחַת הַבְּרִית הָרִאשֹׁנָה לְמַעַן יַשִּׂיגוּ בְחִירֵי-יָהּ אֶת-הַבְטָחַת נַחֲלַת עוֹלָם

15. Ba•a•voor zot mal•ach me•litz hoo la•b`rit ha•cha•da•sha oo•mo•to nim•tza le•cha•pa•rat ha•psh•eem ta•chat ha•b`rit ha•ri•sho•na le•ma•an ya•si•goo ve•chi•rey - Ya et - hav•ta•chat na•cha•lat o•lam.

Rabbinic Jewish Commentary

The Syriac version renders it, "that by his death he might be a redemption for them who transgressed the first testament"; so the Jews say, that the Messiah must die לפדות את אבות "to redeem the fathers" (b)

(b) R. Moses Haddarsan apud Galatin. l. 8. c. 20.

Hebrews 9

16. For where a testament is, there must also of necessity be the death of the testator.

16. Ὅπου γὰρ διαθήκη, θάνατον ἀνάγκη φέρεσθαι τοῦ διαθεμένου.

16. 'Opou gar dyatheikei, thanaton anagkei pheresthai tou dyathemenou.

טז. כִּי בְצַוָּאַת הַמַּנְחִיל יֶחְסַר מוֹת הַמַּנְחִיל:

16. Ki ve•tza•va•at ha•man•chil yech•sar mot ha•man•chil.

Rabbinic Jewish Commentary

For where a testament is,.... The covenant of grace, as administered under the Gospel dispensation, is a testament or will. The Jews have adopted the Greek word, here used, into their language, and pronounce it דייתיקי, and by it understand a dying man's last will and testament (d). Some of them make it to be of Hebrew derivation; as if it was said, דא תהי למיקם, "this shall be to confirm" (e), or this shall be stable and firm; though others own it to be the same with this Greek word διαθηκη (f).

(d) T. Hieros. Peah, fol. 17. 4. & T. Bab. Bava Bathra, fol. 152. 2. (e) T. Bab. Bava Metzia, fol. 19. 1. Maimon & Bartenora in Misn. Moed Katon, c. 3. sect. 3. & in Bava Metzia, c. 1. sect. 7. & in Bava Bathra, c. 8. sect. 6. (f) Cohen de Lara Ir David, p. 30.

---

17. For a testament is of force after men are dead: otherwise it is of no strength at all while the testator liveth.

17. Διαθήκη γὰρ ἐπὶ νεκροῖς βεβαία, ἐπεὶ μήποτε ἰσχύει ὅτε ζῇ ὁ διαθέμενος.

17. Dyatheikei gar epi nekrois bebaia, epei meipote ischuei 'ote zei 'o dyathemenos.

יז. וְצַוָּאַת הַמַּנְחִיל תָּקוּם אַךְ אַחֲרֵי הַמָּוֶת יַעַן אֵין לָה תֹּקֶף בְּחַיֵּי הַמַּנְחִיל:

17. Ve•tza•va•at ha•man•chil ta•koom ach a•cha•rey ha•ma•vet ya•an eyn la to•kef be•cha•yey ha•man•chil.

Hebrews 9

18. Whereupon neither the first testament was dedicated without blood.

18. Ὅθεν οὐδ᾽ ἡ πρώτη χωρὶς αἵματος ἐγκεκαίνισται.

18. 'Othen oud 'ei protei choris 'aimatos egkekainistai.

יח. וְלָכֵן גַּם-חֲנֻכַּת הַבְּרִית הָרִאשׁוֹנָה לֹא נֶעֶשְׂתָה בִּבְלִי-דָם:

18. Ve•la•chen gam - cha•noo•kat ha•b`rit ha•ri•sho•na lo ne•es•ta biv•li - dam.

---

19. For when Moses had spoken every precept to all the people according to the law, he took the blood of calves and of goats, with water, and scarlet wool, and hyssop, and sprinkled both the book, and all the people,

19. Λαληθείσης γὰρ πάσης ἐντολῆς κατὰ νόμον ὑπὸ Μωϋσέως παντὶ τῷ λαῷ, λαβὼν τὸ αἷμα τῶν μόσχων καὶ τράγων, μετὰ ὕδατος καὶ ἐρίου κοκκίνου καὶ ὑσσώπου, αὐτό τε τὸ βιβλίον καὶ πάντα τὸν λαὸν ἐρράντισεν,

19. Laleitheiseis gar paseis entoleis kata nomon 'upo Mouseos panti to lao, labon to 'aima ton moschon kai tragon, meta 'udatos kai eriou kokkinou kai 'ussopou, auto te to biblion kai panta ton laon errantisen,

יט. כִּי כַאֲשֶׁר נֶאֶמְרָה כָל-מִצְוָה כְּפִי הַתּוֹרָה לְכָל-הָעָם בְּיַד-מֹשֶׁה לָקַח דַּם עֲגָלִים וּשְׂעִירִים עִם-מַיִם וּשְׁנִי-תוֹלַעַת וְאֵזוֹב וַיִּזְרֹק עַל-הַסֵּפֶר וְעַל-הָעָם:

19. Ki cha•a•sher ne•em•ra chol - mitz•cha ke•fi ha•Torah le•chol - ha•am be•yad – Moshe la•kach dam a•ga•lim oos•ee•rim eem - ma•yim oosh•ni to•la•at ve•e•zov va•yiz•rok al - ha•se•fer ve•al - ha•am.

Rabbinic Jewish Commentary

he took the blood of calves, and of goats; The Syriac version only reads, "he took the blood of an heifer"; and the Arabic version, "he took the blood of calves"; but all the copies, and other versions, read both. "With water, and scarlet wool, and hyssop."

The apostle Paul calls scarlet, scarlet wool; though whenever the word is used in the Jewish laws of the Old Testament, wool is not expressed, but it is always intended; for it is a rule with the Jews (h), that

"The blue, which is spoken of in every place, is wool dyed of a sky colour; purple is wool dyed red, and scarlet is wool dyed in scarlet."

(h) Ib. Hilchot Cele Hamikdash, c. 8. sect. 13.

Hebrews 9

20. Saying, This is the blood of the testament which God hath enjoined unto you.

20. λέγων, Τοῦτο τὸ αἷμα τῆς διαθήκης ἧς ἐνετείλατο πρὸς ὑμᾶς ὁ Θεός.

20. legon, Touto to 'aima teis dyatheikeis 'eis eneteilato pros 'umas 'o theos.

כ. וַיֹּאמֶר הִנֵּה דַם־הַבְּרִית אֲשֶׁר צִוָּה אֶתְכֶם אֱלֹהִים:

20. Va•yo•mar hee•ne dam - ha•b`rit asher tzi•va et•chem Elohim.

Rabbinic Jewish Commentary

In Judaism, atonement can be made in a variety of ways: Sacrifice, suffering, exile, etc. It has become a major point of contention between Christians and Jews. Christians focus on the last half of the verse, "apart from the shedding of blood, there is no remission" or atonement. However, the first half of the verse limits the application, "almost everything is cleansed by blood." Eleh v'eleh. The harmonization between the two viewpoints is that atonement can be achieved in a variety of ways. First, the entire context of the book of Hebrews is the festival of Yom Kippur. In the presence of the Temple, the Torah requires the shedding of blood on Yom Kippur. Secondly, there are levels of atonement, for the severity of the sin and for a particular time frame. However, there are cases where it requires the blood of the Tzaddik, as Rebbe Nachman of Breslov writes in Likutey Moharan,

"…Israel's spilled blood contains many lofty and hidden matters, be it blood spilled through embarrassment or other, actual spilled blood. For there are very many fallen souls which have no elevation except through the spilled blood of Israel; [that] of a great individual. In some cases, they

have no elevation except through actual spilled blood."
(Likutey Moharan, Volume II, 83:11, Volume XV, Breslov Research Institute, pg 225)

The Breslov Commentary on this passage states, "Rebbe Nachman teaches here that this is the deeper reason – "the lofty and hidden matters" – that Israel's blood has been spilled time and again down through the generations. Whether through embarrassment or murder, the spilled blood of the righteous – a "great individual" – raises the fallen souls and brings to their rectification. The Rebbe has already alluded to this spilled blood of a great individual in the previous section, where he spoke of the tzaddik who must undergo "ritual slaughter" so that God's tasting his mitzvot is not the consumption of the limb of a living creature....In Likutey Moharan 1, 260, Rebbe Nachman teaches that there are times when, to gain forgiveness for the Jewish people, tzaddikim sacrifice their name and honor and willing suffer embarrassment. Other times, the truly great tzaddikim are required to make the ultimate sacrifice and give their lives to effect forgiveness. This related to the tzaddik's spilled blood, and to the elevation of the very many souls which have fallen on account of Adam's blemish of the brit and due to the sins of mankind ever since...The only way to effective unification when sins are prevalent is by the tzaddik's ultimate self-sacrifice. The righteous are required to accept judgment upon themselves, giving up their lives for God. One such time is when the Holy Temple was destroyed. Sin abounded then, and many souls became trapped in the kelipot. The only possibility of releasing the fallen souls was by entering the realm of impurity itself. The Ten Martyrs, all very great and pure tzaddikim, undertook to do this. Accepting the judgment upon themselves, the Ten Martyrs made the ultimate self-sacrifice, submitting their physical bodies to the realm of the kelipot – the Romans, who tortured and murdered them. Through this "exchange" (for the bodies of the tzaddikim were so holy, they were equivalent to the souls of most other people), the Ten Martyrs rescued the trapped souls, whose elevation, an arousal from energy below, brought about a unification of the Holy One and His Shekhinah in the Upper Worlds..."
(Commentary to Likutey Moharan, Volume II, 83:11, Volume XV, Breslov Research Institute, pg 225-226)

---

21. Moreover he sprinkled with blood both the tabernacle, and all the vessels of the ministry.

21. Καὶ τὴν σκηνὴν δὲ καὶ πάντα τὰ σκεύη τῆς λειτουργίας τῷ αἵματι ὁμοίως ἐρράντισεν.

21. Kai tein skeinein de kai panta ta skeuei teis leitourgias to 'aimati 'omoios errantisen.

כא. וְכֵן עַל-הַמִּשְׁכָּן וְעַל-כָּל-כְּלֵי הַשָּׁרֵת זָרַק אֶת-הַדָּם:

21. Ve•chen al - ha•mish•kan ve•al - kol - k`ley ha•sha•ret za•rak et - ha•dam.

Rabbinic Jewish Commentary
Josephus, in agreement with the apostle Paul, asserts (i), that the tabernacle, and its vessels, were not only anointed with oil, but sprinkled with the blood of bulls and goats, as well as the garments of Aaron, and his sons.

(i) Antiq. l. 3. c. 8. sect. 6.

Hebrews 9

22. And almost all things are by the law purged with blood; and without shedding of blood is no remission.

22. Καὶ σχεδὸν ἐν αἵματι πάντα καθαρίζεται κατὰ τὸν νόμον, καὶ χωρὶς αἱματεκχυσίας οὐ γίνεται ἄφεσις.

22. Kai schedon en 'aimati panta katharizetai kata ton nomon, kai choris 'aimatekchusias ou ginetai aphesis.

כב. וְכִמְעַט הַכֹּל לְפִי הַתּוֹרָה יִטְהַר בַּדָּם וּבִבְלִי שְׁפָךְ-דָּם אֵין סְלִיחָה:

22. Ve•chim•at ha•kol le•fi ha•Torah yit•har ba•dam oo•viv•lee sh`foc - dam eyn s`li•cha.

Rabbinic Jewish Commentary
It is a common saying with the Jews, and often to be met with in their writings, אין כפרה אלא בדם, "there is no atonement but by blood" (k); by the shedding of blood; not by the shedding of it, as it flows out of the body of the sacrifice, but as it is poured out on the altar; for the pouring of the blood at the four corners, and at the bottom of the altar, were the chief rites required in sacrifices; nor did they reckon expiation to be expiation, unless the altar was moistened by the blood of the sacrifice (l).

(k) T. Bab. Yoma, fol. 5. 1. Zebachim, fol. 6. 1. & Menachot, fol. 93. 2. (l) Reland. Heb. Antiqu. par. 3. c. 2. sect. 8.

---

23. It was therefore necessary that the patterns of things in the heavens should be purified with these; but the heavenly things themselves with better sacrifices than these.

23. Ἀνάγκη οὖν τὰ μὲν ὑποδείγματα τῶν ἐν τοῖς οὐρανοῖς, τούτοις καθαρίζεσθαι, αὐτὰ δὲ τὰ ἐπουράνια κρείττοσιν θυσίαις παρὰ ταύτας.

23. Anagkei oun ta men 'upodeigmata ton en tois ouranois, toutois katharizesthai, auta de ta epouranya kreittosin thusiais para tautas.

כג. וְלָכֵן נָכוֹן הָיָה לְטַהֵר כָּזֹאת אֶת־הַדְּבָרִים אֲשֶׁר תַּבְנִית הֵם לַאֲשֶׁר בַּמָּרוֹם אֲבָל הַדְּבָרִים עַצְמָם בַּמָּרוֹם:בִּזְבָחִים טוֹבִים מֵאֵלֶּה

23. Ve•la•chen na•chon ha•ya le•ta•her ka•zot et - ha•d`va•rim asher tav•nit hem la•a•sher ba•ma•rom aval ha•d`va•rim atz•mam ba•ma•rom biz•va•chim to•vim me•e•le.

Rabbinic Jewish Commentary
On account of the divine appointment, and that types and antitypes might correspond; and especially it was necessary with respect to the Messiah, the substance and body of all types. So the Targum of Jonathan ben Uzziel paraphrases the text in Exo.40:9,

"And thou shalt take the anointing oil, and thou shalt anoint the tabernacle, and all that is in it; and thou shall sanctify it, מטול, because of the crown of the kingdom of the house of Judah, and the King Messiah, who shall redeem Israel in the latter days."

---

24. For Christ is not entered into the holy places made with hands, which are the figures of the true; but into heaven itself, now to appear in the presence of God for us:

24. Οὐ γὰρ εἰς χειροποίητα ἅγια εἰσῆλθεν ὁ χριστός, ἀντίτυπα τῶν ἀληθινῶν, ἀλλ᾽ εἰς αὐτὸν τὸν οὐρανόν, νῦν ἐμφανισθῆναι τῷ προσώπῳ τοῦ θεοῦ ὑπὲρ ἡμῶν·

24. Ou gar eis cheiropoieita 'agya eiseilthen 'o christos, antitupa ton aleithinon, all eis auton ton ouranon, nun emphanistheinai to prosopo tou theou 'uper 'eimon.

כד. כִּי לֹא בָא הַמָּשִׁיחַ אֶל־הַמִּקְדָּשׁ מַעֲשֵׂה יָדַיִם אֲשֶׁר תַּבְנִית הוּא לְמִקְדָּשׁ אֱמֶת כִּי אִם־בָּא אֶל־עֶצֶם הַשָּׁמַיִם:לְהֵרָאוֹת עַתָּה בַּעֲדֵנוּ לִפְנֵי הָאֱלֹהִים

24. Ki lo va ha•Ma•shi•ach el - ha•mik•dash ma•a•se ya•da•yim asher tav•nit hoo le•mik•dash emet ki eem - ba el - etzem ha•sha•ma•yim le•he•ra•ot ata ba•a•de•noo lif•ney ha•Elohim.

Rabbinic Jewish Commentary
which are the figures of the true; Josephus (m) suggests the same, when speaking of the most holy place; he says, that it was inaccessible to the priests, that it might be as heaven to God.

(m) Antiqu. l. 3. c. 5. sect. 4. & c. 7. sect. 8.

Hebrews 9

25. Nor yet that he should offer himself often, as the high priest entereth into the holy place every year with blood of others;

25. οὐδ᾽ ἵνα πολλάκις προσφέρῃ ἑαυτόν, ὥσπερ ὁ ἀρχιερεὺς εἰσέρχεται εἰς τὰ ἅγια κατ᾽ ἐνιαυτὸν ἐν αἵματι ἀλλοτρίῳ·

25. oud 'ina pollakis prospherei 'eauton, 'osper 'o archiereus eiserchetai eis ta 'agya kat enyauton en 'aimati allotrio.

כה. גַּם־לֹא לְהַקְרִיב אֶת־נַפְשׁוֹ פְּעָמִים רַבּוֹת כַּכֹּהֵן הַגָּדוֹל הַבָּא אֶל־הַקֹּדֶשׁ שָׁנָה בְשָׁנָה בְּדַם לֹא־לוֹ:

25. Gam - lo le•hak•riv et - naf•sho pe•a•mim ra•bot ka•ko•hen ha•ga•dol ha•ba el - ha•ko•desh sha•na ve•sha•na be•dam lo - lo.

26. For then must he often have suffered since the foundation of the world: but now once in the end of the world hath he appeared to put away sin by the sacrifice of himself.

26. ἐπεὶ ἔδει αὐτὸν πολλάκις παθεῖν ἀπὸ καταβολῆς κόσμου· νῦν δὲ ἅπαξ ἐπὶ συντελείᾳ τῶν αἰώνων εἰς ἀθέτησιν ἁμαρτίας διὰ τῆς θυσίας αὐτοῦ πεφανέρωται.

26. epei edei auton pollakis pathein apo kataboleis kosmou. nun de 'apax epi sunteleia ton aionon eis atheteisin 'amartias dya teis thusias autou pephanerotai.

כו. כִּי אִם־כֵּן הָיָה לּוֹ לְהִתְעַנּוֹת פְּעָמִים רַבּוֹת לְמִן הִוָּסֵד אָרֶץ אַךְ עַתָּה בְּקֵץ הַדֹּרוֹת נִגְלָה פַּעַם אַחַת לְהָתֵם:חַטָּאוֹת בְּזֶבַח נַפְשׁוֹ

26. Ki eem - ken ha•ya lo le•hit•a•not pe•a•mim ra•bot le•min hi•va•sed a•retz ach ata be•ketz ha•do•rot nig•la fa•am a•chat le•ha•tem cha•ta•ot be•ze•vach naf•sho.

Rabbinic Jewish Commentary
The Jews expect their Messiah לקץ הימים, "at the end of days" (n): and this appearance was but "once"

(n) Seder Tephillot, Ed. Amstelod. fol. 2. 1.

Hebrews 9

27. And as it is appointed unto men once to die, but after this the judgment:

27. Καὶ καθ᾽ ὅσον ἀπόκειται τοῖς ἀνθρώποις ἅπαξ ἀποθανεῖν, μετὰ δὲ τοῦτο κρίσις·

27. Kai kath 'oson apokeitai tois anthropois 'apax apothanein, meta de touto krisis.

כז. וְכַאֲשֶׁר נִגְזַר עַל־בְּנֵי אָדָם לָמוּת פַּעַם אַחַת וְאַחֲרֵי־כֵן הַמִּשְׁפָּט:

27. Ve•cha•a•sher nig•zar al - b`ney adam la•moot pa•am a•chat ve•a•cha•rey – chen ha•mish•pat.

---

28. So Christ was once offered to bear the sins of many; and unto them that look for him shall he appear the second time without sin unto salvation.

28. οὕτως καὶ ὁ χριστός, ἅπαξ προσενεχθεὶς εἰς τὸ πολλῶν ἀνενεγκεῖν ἁμαρτίας, ἐκ δευτέρου χωρὶς ἁμαρτίας ὀφθήσεται τοῖς αὐτὸν ἀπεκδεχομένοις, εἰς σωτηρίαν.

28. 'outos kai 'o christos, 'apax prosenechtheis eis to pollon anenegkein 'amartias, ek deuterou choris 'amartias ophtheisetai tois auton apekdechomenois, eis soteirian.

כח. כֵּן גַּם-הַמָּשִׁיחַ הִקְרִיב אֶת-נַפְשׁוֹ פַּעַם אַחַת לָשֵׂאת חֵטְא רַבִּים וּבִבְלִי חַטָּאת יֵרָאֶה שֵׁנִית לַמְחַכִּים-לוֹ:לִתְשׁוּעָה

28. Ken gam - ha•Ma•shi•ach hik•riv et - naf•sho fa•am a•chat la•set chet ra•bim oo•viv•li cha•tat ye•ra•eh she•nit lam•cha•kim - lo lit•shoo•ah.

(Hebrews Chapter 9 End)

Hebrews, Chapter 10

1. For the law having a shadow of good things to come, and not the very image of the things, can never with those sacrifices which they offered year by year continually make the comers thereunto perfect.

1. Σκιὰν γὰρ ἔχων ὁ νόμος τῶν μελλόντων ἀγαθῶν, οὐκ αὐτὴν τὴν εἰκόνα τῶν πραγμάτων, κατ᾽ ἐνιαυτὸν ταῖς αὐταῖς θυσίαις ἃς προσφέρουσιν εἰς τὸ διηνεκές, οὐδέποτε δύνανται τοὺς προσερχομένους τελειῶσαι.

1. Skyan gar echon 'o nomos ton mellonton agathon, ouk autein tein eikona ton pragmaton, kat enyauton tais autais thusiais 'as prospherousin eis to dieinekes, oudepote dunantai tous proserchomenous teleiosai.

א. כִּי הַתּוֹרָה אֲשֶׁר בָּהּ רַק צֵל טֹבוֹת הָעֲתִידוֹת וְלֹא פְנֵי עֶצֶם הַטֹּבוֹת הָהֵנָּה אֵין בְּכֹחָהּ לְהָכִין שָׁלֵם לַנִּגָּשִׁים:בַּזְּבָחִים הָאֵלֶּה אֲשֶׁר יַקְרִיבוּ תָּמִיד שָׁנָה בְשָׁנָה

1. Ki ha•Torah asher ba rak tzel to•vot ha•a•ti•dot ve•lo f ney etzem ha•to•vot ha•he•na eyn be•cho•cha le•ha•chin sha•lem la•ni•ga•shim baz•va•chim ha•e•le asher yak•ri•voo ta•mid sha•na ve•sha•na.

Rabbinic Jewish Commentary

The Syriac and Ethiopic versions render it, "perfect them that offer"; and if not one, then not the other: legal sacrifices could not make perfect expiation of sin; there is no proportion between them and sin: nor did they extend to all sin, and at most only typically expiated; nor could they justify and cleanse from sin. Contrary to this, the Jews (p) say,

"When Israel was in the holy land, there was no iniquity found in them, for the sacrifices which they offered every day stoned for them;"

(p) Zohar in Gen. fol. 107. 1.

"R. Phinehas and R. Levi and R. Johanan said in the name of R. Menahem of Gallia: In the Time to Come all sacrifices will be annulled, but that of thanksgiving will not be annulled, and all prayers will be annulled, but that of Thanksgiving will not be annulled. This is indicated by what is written, The voice of joy and the voice of gladness, the voice of the bridegroom and the voice of the bride, the voice of them that say: Give thanks to the L-rd of hosts (Jer. 33:2). . . (Leviticus Rabbah 9:7, Soncino Press Edition)

2. For then would they not have ceased to be offered? because that the worshippers once purged should have had no more conscience of sins.

2. Ἐπεὶ οὐκ ἂν ἐπαύσαντο προσφερόμεναι, διὰ τὸ μηδεμίαν ἔχειν ἔτι συνείδησιν ἁμαρτιῶν τοὺς λατρεύοντας, ἅπαξ κεκαθαρμένους;

2. Epei ouk an epausanto prospheromenai, dya to meidemian echein eti suneideisin 'amartion tous latreuontas, 'apax kekatharmenous?

ב. כִּי אִם-לֹא-כֵן הֲלֹא יֶחְדְּלוּ מֵהַקְרִיבָם עוֹד כִּי אַחֲרֵי אֲשֶׁר הִטַּהֲרוּ הָעֹבְדִים פַּעַם אַחַת אֵין לָהֶם עוֹד מַחְשֶׁבֶת:הַחֵטְא

2. Ki eem - lo - chen ha•lo yech•de•loo me•hak•ri•vam od ki a•cha•rey asher hi•ta•ha•roo ha•ov•dim fa•am a•chat eyn la•hem od mach•she•vet ha•chet.

---

3. But in those sacrifices there is a remembrance again made of sins every year.

3. Ἀλλ' ἐν αὐταῖς ἀνάμνησις ἁμαρτιῶν κατ' ἐνιαυτόν·

3. All en autais anamneisis 'amartion kat enyauton.

ג. אוּלָם בַּקָּרְבָּנוֹת הָאֵלֶּה יֵשׁ-זֵכֶר לַחֲטָאִים שָׁנָה בְשָׁנָה:

3. Oo•lam ba•kor•ba•not ha•e•le yesh - ze•cher la•cha•ta•eem sha•na ve•sha•na.

Rabbinic Jewish Commentary

Though Philo the Jew thinks the contrary, and gives this as a reason why the heart and brain were not offered in sacrifice, because

"It would be foolish, that the sacrifices should cause, not a forgetfulness of sins, but a remembrance of them (q)."

(q) De Victimis, p. 841.

---

4. For it is not possible that the blood of bulls and of goats should take away sins.

4. ἀδύνατον γὰρ αἷμα ταύρων καὶ τράγων ἀφαιρεῖν ἁμαρτίας.

4. adunaton gar 'aima tauron kai tragon aphairein 'amartias.

ד. כִּי אֵין בְּדַם פָּרִים וּשְׂעִירִים לִנְשֹׂא חֲטָאִים:

4. Ki eyn be•dam pa•rim oos•ee•rim lin•so cha•ta•eem.

Rabbinic Jewish Commentary
Compare with this the Septuagint version of Jer.11:15.

"What, has the beloved committed abomination in my house? shall prayers, and the holy flesh take away thy wickednesses from thee, or by these shall thou escape?"

Hebrews 10

5. Wherefore when he cometh into the world, he saith, Sacrifice and offering thou wouldest not, but a body hast thou prepared me:

5. Διὸ εἰσερχόμενος εἰς τὸν κόσμον λέγει, Θυσίαν καὶ προσφορὰν οὐκ ἠθέλησας, σῶμα δὲ κατηρτίσω μοι·

5. Dio eiserchomenos eis ton kosmon legei, Thusian kai prosphoran ouk eitheleisas, soma de kateirtiso moi.

ה. עַל־כֵּן בְּבֹאוֹ אֶל־תֵּבֵל אַרְצָה אָמַר זֶבַח וּמִנְחָה לֹא חָפַצְתָּ גּוּף כּוֹנַנְתָּ לִי:

5. Al - ken be•vo•o el - te•vel ar•tza amar ze•vach oo•min•cha lo cha•fatz•ta goof ko•nan•ta li.

6. In burnt offerings and sacrifices for sin thou hast had no pleasure.

6. ὁλοκαυτώματα καὶ περὶ ἁμαρτίας οὐκ εὐδόκησας·

6. 'olokautomata kai peri 'amartias ouk eudokeisas.

ו. עוֹלָה וַחֲטָאָה לֹא שָׁאַלְתָּ:

6. O•la va•cha•ta•ah lo sha•al•ta.

7. Then said I, Lo, I come (in the volume of the book it is written of me,) to do thy will, O God.

7. τότε εἶπον, Ἰδού, ἥκω- ἐν κεφαλίδι βιβλίου γέγραπται περὶ ἐμοῦ- τοῦ ποιῆσαι, ὁ θεός, τὸ θέλημά σου.

7. tote eipon, Ydou, 'eiko- en kephalidi bibliou gegraptai peri emou- tou poieisai, 'o theos, to theleima sou.

ז. אָז אָמַרְתִּי הִנֵּה־בָאתִי בִּמְגִלַּת־סֵפֶר כָּתוּב עָלָי לַעֲשׂוֹת רְצוֹנְךָ אֱלֹהָי׃

7. Az amar•ti hee•ne - va•ti bim•gi•lat - se•fer ka•toov a•lai la•a•sot r`tzon•cha Elohai.

Rabbinic Jewish Commentary

In the volume of the book it is written of me; In the book of the Torah, as the, Targum and Kimchi on Psa.40:7 interpret it; and which may design the Bible in general, the whole book of the Scriptures of the Old Testament: so ספר, "the book", is used for the whole Bible (r), and it is said (s), all the whole Torah, that is, all Scripture, is called מגילה, "a volume"; accordingly there are things written of Messiah in all the writings of the Old Testament, in the Torah, and in the prophets, and in the psalms. Jarchi interprets it of the Torah of Moses, and so it may design the pentateuch, or the five books of Moses; and there are several places therein, in which it is written of Messiah, and particularly in Genesis, the first of these books, and in the head, the beginning, the frontal piece, the first part of that book.

8. Above when he said, Sacrifice and offering and burnt offerings and offering for sin thou wouldest not, neither hadst pleasure therein; which are offered by the law;

8. Ἀνώτερον λέγων ὅτι Θυσίαν καὶ προσφορὰν καὶ ὁλοκαυτώματα καὶ περὶ ἁμαρτίας οὐκ ἠθέλησας, οὐδὲ εὐδόκησας- αἵτινες κατὰ τὸν νόμον προσφέρονται-

8. Anoteron legon 'oti Thusian kai prosphoran kai 'olokautomata kai peri 'amartias ouk eitheleisas, oude eudokeisas- 'aitines kata ton nomon prospherontai-

ח. בְּאָמְרוֹ מֵרֹאשׁ זֶבַח וּמִנְחָה וְעוֹלָה וַחֲטָאָה לֹא חָפַצְתָּ וְלֹא שָׁאַלְתָּ וְהֵם הֵמָּה הַמּוּבָאִים לְפִי הַתּוֹרָה:

8. Be•om•ro me•rosh ze•vach oo•min•cha ve•o•la va•cha•ta•ah lo cha•fatz•ta ve•lo sha•al•ta ve•hem he•ma ha•moo•va•eem le•fi ha•Torah.

Hebrews 10

9. Then said he, Lo, I come to do thy will, O God. He taketh away the first, that he may establish the second.

9. τότε εἴρηκεν, Ἰδού, ἥκω τοῦ ποιῆσαι, ὁ θεός, τὸ θέλημά σου. Ἀναιρεῖ τὸ πρῶτον, ἵνα τὸ δεύτερον στήσῃ.

9. tote eireiken, Ydou, 'eiko tou poieisai, 'o theos, to theleima sou. Anairei to proton, 'ina to deuteron steisei.

ט. אָז יֹאמַר הִנֵּה-בָאתִי לַעֲשׂוֹת רְצוֹנְךָ הֵסִיר אֶת-הָרִאשֹׁנָה לְמַעַן הָקֵם אֶת-הַשְּׁנִיָּה:

9. Az yo•mar hee•ne - va•ti la•a•sot r`tzon•cha he•sir et - ha•ri•sho•na le•ma•an ha•kem et - hash•ni•ya.

10. By the which will we are sanctified through the offering of the body of Jesus Christ once for all.

10. Ἐν ᾧ θελήματι ἡγιασμένοι ἐσμέν, οἱ διὰ τῆς προσφορᾶς τοῦ σώματος Ἰησοῦ χριστοῦ ἐφάπαξ.

10. En 'o theleimati 'eigyasmenoi esmen, 'oi dya teis prosphoras tou somatos Yeisou christou ephapax.

י. וּבְרָצוֹן הַזֶּה אָנוּ מִתְקַדְּשִׁים בְּקָרְבַּן נֶפֶשׁ יֵשׁוּעַ הַמָּשִׁיחַ אֲשֶׁר הִקְרִיב פַּעַם אֶחָת:

10. Oo•va•ra•tzon ha•ze a•noo mit•kad•shim be•kor•ban ne•fesh Yeshua ha•Ma•shi•ach asher hik•riv pa•am e•chat.

11. And every priest standeth daily ministering and offering oftentimes the same sacrifices, which can never take away sins:

11. Καὶ πᾶς μὲν ἱερεὺς ἕστηκεν καθ᾽ ἡμέραν λειτουργῶν, καὶ τὰς αὐτὰς πολλάκις προσφέρων θυσίας, αἵτινες οὐδέποτε δύνανται περιελεῖν ἁμαρτίας·

11. Kai pas men 'iereus 'esteiken kath 'eimeran leitourgon, kai tas autas pollakis prospheron thusias, 'aitines oudepote dunantai perielein 'amartias.

יא. וְכָל־כֹּהֵן עֹמֵד לְשָׁרֵת יוֹם יוֹם וּלְהַקְרִיב פְּעָמִים שֹׁנוֹת אֶת־הַזְּבָחִים הָהֵמָּה אֲשֶׁר אֵין בָּם - מֵעוֹלָם לְכַפֵּר עַל־חֲטָאִים

11. Ve•chol - co•hen o•med le•sha•ret yom yom ool•hak•riv pe•a•mim sho•not et - haz•va•chim ha•he•ma asher eyn bam me•o•lam le•cha•per al - cha•ta•eem.

Rabbinic Jewish Commentary

Hence the Jews say (t), there is no ministration or service, אלא מעומד, "but standing"; and perhaps some reference may be had to מעמדות, the "stations" (u), or stationary men, who were always upon the spot at Jerusalem, to offer for such as were at a distance.

(t) Jarchi in Deut. xviii. 5. Maimon. Biath Hamikdash, c. 5. sect. 16. (u) Misn. Taanith, c. 4. sect. 2.

---

12. But this man, after he had offered one sacrifice for sins for ever, sat down on the right hand of God;

12. αὐτὸς δὲ μίαν ὑπὲρ ἁμαρτιῶν προσενέγκας θυσίαν εἰς τὸ διηνεκές, ἐκάθισεν ἐν δεξιᾷ τοῦ θεοῦ,

12. autos de mian 'uper 'amartion prosenegkas thusian eis to dieinekes, ekathisen en dexya tou theou,

יב. אֲבָל הוּא הִקְרִיב זֶבַח אֶחָד עַל־הַחֲטָאִים וַיֵּשֶׁב לִימִין אֱלֹהִים עַד־עוֹלָם:

12. Aval hoo hik•riv ze•vach e•chad al - ha•cha•ta•eem va•ye•shev li•y`min Elohim ad - o•lam.

13. From henceforth expecting till his enemies be made his footstool.

13. τὸ λοιπὸν ἐκδεχόμενος ἕως τεθῶσιν οἱ ἐχθροὶ αὐτοῦ ὑποπόδιον τῶν ποδῶν αὐτοῦ.

13. to loipon ekdechomenos 'eos tethosin 'oi echthroi autou 'upopodion ton podon autou.

יג. וּמֵאָז הוּא מְיַחֵל עַד-יוּשְׁתוּ אֹיְבָיו הֲדֹם לְרַגְלָיו:

13. Oo•me•az hoo me•ya•chel ad - yoosh•too oy•vav ha•dom le•rag•lav.

Hebrews 10

14. For by one offering he hath perfected for ever them that are sanctified.

14. Μιᾷ γὰρ προσφορᾷ τετελείωκεν εἰς τὸ διηνεκὲς τοὺς ἁγιαζομένους.

14. Mya gar prosphora teteleioken eis to dieinekes tou 'agyazomenous.

יד. כִּי בְקָרְבָּן אֶחָד הִשְׁלִים אֶת-הַמְקֻדָּשִׁים עַד-עוֹלָם:

14. Ki ve•kor•ban e•chad hish•lim et - ham•koo•da•shim ad - o•lam.

---

15. Whereof the Holy Ghost also is a witness to us: for after that he had said before,

15. Μαρτυρεῖ δὲ ἡμῖν καὶ τὸ πνεῦμα τὸ ἅγιον· μετὰ γὰρ τ προειρηκέναι,

15. Marturei de 'eimin kai to pneuma to 'agion. meta gar to proeireikenai,

טו. וְגַם-רוּחַ הַקֹּדֶשׁ יָעֵד-לָנוּ כָזֹאת כִּי אַחֲרֵי אָמְרוֹ:

15. Ve•gam - Roo•ach ha•Ko•desh ya•ed - la•noo cha•zot ki a•cha•rey om•ro.

---

16. This is the covenant that I will make with them after those days, saith the Lord, I will put my laws into their hearts, and in their minds will I write them;

16. Αὕτη ἡ διαθήκη ἣν διαθήσομαι πρὸς αὐτοὺς μετὰ τὰς ἡμέρας ἐκείνας, λέγει κύριος, διδοὺς νόμους μου ἐπὶ καρδίας αὐτῶν, καὶ ἐπὶ τῶν διανοιῶν αὐτῶν ἐπιγράψω αὐτούς·

16. 'Autei 'ei dyatheikei 'ein dyatheisomai pros autous meta tas 'eimeras ekeinas, legei kurios, didous nomous mou epi kardias auton, kai epi ton dyanoion auton epigrapso autous.

טז. זֹאת הַבְּרִית אֲשֶׁר אֶכְרֹת אִתָּם אַחֲרֵי הַיָּמִים הָהֵם נְאֻם-יְהֹוָה נָתַתִּי אֶת-תּוֹרָתִי בְּקִרְבָּם וְעַל-לִבָּם אֶכְתֲּבֶנָּה:

16. Zot ha•b`rit asher ech•rot ee•tam a•cha•rey ha•ya•mim ha•hem n`oom – Adonai na•ta•ti et - To•ra•ti be•kir•bam ve•al - li•bam ech•to•ve•na.

Hebrews 10

17. And their sins and iniquities will I remember no more.

17. καὶ τῶν ἁμαρτιῶν αὐτῶν καὶ τῶν ἀνομιῶν αὐτῶν οὐ μὴ μνησθῶ ἔτι.

17. kai ton 'amartion auton kai ton anomion auton ou mei mneistho eti.

יז. יוֹסִיף יֹאמַר וְלַעֲוֹנָם וּלְחַטֹּאתָם לֹא אֶזְכָּר-עוֹד:

17. Yo•sif yo•mar ve•la•a•vo•nam ool•cha•ta•tam lo ez•kor - od.

---

18. Now where remission of these is, there is no more offering for sin.

18. Ὅπου δὲ ἄφεσις τούτων, οὐκέτι προσφορὰ περὶ ἁμαρτίας.

18. 'Opou de aphesis touton, ouketi prosphora peri 'amartias.

יח. וּבַאֲשֶׁר יֵשׁ-שָׁם סְלִיחָה לָאֵלֶּה אֵין מָקוֹם לְקָרְבָּן עַל-הַחֵטְא:

18. Oo•va•a•sher yesh - sham s`li•cha la•e•le eyn ma•kom le•kor•ban al - ha•chet.

Rabbinic Jewish Commentary
there is no more offering for sin; There may be other offerings, as of praise and thanksgiving, but none for sin; "there is no need", as the Syriac version; or there is not required, as the Arabic version; there is no need of the reiteration of Messiah's sacrifice, nor will he be offered up any more, nor of the repetition of legal sacrifices, nor ought they to continue any longer. The Jews themselves say (w), that

"In the time to come (i.e. in the times of the Messiah) all offerings shall cease, but the sacrifice of praise."

And one of their writers says (x), when

"The King Messiah, the son of David, shall reign, there will be no need of כפרה, "an atonement", nor of deliverance, or prosperity, for all these things will be had;"

(w) Vajikra Rabba, sect. 9. fol. 153. 1. (x) R. Abendana Not. in Miclol Yophi in Psal. lxxii. 20.

Hebrews 10

19. Having therefore, brethren, boldness to enter into the holiest by the blood of Jesus,

19. Ἔχοντες οὖν, ἀδελφοί, παρρησίαν εἰς τὴν εἴσοδον τῶν ἁγίων ἐν τῷ αἵματι Ἰησοῦ,

19. Echontes oun, adelphoi, parreisian eis tein eisodon ton 'agion en to 'aimati Yeisou,

יט. עַל־כֵּן אֶחָי בִּהְיוֹת לָנוּ בִטָּחוֹן לָבֹא אֶל־הַקֹּדֶשׁ בְּדַם יֵשׁוּעַ:

19. Al - ken e•chai bi•hee•yot la•noo vi•ta•chon la•vo el - ha•ko•desh be•dam Yeshua.

20. By a new and living way, which he hath consecrated for us, through the veil, that is to say, his flesh;

20. ἣν ἐνεκαίνισεν ἡμῖν ὁδὸν πρόσφατον καὶ ζῶσαν, διὰ τοῦ καταπετάσματος, τοῦτ' ἔστιν, τῆς σαρκὸς αὐτοῦ,

20. 'ein enekainisen 'eimin 'odon prosphaton kai zosan, dya tou katapetasmatos, tout estin, teis sarkos autou,

כ. אֲשֶׁר חָנַךְ מְסִלָּה חֲדָשָׁה לָנוּ מְסִלַּת חַיִּים דֶּרֶךְ הַפָּרֹכֶת אֲשֶׁר בְּשָׂרוֹ הוּא:

20. Asher cha•nach me•si•la cha•da•sha la•noo me•si•lat cha•yim de•rech ha•pa•ro•chet asher be•sa•ro hoo.

Rabbinic Jewish Commentary
The Jews (y) say was of thread six times doubled; which may denote the holiness of Messiah's human nature; the strength, courage, and steadfastness of it, under all its sorrows and sufferings; and the purity and duration of his righteousness; the colours of it were blue, purple, and scarlet, which may signify the sufferings of the human nature.

(y) Maimon. Cele Hamikdash, c. 8. sect. 14. Jarchi in Exod. xxvi. 1. Kimchi in Sepher Shorash. rad. שזר.

---

21. And having an high priest over the house of God;

21. καὶ ἱερέα μέγαν ἐπὶ τὸν οἶκον τοῦ θεοῦ,

21. kai 'ierea megan epi ton oikon tou theou,

כא. וּבִהְיוֹת לָנוּ כֹּהֵן גָּדוֹל עַל-בֵּית הָאֱלֹהִים:

21. Oo•vi•hi•yot la•noo co•hen ga•dol al - beit ha•Elohim.

Rabbinic Jewish Commentary
In the Greek text it is, "a great priest"; so the Messiah is called by the Targum on Zec.6:12 כהן רב, "a great priest", as he is; even a great high priest, as in Heb.4:14, and greater than Aaron, and any of his sons.

22. Let us draw near with a true heart in full assurance of faith, having our hearts sprinkled from an evil conscience, and our bodies washed with pure water.

22. προσερχώμεθα μετὰ ἀληθινῆς καρδίας ἐν πληροφορίᾳ πίστεως, ἐρραντισμένοι τὰς καρδίας ἀπὸ συνειδήσεως πονηρᾶς, καὶ λελουμένοι τὸ σῶμα ὕδατι καθαρῷ·

22. proserchometha meta aleithineis kardias en pleirophoria pisteos, errantismenoi tas kardias apo suneideiseos poneiras, kai leloumenoi to soma 'udati katharo.

כב. נִגְּשָׁה בְּלֵב שָׁלֵם וּבֶאֱמוּנָה אֹמֶן מְטֹהָרִים מֵרַעְיוֹן רָע בְּלִבֵּנוּ אֲשֶׁר זֹרַק עָלָיו וּבְשָׂרֵנוּ אֲשֶׁר רֻחַץ בְּמַיִם טְהוֹרִים:

22. Nig•sha be•lev sha•lem oo•ve•e•moo•na o•men me•to•ha•rim me•ra•a•yon ra be•li•be•noo asher zo•rak alav oov•sa•re•noo asher roo•chatz be•ma•yim te•ho•rim.

Rabbinic Jewish Commentary
The allusion is to a custom of the Jews, who were obliged to wash their bodies, and make them clean, when they prayed. So Aben Ezra observes on Gen.35:2

"That every Israelite, when he went to pray at a fixed place, was obliged to have גופו נקי, "his body pure", and his garments pure."

So a priest might not enter into the court for service, though clean, until he had washed himself all over (z); and it is to sacerdotal acts that the reference is here.

(z) Misn. Yoma, c. 3. sect. 3. Vid. Philo de Victimas Offerent. p. 848.

---

23. Let us hold fast the profession of our faith without wavering; (for he is faithful that promised;)

23. κατέχωμεν τὴν ὁμολογίαν τῆς ἐλπίδος ἀκλινῆ, πιστὸς γὰρ ὁ ἐπαγγειλάμενος·

23. katechomen tein 'omologian teis elpidos aklinei, pistos gar 'o epangeilamenos.

:כג. וְנִשְׁמֹר הֵיטֵב שְׁבוּעַת פִּינוּ עַל־דְּבַר תִּקְוָתֵנוּ וְלֹא נֶרֶף כִּי נֶאֱמָן הוּא הַמַּבְטִיחַ

23. Ve•nish•mor hei•tev sh`voo•at pi•noo al - de•var tik•va•te•noo ve•lo ne•ref ki ne•e•man hoo ha•mav•ti•ach.

Hebrews 10

24. And let us consider one another to provoke unto love and to good works:

24. καὶ κατανοῶμεν ἀλλήλους εἰς παροξυσμὸν ἀγάπης καὶ καλῶν ἔργων,

24. kai katanoomen alleilous eis paroxusmon agapeis kai kalon ergon,

:כד. וְנִתְבּוֹנְנָה אִישׁ אֶל־רֵעֵהוּ לְהִתְעוֹרֵר לְאַהֲבָה וּלְמַעֲשִׂים טוֹבִים

24. Ve•nit•bo•ne•na eesh el - re•e•hoo le•hit•o•rer le•a•ha•va ool•ma•a•sim to•vim.

---

25. Not forsaking the assembling of ourselves together, as the manner of some is; but exhorting one another: and so much the more, as ye see the day approaching.

25. μὴ ἐγκαταλείποντες τὴν ἐπισυναγωγὴν ἑαυτῶν, καθὼς ἔθος τισίν, ἀλλὰ παρακαλοῦντες, καὶ τοσούτῳ μᾶλλον, ὅσῳ βλέπετε ἐγγίζουσαν τὴν ἡμέραν.

25. mei egkataleipontes tein episunagogein 'eauton, kathos ethos tisin, alla parakalountes, kai tosouto mallon, 'oso blepete engizousan tein 'eimeran.

כה. וְלֹא נֶחְדַּל מִבֹּא אֶל־קְהִלָּתֵנוּ כְּדֶרֶךְ אֲנָשִׁים אֲחָדִים מִכֶּם כִּי אִם־נוֹכִיחַ אִישׁ אֶת־עֲמִיתוֹ וּמַה גַּם־בִּרְאֹתְכֶם:כִּי־קָרוֹב הַיּוֹם

25. Ve•lo nech•dal mi•bo el - ke•hi•la•te•noo ke•de•rech a•na•shim a•cha•dim mi•kem ki eem - no•chi•ach eesh et - ami•to oo•ma gam - bir•ot•chem ki - ka•rov ha•yom.

Rabbinic Jewish Commentary

The Jews (a) reckon among those that go down to the grave, and perish, and have no part in the world to come, הפורשים מדרכי צבור, "Who separate from the ways of the congregation"

(a) T. Bab. Roshhashanah, fol. 17. 1. Maimon. Hilch. Teshuba, c. 3. sect. 6, 11.

Hebrews 10

26. For if we sin wilfully after that we have received the knowledge of the truth, there remaineth no more sacrifice for sins,

26. Ἐκουσίως γὰρ ἁμαρτανόντων ἡμῶν μετὰ τὸ λαβεῖν τὴν ἐπίγνωσιν τῆς ἀληθείας, οὐκέτι περὶ ἁμαρτιῶν ἀπολείπεται θυσία,

26. 'Ekousios gar 'amartanonton 'eimon meta to labein tein epignosin teis aleitheias, ouketi peri 'amartion apoleipetai thusia,

:כו. כִּי אִם-נֶחֱטָא בְזָדוֹן אַחֲרֵי אֲשֶׁר קָנִינוּ דַעַת הָאֱמֶת לֹא-יִשָּׁאֵר עוֹד קָרְבָּן עַל-חַטָּאתֵנוּ

26. Ki eem - nech•ta ve•za•don a•cha•rey asher ka•ni•noo da•at ha•e•met lo - yi•sha•er od kor•ban al - cha•ta•te•noo.

---

27. But a certain fearful looking for of judgment and fiery indignation, which shall devour the adversaries.

27. φοβερὰ δέ τις ἐκδοχὴ κρίσεως, καὶ πυρὸς ζῆλος ἐσθίειν μέλλοντος τοὺς ὑπεναντίους.

27. phobera de tis ekdochei kriseos, kai puros zeilos esthiein mellontos tous 'upenantious.

:כז. כִּי אִם-מָגוֹר מִפְּנֵי מִשְׁפָּט הַצָּפוּי וְאֵשׁ קִנְאָה אֲשֶׁר תֹּאכַל צָרִים

27. Ki eem - ma•gor mip•ney mish•pat ha•tza•fooy ve•esh kin•ah asher to•chal tza•rim.

28. He that despised Moses' law died without mercy under two or three witnesses:

28. Ἀθετήσας τις νόμον Μωϋσέως χωρὶς οἰκτιρμῶν ἐπὶ δυσὶν ἢ τρισὶν μάρτυσιν ἀποθνῄσκει·

28. Atheteisas tis nomon Mouseos choris oiktirmon epi dusin ei trisin martusin apothneiskei.

כח. הָעֹבֵר תּוֹרַת מֹשֶׁה יוּמַת בְּלִי־חֶמְלָה עַל־פִּי שְׁנַיִם אוֹ־שְׁלֹשָׁה עֵדִים:

28. Ha•o•ver to•rat Moshe yoo•mat b`li - chem•la al - pi sh`na•yim oh - sh`lo•sha e•dim.

Rabbinic Jewish Commentary
Under two or three witnesses; Who "stood by", or were present, as the Arabic version renders it, when the transgression was committed; or that "accused him", as the Ethiopic version; that were witnesses against him, and plainly and fully proved the fact, Deu.17:6.

Hebrews 10

29. Of how much sorer punishment, suppose ye, shall he be thought worthy, who hath trodden under foot the Son of God, and hath counted the blood of the covenant, wherewith he was sanctified, an unholy thing, and hath done despite unto the Spirit of grace?

29. πόσῳ, δοκεῖτε, χείρονος ἀξιωθήσεται τιμωρίας ὁ τὸν υἱὸν τοῦ θεοῦ καταπατήσας, καὶ τὸ αἷμα τῆς διαθήκης κοινὸν ἡγησάμενος ἐν ᾧ ἡγιάσθη, καὶ τὸ πνεῦμα τῆς χάριτος ἐνυβρίσας;

29. poso, dokeite, cheironos axiotheisetai timorias 'o ton 'wion tou theou katapateisas, kai to 'aima teis dyatheikeis koinon 'eigeisamenos en 'o 'eigyasthei, kai to pneuma teis charitos enubrisas?

כט. הִתְבּוֹנְנוּ־נָא מַה־נּוֹרָא הָעֹנֶשׁ אֲשֶׁר יוּשַׁת עַל־רֹמֵס בֶּן־אֱלֹהִים וּמְטַמֵּא דַם בְּרִית אֲשֶׁר נִקְדַּשׁ בּוֹ וּמְגַדֵּף רוּחַ־נְדִיבָה:

29. Hit•bo•ne•noo - na ma - no•ra ha•o•nesh asher yoo•shat al - ro•mes Ben – Elohim oom•ta•me dam b`rit asher nik•dash bo oom•ga•def Roo•ach n`di•va.

30. For we know him that hath said, Vengeance belongeth unto me, I will recompense, saith the Lord. And again, The Lord shall judge his people.

30. Οἴδαμεν γὰρ τὸν εἰπόντα, Ἐμοὶ ἐκδίκησις, ἐγὼ ἀνταποδώσω, λέγει κύριος· καὶ πάλιν, κύριος κρινεῖ τὸν λαὸν αὐτοῦ.

30. Oidamen gar ton eiponta, Emoi ekdikeisis, ego antapodoso, legei kurios. kai palin, kurios krinei ton laon autou.

ל: כִּי־יָדַעְנוּ מִי הוּא הָאֹמֵר לִי נָקָם אֲנִי אֲשַׁלֵּם אָמַר יְהֹוָה וְאֹמֵר עוֹד כִּי יָדִין יְהֹוָה עַמּוֹ

30. Ki - ya•da•a•noo mee hoo ha•o•mer li na•kam ani a•sha•lem amar Adonai ve•o•mer od ki ya•din Adonai amo.

Hebrews 10

31. It is a fearful thing to fall into the hands of the living God.

31. Φοβερὸν τὸ ἐμπεσεῖν εἰς χεῖρας θεοῦ ζῶντος.

31. Phoberon to empesein eis cheiras theou zontos.

לא: מַה־נּוֹרָא לִנְפֹּל בְּיַד אֱלֹהִים חַיִּים

31. Ma - no•ra lin•pol be•yad Elohim cha•yim.

---

32. But call to remembrance the former days, in which, after ye were illuminated, ye endured a great fight of afflictions;

32. Ἀναμιμνῄσκεσθε δὲ τὰς πρότερον ἡμέρας, ἐν αἷς φωτισθέντες πολλὴν ἄθλησιν ὑπεμείνατε παθημάτων·

32. Anamimneiskesthe de tas proteron 'eimeras, en 'ais photisthentes pollein athleisin 'upemeinate patheimaton.

לב: זִכְרוּ־נָא יָמִים מִקֶּדֶם כַּאֲשֶׁר אֹרוּ עֵינֵיכֶם וְשׁוֹט שׁוֹטֵף צָרָה עָבַר עֲלֵיכֶם

32. Zich•roo - na ya•mim mi•ke•dem ka•a•sher o•roo ey•ne•chem ve•shot sho•tef tza•ra avar aley•chem.

Hebrews 10

33. Partly, whilst ye were made a gazingstock both by reproaches and afflictions; and partly, whilst ye became companions of them that were so used.

33. τοῦτο μέν, ὀνειδισμοῖς τε καὶ θλίψεσιν θεατριζόμενοι· τοῦτο δέ, κοινωνοὶ τῶν οὕτως ἀναστρεφομένων γενηθέντες.

33. touto men, oneidismois te kai thlipsesin theatrizomenoi. touto de, koinonoi ton 'outos anastrephomenon geneithentes.

לג. פַּעַם הֱיִיתֶם לְרַאֲוָה מֵעֹנִי וָקֶלֶס וּפַעַם דָּאֲבָה נַפְשְׁכֶם לְסִבְלוֹת אֲחֵיכֶם כָּכֶם:

33. Pa•am he•yi•tem le•ra•a•va me•o•ni ve•ke•les oo•fa•am da•a•va naf•she•chem le•siv•lot a•chey•chem ka•chem.

---

34. For ye had compassion of me in my bonds, and took joyfully the spoiling of your goods, knowing in yourselves that ye have in heaven a better and an enduring substance.

34. Καὶ γὰρ τοῖς δεσμοῖς μου συνεπαθήσατε, καὶ τὴν ἁρπαγὴν τῶν ὑπαρχόντων ὑμῶν μετὰ χαρᾶς προσεδέξασθε, γινώσκοντες ἔχειν ἑαυτοῖς κρείττονα ὕπαρξιν ἐν οὐρανοῖς καὶ μένουσαν.

34. Kai gar tois desmois mou sunepatheisate, kai tein 'arpagein ton 'uparchonton 'umon meta charas prosedexasthe, ginoskontes echein 'eautois kreittona 'uparxin en ouranois kai menousan.

לד. כִּי נִכְמְרוּ רַחֲמֵיכֶם אֶל-מוֹסְרָי וְהוֹנְכֶם הַגָּזוּל מִכֶּם הִנַּחְתֶּם בְּטוֹב-לֵב בְּדַעְתְּכֶם כִּי קִנְיָן גָּדוֹל מִזֶּה יֶשׁ-לָכֶם:בַּשָּׁמַיִם הָעֹמֵד לָעַד

34. Ki nich•me•roo ra•cha•mey•chem el - mo•se•rai ve•hon•chem ha•ga•zool mi•kem hi•nach•tem be•toov - lev be•da•at•chem ki kin•yan ga•dol mi•ze yesh - la•chem ba•sha•ma•yim ha•o•med la•ad.

35. Cast not away therefore your confidence, which hath great recompence of reward.

35. Μὴ ἀποβάλητε οὖν τὴν παρρησίαν ὑμῶν, ἥτις ἔχει μισθαποδοσίαν μεγάλην.

35. Mei apobaleite oun tein parreisian 'umon, 'eitis echei misthapodosian megalein.

לה. עַל־כֵּן אַל־תַּשְׁלִיכוּ מִבְטַחֲכֶם כִּי שְׂכָרוֹ הַרְבֵּה מְאֹד:

35. Al - ken al - tash•li•choo miv•ta•cha•chem ki s`cha•ro har•be me•od.

Hebrews 10

36. For ye have need of patience, that, after ye have done the will of God, ye might receive the promise.

36. Ὑπομονῆς γὰρ ἔχετε χρείαν, ἵνα τὸ θέλημα τοῦ θεοῦ ποιήσαντες κομίσησθε τὴν ἐπαγγελίαν.

36. 'Upomoneis gar echete chreian, 'ina to theleima tou theou poieisantes komiseisthe tein epangelian.

לו. וְכִי גַם־הַתּוֹחֶלֶת נְכוֹנָה לָכֶם בַּעֲבוּר אֲשֶׁר תַּעֲשׂוּ רְצוֹן אֱלֹהִים וְתַשִּׂיגוּ אֵת אֲשֶׁר־דִּבֶּר לָכֶם:

36. Ve•chi gam - ha•to•che•let n`cho•na la•chem ba•a•voor asher ta•a•soo r`tzon Elohim ve•ta•si•goo et asher - di•ber la•chem.

37. For yet a little while, and he that shall come will come, and will not tarry.

37. Ἔτι γὰρ μικρὸν ὅσον ὅσον, Ὁ ἐρχόμενος ἥξει, καὶ οὐ χρονιεῖ.

37. Eti gar mikron 'oson 'oson, 'O erchomenos 'eixei, kai ou chroniei.

לז. כִּי עוֹד מְעַט־רָגַע וְהַבָּא יָבֹא לֹא יְאַחֵר:

37. Ki od me•at - ra•ga ve•ha•ba ya•vo lo ye•a•cher.

135

Hebrews 10

38. Now the just shall live by faith: but if any man draw back, my soul shall have no pleasure in him.

38. Ὁ δὲ δίκαιος ἐκ πίστεως ζήσεται· καὶ ἐὰν ὑποστείληται, οὐκ εὐδοκεῖ ἡ ψυχή μου ἐν αὐτῷ.

38. 'O de dikaios ek pisteos zeisetai. kai ean 'uposteileitai, ouk eudokei 'ei psuchei mou en auto.

לח. וְצַדִּיק בֶּאֱמוּנָתוֹ יִחְיֶה וְאִם-יִסֹּג אָחוֹר לֹא-תִרְצֶה נַפְשִׁי בּוֹ:

38. Ve•tza•dik be•e•moo•na•to yich•ye ve•eem - yi•sog achor lo - ti•retz naf•shi bo.

Rabbinic Jewish Commentary

The Hebrew word עפלה, used in Hab.2:4 and which, by the Septuagint there, and by the apostle here, is translated by υποστειληται, and rendered "draw back", according to R. David Kimchi (c) signifies, pride and haughtiness of heart; and, according to R. Sol. Jarchi (d) it signifies impudence; R. Moses Kimchi (e) takes it to be the same with עפל, which is used for a tower, or fortified place; and thinks it designs one who betakes himself to such a place for safety from the enemy, and seeks not to God for deliverance.

(c) In Hab. ii. 4. (d) In ib. (e) Apud R. David Kimchi in ibid. & in Sepher Shorashim, rad. עפל.

---

39. But we are not of them who draw back unto perdition; but of them that believe to the saving of the soul.

39. Ἡμεῖς δὲ οὐκ ἐσμὲν ὑποστολῆς εἰς ἀπώλειαν, ἀλλὰ πίστεως εἰς περιποίησιν ψυχῆς.

39. 'Eimeis de ouk esmen 'upostoleis eis apoleyan, alla pisteos eis peripoieisin psucheis.

לט. וַאֲנַחְנוּ אֵינֶנּוּ מִן-הַנְּסוֹגִים אָחוֹר לָאֲבַדּוֹן כִּי אִם-מִבְּנֵי אֱמוּנָה לְהַצִּיל אֶת-הַנָּפֶשׁ:

39. Va•a•nach•noo ey•ne•noo min - ha•ne•so•gim achor la•a•va•don ki eem - mi•b`ney e•moo•na le•ha•tzil et - ha•na•fesh.

(Hebrews Chapter 10 End)

Hebrews, Chapter 11

1. Now faith is the substance of things hoped for, the evidence of things not seen.

1. Ἔστιν δὲ πίστις ἐλπιζομένων ὑπόστασις, πραγμάτων ἔλεγχος οὐ βλεπομένων.

1. Estin de pistis elpizomenon 'upostasis, pragmaton elegchos ou blepomenon.

א. וְהָאֱמוּנָה מִבְטַח-עֹז בַּדָּבָר חִכְּנוּ לוֹ דָּבָר בָּחוּן בַּלֵּב וְלֹא תְשׁוּרֶנּוּ עָיִן:

1. Ve•ha•e•moo•na miv•tach - oz ba•da•var chi•ki•noo lo da•var ba•choon ba•lev ve•lo te•shoo•re•noo a•yin.

Rabbinic Jewish Commentary
Philo the Jew (e) says much the same thing of faith;
"The only infallible and certain good thing (says he) is, that faith which is faith towards God; it is the solace of life, πληρωμα χρηστων ελπιδων, "the fulness of good hopes."

(e) De Abrahamo, p. 387.

---

2. For by it the elders obtained a good report.

2. Ἐν ταύτῃ γὰρ ἐμαρτυρήθησαν οἱ πρεσβύτεροι.

2. En tautei gar emartureitheisan 'oi presbuteroi.

ב. כִּי בָזֹאת נִתְּנָה עֵדוּת לַזְּקֵנִים מִדּוֹר דּוֹר:

2. Ki va•zot nit•na e•doot laz•ke•nim mi•dor dor.

---

3. Through faith we understand that the worlds were framed by the word of God, so that things which are seen were not made of things which do appear.

3. Πίστει νοοῦμεν κατηρτίσθαι τοὺς αἰῶνας ῥήματι θεοῦ, εἰς τὸ μὴ ἐκ φαινομένων τὰ βλεπόμενα γεγονέναι.

3. Pistei nooumen kateirtisthai tous aionas 'reimati theou, eis to mei ek phainomenon ta blepomena gegonenai.

ג. בָּאֱמוּנָה נָבִין כִּי בִּדְבַר אֱלֹהִים נַעֲשׂוּ שָׁמַיִם וָאָרֶץ וְכִי הַנִּמְצָאִים לְעֵינֵינוּ לֹא מֵחֹמֶר קַדְמוֹנִי נִבְרָאוּ:

3. Ba•e•moo•na na•vin ki bid•var Elohim na•a•soo sha•ma•yim va•a•retz ve•chi ha•nim•tza•eem le•ey•ney•noo lo me•cho•mer kad•mo•ni niv•ra•oo.

Rabbinic Jewish Commentary

The Jews often speak of three hundred and ten worlds, in all which, they say, there are heavens, earth, stars, planets, &c. (f); and sometimes of eighteen thousand (g); but these notions are rightly charged by Philo (h) with ignorance and folly. However, as many worlds as there are, they are made "by the Word of God"; by Christ, the essential Word of God, to whom the creation of all things is ascribed in Joh.1:1. And this agrees with the sentiments of the Jews, who ascribe the creation of all things to the Word of God, as do the Targumists (i), and Philo the Jew (k). And these are "framed" by the Word, in a very beautiful and convenient order; the heavens before the earth; things less perfect, before those that were more so in the visible world, or terraqueous globe; and things for men, before men, for whom they were; and it is by divine revelation and faith that men form right notions of the creation, and of the author of it, and particularly of the origin of it.

were not made of things which do appear; They were not made from pre-existent matter, but out of nothing, out of which the rude and undigested chaos was formed; and from that invisible mass, covered with darkness, were all visible things brought into a beautiful order; and all from secret and hidden ideas in the divine minds; and this also is the faith of the Jews, that the creation of all things is מאין, "out of nothing" (l). There seems to be an allusion to the word ברא, used for creation, which signifies to make appear a thing unseen; and is rendered in the Septuagint version by δεικνυμι, Num.16:30 and καταδεικνυμι, Isa.40:26 to show, or make appear; and thus God created, or made to appear, the heavens and earth, which before were not in being, and unseen, Gen_1:1 and created to make, as in Gen.2:3 that is, made them to appear, that he might put them into the form and order they now are.

(f) Misn. Oketzim, c. 3. sect. 12. Targum Jon. in Exod. xxviii. 30. Kettoreth Hassamim in Targum Jon. in Gen. fol. 4. 4. Lex. Cabel. p. 60, 61. (g) T. Bab. Avoda Zara, fol. 3. 2. Yalkut, par. 2. fol. 50. 4. (h) De Opificio, p. 39. (i) Targum Oak. in Deut. xxxiii. 27. & Ben Uzziel in Isa.

xlviii. 13. (k) De Opificio, p. 4. & Leg. Alleg. l. 1. p. 44. (l) Tzeror Hammor, fol. 1. 1. Kettoreth Hassamim in Targ. Jon in Gen. fol. 5. 1, 2.

Hebrews 11

4. By faith Abel offered unto God a more excellent sacrifice than Cain, by which he obtained witness that he was righteous, God testifying of his gifts: and by it he being dead yetspeaketh.

4. Πίστει πλείονα θυσίαν Ἄβελ παρὰ Κάϊν προσήνεγκεν τῷ θεῷ, δι᾽ ἧς ἐμαρτυρήθη εἶναι δίκαιος, μαρτυροῦντος ἐπὶ τοῖς δώροις αὐτοῦ τοῦ θεοῦ· καὶ δι᾽ αὐτῆς ἀποθανὼν ἔτι λαλεῖται.

4. Pistei pleiona thusian Abel para Kain proseinegken to theo, di 'eis emartureithei einai dikaios, marturountos epi tois dorois autou tou theou. kai di auteis apothanon eti laleitai.

ד. בֶּאֱמוּנָה הֵבִיא הֶבֶל קָרְבָּן מִנְחָה לֵאלֹהִים מִנְחָה טוֹבָה מִמִּנְחַת קַיִן אֲשֶׁר עַל־יָדָהּ נִתְּנָה לוֹ עֵדוּת כִּי צַדִּיק: הָיָה בְּהָעִיד אֱלֹהִים עַל־מִנְחָתוֹ וְעַל־פִּיהָ עוֹדֶנּוּ דוֹבֵב אַחֲרֵי מֹתוֹ

4. Ba•e•moo•na he•vi he•vel kor•ban min•cha le•Elohim min•cha to•va mi•min•chat Ka•yin asher al - ya•da nit•na lo e•doot ki tza•dik ha•ya be•ha•eed Elohim al - min•cha•to ve•al - pi•ha o•de•noo do•vev a•cha•rey mo•to.

Hebrews 11

5. By faith Enoch was translated that he should not see death; and was not found, because God had translated him: for before his translation he had this testimony, that he pleased God.

5. Πίστει Ἐνὼχ μετετέθη τοῦ μὴ ἰδεῖν θάνατον, καὶ οὐχ εὑρίσκετο, διότι μετέθηκεν αὐτὸν ὁ θεός· πρὸ γὰρ τῆς μεταθέσεως αὐτοῦ μεμαρτύρηται εὐηρεστηκέναι τῷ θεῷ·

5. Pistei 'Enoch metetethei tou mei idein thanaton, kai ouch 'eurisketo, dioti metetheiken auton 'o theos. pro gar teis metatheseos autou memartureitai eueiresteikenai to theo.

ה. בֶּאֱמוּנָה לֻקַּח חֲנוֹךְ מִבְּלִי רְאוֹת מָוֶת וְאֵינֶנּוּ כִּי־לָקַח אֹתוֹ אֱלֹהִים וּבְטֶרֶם הִלָּקְחוֹ נִתְּנָה לּוֹ עֵדוּת כִּי אֶת־הָאֱלֹהִים הִתְהַלֵּךְ

5. Ba•e•moo•na loo•kach Cha•noch mi•b`li r`ot ma•vet ve•ey•ne•noo ki - la•kach o•to Elohim oov•te•rem hi•lak•cho nit•na lo e•doot ki et - ha•Elohim hit•ha•lach.

Rabbinic Jewish Commentary

Jonathan ben Uzziel, in his paraphrase on Gen.5:24 has these words:

"And Enoch worshipped in truth before the Lord; and behold he was not with the inhabitants of the earth, אתנגיד, "he was translated", and ascended to the firmament (or heaven), by the Word before YHVH."

And the Jerusalem Targum to the same purpose;

"And Enoch worshipped in truth before the YHVH; and lo, he was not, for he was translated by the Word from before YHVH."

Or by the Word of YHVH, which went out from him; for this translation was of God, as our apostle afterwards asserts. R. Eleazar says (m):

"The holy blessed God took Enoch, and caused him to ascend to the highest heavens, and delivered into his hands all the superior treasures,"

He is said (n) to be one of the seven which entered into paradise in their life; and some of them say (o), that God took him, בגוף ונפש, body and soul; see the Apocrypha below:

"He pleased God, and was beloved of him: so that living among sinners he was translated." (Wisdom 4:10)

"Enoch pleased the YHVH, and was translated, being an example of repentance to all generations." (Sirach 44:16)

The Targum of Oukelos on Gen.5:24,

"And Enoch walked in the fear of YHVH, and he was not, for the YHVH, לא המית, "did not kill him", or cause, or suffer him to die:"

Though an exemplar of that paraphrase is cited (p), without the negative particle, thus,

"And he was not, for YHVH killed him,"

Or inflicted death on him: and it is the sense of several of the Jewish commentators, that he did die a common death, as Jarchi, Eben Ezra, and others; who by the phrase, "God took him", understand death, for which they cite the following places, 1Ki.19:4.

Some of the Jewish writers very wickedly, and without any ground and foundation, give a different character of him; some of them say that he was a hypocrite, sometimes righteous, and sometimes wicked, and that the holy blessed God removed him, while he was righteous (q); and others (r), that allow him to be a righteous and worthy man, yet represent him as fickle and inconstant; and, therefore, God, foreseeing that he would do wickedly, and to prevent it, made haste, and took him away, by death, before his time.

(m) Zohar in Gen. fol. 44. 3. (n) Derech Eretz Zuta, c. 1. fol. 19. 1. (o) Juchasin, fol. 134. 2. (p) In Tosaphta in T. Bab. Yebamot, fol. 16. 2. & in not. ad triplex Targum in Gen. v. 24. Ed. Hanov. (q) Bereshit Rabba, sect. 25. fol. 21. 3. (r) Zohar in Gen. fol. 44. 2. 3. Jarchi in Gen. v. 24. Wisd. c. iv. 11, 12, 13, 14.

Hebrews 11

6. But without faith it is impossible to please him: for he that cometh to God must believe that he is, and that he is a rewarder of them that diligently seek him.

6. χωρὶς δὲ πίστεως ἀδύνατον εὐαρεστῆσαι· πιστεῦσαι γὰρ δεῖ τὸν προσερχόμενον τῷ θεῷ, ὅτι ἔστιν, καὶ τοῖς ἐκζητοῦσιν αὐτὸν μισθαποδότης γίνεται.

6. choris de pisteos adunaton euaresteisai. pisteusai gar dei ton proserchomenon to theo, 'oti estin, kai tois ekzeitousin auton misthapodoteis ginetai.

ו. וּבְלֹא אֱמוּנָה לֹא-יוּכַל אִישׁ לְהָפִיק רָצוֹן מֵאֱלֹהִים כִּי הַבָּא לִפְנֵי אֱלֹהִים עָלָיו לְהַאֲמִין כִּי הוּא יֵשׁ וּמְשַׁלֵּם גְּמוּל לְדֹרְשָׁיו:

6. Oov•lo e•moo•na lo - yoo•chal eesh le•ha•fik ra•tzon me•Elohim ki ha•ba lif•ney Elohim alav le•ha•a•min ki hoo yesh oom•sha•lem g`mool le•dor•shav.

142

7. By faith Noah, being warned of God of things not seen as yet, moved with fear, prepared an ark to the saving of his house; by the which he condemned the world, and became heir of the righteousness which is by faith.

7. Πίστει χρηματισθεὶς Νῶε περὶ τῶν μηδέπω βλεπομένων, εὐλαβηθεὶς κατεσκεύασεν κιβωτὸν εἰς σωτηρίαν τοῦ οἴκου αὐτοῦ· δι' ἧς κατέκρινεν τὸν κόσμον, καὶ τῆς κατὰ πίστιν δικαιοσύνης ἐγένετο κληρονόμος.

7. Pistei chreimatistheis Noe peri ton meidepo blepomenon, eulabeitheis kateskeuasen kiboton eis soteirian tou oikou autou. di 'eis katekrinen ton kosmon, kai teis kata pistin dikaiosuneis egeneto kleironomos.

ז. בָּאֱמוּנָה עָשָׂה נֹחַ אֶת-הַתֵּבָה וַיַּצֵּל אֶת-בֵּיתוֹ כִּי יָרֵא הָיָה אֶת-אֱלֹהָיו אֲשֶׁר הִזְהִירוֹ עַל-הָעֲתִידוֹת טֶרֶם בָּאוּ: וְעַל-פִּיהָ הִרְשִׁיעַ אֶת-הָאָרֶץ וַיְהִי לְיוֹרֵשׁ הַצְּדָקָה בֶּאֱמוּנָתוֹ

7. Ba•e•moo•na asa no•ach et - ha•te•va va•ya•tzel et - bei•to ki ya•re ha•ya et – Elohav asher hiz•hi•ro al - ha•a•ti•dot te•rem ba•oo ve•al - pi•ha hir•shi•a et - ha•a•retz vay•hi le•yo•resh ha•tz`da•ka be•e•moo•na•to.

Hebrews 11

8. By faith Abraham, when he was called to go out into a place which he should after receive for an inheritance, obeyed; and he went out, not knowing whither he went.

8. Πίστει καλούμενος Ἀβραὰμ ὑπήκουσεν ἐξελθεῖν εἰς τὸν τόπον ὃν ἤμελλεν λαμβάνειν εἰς κληρονομίαν, καὶ ἐξῆλθεν μὴ ἐπιστάμενος ποῦ ἔρχεται.

8. Pistei kaloumenos Abra'am 'upeikousen exelthein eis ton topon 'on eimellen lambanein eis kleironomian, kai exeilthen mei epistamenos pou erchetai.

ח. בָּאֱמוּנָה שָׁמַע אַבְרָהָם כַּאֲשֶׁר נִקְרָא לָלֶכֶת אֶל-הָאָרֶץ אֲשֶׁר עָתַד לְרִשְׁתָּהּ וַיֵּלֶךְ בִּבְלִי-דַעַת אָנָה הוּא בָא:

8. Ba•e•moo•na sha•ma Avraham ka•a•sher nik•ra la•le•chet el - ha•a•retz asher oo•tad le•rish•ta va•ye•lech biv•li - da•at ana hoo va.

Rabbinic Jewish Commentary

unto a land that I will show thee: upon which words a Jewish commentator (r) has this note;

"He (God) did not immediately make known the land unto him, that so it might be lovely in his eyes;"

And it is, elsewhere, said by the Jews (s), that Abraham

"Came from Aspamia (i.e. Mesopotamia), and its companions, ולא היה יודע היכן, "and he knew not where" he was, as a man that is in the dark;"

(r) Jarchi in Gen. xii. 1. (s) Bereshit Rabba, sect. 60. fol. 52. 3.

---

9. By faith he sojourned in the land of promise, as in a strange country, dwelling in tabernacles with Isaac and Jacob, the heirs with him of the same promise:

9. Πίστει παρῴκησεν εἰς γῆν τῆς ἐπαγγελίας, ὡς ἀλλοτρίαν, ἐν σκηναῖς κατοικήσας μετὰ Ἰσαὰκ καὶ Ἰακώβ, τῶν συγκληρονόμων τῆς ἐπαγγελίας τῆς αὐτῆς·

9. Pistei parokeisen eis gein teis epangelias, 'os allotrian, en skeinais katoikeisas meta Ysa'ak kai Yakob, ton sugkleironomon teis epangelias teis auteis.

ט. בָּאֱמוּנָה הִתְגּוֹרֵר בָּאָרֶץ הַנְּתוּנָה לוֹ כִּבְאֶרֶץ נָכְרִיָּה וַיֵּשֶׁב בְּאֹהָלִים הוּא וְיִצְחָק וְיַעֲקֹב יוֹרְשֵׁי הַהַבְטָחָה עִמּוֹ:

9. Ba•e•moo•na hit•go•rer ba•a•retz ha•ne•too•na lo kiv•e•retz noch•ri•ya va•ye•shev be•o•ha•lim hoo ve•Yitzchak ve•Yaakov yor•shey ha•hav•ta•cha ee•mo.

---

10. For he looked for a city which hath foundations, whose builder and maker is God.

10. ἐξεδέχετο γὰρ τὴν τοὺς θεμελίους ἔχουσαν πόλιν, ἧς τεχνίτης καὶ δημιουργὸς ὁ θεός.

10. exedecheto gar tein tous themelious echousan polin, 'eis techniteis kai deimiourgos 'o theos.

י. כִּי-חִכָּה לָעִיר אֲשֶׁר יְסוֹד עוֹלָם לָהּ וַאֲשֶׁר בּוֹנָהּ וְעֹשָׂהּ הוּא הָאֱלֹהִים:

10. Ki - chi•ka la•eer asher ye•sod o•lam la va•a•sher bo•na ve•o•sa hoo ha•Elohim.

Hebrews 11

11. Through faith also Sara herself received strength to conceive seed, and was delivered of a child when she was past age, because she judged him faithful who had promised.

11. Πίστει καὶ αὐτὴ Σάρρα δύναμιν εἰς καταβολὴν σπέρματος ἔλαβεν, καὶ παρὰ καιρὸν ἡλικίας ἔτεκεν, ἐπεὶ πιστὸν ἡγήσατο τὸν ἐπαγγειλάμενον.

11. Pistei kai autei Sarra dunamin eis katabolein spermatos elaben, kai para kairon 'eilikias eteken, epei piston 'eigeisato ton epangeilamenon.

יא. בָּאֱמוּנָה גַם-שָׂרָה הַחֲלִיפָה-כֹּחַ לְהַזְרִיעַ וַתֵּלֶד אַחֲרֵי בִלֹתָהּ עֵקֶב אֲשֶׁר חָרְצָה כִּי הַמַּבְטִיחַ נֶאֱמָן הוּא:

11. Ba•e•moo•na gam - sa•ra he•che•li•fa - cho•ach le•haz•ri•a va•te•led a•cha•rey be•lo•ta e•kev asher char•tza ki ha•mav•ti•ach ne•e•man hoo.

Rabbinic Jewish Commentary

received strength to conceive seed: Sometimes "strength" itself signifies seed, as in Pro.31:3 and so to receive strength is to receive seed; which the female does from the male; hence that saying of the Jews (t), the male does not receive strength from another, but the female מקבלת כח "receiveth strength" from another; but here it is to be understood of receiving power from God to retain seed, received from men, and conceive by it; which Sarah, in her circumstances, without the interposition of the almighty power, could never have done. The nymph Anobret is so called, in imitation of this conception of Sarah's; or as she is called in the Phoenician language, חן ענברת, which signifies "conceiving by grace": as this conception must be entirely ascribed to the power and grace of God.

(t) Caphtor, fol. 21. 2.

Hebrews 11

12. Therefore sprang there even of one, and him as good as dead, so many as the stars of the sky in multitude, and as the sand which is by the sea shore innumerable.

12. Διὸ καὶ ἀφ᾽ ἑνὸς ἐγεννήθησαν, καὶ ταῦτα νενεκρωμένου, καθὼς τὰ ἄστρα τοῦ οὐρανοῦ τῷ πλήθει, καὶ ὡς ἡ ἄμμος ἡ παρὰ τὸ χεῖλος τῆς θαλάσσης ἡ ἀναρίθμητος.

12. Dio kai aph 'enos egenneitheisan, kai tauta nenekromenou, kathos ta astra tou ouranou to pleithei, kai 'os 'ei ammos 'ei para to cheilos teis thalasseis 'ei anarithmeitos.

יב. וְעַל-כֵּן מֵאֶחָד הַהוּא הַקָּרוֹב לָמָוֶת נוֹלְדוּ כְּכוֹכְבֵי הַשָּׁמַיִם לָרֹב וְכַחוֹל אֲשֶׁר עַל-שְׂפַת הַיָּם אֲשֶׁר לֹא יִסָּפֵר:

12. Ve•al - ken me•e•chad ha•hoo ha•ka•rov la•ma•vet nol•doo ke•choch•vey ha•sha•ma•yim la•rov ve•cha•chol asher al - s`fat ha•yam asher lo yi•sa•fer.

Rabbinic Jewish Commentary

That is, Abraham: the Arabic version has here a strange interpolation;

"This faith Isaac and Rebecca conceived in mind, and so there were born of one, Esau and Jacob."

The Ethiopic version reads, "The bodies of both were like a dead carcass"; both of Abraham and Sarah.

---

13. These all died in faith, not having received the promises, but having seen them afar off, and were persuaded of them, and embraced them, and confessed that they were strangers and pilgrims on the earth.

13. Κατὰ πίστιν ἀπέθανον οὗτοι πάντες, μὴ λαβόντες τὰς ἐπαγγελίας, ἀλλὰ πόρρωθεν αὐτὰς ἰδόντες, καὶ ἀσπασάμενοι, καὶ ὁμολογήσαντες ὅτι ξένοι καὶ παρεπίδημοί εἰσιν ἐπὶ τῆς γῆς.

13. Kata pistin apethanon 'outoi pantes, mei labontes tas epangelias, alla porrothen autas idontes, kai aspasamenoi, kai 'omologeisantes 'oti xenoi kai parepideimoi eisin epi teis geis.

יג. בָּאֱמוּנָה מֵתוּ כָל-אֵלֶּה וְלֹא רָאוּ אֶת-הַהַבְטָחוֹת בְּקִיּוּמָן כִּי אִם-מֵרָחוֹק חָזוּ אֹתָן וַיַּאֲמִינוּ וַיִּצְהֲלוּ לִקְרָאתָן: וַיּוֹדוּ כִּי-גֵרִים וְתוֹשָׁבִים הֵם בָּאָרֶץ

13. Ba•e•moo•na me•too chol - ele ve•lo ra•oo et - ha•hav•ta•chot be•ki•yoo•man ki eem - me•ra•chok cha•zoo o•tan va•ya•a•mi•noo va•yitz•ha•loo lik•ra•tan va•yo•doo ki - ge•rim ve•to•sha•vim hem ba•a•retz.

Hebrews 11

14. For they that say such things declare plainly that they seek a country.

14. Οἱ γὰρ τοιαῦτα λέγοντες ἐμφανίζουσιν ὅτι πατρίδα ἐπιζητοῦσιν.

14. 'Oi gar toyauta legontes emphanizousin 'oti patrida epizeitousin.

יד. וְאֵלֶּה הָאֹמְרִים כָּזֹאת מוֹדִיעִים כִּי אֶרֶץ אֲשֶׁר לָהֶם הֵם מְבַקְשִׁים:

14. Ve•e•le ha•om•rim ka•zot mo•di•eem ki e•retz asher la•hem hem me•vak•shim.

15. And truly, if they had been mindful of that country from whence they came out, they might have had opportunity to have returned.

15. Καὶ εἰ μὲν ἐκείνης ἐμνημόνευον ἀφ᾽ ἧς ἐξῆλθον, εἶχον ἂν καιρὸν ἀνακάμψαι.

15. Kai ei men ekeineis emneimoneuon aph 'eis exeilthon, eichon an kairon anakampsai.

טו. וְאִם הָאָרֶץ הַהִיא אֲשֶׁר יָצְאוּ מִמֶּנָּה עָלְתָה עַל-לִבָּם הֲלֹא הָיָה בְיָדָם לָשׁוּב אֵלֶיהָ:

15. Ve•eem ha•a•retz ha•hee asher yatz•oo mi•me•na al•ta al - li•bam ha•lo ha•ya ve•ya•dam la•shoov e•le•ha.

Hebrews 11

16. But now they desire a better country, that is, an heavenly: wherefore God is not ashamed to be called their God: for he hath prepared for them a city.

16. Νῦν δὲ κρείττονος ὀρέγονται, τοῦτ' ἔστιν, ἐπουρανίου· διὸ οὐκ ἐπαισχύνεται αὐτοὺς ὁ θεός, θεὸς ἐπικαλεῖσθαι αὐτῶν· ἡτοίμασεν γὰρ αὐτοῖς πόλιν.

16. Nun de kreittonos oregontai, tout estin, epouraniou. dio ouk epaischunetai autous 'o theos, theos epikaleisthai auton. 'eitoimasen gar autois polin.

טז. אוּלָם טוֹבָה מִמֶּנָּה הִתְאַוּוּ וְהִיא בִשְׁמֵי מָעַל וְעַל-כֵּן לֹא בוֹשׁ הָאֱלֹהִים מֵהֶם לְהִקָּרֵא אֱלֹהֵיהֶם וַיָּכֶן-לָהֶם:עִיר שָׁמָּה

16. Oo•lam to•va mi•me•na hit•a•voo ve•hee vish•mey ma•al ve•al - ken lo vosh ha•Elohim me•hem le•hi•ka•re Elohey•hem va•ya•chen - la•hem eer sha•ma.

Rabbinic Jewish Commentary

Remarkable is the saying of Anaxagoras (u) who, when one said to him, hast thou no regard to thy country? answered, I have, and that the greatest, pointing with his fingers towards heaven; and, says Philo the Jew (w), the soul of every wise man has heaven for his country, and the earth as a strange place.

(u) Laert. in Vit. Anaxag. p. 92. (w) De Agricultura, p. 196. Vid. ib. de Confus. Ling. p. 331.

---

17. By faith Abraham, when he was tried, offered up Isaac: and he that had received the promises offered up his only begotten son,

17. Πίστει προσενήνοχεν Ἀβραὰμ τὸν Ἰσαὰκ πειραζόμενος, καὶ τὸν μονογενῆ προσέφερεν ὁ τὰς ἐπαγγελίας ἀναδεξάμενος,

17. Pistei proseneinochen Abra'am ton Ysa'ak peirazomenos, kai ton monogenei prospheren 'o tas epangelias anadexamenos,

יז. בָּאֱמוּנָה הֶעֱלָה אַבְרָהָם אֶת-יִצְחָק בְּיוֹם מֻסָּה וְיֹרֵשׁ הַהַבְטָחוֹת הִקְרִיב אֶת-יְחִידוֹ לְעֹלָה:

17. Ba•e•moo•na he•e•la Avraham et - Yitzchak be•yom ma•sa ve•yo•resh ha•hav•ta•chot hik•riv et - ye•chi•do le•o•la.

Rabbinic Jewish Commentary

The Jews speak (x) of ten temptations, with which Abraham was tried, and in all which he stood; and say, that this of the binding of Isaac was the tenth and last.

The Jews are divided about the age of Isaac at his binding: Josephus (y) says he was twenty five years of age; others say twenty six (z); some say (a) thirty six: but the more prevailing opinion is (b), that he was thirty seven years of age; only Aben (c) Ezra makes him to be about thirteen; rejecting the more commonly received account, as well as that he was but five years old, that being an age unfit to carry wood. Some Christian writers have thought he might be about thirty three years of age, the age of Yeshua when he suffered, of whom he was a type.

(x) Targum in Cant. vii. 8. Pirke Eliezer, c. 26. & c. 31. Maimon. Jarchi & Bartenora in Misn. Abot, c. 5. sect. 3. (y) Antiqu. l. 1. c. 13. sect. 2. (z) Tzemach David, par. 1. fol. 6. 1. (a) Targum Jon. in Gen. xxii. 1. (b) Zohar in Gen. fol. 68. 2. & 74. 4. & 76. 2. Targ. Hieros. in Ex. xii. 42. Pirke Eliezer, c. 31, Juchasin, fol. 9. 1. Prefat. Echa Rabbati, fol. 40. 2. Seder Olam Rabba, c. 1. p. 3. Shalshelet Hakabala, fol. 3. 1. (c) In Gen. xxii. 4.

Hebrews 11

18. Of whom it was said, That in Isaac shall thy seed be called:

18. πρὸς ὃν ἐλαλήθη, ὅτι Ἐν Ἰσαὰκ κληθήσεταί σοι σπέρμα·

18. pros 'on elaleithei, 'oti En Ysa'ak kleitheisetai soi sperma.

יח. אֲשֶׁר נֶאֱמַר עָלָיו כִּי בְיִצְחָק יִקָּרֵא לְךָ זָרַע:

18. Asher ne•e•mar alav ki ve•Yitzchak yi•ka•re le•cha za•ra.

---

19. Accounting that God was able to raise him up, even from the dead; from whence also he received him in a figure.

19. λογισάμενος ὅτι καὶ ἐκ νεκρῶν ἐγείρειν δυνατὸς ὁ θεός· ὅθεν αὐτὸν καὶ ἐν παραβολῇ ἐκομίσατο.

19. logisamenos 'oti kai ek nekron egeirein dunatos 'o theos. 'othen auton kai en parabolei ekomisato.

יט. וּבְלִבּוֹ אָמַר כִּי תַשִּׂיג יַד אֱלֹהִים לַהֲקִימוֹ מִן-הַמֵּתִים וְכֵן גַּם-הֱשִׁיבוֹ אֵלָיו וַיְהִי לְמוֹפֵת:

19. Oov•li•bo amar ki ta•sig yad Elohim la•ha•ki•mo min - ha•me•tim ve•chen gam - he•shi•vo elav vay•hi le•mo•fet.

Rabbinic Jewish Commentary

"Rabbi Yehudah says: As the knife touched Yitzchak's throat, his soul left hijm, but when G-d's Voice emerged from between the two keruvim, saying Do not harm the boy, do not do anything to him (Bereshis 22:12), his soul came back into his body. He was untied, and stood up, experiencing the revival of the dead. Immediately he realized that the dead will be revived in the time to come and he recited [the berachah]: "Blessed are You HaShem, who revives the dead."
(Pirkei D'Rebbi Eliezer, Chapter 31, translated by Avraham Yaakov Finkel, Yeshivath Beth Moshe, pg 22)

The Jews speak of this matter agreeably to the apostle; they say, a man has two breaths or souls, one in this world, and another in the world to come; and of Isaac they say (d), that

"In the time that he was offered upon the altar, his soul (or "breath"), which he had in this world, "went out"; and when it was said to Abraham (or by him) blessed be he that quickeneth the dead, his soul (or breath), which he had in the world to come, returned to him--for אתחשב כמת, "he was accounted as dead"."

They speak of him as if he was just dead; they say (e),

"When he saw the sword over his neck, his breath fled from him, and came to the place of the soul, כאילו היה, "as if he was at the point of giving up the ghost"."

So that a Jew cannot find fault with the apostle for expressing himself in this manner.

(d) Tosaphta in Zohar in Gen. fol. 46. 21. (e) Tzeror Hammor, fol. 58. 2. Pirke Eliezer, c. 31.

20. By faith Isaac blessed Jacob and Esau concerning things to come.

20. Πίστει περὶ μελλόντων εὐλόγησεν Ἰσαὰκ τὸν Ἰακὼβ καὶ τὸν Ἡσαῦ.

20. Pistei peri mellonton eulogeisen Ysa'ak ton Yakob kai ton Eisau.

:כ. בָּאֱמוּנָה בֵּרַךְ יִצְחָק אֶת-יַעֲקֹב וְאֶת-עֵשָׂו וַיְדַבֵּר עַל-עֲתִדֹתָם

20. Ba•e•moo•na be•rach Yitzchak et - Yaakov ve•et - Esav va•y`da•ber al - a•ti•do•tam.

Hebrews 11

21. By faith Jacob, when he was a dying, blessed both the sons of Joseph; and worshipped, leaning upon the top of his staff.

21. Πίστει Ἰακὼβ ἀποθνῄσκων ἕκαστον τῶν υἱῶν Ἰωσὴφ εὐλόγησεν, καὶ προσεκύνησεν ἐπὶ τὸ ἄκρον τῆς ῥάβδου αὐτοῦ.

21. Pistei Yakob apothneiskon 'ekaston ton 'wion Yoseiph eulogeisen, kai prosekuneisen epi to akron teis 'rabdou autou.

:כא. בָּאֱמוּנָה בֵּרַךְ יַעֲקֹב בְּמֹתוֹ אֶת-שְׁנֵי בְנֵי-יוֹסֵף וַיִּשְׁתַּח עַל-רֹאשׁ הַמַּטֶּה

21. Ba•e•moo•na be•rach Yaakov be•mo•to et - sh`ney v`ney - Yo•sef va•yish•tach al – rosh ha•ma•te.

Rabbinic Jewish Commentary
and worshipped, leaning upon the top of his staff; not that he "worshipped the top of his staff", as the Vulgate Latin version renders it, either his own, or Joseph's, or any little image upon the top of it; which would be an instance of idolatry, and not faith, contrary to the scope of the apostle; nor is there any need to interpret this of civil worship and respect paid to Joseph, as a fulfilment of his dream, and with a peculiar regard to Messiah, of whom Joseph was a type; whereas, on the contrary, Joseph at this time bowed to his father, as was most natural and proper, Gen.48:12
nor is there any necessity of supposing a different punctuation of Gen.47:31 and that the true reading is not "mittah", a bed, but "matteh"; a staff, contrary to all the Targums (f), and the Talmud (g), which read "mittah", a bed, seeing it is not that place the apostle cites or refers to; for that was before the blessing of the sons of Joseph, but this was at the same time; and the apostle relates what is nowhere recorded in Genesis, but what

he had either from tradition, or immediate revelation; or else he concludes it from the general account in Gen.48:1 and the sense is, that Jacob, having blessed the two sons of Joseph, being sat upon his bed, and weak, he leaned upon the top of his staff, and worshipped God, and gave praise and glory to him, that he had lived to see not only his son Joseph, but his seed also, see Gen.48:2.

(f) Onkelos, Jonathan & Jerusalem in Gen. xlvii. 31. (g) T. Bab. Megilla, fol. 16. 2.

Hebrews 11

22. By faith Joseph, when he died, made mention of the departing of the children of Israel; and gave commandment concerning his bones.

22. Πίστει Ἰωσὴφ τελευτῶν περὶ τῆς ἐξόδου τῶν υἱῶν Ἰσραὴλ ἐμνημόνευσεν, καὶ περὶ τῶν ὀστέων αὐτοῦ ἐνετείλατο.

22. Pistei Yoseiph teleuton peri teis exodou ton 'wion Ysraeil emneimoneusen, kai peri ton osteon autou eneteilato.

:כב. בָּאֱמוּנָה הִזְכִּיר יוֹסֵף לִפְנֵי מוֹתוֹ אֶת-צֵאת בְּנֵי יִשְׂרָאֵל וַיְצַו עַל-אֹדוֹת עַצְמוֹתָיו

22. Ba•e•moo•na hiz•kir Yo•sef lif•ney mo•to et - tzet b`ney Israel vay•tzav al - o•dot atz•mo•tav.

Rabbinic Jewish Commentary

Joseph's coffin, the Jews say (h), was put into the river Nile; and so says Patricides (i), an Arabic writer: others say it was in the buryingplace of the kings, until it was taken up and removed by Moses.

(h) T. Bab. Sota, fol. 13. 1. (i) Apud Hottinger. Smegma Oriental. l. 1. c. 8. p. 379.

23. By faith Moses, when he was born, was hid three months of his parents, because they saw he was a proper child; and they were not afraid of the king's commandment.

23. Πίστει Μωϋσῆς γεννηθεὶς ἐκρύβη τρίμηνον ὑπὸ τῶν πατέρων αὐτοῦ, διότι εἶδον ἀστεῖον τὸ παιδίον· καὶ οὐκ ἐφοβήθησαν τὸ διάταγμα τοῦ βασιλέως.

23. Pistei Mouseis genneitheis ekrubei trimeinon 'upo ton pateron autou, dioti eidon asteion to paidion. kai ouk ephobeitheisan to dyatagma tou basileos.

כג. בָּאֱמוּנָה נִצְפַּן מֹשֶׁה שְׁלֹשָׁה יְרָחִים עַל-יְדֵי אֲבוֹתָיו בְּהִוָּלְדוֹ כִּי רָאוּ כִּי-טוֹב הַיֶּלֶד וְלֹא יָרְאוּ מִדַּת הַמֶּלֶךְ:

23. Ba•e•moo•na nitz•pan Moshe sh`lo•sha ye•ra•chim al - ye•dey avo•tav be•hi•val•do ki ra•oo ki - tov ha•ye•led ve•lo yar•oo mi•dat ha•me•lech.

Rabbinic Jewish Commentary
According to the Targumist (k), his mother went with him but six months, at the end of which he was born, and that she hid him three months, which made up the nine, the time in which a woman usually goes with child; and after that she could conceal him no longer: the hiding of him is here ascribed to both his parents, though in Exo.2:2 it is represented as the act of his mother; which, no doubt, was done, with the knowledge, advice, and consent of his father; and the Septuagint there renders it, εσκεπασαν, "they hid him"; though the order of the history makes it necessary that it should be read in the singular.

(k) Jonathan ben Uzziel in Exod. ii. 2.

---

24. By faith Moses, when he was come to years, refused to be called the son of Pharaoh's daughter;

24. Πίστει Μωϋσῆς μέγας γενόμενος ἠρνήσατο λέγεσθαι υἱὸς θυγατρὸς Φαραώ,

24. Pistei Mouseis megas genomenos eirneisato legesthai 'wios thugatros Pharao,

כד. בָּאֱמוּנָה מֵאֵן מֹשֶׁה בְגָדְלוֹ לְהִקָּרֵא בֶן לְבַת-פַּרְעֹה:

24. Ba•e•moo•na me•en Moshe ve•god•lo le•hi•ka•re ven le•vat - Par•oh.

Rabbinic Jewish Commentary

refused to be called the son of Pharaoh's daughter; by whom Moses was taken up out of the water; by whom he was named, and provided for; she reckoned him as her own son, and designed him for Pharaoh's successor, as Josephus reports (l).

(l) Antiqu. l. 2. c. 9. sect. 7.

Hebrews 11

25. Choosing rather to suffer affliction with the people of God, than to enjoy the pleasures of sin for a season;

25. μᾶλλον ἑλόμενος συγκακουχεῖσθαι τῷ λαῷ τοῦ θεοῦ ἢ πρόσκαιρον ἔχειν ἁμαρτίας ἀπόλαυσιν·

25. mallon 'elomenos sugkakoucheisthai to lao tou theou ei proskairon echein 'amartias apolausin.

כה: וַיִּבְחַר-לוֹ לְהִתְעַנּוֹת עִם-עַם אֱלֹהִים מֵהִתְעַנֵּג בְּתַעֲנוּגֵי הַחֵטְא בִּימֵי חָלֶד.

25. Va•yiv•char - lo le•hit•a•not eem - am Elohim me•hit•a•neg be•ta•a•noo•gey ha•chet bi•mey cha•led.

Rabbinic Jewish Commentary

The Jews call (m) תענוגי רגע, "pleasures for a moment", or momentary ones.

(m) Aben Ezra in Psal. xxiii. 4.

---

26. Esteeming the reproach of Christ greater riches than the treasures in Egypt: for he had respect unto the recompence of the reward.

26. μείζονα πλοῦτον ἡγησάμενος τῶν Αἰγύπτου θησαυρῶν τὸν ὀνειδισμὸν τοῦ χριστοῦ· ἀπέβλεπεν γὰρ εἰς τὴν μισθαποδοσίαν.

26. meizona plouton 'eigeisamenos ton Aiguptou theisauron ton oneidismon tou christou. apeblepen gar eis tein misthapodosian.

כו: וְאֶת-חֶרְפָּתוֹ כְּחֶרְפַּת הַמָּשִׁיחַ חָשַׁב לְעֹשֶׁר גָּדוֹל מֵאֹצְרוֹת מִצְרָיִם כִּי צָפָה אֶל-הַגְּמוּל.

26. Ve•et - cher•pa•to ke•cher•pat ha•Ma•shi•ach cha•shav le•o•sher ga•dol me•otz`rot Mitz•ra•yim ki tza•fa el - ha•g`mool.

Hebrews 11

27. By faith he forsook Egypt, not fearing the wrath of the king: for he endured, as seeing him who is invisible.

27. Πίστει κατέλιπεν Αἴγυπτον, μὴ φοβηθεὶς τὸν θυμὸν τοῦ βασιλέως· τὸν γὰρ ἀόρατον ὡς ὁρῶν ἐκαρτέρησεν.

27. Pistei katelipen Aigupton, mei phobeitheis ton thumon tou basileos. ton gar aoraton 'os 'oron ekartereisen.

כז. בָּאֱמוּנָה עָזַב אֶת-מִצְרַיִם וְלֹא יָרֵא מֵחֲמַת מַלְכָּה כִּי נָשָׂא אֶת-נַפְשׁוֹ אֵלָיו כִּרְאֹה אֹתוֹ אֲשֶׁר פָּנָיו לֹא יֵרָאוּ:

27. Ba•e•moo•na azav et - Mitz•ra•yim ve•lo ya•re me•cha•mat mal•ka ki na•sa et - naf•sho elav ke•ro•eh o•to asher pa•nav lo ye•ra•oo.

28. Through faith he kept the passover, and the sprinkling of blood, lest he that destroyed the firstborn should touch them.

28. Πίστει πεποίηκεν τὸ Πάσχα καὶ τὴν πρόσχυσιν τοῦ αἵματος, ἵνα μὴ ὁ ὀλοθρεύων τὰ πρωτότοκα θίγῃ αὐτῶν.

28. Pistei pepoieiken to Pascha kai tein proschusin tou 'aimatos, 'ina mei 'o olothreuon ta prototoka thigei auton.

כח. בָּאֱמוּנָה עָשָׂה אֶת-הַפֶּסַח וְנָתוֹן אֶת-הַדָּם עַל-הַבָּתִים לְבִלְתִּי יִגַּע בָּם הַמַּשְׁחִית אֶת-הַבְּכֹרִים:

28. Ba•e•moo•na asa et - ha•Pe•sach ve•na•ton et - ha•dam al - ha•ba•tim le•vil•ti yi•ga bam ha•mash•chit et - ha•b`cho•rim.

29. By faith they passed through the Red sea as by dry land: which the Egyptians assaying to do were drowned.

29. Πίστει διέβησαν τὴν Ἐρυθρὰν Θάλασσαν ὡς διὰ ξηρᾶς· ἧς πεῖραν λαβόντες οἱ Αἰγύπτιοι κατεπόθησαν.

29. Pistei diebeisan tein Eruthran Thalassan 'os dya xeiras. 'eis peiran labontes 'oi Aiguptioi katepotheisan.

כט: בָּאֱמוּנָה הָלְכוּ בְיַם-סוּף כְּמוֹ בַיַּבָּשָׁה וְהַמִּצְרִים הָלְכוּ אַחֲרֵיהֶם וַיִּשְׁקָעוּ

29. Ba•e•moo•na hal•choo ve•yam - soof k`mo va•ya•ba•sha ve•ha•Mitz•rim hal•choo a•cha•rey•hem va•yish•ka•oo.

Hebrews 11

30. By faith the walls of Jericho fell down, after they were compassed about seven days.

30. Πίστει τὰ τείχη Ἰεριχὼ ἔπεσεν, κυκλωθέντα ἐπὶ ἑπτὰ ἡμέρας.

30. Pistei ta teichei Yericho epesen, kuklothenta epi 'epta 'eimeras.

ל: בָּאֱמוּנָה נָפְלוּ חוֹמוֹת יְרִיחוֹ בְּהִסֵּב אוֹתָן שִׁבְעַת יָמִים

30. Ba•e•moo•na naf•loo cho•mot Ye•ri•cho be•ha•sev o•tan shiv•at ya•mim.

Rabbinic Jewish Commentary

Of themselves, not from any natural cause: the Jews say (n) they sunk right down into the ground, and were swallowed up; even the whole wall fell round about, as the Septuagint version in Jos.6:20 expresses it: or, it may be, only that which was over against the camp of Israel, as Kimchi observes; since Rahab's house was built upon the wall, and yet fell not. And this was by the faith of Joshua, and the Israelites, who believed the walls would fall, at the sound of the rams' horns, as God said they should: after they were compassed about seven days; which was a trial of their faith and patience: the Jews say (o) it was on the sabbath day that they fell: this was a preternatural act, and cannot be ascribed to any second cause; nothing is impossible with God.

(n) Targum Jon. Jarchi & Kimchi in Josh. vi. 5. (o) Jarchi & Kimchi in ver. 15.

31. By faith the harlot Rahab perished not with them that believed not, when she had received the spies with peace.

31. Πίστει Ῥαὰβ ἡ πόρνη οὐ συναπώλετο τοῖς ἀπειθήσασιν, δεξαμένη τοὺς κατασκόπους μετ᾽ εἰρήνης.

31. Pistei 'Ra'ab 'ei pornei ou sunapoleto tois apeitheisasin, dexamenei tous kataskopous met eireineis.

לֹא. בֶּאֱמוּנָה לֹא אָבְדָה רָחָב הַזּוֹנָה עִם-בְּנֵי בְלִיַּעַל כַּאֲשֶׁר אָסְפָה אֶת-הַמְרַגְּלִים אֶל-בֵּיתָהּ בְּשָׁלוֹם:

31. Ba•e•moo•na lo av•da ra•chav ha•zo•na eem - b`ney ve•li•yaal ka•a•sher as•fa et - ha•me•rag•lim el - bey•ta be•sha•lom.

Rabbinic Jewish Commentary

The Targum on Jos.2:1 calls her אתתא פונדקיתא, "a woman, that kept a victualling house": this paraphrase is taken notice of by Jarchi and Kimchi on the place, who interpret it, "a seller of food": and even the Hebrew word זונה, is so explained by a considerable Jewish writer (p); and this may rather seem to be the sense of the word, and to be her proper business, from the spies going to her house, as being an house of entertainment; and from Salmon's marrying her, which might be thought strange that a prince of Israel would, had she been a person of ill fame; to which may be added, the encomiums of her for her faith and works, both by our apostle, and by James: but yet, the constant use of the word, in this form, the testimonies of two apostles, and her making no mention of her husband and children, when she agreed with the spies, confirm the generally received character of her, that she was an harlot. Some Jewish writers say (q) that she was ten years of age when the Israelites came out of Egypt; and that all the forty years they were in the wilderness, זנתה, "she played the harlot"; and was one and fifty years of age when she was proselyted. She is called an harlot; not with respect to her present, but past life. In the Greek text, she is here called Raab, as also in Jas.2:25 and so in the Septuagint in Jos.2:1. Rachab, which exactly answers to the Hebrew word רחב, Jos.2:1 and by Josephus (r) "Rachabe".

when she had received the spies with peace; And had hid them, for some time, in her house, and then let them down by the wall; and who, at the taking of the city, saved her, and hers, according to their promise and oath: the number of these spies were two, according to Jos.2:1. The Jews (s) say one of them was Phinehas, the son of Eleazar, the high priest; and others (t) of them say they were Phinehas and Caleb.

(p) R. Sol. Urbin. Ohel Moed, fol. 24. 1. (q) T. Bab. Zebachin. fol. 116. 2. Shalshalet Hakabala, fol. 7. 2. (r) Antiqu. l. 5. c. 1. sect. 2. (s) Laniado in Josh. ii. 1. (t) Tanchuma apud Masum in ib.

Hebrews 11

32. And what shall I more say? for the time would fail me to tell of Gedeon, and of Barak, and of Samson, and of Jephthae; of David also, and Samuel, and of the prophets:

32. Καὶ τί ἔτι λέγω; Ἐπιλείψει γάρ με διηγούμενον ὁ χρόνος περὶ Γεδεών, Βαράκ τε καὶ Σαμψὼν καὶ Ἰεφθάε, Δαυίδ τε καὶ Σαμουὴλ καὶ τῶν προφητῶν·

32. Kai ti eti lego? Epileipsei gar me dieigoumenon 'o chronos peri Gedeon, Barak te kai Sampson kai Yephthae, Dauid te kai Samoueil kai ton propheiton.

לב. וּמָה אמַר עוֹד הֲלֹא תִקְצַר-לִי הָעֵת כִּי-אֲסַפֵּר מִדִּבְרֵי גִדְעוֹן בָּרָק שִׁמְשׁוֹן וְיִפְתָּח דָּוִד שְׁמוּאֵל וְהַנְּבִיאִים:

32. Oo•ma o•mar od ha•lo tik•tzar - li ha•et ki - asa•per mi•div•rey Gid•on Ba•rak Shim•shon ve•Yif•tach David Sh`moo•el ve•ha•n`vi•eem.

Rabbinic Jewish Commentary

for the time would fail me; either the time of life, and so it is an hyperbolical expression; or the time convenient for the writing this epistle; to enumerate all the instances of faith, and enlarge upon them, would take up too much of his time, and make the epistle prolix and tedious: this form of speech is often used by Philo the Jew (u), and by Julian the emperor (w). It may be observed, that many, who are not mentioned by name, do not stand excluded from being believers; and that the number of believers, under the Old Testament, was very large.

to tell of Gedeon; so Gideon is called in the Septuagint version of Jdg.6:11 and other places; and by Josephus (x), and Philo (y) the Jew, as here: he was a man, but of a mean extract, and had his infirmities; and even in the exercise of that particular grace, for which he is mentioned; but was, no doubt, a good man, and is commended for his faith.

(u) De Creat. Princip. p. 735. Merced. Meret. p. 863. De Legat. ad Caium, p. 1037. De Somniis, p. 1116. (w) Orat l. p. 50, 62, 75. (x) Antiqu. Jud. l. 5. c. 6. sect. 2. &c. (y) De Confusione Ling. p. 339.

Hebrews 11

33. Who through faith subdued kingdoms, wrought righteousness, obtained promises, stopped the mouths of lions,

33. οἳ διὰ πίστεως κατηγωνίσαντο βασιλείας, εἰργάσαντο δικαιοσύνην, ἐπέτυχον ἐπαγγελιῶν, ἔφραξαν στόματα λεόντων,

33. 'oi dya pisteos kateigonisanto basileias, eirgasanto dikaiosunein, epetuchon epangelion, ephraxan stomata leonton,

לג: אֲשֶׁר בָּאֱמוּנָה כָּבְשׁוּ מַמְלָכוֹת פָּעֲלוּ צְדָקוֹת הִשִּׂיגוּ הַבְטָחוֹת וְסָכְרוּ פִּי אֲרָיוֹת

33. Asher ba•e•moo•na kav•shoo mam•la•chot pa•a•loo tze•da•kot hi•si•goo hav•ta•chot ve•sach•roo pi ara•yot.

---

34. Quenched the violence of fire, escaped the edge of the sword, out of weakness were made strong, waxed valiant in fight, turned to flight the armies of the aliens.

34. ἔσβεσαν δύναμιν πυρός, ἔφυγον στόματα μαχαίρας, ἐνεδυναμώθησαν ἀπὸ ἀσθενείας, ἐγενήθησαν ἰσχυροὶ ἐν πολέμῳ, παρεμβολὰς ἔκλιναν ἀλλοτρίων.

34. esbesan dunamin puros, ephugon stomata machairas, enedunamotheisan apo astheneias, egeneitheisan ischuroi en polemo, parembolas eklinan allotrion.

לד. כִּבּוּ חֲמַת אֵשׁ נִמְלְטוּ מִפִּי חֶרֶב מָצְאוּ אוֹן לָהֶם מִתּוֹךְ רִפְיוֹנָם עָשׂוּ חַיִל בַּמִּלְחָמָה וַיָּנִיסוּ מַחֲנוֹת זָרִים:

34. Ki•boo cha•mat esh nim•le•too mi•pi che•rev matz•oo on la•hem mi•toch rif•yo•nam a•soo cha•yil ba•mil•cha•ma va•ya•ni•soo ma•cha•not za•rim.

35. Women received their dead raised to life again: and others were tortured, not accepting deliverance; that they might obtain a better resurrection:

35. Ἔλαβον γυναῖκες ἐξ ἀναστάσεως τοὺς νεκροὺς αὐτῶν· ἄλλοι δὲ ἐτυμπανίσθησαν, οὐ προσδεξάμενοι τὴν ἀπολύτρωσιν, ἵνα κρείττονος ἀναστάσεως τύχωσιν·

35. Elabon gunaikes ex anastaseos tous nekrous auton. alloi de etumpanistheisan, ou prosdexamenoi tein apolutrosin, 'ina kreittonos anastaseos tuchosin.

לה. נָשִׁים מָצְאוּ אֶת־מֵתֵיהֶן כִּי קָמוּ מִן־הַמֵּתִים וְרַבִּים הִתְעַנּוּ וְלֹא מָצְאוּ פְלֵיטָה לְמַעַן יָקוּמוּ בְּיוֹם הַתְּקוּמָה:בְּיֶתֶר עֹז

35. Na•shim matz•oo et - me•tey•hen ki ka•moo min - ha•me•tim ve•ra•bim hit•a•noo ve•lo matz•oo fe•ley•ta le•ma•an ya•koo•moo ve•yom ha•t`koo•ma be•ye•ter oz.

Rabbinic Jewish Commentary

not accepting deliverance; when offered them by the king, see the Apocrypha:

"24. Now Antiochus, thinking himself despised, and suspecting it to be a reproachful speech, whilst the youngest was yet alive, did not only exhort him by words, but also assured him with oaths, that he would make him both a rich and a happy man, if he would turn from the laws of his fathers; and that also he would take him for his friend, and trust him with affairs. 25. But when the young man would in no case hearken unto him, the king called his mother, and exhorted her that she would counsel the young man to save his life." (2 Maccabees 7)

that they might obtain a better resurrection; which they died in the faith of, see the Apocryha:

"7. And him he sent with that wicked Alcimus, whom he made high priest, and commanded that he should take vengeance of the children of Israel. 11 And said courageously, These I had from heaven; and for his laws I despise them; and from him I hope to receive them again. 14 So when he was ready to die he said thus, It is good, being put to death by men, to look for hope from God to be raised up again by him: as for thee, thou shalt have no resurrection to life. (2 Maccabees)

36. And others had trial of cruel mockings and scourgings, yea, moreover of bonds and imprisonment:

36. ἕτεροι δὲ ἐμπαιγμῶν καὶ μαστίγων πεῖραν ἔλαβον, ἔτι δὲ δεσμῶν καὶ φυλακῆς·

36. 'eteroi de empaigmon kai mastigon peiran elabon, eti de desmon kai phulakeis.

לו. מִקְצוֹתָם נָשְׂאוּ קָלוֹן וּמַהֲלֻמוֹת וְגַם-כְּבָלִים וּכְלָאִים:

36. Mik•tzo•tam nas•oo ka•lon oo•ma•ha•loo•mot ve•gam - k`va•lim ooch•la•eem.

Hebrews 11

37. They were stoned, they were sawn asunder, were tempted, were slain with the sword: they wandered about in sheepskins and goatskins; being destitute, afflicted, tormented;

37. ἐλιθάσθησαν, ἐπρίσθησαν, ἐπειράσθησαν, ἐν φόνῳ μαχαίρας ἀπέθανον· περιῆλθον ἐν μηλωταῖς, ἐν αἰγείοις δέρμασιν, ὑστερούμενοι, θλιβόμενοι, κακουχούμενοι-

37. elithastheisan, epristheisan, epeirastheisan, en phono machairas apethanon. perieilthon en meilotais, en aigeiois dermasin, 'usteroumenoi, thlibomenoi, kakouchoumenoi-

לז. נִסְקְלוּ בָאֲבָנִים גֹּרְרוּ בַמְּגֵרוֹת נִצְרְפוּ בְמַסָּה וְהוֹצִיאוּ נַפְשָׁם לְטִבְחַת חָרֶב נָעוּ בְּעוֹרֹת כְּבָשִׂים וְעִזִּים וְנָמֹגוּ:בְחֹסֶר כֹּל בְּלַחַץ בְּמָצוֹק

37. Nis•ke•loo va•a•va•nim go•re•roo vam•ge•rot nitz•re•foo ve•ma•sa ve•ho•tzi•oo naf•sham le•tiv•chat cha•rev na•oo be•o•rot ke•va•sim ve•ee•zim ve•na•mo•goo ve•cho•ser kol be•la•chatz ve•ma•tzok.

Rabbinic Jewish Commentary
The tradition is in both Talmuds: in the one, the account is this: (z) that "Manasseh sought to kill Isaiah, and he fled from him, and fled to a cedar, and the cedar swallowed him up, all but the fringe of his garment; they came and told him (Manasseh), he said unto them, go and saw the cedar, ונסרו, "and they sawed the cedar", and blood was seen to come out."

And in the other (a) thus,

"Says R. Simeon ben Azzai, I found a book of genealogies in Jerusalem, and in it was written that Manasseh slew Isaiah."

And after relating the occasion of it, being some passages in Isaiah Manasseh was displeased with and objected to; and the prophet not thinking it worth his while to return an answer, or attempt to reconcile them with other passages, objected, knowing that the king would use him contemptuously; he is made to say,

"I will swallow (or put myself into) a cedar, they brought the cedar, ונסרו, "and sawed it asunder", and when it (the saw) came to his mouth, he expired."

Another Jewish writer (b) out of the Midrash, reports it thus;

"Manasseh sought to slay him, and Isaiah fled, and the Lord remembered him, and he was swallowed up in the middle of a tree; but there remained without the tree the fringe of his garment; and then Manasseh ordered the tree to be cut down, and Isaiah died."

And it is become a generally received opinion of the ancient Christian writers, that Isaiah was sawn asunder; as of Justin Martyr (c), Origen (d), Tertullian (e), Lactantius (f), Athanasius (g), Hilary (h), Cyril of Jerusalem (i), Gregory Nyssene (k), Jerom (l), Isidorus Pelusiota (m), Gregentius (n), Procopius Gazaeus (o), and others; but more persons seem to be designed:

were tempted; either by God, as Abraham, and Job; or by the devil, as all the saints are; or rather by cruel tyrants, to deny the faith, and renounce the worship of God, as Eleazar, and the seven brethren with their mother; at least some of them were, 2 Maccabees 6,7. Some think the true reading is επρηθησαν, "were burned"; as one of the seven brethren were in the Apocrytha,

"Now when he was thus maimed in all his members, he commanded him being yet alive to be brought to the fire, and to be fried in the pan: and as the vapour of the pan was for a good space dispersed, they exhorted one another with the mother to die manfully, saying thus," (2 Maccabees 7:5)

And as Zedekiah and Ahab were roasted in the fire, by the king of Babylon, Jer.29:22 though they were lying prophets, and cannot be referred to here; see Dan.11:33. This clause is wanting in the Syriac version.

were slain with the sword; As the priests at Nob, by the order of Saul; 1Sa.22:18. The prophets of the Lord by Jezebel, 1Ki.18:22 and many in the times of the Maccabees; Dan.11:33 and in the Apocrypha:

"And there were destroyed within the space of three whole days fourscore thousand, whereof forty thousand were slain in the conflict; and no fewer sold than slain." (2 Maccabees 5:14)

(z) T. Hieros. Sanhedrin, fol. 28. 3. (a) T. Bab. Yebamot, fol. 49. 2. (b) Shalshelet Hakabala, fol. 12. 2. (c) Dialog. cum Tryph. p. 249. (d) In Jer. Homil. 19. p. 197. in Isa. Homil. 1. fol. 101. & in Matt. Homil. 26. fol. 51. (e) De Patientia, c. 14. Scorpiace, c. 8. (f) De vera sapientia, l. 4. c. 11. (g) Vol. I. de Incarnat. p. 55, 65. Vol. II. dicta & Interpret. Parab. p. 325, 353. (h) Contr. Constant, p. 199. & enarrat. in Psal. cxviii. p. 465. (i) Cateches. 2. sect. 9. p. 29. & Cateches. 13. sect. 3. p. 169. (k) Vol. II. de Castigat. p. 749. (l) In Isa. lvii. 2. (m) L. 4. Ep. 205. (n) Disputat. cum Herbano Judaeo, p. 19. (o) In Reg. l. 4. c. 21. 16.

Hebrews 11

38. (Of whom the world was not worthy:) they wandered in deserts, and in mountains, and in dens and caves of the earth.

38. ὧν οὐκ ἦν ἄξιος ὁ κόσμος- ἐν ἐρημίαις πλανώμενοι καὶ ὄρεσιν καὶ σπηλαίοις καὶ ταῖς ὀπαῖς τῆς γῆς.

38. 'on ouk ein axios 'o kosmos- en ereimiais planomenoi kai oresin kai speilaiois kai tais opais teis geis.

לח: וְהָאָרֶץ לֹא שָׁוָה לָהֶם תָּעוּ בַמִּדְבָּר בֶּהָרִים בִּמְעָרוֹת וּבִמְחִילוֹת עָפָר

38. Ve•ha•a•retz lo sho•va la•hem ta•oo va•mid•bar be•ha•rim bim•a•rot oo•vim•chi•lot afar.

Rabbinic Jewish Commentary

As Elijah did; 1Ki.18:4, and many in the times of the Maccabees;

"And they kept the eight days with gladness, as in the feast of the tabernacles, remembering that not long afore they had held the feast of the tabernacles, when as they wandered in the mountains and dens like beasts." (2 Maccabees 10:6)

39. And these all, having obtained a good report through faith, received not the promise:

39. Καὶ οὗτοι πάντες, μαρτυρηθέντες διὰ τῆς πίστεως, οὐκ ἐκομίσαντο τὴν ἐπαγγελίαν,

39. Kai 'outoi pantes, martureithentes dya teis pisteos, ouk ekomisanto tein epangelian,

לט: וְכָל-אֵלֶּה עֵדוּת לָהֶם עַל-אֱמוּנָתָם וְלֹא רָאוּ אֶת-הַהַבְטָחוֹת בְּקִיּוּמָן

39. Ve•chol - ele e•doot la•hem al - emoo•na•tam ve•lo ra•oo et - ha•hav•ta•chot be•ki•yoo•man.

Hebrews 11

40. God having provided some better thing for us, that they without us should not be made perfect.

40. τοῦ θεοῦ περὶ ἡμῶν κρεῖττόν τι προβλεψαμένου, ἵνα μὴ χωρὶς ἡμῶν τελειωθῶσιν.

40. tou theou peri 'eimon kreitton ti problepsamenou, 'ina mei choris 'eimon teleiothosin.

מ: יַעַן הֵכִין אֱלֹהִים לָנוּ אֶת-הַטּוֹב מִקֶּדֶם לְבִלְתִּי יַגִּיעוּ הֵם לְכָל-תַּכְלִיתָם מִבַּלְעָדֵינוּ

40. Ya•an he•chin Elohim la•noo et - ha•tov mi•ke•dem le•vil•ti ya•gi•oo hem le•chol - tach•li•tam mi•bal•a•dey•noo.

(Hebrews Chapter 11 End)

Hebrews, Chapter 12

1. Wherefore seeing we also are compassed about with so great a cloud of witnesses, let us lay aside every weight, and the sin which doth so easily beset us, and let us run with patience the race that is set before us,

1. Τοιγαροῦν καὶ ἡμεῖς, τοσοῦτον ἔχοντες περικείμενον ἡμῖν νέφος μαρτύρων, ὄγκον ἀποθέμενοι πάντα καὶ τὴν εὐπερίστατον ἁμαρτίαν, δι᾽ ὑπομονῆς τρέχωμεν τὸν προκείμενον ἡμῖν ἀγῶνα,

1. Toigaroun kai 'eimeis, tosouton echontes perikeimenon 'eimin nephos marturon, ogkon apothemenoi panta kai tein euperistaton 'amartian, di 'upomoneis trechomen ton prokeimenon 'eimin agona,

א. לָכֵן גַּם-אֲנַחְנוּ אַחֲרֵי אֲשֶׁר הֲמוֹן עֵדִים כָּאֵלֶּה עֹטְרִים אֹתָנוּ כַּעֲנָנִים מִסָּבִיב נַשְׁלִיכָה מִמֶּנּוּ כָּל-מַשָּׂא וְחֵטְא:אֲשֶׁר יִגְדְּרוּ בַעֲדֵנוּ תָּמִיד וְעַל-גַּב תּוֹחֶלֶת נָרוּצָה בִּמְרוֹץ הֶעָרוּךְ לְפָנֵינוּ

1. La•chen gam - a•nach•noo a•cha•rey asher ha•mon e•dim ka•e•le ot•rim o•ta•noo ka•a•na•nim mi•sa•viv nash•li•cha mi•me•noo kol - ma•sa ve•chet asher yig•de•roo va•a•de•noo ta•mid ve•al - gav to•che•let na•roo•tza va•me•rotz he•a•rooch le•fa•ney•noo.

---

2. Looking unto Jesus the author and finisher of our faith; who for the joy that was set before him endured the cross, despising the shame, and is set down at the right hand of the throne of God.

2. ἀφορῶντες εἰς τὸν τῆς πίστεως ἀρχηγὸν καὶ τελειωτὴν Ἰησοῦν, ὅς, ἀντὶ τῆς προκειμένης αὐτῷ χαρᾶς, ὑπέμεινεν σταυρόν, αἰσχύνης καταφρονήσας, ἐν δεξιᾷ τε τοῦ θρόνου τοῦ θεοῦ κεκάθικεν.

2. aphorontes eis ton teis pisteos archeigon kai teleiotein Yeisoun, 'os, anti teis prokeimeneis auto charas, 'upemeinen stauron, aischuneis kataphroneisas, en dexya te tou thronou tou theou kekathiken.

ב. וְעֵינֵינוּ אֶל-יֵשׁוּעַ צוּר אֱמוּנָתֵנוּ הַגֹּמֵר עָלֵינוּ אֲשֶׁר בַּעֲבוּר הַשִּׂמְחָה הַזְּרוּעָה לוֹ נָשָׂא עֵץ סִבְלוֹ וְאֶת-הַחֶרְפָּה:בָּזָה וַיֵּשֶׁב לִימִין כִּסֵּא הָאֱלֹהִים.

2. Ve•ey•ney•noo el - Yeshua tzoor emoo•na•te•noo ha•go•mer aley•noo asher ba•a•voor ha•sim•cha ha•z`roo•ah lo na•sa etz soo•bo•lo ve•et - ha•cher•pa va•za va•ye•shev li•y`min ki•se ha•Elohim.

Rabbinic Jewish Commentary
And to this agrees the Chaldee paraphrase of Psa.21:1.

"O YHVH, in thy power shall the King Messiah יחדי, "rejoice", and in thy redemption how greatly will he exult!"

Hebrews 12

3. For consider him that endured such contradiction of sinners against himself, lest ye be wearied and faint in your minds.

3. Ἀναλογίσασθε γὰρ τὸν τοιαύτην ὑπομεμενηκότα ὑπὸ τῶν ἁμαρτωλῶν εἰς αὐτὸν ἀντιλογίαν, ἵνα μὴ κάμητε ταῖς ψυχαῖς ὑμῶν ἐκλυόμενοι.

3. Analogisasthe gar ton toyautein 'upomemeneikota 'upo ton 'amartolon eis auton antilogian, 'ina mei kameite tais psuchais 'umon ekluomenoi.

ג: הִתְבּוֹנְנוּ אֵלָיו אֲשֶׁר-נָשָׂא תִגְרָה כָזֹאת מִיַּד הַחַטָּאִים בְּנַפְשׁוֹ פֶּן-תִּתְרַפּוּ וְעָיְפָה נַפְשְׁכֶם

3. Hit•bo•ne•noo elav asher - na•sa tig•ra cha•zot mi•yad ha•cha•ta•eem be•naf•sho pen - tit•ra•poo ve•ai•fa naf•she•chem.

---

4. Ye have not yet resisted unto blood, striving against sin.

4. Οὔπω μέχρι αἵματος ἀντικατέστητε πρὸς τὴν ἁμαρτίαν ἀνταγωνιζόμενοι·

4. Oupo mechri 'aimatos antikatesteite pros tein 'amartian antagonizomenoi.

ד: עַד-כֹּה עוֹד לֹא קַמְתֶּם לְהִלָּחֵם בַּחֵטְא עַד-הַדָּם

4. Ad - ko od lo kam•tem le•hi•la•chem ba•chet ad - ha•dam.

---

5. And ye have forgotten the exhortation which speaketh unto you as unto children, My son, despise not thou the chastening of the Lord, nor faint when thou art rebuked of him:

5. καὶ ἐκλέλησθε τῆς παρακλήσεως, ἥτις ὑμῖν ὡς υἱοῖς διαλέγεται, Υἱέ μου, μὴ ὀλιγώρει παιδείας κυρίου, μηδὲ ἐκλύου ὑπ᾽ αὐτοῦ ἐλεγχόμενος·

5. kai ekleleisthe teis parakleiseos, 'eitis 'umin 'os 'wiois dyalegetai, 'Wie mou, mei oligorei paideias kuriou, meide ekluou 'up autou elegchomenos.

ה. וַתִּשְׁכְּחוּ אֶת-הַתּוֹכֵחָה אֲשֶׁר נוֹכַחְתֶּם כְּבָנִים לֵאמֹר מוּסַר יְהֹוָה בְּנִי אַל-תִּמְאָס וְאַל-תָּקֹץ בְּתוֹכַחְתּוֹ:

5. Va•tish•ke•choo et - ha•to•che•cha asher no•chach•tem ke•va•nim le•mor moo•sar Adonai B`ni al - tim•as ve•al - ta•kotz be•to•chach•to.

Hebrews 12

6. For whom the Lord loveth he chasteneth, and scourgeth every son whom he receiveth.

6. ὃν γὰρ ἀγαπᾷ κύριος παιδεύει· μαστιγοῖ δὲ πάντα υἱὸν ὃν παραδέχεται.

6. 'on gar agapa kurios paideuei. mastigoi de panta 'wion 'on paradechetai.

ו. כִּי אֶת אֲשֶׁר-יֶאֱהַב יְהֹוָה יוֹכִיחַ יַכְאִיב אֶת-בֵּן יִרְצֶה:

6. Ki et asher - ye•e•hav Adonai yo•chi•ach yach•eev et - ben yir•tze.

Rabbinic Jewish Commentary
So the Jews (p) often speak of יסורין של אהבה, "chastisements of love", in distinction from evil "chastisement", or vindictive ones.

(p) Zohar in Gen. fol. 39. 3. & 102. 4. & in Exod. fol. 98. 2. & 102. 2. & in Lev. fol. 19. 3.

---

7. If ye endure chastening, God dealeth with you as with sons; for what son is he whom the father chasteneth not?

7. Εἰς παιδείαν ὑπομένετε, ὡς υἱοῖς ὑμῖν προσφέρεται ὁ θεός· τίς γάρ ἐστιν υἱὸς ὃν οὐ παιδεύει πατήρ;

7. Eis paideian 'upomenete, 'os 'wiois 'umin prospheretai 'o theos. tis gar estin 'wios 'on ou paideuei pateir?

ז. אִם-תִּשְׂאוּ אֶת-מוּסָרוֹ הוּא לְאוֹת כִּי עֵינֵי אֱלֹהֵיכֶם עֲלֵיכֶם כְּבָנִים כִּי מִי הוּא הַבֵּן אֲשֶׁר אָבִיו לֹא יְיַסְּרֶנּוּ:

7. Eem - tis•oo et - moo•sa•ro hoo le•ot ki ey•ney Elohey•chem aley•chem ke•va•nim ki mee hoo ha•ben asher aviv lo ye•yas•re•noo.

Rabbinic Jewish Commentary
The Jews have a saying (q), that

"The doctrine of chastisements is silence;"

That is, they are to be patiently bore, and not murmured at. The Vulgate Latin, and all the Oriental versions, read the words as an exhortation; the former of these renders it, "persevere in discipline"; the Syriac version, "endure correction"; the Arabic version, "be ye patient in chastisement"; and the Ethiopic version, "endure your chastening": but then the word, "for", should be supplied in the next clause, as it is in the Syriac and Ethiopic versions.

(q) T. Bab. Beracot, fol. 62. 1.

Hebrews 12

8. But if ye be without chastisement, whereof all are partakers, then are ye bastards, and not sons.

8. Εἰ δὲ χωρίς ἐστε παιδείας, ἧς μέτοχοι γεγόνασιν πάντες, ἄρα νόθοι ἐστὲ καὶ οὐχ υἱοί.

8. Ei de choris este paideias, 'eis metochoi gegonasin pantes, ara nothoi este kai ouch 'wioi.

ח. אֶפֶס אִם-תִּהְיוּ בְאֵין-מוּסָר אֲשֶׁר הוּא מְנָת כֻּלָּם הֲלֹא זָרִים אַתֶּם וְלֹא בָנִים:

8. E•fes eem - ti•hi•yoo be•eyn - moo•sar asher hoo m`nat koo•lam ha•lo za•rim atem ve•lo va•nim.

Hebrews 12

9. Furthermore we have had fathers of our flesh which corrected us, and we gave them reverence: shall we not much rather be in subjection unto the Father of spirits, and live?

9. Εἶτα τοὺς μὲν τῆς σαρκὸς ἡμῶν πατέρας εἴχομεν παιδευτάς, καὶ ἐνετρεπόμεθα· οὐ πολλῷ μᾶλλον ὑποταγησόμεθα τῷ πατρὶ τῶν πνευμάτων, καὶ ζήσομεν;

9. Eita tous men teis sarkos 'eimon pateras eichomen paideutas, kai enetrepometha. ou pollo mallon 'upotageisometha to patri ton pneumaton, kai zeisomen?

ט. הֵן יֶשׁ-לָנוּ אָבוֹת בִּשָׂרֵנוּ אֲשֶׁר יִסְּרוּנוּ וַנִּירָא מִפְּנֵיהֶם אַף כִּי-עָלֵינוּ לְהִכָּנַע מִפְּנֵי אֲבִי הָרוּחוֹת לְמַעַן חָיֹה־נִחְיֶה

9. Hen yesh - la•noo avot be•sa•re•noo asher yis•roo•noo va•ni•ra mip•ney•hem af ki - aley•noo le•hi•ka•na mip•ney Avi ha•roo•chot le•ma•an cha•yo nich•ye.

---

10. For they verily for a few days chastened us after their own pleasure; but he for our profit, that we might be partakers of his holiness.

10. Οἱ μὲν γὰρ πρὸς ὀλίγας ἡμέρας κατὰ τὸ δοκοῦν αὐτοῖς ἐπαίδευον· ὁ δὲ ἐπὶ τὸ συμφέρον, εἰς τὸ μεταλαβεῖν τῆς ἁγιότητος αὐτοῦ.

10. 'Oi men gar pros oligas 'eimeras kata to dokoun autois epaideuon. 'o de epi to sumpheron, eis to metalabein teis 'agioteitos autou.

י. וְהֵמָּה יִסְּרוּנוּ לְיָמִים מְעַטִּים כַּטּוֹב בְּעֵינֵיהֶם אַךְ הוּא לְטוֹב לָנוּ לָתֶת-לָנוּ חֵלֶק בְּקָדְשׁוֹ:

10. Ve•he•ma yis•roo•noo le•ya•mim me•a•tim ka•tov be•ey•ne•hem ach hoo le•tov la•noo la•tet - la•noo che•lek be•kod•sho.

Rabbinic Jewish Commentary
The Alexandrian copy reads in the plural number, "profits."

11. Now no chastening for the present seemeth to be joyous, but grievous: nevertheless afterward it yieldeth the peaceable fruit of righteousness unto them which are exercised thereby.

11. Πᾶσα δὲ παιδεία πρὸς μὲν τὸ παρὸν οὐ δοκεῖ χαρᾶς εἶναι, ἀλλὰ λύπης· ὕστερον δὲ καρπὸν εἰρηνικὸν τοῖς δι᾽ αὐτῆς γεγυμνασμένοις ἀποδίδωσιν δικαιοσύνης.

11. Pasa de paideia pros men to paron ou dokei charas einai, alla lupeis. 'usteron de karpon eireinikon tois di auteis gegumnasmenois apodidosin dikaiosuneis.

יא. וְכָל-מוּסָר לֹא יִמָּצֵא לְשָׂשׂוֹן בְּעִתּוֹ כִּי יוֹסִף עֶצֶב עִמּוֹ אַךְ אַחֲרֵי-כֵן יִתֵּן פְּרִי שָׁלוֹם לַאֲשֶׁר יְצָרְפוּ בוֹ לִצְדָקָה:

11. Ve•chol - moo•sar lo yi•ma•tze le•sa•son be•ee•to ki yo•sif etzev ee•mo ach a•cha•rey - chen yi•ten p`ri sha•lom la•a•sher yi•tzar•foo vo litz•da•ka.

---

12. Wherefore lift up the hands which hang down, and the feeble knees;

12. Διὸ τὰς παρειμένας χεῖρας καὶ τὰ παραλελυμένα γόνατα ἀνορθώσατε·

12. Dio tas pareimenas cheiras kai ta paralelumena gonata anorthosate.

יב. עַל-כֵּן חַזְּקוּ יָדַיִם רָפוֹת וּבִרְכַּיִם כֹּשְׁלוֹת אַמֵּצוּ:

12. Al - ken chaz•koo ya•da•yim ra•fot oo•vir•ka•yim kosh•lot a•me•tzoo.

---

13. And make straight paths for your feet, lest that which is lame be turned out of the way; but let it rather be healed.

13. καὶ τροχιὰς ὀρθὰς ποιήσατε τοῖς ποσὶν ὑμῶν, ἵνα μὴ τὸ χωλὸν ἐκτραπῇ, ἰαθῇ δὲ μᾶλλον.

13. kai trochyas orthas poieisate tois posin 'umon, 'ina mei to cholon ektrapei, iathei de mallon.

יג. וְיַשְּׁרוּ מְסִלּוֹת לְרַגְלֵיכֶם לְבִלְתִּי תֵקַע כַּף יֶרֶךְ הַצֹּלֵעַ כִּי אִם-תֵּרָפֵא:

13. Ve•yash•roo me•si•lot le•rag•ley•chem le•vil•ti te•ka kaf ye•rech ha•tzo•le•a ki eem - te•ra•fe.

Hebrews 12

14. Follow peace with all men, and holiness, without which no man shall see the Lord:

14. Εἰρήνην διώκετε μετὰ πάντων, καὶ τὸν ἁγιασμόν, οὗ χωρὶς οὐδεὶς ὄψεται τὸν κύριον·

14. Eireinein diokete meta panton, kai ton 'agyasmon, 'ou choris oudeis opsetai ton kurion.

יד. בַּקְּשׁוּ שָׁלוֹם עִם-כָּל-אָדָם וּקְדֻשָּׁה אֲשֶׁר מִבַּלְעָדֶיהָ לֹא-יִרְאֶה אִישׁ אֶת-הָאָדוֹן:

14. Bak•shoo sha•lom eem - kol - adam ook•doo•sha asher mi•bal•a•de•ha lo - yir•eh eesh et - ha•Adon.

Rabbinic Jewish Commentary

It was a saying of Hillell (r), who lived about the times of Messiah;

"Be thou one of the disciples of Aaron, who loved peace, ורודף שלום, "and followed peace"."

This is said of Aaron in the Talmud (s), that

"He loved peace, and followed peace, and made peace between a man and his neighbour, as is said, Mal.2:6."

They recommend peace on many accounts, and say, great is peace, and among the rest, because it is one of the names of God (t)

(r) Pirke Abot, c. 1. sect. 12. (s) T. Bab. Sanhedrin, fol. 6. 2. & Gloss. in T. Bab. Yoma, fol. 71. 2. (t) Vajikra Rabba, sect. 9. fol. 153. 1, 2.

15. Looking diligently lest any man fail of the grace of God; lest any root of bitterness springing up trouble you, and thereby many be defiled;

15. ἐπισκοποῦντες μή τις ὑστερῶν ἀπὸ τῆς χάριτος τοῦ θεοῦ· μή τις ῥίζα πικρίας ἄνω φύουσα ἐνοχλῇ, καὶ διὰ ταύτης μιανθῶσιν πολλοί·

15. episkopountes mei tis 'usteron apo teis charitos tou theou. mei tis 'riza pikrias ano phuousa enochlei, kai dya tauteis myanthosin polloi.

טו. הִשָּׁמְרוּ לָכֶם פֶּן-יִגָּרַע אִישׁ מֵחֶסֶד אֱלֹהִים פֶּן-יֵשׁ בָּכֶם שֹׁרֶשׁ פֹּרֶה רֹאשׁ וְלַעֲנָה וְחֻלְּלוּ בוֹ רַבִּים:

15. Hi•sham•roo la•chem pen - yi•ga•ra eesh me•che•sed Elohim pen - yesh ba•chem sho•resh po•re rosh ve•la•a•na ve•choo•le•loo vo ra•bim.

Rabbinic Jewish Commentary

So ριζα αμαρτωλος, "a sinful root", is used for a "wicked man", in the Apocrypha:

"In those days went there out of Israel wicked men, who persuaded many, saying, Let us go and make a covenant with the heathen that are round about us: for since we departed from them we have had much sorrow." (1 Maccabees 1:11)

And שורש המרי, "a root of bitterness", signifies, in Jewish writings (u), an error, or heresy, in opposition to a root of faith, or a fundamental doctrine.

(u) Cosri, Orat. 1. fol. 35. 1.

---

16. Lest there be any fornicator, or profane person, as Esau, who for one morsel of meat sold his birthright.

16. μή τις πόρνος, ἢ βέβηλος, ὡς Ἡσαῦ, ὃς ἀντὶ βρώσεως μιᾶς ἀπέδοτο τὰ πρωτοτόκια αὐτοῦ.

16. mei tis pornos, ei bebeilos, 'os Eisau, 'os anti broseos myas apedoto ta prototokya autou.

טז. פֶּן-יִהְיֶה בָכֶם אִישׁ זֹנֶה וְחָלָל כְּעֵשָׂו אֲשֶׁר מָכַר אֶת-בְּכֹרָתוֹ בְּעַד נְזִיד עֲדָשִׁים:

16. Pen - yi•hee•ye va•chem eesh zo•ne ve•cha•lal ke•Esav asher ma•char et - be•cho•ra•to be•ad n`zid a•da•shim.

Rabbinic Jewish Commentary

The Jews have a tradition (w), that he committed five transgressions on the day he came out of the field weary.

"He committed idolatry: he shed innocent blood; and lay with a virgin betrothed; and denied the life of the world to come (or a future state); and despised his birthright."

It is elsewhere (x) a little differently expressed.

"Esau, the wicked, committed five transgressions on that day: he lay with a virgin betrothed; and killed a person; and denied the resurrection of the dead; and denied the root, or foundation, (i.e. that there is a God,) and despised his birthright; and besides, he desired his father's death, and sought to slay his brother."

It is common for them to say of him, that he was an ungodly man; and particularly, that he was a murderer, a robber, ונואף, "and an adulterer" (y); and that he has no part in the world to come (z): who for one morsel of meat sold his birthright; the account of which is in Gen.25:29 this includes all the privileges which he had a right unto by being the firstborn; as a peculiar blessing from his father; a double portion of goods; and dominion over his brethren: and it is commonly said by the Jews, that the priesthood belonged to the firstborn, before the Levitical dispensation; and that for this reason, Jacob coveted the birthright (a), Esau being a wicked man, and unfit for it. The birthright was reckoned sacred; it was typical of the primogeniture of Messiah; of the adoption of saints, and of the heavenly inheritance belonging thereunto; all which were despised by Esau: and so the Jewish paraphrases (b) interpret the contempt of his birthright, a despising of his part in the world to come, and a denial of the resurrection of the dead: and his contempt of it was shown in his selling it; and this was aggravated by his selling it for "one morsel of meat"; which was bread, and pottage of lentiles, Gen.25:34. The Jewish writers speak of this bargain and sale much in the same language as the apostle here does; they say (c) of him, this is the man that sold his birthright בעד ככר להם, "for a morsel of bread"; and apply to him the passage in Pro.28:21 "for a piece of bread that man will transgress".

(w) Targum Jon. ben Uzziel in Gen. xxv. 29. (x) Shemot Rabba, sect. I. fol. 89. 3. T. Bab. Bava Bathra, fol. 16. 2. (y) Tzeror Hammor, fol. 27. 1. (z) Tzeror Hammor, fol. 26. 3. (a) Bereshit Rabba, sect. 63. fol. 56. 2. (b)

Targum Hieros. & Jon. in Gen. 25. 34. Bereshit Rabba, ib. (c) Tzeror Hammor, fol. 26. 4. & 27. 1.

Hebrews 12

17. For ye know how that afterward, when he would have inherited the blessing, he was rejected: for he found no place of repentance, though he sought it carefully with tears.

17. Ἴστε γὰρ ὅτι καὶ μετέπειτα, θέλων κληρονομῆσαι τὴν εὐλογίαν, ἀπεδοκιμάσθη· μετανοίας γὰρ τόπον οὐχ εὗρεν, καίπερ μετὰ δακρύων ἐκζητήσας αὐτήν.

17. Yste gar 'oti kai metepeita, thelon kleironomeisai tein eulogian, apedokimasthei. Metanoias gar topon ouch 'euren, kaiper meta dakruon ekzeiteisas autein.

יז. הֲלֹא יְדַעְתֶּם כִּי חָפֵץ אַחֲרֵי-כֵן לָרֶשֶׁת אֶת-הַבְּרָכָה וְשֹׁמֵעַ לֹא הָיָה לוֹ וְאַף כִּי-בִקֵּשׁ בְּדִמְעָה לֹא מָצָא מָקוֹם לִתְשׁוּבָתוֹ:

17. Ha•lo ye•da•a•tem ki cha•fetz a•cha•rey - chen la•re•shet et - ha•b`ra•cha ve•sho•me•a lo ha•ya lo ve•af ki - vi•kesh be•dim•ah lo ma•tza ma•kom lit•shoo•va•to.

Rabbinic Jewish Commentary

This latter seems to be the better interpretation of the words, though the former agrees with the Targum on Job.15:20

"All the days of Esau the ungodly, they expected that he would have repented, but he repented not."

---

18. For ye are not come unto the mount that might be touched, and that burned with fire, nor unto blackness, and darkness, and tempest,

18. Οὐ γὰρ προσεληλύθατε ψηλαφωμένῳ ὄρει, καὶ κεκαυμένῳ πυρί, καὶ γνόφῳ, καὶ σκότῳ, καὶ θυέλλῃ,

18. Ou gar proseleiluthate pseilaphomeno orei, kai kekaumeno puri, kai gnopho, kai skoto, kai thuellei,

יח. כִּי הִנֵּה לֹא בָאתֶם אֶל-הַר אֲשֶׁר תִּגַּע בּוֹ יָד וַאֲשֶׁר אֵשׁ תְּלַהֵט אֹתוֹ וְלֹא אֶל-עָנָן וַעֲרָפֶל וָרָעַשׁ:

18. Ki hee•ne lo va•tem el - har asher ti•ga bo yad va•a•sher esh te•la•het o•to ve•lo el - anan va•a•ra•fel va•ra•ash.

Rabbinic Jewish Commentary
and tempest; there being thunderings and lightnings, which were very terrible, Exo.19:16 and though there is no express mention made of a tempest by Moses, yet Josephus (d) speaks not only of very terrible thunderings and lightnings, but of violent storms of wind, which produced exceeding great rains: and the Septuagint on Deu.4:11 use the same words as the apostle does here, "blackness, darkness, and tempest". This also may denote the majesty of God, who was then present; the terror of that dispensation; the horrible curses of the law; and the great confusion and disquietude raised by it in the conscience of a sinner.

(d) Antiqu. l. 3. c. 5. sect. 2.

Hebrews 12

19. And the sound of a trumpet, and the voice of words; which voice they that heard intreated that the word should not be spoken to them any more:

19. καὶ σάλπιγγος ἤχῳ, καὶ φωνῇ ῥημάτων, ἧς οἱ ἀκούσαντες παρῃτήσαντο μὴ προστεθῆναι αὐτοῖς λόγον·

19. kai salpingos eicho, kai phonei 'reimaton, 'eis 'oi akousantes pareiteisanto mei prostetheinai autois logon.

יט. וְלֹא לְקוֹל שׁוֹפָר וְקוֹל דְּבָרִים אֲשֶׁר שֹׁמְעָיו שָׁאֲלוּ לְבִלְתִּי יוֹסֵף דַּבֵּר עִמָּהֶם:

19. Ve•lo le•kol sho•far ve•kol d`va•rim asher shom•av sha•a•loo le•vil•ti Yo•sef da•ber ee•ma•hem.

Rabbinic Jewish Commentary
and the voice of words; of the ten words, or decalogue; which was as an articulate voice, formed by angels; and, therefore, the Torah is called the word spoken by messengers, Heb.2:2 and is represented, as the voice of God himself, Exo.20:1 who made use of the ministry of messengers to deliver the Torah to Moses; "which" voice is called קוֹל דברים, "the voice of words", in Deu.4:12, and this voice.

Hebrews 12

20. (For they could not endure that which was commanded, And if so much as a beast touch the mountain, it shall be stoned, or thrust through with a dart:

20. οὐκ ἔφερον γὰρ τὸ διαστελλόμενον, Κἂν θηρίον θίγῃ τοῦ ὄρους, λιθοβοληθήσεται·

20. ouk epheron gar to dyastellomenon, Kan theirion thigei tou orous, lithoboleitheisetai.

כ. כִּי קָשְׁתָה עֲלֵיהֶם הַמִּצְוָה מִנְּשֹׂא לֵאמֹר וְאַף גַּם-בְּהֵמָה תִּגַּע בָּהָר סָקֹל תִּסָּקֵל אוֹ-יָרֹה תִיָּרֶה בַּחִצִּים:

20. Ki kash•ta aley•hem ha•mitz•va min•so le•mor ve•af gam - be•he•ma ti•ga ba•har sa•kol ti•sa•kel oh - ya•ro ti•ya•re ba•chi•tzim.

---

21. And so terrible was the sight, that Moses said, I exceedingly fear and quake:

21. καί, οὕτως φοβερὸν ἦν τὸ φανταζόμενον, Μωϋσῆς εἶπεν, Ἔκφοβός εἰμι καὶ ἔντρομος.

21. kai, 'outos phoberon ein to phantazomenon, Mouseis eipen, Ekphobos eimi kai entromos.

כא. וּמַה-נּוֹרָא הָיָה הַמַּחֲזֶה עַד שֶׁגַּם מֹשֶׁה אָמַר פַּחַד קְרָאַנִי וּרְעָדָה:

21. Oo•ma - no•ra ha•ya ha•ma•cha•ze ad she•gam Moshe amar pa•chad ke•ra•a•ni oor•a•da.

Rabbinc Jewish Commentary

The Jews have a notion that Moses did quake and tremble, and when upon the mount; and that he expressed his fear and dread. They have such a tradition as this (e);

"When Moses ascended on high, the ministering messengers said before the holy blessed God, YHVH of the world, what has this man, born of a woman, to do among us? he said unto them, to receive the law he is come; they replied before him, that desirable treasure, which is treasured up with thee, nine hundred, and seventy, and four generations, before the world was created, dost thou seek to give to flesh and blood? "What is man, that thou art mindful of him, and the son of man, that thou visitest him? who hast set thy glory above the heavens!" The holy blessed God said to Moses, return them an answer; he said, before him, YHVH of the world, מתיירא ענא, "I am afraid", lest they should burn, (or consume) me, with the breath of their mouth."

Compare this last clause with 2Th.2:8 and elsewhere (f) those words being cited, he called unto Moses, Exo.25:16 it is observed:

"This Scripture comes not, but לאיים עליו "to terrify him"; that so the Torah might be given with fear, fervour, and trembling; as it is said, Psa.2:11" Once more (g),

"At the time that the holy blessed God said to Moses, "go, get thee down, for thy people have corrupted themselves", Exo.32:7 אזדעזע משה, "Moses trembled"; and he could not speak."

And again, it is said (h), that when Moses was on Mount Sinai, supplicating for the people of Israel, five destroying angels appeared, and immediately נתיירא משה, "Moses was afraid".

(e) T. Bab. Sabbat, fol. 88. 2. Yalkut, 2. par. 2. fol. 92. (f) T. Bab. Yoma, fol. 4. 2. (g) Zohar in Exod. fol. 84. 4. (h) Midrash Kohelet, fol. 69. 4.

---

22. But ye are come unto mount Sion, and unto the city of the living God, the heavenly Jerusalem, and to an innumerable company of angels,

22. Ἀλλὰ προσεληλύθατε Σιὼν ὄρει, καὶ πόλει θεοῦ ζῶντος, Ἰερουσαλὴμ ἐπουρανίῳ, καὶ μυριάσιν ἀγγέλων,

22. Alla proseleiluthate Sion orei, kai polei theou zontos, 'Yerousaleim epouranio, kai muryasin angelon,

כב. כִּי אִם-בָּאתֶם אֶל-הַר צִיּוֹן אֶל-עִיר אֵל חָי אֶל-יְרוּשָׁלַיִם הָעֶלְיוֹנָה וְאֶל-רִבֲבוֹת צְבָא מַלְאָכִים:

22. Ki eem - ba•tem el - har Tzi•yon el - eer El chai el - Ye•roo•sha•la•yim ha•el•yo•na ve•el - ri•va•vot tz`va mal•a•chim.

Rabbinic Jewish Commentary
A like phrase is used in the Apocrypha:

"Before the fair flowers were seen, or ever the moveable powers were established, before the innumerable multitude of angels were gathered together," (2 Esdras 6:3)

Hebrews 12

23. To the general assembly and church of the firstborn, which are written in heaven, and to God the Judge of all, and to the spirits of just men made perfect,

23. πανηγύρει καὶ ἐκκλησίᾳ πρωτοτόκων ἐν οὐρανοῖς ἀπογεγραμμένων, καὶ κριτῇ θεῷ πάντων, καὶ πνεύμασιν δικαίων τετελειωμένων,

23. paneigurei kai ekkleisia prototokon en ouranois apogegrammenon, kai kritei theo panton, kai pneumasin dikaion teteleiomenon,

כג. וְאֶל-עֲדַת הַבְּכוֹרִים אֲשֶׁר הֵמָּה בַּכְּתוּבִים בַּשָּׁמַיִם וְאֶל-אֱלֹהִים שֹׁפֵט הַכֹּל וְאֶל-רוּחוֹת הַצַּדִּיקִים אֲשֶׁר נַעֲשׂוּ שְׁלֵמִים׃

23. Ve•el - adat ha•b`cho•rim asher he•ma va•k`too•vim ba•sha•ma•yim ve•el – Elohim sho•fet ha•kol ve•el - roo•chot ha•tza•di•kim asher na•a•soo sh`le•mim.

Rabbinic Jewish Commentary
The apostle seems to have respect to some distinctions among the Jews: they divide mankind into three sorts; some are perfectly wicked; and some are perfectly righteous; and there are others that are between both (k): they often speak of צדיקים גמורים, "just men perfect" (l); and distinguish between a just man perfect, and a just man that is not perfect (m); as they do also between penitents and just men perfect;

(k) T. Hieros. Roshhashanah, fol. 57. 1. & T. Bab. Roshhashanah, fol. 16. 2. Derech Eretz, fol. 19. 4. (l) Zohar in Gen. fol. 28. 2. & 29. 1. & 39. 3. T. Bab. Taanith, fol. 18. 2. & Roshbahanah, fol. 4. 1. Pesachim, fol. 8. 1. 2. (m) T. Bab. Megilla, fol. 6. 2. & Avoda Zora, fol. 4. 1.

24. And to Jesus the mediator of the new covenant, and to the blood of sprinkling, that speaketh better things than that of Abel.

24. καὶ διαθήκης νέας μεσίτῃ Ἰησοῦ, καὶ αἵματι ῥαντισμοῦ κρεῖττον λαλοῦντι παρὰ τὸν Ἄβελ.

24. kai dyatheikeis neas mesitei Yeisou, kai 'aimati 'rantismou kreitton lalounti para ton 'Abel.

כד. וְאֶל-יֵשׁוּעַ מֵלִיץ לִבְרִית חֲדָשָׁה וְאֶל-דָּמוֹ הַנִּזְרָק אֲשֶׁר קוֹל קְרִיאָתוֹ טוֹב מִקּוֹל דְּמֵי הָבֶל׃

24. Ve•el - Yeshua me•litz liv•rit cha•da•sha ve•el - da•mo ha•niz•rak asher kol k`ri•a•to tov mi•kol d`mey ha•vel.

Hebrews 12

25. See that ye refuse not him that speaketh. For if they escaped not who refused him that spake on earth, much more shall not we escape, if we turn away from him that speaketh from heaven:

25. Βλέπετε μὴ παραιτήσησθε τὸν λαλοῦντα. Εἰ γὰρ ἐκεῖνοι οὐκ ἔφυγον, τὸν ἐπὶ γῆς παραιτησάμενοι χρηματίζοντα, πολλῷ μᾶλλον ἡμεῖς οἱ τὸν ἀπ᾽ οὐρανῶν ἀποστρεφόμενοι·

25. Blepete mei paraiteiseisthe ton lalounta. Ei gar ekeinoi ouk ephugon, ton epi geis paraiteisamenoi chreimatizonta, pollo mallon 'eimeis 'oi ton ap ouranon apostrephomenoi.

כה. הִשָּׁמְרוּ לָכֶם פֶּן-תָּסוּרוּ מִן-הַדֹּבֵר בָּכֶם כִּי אִם-לֹא נִמְלְטוּ הַסָּרִים מִן-מַזְהִירָם בָּאָרֶץ אֵיךְ נִמָּלֵט אֲנַחְנוּ אִם-נָסוּר מִן-מַזְהִירֵנוּ מִשָּׁמָיִם׃

25. Hi•sham•roo la•chem pen - ta•soo•roo min - ha•do•ver ba•chem ki eem - lo nim•le•too ha•sa•rim min - maz•hi•ram ba•a•retz eych ni•ma•let a•nach•noo eem na•soor min - maz•hi•re•noo mi•sha•ma•yim.

---

26. Whose voice then shook the earth: but now he hath promised, saying, Yet once more I shake not the earth only, but also heaven.

179

26. οὗ ἡ φωνὴ τὴν γῆν ἐσάλευσεν τότε, νῦν δὲ ἐπήγγελται, λέγων, Ἔτι ἅπαξ ἐγὼ σείω οὐ μόνον τὴν γῆν, ἀλλὰ καὶ τὸν οὐρανόν.

26. 'ou 'ei phonei tein gein esaleusen tote, nun de epeingeltai, legon, Eti 'apax ego seio ou monon tein gein, alla kai ton ouranon.

כו. אֲשֶׁר קֹלוֹ אָז הִרְעִישׁ אֶת־הָאָרֶץ וְעַתָּה הֻגַּד לֵאמֹר עוֹד אַחַת מְעַט הִיא וַאֲנִי מַרְעִישׁ לֹא לְבַד אֶת־הָאָרֶץ כִּי־אִם־גַּם אֶת־הַשָּׁמָיִם

26. Asher ko•lo az hir•eesh et - ha•a•retz ve•a•ta hoo•gad le•mor od a•chat me•at hee va•a•ni mar•eesh lo le•vad et - ha•a•retz ki eem - gam et - ha•sha•ma•yim.

Hebrews 12

27. And this word, Yet once more, signifieth the removing of those things that are shaken, as of things that are made, that those things which cannot be shaken may remain.

27. Τὸ δέ, Ἔτι ἅπαξ, δηλοῖ τῶν σαλευομένων τὴν μετάθεσιν, ὡς πεποιημένων, ἵνα μείνῃ τὰ μὴ σαλευόμενα.

27. To de, Eti 'apax, deiloi ton saleuomenon tein metathesin, 'os pepoieimenon, 'ina meinei ta mei saleuomena.

כז. וּמַה שֶּׁאָמַר עוֹד אַחַת מְעַט הוּא מַגִּיד חֲלִיפַת־כֹּל אֲשֶׁר יִמּוֹט מִן־הָרַעַשׁ כְּדָבָר נִבְרָא רַק לְמַעְנוֹ וַאֲשֶׁר לֹא־יִמּוֹט מִן־הָרַעַשׁ יַעֲמֹד לָעַד

27. Oo•ma she•a•mar od a•chat me•at hoo ma•gid cha•li•fat - kol asher yi•mot min - ha•ra•ash ke•da•var niv•ra rak liz•ma•no va•a•sher lo yi•mot min - ha•ra•ash ya•a•mod la•ad.

28. Wherefore we receiving a kingdom which cannot be moved, let us have grace, whereby we may serve God acceptably with reverence and godly fear:

28. Διὸ βασιλείαν ἀσάλευτον παραλαμβάνοντες, ἔχωμεν χάριν, δι' ἧς λατρεύομεν εὐαρέστως τῷ θεῷ μετὰ αἰδοῦς καὶ εὐλαβείας·

28. Dio basileian asaleuton paralambanontes, echomen charin, di 'eis latreuomen euarestos to theo meta aidous kai eulabeias.

כח. לָכֵן בִּהְיוֹת לָנוּ מַלְכוּת אֲשֶׁר לֹא תִמּוֹט נָבוֹאָה בְתוֹדָה וְנַעַבְדָה אֶת-הָאֱלֹהִים לְרָצוֹן לוֹ בְּאֵימָה וּבְיִרְאָה:

28. La•chen bi•hee•yot la•noo mal•choot asher lo ti•mot na•vo•ah ve•to•da ve•na•av•da et - ha•Elohim le•ra•tzon lo be•ey•ma oov•yir•ah.

---

29. For our God is a consuming fire.

29. καὶ γὰρ ὁ θεὸς ἡμῶν πῦρ καταναλίσκον.

29. kai gar 'o theos 'eimon pur kataναliskon.

כט. כִּי אֱלֹהֵינוּ אֵשׁ אֹכְלָה הוּא:

29. Ki Elohey•noo esh och•la hoo.

Rabbinic Jewish Commentary
So the Shechinah, with the Jews, is called a consuming fire (n). So the Jews interpret Deu.4:24 of a fire consuming fire (o); and observe, that Moses says, thy God, and not our God (p); but the apostle here uses the latter phrase.

(n) Tzeror Hammor, fol. 21. 4. (o) Zohar in Gen. fol. 35. 3. & 51. 1. & in Exod. fol. 91. 1. & in Lev. fol. 11. 1. (p) Lexic. Cabalist, p. 111.

(Hebrews Chapter 12 End)

Hebrews, Chapter 13

1. Let brotherly love continue.

1. Ἡ φιλαδελφία μενέτω.

1. 'Ei philadelphia meneto.

א: שִׁמְרוּ אַהֲבַת אַחִים בֵּינֵיכֶם תָּמִיד.

1. Shim•roo a•ha•vat a•chim bey•ney•chem ta•mid.

Rabbinic Jewish Commentary
One of the Jewish prayers is to this purpose (q);

"He that dwells in this house, let him plant among you אחוה ואהבה, "brotherhood and love", (or brotherly love,) peace and friendship."

(q) T. Hieros. Beracot, fol. 3. 3.

---

2. Be not forgetful to entertain strangers: for thereby some have entertained angels unawares.

2. Τῆς φιλοξενίας μὴ ἐπιλανθάνεσθε· διὰ ταύτης γὰρ ἔλαθόν τινες ξενίσαντες ἀγγέλους.

2. Teis philoxenias mei epilanthanesthe. dya tauteis gar elathon tines xenisantes angelous.

ב. וְאַל־תִּשְׁכְּחוּ מֵהַכְנִיס אֹרְחִים מֵאַהֲבָה כִּי בְאַהֲבָה זוּ יֵשׁ אֲשֶׁר בִּבְלִי־דַעַת הִכְנִיסוּ מַלְאָכִים אֶת־בָּתֵּיהֶם:

2. Ve•al - tish•ke•choo me•hach•nis or•chim me•a•ha•va ki ve•a•ha•va zoo yesh asher biv•li - da•at hich•ni•soo mal•a•chim et - ba•tey•hem.

Rabbinic Jewish Commentary
It is an observation of a Jewish writer (r) upon the first of these instances; "from hence we learn (says he) how great is the strength (or virtue) of the reception of travellers (or hospitality), as the Rabbis of blessed memory say, greater is הכנסת אורחים, "hospitality", than the reception of the face of the Shechinah."

And this is said to be one of the six things which a man enjoys the fruit of in this world, and for which there remains a reward in the world to come (s).

(r) R. Abraham Seba in Tzeror Hammor, fol. 18, 4. (s) T. Bab. Sabbat, fol. 127. 1.

Hebrews 13

3. Remember them that are in bonds, as bound with them; and them which suffer adversity, as being yourselves also in the body.

3. Μιμνήσκεσθε τῶν δεσμίων, ὡς συνδεδεμένοι· τῶν κακουχουμένων, ὡς καὶ αὐτοὶ ὄντες ἐν σώματι.

3. Mimneiskesthe ton desmion, 'os sundedemenoi. ton kakouchoumenon, 'os kai autoi ontes en somati.

ג. זִכְרוּ אֶת-הָאֲסִירִים כְּמוֹ אִם-אַתֶּם אֲסוּרִים עִמָּהֶם וְאֶת-הַנִּלְחָצִים כַּאֲשֶׁר גַּם-אַתֶּם עִמָּהֶם בְּבָשָׂר אֶחָד:

3. Zich•roo et - ha•a•si•rim k`mo eem - atem asoo•rim ee•ma•hem ve•et - ha•nil•cha•tzim ka•a•sher gam - atem ee•ma•hem be•va•sar e•chad.

---

4. Marriage is honourable in all, and the bed undefiled: but whoremongers and adulterers God will judge.

4. Τίμιος ὁ γάμος ἐν πᾶσιν, καὶ ἡ κοίτη ἀμίαντος· πόρνους δὲ καὶ μοιχοὺς κρινεῖ ὁ θεός.

4. Timios 'o gamos en pasin, kai 'ei koitei amiantos. pornous de kai moichous krinei 'o theos.

ד. קֹדֶשׁ תִּהְיֶה הָאִישׁוּת לְכָל-אִישׁ מִכֶּם לֹא תְחַלְּלוּ אֶת-יְצוּעַ אִישׁ וְאֶת-זֹנִים וְנֹאֲפִים יִשְׁפֹּט אֱלֹהִים:

4. Ko•desh ti•hi•ye ha•ee•shoot le•chol - eesh mi•kem lo te•cha•le•loo et - ye•tzoo•a eesh ve•et - zo•nim ve•no•a•fim yish•pot Elohim.

Rabbinic Jewish Commentary
The Jews say,
"Whoever lies with another man's wife, shall not escape דינה, "the judgment", or damnation of Gehenna (t)"

(t) T. Bab. Sota. fol. 4. 2.

Hebrews 13

5. Let your conversation be without covetousness; and be content with such things as ye have: for he hath said, I will never leave thee, nor forsake thee.

5. Ἀφιλάργυρος ὁ τρόπος, ἀρκούμενοι τοῖς παροῦσιν· αὐτὸς γὰρ εἴρηκεν, Οὐ μή σε ἀνῶ, οὐδ' οὐ μή σε ἐγκαταλείπω.

5. Aphilarguros 'o tropos, arkoumenoi tois parousin. autos gar eireiken, Ou mei se ano, oud ou mei se egkataleipo.

ה. הַרְחִיקוּ דַרְכְּכֶם מֵאַהֲבַת כֶּסֶף וְשִׂמְחוּ בְדֵי חֶלְקְכֶם כִּי הוּא אָמַר לֹא אַרְפְּךָ וְלֹא אֶעֶזְבֶךָ:

5. Har•chi•koo dar•ke•chem me•a•ha•vat ke•sef ve•sim•choo ve•dey chel•ke•chem ki hoo amar lo ar•pe•cha ve•lo e•ez•ve•cha.

Rabbinic Jewish Commentary
For the Jews explain such places as speak of God's not forsaking men, of the sustenance of them, as Psa.37:25 and observe that the word עזיבה, "forsaking", is never used but with respect to פרנסה, "sustenance" (u); though the words may also relate to things spiritual, as that God will not leave them to themselves, to their own corruptions, which would overpower them; nor to their own strength, which is but weakness; nor to their own wisdom, which is folly.

(u) Bereshit Rabba, sect. 69. fol. 61. 4. Vajikra Rabba, sect. 35. fol. 175. 2. Yalkut, par. 2. fol. 103. 2.

---

6. So that we may boldly say, The Lord is my helper, and I will not fear what man shall do unto me.

6. Ὥστε θαρροῦντας ἡμᾶς λέγειν, Κύριος ἐμοὶ βοηθός, καὶ οὐ φοβηθήσομαι τί ποιήσει μοι ἄνθρωπος.

6. 'Oste tharrountas 'eimas legein, Kurios emoi boeithos, kai ou phobeitheisomai ti poieisei moi anthropos.

:ו. עַל־כֵּן נִבְטַח וְנֹאמַר יְהֹוָה לִי בְּעֹזְרָי לֹא אִירָא מַה־יַּעֲשֶׂה לִי אָדָם

6. Al - ken niv•tach ve•no•mar Adonai li be•oz•rai lo ee•ra ma - ya•a•se li adam.

Hebrews 13

7. Remember them which have the rule over you, who have spoken unto you the word of God: whose faith follow, considering the end of their conversation.

7. Μνημονεύετε τῶν ἡγουμένων ὑμῶν, οἵτινες ἐλάλησαν ὑμῖν τὸν λόγον τοῦ θεοῦ· ὧν ἀναθεωροῦντες τὴν ἔκβασιν τῆς ἀναστροφῆς, μιμεῖσθε τὴν πίστιν.

7. Mneimoneuete ton 'eigoumenon 'umon, 'oitines elaleisan 'umin ton logon tou theou. 'on anatheorountes tein ekbasin teis anastropheis, mimeisthe tein pistin.

:ז. זִכְרוּ אֶת־מְאַשְּׁרֵיכֶם אֲשֶׁר־הִגִּידוּ לָכֶם דְּבַר הָאֱלֹהִים בִּינוּ לְתַכְלִית דַּרְכָּם וּלְכוּ בֶּאֱמוּנָתָם

7. Zich•roo et - me•ash•rey•chem asher - hi•gi•doo la•chem de•var ha•Elohim bi•noo le•tach•lit dar•kam ool•choo ve•e•moo•na•tam.

Rabbinic Jewish Commentary

The word may be rendered "guides" or "leaders"; for such point out the way of peace, life, and salvation to men, and direct them to Christ; and guide them into the understanding of the Scriptures, and the truths of the Gospel; and lead them in the paths of faith and holiness, and are examples to them. The Greek word, here used, is what the Jews call Christian bishops by; and ηγεμονια, is, by Maimonides (w), said to be the same as פקידות, "a bishopric": to "remember" them is to know, own, acknowledge, and respect them as their governors; to obey them, and submit to them.

(w) In Misn. Gittin, c. 1. sect. 1.

8. Jesus Christ the same yesterday, and to day, and for ever.

8. Ἰησοῦς χριστὸς χθὲς καὶ σήμερον ὁ αὐτός, καὶ εἰς τοὺς αἰῶνας.

8. Yeisous christos chthes kai seimeron 'o autos, kai eis tous aionas.

ח. יֵשׁוּעַ הַמָּשִׁיחַ הִנּוֹ הוּא אֶתְמֹל וְהוּא הַיּוֹם וְהוּא לְעוֹלָם וָעֶד:

8. Yeshua ha•Ma•shi•ach hi•no hoo et•mol ve•hoo ha•yom ve•hoo le•o•lam va•ed.

Rabbinic Jewish Commentary

It may be observed, that ο αυτος, translated "the same", answers to הוא, "he", a name of God, Psa.102:27 and which is used in Jewish writings (x) for a name of God; and so it is among the Turks (y): and it is expressive of his eternity, immutability, and independence; and well agrees with Messiah, who is God over all, blessed for ever.

(x) Seder Tephillot, fol. 2. 1. & 4. 1. Ed. Basil. fol. 6. 2. & 7. 1. Ed. Amstelod. Zehar in Exod. fol. 35. 4. Maimonides in Misn. Succa, c. 4. sect. 5. (y) Smith de Moribus Turc. p. 40.

Hebrews 13

9. Be not carried about with divers and strange doctrines. For it is a good thing that the heart be established with grace; not with meats, which have not profited them that have been occupied therein.

9. Διδαχαῖς ποικίλαις καὶ ξέναις μὴ παραφέρεσθε· καλὸν γὰρ χάριτι βεβαιοῦσθαι τὴν καρδίαν, οὐ βρώμασιν, ἐν οἷς οὐκ ὠφελήθησαν οἱ περιπατήσαντες.

9. Didachais poikilais kai xenais mei parapheresthe. kalon gar chariti bebaiousthai tein kardian, ou bromasin, en 'ois ouk opheleitheisan 'oi peripateisantes.

ט. אַל-תִּמּוֹטוּ מִפְּנֵי תוֹרֹת שֹׁנוֹת וְזָרוֹת כִּי טוֹב לַלֵּב אֲשֶׁר חֶסֶד יִסְעָדֶנּוּ לֹא חֻקֵּי מַאֲכָלִים חֻקִּים לֹא-טוֹבִים לְבַעֲלֵיהֶם:

9. Al - ti•mo•too mip•ney to•rot sho•not ve•za•rot ki tov la•lev asher che•sed yis•a•de•noo lo choo•key ma•a•cha•lim choo•kim lo - to•vim le•va•a•ley•hem.

10. We have an altar, whereof they have no right to eat which serve the tabernacle.

10. Ἔχομεν θυσιαστήριον, ἐξ οὗ φαγεῖν οὐκ ἔχουσιν ἐξουσίαν οἱ τῇ σκηνῇ λατρεύοντες.

10. Echomen thusyasteirion, ex 'ou phagein ouk echousin exousian 'oi tei skeinei latreuontes.

י. יֶשׁ־לָנוּ מִזְבֵּחַ אֲשֶׁר לֶאֱכֹל מֵעָלָיו אֵין מִשְׁפָּט לִמְשָׁרְתֵי הַמִּשְׁכָּן:

10. Yesh - la•noo miz•beach asher le•e•chol me•a•lav eyn mish•pat lim•shar•tey ha•mish•kan.

Hebrews 13

11. For the bodies of those beasts, whose blood is brought into the sanctuary by the high priest for sin, are burned without the camp.

11. Ὧν γὰρ εἰσφέρεται ζῴων τὸ αἷμα περὶ ἁμαρτίας εἰς τὰ ἅγια διὰ τοῦ ἀρχιερέως, τούτων τὰ σώματα κατακαίεται ἔξω τῆς παρεμβολῆς.

11. 'On gar eispheretai zoon to 'aima peri 'amartias eis ta 'agya dya tou archiereos, touton ta somata katakaietai exo teis paremboleis.

יא. כִּי־פִגְרֵי הַזְּבָחִים אֲשֶׁר דָּמָם הוּבָא אֶל־הַקֹּדֶשׁ בְּיַד הַכֹּהֵן הַגָּדוֹל לְכַפֵּר עָוֹן נִשְׂרְפוּ מִחוּץ לַמַּחֲנֶה:

11. Ki - fig•rey haz•va•chim asher da•mam hoo•va el - ha•ko•desh be•yad ha•ko•hen ha•ga•dol le•cha•per a•von nis•re•foo mi•choo•tz la•ma•cha•ne.

---

12. Wherefore Jesus also, that he might sanctify the people with his own blood, suffered without the gate.

12. Διὸ καὶ Ἰησοῦς, ἵνα ἁγιάσῃ διὰ τοῦ ἰδίου αἵματος τὸν λαόν, ἔξω τῆς πύλης ἔπαθεν.

12. Dio kai Yeisous, 'ina 'agyasei dya tou idiou 'aimatos ton laon, exo teis puleis epathen.

יב. בַּעֲבוּר זֹאת גַּם-יֵשׁוּעַ לַאֲשֶׁר יְקַדֵּשׁ אֶת-הָעָם בְּדָמוֹ עֻנָּה מִחוּץ לַשָּׁעַר:

12. Ba•a•voor zot gam - Yeshua la•a•sher ye•ka•desh et - ha•am be•da•mo oo•na mi•choo•tz la•sha•ar.

Rabbinic Jewish Commentary

suffered without the gate; That is, of Jerusalem: the Syriac version reads, "without the city"; meaning Jerusalem; which answered to the camp of Israel, in the wilderness; without which, the bodies of beasts were burnt, on the day of atonement: for so say (z) the Jews;

"As was the camp in the wilderness, so was the camp in Jerusalem; from Jerusalem to the mountain of the house, was the camp of Israel; from the mountain of the house to the gate of Nicanor, was the camp of the Levites; and from thence forward, the camp of the Shechinah, or the divine Majesty:"

And so Josephus (a) renders the phrase, without the camp, in Lev.16:27 by εν τοις προαστειοις; "in the suburbs"; that is, of Jerusalem, where Messiah suffered,

(z) T. Bab. Zebachim, fol. 116. 2. Bemidbar Rabba, sect. 7. fol. 188. 3. 4. Maimon. Beth Habbechira, c. 7. sect. 11. (a) Antiqu. l. 3. c. 10. sect. 3.

Hebrews 13

13. Let us go forth therefore unto him without the camp, bearing his reproach.

13. Τοίνυν ἐξερχώμεθα πρὸς αὐτὸν ἔξω τῆς παρεμβολῆς, τὸν ὀνειδισμὸν αὐτοῦ φέροντες.

13. Toinun exerchometha pros auton exo teis paremboleis, ton oneidismon autou pherontes.

יג. עַל-כֵּן נֵצְאָה-נָּא אֵלָיו אֶל-מִחוּץ לַמַּחֲנֶה וְנִשָּׂא אֶת-חֶרְפָּתוֹ:

13. Al - ken netz•ah - na elav el - mi•choo•tz la•ma•cha•ne ve•ni•sa et - cher•pa•to.

14. For here have we no continuing city, but we seek one to come.

14. Οὐ γὰρ ἔχομεν ὧδε μένουσαν πόλιν, ἀλλὰ τὴν μέλλουσαν ἐπιζητοῦμεν.

14. Ou gar echomen 'ode menousan polin, alla tein mellousan epizeitoumen.

יד. פֹּה אֵין־לָנוּ עִיר עֹמֶדֶת לָעַד אַךְ הָעִיר הָעֲתִידָה אָנוּ מְבַקְשִׁים:

14. Po eyn - la•noo eer o•me•det la•ad ach ha•eer ha•a•ti•da a•noo me•vak•shim.

Hebrews 13

15. By him therefore let us offer the sacrifice of praise to God continually, that is, the fruit of our lips giving thanks to his name.

15. Δι' αὐτοῦ οὖν ἀναφέρωμεν θυσίαν αἰνέσεως διὰ παντὸς τῷ θεῷ, τοῦτ' ἔστιν, καρπὸν χειλέων ὁμολογούντων τῷ ὀνόματι αὐτοῦ.

15. Di autou oun anapheromen thusian aineseos dya pantos to theo, tout estin, karpon cheileon 'omologounton to onomati autou.

טו. וְעַתָּה נַקְרִיב עַל־יָדוֹ זִבְחֵי תוֹדָה לֵאלֹהִים תָּמִיד הֲלֹא הֵם פְּרִי שְׂפָתֵינוּ הַנֹּתְנוֹת תּוֹדָה לִשְׁמוֹ:

15. Ve•a•ta nak•riv al - ya•do ziv•chey to•da le•Elohim ta•mid ha•lo hem p`ri s`fa•tey•noo ha•not•not to•da lish•mo.

Rabbinic Jewish Commentary

that is, the fruit of our lips; The sacrifice of praise is so called, in allusion to the offering of the firstfruits under the Torah; and to distinguish it from legal sacrifices; and to show in what way and manner we are to praise God, namely, with our lips: in Hos.14:2 which is thought to be referred to here, it is, "the calves of our lips"; sacrifices of praise being instead of calves: and the apostle interprets it in great agreement with the Jewish writers; the Chaldee paraphrase explains it by מלי ספותנא, "the words of their lips": and so Jarchi, דברי שפתינו, "the words of our lips"; and Kimchi, וידוי שפתינו, "the confession of our lips": and it may be observed, that there is a great nearness in פרים, "calves", and פרי, "fruit"; though perhaps rather the phrase is borrowed from Isa.57:19 where it is expressly had; the Septuagint indeed have it in Hos.14:2.

The phrase θυσια αινεσεως, "the sacrifice of praise", is used by the Septuagint in 2Ch.29:31. The apostle having shown that legal sacrifices were all superseded and abolished by the sacrifice of the Messiah, which is the design of this epistle, points out what sacrifice believers should offer up to God, under the Gospel dispensation; and the Jews themselves say, that,

"In future time (i.e. in the days of the Messiah) all sacrifices shall cease, but קרבן תודה, "the sacrifice of praise" shall not cease (b)."

(b) Vajikra Rabba, sect. 9. fol. 153. 1. & sect 27. fol. 168. 4.

Hebrews 13

16. But to do good and to communicate forget not: for with such sacrifices God is well pleased.

16. Τῆς δὲ εὐποιΐας καὶ κοινωνίας μὴ ἐπιλανθάνεσθε· τοιαύταις γὰρ θυσίαις εὐαρεστεῖται ὁ θεός.

16. Teis de eupoi'ias kai koinonias mei epilanthanesthe. toyautais gar thusiais euaresteitai 'o theos.

טז. אַךְ לִגְמָל-טוֹב וּלְפַזֵּר לָאֶבְיוֹנִים אַל-תִּשְׁכָּחוּ כִּי-זְבָחִים כָּאֵלֶּה הֵם לְרֵיחַ נִיחֹחַ לֵאלֹהִים:

16. Ach lig•mol - tov ool•fa•zer la•ev•yo•nim al - tish•ka•choo ki - z`va•chim ka•e•le hem le•re•ach ni•cho•ach le•Elohim.

Rabbinic Jewish Commentary
These sacrifices are preferred by him to legal ones, Hos.6:6 and the Jews also say, that

"Greater is he who does alms than (if he offered) all sacrifices (c)."

(c) T. Bab. Succa, fol. 49. 2.

17. Obey them that have the rule over you, and submit yourselves: for they watch for your souls, as they that must give account, that they may do it with joy, and not with grief: for that is unprofitable for you.

17. Πείθεσθε τοῖς ἡγουμένοις ὑμῶν, καὶ ὑπείκετε· αὐτοὶ γὰρ ἀγρυπνοῦσιν ὑπὲρ τῶν ψυχῶν ὑμῶν, ὡς λόγον ἀποδώσοντες· ἵνα μετὰ χαρᾶς τοῦτο ποιῶσιν, καὶ μὴ στενάζοντες· ἀλυσιτελὲς γὰρ ὑμῖν τοῦτο.

17. Peithesthe tois 'eigoumenois 'umon, kai 'upeikete. autoi gar agrupnousin 'uper ton psuchon 'umon, 'os logon apodosontes. 'ina meta charas touto poiosin, kai mei stenazontes. Alusiteles gar 'umin touto.

יז. שִׁמְעוּ אֶל-מְאַשְּׁרֵיכֶם וְהִכָּנְעוּ מִפְּנֵיהֶם כִּי-שֹׁקְדִים הֵם עַל-נַפְשֹׁתֵיכֶם כְּעֹמְדִים לָתֵת דִּין וְחֶשְׁבּוֹן בַּעֲבוּר: יַעֲשׂוּ כָזֹאת בְּחֶדְוָה וְלֹא בַאֲנָחָה כִּי לוּלֵא כֵן לֹא-טוֹב לָכֶם הַדָּבָר הַזֶּה

17. Shim•oo el - me•ash•rey•chem ve•hi•kan•oo mip•ney•hem ki - shok•dim hem al - naf•sho•tey•chem ke•om•dim la•tet din ve•chesh•bon ba•a•voor ya•a•soo cha•zot be•ched•va ve•lo va•a•na•cha ki loo•le chen lo - tov la•chem ha•da•var ha•ze.

Hebrews 13

18. Pray for us: for we trust we have a good conscience, in all things willing to live honestly.

18. Προσεύχεσθε περὶ ἡμῶν· πεποίθαμεν γὰρ ὅτι καλὴν συνείδησιν ἔχομεν, ἐν πᾶσιν καλῶς θέλοντες ἀναστρέφεσθαι.

18. Proseuchesthe peri 'eimon. pepoithamen gar 'oti kalein suneideisin echomen, en pasin kalos thelontes anastrephesthai.

יח. הִתְפַּלְלוּ עָלֵינוּ כִּי-יָדַעְנוּ מְאֹד כִּי נָכוֹן לִבֵּנוּ וּלְהִתְהַלֵּךְ בְּמֵישָׁרִים תָּמִיד כָּל-חֶפְצֵנוּ:

18. Hit•pa•le•loo aley•noo ki - ya•da•a•noo me•od ki na•chon li•be•noo ool•hit•ha•lech be•mey•sha•rim ta•mid kol - chef•tze•noo.

---

19. But I beseech you the rather to do this, that I may be restored to you the sooner.

19. Περισσοτέρως δὲ παρακαλῶ τοῦτο ποιῆσαι, ἵνα τάχιον ἀποκατασταθῶ ὑμῖν.

19. Perissoteros de parakalo touto poieisai, 'ina tachion apokatastatho 'umin.

יט. וּבְחֵפֶץ יֶתֶר אֲנִי שֹׁאֵל מֵעִמָּכֶם לַעֲשׂוֹת זֹאת לְבַעֲבוּר יֻתַּן לִי לָשׁוּב אֲלֵיכֶם עַד-מְהֵרָה.

19. Oov•che•fetz ye•ter ani sho•el me•ee•ma•chem la•a•sot zot le•va•a•voor yoo•tan li la•shoov aley•chem ad - me•he•ra.

Hebrews 13

20. Now the God of peace, that brought again from the dead our Lord Jesus, that great shepherd of the sheep, through the blood of the everlasting covenant,

20. Ὁ δὲ θεὸς τῆς εἰρήνης, ὁ ἀναγαγὼν ἐκ νεκρῶν τὸν ποιμένα τῶν προβάτων τὸν μέγαν ἐν αἵματι διαθήκης αἰωνίου, τὸν κύριον ἡμῶν Ἰησοῦν,

20. 'O de theos teis eireineis, 'o anagagon ek nekron ton poimena ton probaton ton megan en 'aimati dyatheikeis aioniou, ton kurion 'eimon Yeisoun,

כ. וֵאלֹהֵי הַשָּׁלוֹם אֲשֶׁר בְּדַם בְּרִית עוֹלָם הֵקִים מִן-הַמֵּתִים אֶת-רֹעֵה הַצֹּאן הַגָּדוֹל אֶת-יֵשׁוּעַ אֲדֹנֵינוּ:

20. Ve•Elohey ha•sha•lom asher be•dam b`rit o•lam he•kim min - ha•me•tim et - ro•eh ha•tzon ha•ga•dol et - Yeshua Ado•ney•noo.

Rabbinic Jewish Commentary

The "covenant" spoken of is not the covenant of works made with Adam, as the federal head of his natural seed; there was no mediator or shepherd of the sheep that had any concern therein; there was no blood in that covenant; nor was it an everlasting one: nor the covenant of circumcision given to Abraham; though possibly there may be some reference to it; or this may be opposed to that, since the blood of circumcision is often called by the Jews דם ברית, "the blood of the covenant" (d): nor the covenant on Mount Sinai, though there may be an allusion to it; since the blood which was then shed, and sprinkled on the people, is called the blood of the covenant, Exo.24:8 but that was not an everlasting covenant, that has waxed old, and vanished away; but the covenant of grace is meant, before called the new and better covenant, of which the Messiah is the surety and Mediator.

(d) T. Bab. Sabbat, fol. 135. 1. & T. Hieros. Yebamot, fol. 9. 1.

21. Make you perfect in every good work to do his will, working in you that which is wellpleasing in his sight, through Jesus Christ; to whom be glory for ever and ever. Amen.

21. καταρτίσαι ὑμᾶς ἐν παντὶ ἔργῳ ἀγαθῷ εἰς τὸ ποιῆσαι τὸ θέλημα αὐτοῦ, ποιῶν ἐν ὑμῖν τὸ εὐάρεστον ἐνώπιον αὐτοῦ, διὰ Ἰησοῦ χριστοῦ· ᾧ ἡ δόξα εἰς τοὺς αἰῶνας τῶν αἰώνων. Ἀμήν.

21. katartisai 'umas en panti ergo agatho eis to poieisai to theleima autou, poion en 'umin to euareston enopion autou, dya Yeisou christou. 'o 'ei doxa eis tous aionas ton aionon. Amein.

כא. הוּא יְכוֹנֵן אֶתְכֶם בְּכָל-מַעֲשֶׂה טוֹב לְמַלֹּא אֶת-חֶפְצוֹ וְיִפְעַל עִמָּכֶם כַּטּוֹב בְּעֵינָיו בְּיַד- יֵשׁוּעַ הַמָּשִׁיחַ אֲשֶׁר:לוֹ הַכָּבוֹד לְעוֹלָם וָעֶד אָמֵן

21. Hoo ye•cho•nen et•chem be•chol - ma•a•se tov le•ma•le et - chef•tzo ve•yif•al ee•ma•chem ka•tov be•ey•nav be•yad - Yeshua ha•Ma•shi•ach asher - lo ha•ka•vod le•o•lam va•ed Amen.

Hebrews 13

22. And I beseech you, brethren, suffer the word of exhortation: for I have written a letter unto you in few words.

22. Παρακαλῶ δὲ ὑμᾶς, ἀδελφοί, ἀνέχεσθε τοῦ λόγου τῆς παρακλήσεως· καὶ γὰρ διὰ βραχέων ἐπέστειλα ὑμῖν.

22. Parakalo de 'umas, adelphoi, anechesthe tou logou teis parakleiseos. kai gar dya bracheon epesteila 'umin.

כב. וַאֲנִי שֹׁאֵל מֵעִמָּכֶם אַחַי שְׂאוּ-נָא דִּבְרֵי מוּסָרִי כִּי-מְעַט מִזְעָר כָּתַבְתִּי אֲלֵיכֶם:

22. Va•a•ni sho•el me•ee•ma•chem a•chai s`oo - na div•rey moo•sa•ri ki - me•at miz•ar ka•tav•ti aley•chem.

23. Know ye that our brother Timothy is set at liberty; with whom, if he come shortly, I will see you.

23. Γινώσκετε τὸν ἀδελφὸν Τιμόθεον ἀπολελυμένον, μεθ᾽ οὗ, ἐὰν τάχιον ἔρχηται, ὄψομαι ὑμᾶς.

23. Ginoskete ton adelphon Timotheon apolelumenon, meth 'ou, ean tachion ercheitai, opsomai 'umas.

:כג. וּדְעוּ כִּי טִימוֹתִיוֹס אָחִינוּ יָצָא לַחָפְשִׁי וְאִם-יָבֹא בְּקֶרֶב הַיָּמִים אֶרְאֶה אִתּוֹ אֶת-פְּנֵיכֶם

23. Ood•oo ki Ti•mo•ti•yos achi•noo ya•tza la•chof•shi ve•eem - ya•vo ve•ke•rev ha•ya•mim er•eh ee•to et - p`ney•chem.

Hebrews 13

24. Salute all them that have the rule over you, and all the saints. They of Italy salute you.

24. Ἀσπάσασθε πάντας τοὺς ἡγουμένους ὑμῶν, καὶ πάντας τοὺς ἁγίους. Ἀσπάζονται ὑμᾶς οἱ ἀπὸ τῆς Ἰταλίας.

24. Aspasasthe pantas tous 'eigoumenous 'umon, kai pantas tous 'agious. Aspazontai 'umas 'oi apo teis Ytalias.

כד. שַׁאֲלוּ לְשָׁלוֹם כָּל-מְאַשְּׁרֵיכֶם וְכָל-הַקְּדוֹשִׁים וְאֵלֶּה אֲשֶׁר מֵאִיטַלְיָא פֹּקְדִים לְשָׁלוֹם לָכֶם:

24. Sha•a•loo lish•lom kol - me•ash•rey•chem ve•chol - ha•k`do•shim ve•e•le asher me•Ee•talia pok•dim le•sha•lom la•chem.

Rabbinic Jewish Commentary

Italy is a famous and well known country in Europe; a very fruitful and delightful one; of which Rome, where the apostle very likely now was, is the chief city: it has been called by different names, as Saturnia from Saturn; and Ausonia, Aenotria, and Hesperia Magna; and it had its name Italy, some say, from Italus, the son of Penelope and Telegonus; others, from Italus, a king of the Arcadians, or, as some say, the Sicilians; but, according to Timsaeus and Varro (e), it was so called from the multitude of oxen in it, which in the old Greek language were called ιταλοι, "Italoi", to which comes near in sound the Latin word "vituli", used for "calves"; and Italy is frequently, by Jewish writers (f) called איטליא של יון, "Italy of Greece"; and formerly it was inhabited by Greeks, and was called Great Greece (g): it is bounded on the east with the Adriatic sea; and on the west by the river Var, with the Alps, which separate France from Italy; and on the south with the Tyrrhene, or Tuscan sea, called the lower, and on the north, partly with the Alps, which are on the borders of Germany, and partly with the Adriatic sea, called the higher. There were Christians in this country before the Apostle Paul came to Rome, both at Rome, and other places, as before observed. It is said (h), that Barnabas was first at Rome, and planted the church there; that he went round Lombardy, and lived at Milain; that in the "first" century, Apollinaris preached at Ravenna, and Hermagoras at Aquileia; and there were Christian churches in the "second" century, not only at Rome, but in many other cities and places; and so likewise in the "third" century, as at Verona, Spoletum, Beneventum, &c. and in the "fourth" century, there were great numbers of churches in this country; as at Verona, and Capua, in Calabria, Campania, and Apulia; and which might be traced in following centuries.

(e) Apud Aul. Gell. Noct. Attic. l. 11. c. 1. Vid. Apollodor. de Orig. Deorum, l. 2. p. 101. (f) Bereshit Rabba, sect. 67. fol. 59. 4. T. Bab. Sabbat, fol. 56. 2. R. Sol. Jarchi in Gen. xxvii. 39. (g) lsidor. Hispal. Origin. l. 14. c. 4. (h) Hist. Eccl. Magdeburg. cent. 1. l. 2. c. 2. p. 17. cent. 2. c. 2. p. 4. cent. 3. c. 2. p. 4. cent. 4. c. 2. p. 6.

---

25. Grace be with you all. Amen.

25. Ἡ χάρις μετὰ πάντων ὑμῶν. Ἀμήν.

25. 'Ei charis meta panton 'umon. Amein.

כה. הַחֶסֶד עִם-כֻּלְכֶם אָמֵן:

25. Ha•che•sed eem - kool•chem Amen.

Rabbinic Jewish Commentary
In the Alexandrian copy it is, "written to the Hebrews from Rome."

(Hebrews Chapter 13 End)

THE GENERAL EPISTLE OF JAMES

James, Chapter 1

1. James, a servant of God and of the Lord Jesus Christ, to the twelve tribes which are scattered abroad, greeting.

1. Ἰάκωβος, θεοῦ καὶ κυρίου Ἰησοῦ χριστοῦ δοῦλος, ταῖς δώδεκα φυλαῖς ταῖς ἐν τῇ διασπορᾷ, χαίρειν.

1. Yakobos, theou kai kuriou Yeisou christou doulos, tais dodeka phulais tais en tei dyaspora, chairein.

א. יַעֲקֹב עֶבֶד לֵאלֹהִים וּלְאָדוֹן יֵשׁוּעַ הַמָּשִׁיחַ אֶל־הָעֵדָה הַפְּזוּרָה מִשְּׁנֵים עָשָׂר הַשְּׁבָטִים שָׁלוֹם:

1. Ya•a•kov eved le•Elohim ool•Adon Yeshua ha•Ma•shi•ach el - ha•e•da ha•p`zoo•ra mi•sh`neim asar hash•va•tim sha•lom.

Rabbinic Jewish Commentary
The Jews say (f), that the ten tribes will never return, and that they will have no part nor portion in the world to come.

(f) T. Bab. Sanhedrin, fol. 110. 2.

---

2. My brethren, count it all joy when ye fall into divers temptations;

2. Πᾶσαν χαρὰν ἡγήσασθε, ἀδελφοί μου, ὅταν πειρασμοῖς περιπέσητε ποικίλοις,

2. Pasan charan 'eigeisasthe, adelphoi mou, 'otan peirasmois peripeseite poikilois,

:ב. חִשְׁבוּ לָכֶם אַחַי אַךְ לְשִׂמְחָה אִם מַסּוֹת שֹׁנוֹת תִּקְרֶינָה אֶתְכֶם

2. Chish•voo la•chem a•chai ach le•sim•cha eem ma•sot sho•not tik•re•na et•chem.

Rabbinic Jewish Commentary
The Jews have a saying (g),

"Whoever rejoices in afflictions that come upon him, brings salvation to the world."

(g) T. Bab. Taanith, fol. 8. 1.

James 1

3. Knowing this, that the trying of your faith worketh patience.

3. γινώσκοντες ὅτι τὸ δοκίμιον ὑμῶν τῆς πίστεως κατεργάζεται ὑπομονήν·

3. ginoskontes 'oti to dokimion 'umon teis pisteos katergazetai 'upomonein.

ג: בְּדַעְתְּכֶם כִּי כוּר בֹּחֵן אֱמוּנַתְכֶם יִתֵּן לָכֶם אֶת-כֹּחַ הַסַּבָּל

3. Be•da•at•chem ki choor bo•chen emoo•nat•chem yi•ten la•chem et - ko•ach ha•sa•bal.

---

4. But let patience have her perfect work, that ye may be perfect and entire, wanting nothing.

4. ἡ δὲ ὑπομονὴ ἔργον τέλειον ἐχέτω, ἵνα ἦτε τέλειοι καὶ ὁλόκληροι, ἐν μηδενὶ λειπόμενοι.

4. 'ei de 'upomonei ergon teleion echeto, 'ina eite teleioi kai 'olokleiroi, en meideni leipomenoi.

ד: וּפְעֻלַּת כֹּחַ הַסַּבָּל תִּהְיֶה שְׁלֵמָה לַבַעֲבוּר תִּהְיוּ שְׁלֵמִים וּתְמִימִים וְלֹא יֶחְסַר לָכֶם דָּבָר

4. Oof•oo•lat ko•ach ha•sa•bal ti•hi•ye sh`le•ma le•va•a•voor ti•hi•yoo sh`le•mim oot•mi•mim ve•lo yech•sar la•chem da•var.

---

5. If any of you lack wisdom, let him ask of God, that giveth to all men liberally, and upbraideth not; and it shall be given him.

5. Εἰ δέ τις ὑμῶν λείπεται σοφίας, αἰτείτω παρὰ τοῦ διδόντος θεοῦ πᾶσιν ἁπλῶς, καὶ οὐκ ὀνειδίζοντος, καὶ δοθήσεται αὐτῷ.

5. Ei de tis 'umon leipetai sophias, aiteito para tou didontos theou pasin 'aplos, kai ouk oneidizontos, kai dotheisetai auto.

ה. וְאִישׁ מִכֶּם כִּי יֶחְסַר חָכְמָה יְבַקְשֶׁנָּה וְתִנָּתֶן-לוֹ מֵאֵת הָאֱלֹהִים הַנֹּתֵן לַכֹּל בְּרוּחַ נְדִיבָה וְאֵין-מַכְלִים דָּבָר:

5. Ve•eesh mi•kem ki yech•sar choch•ma ye•vak•she•na ve•ti•na•ten - lo me•et ha•Elohim ha•no•ten la•kol be•roo•ach n`di•va ve•eyn - mach•lim da•var.

James 1

6. But let him ask in faith, nothing wavering. For he that wavereth is like a wave of the sea driven with the wind and tossed.

6. Αἰτείτω δὲ ἐν πίστει, μηδὲν διακρινόμενος· ὁ γὰρ διακρινόμενος ἔοικεν κλύδωνι θαλάσσης ἀνεμιζομένῳ καὶ ῥιπιζομένῳ.

6. Aiteito de en pistei, meiden dyakrinomenos. 'o gar dyakrinomenos eoiken kludoni thalasseis anemizomeno kai 'ripizomeno.

ו. אַךְ יְבַקֵּשׁ בֶּאֱמוּנָה וְלֹא יִפְסַח עַל-שְׁתֵּי סְעִפִּים כִּי הַפֹּסֵחַ עַל-שְׁתֵּי סְעִפִּים דּוֹמֶה הוּא לְגַלֵּי הַיָּם אֲשֶׁר הֵם:עֹלִים וְיֹרְדִים מִפְּנֵי-רוּחַ

6. Ach ye•va•kesh be•e•moo•na ve•lo yif•sach al - sh`tey s`ee•pim ki ha•po•se•ach al - sh`tey s`ee•pim do•me hoo le•ga•ley ha•yam asher hem o•lim ve•yor•dim mip•ney - roo•ach.

7. For let not that man think that he shall receive any thing of the Lord.

7. Μὴ γὰρ οἰέσθω ὁ ἄνθρωπος ἐκεῖνος ὅτι λήψεταί τι παρὰ τοῦ κυρίου.

7. Mei gar oiestho 'o anthropos ekeinos 'oti leipsetai ti para tou kuriou.

ז. וְהָאִישׁ הַהוּא אַל-יְדַמֶּה בְנַפְשׁוֹ כִּי-יִשָּׂא דָבָר מֵאֵת יְהוָֹה:

7. Ve•ha•eesh ha•hoo al - ye•da•me ve•naf•sho ki - yi•sa da•var me•et Adonai.

8. A double minded man is unstable in all his ways.

8. Ἀνὴρ δίψυχος, ἀκατάστατος ἐν πάσαις ταῖς ὁδοῖς αὐτοῦ.

8. Aneir dipsuchos, akatastatos en pasais tais 'odois autou.

:ח. אִישׁ אֲשֶׁר חָלַק לִבּוֹ פֹּחֵז הוּא בְּכָל־נְתִיבֹתָיו

8. Eesh asher cha•lak li•bo po•chez hoo be•chol - n`ti•vo•tav.

James 1

9. Let the brother of low degree rejoice in that he is exalted:

9. Καυχάσθω δὲ ὁ ἀδελφὸς ὁ ταπεινὸς ἐν τῷ ὕψει αὐτοῦ·

9. Kauchastho de 'o adelphos 'o tapeinos en to 'upsei autou.

:ט. אוּלָם אָח שָׁפָל יִתְהַלֵּל בְּרוֹמְמוֹת נַפְשׁוֹ

9. Oo•lam ach sha•fel yit•ha•lel be•ro•me•mot naf•sho.

---

10. But the rich, in that he is made low: because as the flower of the grass he shall pass away.

10. ὁ δὲ πλούσιος ἐν τῇ ταπεινώσει αὐτοῦ· ὅτι ὡς ἄνθος χόρτου παρελεύσεται.

10. 'o de plousios en tei tapeinosei autou. 'oti 'os anthos chortou pareleusetai.

:י. וְעָשִׁיר בְּשִׁפְלוּת נַפְשׁוֹ כִּי כְצִיץ חָצִיר כֵּן יַעֲבֹר

10. Ve•a•shir be•shif•loot naf•sho ki che•tzitz cha•tzir ken ya•a•vor.

---

11. For the sun is no sooner risen with a burning heat, but it withereth the grass, and the flower thereof falleth, and the grace of the fashion of it perisheth: so also shall the rich man fade away in his ways.

11. Ἀνέτειλεν γὰρ ὁ ἥλιος σὺν τῷ καύσωνι, καὶ ἐξήρανεν τὸν χόρτον, καὶ τὸ ἄνθος αὐτοῦ ἐξέπεσεν, καὶ ἡ εὐπρέπεια τοῦ προσώπου αὐτοῦ ἀπώλετο· οὕτως καὶ ὁ πλούσιος ἐν ταῖς πορείαις αὐτοῦ μαρανθήσεται.

11. Aneteilen gar 'o 'eilios sun to kausoni, kai exeiranen ton chorton, kai to anthos autou exepesen, kai 'ei euprepeya tou prosopou autou apoleto. 'outos kai 'o plousios en tais poreiais autou marantheisetai.

יא. כִּי כְצֵאת הַשֶּׁמֶשׁ בִּגְבֻרָתוֹ יִיבַשׁ חָצִיר אֻמְלַל צִיץ וּצְבִי תִפְאַרְתּוֹ נֹבֵל כֵּן יִבֹּל הֶעָשִׁיר עֲלֵי-שְׁבִיל מְרוּצָתוֹ:

11. Ki che•tzet ha•she•mesh big•voo•ra•to yi•vash cha•tzir oom•lal tzitz ootz•vi tif•ar•to no•vel ken yi•bol he•a•shir aley - sh`vil me•roo•tza•to.

James 1

12. Blessed is the man that endureth temptation: for when he is tried, he shall receive the crown of life, which the Lord hath promised to them that love him.

12. Μακάριος ἀνὴρ ὃς ὑπομένει πειρασμόν· ὅτι δόκιμος γενόμενος λήψεται τὸν στέφανον τῆς ζωῆς, ὃν ἐπηγγείλατο ὁ κύριος τοῖς ἀγαπῶσιν αὐτόν.

12. Makarios aneir 'os 'upomenei peirasmon. 'oti dokimos genomenos leipsetai ton stephanon teis zoeis, 'on epeingeilato 'o kurios tois agaposin auton.

:יב. אַשְׁרֵי הָאִישׁ הַנִּבְחַן בְּמַסָּה כִּי בְהִבָּחֲנוֹ יִשָּׂא עֲטֶרֶת הַחַיִּים אֲשֶׁר-דִּבֶּר אֲדֹנָי לְאֹהֲבָיו

12. Ash•rey ha•eesh ha•niv•chan be•ma•sa ki ve•hi•ba•cha•no yi•sa ate•ret ha•cha•yim asher - di•ber Adonai le•o•ha•vav.

Rabbinic Jewish Commentary
The Jews have a saying (h) much like this,

""Blessed" is the man, שהוא עומד בנסיונו, "who stands in his temptation", for there is no creature whom the holy blessed God does not tempt."

(h) Shemot. Rabba, sect. 34. fol. 133. 3.

13. Let no man say when he is tempted, I am tempted of God: for God cannot be tempted with evil, neither tempteth he any man:

13. Μηδεὶς πειραζόμενος λεγέτω ὅτι Ἀπὸ θεοῦ πειράζομαι· ὁ γὰρ θεὸς ἀπείραστός ἐστιν κακῶν, πειράζει δὲ αὐτὸς οὐδένα·

13. Meideis peirazomenos legeto 'oti Apo theou peirazomai. 'o gar theos apeirastos estin kakon, peirazei de autos oudena.

יג. אַל-יֹאמַר הַנִּכְשָׁל בְּמַסָּה בְּאֱלֹהִים נֻסָּה אֹתִי כִּי כַאֲשֶׁר אֵין מְנַסֶּה אֶת-הָאֱלֹהִים בְּרָע כֵּן גַּם-הוּא לֹא-יְנַסֶּה אִישׁ:

13. Al - yo•mar ha•nich•shal be•ma•sa ha•Elohim ni•sa o•ti ki cha•a•sher eyn me•na•se et - ha•Elohim be•ra ken gam - hoo lo - ye•na•se eesh.

James 1

14. But every man is tempted, when he is drawn away of his own lust, and enticed.

14. ἕκαστος δὲ πειράζεται, ὑπὸ τῆς ἰδίας ἐπιθυμίας ἐξελκόμενος καὶ δελεαζόμενος.

14. 'ekastos de peirazetai, 'upo teis idias epithumias exelkomenos kai deleazomenos.

יד. אַךְ כָּל-אִישׁ תַּאֲוַת נַפְשׁוֹ תְּנַסֵּהוּ כִּי יִמְשְׁךָ וְיִלָּכֶד-בָּהּ:

14. Ach kol - eesh ta•a•vat naf•sho te•na•se•hoo ki yi•ma•shech ve•yi•la•ched - ba.

---

15. Then when lust hath conceived, it bringeth forth sin: and sin, when it is finished, bringeth forth death.

15. Εἶτα ἡ ἐπιθυμία συλλαβοῦσα τίκτει ἁμαρτίαν· ἡ δὲ ἁμαρτία ἀποτελεσθεῖσα ἀποκύει θάνατον.

15. Eita 'ei epithumia sullabousa tiktei 'amartian. 'ei de 'amartia apotelestheisa apokuei thanaton.

טו. וְהַתַּאֲוָה אַחֲרֵי אֲשֶׁר הָרָתָה תֵּלֵד חֵטְא וְהַחֵטְא כַּאֲשֶׁר הוּא שָׁלֵם הוּא יוֹלִיד מָוֶת:

15. Ve•ha•ta•a•va a•cha•rey asher har•ta te•led chet ve•ha•chet ka•a•sher hoo sha•lem yo•lid ma•vet.

Rabbinic Jewish Commentary

The figure is used in Psa.7:14 on which Kimchi, a Jewish commentator, has this note;

"He (the psalmist) compares the thoughts of the heart להריון, "to a conception", and when they go out in word, this is "travail", and in work or act, this is "bringing forth"."

bringeth forth death; Something like these several gradual steps, in which sin proceeds, is observed by the Jews, and expressed in much the like language, in allegorizing the case of Lot, and his two daughters (i);

"The concupiscent soul (or "lust") stirs up the evil figment, and imagines by it, and it cleaves to every evil imagination, שמתעברת, "until it conceives a little", and produces in the heart of man the evil thought, and cleaves to it; and as yet it is in his heart, and is not "finished" to do it, until this desire or lust stirs up the strength of the body, first to cleave to the evil figment, and then תשלום הרעה, "sin is finished"; as it is said, Gen.19:36."

(i) Midrash Haneelam in Zohar in Gen. fol. 67. 4.

James 1

16. Do not err, my beloved brethren.

16. Μὴ πλανᾶσθε, ἀδελφοί μου ἀγαπητοί.

16. Mei planasthe, adelphoi mou agapeitoi.

טז. אַל-תִּתְעוּ אֶת-נַפְשְׁכֶם אַחַי הַיְקָרִים:

16. Al - tat•oo et - naf•she•chem a•chai hay•ka•rim.

---

17. Every good gift and every perfect gift is from above, and cometh down from the Father of lights, with whom is no variableness, neither shadow of turning.

17. Πᾶσα δόσις ἀγαθὴ καὶ πᾶν δώρημα τέλειον ἄνωθέν ἐστιν, καταβαῖνον ἀπὸ τοῦ πατρὸς τῶν φώτων, παρ᾽ ᾧ οὐκ ἔνι παραλλαγή, ἢ τροπῆς ἀποσκίασμα.

17. Pasa dosis agathei kai pan doreima teleion anothen estin, katabainon apo tou patros ton photon, par 'o ouk eni parallagei, ei tropeis aposkiasma.

יז. כָּל-מַתָּנָה טוֹבָה וְכָל-תְּשׁוּרָה שְׁלֵמָה יֹרֶדֶת מֵעַל מֵאֵת אֲבִי הַמְּאֹרֹת אֲשֶׁר אֵין-חֲלִיפוֹת לוֹ אַף לֹא צֵל:תְּמוּרָה

17. Kol - ma•ta•na to•va ve•chol - t`shoo•ra sh`le•ma yo•re•det me•al me•et Avi ham•o•rot asher eyn - cha•li•fot lo af lo tzel t`moo•ra.

Rabbinic Jewish Commentary
The Jews say (k), that the good things of this world are not truly good, in comparison of the good things of the world to come, and are not גמור טוב, "a perfect good." And every such an one is from above; is not from a man's self, from the creature, or from below, but from heaven, and from God who dwells there

(k) Tzeror Hammor, fol. 23. 2, 3.

James 1

18. Of his own will begat he us with the word of truth, that we should be a kind of firstfruits of his creatures.

18. Βουληθεὶς ἀπεκύησεν ἡμᾶς λόγῳ ἀληθείας, εἰς τὸ εἶναι ἡμᾶς ἀπαρχήν τινα τῶν αὐτοῦ κτισμάτων.

18. Bouleitheis apekueisen 'eimas logo aleitheias, eis to einai 'eimas aparchein tina ton autou ktismaton.

יח. וְהוּא בַּאֲוַת נַפְשׁוֹ הוֹלִיד אֹתָנוּ בִּדְבַר אֲמִתּוֹ לִהְיוֹת לוֹ כְּרֵאשִׁית תְּבוּאָתוֹ בְּתוֹךְ יְצוּרָיו:

18. Ve•hoo be•a•vat naf•sho ho•lid o•ta•noo bid•var ami•to li•hee•yot lo ke•re•sheet t`voo•a•to be•toch ye•tzoo•rav.

---

19. Wherefore, my beloved brethren, let every man be swift to hear, slow to speak, slow to wrath:

19. Ὥστε, ἀδελφοί μου ἀγαπητοί, ἔστω πᾶς ἄνθρωπος ταχὺς εἰς τὸ ἀκοῦσαι, βραδὺς εἰς τὸ λαλῆσαι, βραδὺς εἰς ὀργήν·

19. 'Oste, adelphoi mou agapeitoi, esto pas anthropos tachus eis to akousai, bradus eis to laleisai, bradus eis orgein.

יט. לָכֵן אַחַי הַיְקָרִים יְהִי כָל־אִישׁ מִכֶּם מָהִיר לִשְׁמֹעַ בְּשֵׁשׁ לְדַבֵּר וּבְשֵׁשׁ לִקְצֹף־קָצֶף:

19. La•chen a•chai hay•ka•rim ye•hee chol - eesh mi•kem ma•hir lish•mo•a bshesh le•da•ber oo•vo•shesh lik•tzof - ka•tzef.

Rabbinic Jewish Commentary

The phrase is Jewish; things easy and smooth, a man is מהיר לשמען, "swift to hear them (l): slow to speak"; against what is heard, without thoroughly weighing and considering what is said; and this may regard silence under hearing the word, and is also a rule to be observed in private conversation: or the sense may be, be content to be hearers of the word, and not forward to be preachers of it; and if called to that work, think before you speak, meditate on the word, and study to be approved to God and men. Silence is not only highly commended by the Pythagoreans, among whom it was enjoined their disciples five years (m); but also by the Jews: they say, nothing is better for the body than silence; that if a word is worth one shekel, silence is worth two, or worth a precious stone; that it is the spice of speech, and the chief of all spices; that it is the hedge of wisdom; hence it is the advice of Shammai; "say little, and do much" (n): and they cry up, as a very excellent precept, "be silent, and hear"; and as containing more than persons are aware of (o):

(l) Gloss. in T. Bab. Megilla, fol. 21. 1. (m) Alex. ab Alex. Genial. Dier. l. 2. c. 25. (n) Pirke Abot, c. 1. sect. 15. 17. & 3. 13. T. Bab. Megilla. fol. 18. 1. Vajikra Rabba, sect. 16. fol. 158. 3. Midrash Kohelet, fol. 71. 1. (o) Philo Zuis Rer. Divin. Haeres. p. 482. Vid. T. Bab. Sanhedrin, fol. 7. 1.

---

20. For the wrath of man worketh not the righteousness of God.

20. ὀργὴ γὰρ ἀνδρὸς δικαιοσύνην θεοῦ οὐ κατεργάζεται.

20. orgei gar andros dikaiosunein theou ou katergazetai.

כ. כִּי־קֶצֶף אָדָם לֹא יִפְעַל צִדְקַת אֱלֹהִים:

20. Ki - ke•tzef adam lo yif•al tzid•kat Elohim.

James 1

21. Wherefore lay apart all filthiness and superfluity of naughtiness, and receive with meekness the engrafted word, which is able to save your souls.

21. Διὸ ἀποθέμενοι πᾶσαν ῥυπαρίαν καὶ περισσείαν κακίας, ἐν πραΰτητι δέξασθε τὸν ἔμφυτον λόγον, τὸν δυνάμενον σῶσαι τὰς ψυχὰς ὑμῶν.

21. Dio apothemenoi pasan 'ruparian kai perisseian kakias, en prauteiti dexasthe ton emphuton logon, ton dunamenon sosai tas psuchas 'umon.

כא. עַל-כֵּן הָסִירוּ מֵעֲלֵיכֶם כָּל-גִּלּוּלִים וְכֹבֶד רִשְׁעָה וּבַעֲנָוָה הַחֲזִיקוּ בַּתּוֹרָה הַנְּטוּעָה בְּתוֹכֲכֶם אֲשֶׁר יֶשׁ-בָּהּ:לְהוֹשִׁיעַ לְנַפְשֹׁתֵיכֶם

21. Al - ken ha•si•roo me•a•ley•chem kol - gi•loo•lim ve•cho•ved rish•ah oo•va•ana•va ha•cha•zi•koo va•Torah ha•ne•too•ah ve•to•cha•chem asher yesh - ba le•ho•shi•a le•naf•sho•tey•chem.

Rabbinic Jewish Commentary

of the foreskin of the heart, spoken of in Jer.4:4 which the Targum, in that place, calls רשע לבכון, "the wickedness", or "naughtiness of your hearts" to be removed.

---

22. But be ye doers of the word, and not hearers only, deceiving your own selves.

22. Γίνεσθε δὲ ποιηταὶ λόγου, καὶ μὴ μόνον ἀκροαταί, παραλογιζόμενοι ἑαυτούς.

22. Ginesthe de poieitai logou, kai mei monon akroatai, paralogizomenoi 'eautous.

כב. וּרְאוּ לִהְיוֹת עֹשִׂים דְּבַר הַמִּצְוָה וְלֹא רַק שֹׁמְעִים לְאֹזֶן לְהַתְעוֹת אֶת-נַפְשְׁכֶם:

22. Oor•oo li•hee•yot o•sim de•var ha•mitz•va ve•lo rak shom•eem le•o•zen le•hat•ot et - naf•she•chem.

James 1

23. For if any be a hearer of the word, and not a doer, he is like unto a man beholding his natural face in a glass:

23. Ὅτι εἴ τις ἀκροατὴς λόγου ἐστὶν καὶ οὐ ποιητής, οὗτος ἔοικεν ἀνδρὶ κατανοοῦντι τὸ πρόσωπον τῆς γενέσεως αὐτοῦ ἐν ἐσόπτρῳ·

23. 'Oti ei tis akroateis logou estin kai ou poieiteis, 'outos eoiken andri katanoounti to prosopon teis geneseos autou en esoptro.

כג: כִּי הַשֹּׁמֵעַ דָּבָר וְלֹא יַעֲשֵׂנוּ נִמְשַׁל הוּא לְאִישׁ הַמַּבִּיט תֹּאַר פָּנָיו בִּרְאִי מְלֻטָּשׁ

23. Ki ha•sho•me•a da•var ve•lo ya•a•se•noo nim•shal hoo le•eesh ha•ma•bit to•ar pa•nav bir•ee me•loo•tash.

Rabbinic Jewish Commentary

The Arabic version here again reads, "a hearer of the Torah", and so some copies; not hearing, but practice, is the main thing; not theory, but action: hence, says R. Simeon, not the word, or the searching into it, and the explanation of it, is the root, or principal thing, אלא המעשה, "but the work" (p)

(p) Pirke Abot, c. 1. sect. 17.

---

24. For he beholdeth himself, and goeth his way, and straightway forgetteth what manner of man he was.

24. κατενόησεν γὰρ ἑαυτὸν καὶ ἀπελήλυθεν, καὶ εὐθέως ἐπελάθετο ὁποῖος ἦν.

24. katenoeisen gar 'eauton kai apeleiluthen, kai eutheos epelatheto 'opoios ein.

כד. כִּי הוּא מַבִּיט בְּפָנָיו וּכְרֶגַע הוֹלֵךְ וְשֹׁכֵחַ מַה-תָּאֲרוֹ:

24. Ki hoo ma•bit be•fa•nav ooch•re•ga ho•lech ve•sho•che•ach ma-to•o•ro.

25. But whoso looketh into the perfect law of liberty, and continueth therein, he being not a forgetful hearer, but a doer of the work, this man shall be blessed in his deed.

25. Ὁ δὲ παρακύψας εἰς νόμον τέλειον τὸν τῆς ἐλευθερίας καὶ παραμείνας, οὗτος οὐκ ἀκροατὴς ἐπιλησμονῆς γενόμενος ἀλλὰ ποιητὴς ἔργου, οὗτος μακάριος ἐν τῇ ποιήσει αὐτοῦ ἔσται.

25. 'O de parakupsas eis nomon teleion ton teis eleutherias kai parameinas, 'outos ouk akroateis epileismoneis genomenos alla poieiteis ergou, 'outos makarios en tei poieisei autou estai.

כה. אַךְ הַשָּׂם עֵינוֹ בַּתּוֹרָה הַתְּמִימָה אֲשֶׁר חֹפֶשׁ בָּהּ וְהָגָה בָּהּ תָּמִיד וְאֵינֶנּוּ שֹׁמֵעַ וְשֹׁכֵחַ כִּי אִם-עֹשֶׂה הַדָּבָר: לְמַעֲנֵהוּ הָאִישׁ הַהוּא יְאֻשַּׁר בְּמַעֲשֵׂהוּ

25. Ach ha•sam ey•no va•Torah hat•mi•ma asher cho•fesh ba ve•ho•ge va ta•mid ve•ey•ne•noo sho•me•a ve•sho•che•ach ki eem - o•se ha•da•var le•ma•a•ne•hoo ha•eesh ha•hoo ye•oo•shar be•ma•a•se•hoo.

Rabbinic Jewish Commentary

The Torah with the Jews is called תורה, because it is teaching and instructive; and everything that is so is by them called by this name: hence we find the doctrine of the Messiah, which is no other than the Gospel, is in the Old Testament called the Torah of the Lord, and his Torah, Isa.2:2 and in the New Testament it is called the Torah, or doctrine of faith, Rom.3:27 and this doctrine is perfect, as in Psa.19:7, it being a perfect plan of truths, containing in it all truth, as it is in Yeshua, even all the treasures of wisdom and knowledge; and because it is a revelation of things perfect; of the perfect righteousness of Messiah, and of perfect justification by it, and of free and full pardon of sins through him, and of complete salvation by him; and because it directs to Messiah, in whom perfection is: and it is a Torah or doctrine of liberty; τον της ελευθηριας, "that which is if liberty."

---

26. If any man among you seem to be religious, and bridleth not his tongue, but deceiveth his own heart, this man's religion is vain.

26. Εἴ τις δοκεῖ θρῆσκος εἶναι ἐν ὑμῖν, μὴ χαλιναγωγῶν γλῶσσαν αὐτοῦ, ἀλλὰ ἀπατῶν καρδίαν αὐτοῦ, τούτου μάταιος ἡ θρησκεία.

26. Ei tis dokei threiskos einai en 'umin, mei chalinagogon glossan autou, alla apaton kardian autou, toutou mataios 'ei threiskeia.

כו. וְאִם-יְדַמֶּה אִישׁ מִכֶּם לִהְיוֹת עֹבֵד אֱלֹהִים וְלֹא יִשְׁמֹר רֶסֶן לְשׁוֹנוֹ כִּי אִם-יַתְעֶה אֶת-לְבָבוֹ עֲבֹדָתוֹ הֶבֶל הִיא:

26. Ve•eem - ye•da•me eesh mi•kem li•hee•yot o•ved Elohim ve•lo yish•mor re•sen le•sho•no ki eem - yat•eh et - le•va•vo avo•da•to he•vel hee.

James 1

27. Pure religion and undefiled before God and the Father is this, To visit the fatherless and widows in their affliction, and to keep himself unspotted from the world.

27. Θρησκεία καθαρὰ καὶ ἀμίαντος παρὰ θεῷ καὶ πατρὶ αὕτη ἐστίν, ἐπισκέπτεσθαι ὀρφανοὺς καὶ χήρας ἐν τῇ θλίψει αὐτῶν, ἄσπιλον ἑαυτὸν τηρεῖν ἀπὸ τοῦ κόσμου.

27. Threiskeia kathara kai amiantos para theo kai patri 'autei estin, episkeptesthai orphanous kai cheiras en tei thlipsei auton, aspilon 'eauton teirein apo tou kosmou.

כז. זֹאת הִיא עֲבֹדָה טְהוֹרָה וּתְמִימָה לִפְנֵי אֱלֹהֵינוּ אָבִינוּ לְבַקֵּר יְתוֹמִים וְאַלְמָנוֹת בִּמְצוּקוֹתֵיהֶם וּלְהִשְׁתַּמֵּר מִן: שֶׁמֶץ דָּבָר מִן-עֶרְוַת הָאָרֶץ

27. Zot hee avo•da te•ho•ra oot•mi•ma lif•ney Elohey•noo Avi•noo le•va•ker ye•to•mim ve•al•ma•not bim•tzoo•ko•tey•hem ool•hish•ta•mer min - she•metz da•var min - er•vat ha•a•retz.

(James Chapter 1 End)

James, Chapter 2

1. My brethren, have not the faith of our Lord Jesus Christ, the Lord of glory, with respect of persons.

1. Ἀδελφοί μου, μὴ ἐν προσωποληψίαις ἔχετε τὴν πίστιν τοῦ κυρίου ἡμῶν Ἰησοῦ χριστοῦ τῆς δόξης.

1. Adelphoi mou, mei en prosopoleipsiais echete tein pistin tou kuriou 'eimon Yeisou christou teis doxeis.

א. אַל־תַּכִּירוּ פָנִים אַחַי בֶּאֱמוּנַת יֵשׁוּעַ הַמָּשִׁיחַ אֲדֹנֵינוּ אֲדוֹן הַכָּבוֹד:

1. Al - ta•ki•roo fa•nim a•chai be•e•moo•nat Yeshua ha•Ma•shi•ach Ado•ney•noo Adon ha•ka•vod.

---

2. For if there come unto your assembly a man with a gold ring, in goodly apparel, and there come in also a poor man in vile raiment;

2. Ἐὰν γὰρ εἰσέλθῃ εἰς τὴν συναγωγὴν ὑμῶν ἀνὴρ χρυσοδακτύλιος ἐν ἐσθῆτι λαμπρᾷ, εἰσέλθῃ δὲ καὶ πτωχὸς ἐν ῥυπαρᾷ ἐσθῆτι,

2. Ean gar eiselthei eis tein sunagogein 'umon aneir chrusodaktulios en estheiti lampra, eiselthei de kai ptochos en 'rupara estheiti,

ב. כִּי אִם־יָבֹא אִישׁ אֶל־בֵּית הַכְּנֵסֶת לָכֶם הָדוּר בְּטַבְּעוֹת זָהָב וְלָבוּשׁ מַחֲלָצוֹת וּבָא שָׁם גַּם־עָנִי בִּבְגָדִים צוֹאִים:

2. Ki eem - ya•vo eesh el - beit ha•k`ne•set la•chem ha•door be•tab•ot za•hav ve•la•voosh ma•cha•la•tzot oo•va sham gam - ani biv•ga•dim tzo•eem.

Rabbinic Jewish Commentary

a man with a gold ring; On his finger, which shows him to be a man of dignity and wealth; so those of the senatorian and equestrian orders among the Romans were distinguished from the common people by wearing gold rings; though in time the use of them became promiscuous (q); the ancients used to wear but one (r), as here but one is mentioned; and only freemen, not servants, might wear it.

and there come in also a poor man in vile raiment; Mean and despicable, filthy and ragged: in the courts of judicature with the Jews, two men, who were at law with one another, might not have different apparel on while they were in court, and their cause was trying: their law runs thus (s);

"Two adversaries (at law with each other), if one of them is clothed "with precious garments", (Myrqy Mydgb, "goodly apparel",) and the other is clothed with בגדים בזויין, "vile raiment", (the judge) says to the honourable person, either clothe him as thou art, while thou contendest with him, or be clothed as he is, that ye may be alike, or on an equal foot."

(q) Alex. ab Alex. Genial. Dier. l. 2. c. 29. (r) Isidor. Hispal. Originum, l. 19. c. 32. p. 171. (s) Maimon. Hilchot Sanhedrin, c. 21. sect. 2.

James 2

3. And ye have respect to him that weareth the gay clothing, and say unto him, Sit thou here in a good place; and say to the poor, Stand thou there, or sit here under my footstool:

3. καὶ ἐπιβλέψητε ἐπὶ τὸν φοροῦντα τὴν ἐσθῆτα τὴν λαμπράν, καὶ εἴπητε αὐτῷ, Σὺ κάθου ὧδε καλῶς, καὶ τῷ πτωχῷ εἴπητε, Σὺ στῆθι ἐκεῖ, ἢ κάθου ὧδε ὑπὸ τὸ ὑποπόδιόν μου·

3. kai epiblepseite epi ton phorounta tein estheita tein lampran, kai eipeite auto, Su kathou 'ode kalos, kai to ptocho eipeite, Su steithi ekei, ei kathou 'ode 'upo to 'upopodion mou.

ג. וּפְנִיתֶם אֶל־הַלָּבוּשׁ מַחֲלָצוֹת לֵאמֹר שְׁבָה־נָּא פֹה בְּמוֹשָׁב נִכְבָּד וְאֶל־הֶעָנִי תֹאמְרוּן אַתָּה עֲמֹד שָׁם אוֹ שֵׁב־לַהֲדֹם רַגְלָי:

3. Oof•ni•tem el - ha•la•voosh ma•cha•la•tzot le•mor sh`va - na fo be•mo•shav nich•bad ve•el - he•a•ni tom•roon ata amod sham oh shev la•ha•dom rag•lai.

Rabbinic Jewish Commentary
or sit thou here under my footstool; this also was contrary to the Jewish canons (t), that one should sit, and another stand, while their cause was trying; the Torah runs thus:

"One shall not sit, and another stand, but both shall stand; but if the sanhedrim, or court, please to let them sit, they sit; but one does not sit above, and the other below; but one by the side of the other."

(t) Maimon. ib. sect. 3. vid. T. Bab. Shebuot, fol. 30. 1.

James 2

4. Are ye not then partial in yourselves, and are become judges of evil thoughts?

4. καὶ οὐ διεκρίθητε ἐν ἑαυτοῖς, καὶ ἐγένεσθε κριταὶ διαλογισμῶν πονηρῶν;

4. kai ou diekritheite en 'eautois, kai egenesthe kritai dyalogismon poneiron?

ד. הַאִם לֹא לֵב וָלֵב בְּקִרְבְּכֶם וְאִם לֹא כְשׁוֹפְטִים חוֹרְשֵׁי רַע אַתֶּם:

4. Ha•eem lo lev va•lev be•kir•be•chem ve•eem lo che•shof•tim chor•shey ra atem.

---

5. Hearken, my beloved brethren, Hath not God chosen the poor of this world rich in faith, and heirs of the kingdom which he hath promised to them that love him?

5. Ἀκούσατε, ἀδελφοί μου ἀγαπητοί. Οὐχ ὁ θεὸς ἐξελέξατο τοὺς πτωχοὺς τοῦ κόσμου πλουσίους ἐν πίστει, καὶ κληρονόμους τῆς βασιλείας ἧς ἐπηγγείλατο τοῖς ἀγαπῶσιν αὐτόν;

5. Akousate, adelphoi mou agapeitoi. Ouch 'o theos exelexato tous ptochous tou kosmou plousious en pistei, kai kleironomous teis basileias 'eis epeingeilato tois agaposin auton?

ה. שִׁמְעוּנִי אַחַי הַיְקָרִים הֲלֹא אֱלֹהִים בָּחַר בַּעֲנִיֵּי הָאָרֶץ לִהְיוֹת עֲשִׁירֵי אֱמוּנָה וְיוֹרְשֵׁי מַלְכוּת כַּאֲשֶׁר דִּבֶּר לְאֹהֲבָיו:

5. Sh`ma•oo•ni a•chai hay•ka•rim ha•lo Elohim ba•char ba•a•ni•ey ha•a•retz li•hee•yot a•shi•rey e•moo•na ve•yor•shey mal•choot ka•a•sher di•ber le•o•ha•vav.

Rabbinic Jewish Commentary

It may be the apostle has some peculiar respect to the poor among the Gentiles, whom God had chosen; it was usual with the Jews to call the Gentiles the world, and they were Jews the apostle now writes to, and who were scattered abroad among the Gentiles; and therefore he might very aptly call them "this world", among whom they lived; and suggest to them, that God had chosen some of the Gentiles, as well as of the Jews, and even some of the poorer sort of them; and it was usual with the Jews to distinguish between עניי ישראל, "the poor of Israel", and עניי עולם, "the poor of the world", or עניי אומות העולם "the poor of the nations of the world" (u): the Alexandrian copy, and some others, leave out the word "this", and so the Syriac and Arabic versions, which makes the phrase more agreeable to the Jewish way of speaking.

(u) T. Bab. Gittin, fol. 30. 1. & Bava Bathra, fol. 10. 2.

---

6. But ye have despised the poor. Do not rich men oppress you, and draw you before the judgment seats?

6. Ὑμεῖς δὲ ἠτιμάσατε τὸν πτωχόν. Οὐχ οἱ πλούσιοι καταδυναστεύουσιν ὑμῶν, καὶ αὐτοὶ ἕλκουσιν ὑμᾶς εἰς κριτήρια;

6. 'Umeis de eitimasate ton ptochon. Ouch 'oi plousioi katadunasteuousin 'umon, kai autoi 'elkousin 'umas eis kriteirya?

ו: וְאַתֶּם הוֹבַשְׁתֶּם פְּנֵי הֶעָנִי הֲלֹא הָעֲשִׁירִים הֵם יַעֲשְׁקוּן וְיִסְחֲבוּן אֶתְכֶם לִמְקוֹם הַמִּשְׁפָּט

6. Ve•a•tem ho•vash•tem p`ney he•a•ni ha•lo ha•a•shi•rim hem ya•ash•koon ve•yis•cha•voon et•chem lim•kom ha•mish•pat.

---

7. Do not they blaspheme that worthy name by the which ye are called?

7. Οὐκ αὐτοὶ βλασφημοῦσιν τὸ καλὸν ὄνομα τὸ ἐπικληθὲν ἐφ᾽ ὑμᾶς;

7. Ouk autoi blaspheimousin to kalon onoma to epikleithen eph 'umas?

ז: וְגַם הַשֵּׁם הַטּוֹב אֲשֶׁר נִקְרָא עֲלֵיכֶם יָשִׂימוּ אֹתוֹ לַחֲרָפוֹת

7. Ve•gam ha•shem ha•tov asher nik•ra aley•chem ya•si•moo o•to la•cha•ra•fot.

8. If ye fulfill the royal law according to the scripture, Thou shalt love thy neighbour as thyself, ye do well:

8. Εἰ μέντοι νόμον τελεῖτε βασιλικόν, κατὰ τὴν γραφήν, Ἀγαπήσεις τὸν πλησίον σου ὡς σεαυτόν, καλῶς ποιεῖτε·

8. Ei mentoi nomon teleite basilikon, kata tein graphein, Agapeiseis ton pleision sou 'os seauton, kalos poieite.

ח. הִנֵּה אִם תִּשְׁמְרוּ דָת הַמַּלְכוּת כַּכָּתוּב בַּתּוֹרָה וְאָהַבְתָּ לְרֵעֲךָ כָּמוֹךָ תֵּיטִיבוּ לַעֲשׂוֹת:

8. Hee•ne eem tish•me•roo dat ha•mal•choot ka•ka•toov ba•To•rah ve•a•hav•ta le•re•a•cha ka•mo•cha tey•ti•voo la•a•sot.

Rabbinic Jewish Commentary

The Jews frequently ascribe royalty to the Torah, and often speak of כתר תורה, "The crown of the Torah" (w); and they suppose the Israelites had crowns upon their heads, when the Torah was given them on Mount Sinai, in which were engraven the name of God, and which they were stripped of when they made the golden calf (x): now this royal Torah is fulfilled, when it is regarded without respect of persons.

(w) Pirke Abot, c. 4. sect. 13. & Abot R. Nathan, c. 41. T. Bab. Megilla, fol. 28. 2. Bemidbar Rabba, sect. 4. fol. 183. 2. & sect. 14. fol. 215. 2. & Midrash Kohelet, fol. 73. 4. Targum Jon in Deut. xxxiv. 5. (x) Vid. Targum. Jon. & Jerus. in Exod. xxxii. 25. & xxxiii. 4.

James 2

9. But if ye have respect to persons, ye commit sin, and are convinced of the law as transgressors.

9. εἰ δὲ προσωποληπτεῖτε, ἁμαρτίαν ἐργάζεσθε, ἐλεγχόμενοι ὑπὸ τοῦ νόμου ὡς παραβάται.

9. ei de prosopoleipteite, 'amartian ergazesthe, elegchomenoi 'upo tou nomou 'os parabatai.

ט. אוּלָם אִם-תִּשְׂאוּ פָנִים תֶּחֱטָאוּ בְמַעֲשֵׂיכֶם וְעַל-פִּי הַתּוֹרָה תִּשָּׁפְטוּ כְּפֹשְׁעִים בָּה:

9. Oo•lam eem - tis•oo fa•nim te•chet•oo ve•ma•a•sey•chem ve•al - pi ha•Torah ti•shaf•too ke•fosh•eem ba.

James 2

10. For whosoever shall keep the whole law, and yet offend in one point, he is guilty of all.

10. Ὅστις γὰρ ὅλον τὸν νόμον τηρήσει, πταίσει δὲ ἐν ἑνί, γέγονεν πάντων ἔνοχος.

10. 'Ostis gar 'olon ton nomon teireisei, ptaisei de en 'eni, gegonen panton enochos.

:י. כִּי הַשֹּׁמֵר אֶת-כָּל-הַתּוֹרָה וְעָבַר אַחַת מִמִּצְוֹתֶיהָ הוּא אָשֵׁם כְּעֹבֵר כָּל-מִצְוֹתֶיהָ

10. Ki ha•sho•mer et - kol - ha•Torah ve•o•ver a•chat mi•mitz•vo•te•ha hoo a•shem ke•o•ver kol - mitz•vo•te•ha.

Rabbinic Jewish Commentary

he is guilty of all: this seems to agree with some common sayings of the Jews, that he that is suspected in one thing, is suspected in the whole Torah (y); and he that keeps this or the other command, keeps the whole Torah; and he that breaks this, or the other command, breaks the whole Torah; as whether it respects the sabbath, or adultery, or that command. Thou shall not covet, or any other (z).

But it does not follow from hence, that all sins are equal, as the Stoics say (a).

(y) T. Bab. Erubin, fol. 69. 1. (z) Bemidbar Rabba, sect. 9. fol. 192. 3. Zohar in Exod. fol. 20. 2. & 37. 1. & in Lev. fol. 32. 3. Shemot Rabba, sect. 25. fol. 109. 3. T. Bab. Kiddushin, fol. 39. 2. & Menachot, fol. 43. 2. & Abkath Rochel, par. 1. p. 3. (a) Zeno & Chrysippus apud Laert. Vit. Zeno, p. 510.

---

11. For he that said, Do not commit adultery, said also, Do not kill. Now if thou commit no adultery, yet if thou kill, thou art become a transgressor of the law.

11. Ὁ γὰρ εἰπών, Μὴ μοιχεύσεις, εἶπεν καί, Μὴ φονεύσεις· εἰ δὲ οὐ μοιχεύσεις, φονεύσεις δέ, γέγονας παραβάτης νόμου.

11. 'O gar eipon, Mei moicheuseis, eipen kai, Mei phoneuseis. ei de ou moicheuseis, phoneuseis de, gegonas parabateis nomou.

יא. כִּי הָאֹמֵר לֹא תִנְאָף גַּם-הוּא אֹמֵר לֹא תִּרְצָח וְאִם-אַתָּה לֹא נָאַפְתָּ אַךְ רָצַחְתָּ פֹּשֵׁעַ בַּתּוֹרָה הִנֶּךָ:

11. Ki ha•o•mer lo tin•af gam - hoo o•mer lo tir•tzach ve•eem - ata lo na•af•ta ach ra•tzach•ta po•she•a ba•To•rah hi•ne•cha.

James 2

12. So speak ye, and so do, as they that shall be judged by the law of liberty.

12. Οὕτως λαλεῖτε καὶ οὕτως ποιεῖτε, ὡς διὰ νόμου ἐλευθερίας μέλλοντες κρίνεσθαι.

12. 'Outos laleite kai 'outos poieite, 'os dya nomou eleutherias mellontes krinesthai.

יב. וְאַתֶּם כֹּה תְדַבְּרוּן וְכֹה תַעֲשׂוּן כַּעֲתִידִים לְהִשָּׁפֵט עַל-פִּי הַתּוֹרָה אֲשֶׁר חֹפֶשׁ בָּהּ:

12. Ve•a•tem ko te•dab•roon ve•cho ta•a•soon ka•a•ti•dim le•hi•sha•fet al - pi ha•Torah asher cho•fesh ba.

---

13. For he shall have judgment without mercy, that hath shewed no mercy; and mercy rejoiceth against judgment.

13. Ἡ γὰρ κρίσις ἀνέλεος τῷ μὴ ποιήσαντι ἔλεος· κατακαυχᾶται ἔλεον κρίσεως.

13. 'Ei gar krisis aneleos to mei poieisanti eleos. katakauchatai eleon kriseos.

יג. כִּי אֵין חֶסֶד בַּדִּין לְלֹא חָסֵד אַךְ כֹּחַ הַחֶסֶד יָעֹז עַל-כֹּחַ הַדִּין:

13. Ki eyn che•sed ba•din le•lo cha•sed ach ko•ach ha•che•sed ya•oz al - ko•ach ha•din.

14. What doth it profit, my brethren, though a man say he hath faith, and have not works? Can faith save him?

14. Τί τὸ ὄφελος, ἀδελφοί μου, ἐὰν πίστιν λέγῃ τις ἔχειν, ἔργα δὲ μὴ ἔχῃ; Μὴ δύναται ἡ πίστις σῶσαι αὐτόν;

14. Ti to ophelos, adelphoi mou, ean pistin legei tis echein, erga de mei echei? Mei dunatai 'ei pistis sosai auton?

:יד. אַחַי מַה-יּוֹעִיל לְאִישׁ הָאֹמֵר כִּי אֱמוּנָה בּוֹ וּמַעֲשִׂים אֵין לוֹ הֲתוּכַל אֱמוּנָה לְהוֹשִׁיעַ-לּוֹ

14. A•chai ma - yo•eel le•eesh ha•o•mer ki e•moo•na vo oo•ma•a•sim eyn lo ha•too•chal e•moo•na le•ho•shi•a - lo.

James 2

15. If a brother or sister be naked, and destitute of daily food,

15. Ἐὰν δὲ ἀδελφὸς ἢ ἀδελφὴ γυμνοὶ ὑπάρχωσιν καὶ λειπόμενοι ὦσιν τῆς ἐφημέρου τροφῆς,

15. Ean de adelphos ei adelphei gumnoi 'uparchosin kai leipomenoi osin teis epheimerou tropheis,

:טו. אִם אָח אוֹ-אָחוֹת יִהְיוּ עֵירֻמִּים וְאֵין לָהֶם לֶחֶם חֻקָּם

15. Eem ach oh - a•chot yi•hee•yoo ey•roo•mim ve•eyn la•hem le•chem choo•kam.

---

16. And one of you say unto them, Depart in peace, be ye warmed and filled; notwithstanding ye give them not those things which are needful to the body; what doth it profit?

16. εἴπῃ δέ τις αὐτοῖς ἐξ ὑμῶν, Ὑπάγετε ἐν εἰρήνῃ, θερμαίνεσθε καὶ χορτάζεσθε, μὴ δῶτε δὲ αὐτοῖς τὰ ἐπιτήδεια τοῦ σώματος, τί τὸ ὄφελος;

16. eipei de tis autois ex 'umon, 'Upagete en eireinei, thermainesthe kai chortazesthe, mei dote de autois ta epiteideya tou somatos, ti to ophelos?

טז. וְאִישׁ מִכֶּם יֹאמַר אֲלֵיהֶם לְכוּ לְשָׁלוֹם וְחַם-לָכֶם וּשְׂבַעְתֶּם וְלֹא-תִתְּנוּ לְנַפְשָׁם דֵּי-מַחְסֹרָם מַה-יִּתֵּן לָהֶם:דְּבַר שְׂפָתָיִם

16. Ve•eesh mi•kem yo•mar aley•hem le•choo le•sha•lom ve•cham - la•chem oos•va•a•tem ve•lo - tit•noo le•naf•sham dey - mach•so•ram ma - yi•ten la•hem de•var s`fa•ta•yim.

James 2

17. Even so faith, if it hath not works, is dead, being alone.

17. Οὕτως καὶ ἡ πίστις, ἐὰν μὴ ἔργα ἔχῃ, νεκρά ἐστιν καθ᾽ ἑαυτήν.

17. 'Outos kai 'ei pistis, ean mei erga echei, nekra estin kath 'eautein.

יז. כֵּן גַּם-הָאֱמוּנָה אִם מַעֲשִׂים אֵין עִמָּהּ מֵתָה הִיא לְבַדָּהּ:

17. Ken gam - ha•e•moo•na eem ma•a•sim eyn ee•ma me•ta hee le•va•da.

Rabbinic Jewish Commentary
Dr. Ames observes (b), good works are second acts, necessarily flowing from the life of faith; to which may be added, and by these faith appears to be living, lively and active, or such who perform them appear to be true and living believers.

(b) Medulla Theolog. l. 2. c. 7. sect. 35.

---

18. Yea, a man may say, Thou hast faith, and I have works: shew me thy faith without thy works, and I will shew thee my faith by my works.

18. Ἀλλ᾽ ἐρεῖ τις, Σὺ πίστιν ἔχεις, κἀγὼ ἔργα ἔχω· δεῖξόν μοι τὴν πίστιν σου ἐκ τῶν ἔργων σου, κἀγὼ δείξω σοι ἐκ τῶν ἔργων μου τὴν πίστιν μου.

18. All erei tis, Su pistin echeis, kago erga echo. deixon moi tein pistin sou ek ton ergon sou, kago deixo soi ek ton ergon mou tein pistin mou.

יח. אֲבָל יֹאמַר אִישׁ הֵן אַתָּה יֶשׁ אֱמוּנָה בְּךָ וַאֲנִי יֶשׁ-לִי מַעֲשִׂים הַרְאֵנִי אֶת-אֱמוּנָתְךָ בִּבְלִי מַעֲשֶׂיךָ וַאֲנִי מִתּוֹךְ:מַעֲשַׂי אַרְאֲךָ אֶת-אֱמוּנָתִי

18. Aval yo•mar eesh hen ata yesh e•moo•na ve•cha va•a•ni yesh - li ma•a•sim har•e•ni et - emoo•nat•cha biv•li ma•a•se•cha va•a•ni mi•toch ma•a•sai ar•a•cha et - emoo•na•ti.

James 2

19. Thou believest that there is one God; thou doest well: the devils also believe, and tremble.

19. Σὺ πιστεύεις ὅτι ὁ θεὸς εἷς ἐστίν· καλῶς ποιεῖς· καὶ τὰ δαιμόνια πιστεύουσιν, καὶ φρίσσουσιν.

19. Su pisteueis 'oti 'o theos 'eis estin. kalos poieis. kai ta daimonya pisteuousin, kai phrissousin.

יט. אַתָּה מַאֲמִין כִּי אֱלֹהִים אֶחָד הוּא וְהֵיטַבְתָּ לְהַאֲמִין וְגַם הַשֵּׁדִים כֵּן יַאֲמִינוּ וְיָחִילוּן:

19. Ata ma•a•min ki Elohim e•chad hoo ve•hey•tav•ta le•ha•a•min ve•gam ha•she•dim ken ya•a•mi•noo ve•ya•chi•loon.

20. But wilt thou know, O vain man, that faith without works is dead?

20. Θέλεις δὲ γνῶναι, ὦ ἄνθρωπε κενέ, ὅτι ἡ πίστις χωρὶς τῶν ἔργων νεκρά ἐστιν;

20. Theleis de gnonai, o anthrope kene, 'oti 'ei pistis choris ton ergon nekra estin?

כ. אַךְ עַתָּה רֹעֵה רוּחַ אִם חָפַצְתָּ לָדַעַת כִּי אֱמוּנָה בִּבְלִי מַעֲשִׂים מֵתָה הִיא:

20. Ach ata ro•eh roo•ach eem cha•fatz•ta la•da•at ki e•moo•na biv•li ma•a•sim me•ta hee.

Rabbinic Jewish Commentary
The phrase, "vain man", is a proper interpretation of the word ריקא, "Raca", or Reka, used in Mat.5:22; which though not to be said to a man in an angry way, yet may be applied to men of such a character as here described; who were empty of solid good, and yet boasted of their knowledge. "Wilt thou know?" dost thou require proofs.

21. Was not Abraham our father justified by works, when he had offered Isaac his son upon the altar?

21. Ἀβραὰμ ὁ πατὴρ ἡμῶν οὐκ ἐξ ἔργων ἐδικαιώθη, ἀνενέγκας Ἰσαὰκ τὸν υἱὸν αὐτοῦ ἐπὶ τὸ θυσιαστήριον;

21. Abra'am 'o pateir 'eimon ouk ex ergon edikaiothei, anenegkas Ysa'ak ton 'wion autou epi to thusyasteirion?

כא: הֲלֹא בְמַעֲשָׂיו נִצְדַּק אַבְרָהָם אָבִינוּ בְּהַעֲלֹתוֹ אֶת-יִצְחָק בְּנוֹ עַל-גַּב הַמִּזְבֵּחַ.

21. Ha•lo ve•ma•a•sav nitz•dak Avraham avi•noo be•ha•a•lo•to et - Yitzchak b`no al – gav ha•miz•be•ach.

James 2

22. Seest thou how faith wrought with his works, and by works was faith made perfect?

22. Βλέπεις ὅτι ἡ πίστις συνήργει τοῖς ἔργοις αὐτοῦ, καὶ ἐκ τῶν ἔργων ἡ πίστις ἐτελειώθη;

22. Blepeis 'oti 'ei pistis suneirgei tois ergois autou, kai ek ton ergon 'ei pistis eteleiothei?

כב: הִנְּךָ רֹאֶה כִּי-הָאֱמוּנָה נָתְנָה-כֹּחַ לְמַעֲשָׂיו וּמִתּוֹךְ מַעֲשָׂיו נֶעֶשְׂתָה אֱמוּנָתוֹ שְׁלֵמָה.

22. Hin•cha ro•eh ki - ha•e•moo•na nat•na - ko•ach le•ma•a•sav oo•mi•toch ma•a•sav ne•es•ta emoo•na•to sh`le•ma.

---

23. And the scripture was fulfilled which saith, Abraham believed God, and it was imputed unto him for righteousness: and he was called the Friend of God.

23. Καὶ ἐπληρώθη ἡ γραφὴ ἡ λέγουσα, Ἐπίστευσεν δὲ Ἀβραὰμ τῷ θεῷ, καὶ ἐλογίσθη αὐτῷ εἰς δικαιοσύνην, καὶ φίλος θεοῦ ἐκλήθη.

23. Kai epleirothei 'ei graphei 'ei legousa, Episteusen de Abra'am to theo, kai elogisthei auto eis dikaiosunein, kai philos theou ekleithei.

:כג. וְהוּקַם הַכָּתוּב הָאוֹמֵר וְהֶאֱמִן אַבְרָהָם בַּיהוָה וַתֵּחָשֶׁב-לוֹ צְדָקָה וְגַם נִקְרָא אֹהֵב אֱלֹהִים

23. Ve•hoo•kam ha•ka•toov ha•o•mer ve•he•e•min Avraham ba•Adonai va•te•cha•shev - lo tze•da•ka ve•gam nik•ra O•hev Elohim.

Rabbinic Jewish Commentary

Gen.12:8 and Abraham, on the other hand, loved God, and showed himself friendly to him; trusted in him, and believed every word of his; readily complied with his will, and not only yielded a cheerful obedience to his commands, but enjoined his children after him to observe them: this was a name which Abraham was well known by among the eastern nations; hence he is called by the Mahometans, חליל אללה, "Khalil Allah", the friend of God; and Mahomet says himself (c),

"God took Abraham for his friend."

(c) Koran, Sura 4:125.

---

24. Ye see then how that by works a man is justified, and not by faith only.

24. Ὁρᾶτε τοίνυν ὅτι ἐξ ἔργων δικαιοῦται ἄνθρωπος, καὶ οὐκ ἐκ πίστεως μόνον.

24. 'Orate toinun 'oti ex ergon dikaioutai anthropos, kai ouk ek pisteos monon.

:כד. הִנֵּה רֹאִים אַתֶּם כִּי בְמַעֲשִׂים יִצְדַּק אִישׁ וְלֹא בֶאֱמוּנָה לְבַדָּהּ

24. Hee•ne ro•eem atem ki ve•ma•a•sim yitz•dak eesh ve•lo ve•e•moo•na le•va•da.

---

25. Likewise also was not Rahab the harlot justified by works, when she had received the messengers, and had sent them out another way?

25. Ὁμοίως δὲ καὶ Ῥαὰβ ἡ πόρνη οὐκ ἐξ ἔργων ἐδικαιώθη, ὑποδεξαμένη τοὺς ἀγγέλους, καὶ ἑτέρᾳ ὁδῷ ἐκβαλοῦσα;

25. 'Omoios de kai 'Ra'ab 'ei pornei ouk ex ergon edikaiothei, 'upodexamenei tous angelous, kai 'etera 'odo ekbalousa?

כה. וְכֵן גַּם-רָחָב הַזּוֹנָה נִצְדְּקָה בְּמַעֲשֶׂיהָ כַּאֲשֶׁר הֵבִיאָה אֶת-הַמַּלְאָכִים אֶל-בֵּיתָהּ וַתְּשַׁלְּחֵם בְּדֶרֶךְ אַחֶרֶת:

25. Ve•chen gam - ra•chav ha•zo•na nitz•de•ka ve•ma•a•se•ha ka•a•sher he•vi•ah et - ha•mal•a•chim el - bey•ta vat•shal•chem be•de•rech a•che•ret.

James 2

26. For as the body without the spirit is dead, so faith without works is dead also.

26. Ὥσπερ γὰρ τὸ σῶμα χωρὶς πνεύματος νεκρόν ἐστιν, οὕτως καὶ ἡ πίστις χωρὶς τῶν ἔργων νεκρά ἐστιν.

26. 'Osper gar to soma choris pneumatos nekron estin, 'outos kai 'ei pistis choris ton ergon nekra estin.

כו. כִּי כְמוֹ-גוּף בְּלֹא נְשָׁמָה מֵת הוּא כֵּן גַּם-אֱמוּנָה בִּבְלִי מַעֲשִׂים מֵתָה הִיא:

26. Ki che•mo - goof be•lo n`sha•ma met hoo ken gam - e•moo•na biv•li ma•a•sim me•ta hee.

Rabbinic Jewish Commentary
This simile is made use of to illustrate what the apostle had asserted in Jas.2:17 that as a body, when the spirit or soul is departed from it, or the breath is gone out of it, is dead, and without motion, and useless; which the Jews (d) express in like manner, פגר גוף בלא רוח, "the body without the spirit", or "breath, is a carcass".

(d) Ohel. Moed, fol. 15. 1.

(James Chapter 2 End)

James, Chapter 3

1. My brethren, be not many masters, knowing that we shall receive the greater condemnation.

1. Μὴ πολλοὶ διδάσκαλοι γίνεσθε, ἀδελφοί μου, εἰδότες ὅτι μεῖζον κρίμα ληψόμεθα.

1. Mei polloi didaskaloi ginesthe, adelphoi mou, eidotes 'oti meizon krima leipsometha.

א: לֹא תָקִימוּ מִכֶּם אַחַי מוֹרִים רַבִּים בְּדַעְתְּכֶם כִּי תִכְבַּד עָלֵינוּ יַד-הַמִּשְׁפָּט

1. Lo ta•ki•moo mi•kem a•chai mo•rim ra•bim be•da•at•chem ki tich•bad aley•noo yad - ha•mish•pat.

---

2. For in many things we offend all. If any man offend not in word, the same is a perfect man, and able also to bridle the whole body.

2. Πολλὰ γὰρ πταίομεν ἅπαντες. Εἴ τις ἐν λόγῳ οὐ πταίει, οὗτος τέλειος ἀνήρ, δυνατὸς χαλιναγωγῆσαι καὶ ὅλον τὸ σῶμα.

2. Polla gar ptaiomen 'apantes. Ei tis en logo ou ptaiei, 'outos teleios aneir, dunatos chalinagogeisai kai 'olon to soma.

ב. כִּי רַבּוֹת נִכְשַׁלְנוּ כֻלָּנוּ וּמִי אֲשֶׁר לֹא-יִכָּשֵׁל בִּשְׂפָתָיו אִישׁ תָּמִים הוּא וְיָדָיו רַב-לוֹ לָשִׂים מַעֲצוֹר לְכָל-בְּשָׂרוֹ:

2. Ki ra•bot nich•shal•noo choo•la•noo oo•mi asher lo - yi•ka•shel bis•fa•tav eesh ta•mim hoo ve•ya•dav rav - lo la•sim ma•a•tzor le•chol - be•sa•ro.

---

3. Behold, we put bits in the horses' mouths, that they may obey us; and we turn about their whole body.

3. Ἴδε, τῶν ἵππων τοὺς χαλινοὺς εἰς τὰ στόματα βάλλομεν πρὸς τὸ πείθεσθαι αὐτοὺς ἡμῖν, καὶ ὅλον τὸ σῶμα αὐτῶν μετάγομεν.

3. Yde, ton 'ippon tous chalinous eis ta stomata ballomen pros to peithesthai autous 'eimin, kai 'olon to soma auton metagomen.

ג. הִנֵּה פִּי הַסּוּס נִבְלֹם בְּמֶתֶג לַעֲבוּר יִשְׁמַע וְיִנָּטֶה לְפִי רְצוֹנֵנוּ:

3. Hee•ne fi ha•soos niv•lom be•me•teg le•va•a•voor yish•ma ve•yi•na•te le•fi r`tzo•ne•noo.

James 3

4. Behold also the ships, which though they be so great, and are driven of fierce winds, yet are they turned about with a very small helm, whithersoever the governor listeth.

4. Ἰδού, καὶ τὰ πλοῖα, τηλικαῦτα ὄντα, καὶ ὑπὸ σκληρῶν ἀνέμων ἐλαυνόμενα, μετάγεται ὑπὸ ἐλαχίστου πηδαλίου, ὅπου ἂν ἡ ὁρμὴ τοῦ εὐθύνοντος βούληται.

4. Ydou, kai ta ploia, teilikauta onta, kai 'upo skleiron anemon elaunomena, metagetai 'upo elachistou peidaliou, 'opou an 'ei 'ormei tou euthunontos bouleitai.

ד. וְהִנֵּה גַּם-אֳנִיּוֹת גְּדֹלֹת הַנֶּהְדָּפוֹת בְּרוּחַ עַזָּה יַטֶּה אֹתָן מָשׁוֹט קָטֹן אֶל-אֲשֶׁר יַחְפֹּץ רוּחַ הַחֹבֵל:

4. Ve•hee•ne gam - o•ni•yot ge•do•lot ha•ne•he•da•fot be•roo•ach a•za ya•te o•tan ma•shot ka•ton el - asher yach•potz roo•ach ha•cho•vel.

Rabbinic Jewish Commentary
The helm, or tiller of a ship, is a beam or piece of timber fastened into the rudder, and so coming forward into the steerage, where he that stands at helm steers the ship (e), who is here called the governor; or "he that directs", as the word may be rendered; that is, that steers; the word for "helm" is translated rudder in Act.27:40, and the helm or tiller is sometimes, though improperly, called the rudder itself (f); and this is very small, in comparison of the bulk of the ship that is guided by it (g). Aristotle calls it πηδαλιον μικρον, "a small helm", as the apostle here does, and accounts for it how large ships should be moved and steered by it.

(e) Chambers's Cyclopedia, in the word "Helm". (f) Ib. in the word "Rudder". (g) Quaest. Mechanic. c. 5.

5. Even so the tongue is a little member, and boasteth great things. Behold, how great a matter a little fire kindleth!

5. Οὕτως καὶ ἡ γλῶσσα μικρὸν μέλος ἐστίν, καὶ μεγαλαυχεῖ. Ἰδού, ὀλίγον πῦρ ἡλίκην ὕλην ἀνάπτει.

5. 'Outos kai 'ei glossa mikron melos estin, kai megalauchei. Ydou, oligon pur 'eilikein 'ulein anaptei.

ה. כֵּן גַּם-הַלָּשׁוֹן אֵבֶר קָטֹן וּמְדַבֶּרֶת גְּדֹלוֹת אֵיךְ מְעַט אֵשׁ תִּבְעַר יַעַר גָּדוֹל:

5. Ken gam - ha•la•shon evar ka•ton oom•da•be•ret ge•do•lot eych me•at esh tiv•ar ya•ar ga•dol.

Rabbinic Jewish Commentary

Behold, how great a matter a little fire kindleth; what vast quantities of wood, large forests, stately buildings, and populous towns and cities, are at once seized on by a little fire, a few sparks, and in a short time burnt down, and utterly destroyed. One of the proverbs of Ben Syra is,

"Burning fire kindles great heaps;"

suggesting, that an evil tongue does great mischief, as did the tongue of Doeg the Edomite, as the gloss upon it observes: from hence the apostle passes to consider the abuse or vices of the tongue.

---

6. And the tongue is a fire, a world of iniquity: so is the tongue among our members, that it defileth the whole body, and setteth on fire the course of nature; and it is set on fire of hell.

6. Καὶ ἡ γλῶσσα πῦρ, ὁ κόσμος τῆς ἀδικίας· οὕτως ἡ γλῶσσα καθίσταται ἐν τοῖς μέλεσιν ἡμῶν, ἡ σπιλοῦσα ὅλον τὸ σῶμα, καὶ φλογίζουσα τὸν τροχὸν τῆς γενέσεως, καὶ φλογιζομένη ὑπὸ τῆς γεέννης.

6. Kai 'ei glossa pur, 'o kosmos teis adikias. 'outos 'ei glossa kathistatai en tois melesin 'eimon, 'ei spilousa 'olon to soma, kai phlogizousa ton trochon teis geneseos, kai phlogizomenei 'upo teis ge'enneis.

ו. וְהַלָּשׁוֹן אֵשׁ הִיא הַלָּשׁוֹן עוֹלָם קָטֹן וּמִלֹּאוֹ אָוֶן נְתוּנָה בְּתוֹךְ אֲבָרֵינוּ מְחַלֶּלֶת כָּל-הַבָּשָׂר מְלַהֶטֶת גַּלְגַּל הַשֶּׁבַע:וִיקָדַת מֵאֵשׁ גֵּיהִנֹּם

6. Ve•ha•la•shon esh hee ha•la•shon o•lam ka•ton oom•lo•o aven n`too•na ve•toch eva•rey•noo me•cho•le•let kol - ha•ba•sar me•la•he•tet gal•gal ha•te•va ve•yo•ke•det me•esh Gey•hi•nom.

Rabbinic Jewish Commentary

The Jews say, that he that uses an evil tongue multiplies transgression, and that it is equal to idolatry, adultery, and murder (h), and the cause of all sin; and which they express by way of fable, in this manner (i):

"When Adam sinned, God laid hold on him, and slit his tongue into two parts, and said unto him, the wickedness which is, or shall be in the world, thou hast begun with an evil tongue; wherefore I will make all that come into the world know that thy tongue is the cause of all this."

The Syriac version renders this clause thus, "and the world of iniquity is as wood"; or the branch of a tree; the tongue is fire, and a wicked world is fuel to it.

To which purpose are those words of the Talmud (k);

"Whoever uses an evil tongue, the holy blessed God says to Gehenna, I concerning him above, and thou concerning him below, will judge him, as it is said, Psa.120:3. "What shall be done to thee, thou false tongue? sharp arrows of the mighty, with coals of juniper", there is no arrow but the tongue, according to Jer.9:8 and there is no mighty one but God, Isa.42:13 "coals of juniper", היינו גיהנם, these are Gehennim."

(h) T. Bab. Erachin, fol. 15. 2. Tzeror Hammor, fol. 100. 1. (i) Otiot R. Aquiba in Ketoreth Hassammim in Gen. fol. 12. 4. (k) T. Bab. Erachin, fol. 15. 2. Yalkut, par. 2. fol. 127. 2.

---

7. For every kind of beasts, and of birds, and of serpents, and of things in the sea, is tamed, and hath been tamed of mankind:

7. Πᾶσα γὰρ φύσις θηρίων τε καὶ πετεινῶν, ἑρπετῶν τε καὶ ἐναλίων, δαμάζεται καὶ δεδάμασται τῇ φύσει τῇ ἀνθρωπίνῃ·

7. Pasa gar phusis theirion te kai peteinon, 'erpeton te kai enalion, damazetai kai dedamastai tei phusei tei anthropinei.

ז. כָּל-מִין בְּהֵמָה וְעוֹף וָרֶמֶשׂ וְחַיָּתוֹ-יָם נִכְבָּשִׁים הֵם כֻּלָּם כִּי הָאָדָם לְמִינֵהוּ כֹּבֵשׁ אֹתָם:

7. Kol - min be•he•ma ve•of ve•re•mes ve•chai•to - yam nich•ba•shim hem koo•lam ki ha•a•dam le•mi•ne•hoo ko•vesh o•tam.

Rabbinic Jewish Commentary
So Pliny (l) relates, that elephants lions and tigers among beasts, and the eagle among birds, and crocodiles, asps, and other serpents, and fishes of the sea, have been tamed: though some think this is only to be understood of their being mastered and subdued, by one means or another; or of their being despoiled of their power, or of their poison: and the Syriac and Ethiopic versions render it, "subjected to human nature".

(l) Nat. Hist. l. 8. c. 9. 16, 17. & 10. 5, 44.

James 3

8. But the tongue can no man tame; it is an unruly evil, full of deadly poison.

8. τὴν δὲ γλῶσσαν οὐδεὶς δύναται ἀνθρώπων δαμάσαι· ἀκατάσχετον κακόν, μεστὴ ἰοῦ θανατηφόρου.

8. tein de glossan oudeis dunatai anthropon damasai. akatascheton kakon, mestei iou thanateiphorou.

:ח. אַךְ הַלָּשׁוֹן לְבַדָּהּ אֵין לְאֵל יַד אָדָם לְכָבְשָׁהּ רָעָה הִיא מֵאֵין מַעְצוֹר וּמְלֵאָה חֲמַת מָוֶת

8. Ach ha•la•shon le•va•da eyn le•el yad adam le•chov•sha ra•ah hee me•eyn ma•a•tzor oom•le•ah cha•mat ma•vet.

---

9. Therewith bless we God, even the Father; and therewith curse we men, which are made after the similitude of God.

9. Ἐν αὐτῇ εὐλογοῦμεν τὸν θεὸν καὶ πατέρα, καὶ ἐν αὐτῇ καταρώμεθα τοὺς ἀνθρώπους τοὺς καθ' ὁμοίωσιν θεοῦ γεγονότας·

9. En autei eulogoumen ton theon kai patera, kai en autei katarometha tous anthropous tous kath 'omoiosin theou gegonotas.

:ט. בָּהּ נְבָרֵךְ יְהֹוָה אָבִינוּ וּבָהּ נְקַלֵּל אֲנָשִׁים אֲשֶׁר נַעֲשׂוּ בְּצֶלֶם אֱלֹהִים

9. Ba n`va•rech Adonai Avi•noo oo•va n`ka•lel a•na•shim asher na•a•soo be•tze•lem Elohim.

James 3

10. Out of the same mouth proceedeth blessing and cursing. My brethren, these things ought not so to be.

10. ἐκ τοῦ αὐτοῦ στόματος ἐξέρχεται εὐλογία καὶ κατάρα. Οὐ χρή, ἀδελφοί μου, ταῦτα οὕτως γίνεσθαι.

10. ek tou autou stomatos exerchetai eulogia kai katara. Ou chrei, adelphoi mou, tauta 'outos ginesthai.

י. מִפֶּה אֶחָד תֵּצֵא בְרָכָה וּקְלָלָה לֹא־כֵן אַחַי לֹא־יֵעָשֶׂה כֵן בָּכֶם:

10. Mi•pe e•chad te•tze v`ra•cha ook•la•la lo - chen a•chai lo - ye•a•se chen ba•chem.

---

11. Doth a fountain send forth at the same place sweet water and bitter?

11. Μήτι ἡ πηγὴ ἐκ τῆς αὐτῆς ὀπῆς βρύει τὸ γλυκὺ καὶ τὸ πικρόν;

11. Meiti 'ei peigei ek teis auteis opeis bruei to gluku kai to pikron?

יא. הֲתָקִיר בְּאֵר מֵימֶיהָ מְתוּקִים וּמָרִים מִמּוֹצָא אֶחָד:

11. Ha•ta•kir be•er mey•mey•ha me•too•kim oo•ma•rim mi•mo•tza e•chad?

Rabbinic Jewish Commentary
"Or hole"; for at divers places, and at different times, as Pliny (m) observes, it may send forth,

sweet water and bitter: and it is reported (n), there is a lake with the Trogloditae, a people in Ethiopia, which becomes thrice a day bitter, and then as often sweet; but then it does not yield sweet water and bitter at the same time: this simile is used to show how unnatural it is that blessing and cursing should proceed out of the same mouth.

(m) Nat. Hist. l. 2. c. 103. (n) Isodor. Hispal. Originum, l. 13. c. 13. p. 115.

James 3

12. Can the fig tree, my brethren, bear olive berries? either a vine, figs? so can no fountain both yield salt water and fresh.

12. Μὴ δύναται, ἀδελφοί μου, συκῆ ἐλαίας ποιῆσαι, ἢ ἄμπελος σῦκα; Οὕτως οὐδεμία πηγὴ ἁλυκὸν καὶ γλυκὺ ποιῆσαι ὕδωρ.

12. Mei dunatai, adelphoi mou, sukei elaias poieisai, ei ampelos suka? 'Outos oudemia peigei 'alukon kai gluku poieisai 'udor.

יב. הֲתַעֲשֶׂה תְאֵנָה אַחַי עִנְבֵי גֶפֶן וְהַגֶּפֶן הֲתוֹצִיא תְאֵנִים כֵּן מִמַּיִם מְלוּחִים לֹא יֵצְאוּ מְתוּקִים:

12. Ha•ta•a•se te•e•na a•chai een•vey ge•fen ve•ha•ge•fen ha•to•tzi te•e•nim ken mi•ma•yim me•loo•chim lo yetz•oo me•too•kim.

Rabbinic Jewish Commentary
so can no fountain both yield salt water and fresh. The Alexandrian copy reads, "neither can the salt water yield sweet water"; that is, the sea cannot yield sweet or fresh water: the Syriac version renders it, "neither can salt water be made sweet": but naturalists say, it may be made sweet, by being strained through sand: the design of these similes is to observe how absurd a thing it is that a man should both bless and curse with his tongue.

---

13. Who is a wise man and endued with knowledge among you? let him shew out of a good conversation his works with meekness of wisdom.

13. Τίς σοφὸς καὶ ἐπιστήμων ἐν ὑμῖν; Δειξάτω ἐκ τῆς καλῆς ἀναστροφῆς τὰ ἔργα αὐτοῦ ἐν πραΰτητι σοφίας.

13. Tis sophos kai episteimon en 'umin? Deixato ek teis kaleis anastropheis ta erga autou en prauteiti sophias.

יג. מִי חָכָם וְנָבוֹן בָּכֶם יַרְאֵנוּ אֶת-מַעֲשָׂיו מִתּוֹךְ מַעְגְּלֵי חַיָּיו הַטּוֹבִים בְּעַנְוַת חָכְמָתוֹ:

13. Mee cha•cham ve•na•von ba•chem yar•e•noo et - ma•a•sav mi•toch ma•ag•ley cha•yav ha•to•vim be•an•vat choch•ma•to.

James 3

14. But if ye have bitter envying and strife in your hearts, glory not, and lie not against the truth.

14. Εἰ δὲ ζῆλον πικρὸν ἔχετε καὶ ἐριθείαν ἐν τῇ καρδίᾳ ὑμῶν, μὴ κατακαυχᾶσθε καὶ ψεύδεσθε κατὰ τῆς ἀληθείας.

14. Ei de zeilon pikron echete kai eritheian en tei kardia 'umon, mei katakauchasthe kai pseudesthe kata teis aleitheias.

יד: וְאִם-חֲמַת קִנְאָה בָכֶם וּלְבַבְכֶם יִגְרֶה מָדוֹן לָמָּה תִּתְהַלָּלוּ וּתְכַחֲשׁוּ נֶגֶד פְּנֵי הָאֱמֶת

14. Ve•eem - cha•mat kin•ah va•chem ve•lib•chem ye•ga•re ma•don la•ma tit•ha•le•loo oot•cha•che•shoo ne•ged p`ney ha•e•met.

---

15. This wisdom descendeth not from above, but is earthly, sensual, devilish.

15. Οὐκ ἔστιν αὕτη ἡ σοφία ἄνωθεν κατερχομένη, ἀλλ᾽ ἐπίγειος, ψυχική, δαιμονιώδης.

15. Ouk estin 'autei 'ei sophia anothen katerchomenei, all epigeios, psuchikei, daimoniodeis.

טו: לֹא זוּ הַחָכְמָה הַבָּאָה מֵעָל כִּי הִיא מִלְמַטָּה לָאָרֶץ מִטֶּבַע הַבָּשָׂר אוֹ הַשֵּׁדִים

15. Lo zoo ha•choch•ma ha•ba•ah me•al ki hee mil•ma•ta la•a•retz mi•te•va ha•ba•sar oh ha•she•dim.

Rabbinic Jewish Commentary

The Jews say (o) of the wisdom of Egypt, may be said of this, that it is חכמה תתאה "wisdom from below"

(o) Zohar in Gen. fol. 119. 2.

---

16. For where envying and strife is, there is confusion and every evil work.

16. Ὅπου γὰρ ζῆλος καὶ ἐριθεία, ἐκεῖ ἀκαταστασία καὶ πᾶν φαῦλον πρᾶγμα.

16. 'Opou gar zeilos kai eritheia, ekei akatastasia kai pan phaulon pragma.

טז. כִּי-בִמְקוֹם קִנְאָה וּמְדָנִים שָׁם מְהוּמָה וְכָל-דְּבַר בְּלִיָּעַל:

16. Ki - vim•kom kin•ah oom•da•nim sham me•hoo•ma ve•chol - de•var be•li•ya•al.

James 3

17. But the wisdom that is from above is first pure, then peaceable, gentle, and easy to be intreated, full of mercy and good fruits, without partiality, and without hypocrisy.

17. Ἡ δὲ ἄνωθεν σοφία πρῶτον μὲν ἁγνή ἐστιν, ἔπειτα εἰρηνική, ἐπιεικής, εὐπειθής, μεστὴ ἐλέους καὶ καρπῶν ἀγαθῶν, ἀδιάκριτος καὶ ἀνυπόκριτος.

17. 'Ei de anothen sophia proton men 'agnei estin, epeita eireinikei, epieikeis, eupeitheis, mestei eleous kai karpon agathon, adyakritos kai anupokritos.

יז. אַךְ הַחָכְמָה הַיֹּרֶדֶת מֵעַל טְהוֹרָה הִיא פִּיהָ תִּפְתַּח לְשָׁלוֹם וּבַעֲנָוָה דְבָרֶיהָ נֹחָה הִיא לְהִתְרַצּוֹת מְלֵאָה:רַחֲמִים וּפִרְיָהּ טוֹב אֵין עִמָּהּ מַשּׂא פָנִים וְאֵין חֲנֻפָּה בָּהּ

17. Ach ha•choch•ma ha•yo•re•det me•al te•ho•ra hee pi•ha tif•tach le•sha•lom oo•va•ana•va d`va•re•ha no•cha hee le•hit•ra•tzot me•le•ah ra•cha•mim oo•fir•ya tov eyn ee•ma ma•so fa•nim ve•eyn cha•noo•pa ba.

---

18. And the fruit of righteousness is sown in peace of them that make peace.

18. Καρπὸς δὲ τῆς δικαιοσύνης ἐν εἰρήνῃ σπείρεται τοῖς ποιοῦσιν εἰρήνην.

18. Karpos de teis dikaiosuneis en eireinei speiretai tois poiousin eireinein.

:יח. זֶה פְּרִי הַצְּדָקָה זֶרַע לָבֶטַח לְעֹשֵׂי שָׁלוֹם

18. Ze p`ri ha•tz`da•ka za•roo•a la•ve•tach le•o•sey sha•lom.

(James Chapter 3 End)

James, Chapter 4

1. From whence come wars and fightings among you? come they not hence, even of your lusts that war in your members?

1. Πόθεν πόλεμοι καὶ μάχαι ἐν ὑμῖν; Οὐκ ἐντεῦθεν, ἐκ τῶν ἡδονῶν ὑμῶν τῶν στρατευομένων ἐν τοῖς μέλεσιν ὑμῶν;

1. Pothen polemoi kai machai en 'umin? Ouk enteuthen, ek ton 'eidonon 'umon ton strateuomenon en tois melesin 'umon?

א. מֵאַיִן תִּגְרָה וּמִלְחָמוֹת בֵּינֵיכֶם אִם לֹא מִתּוֹךְ הַתַּאֲוֹת הַפֹּרְצוֹת בְּאֵבָרֵיכֶם:

1. Me•a•yin tig•ra oo•mil•cha•mot bey•ney•chem eem lo mi•toch ha•ta•a•vot ha•por•tzot be•e•va•rey•chem?

---

2. Ye lust, and have not: ye kill, and desire to have, and cannot obtain: ye fight and war, yet ye have not, because ye ask not.

2. Ἐπιθυμεῖτε, καὶ οὐκ ἔχετε· φονεύετε καὶ ζηλοῦτε, καὶ οὐ δύνασθε ἐπιτυχεῖν· μάχεσθε καὶ πολεμεῖτε, οὐκ ἔχετε διὰ τὸ μὴ αἰτεῖσθαι ὑμᾶς·

2. Epithumeite, kai ouk echete. phoneuete kai zeiloute, kai ou dunasthe epituchein. Machesthe kai polemeite, ouk echete dya to mei aiteisthai 'umas.

ב. תִּתְאַוּוּ וְאֵין לָכֶם תְּרַצְּחוּ וּתְקַנְאוּ וִידֵיכֶם לֹא תַעֲשֶׂינָה תּוּשִׁיָּה תִּתְגָּרוּ וְתִלָּחֲמוּ וְאֵין לָכֶם מְאוּמָה יַעַן לֹא שְׁאֶלְתֶּם:

2. Tit•a•voo ve•eyn la•chem te•ratz•choo oot•kan•oo viy•dey•chem lo ta•a•sei•na too•shi•ya tit•ge•roo ve•ti•la•cha•moo ve•eyn la•chem me•oo•ma ya•an lo sh`el•tem.

---

3. Ye ask, and receive not, because ye ask amiss, that ye may consume it upon your lusts.

3. αἰτεῖτε, καὶ οὐ λαμβάνετε, διότι κακῶς αἰτεῖσθε, ἵνα ἐν ταῖς ἡδοναῖς ὑμῶν δαπανήσητε.

3. aiteite, kai ou lambanete, dioti kakos aiteisthe, 'ina en tais 'eidonais 'umon dapaneiseite.

ג. שְׁאֶלְתֶּם וְלֹא הִשַּׂגְתֶּם יַעַן בְּרָעָה שְׁאֶלְתֶּם לְמַלֵּא מִשְׁאֲלוֹת תַּאֲוַתְכֶם:

3. Sh`el•tem ve•lo hi•sag•tem ya•an be•ra•ah sh`el•tem le•ma•le mish•a•lot ta•a•vat•chem.

James 4

4. Ye adulterers and adulteresses, know ye not that the friendship of the world is enmity with God? whosoever therefore will be a friend of the world is the enemy of God.

4. Μοιχοὶ καὶ μοιχαλίδες, οὐκ οἴδατε ὅτι ἡ φιλία τοῦ κόσμου ἔχθρα τοῦ θεοῦ ἐστιν; Ὃς ἂν οὖν βουληθῇ φίλος εἶναι τοῦ κόσμου, ἐχθρὸς τοῦ θεοῦ καθίσταται.

4. Moichoi kai moichalides, ouk oidate 'oti 'ei philia tou kosmou echthra tou theou estin? 'Os an oun bouleithei philos einai tou kosmou, echthros tou theou kathistatai.

ד. הַאִם לֹא יְדַעְתֶּם נֹאֲפִים וְנֹאֲפוֹת כִּי-אַהֲבַת הָעוֹלָם אֵיבָה הִיא לֵאלֹהִים לָזֹאת אֵפוֹא מִי הוּא הֶחָפֵץ לִהְיוֹת:אֹהֵב הָעוֹלָם אֹיֵב לֵאלֹהִים יֵחָשֵׁב

4. Ha•eem lo ye•da•a•tem no•a•fim ve•no•a•fot ki - a•ha•vat ha•o•lam ey•va hee le•Elohim le•zot e•fo mee hoo he•cha•fetz li•hee•yot o•hev ha•o•lam o•yev le•Elohim ye•cha•shev.

---

5. Do ye think that the scripture saith in vain, The spirit that dwelleth in us lusteth to envy?

5. Ἦ δοκεῖτε ὅτι κενῶς ἡ γραφὴ λέγει; Πρὸς φθόνον ἐπιποθεῖ τὸ πνεῦμα ὃ κατῴκησεν ἐν ἡμῖν.

5. Ei dokeite 'oti kenos 'ei graphei legei? Pros phthonon epipothei to pneuma 'o katokeisen en 'eimin.

ה. הַאִם תַּחְשְׁבוּן כִּי הַמִּקְרָא יַזְהִיר לָרִיק וְהָרוּחַ הַשֹּׁכֵן בְּקִרְבֵּנוּ הַאִם תַּאֲוָתוֹ קִנְאָה:

5. Ha•eem tach•she•voon ki ha•mik•ra yaz•hir la•rik ve•ha•roo•ach ha•sho•chen be•kir•be•noo ha•eem ta•a•va•to kin•ah.

Rabbinic Jewish Commentary

Some think that the apostle refers to a particular passage of Scripture in the Old Testament, and that he took it from Gen.6:3 as some; or from Exo.20:5, as others; or from Deu.7:2 or from Job.5:6 or from Pro.21:10 others think he had in view some text in the New Testament; either Rom.12:2 or Gal.5:17 and some have imagined that he refers to a passage in the apocryphal book:

"For into a malicious soul wisdom shall not enter; nor dwell in the body that is subject unto sin." (Wisdom 1:4)

James 4

6. But he giveth more grace. Wherefore he saith, God resisteth the proud, but giveth grace unto the humble.

6. Μείζονα δὲ δίδωσιν χάριν· διὸ λέγει, Ὁ θεὸς ὑπερηφάνοις ἀντιτάσσεται, ταπεινοῖς δὲ δίδωσιν χάριν.

6. Meizona de didosin charin. dio legei, 'O theos 'upereiphanois antitassetai, tapeinois de didosin charin.

:ו. אָכֵן הוּא נֹתֵן יֶתֶר חֵן עַל-כֵּן הוּא אֹמֵר יְהֹוָה לַלֵּצִים יָלִיץ וְלַעֲנָוִים יִתֶּן-חֵן

6. A•chen hoo no•ten ye•ter chen al - ken hoo o•mer Adonai la•le•tzim ya•litz ve•la•a•na•vim yi•ten - chen.

---

7. Submit yourselves therefore to God. Resist the devil, and he will flee from you.

7. Ὑποτάγητε οὖν τῷ θεῷ· ἀντίστητε δὲ τῷ διαβόλῳ, καὶ φεύξεται ἀφ᾽ ὑμῶν.

7. 'Upotageite oun to theo. antisteite de to dyabolo, kai pheuxetai aph 'umon.

:ז. לָכֵן הִכָּנְעוּ מִפְּנֵי אֱלֹהִים הִתְיַצְּבוּ בִּפְנֵי הַשָּׂטָן וְיָנוּס מִפְּנֵיכֶם

7. La·chen hi·kan·oo mip·ney Elohim hit·yatz·voo bif·ney ha·Satan ve·ya·noos mip·ney·chem.

James 4

8. Draw nigh to God, and he will draw nigh to you. Cleanse your hands, ye sinners; and purify your hearts, ye double minded.

8. Ἐγγίσατε τῷ θεῷ, καὶ ἐγγιεῖ ὑμῖν· καθαρίσατε χεῖρας, ἁμαρτωλοί, καὶ ἁγνίσατε καρδίας, δίψυχοι.

8. Engisate to theo, kai engiei 'umin. katharisate cheiras, 'amartoloi, kai 'agnisate kardias, dipsuchoi.

ח. קִרְבוּ אֶל-אֱלֹהִים וְיִקְרַב אֲלֵיכֶם רַחֲצוּ יְדֵיכֶם מְתֵי-אָוֶן הִזַּכּוּ בִלְבַבְכֶם בַּעֲלֵי לֵב וָלֵב:

8. Kir·voo el - Elohim ve·yik·rav aley·chem ra·cha·tzoo ye·dey·chem me·tey – aven hi·za·koo vil·vav·chem ba·a·ley lev va·lev.

9. Be afflicted, and mourn, and weep: let your laughter be turned to mourning, and your joy to heaviness.

9. Ταλαιπωρήσατε καὶ πενθήσατε καὶ κλαύσατε· ὁ γέλως ὑμῶν εἰς πένθος μεταστραφήτω, καὶ ἡ χαρὰ εἰς κατήφειαν.

9. Talaiporeisate kai pentheisate kai klausate. 'o gelos 'umon eis penthos metastrapheito, kai 'ei chara eis kateipheyan.

ט. הִתְעַצְּבוּ הִתְאַבְּלוּ וְהֵילִילוּ שְׂחוֹק יֵהָפֵךְ לָכֶם לְאֵבֶל וְשִׂמְחָה לְתוּגָה:

9. Hit·atz·voo hit·ab·loo ve·hey·li·loo s`chok ye·ha·fech la·chem le·e·vel ve·sim·cha le·too·ga.

10. Humble yourselves in the sight of the Lord, and he shall lift you up.

10. Ταπεινώθητε ἐνώπιον τοῦ κυρίου, καὶ ὑψώσει ὑμᾶς.

10. Tapeinotheite enopion tou kuriou, kai 'upsosei 'umas.

:י. הַשְׁפִּילוּ נַפְשְׁכֶם לִפְנֵי יְהֹוָה וְהוּא יָרִים אֶתְכֶם

10. Hash•pi•loo naf•she•chem lif•ney Adonai ve•hoo ya•rim et•chem.

James 4

11. Speak not evil one of another, brethren. He that speaketh evil of his brother, and judgeth his brother, speaketh evil of the law, and judgeth the law: but if thou judge the law, thou art not a doer of the law, but a judge.

11. Μὴ καταλαλεῖτε ἀλλήλων, ἀδελφοί. Ὁ καταλαλῶν ἀδελφοῦ, καὶ κρίνων τὸν ἀδελφὸν αὐτοῦ, καταλαλεῖ νόμου, καὶ κρίνει νόμον· εἰ δὲ νόμον κρίνεις, οὐκ εἶ ποιητὴς νόμου, ἀλλὰ κριτής.

11. Mei katalaleite alleilon, adelphoi. 'O katalalon adelphou, kai krinon ton adelphon autou, katalalei nomou, kai krinei nomon. ei de nomon krineis, ouk ei poieiteis nomou, alla kriteis.

יא. אַחַי לֹא תְדַבְּרוּ אִישׁ בַּעֲמִיתוֹ הַמְדַבֵּר בְּאָחִיו וְהַדָּן אֶת-אָחִיו הוּא מְדַבֵּר בַּתּוֹרָה וְדָן אֶת-הַתּוֹרָה וְאִם אֶת:הַתּוֹרָה תָדִין אֵינְךָ עֹשֶׂה הַתּוֹרָה כִּי אִם-שֹׁפְטָהּ

11. A•chai lo te•dab•roo eesh ba•a•mi•to ha•me•da•ber be•a•chiv ve•ha•dan et - a•chiv hoo me•da•ber ba•To•rah ve•dan et - ha•Torah ve•eem et - ha•Torah ta•din eyn•cha o•se ha•Torah ki eem - shof•ta.

---

12. There is one lawgiver, who is able to save and to destroy: who art thou that judgest another?

12. Εἷς ἐστιν ὁ νομοθέτης, ὁ δυνάμενος σῶσαι καὶ ἀπολέσαι· σὺ δὲ τίς εἶ ὃς κρίνεις τὸν ἕτερον;

12. 'Eis estin 'o nomotheteis, 'o dunamenos sosai kai apolesai. su de tis ei 'os krineis ton 'eteron?

יב. אֶחָד הוּא הַמְחֹקֵק וְהַשֹׁפֵט הוּא אֲשֶׁר הַכֹּחַ בְּיָדוֹ לְהַצִּיל וּלְאַבֵּד וּמִי אַתָּה הוּא כִּי תִשְׁפֹּט אֶת-עֲמִיתֶךָ:

12. E•chad hoo ham•cho•kek ve•ha•sho•fet hoo asher ha•ko•ach be•ya•do le•ha•tzil ool•a•bed oo•mi ata hoo ki tish•pot et - ami•te•cha.

Rabbinic Jewish Commentary

There is one lawgiver,.... The Alexandrian copy, and others, and the Syriac, Ethiopic, and Vulgate Latin versions, add, "and judge". Who is the one only Lord God, Isa.33:22.

who art thou that judgest another? another man's servant, as in Rom.14:4 or "thy neighbour", as the Syriac and Ethiopic versions read; or "the neighbour", as the Alexandrian copy, and the Vulgate Latin version; that is, any brother, friend, or neighbour, in the manner as before observed in the preceding verse.

James 4

13. Go to now, ye that say, To day or to morrow we will go into such a city, and continue there a year, and buy and sell, and get gain:

13. Ἄγε νῦν οἱ λέγοντες, Σήμερον καὶ αὔριον πορευσώμεθα εἰς τήνδε τὴν πόλιν, καὶ ποιήσωμεν ἐκεῖ ἐνιαυτὸν ἕνα, καὶ ἐμπορευσώμεθα, καὶ κερδήσωμεν·

13. Age nun 'oi legontes, Seimeron kai aurion poreusometha eis teinde tein polin, kai poieisomen ekei enyauton 'ena, kai emporeusometha, kai kerdeisomen.

יג. הוֹי הָאוֹמְרִים נֵלְכָה לָּנוּ הַיּוֹם אוֹ לְמָחָר לָעִיר הַהִיא וְנִסְחַר שָׁם שָׁנָה אַחַת וְנַעֲשֶׂה לָּנוּ חָיִל:

13. Hoy ha•om•rim nel•cha la•noo ha•yom oh le•ma•char la•eer ha•hee ve•nis•char sham sha•na a•chat ve•na•a•se la•noo cha•yil.

---

14. Whereas ye know not what shall be on the morrow. For what is your life? It is even a vapour, that appeareth for a little time, and then vanisheth away.

14. οἵτινες οὐκ ἐπίστασθε τὸ τῆς αὔριον. Ποία γὰρ ἡ ζωὴ ὑμῶν; Ἀτμὶς γὰρ ἔσται ἡ πρὸς ὀλίγον φαινομένη, ἔπειτα δὲ καὶ ἀφανιζομένη.

14. 'oitines ouk epistasthe to teis aurion. Poia gar 'ei zoei 'umon? Atmis gar estai 'ei pros oligon phainomenei, epeita de kai aphanizomenei.

יד. וְאַתֶּם לֹא תֵדְעוּן מַה-יֵּלֶד יוֹם מָחָר כִּי מֶה חַיֵּיכֶם כִּיתוֹר יֵרָאֶה כְּרֶגַע וְאַחַר יַעֲלֶה בַתֹּהוּ:

14. Ve•a•tem lo ted•oon ma - ye•led yom ma•char ki me cha•yey•chem ki•tor ye•ra•eh ke•re•ga ve•a•char ya•a•le va•to•hoo.

James 4

15. For that ye ought to say, If the Lord will, we shall live, and do this, or that.

15. Ἀντὶ τοῦ λέγειν ὑμᾶς, Ἐὰν ὁ κύριος θελήσῃ, καὶ ζήσωμεν, καὶ ποιήσωμεν τοῦτο ἢ ἐκεῖνο.

15. Anti tou legein 'umas, Ean 'o kurios theleisei, kai zeisomen, kai poieisomen touto ei ekeino.

טו. אַךְ כָּזֹאת עֲלֵיכֶם לֵאמֹר אִם-יִרְצֶה יְהֹוָה וְנִחְיֶה נַעֲשֶׂה כָזֹאת אוֹ כָזֹאת:

15. Ach ka•zot aley•chem le•mor eem - yir•tze Adonai ve•nich•ye na•a•se cha•zot oh ka•zot.

Rabbinic Jewish Commentary

if the Lord will, and we shall live, and do this and that; The last "and" is left out in the Vulgate Latin, Syriac, Arabic, and Ethiopic versions; and the passage rendered thus, "If the Lord will, and we shall live, we will do this"

It is a saying of Ben Syra, the Jew (p),

"Let a man never say he will do anything, before he says אם גוזר השם, "if God will""

So Cyrus, king of Persia, when, under pretence of hunting, he designed an expedition into Armenia, upon which an hare started, and was caught by an eagle, said to his friends, this will be a good or prosperous hunting to us, ην θεος θελη, "if God will" (q). And very remarkable are the words of Socrates to Alcibiades, inquiring of him how he ought to speak; says Socrates, εας θεος εθελη, "if God will" (r); and says he, in another place (s),

"But I will do this, and come unto thee tomorrow, "if God will"."
And it is reported of the Turks (t), that they submit everything to the divine will; as the success of war, or a journey, or anything, even of the least

moment, they desire to be done; and never promise themselves, or others, anything, but under this condition, "In Shallah", if God will.

(p) Sentent. 11. (q) Xenophon. Cyropaed. l. 2. c. 25. (r) Plato in Aleibiade, p. 135. (s) Plato in Laches. (t) Smith de Moribus Turc. p. 74.

James 4

16. But now ye rejoice in your boastings: all such rejoicing is evil.

16. Νῦν δὲ καυχᾶσθε ἐν ταῖς ἀλαζονείαις ὑμῶν· πᾶσα καύχησις τοιαύτη πονηρά ἐστιν.

16. Nun de kauchasthe en tais alazoneiais 'umon. pasa kaucheisis toyautei poneira estin.

טז. רַק אַתֶּם מִתְהַלֲלִים בְּגַאֲוַתְכֶם כָּל־תְּהִלָה כָזֹאת רָעָה הִיא:

16. Rak atem mit•ha•le•lim be•ge•oot•chem kol - te•hi•la cha•zot ra•ah hee.

17. Therefore to him that knoweth to do good, and doeth it not, to him it is sin.

17. Εἰδότι οὖν καλὸν ποιεῖν καὶ μὴ ποιοῦντι, ἁμαρτία αὐτῷ ἐστιν.

17. Eidoti oun kalon poiein kai mei poiounti, 'amartia auto estin.

יז. וְכָל־הַיּוֹדֵעַ לַעֲשׂוֹת טוֹב וְכַיָּשָׁר וְלֹא יַעֲשֶׂנּוּ חֶטְאוֹ יִשָּׂא:

17. Ve•chol - ha•yo•dea la•a•sot ka•tov ve•cha•ya•shar ve•lo ya•a•se•noo chet•oh yi•sa.

(James Chapter 4 End)

James, Chapter 5

1. Go to now, ye rich men, weep and howl for your miseries that shall come upon you.

1. Ἄγε νῦν οἱ πλούσιοι, κλαύσατε ὀλολύζοντες ἐπὶ ταῖς ταλαιπωρίαις ὑμῶν ταῖς ἐπερχομέναις.

1. Age nun 'oi plousioi, klausate ololuzontes epi tais talaiporiais 'umon tais eperchomenais.

א: הוֹי עֲשִׁירֵי עָם זַעֲקוּ הֵילִילוּ לַצָּרוֹת אֲשֶׁר תִּקְרֶינָה אֶתְכֶם

1. Hoy ashi•rey am za•a•koo hey•li•loo la•tza•rot asher tik•re•na et•chem.

---

2. Your riches are corrupted, and your garments are motheaten.

2. Ὁ πλοῦτος ὑμῶν σέσηπεν, καὶ τὰ ἱμάτια ὑμῶν σητόβρωτα γέγονεν·

2. 'O ploutos 'umon seseipen, kai ta 'imatya 'umon seitobrota gegonen.

ב: עָשְׁרְכֶם רָקַב וּבִגְדֵיכֶם יֹאכַל עָשׁ

2. Osh•re•chem ra•kav oo•vig•dey•chem yo•chal ash.

---

3. Your gold and silver is cankered; and the rust of them shall be a witness against you, and shall eat your flesh as it were fire. Ye have heaped treasure together for the last days.

3. ὁ χρυσὸς ὑμῶν καὶ ὁ ἄργυρος κατίωται, καὶ ὁ ἰὸς αὐτῶν εἰς μαρτύριον ὑμῖν ἔσται, καὶ φάγεται τὰς σάρκας ὑμῶν ὡς πῦρ. Ἐθησαυρίσατε ἐν ἐσχάταις ἡμέραις.

3. 'o chrusos 'umon kai 'o arguros katiotai, kai 'o ios auton eis marturion 'umin estai, kai phagetai tas sarkas 'umon 'os pur. Etheisaurisate en eschatais 'eimerais.

ג. הַזָּהָב יוּעַם הַכֶּסֶף יִשָּׂנֵא וְהוֹן נִמְאָס הַזֶּה יַעֲנֶה בָכֶם לְעֵד וְאָכַל בִּשְׂרְכֶם כָּאֵשׁ זֶה הוּא הָאוֹצָר אֲצַרְתֶּם לָכֶם:לְיוֹם אַחֲרוֹן

3. Ha•za•hav yoo•am ha•ke•sef yish•ne ve•hon nim•as ha•ze ya•a•ne va•chem le•ed ve•a•chal be•sar•chem ka•esh ze hoo ha•o•tzar atzar•tem la•chem le•yom acha•ron.

James 5

4. Behold, the hire of the labourers who have reaped down your fields, which is of you kept back by fraud, crieth: and the cries of them which have reaped are entered into the ears of the Lord of sabaoth.

4. Ἰδού, ὁ μισθὸς τῶν ἐργατῶν τῶν ἀμησάντων τὰς χώρας ὑμῶν, ὁ ἀπεστερημένος ἀφ᾽ ὑμῶν, κράζει· καὶ αἱ βοαὶ τῶν θερισάντων εἰς τὰ ὦτα κυρίου Σαβαὼθ εἰσεληλύθασιν.

4. Ydou, 'o misthos ton ergaton ton ameisanton tas choras 'umon, 'o apestereimenos aph 'umon, krazei. kai 'ai boai ton therisanton eis ta ota kuriou Sabaoth eiseleiluthasin.

ד. הִנֵּה שְׂכַר הַפֹּעֲלִים יִזְעַק שְׂכַר קֹצְרֵי שְׂדֹתֵיכֶם אֲשֶׁר עֲשַׁקְתֶּם וְזַעֲקַת הַקֹּצְרִים בָּאָה בְּאָזְנֵי יְהוָה צְבָאוֹת:

4. Hee•ne s`char ha•po•a•lim yiz•ak s`char kotz•rey s`do•tey•chem asher a•shak•tem ve•za•a•kat ha•kotz•rim ba•ah ve•oz•ney Adonai Tz`va•ot.

---

5. Ye have lived in pleasure on the earth, and been wanton; ye have nourished your hearts, as in a day of slaughter.

5. Ἐτρυφήσατε ἐπὶ τῆς γῆς καὶ ἐσπαταλήσατε· ἐθρέψατε τὰς καρδίας ὑμῶν ὡς ἐν ἡμέρᾳ σφαγῆς.

5. Etrupheisate epi teis geis kai espataleisate. ethrepsate tas kardias 'umon 'os en 'eimera sphageis.

ה. הִתְעַנַּגְתֶּם בָּאָרֶץ הִתְעַדַּנְתֶּם וַיִּשְׁמַן לִבְּכֶם כְּמוֹ לְיוֹם טִבְחָה:

5. Hit•a•nag•tem ba•a•retz hit•a•dan•tem va•yish•man lib•chem k`mo le•yom tiv•cha.

6. Ye have condemned and killed the just; and he doth not resist you.

6. Κατεδικάσατε, ἐφονεύσατε τὸν δίκαιον· οὐκ ἀντιτάσσεται ὑμῖν.

6. Katedikasate, ephoneusate ton dikaion. ouk antitassetai 'umin.

ו. הִרְשַׁעְתֶּם הֲמִיתֶּם אֶת-הַצַּדִּיק וְהוּא לֹא-עָמַד בִּפְנֵיכֶם:

6. Hir•sha•a•tem ha•mi•tem et - ha•tza•dik ve•hoo lo - amad bif•ney•chem.

James 5

7. Be patient therefore, brethren, unto the coming of the Lord. Behold, the husbandman waiteth for the precious fruit of the earth, and hath long patience for it, until he receive the early and latter rain.

7. Μακροθυμήσατε οὖν, ἀδελφοί, ἕως τῆς παρουσίας τοῦ κυρίου. Ἰδού, ὁ γεωργὸς ἐκδέχεται τὸν τίμιον καρπὸν τῆς γῆς, μακροθυμῶν ἐπ᾽ αὐτόν, ἕως λάβῃ ὑετὸν πρώϊμον καὶ ὄψιμον.

7. Makrothumeisate oun, adelphoi, 'eos teis parousias tou kuriou. Ydou, 'o georgos ekdechetai ton timion karpon teis geis, makrothumon ep auton, 'eos labei 'ueton proimon kai opsimon.

ז. עַל-כֵּן דֹּמוּ אַחַי עַד-בֹּא הָאָדוֹן הִנֵּה הָאִכָּר יְחַכֶּה לִתְבוּאַת הָאֲדָמָה הַטּוֹבָה יְיַחֵל עַד-אֲשֶׁר יָבוֹא יוֹרֶה:וּמַלְקוֹשׁ

7. Al - ken do•moo a•chai ad - bo ha•Adon hee•ne ha•ee•kar ye•cha•ke lit•voo•at ha•a•da•ma ha•to•va ye•ya•chel ad - asher ya•vo yo•re oo•mal•kosh.

Rabbinic Jewish Commentary

The Jews had seldom rains any more than twice a year; the early, or former rain, was shortly after the feast of tabernacles (u), in the month Marchesvan, or October, when the seed was sown in the earth; and if it did not rain, they prayed for it, on the third or seventh day of the month (w); and the latter rain was in Nisan, or March (x), just before harvest; and to this distinction the passage refers.

(u) Bartenora in Misn. Taanith, c. 1. sect. 2. (w) T. Bab. Taanith, fol. 4. 2. & 6. 1. & 10. 1. & Bava Metzia, fol. 28. 1. Maimon. Tephilla, c. 2. sect.

16. (x) Targum, Jarchi, Kimchi, & Miclol Jophi in Joel ii. 23. Vajikra Rabba, sect. 35. fol. 175. 3.

James 5

8. Be ye also patient; stablish your hearts: for the coming of the Lord draweth nigh.

8. Μακροθυμήσατε καὶ ὑμεῖς, στηρίξατε τὰς καρδίας ὑμῶν, ὅτι ἡ παρουσία τοῦ κυρίου ἤγγικεν.

8. Makrothumeisate kai 'umeis, steirixate tas kardias 'umon, 'oti 'ei parousia tou kuriou eingiken.

‎:ח. כֵּן הוֹחִילוּ גַם-אַתֶּם אַמְּצוּ אֶת-לִבְכֶם כִּי פְּנֵי הָאָדוֹן הִנֵּה בָּאִים

8. Ken ho•chi•loo gam - atem am•tzoo et - lib•chem ki f ney ha•Adon hee•ne ba•eem.

9. Grudge not one against another, brethren, lest ye be condemned: behold, the judge standeth before the door.

9. Μὴ στενάζετε κατ᾽ ἀλλήλων, ἀδελφοί, ἵνα μὴ κριθῆτε· ἰδού, ὁ κριτὴς πρὸ τῶν θυρῶν ἕστηκεν.

9. Mei stenazete kat alleilon, adelphoi, 'ina mei kritheite. idou, 'o kriteis pro ton thuron 'esteiken.

‎:ט. אַל-תִּלּוֹנוּ אַחַי אִישׁ עַל-רֵעֵהוּ וְלֹא תֵאָשְׁמוּ בַּמִּשְׁפָּט הִנֵּה הַשֹּׁפֵט עֹמֵד לַפָּתַח

9. Al - ti•lo•noo a•chai eesh al - re•e•hoo ve•lo te•esh•moo va•mish•pat hee•ne ha•sho•fet o•med la•pe•tach.

10. Take, my brethren, the prophets, who have spoken in the name of the Lord, for an example of suffering affliction, and of patience.

10. Ὑπόδειγμα λάβετε, ἀδελφοί μου, τῆς κακοπαθείας, καὶ τῆς μακροθυμίας, τοὺς προφήτας οἳ ἐλάλησαν τῷ ὀνόματι κυρίου.

10. 'Upodeigma labete, adelphoi mou, teis kakopatheias, kai teis makrothumias, tous propheitas 'oi elaleisan to onomati kuriou.

י. קְחוּ לָכֶם אַחַי לְמוֹפֵת צָרוֹת הַנְּבִיאִים וְאֹרֶךְ רוּחָם הַנְּבִיאִים אֲשֶׁר דִּבְּרוּ בְּשֵׁם יְהֹוָה:

10. Ke•choo la•chem a•chai le•mo•fet tza•rot ha•n`vi•eem ve•o•rech roo•cham ha•n`vi•eem asher dib•roo be•shem Adonai.

James 5

11. Behold, we count them happy which endure. Ye have heard of the patience of Job, and have seen the end of the Lord; that the Lord is very pitiful, and of tender mercy.

11. Ἰδού, μακαρίζομεν τοὺς ὑπομένοντας· τὴν ὑπομονὴν Ἰὼβ ἠκούσατε, καὶ τὸ τέλος κυρίου ἴδετε, ὅτι πολύσπλαγχνός ἐστιν καὶ οἰκτίρμων.

11. Ydou, makarizomen tous 'upomenontas. tein 'upomonein Yob eikousate, kai to telos kuriou idete, 'oti polusplagchnos estin kai oiktirmon.

יא. הִנֵּה אֲנַחְנוּ מְאַשְּׁרִים כֹּחַ הַסַּבָּל וְכֹחַ סִבְלוֹת אִיּוֹב הֲלֹא שְׁמַעְתֶּם וְגַם רְאִיתֶם מֶה-הָיְתָה אַחֲרִיתוֹ מֵאֵת:יְהֹוָה כִּי יְהֹוָה רַחוּם וְחַנּוּן הוּא

11. Hee•ne a•nach•noo me•ash•rim ko•ach ha•sa•bal ve•cho•ach siv•lot Ee•yov ha•lo sh`ma•a•tem ve•gam r`ee•tem me - hai•ta acha•ri•to me•et Adonai ki Adonai ra•choom ve•cha•noon hoo.

Rabbinic Jewish Commentary

Ye have heard of the patience of Job; from the account which is given of him, and his patience, in the book that bears his name; how he behaved under every trial, which came one upon the back of another; as the plundering of his substance, the loss of his children, and of the health of his body; and yet in all this Job sinned not, nor murmured against God, nor charged him foolishly, and was a mirror of patience; and though he afterwards let fall some expressions of impatience, yet he was humbled for them, and brought to repentance: this shows, that as the Apostle James, so the Jews, to whom he writes, believed that there had been really such a man as Job; and that the book which bears his name is an authentic piece of holy Scripture, and contains a narrative of matters of fact; or otherwise this reference to him would have been impertinent. How long Job endured the chastenings of YHVH cannot be said. The Jews (y) say they continued on him twelve months, which they gather from Job.7:3.

(y) Seder Olam Rabba, c. 3. p. 9.

James 5

12. But above all things, my brethren, swear not, neither by heaven, neither by the earth, neither by any other oath: but let your yea be yea; and your nay, nay; lest ye fall into condemnation.

12. Πρὸ πάντων δέ, ἀδελφοί μου, μὴ ὀμνύετε, μήτε τὸν οὐρανόν, μήτε τὴν γῆν, μήτε ἄλλον τινὰ ὅρκον· ἤτω δὲ ὑμῶν τὸ ναί, ναί, καὶ τὸ οὔ, οὔ· ἵνα μὴ εἰς ὑπόκρισιν πέσητε.

12. Pro panton de, adelphoi mou, mei omnuete, meite ton ouranon, meite tein gein, meite allon tina 'orkon. eito de 'umon to nai, nai, kai to ou, ou. 'ina mei eis 'upokrisin peseite.

יב. וְעַתָּה אַחַי לִפְנֵי כָל־דָּבָר אַל־תִּשָּׁבְעוּ לֹא בַשָּׁמַיִם וְלֹא בָאָרֶץ וְלֹא כָל־שְׁבוּעָה אַחֶרֶת הֵן וְכֹה יִהְיֶה דְבַרְכֶם הֵן:אוֹ לֹא לֹא פֶּן־תֵּעָנְשׁוּ בַּמִּשְׁפָּט

12. Ve•a•ta a•chai lif•ney chol - da•var al - ti•shav•oo lo va•sha•ma•yim ve•lo va•a•retz ve•lo chol - sh`voo•ah a•che•ret ve•cho yi•hee•ye d`var•chem hen hen oh lo lo pen - te•an•shoo ba•mish•pat.

---

13. Is any among you afflicted? let him pray. Is any merry? let him sing psalms.

13. Κακοπαθεῖ τις ἐν ὑμῖν; Προσευχέσθω. Εὐθυμεῖ τις; Ψαλλέτω.

13. Kakopathei tis en 'umin? Proseuchestho. Euthumei tis? Psalleto.

יג. אִם־יֵצֶר לְאִישׁ מִכֶּם יִתְפַּלֵּל וְאִם לִבּוֹ טוֹב עָלָיו יְזַמֵּר:

13. Eem - ye•tzar le•eesh mi•kem yit•pa•lel ve•eem li•bo tov alav ye•za•mer.

Rabbinic Jewish Commentary

Weeping, and singing of psalms, were thought, by the Jews, inconsistent. Kimchi, on the title of the third psalm, observes, that their Rabbins say, that when David went up the ascent of the Mount of Olives, he wept; and if he wept, why is this called a psalm? and if a psalm, למה בכה, "why did he weep?"

James 5

14. Is any sick among you? let him call for the elders of the church; and let them pray over him, anointing him with oil in the name of the Lord:

14. Ἀσθενεῖ τις ἐν ὑμῖν; Προσκαλεσάσθω τοὺς πρεσβυτέρους τῆς ἐκκλησίας, καὶ προσευξάσθωσαν ἐπ᾽ αὐτόν, ἀλείψαντες αὐτὸν ἐλαίῳ ἐν τῷ ὀνόματι τοῦ κυρίου·

14. Asthenei tis en 'umin? Proskalesastho tous presbuterous teis ekkleisias, kai proseuxasthosan ep auton, aleipsantes auton elaio en to onomati tou kuriou.

יד. אִם-יִהְיֶה בָכֶם חֹלֶה יִקְרָא לְזִקְנֵי הָעֵדָה וְהִתְפַּלְלוּ עָלָיו וּמָשְׁחוּ אֹתוֹ שֶׁמֶן בְּשֵׁם יְהוָה:

14. Eem - yi•hee•ye ba•chem cho•le yik•ra le•zik•ney ha•e•da ve•hit•pa•le•loo alav oo•mash•choo o•to she•men be•shem Adonai.

Rabbinic Jewish Commentary

It was a kind of proverbial saying of Aristophanes the grammarian;

"The works of young men, the counsels of middle aged persons, and ευχαι γεροντων, "the prayers of ancient men" (z):"

Or rather officers of churches are meant, particularly pastors, who are so called in Scripture; these should be sent for in times of sickness, as well as physicians; and rather than they, since their prayers may be the means of healing both soul and body: so in former times, the prophets of God were sent to in times of sickness, for advice and assistance. It is a saying of R. Phinehas ben Chama (a) that

"Whoever has a sick person in his house, let him go to a wise man, and he will seek mercy for him."

(z) Apud Harpocratian. Lex. p. 125. (a) T. Bab. Bava Bathra, fol. 116. 1.

15. And the prayer of faith shall save the sick, and the Lord shall raise him up; and if he have committed sins, they shall be forgiven him.

15. καὶ ἡ εὐχὴ τῆς πίστεως σώσει τὸν κάμνοντα, καὶ ἐγερεῖ αὐτὸν ὁ κύριος· κἂν ἁμαρτίας ᾖ πεποιηκώς, ἀφεθήσεται αὐτῷ.

15. kai 'ei euchei teis pisteos sosei ton kamnonta, kai egerei auton 'o kurios. kan 'amartias ei pepoieikos, aphetheisetai auto.

טו. וּתְפִלָּה עִם-אֱמוּנָה תַּעֲזֹר לַחֹלֶה וַיהוָה יְקִימֶנּוּ וְאִם חָטָא וְנִסְלַח-לוֹ:

15. Oot•fi•la eem - e•moo•na ta•a•zor la•cho•le va•Adona ye•ki•me•noo ve•eem cha•ta ve•nis•lach - lo.

James 5

16. Confess your faults one to another, and pray one for another, that ye may be healed. The effectual fervent prayer of a righteous man availeth much.

16. Ἐξομολογεῖσθε ἀλλήλοις τὰ παραπτώματα, καὶ εὔχεσθε ὑπὲρ ἀλλήλων, ὅπως ἰαθῆτε. Πολὺ ἰσχύει δέησις δικαίου ἐνεργουμένη.

16. Exomologeisthe alleilois ta paraptomata, kai euchesthe 'uper alleilon, 'opos iatheite. Polu ischuei deeisis dikaiou energoumenei.

טז. לָכֵן הִתְוַדּוּ עֲוֹנוֹתֵיכֶם אִישׁ אֶל-רֵעֵהוּ וְהִתְפַּלְלוּ אִישׁ בְּעַד רֵעֵהוּ וְרָפָא לָכֶם כִּי-תְפִלַּת צַדִּיק רַב כֹּחָהּ:בִּפְעֻלָּתָהּ

16. La•chen hit•va•doo ao•no•tey•chem eesh el - re•e•hoo ve•hit•pa•le•loo eesh be•ad re•e•hoo ve•ra•fa la•chem ki - t`fi•lat tza•dik rav ko•cha bif•oo•la•ta.

Rabbinic Jewish Commentary

The Jews have had formerly a great notion of prayer: the power of prayer, they say (b), is strong; and extol it above all other services: they say (c), it is better than good works, or than offerings and sacrifices; and particularly, the prayer of righteous men: says R. Eliezar (d).

"To what is תפלתן של צדיקים, "prayer of righteous men" like? it is like a shovel: the sense is, that as the shovel turns the corn on the floor, from one place to another, so prayer turns the holy blessed God from wrath to mercy."

(b) Zohar in Exod. fol. 100. 1. (c) T. Bab. Beracot, fol. 32. 2. (d) T. Bab. Succa, fol. 14. 1. & Yebamot, fol. 64. 1.

James 5

17. Elias was a man subject to like passions as we are, and he prayed earnestly that it might not rain: and it rained not on the earth by the space of three years and six months.

17. Ἠλίας ἄνθρωπος ἦν ὁμοιοπαθὴς ἡμῖν, καὶ προσευχῇ προσηύξατο τοῦ μὴ βρέξαι· καὶ οὐκ ἔβρεξεν ἐπὶ τῆς γῆς ἐνιαυτοὺς τρεῖς καὶ μῆνας ἕξ.

17. Eilias anthropos ein 'omoiopatheis 'eimin, kai proseuchei proseiuxato tou mei brexai. kai ouk ebrexen epi teis geis enyautous treis kai meinas 'ex.

יז. אֵלִיָּהוּ הָיָה בַּעַל נֶפֶשׁ כָּמֹנוּ וְהִתְפַּלֵּל לְבִלְתִּי הֱיוֹת מָטָר וְלֹא-הָיָה מָטָר עַל-הָאָרֶץ שָׁלֹשׁ שָׁנִים וְשִׁשָּׁה חֳדָשִׁים:

17. Eli•yahoo ha•ya ba•al ne•fesh ka•mo•noo ve•hit•pa•lel le•vil•ti he•yot ma•tar ve•lo - ha•ya ma•tar al - ha•a•retz sha•losh sha•nim ve•shi•sha cho•da•shim.

Rabbinic Jewish Commentary

The apostle gives an instance of earnest and fervent prayer, and of the efficacy of it in Elias; who is the same with the prophet Elijah, or Elijah the Tishbite; who, by the Septuagint in Mal.4:5 is called Elias, as here, and elsewhere, in the New Testament: of him James says, that he was a "man", contrary to the notion of some of the Jewish writers, who affirm, that Elijah was not born of a father and mother, but was an angel, who was clothed with the four elements of the world (e); but he was not only born, but born in sin, as others are, and was by nature no better than others; and he himself confesses that he was no better than his fathers, 1Ki.19:4.

And he prayed earnestly; or prayed in prayer; an Hebraism: it is said (f) of one, that צלי צלותיה, "he prayed his prayer"; and of others, that צלאן צלותין, "they prayed prayers"; though the phrase here seems to design something more than bare praying; a praying, not merely externally, or formally, and with the lip only, but with the Spirit, and with the understanding, and with the heart engaged in it, with inwrought prayer. The prophet prayed with much earnestness, with great vehemence and intenseness of Spirit, as this Hebraism denotes.

that it might not rain; this is not recorded in express words, but may be gathered from 1Ki.17:1 where he says, "as the Lord God of Israel liveth, before whom I stand, there shall not be dew, nor rain, these years, but according to my word"; so the passage is understood by the Jewish interpreters: the phrase, "before whom I stand", is paraphrased by one of them (g) thus; before whom I am used to stand, בתפילה, "in prayer"; and it is a common saying with the Jews, there is no standing ever mentioned, but prayer is intended; And the other phrase, "according to my word", is, by another (h), interpreted to this sense, that the rain should not descend naturally, according to the custom of the world, but it should descend when Elijah יתפלל עליו, "prayed for it", and so it was.

(e) Zohar in Gen. fol. 31. 1. & Imre Binah in ib. (f) Ib. in Exod. fol. 4. 2. & in Numb. fol. 79. 2. (g) R. David, Kimchi in loc. (h) Vid. Laniado in loc.

James 5

18. And he prayed again, and the heaven gave rain, and the earth brought forth her fruit.

18. Καὶ πάλιν προσηύξατο, καὶ ὁ οὐρανὸς ὑετὸν ἔδωκεν, καὶ ἡ γῆ ἐβλάστησεν τὸν καρπὸν αὐτῆς.

18. Kai palin proseiuxato, kai 'o ouranos 'ueton edoken, kai 'ei gei eblasteisen ton karpon auteis.

יח. וַיָּשָׁב וַיִּתְפַּלֵּל וְהַשָּׁמַיִם הֵרִיפוּ מָטָר וְהָאָרֶץ נָתְנָה אֶת-יְבוּלָהּ:

18. Va•ya•shov va•yit•pa•lel ve•ha•sha•ma•yim he•e•ri•foo ma•tar ve•ha•a•retz nat•na et - ye•voo•la.

Rabbinic Jewish Commentary
1Ki.18:42. Here also is no express mention of his prayer, but it may be concluded from his gestures; and so the Jewish interpreters understand these words, "Elijah went up to the top of Carmel", להתפלל, "to pray, and he cast himself down upon the earth", להתפלל על הגשמים, "to pray for rain; and he put his face between his knees", והתפלל, "and prayed, and said to his servant, go up now, look toward the sea"; and this he said while he was בתפילתו, "in his prayers" (i).

And the earth brought forth her fruit: which for the years past it had not; hence there was a sore famine in the land, 1Ki.18:2. Now the apostle chose to give this example, because it was a common thing for the Jews to ask for rain: we often read of such a doctor, that he prayed for rain, and it came; and of another, that he asked for the rains, and they descended (k): and his view is to observe, that the weakness and infirmities of the saints ought not to discourage them from prayer; and that they should be earnest and fervent in it, as was Elias, a man of like passions with themselves.

(i) Jarchi, Kimchi, Ralbag, & Laniado in loc. (k) T. Bab. Moed Katon, fol. 28. 1. & Taanith, fol. 19. 1. 23. 1. 24. 2. 25. 2. & Yoma, fol. 53. 2.

James 5

19. Brethren, if any of you do err from the truth, and one convert him;

19. Ἀδελφοί, ἐάν τις ἐν ὑμῖν πλανηθῇ ἀπὸ τῆς ἀληθείας, καὶ ἐπιστρέψῃ τις αὐτόν,

19. Adelphoi, ean tis en 'umin planeithei apo teis aleitheias, kai epistrepsei tis auton,

יט. אַחַי אִם אֶחָד מִכֶּם יָסוּר מִדֶּרֶךְ הָאֱמֶת וְאִישׁ אַחֵר יְשִׁיבֶנּוּ:

19. A•chai eem e•chad mi•kem ya•soor mi•de•rech ha•e•met ve•eesh a•cher ye•shi•ve•noo.

20. Let him know, that he which converteth the sinner from the error of his way shall save a soul from death, and shall hide a multitude of sins.

20. γινωσκέτω ὅτι ὁ ἐπιστρέψας ἁμαρτωλὸν ἐκ πλάνης ὁδοῦ αὐτοῦ σώσει ψυχὴν ἐκ θανάτου, καὶ καλύψει πλῆθος ἁμαρτιῶν.

20. ginosketo 'oti 'o epistrepsas 'amartolon ek planeis 'odou autou sosei psuchein ek thanatou, kai kalupsei pleithos 'amartion.

כ. יֵדַע-נָא כִּי הַמֵּשִׁיב אֶת-הַחוֹטֵא מִדֶּרֶךְ פִּשְׁעוֹ יַצִּיל נֶפֶשׁ מִמָּוֶת וִיכַסֶּה עַל-פְּשָׁעִים רַבִּים:

20. Ye•da - na ki ha•me•shiv et - ha•cho•te mi•de•rech pish•oh ya•tzil ne•fesh mi•ma•vet vi•cha•se al - pe•sha•eem ra•bim.

Rabbinic Jewish Commentary

shall save a soul from death;The Alexandrian copy and others, and the Vulgate Latin version read, "his soul"; but the common reading is more emphatic; the Syriac and Arabic versions render it, "his own soul"; and the Ethiopic version, "himself", as respecting him that is the instrument of the conversion of the other, and not the person converted

---

(James Chapter 5 End)

THE FIRST EPISTLE GENERAL OF PETER

1 Peter, Chapter 1

1. Peter, an apostle of Jesus Christ, to the strangers scattered throughout Pontus, Galatia, Cappadocia, Asia, and Bithynia,

1. Πέτρος, ἀπόστολος Ἰησοῦ χριστοῦ, ἐκλεκτοῖς παρεπιδήμοις διασπορᾶς Πόντου, Γαλατίας, Καππαδοκίας, Ἀσίας, καὶ Βιθυνίας,

1. Petros, apostolos Yeisou christou, eklektois parepideimois dyasporas Pontou, Galatias, Kappadokias, Asias, kai Bithunias,

א. פֶּטְרוֹס שְׁלִיחַ יֵשׁוּעַ הַמָּשִׁיחַ אֶל-הַבְּחִירִים הַפְּזוּרִים הַגָּרִים בְּפָנְטוֹס גָּלַטְיָא קַפּוֹדְקִיָּא אַסְיָא וּבִיתוּנְיָא:

1. Petros sh`li•ach Yeshua ha•Ma•shi•ach el - ha•b`chi•rim ha•p`zoo•rim ha•ga•rim be•Fantos Ga•lat•ya Ka•pod•kiya Asia oo•Vi•toonya.

Rabbinic Jewish Commentary
In these places however, it seems, dwelt many Jews, who were converted to Messiah Yeshua, to whom the apostle inscribes this epistle.

---

2. Elect according to the foreknowledge of God the Father, through sanctification of the Spirit, unto obedience and sprinkling of the blood of Jesus Christ: Grace unto you, and peace, be multiplied.

2. κατὰ πρόγνωσιν θεοῦ πατρός, ἐν ἁγιασμῷ πνεύματος, εἰς ὑπακοὴν καὶ ῥαντισμὸν αἵματος Ἰησοῦ χριστοῦ· χάρις ὑμῖν καὶ εἰρήνη πληθυνθείη.

2. kata prognosin theou patros, en 'agyasmo pneumatos, eis 'upakoein kai 'rantismon 'aimatos Yeisou christou. charis 'umin kai eireinei pleithuntheiei.

ב. אֲשֶׁר נִבְחֲרוּ מִקֶּדֶם מִטַּעַם אֱלֹהִים הָאָב לְקַדְּשָׁם בְּרוּחוֹ וּלְהָכִין לִבָּם לִשְׁמֹעַ לְיֵשׁוּעַ הַמָּשִׁיחַ וְיֵז דָּמוֹ עֲלֵיהֶם: חַסְדְּכֶם וּשְׁלוֹמְכֶם יִשְׂגֶּא

2. Asher niv•cha•roo mi•ke•dem mi•ta•am Elohim ha•Av le•kad•sham be•roo•cho ool•ha•chin li•bam lish•mo•a le•Yeshua ha•Ma•shi•ach va•yez da•mo aley•hem chas•de•chem oosh•lom•chem yis•ge.

Rabbinic Jewish Commentary

The phrase is Jewish, and is used in their salutations in this form, שלמכון יסגי, "let your peace be multiplied" (t),

(t) T. Hieros. Masser Sheni, fol. 56. 3. T. Bab. Sanhedrin, fol. 11. 2.

---

1 Peter 1

3. Blessed be the God and Father of our Lord Jesus Christ, which according to his abundant mercy hath begotten us again unto a lively hope by the resurrection of Jesus Christ from the dead,

3. Εὐλογητὸς ὁ θεὸς καὶ πατὴρ τοῦ κυρίου ἡμῶν Ἰησοῦ χριστοῦ, ὁ κατὰ τὸ πολὺ αὐτοῦ ἔλεος ἀναγεννήσας ἡμᾶς εἰς ἐλπίδα ζῶσαν δι᾽ ἀναστάσεως Ἰησοῦ χριστοῦ ἐκ νεκρῶν,

3. Eulogeitos 'o theos kai pateir tou kuriou 'eimon Yeisou christou, 'o kata to polu autou eleos anagenneisas 'eimas eis elpida zosan di anastaseos Yeisou christou ek nekron,

ג. בָּרוּךְ הוּא הָאֱלֹהִים אֲבִי אֲדֹנֵינוּ יֵשׁוּעַ הַמָּשִׁיחַ אֲשֶׁר כְּגֹדֶל חַסְדּוֹ הוֹלִיד אֹתָנוּ שֵׁנִית לְתִקְוַת חַיִּים בִּתְקוּמַת:יֵשׁוּעַ הַמָּשִׁיחַ מִן-הַמֵּתִים

3. Ba•rooch hoo ha•Elohim Avi Ado•ney•noo Yeshua ha•Ma•shi•ach asher ke•go•del chas•do ho•lid o•ta•noo she•nit le•tik•vat cha•yim bit•koo•mat Yeshua ha•Ma•shi•ach min - ha•me•tim.

Rabbinic Jewish Commentary

By "God" is meant, not God essentially, but personally considered, even God the Father, as is clearly expressed: the words are rendered in the Arabic and Ethiopic versions without the copulative "and", thus, "blessed be God the Father"; and if that is retained, they, may be rendered thus, "Blessed be God, even the Father"

4. To an inheritance incorruptible, and undefiled, and that fadeth not away, reserved in heaven for you,

4. εἰς κληρονομίαν ἄφθαρτον καὶ ἀμίαντον καὶ ἀμάραντον, τετηρημένην ἐν οὐρανοῖς εἰς ὑμᾶς,

4. eis kleironomian aphtharton kai amianton kai amaranton, teteireimenein en ouranois eis 'umas,

ד. לְנַחֲלָה אֲשֶׁר לֹא תִשָּׁחֵת וְלֹא תֵחָלֵל וְלֹא תִבּוֹל הַצְּפוּנָה לָכֶם בַּשָּׁמָיִם:

4. Le•na•cha•la asher lo ti•sha•chet ve•lo te•choo•lal ve•lo ti•bol hatz•foo•na la•chem ba•sha•ma•yim.

Rabbinic Jewish Commentary

The Jews are wont to call the future state an inheritance of the land of the living: they say (u).

"This is called נחלה, "an inheritance"; and add, but in this world a man has no inheritance, nor continuance;

So they interpret that phrase, "by the God of thy father", in Gen.49:25 thus (w).

"This is אחסנא, "the inheritance" of the superior place, which is called "heaven";

And sometimes they style it אחסנתא עלאה, "the superior inheritance", or "the inheritance above" (x); all which agrees with Peter's language,

(u) Tzeror Hammor, fol. 150. 3. (w) Zohar in Gen. fol. 131. 2. (x) Zohar in Exod. fol. 34. 3.

---

5. Who are kept by the power of God through faith unto salvation ready to be revealed in the last time.

5. τοὺς ἐν δυνάμει θεοῦ φρουρουμένους διὰ πίστεως εἰς σωτηρίαν ἑτοίμην ἀποκαλυφθῆναι ἐν καιρῷ ἐσχάτῳ.

5. tous en dunamei theou phrouroumenous dya pisteos eis soteirian 'etoimein apokaluphtheinai en kairo eschato.

ה: כִּי שְׁמוּרִים אַתֶּם בְּכֹחַ אֵל עַל-יְדֵי אֱמוּנַתְכֶם לַתְּשׁוּעָה אֲשֶׁר תִּגָּלֶה לְקֵץ הַיָּמִים.

5. Ki sh`moo•rim atem be•cho•ach El al - ye•dey emoo•nat•chem lat•shoo•ah asher ti•ga•le le•ketz ha•ya•mim.

1 Peter 1

6. Wherein ye greatly rejoice, though now for a season, if need be, ye are in heaviness through manifold temptations:

6. Ἐν ᾧ ἀγαλλιᾶσθε, ὀλίγον ἄρτι, εἰ δέον ἐστίν, λυπηθέντες ἐν ποικίλοις πειρασμοῖς,

6. En 'o agallyasthe, oligon arti, ei deon estin, lupeithentes en poikilois peirasmois,

ו. אֲשֶׁר בָּהּ תָּגִילוּ עַד-מְאֹד אַף כִּי-עַתָּה תִתְאַבְּלוּ לַמִּצְעָר לְרַגְלֵי מַסּוֹת שֹׁנוֹת אֲשֶׁר בֹּאָן נָחוּץ:

6. Asher ba ta•gi•loo ad - me•od af ki - ata tit•ab•loo la•mitz•ar le•rag•ley ma•sot sho•not asher bo•an na•chootz.

Rabbinic Jewish Commentary

The Vulgate Latin version reads, "in which ye shall rejoice": and so the Syriac version, adding, "for ever"; and refer these words to the "last time"; or, times spoken of in the preceding verse; when the saints will greatly rejoice, being in full possession of eternal salvation.

The Syriac version renders it, "though at this time" קְלִיל, "ye are a little made sorrowful"; and then it is only "now", for the present time, and but for a short time; for a little season, even for a moment, comparatively speaking; and also, "if need be", which the Syriac version omits, though by all means to be retained.

See Lam.3:33 so the Jews say (y), that הוצרך, "there was a necessity" of God's tempting Abraham as he did, to humble and purify him,

(y) Tzeror Hammor, fol. 22. 1.

7. That the trial of your faith, being much more precious than of gold that perisheth, though it be tried with fire, might be found unto praise and honour and glory at the appearing of Jesus Christ:

7. ἵνα τὸ δοκίμιον ὑμῶν τῆς πίστεως πολὺ τιμιώτερον χρυσίου τοῦ ἀπολλυμένου, διὰ πυρὸς δὲ δοκιμαζομένου, εὑρεθῇ εἰς ἔπαινον καὶ τιμὴν καὶ εἰς δόξαν ἐν ἀποκαλύψει Ἰησοῦ χριστοῦ·

7. 'ina to dokimion 'umon teis pisteos polu timioteron chrusiou tou apollumenou, dya puros de dokimazomenou, 'eurethei eis epainon kai timein kai eis doxan en apokalupsei Yeisou christou.

ז. לְצָרֵף אֱמוּנַתְכֶם אֲשֶׁר רָחוֹק מְחִירָהּ מִזָּהָב מְזֻקָּק בָּאֵשׁ אֲשֶׁר אַחֲרִיתוֹ עֲדֵי-אֹבֵד וֶאֱמוּנַתְכֶם תִּהְיֶה לִתְהִלָּה:לְכָבוֹד וּלְתִפְאֶרֶת בְּהִתְגַּלּוֹת יֵשׁוּעַ הַמָּשִׁיחַ

7. Le•tza•ref emoo•nat•chem asher ra•chok me•chi•ra mi•za•hav me•zoo•kak ba•esh asher acha•ri•to adey - o•ved ve•e•moo•nat•chem ti•hi•ye lit•hi•la le•cha•vod ool•tif•e•ret be•hit•ga•lot Yeshua ha•Ma•shi•ach.

---

1 Peter 1

8. Whom having not seen, ye love; in whom, though now ye see him not, yet believing, ye rejoice with joy unspeakable and full of glory:

8. ὃν οὐκ εἰδότες ἀγαπᾶτε, εἰς ὃν ἄρτι μὴ ὁρῶντες, πιστεύοντες δέ, ἀγαλλιᾶσθε χαρᾷ ἀνεκλαλήτῳ καὶ δεδοξασμένῃ,

8. 'on ouk eidotes agapate, eis 'on arti mei 'orontes, pisteuontes de, agallyasthe chara aneklaleito kai dedoxasmenei,

ח. אֲשֶׁר אֹתוֹ אֲהַבְתֶּם אַף כִּי לֹא חֲזִיתֶם פָּנָיו וַתַּאֲמִינוּ-בוֹ אַף כִּי עַד-עַתָּה לֹא רְאִיתֶם אֹתוֹ בְּעֵינֵיכֶם וּבוֹ תָשִׂישׂוּ:בְּשָׂשׂוֹן עָצוּם מִסַּפֵּר וְכָלִיל בַּהֲדָרוֹ

8. Asher o•to ahav•tem af ki lo cha•zi•tem pa•nav va•ta•a•mi•noo - vo af ki ad - ata lo r`ee•tem o•to be•ey•ne•chem oo•vo ta•si•soo ve•sa•son a•tzoom mi•sa•per ve•cha•lil ba•ha•da•ro.

---

9. Receiving the end of your faith, even the salvation of your souls.

9. κομιζόμενοι τὸ τέλος τῆς πίστεως ὑμῶν, σωτηρίαν ψυχῶν.

9. komizomenoi to telos teis pisteos 'umon, soteirian psuchon.

ט. כַּאֲשֶׁר תִּמְצְאוּ אֶת-פְּרִי אֱמוּנַתְכֶם וְאֶת-תְּשׁוּעַת נַפְשְׁכֶם:

9. Ka•a•sher tim•tze•oo et - p`ri emoo•nat•chem ve•et - te•shoo•at naf•she•chem.

Rabbinic Jewish Commentary
It is rightly supplied in our version by "your", as in the Syriac, Arabic, and Ethiopic versions; though the Vulgate Latin version only reads, "the salvation of souls"; and which is to be understood, not to the exclusion of bodies, for God has designed the salvation of them; and Yeshua has procured the redemption of them; and these will be preserved unto the coming of Messiah, being united to him; and will be raised by him, and with their souls enjoy everlasting happiness with him; though, in the present state of things, salvation rather takes place in the soul than in the body, which is exposed to various labours, afflictions, and diseases; but the chief design of the phrase is, to distinguish this salvation from a corporeal and temporal one: and so the Jews use the phrase תשועת הנפש, "the salvation of the soul" (z), in opposition to, and distinction from, a mere bodily one; and it intends a salvation from sin, the Torah, and its curses; from the second death, and wrath to come, and every spiritual enemy: which is the end of faith; or, as the Syriac version renders it, פורענא, "the reward of faith"; not that faith is the cause of salvation, or meritorious of it.

(z) Tzeror Hammor, fol. 168. 4.

---

1 Peter 1

10. Of which salvation the prophets have inquired and searched diligently, who prophesied of the grace that should come unto you:

10. Περὶ ἧς σωτηρίας ἐξεζήτησαν καὶ ἐξηρεύνησαν προφῆται οἱ περὶ τῆς εἰς ὑμᾶς χάριτος προφητεύσαντες·

10. Peri 'eis soteirias exezeiteisan kai exeireuneisan propheitai 'oi peri teis eis 'umas charitos propheiteusantes.

י. אֶת הַתְּשׁוּעָה אֲשֶׁר עָלֶיהָ חָקְרוּ וְדָרְשׁוּ הַנְּבִיאִים אֲשֶׁר נִבְּאוּ עַל-הַחֶסֶד הַצָּפוּן לָכֶם:

10. Et hat•shoo•ah asher a•le•ha chak•roo ve•dar•shoo ha•n`vi•eem asher nib•oo al - ha•che•sed ha•tza•foon la•chem.

11. Searching what, or what manner of time the Spirit of Christ which was in them did signify, when it testified beforehand the sufferings of Christ, and the glory that should follow.

11. ἐρευνῶντες εἰς τίνα ἢ ποῖον καιρὸν ἐδήλου τὸ ἐν αὐτοῖς πνεῦμα χριστοῦ, προμαρτυρόμενον τὰ εἰς χριστὸν παθήματα, καὶ τὰς μετὰ ταῦτα δόξας.

11. ereunontes eis tina ei poion kairon edeilou to en autois pneuma christou, promarturomenon ta eis christon patheimata, kai tas meta tauta doxas.

יא. וַיַּחְתְּרוּ לָדַעַת מָתַי וְאֵיךְ יָבוֹא הַמּוֹעֵד אֲשֶׁר הוֹדִיעָם רוּחַ הַמָּשִׁיחַ אֲשֶׁר שָׁכַן בְּקִרְבָּם כַּאֲשֶׁר הִגִּיד לָהֶם:מֵרֹאשׁ חֶבְלֵי הַמָּשִׁיחַ וְהַכָּבוֹד אֲשֶׁר בְּעָקְבָם

11. Va•yach•te•roo la•da•at ma•tai ve•eych ya•vo ha•mo•ed asher ho•di•am Roo•ach ha•Ma•shi•ach asher sha•chan be•kir•bam ka•a•sher hi•gid la•hem me•rosh chev•ley ha•Ma•shi•ach ve•ha•ka•vod asher ba•a•ke•vam.

Rabbinic Jewish Commentary
the Spirit of Christ in them did signify; or "make manifest": from whence it appears, that Messiah then existed, as he did before there were any prophets, and even from everlasting, being the eternal God; and that the Spirit is from him, as well as from the Father; and as here, so he is often by the Jews (a) called רוחא משיחא, "the Spirit of the Messiah", or "Christ"; and that the Spirit is truly God.

The "sufferings of Christ" are what the Jews call (b) חבלי משיח, "the sorrows of the Messiah". These are particularly testified of in Psa.22:1. The glory, or "glories", as it may be rendered, design his resurrection from the dead, his ascension to heaven, his session at the right hand of God, and having all power, authority, and judgment committed to him; and which are eminently and distinctly prophesied of in Psa.16:10.

(a) Zohar in Gen. fol. 19. 3. & passim. (b) T. Bab. Sabbat, fol. 118. 1. & passim.

12. Unto whom it was revealed, that not unto themselves, but unto us they did minister the things, which are now reported unto you by them that have preached the gospel unto you with the Holy Ghost sent down from heaven; which things the angels desire to look into.

12. Οἷς ἀπεκαλύφθη ὅτι οὐχ ἑαυτοῖς, ὑμῖν δὲ διηκόνουν αὐτά, ἃ νῦν ἀνηγγέλη ὑμῖν διὰ τῶν εὐαγγελισαμένων ὑμᾶς ἐν πνεύματι ἁγίῳ ἀποσταλέντι ἀπ' οὐρανοῦ, εἰς ἃ ἐπιθυμοῦσιν ἄγγελοι παρακύψαι.

12. 'Ois apekaluphthei 'oti ouch 'eautois, 'umin de dieikonoun auta, 'a nun aneingelei 'umin dya ton euangelisamenon 'umas en pneumati 'agio apostalenti ap ouranou, eis 'a epithumousin angeloi parakupsai.

יב. וְנִגְלָה לָהֶם כִּי לֹא לְנַפְשָׁם כִּי אִם-לְנַפְשְׁכֶם חָזוּ הַדְּבָרִים הָהֵם אֲשֶׁר הֻגַּד לָכֶם הַיּוֹם מִפִּי הַמְבַשְּׂרִים בְּרוּחַ הַקֹּדֶשׁ הַשָּׁלוּחַ מִשָּׁמַיִם דְּבָרִים אֲשֶׁר מַלְאֲכֵי-יָהּ נִכְסָפִים לְהַבֵּט-בָּם

12. Ve•nig•la la•hem ki lo le•naf•sham ki eem - le•naf•she•chem cha•zoo ha•d`va•rim ha•hem asher hoo•gad la•chem ha•yom mi•pi ham•vas•rim be•Roo•ach ha•Ko•desh ha•sha•loo•ach mi•sha•ma•yim d`va•rim asher mal•a•chey - Ya nich•sa•fim le•ha•bet - bam.

Rabbinic Jewish Commentary
that not unto themselves, but unto us they did minister. The Vulgate Latin, Arabic, and Ethiopic versions, read "unto you"; and so do some copies. Not that they were ignorant of the things they searched into, and were revealed unto them, and they prophesied of; as the Jews sometimes say (c) of them,

"That they prophesied, and knew not what they prophesied of

(c) T. Bab. Bava Bathra, fol. 119. 2.

---

1 Peter 1

13. Wherefore gird up the loins of your mind, be sober, and hope to the end for the grace that is to be brought unto you at the revelation of Jesus Christ;

13. Διὸ ἀναζωσάμενοι τὰς ὀσφύας τῆς διανοίας ὑμῶν, νήφοντες, τελείως ἐλπίσατε ἐπὶ τὴν φερομένην ὑμῖν χάριν ἐν ἀποκαλύψει Ἰησοῦ χριστοῦ·

13. Dio anazosamenoi tas osphuas teis dyanoias 'umon, neiphontes, teleios elpisate epi tein pheromenein 'umin charin en apokalupsei Yeisou christou.

יג. עַל־כֵּן חִגְרוּ מָתְנֵיכֶם וְיַאֲמֵץ לִבְּכֶם הִתְעוֹרְרוּ וְיַחְלוּ בְכָל־מְאֹדְכֶם לַחֶסֶד אֲשֶׁר יְסוֹבֵב אֶתְכֶם בְּהִתְגַּלוֹת יֵשׁוּעַ הַמָּשִׁיחַ:

13. Al - ken chig•roo mot•ney•chem ve•ya•a•metz lib•chem hit•o•re•roo ve•yach•loo ve•chol - me•od•chem la•che•sed asher ye•so•vev et•chem be•hit•ga•lot Yeshua ha•Ma•shi•ach.

Rabbinic Jewish Commentary
The Syriac and Ethiopic versions, instead of "grace", read "joy"; and is the same with eternal glory, the joy of YHVH prepared for them, and which they shall enter into.

---

1 Peter 1

14. As obedient children, not fashioning yourselves according to the former lusts in your ignorance:

14. ὡς τέκνα ὑπακοῆς, μὴ συσχηματιζόμενοι ταῖς πρότερον ἐν τῇ ἀγνοίᾳ ὑμῶν ἐπιθυμίαις,

14. 'os tekna 'upakoeis, mei suscheimatizomenoi tais proteron en tei agnoia 'umon epithumiais,

יד. וּכְבָנִים מַקְשִׁיבִים אַל־תְּשַׁוּוּ נַפְשְׁכֶם לְנֶפֶשׁ תַּאֲוָה אֲשֶׁר הָיְתָה לָכֶם לְפָנִים מִבְּלִי־דָעַת:

14. Ooch•va•nim mak•shi•vim al - te•sha•voo naf•she•chem le•ne•fesh ta•a•va asher hai•ta la•chem le•fa•nim mi•b`li - da•at.

---

15. But as he which hath called you is holy, so be ye holy in all manner of conversation;

15. ἀλλὰ κατὰ τὸν καλέσαντα ὑμᾶς ἅγιον καὶ αὐτοὶ ἅγιοι ἐν πάσῃ ἀναστροφῇ γενήθητε·

15. alla kata ton kalesanta 'umas 'agion kai autoi 'agioi en pasei anastrophei geneitheite.

טו. כִּי אִם-קְדֹשִׁים תִּהְיוּ בְּכָל-דַּרְכֵיכֶם כַּאֲשֶׁר הַקֹּרֵא אֶתְכֶם קָדוֹשׁ הוּא:

15. Ki eem - k`do•shim ti•hi•yoo ve•chol - dar•chey•chem ka•a•sher ha•ko•re et•chem ka•dosh hoo.

---

1 Peter 1

16. Because it is written, Be ye holy; for I am holy.

16. διότι γέγραπται, Ἅγιοι γίνεσθε, ὅτι ἐγὼ ἅγιός εἰμι.

16. dioti gegraptai, 'Agioi ginesthe, 'oti ego 'agios eimi.

טז. כִּי כֵן כָּתוּב וִהְיִיתֶם קְדֹשִׁים כִּי קָדוֹשׁ אָנִי:

16. Ki chen ka`toov vi•hi•yee•tem k`do•shim ki ka•dosh ani.

---

17. And if ye call on the Father, who without respect of persons judgeth according to every man's work, pass the time of your sojourning here in fear:

17. Καὶ εἰ πατέρα ἐπικαλεῖσθε τὸν ἀπροσωπολήπτως κρίνοντα κατὰ τὸ ἑκάστου ἔργον, ἐν φόβῳ τὸν τῆς παροικίας ὑμῶν χρόνον ἀναστράφητε·

17. Kai ei patera epikaleisthe ton aprosopoleiptos krinonta kata to 'ekastou ergon, en phobo ton teis paroikias 'umon chronon anastrapheite.

יז. וְאִם הַשֹּׁפֵט אִישׁ אִישׁ לְפִי מַעֲלָלָיו אֲשֶׁר לֹא יִשָּׂא פָנִים אִם-אֹתוֹ תִקְרְאוּ אֲבִיכֶם - הִתְהַלְּכוּ לְפָנָיו בְּיִרְאָה כָּל-יְמֵי מְגוּרֵיכֶם:

17. Ve•eem ha•sho•fet eesh eesh le•fi ma•a•la•lav asher lo yi•sa fa•nim eem - o•to tik•re•oo Avi•chem hit•hal•choo le•fa•nav be•yir•ah kol - ye•mey me•goo•rey•chem.

---

18. Forasmuch as ye know that ye were not redeemed with corruptible things, as silver and gold, from your vain conversation received by tradition from your fathers;

18. εἰδότες ὅτι οὐ φθαρτοῖς, ἀργυρίῳ ἢ χρυσίῳ, ἐλυτρώθητε ἐκ τῆς ματαίας ὑμῶν ἀναστροφῆς πατροπαραδότου,

18. eidotes 'oti ou phthartois, argurio ei chrusio, elutrotheite ek teis mataias 'umon anastropheis patroparadotou,

יח. הֵן יְדַעְתֶּם כִּי לֹא-בְכֶסֶף וּבְזָהָב אֲשֶׁר יִכְלוּ בְּאַחֲרִיתָם נִפְדֵּיתֶם מֵאָרְחוֹת שָׁוְא אֲשֶׁר נִחֲלוּ לָכֶם אֲבוֹתֵיכֶם:

18. Hen ye•da•a•tem ki lo - ve•che•sef oov•za•hav asher yich•loo ve•a•cha•ri•tam nif•dey•tem me•or•chot shav asher ni•cha•loo la•chem avo•tei•chem.

Rabbinic Jewish Commentary

The allusion is to the redemption of the people of Israel, and of the firstborn, by shekels, Exo.30:12. Gold and silver do not mean pieces of gold and silver, but gold and silver coined; for only by such could redemption of anything be obtained (d) but these are insufficient for the redemption of the spirit.

These were the inventions and decrees of them they called אבות, "fathers", to whose dogmas and decisions they paid the utmost respect. These made up their oral Torah, which the Jews say (e) Moses received from Sinai, and delivered to Joshua; and Joshua to the elders; and the elders to the prophets; and the prophets to the men of the great synagogue, the last of which was Simeon the just; and from him it was delivered to another.

(d) Maimon. & Bartenora in Misn. Beracot, c. 7. sect. 1. (e) Pirke Abot, c. 1. sect. 1, 2, &c.

---

19. But with the precious blood of Christ, as of a lamb without blemish and without spot:

19. ἀλλὰ τιμίῳ αἵματι ὡς ἀμνοῦ ἀμώμου καὶ ἀσπίλου χριστοῦ,

19. alla timio 'aimati 'os amnou amomou kai aspilou christou,

יט. כִּי אִם-בְּדָם יָקָר בְּדַם הַמָּשִׁיחַ שֶׂה תָּמִים וּמוּם אֵין-בּוֹ:

19. Ki eem - be•dam ya•kar be•dam ha•Ma•shi•ach se ta•mim oo•moom eyn - bo.

Rabbinic Jewish Commentary
But with the precious blood of Christ,.... Messiah was prophesied of as a Redeemer under the Old Testament, Isa.59:20 and the Jews frequently ascribe redemption to the Word of YHVH God (f).

The Jews have a notion, that the redemption of the Israelites out of Egypt, when a lamb without blemish was taken, and sacrificed and eaten, had a respect to the future redemption by the Messiah; and which, they say (g), was to be in the same time of the year; that as they were redeemed in Nisan, the month in which the passover was kept, so they were to be redeemed in the same month: and indeed at that time, and in that month, was redemption obtained by the blood of Messiah. Of the former, the Targumist in Hos.3:2 says,

"I have redeemed them by my Word, on the fifteenth day of the month Nisan, and have given silver shekels, the atonement of their souls. It is observable that the Hebrew word דם signifies both "blood" and "money", or price; whether some reference may not be had to this here, since both are included here, may be considered.

(f) Targum in Hos. i. 7. & iii. 2. & in Joel ii. 17. (g) Zohar in Numb. fol. 102. 3.

---

1 Peter 1

20. Who verily was foreordained before the foundation of the world, but was manifest in these last times for you,

20. προεγνωσμένου μὲν πρὸ καταβολῆς κόσμου, φανερωθέντος δὲ ἐπ᾽ ἐσχάτων τῶν χρόνων δι᾽ ὑμᾶς,

20. proegnosmenou men pro kataboleis kosmou, phanerothentos de ep eschaton ton chronon di 'umas,

כ. וְהוּא הוּכַן מִקֶּדֶם טֶרֶם הִוָּסֵד אָרֶץ וְנִגְלָה בְּאַחֲרִית הַיָּמִים לְמַעַנְכֶם:

20. Ve•hoo hoo•chan mi•ke•dem te•rem hi•va•sed a•retz ve•nig•la ve•a•cha•rit ha•ya•mim le•ma•an•chem.

Rabbinic Jewish Commentary
The Jews (h) reckon the name of the Messiah among the seven things that were created before the world was; in proof of which they mention, Psa.72:17 but was manifest in these last times for you; he was before, he

existed from everlasting; he lay in the bosom of his Father from all eternity: and was veiled and hid under the shadows of the ceremonial law, during the legal dispensation; but in the fulness of time was manifest in the flesh, and more clearly revealed in the Gospel, and to the souls of men; his manifestation in human nature is principally intended.

It is a rule with the Jews (i), that whenever the last days or times are mentioned, the times of the Messiah are designed: and this manifestation of Messiah was for the sake of some particular persons, even for all God's people, whether among Jews or Gentiles, and who are described in the following verse. The Alexandrian copy reads, "for us"; and the Ethiopic version, "for him",

(h) T. Bab. Pesachim, fol. 59. 1. & Nedarim, fol. 89. 2. (i) Kimchi in Isa. ii. 2.

---

1 Peter 1

21. Who by him do believe in God, that raised him up from the dead, and gave him glory; that your faith and hope might be in God.

21. τοὺς δι' αὐτοῦ πιστεύοντας εἰς θεόν, τὸν ἐγείραντα αὐτὸν ἐκ νεκρῶν, καὶ δόξαν αὐτῷ δόντα, ὥστε τὴν πίστιν ὑμῶν καὶ ἐλπίδα εἶναι εἰς θεόν.

21. tous di autou pisteuontas eis theon, ton egeiranta auton ek nekron, kai doxan auto donta, 'oste tein pistin 'umon kai elpida einai eis theon.

כא. אֲשֶׁר עַל־יָדוֹ מַאֲמִינִים אַתֶּם בֵּאלֹהִים אֲשֶׁר הֲקִימוֹ מִן־הַמֵּתִים וַיִּתֶּן־לוֹ כָבוֹד לְבַעֲבוּר תִּמָּצֵא אֱמוּנַתְכֶם: וְתִקְוַתְכֶם בֵּאלֹהִים

21. Asher al - ya•do ma•a•mi•nim atem be•Elohim asher ha•ki•mo min - ha•me•tim va•yi•ten - lo cha•vod le•va•a•voor ti•ma•tze emoo•nat•chem ve•tik•vat•chem be•Elohim.

---

22. Seeing ye have purified your souls in obeying the truth through the Spirit unto unfeigned love of the brethren, see that ye love one another with a pure heart fervently:

22. Τὰς ψυχὰς ὑμῶν ἡγνικότες ἐν τῇ ὑπακοῇ τῆς ἀληθείας διὰ πνεύματος εἰς φιλαδελφίαν ἀνυπόκριτον, ἐκ καθαρᾶς καρδίας ἀλλήλους ἀγαπήσατε ἐκτενῶς·

22. Tas psuchas 'umon 'eignikotes en tei 'upakoei teis aleitheias dya pneumatos eis philadelphian anupokriton, ek katharas kardias alleilous agapeisate ektenos.

כב. וְאַחֲרֵי אֲשֶׁר זִכִּיתֶם אֶת-נַפְשֹׁתֵיכֶם לִשְׁמֹעַ אֶל-הָאֱמֶת עַל-יְדֵי הָרוּחַ וּלְאַהֲבָה אִישׁ אֶת-אָחִיו בְּלֹא שִׂפְתֵי מִרְמָה:מֵרָמָה הִתְאַמְּצוּ וַאֲהַבְתֶּם אֶת-אֲחֵיכֶם בְּתָם-לֵב

22. Ve•a•cha•rey asher zi•ki•tem et - naf•sho•tey•chem lish•mo•a el - ha•e•met al - ye•dey ha•Roo•ach ool•a•ha•va eesh et - a•chiv be•lo sif•tey mir•ma hit•am•tzoo va•a•hav•tem et - a•chey•chem be•tom - lev.

---

1 Peter 1

23. Being born again, not of corruptible seed, but of incorruptible, by the word of God, which liveth and abideth for ever.

23. ἀναγεγεννημένοι οὐκ ἐκ σπορᾶς φθαρτῆς, ἀλλὰ ἀφθάρτου, διὰ λόγου ζῶντος θεοῦ καὶ μένοντος εἰς τὸν αἰῶνα.

23. anagegenneimenoi ouk ek sporas phtharteis, alla aphthartou, dya logou zontos theou kai menontos eis ton aiona.

כג. כַּאֲנָשִׁים אֲשֶׁר נוֹלְדוּ שֵׁנִית וְלֹא מִזֶּרַע אַכְזָב כִּי אִם-מִמָּקוֹר נֶאֱמָן בִּדְבַר אֱלֹהִים אֲשֶׁר הוּא חַי וְנִצָּב לְעוֹלָם:

23. Ka•a•na•shim asher nol•doo she•nit ve•lo mi•ze•ra ach•zav ki eem - mi•ma•kor ne•e•man bid•var Elohim asher hoo chai ve•ni•tzav le•o•lam.

Rabbinic Jewish Commentary

not of corruptible seed, but of incorruptible; referring not to seed cast into the earth, which first corrupts and dies, and then is quickened, and rises, and brings forth fruit; but to human seed, and which the Jews call טפה סרוחה, "the filthy drop" (k); which is in itself corrupt, and is corrupted, and whereby the corruption of human nature is propagated; for whatsoever is born of the flesh is carnal and corrupt.

The phrases, "which liveth and abideth forever", may be either read in connection only with "God", and as descriptive of him, who is the living

God, is from everlasting to everlasting, in distinction from idols; and here added, to show that he can give power and efficacy to his word, to regenerate and quicken, and will continue to preserve and make it useful to all his saving purposes; so Jarchi explains the passage in Isa.40:8 after referred to, "The Word of our God shall stand for ever",

"Because he lives and abides, and it is in his power to confirm it therefore it follows, "O Zion, that bringeth good tidings, get thee up into the high mountain"; for because he lives forever, this promise is published.

The same is said of the "Memra", or Word of God, in the Chaldee paraphrase on Hos.11:9 "I am God", מימרי, "my Word abideth for ever" The Syriac version renders it, "the living Word of God"

(k) Pirke Abot, c. 3. sect. 1. & Bartenora in ib. Zohar in Exod. fol. 62. 1. & 78. 2.

---

24. For all flesh is as grass, and all the glory of man as the flower of grass. The grass withereth, and the flower thereof falleth away:

24. Διότι, Πᾶσα σὰρξ ὡς χόρτος, καὶ πᾶσα δόξα ἀνθρώπου ὡς ἄνθος χόρτου. Ἐξηράνθη ὁ χόρτος, καὶ τὸ ἄνθος αὐτοῦ ἐξέπεσεν·

24. Dioti, Pasa sarx 'os chortos, kai pasa doxa anthropou 'os anthos chortou. Exeiranthei 'o chortos, kai to anthos autou exepesen.

כד. כִּי כָל-הַבָּשָׂר חָצִיר וְכָל-כְּבוֹד-אִישׁ כְּצִיץ חָצִיר יָבֵשׁ חָצִיר נָבֵל צִיץ:

24. Ki kol - ha•ba•sar cha•tzir ve•chol - k`vod - eesh ke•tzitz cha•tzir ya•vesh cha•tzir na•vel tzitz.

Rabbinic Jewish Commentary

All men, as born of corruptible seed, are frail, mortal, and perishing; they spring up like grass, and look beautiful for a while, but are very weak and tender, and in a little time they are cut down by death, and wither away; and while they live, are, in a good measure, nothing but grass in another form; the substance of their life is greatly by it; what is the flesh they eat, but grass turned into it? and this mortality is not only the case of wicked men, as the Jews (l) interpret the word, but of good men; even of the prophets, and preachers of the Gospel; and yet the word of God spoken by them continues for ever: the passage referred to is in Isa.40:6.

(l) Targum, Jarchi, & Kimchi, in Isa. xl. 6.

1 Peter 1

25. But the word of the Lord endureth for ever. And this is the word which by the gospel is preached unto you.

25. τὸ δὲ ῥῆμα κυρίου μένει εἰς τὸν αἰῶνα. Τοῦτο δέ ἐστιν τὸ ῥῆμα τὸ εὐαγγελισθὲν εἰς ὑμᾶς.

25. to de 'reima kuriou menei eis ton aiona. Touto de estin to 'reima to euangelisthen eis 'umas.

כה. וּדְבַר יְהֹוָה יָקוּם לְעוֹלָם וְהוּא הַדָּבָר אֲשֶׁר בִּשְׂרוּ לָכֶם הַמְבַשְּׂרִים:

25. Oo•d`var Adonai ya•koom le•o•lam ve•hoo ha•da•var asher bis•roo la•chem ham•vas•rim.

(1Peter Chapter 1 End)

1 Peter, Chapter 2

1. Wherefore laying aside all malice, and all guile, and hypocrisies, and envies, and all evil speakings,

1. Ἀποθέμενοι οὖν πᾶσαν κακίαν καὶ πάντα δόλον καὶ ὑποκρίσεις καὶ φθόνους καὶ πάσας καταλαλιάς,

1. Apothemenoi oun pasan kakian kai panta dolon kai 'upokriseis kai phthonous kai pasas katalalyas,

א. וְעַתָּה הָסִירוּ מִכֶּם כָּל-רִשְׁעָה וְכָל-מִרְמָה וַחֲנֻפָּה וְקִנְאָה וְכָל-שְׂפַת רָכִיל:

1. Ve•a•ta ha•si•roo mi•kem kol - rish•ah ve•chol - mir•ma va•cha•noo•pa ve•kin•ah ve•chol - s`fat ra•chil.

---

2. As newborn babes, desire the sincere milk of the word, that ye may grow thereby:

2. ὡς ἀρτιγέννητα βρέφη, τὸ λογικὸν ἄδολον γάλα ἐπιποθήσατε, ἵνα ἐν αὐτῷ αὐξηθῆτε,

2. 'os artigenneita brephei, to logikon adolon gala epipotheisate, 'ina en auto auxeitheite,

ב. וּכְעוֹלָלִים אֲשֶׁר נוֹלְדוּ מִקָּרוֹב בַּקְּשׁוּ לִשְׂבֹּעַ חָלָב זַךְ מִשְּׁדֵי בִינָה אֲשֶׁר עָלָיו תִּגְדְּלוּ לִישׁוּעָה:

2. Ooch•o•la•lim asher nol•doo mi•ka•rov bak•shoo lis•bo•a cha•lav zach mish•dey vi•na asher alav tig•de•loo li•shoo•ah.

Rabbinic Jewish Commentary

The proselytes to the Jews' religion are often said (m) to be כקטון שנולד דמי, "as an infant just born", or a new born babe; to which the allusion may here be made. The Jewish writers speak of חלב של תורה, "the milk of the Torah" (n), of which they generally interpret (o) the passage in Isa.55:1 so it is much better applied to the Torah, which is the milk of the word, or "rational milk" that leads to Messiah.

The Alexandrian copy, and several others, and also the Vulgate Latin, Syriac, and Ethiopic versions, add, "unto salvation"

(m) T. Bab. Yebamot, fol. 22. 1. & 48. 2. & 62. 1. & 97. 2. Maimon. Hilch. Issure Bia, c. 14. sect. 11. & Eduth, c. 13. sect. 2. (n) Jarchi in Cant. 5. 12. (o) Jarchi, Aben Ezra, & Kimchi, in Isa. lv. 1. Abarbinel, Mashmia Jeshua, fol. 26. 1.

---

1 Peter 2

3. If so be ye have tasted that the Lord is gracious.

3. εἴπερ ἐγεύσασθε ὅτι χρηστὸς ὁ κύριος·

3. eiper egeusasthe 'oti chreistos 'o kurios.

ג. אִם-רַק בֶּאֱמֶת וּבְתָמִים טְעַמְתֶּם כִּי-טוֹב אֲדֹנֵינוּ:

3. Eem - rak be•e•met oov•ta•mim te•am•tem ki - tov Ado•ney•noo.

Rabbinic Jewish Commentary
Reference is had to Psa.34:8, "O taste and see that YHVH is good"; and the Syriac version here adds, "if ye have seen."

---

4. To whom coming, as unto a living stone, disallowed indeed of men, but chosen of God, and precious,

4. πρὸς ὃν προσερχόμενοι, λίθον ζῶντα, ὑπὸ ἀνθρώπων μὲν ἀποδεδοκιμασμένον, παρὰ δὲ Θεῷ ἐκλεκτόν, ἔντιμον,

4. pros 'on proserchomenoi, lithon zonta, 'upo anthropon men apodedokimasmenon, para de theo eklekton, entimon,

ד. וְאֵלָיו בָּאתֶם כְּמוֹ אֶל-אֶבֶן חַיִּים אֲשֶׁר מָאֲסוּ בְנֵי אָדָם אַךְ נִבְחֶרֶת הִיא וִיקָרָה לֵאלֹהִים:

4. Ve•e•lav ba•tem k`mo el - even cha•yim asher ma•a•soo v`ney adam ach niv•che•ret hee viy•ka•ra le•Elohim.

---

5. Ye also, as lively stones, are built up a spiritual house, an holy priesthood, to offer up spiritual sacrifices, acceptable to God by Jesus Christ.

5. καὶ αὐτοὶ ὡς λίθοι ζῶντες οἰκοδομεῖσθε οἶκος πνευματικός, ἱεράτευμα ἅγιον, ἀνενέγκαι πνευματικὰς θυσίας εὐπροσδέκτους τῷ θεῷ διὰ Ἰησοῦ χριστοῦ.

5. kai autoi 'os lithoi zontes oikodomeisthe oikos pneumatikos, 'ierateuma 'agion, anenegkai pneumatikas thusias euprosdektous to theo dya Yeisou christou.

ה. וְגַם-אַתֶּם אַבְנֵי חַיִּים לְהִבָּנוֹת הֵיכָל עֶלְיוֹן לִכְהֻנַּת קֹדֶשׁ לְהַקְרִיב זִבְחֵי-רוּחַ לְרֵיחַ נִיחֹחַ לֵאלֹהִים בְּיַד יֵשׁוּעַ הַמָּשִׁיחַ:

5. Ve•gam - atem av•ney cha•yim le•hi•ba•not hey•chal el•yon lich•hoo•nat ko•desh le•hak•riv ziv•chey - roo•ach le•re•ach ni•cho•ach le•Elohim be•yad Yeshua ha•Ma•shi•ach.

Rabbinic Jewish Commentary

Some read these words in the imperative, as an exhortation, "be ye built up as lively stones; and be ye spiritual temples and holy priests", as the Syriac version. A synagogue with the Jews is called בית רוחני, "a spiritual house" (r); and so is the third temple which the Jews expect in the times of the Messiah; of which one of their writers (s) thus says:

"It is known from the ancient wise men, that the future redemption, with which shall be the third רוחני, "spiritual" sanctuary, is the work of God, and will not be as the former redemptions: "I will fill this house with glory"; this is רוחני, "a spiritual" one, for even the walls shall be רוחניים, "spiritual"--for even all this "house" shall be "spiritual"; for that which was then built, which is the second, shall be turned into another a "spiritual" one. So the Jews speak of spiritual sacrifices, as distinct from material ones:

"The intellectual sacrifice (they say (t)) is before the material sacrifices, both in time and excellency.--Cain brought an offering to YHVH of the fruit of the earth, and behold the intellectual attention did not agree with it, which is קרבן הרוחני, "the spiritual sacrifice."

(r) Neve Shalom apud Caphtor, fol. 14. 1. (s) R. Alshech. in Hagg. ii. 7, 8, 9, 10. (t) Neve Shalom apud Caphtor, fol. 88. 2. Vid. Raziel. fol. 33. 1.

---

6. Wherefore also it is contained in the scripture, Behold, I lay in Sion a chief corner stone, elect, precious: and he that believeth on him shall not be confounded.

6. Διότι περιέχει ἐν τῇ γραφῇ, Ἰδού, τίθημι ἐν Σιὼν λίθον ἀκρογωνιαῖον, ἐκλεκτόν, ἔντιμον· καὶ ὁ πιστεύων ἐπ᾽ αὐτῷ οὐ μὴ καταισχυνθῇ.

6. Dioti periechei en tei graphei, Ydou, titheimi en Sion lithon akrogonyaion, eklekton, entimon. kai 'o pisteuon ep auto ou mei kataischunthei.

ו. וְזֶה הוּא שֶׁאָמַר בַּמִּקְרָא הִנְנִי יִסַּד בְּצִיּוֹן אֶבֶן בֹּחַן פִּנָּה וִיקָרָה וְהַמַּאֲמִין בָּהּ לֹא יֵבוֹשׁ:

6. Ve•ze hoo she•a•mar ba•mik•ra hi•ne•ni yi•sad be•Tziyon even bo•chan pi•na viy•ka•ra ve•ha•ma•a•min ba lo ye•vosh.

Rabbinic Jewish Commentary

Wherefore also it is contained in the Scripture,.... Isa.28:16. This is produced as a proof of the excellency of Yeshua, as compared to a stone; and of his usefulness in the spiritual building; and of his being chosen of God, and precious, though rejected by men; and of the happiness, comfort, and safety of those that believe in him. That this prophecy belongs to the Messiah, is the sense of some of the Jewish writers: the Targum on it applies it to a mighty king; it does not mention the King Messiah, as Galatinus (u) cites it; but Jarchi expressly names him, and interprets it of him.

(u) De Aroan. Cathol. Ver. l. 3. c. 21.

---

1 Peter 2

7. Unto you therefore which believe he is precious: but unto them which be disobedient, the stone which the builders disallowed, the same is made the head of the corner,

7. Ὑμῖν οὖν ἡ τιμὴ τοῖς πιστεύουσιν· ἀπειθοῦσιν δέ, Λίθον ὃν ἀπεδοκίμασαν οἱ οἰκοδομοῦντες, οὗτος ἐγενήθη εἰς κεφαλὴν γωνίας,

7. 'Umin oun 'ei timei tois pisteuousin. apeithousin de, Lithon 'on apedokimasan 'oi oikodomountes, 'outos egeneithei eis kephalein gonias,

ז. עַל־כֵּן לָכֶם הַמַּאֲמִינִים הוּא לְאֶבֶן חֵפֶץ וְלַאֲשֶׁר אֵינָם מַאֲמִינִים הוּא אֶבֶן מָאֲסוּ הַבּוֹנִים הָיְתָה לְרֹאשׁ פִּנָּה:

7. Al - ken la•chem ha•ma•a•mi•nim hoo le•e•ven che•fetz ve•la•a•sher ey•nam ma•a•mi•nim hoo even ma•a•soo ha•bo•nim hai•ta le•rosh pi•na.

Rabbinic Jewish Commentary

The Septuagint use the word in Isa.11:10 where it is prophesied of the Messiah, that his rest shall be glorious; they render it τιμη, "honour", or "precious". The Jewish writers have adopted the word טימי into their language, and use it for profit and gain (w); in which sense it is applicable to Yeshua, who is gain to believers, both in life and in death; they being blessed with all spiritual blessings in him, and he being all in all to them: and also they use it, as denoting the intrinsic price and value of anything (x), and which is a right sense of the word.

(w) Targum in Esther iii. 8. & v. 13. & vii. 4. (x) Targum Hierosol. in Gen. xxi. 33. Targum Jon. in Gen. xxiii. 15. Targum in Prov. xxxi. 10. Bereshit Rabba, sect. 2. fol. 2. 3. & sect. 11. fol. 9. 3.

---

8. And a stone of stumbling, and a rock of offence, even to them which stumble at the word, being disobedient: whereunto also they were appointed.

8. καί, Λίθος προσκόμματος καὶ πέτρα σκανδάλου· οἳ προσκόπτουσιν τῷ λόγῳ ἀπειθοῦντες· εἰς ὃ καὶ ἐτέθησαν.

8. kai, Lithos proskommatos kai petra skandalou. 'oi proskoptousin to logo apeithountes. eis 'o kai etetheisan.

ח. וּלְאֶבֶן נֶגֶף וּלְצוּר מִכְשׁוֹל כִּי נִכְשְׁלוּ-בוֹ בְּחֹסֶר אֱמוּנָתָם כַּאֲשֶׁר גַּם-לְהִכָּשֵׁל נוֹעֲדוּ מֵאָז:

8. Ool•e•ven ne•gef ool•tzoor mich•shol ki nich•she•loo - vo be•cho•ser emoo•na•tam ka•a•sher gam - le•hi•ka•shel no•a•doo me•az.

Rabbinic Jewish Commentary

It is worth while to compare this with the paraphrase of Isa.8:14 which passage is here referred to; and the paraphrase of it runs thus,

""If ye obey not", his word shall be among you for revenge, and for a stone smiting, and for a rock of offence to both houses of the princes of Israel, and for destruction and offence to those who are divided upon the house of Judah..."

9. But ye are a chosen generation, a royal priesthood, an holy nation, a peculiar people; that ye should shew forth the praises of him who hath called you out of darkness into his marvellous light:

9. Ὑμεῖς δὲ γένος ἐκλεκτόν, βασίλειον ἱεράτευμα, ἔθνος ἅγιον, λαὸς εἰς περιποίησιν, ὅπως τὰς ἀρετὰς ἐξαγγείλητε τοῦ ἐκ σκότους ὑμᾶς καλέσαντος εἰς τὸ θαυμαστὸν αὐτοῦ φῶς·

9. 'Umeis de genos eklekton, basileion 'ierateuma, ethnos 'agion, laos eis peripoieisin, 'opos tas aretas exangeileite tou ek skotous 'umas kalesantos eis to thaumaston autou phos.

ט. וְאַתֶּם הִנְּכֶם בְּחִירֵי-יָה מַמְלֶכֶת כֹּהֲנִים גּוֹי קָדוֹשׁ וְעַם סְגֻלָּה לוֹ לְסַפֵּר תְּהִלָּתוֹ אֲשֶׁר קָרָא אֶתְכֶם מֵחשֶׁךְ:לְאוֹר פֶּלְאִי

9. Ve•a•tem hin•chem be•chi•rey - Ya mam•le•chet Co•ha•nim goy ka•dosh ve•am se•goo•la lo le•sa•per te•hi•la•to asher ka•ra et•chem me•cho•shech le•or pel•ee.

Rabbinic Jewish Commentary

But ye are a chosen generation,.... Or "kindred"; the phrase is to be seen in the Septuagint, on Isa.43:20, to which, and the following verse, the apostle refers here, and in another part of this text. The allusion is throughout to the people of Israel in general, who, in an external way, were all that is here said; but was only true in a spiritual sense of such as were chosen and called among the Jews: and who were a "generation or kindred"

a royal priesthood; referring to Exo.19:6, where the Israelites are called a "kingdom of priests"; which the Chaldee paraphrase renders, kings, priests; a character which one of the Jewish commentators says (y) shall return to the Jews לעתיד לבא, "in time to come". The Jews were wont to call the priestly dignity and office כתר כהנה, "the crown of the priesthood" (z)

a peculiar people; as the Israelites are called a "peculiar treasure", Exo.19:5 to which the reference is: God's elect are a peculiar people, to whom he bears a peculiar love; they are chosen by him to be a special people above all others, and have peculiar blessings bestowed on them, and peculiar care is taken of them; they are the Lord's, סגלה, his treasure, his jewels, his portion and inheritance, and therefore he will preserve and save them; they are a people for acquisition, purchase, and possession, as the words may be rendered; whom God has obtained, procured, and purchased for himself, with the precious blood of his Son; hence the Syriac version renders them, כנשא פריקא, "a redeemed company."

into his marvellous light: The Syriac version renders it, "his most excellent light"; the apostle seems to refer to the form of praise and thanksgiving used by the Jews, at the time of the passover; who say (a), "we are bound to confess, to praise, to glorify, &c. him who hath done for our fathers, and for us, all these wonders; he hath brought us out of bondage to liberty; from sorrow to joy, and from mourning to a good day, ומאפילה לאור גדול, "and out of darkness into great light"; and from subjection unto redemption.

This was also part of their morning prayer (b), "I confess before thee, O my God, and the God of my fathers, that thou hast brought me out of darkness into light.

And it is to be observed, that the third Sephira, or number, in the Jewish Cabalistic tree, which answers to the third Person in the Trinity, among other names, is called, "marvellous light" (c),

(y) Baal Hatturim in loc. (z) Pirke Abot, c. 4. sect. 13. Tzeror Hammot, fol. 78. 3. (a) Misn. Pesachim, c. 10. sect. 5. Haggada Shel Pesach, p. 23. Maimon. Hilchot Chametz Umetzah, c. 8. sect. 5. (b) T. Hieros. Beracot, c. 4. fol. 7. 1. (c) Cabala Denudata, par. 2. p. 8.

---

1 Peter 2

10. Which in time past were not a people, but are now the people of God: which had not obtained mercy, but now have obtained mercy.

10. οἱ ποτὲ οὐ λαός, νῦν δὲ λαὸς Θεοῦ· οἱ οὐκ ἠλεημένοι, νῦν δὲ ἐλεηθέντες.

10. 'oi pote ou laos, nun de laos theou. 'oi ouk eileeimenoi, nun de eleeithentes.

י. אֲשֶׁר לְפָנִים לֹא-עָם הֱיִיתֶם וְעַתָּה עַם אֱלֹהִים לְפָנִים בָּנִים לֹא-רֻחָמוּ וְעַתָּה מְרֻחָמִים:

10. Asher le•fa•nim lo - am he•yi•tem ve•a•ta am Elohim le•fa•nim ba•nim lo - roo•cha•moo ve•a•ta me•roo•cha•mim.

Rabbinic Jewish Commentary

Which in time were not a people*,....* A "Lo ammi" being put upon them; see Hos.1:9 to which the apostle here refers: God's elect, the Jews. the Syriac version gives the true sense of the phrase, by rendering it "these who before were not" חשבון, "reckoned or accounted a people."

11. Dearly beloved, I beseech you as strangers and pilgrims, abstain from fleshly lusts, which war against the soul;

11. Ἀγαπητοί, παρακαλῶ ὡς παροίκους καὶ παρεπιδήμους, ἀπέχεσθαι τῶν σαρκικῶν ἐπιθυμιῶν, αἵτινες στρατεύονται κατὰ τῆς ψυχῆς·

11. Agapeitoi, parakalo 'os paroikous kai parepideimous, apechesthai ton sarkikon epithumion, 'aitines strateuontai kata teis psucheis.

יא. וַאֲנִי שׁוֹאֵל מִכֶּם יְדִידִים כְּגֵרִים וְתוֹשָׁבִים לְהִנָּזֵר מִתַּאֲוֹת הַבָּשָׂר הַנִּלְחָמוֹת בַּנֶּפֶשׁ:

11. Va•a•ni sho•el mi•kem ye•di•dim ke•ge•rim ve•to•sha•vim le•hi•na•zer mi•ta•a•vot ha•ba•sar ha•nil•cha•mot ba•na•fesh.

---

1 Peter 2

12. Having your conversation honest among the Gentiles: that, whereas they speak against you as evildoers, they may by your good works, which they shall behold, glorify God in the day of visitation.

12. τὴν ἀναστροφὴν ὑμῶν ἔχοντες καλὴν ἐν τοῖς ἔθνεσιν, ἵνα, ἐν ᾧ καταλαλοῦσιν ὑμῶν ὡς κακοποιῶν, ἐκ τῶν καλῶν ἔργων, ἐποπτεύσαντες, δοξάσωσιν τὸν θεὸν ἐν ἡμέρᾳ ἐπισκοπῆς.

12. tein anastrophein 'umon echontes kalein en tois ethnesin, 'ina, en 'o katalalousin 'umon 'os kakopoion, ek ton kalon ergon, epopteusantes, doxasosin ton theon en 'eimera episkopeis.

יב. וּלְהִתְהַלֵּךְ בְּמֵישָׁרִים בֵּין הַגּוֹיִם אֲשֶׁר דִּבְּרוּ עֲלֵיכֶם סָרָה כְּפֹעֲלֵי אָוֶן וְעַתָּה יִתְבּוֹנְנוּ בְמַעֲשֵׂיכֶם הַטּוֹבִים וִיכַבְּדוּ אֶת-אֱלֹהִים בְּיוֹם פְּקֻדּוֹ

12. Ool•hit•ha•lech be•mey•sha•rim bein ha•go•yim asher dib•roo aley•chem sa•ra ke•fo•a•ley aven ve•a•ta yit•bo•ne•noo ve•ma•a•sey•chem ha•to•vim vi•chab•doo et - Elohim be•yom pok•do.

Rabbinic Jewish Commentary

...*glorify God in the day of visitation*; or "trial", or "examination", as the Syriac version renders it. this must either design a visitation by way of judgment, or of mercy; for as the Jews say (d), there is פקידה, "a visitation", for good, and a visitation for evil: God sometimes visits in a way of punishment for sin, and sometimes in away of grace.

(d) Zohar in Gen. fol. 93. 3.

13. Submit yourselves to every ordinance of man for the Lord's sake: whether it be to the king, as supreme;

13. Ὑποτάγητε οὖν πάσῃ ἀνθρωπίνῃ κτίσει διὰ τὸν κύριον· εἴτε βασιλεῖ, ὡς ὑπερέχοντι·

13. 'Upotageite oun pasei anthropinei ktisei dya ton kurion. eite basilei, 'os 'uperechonti.

יג. וְהִכָּנְעוּ לְכָל-מִשְׂרָה אֲשֶׁר לִבְנֵי-אָדָם לְמַעַן הָאָדוֹן אִם-לַמֶּלֶךְ כַּאֲשֶׁר הוּא הָרֹאשׁ:

13. Ve•hi•kan•oo le•chol - mis•ra asher liv•ney - adam le•ma•an ha•Adon eem - la•me•lech ka•a•sher hoo ha•rosh.

---

1 Peter 2

14. Or unto governors, as unto them that are sent by him for the punishment of evildoers, and for the praise of them that do well.

14. εἴτε ἡγεμόσιν, ὡς δι' αὐτοῦ πεμπομένοις εἰς ἐκδίκησιν κακοποιῶν, ἔπαινον δὲ ἀγαθοποιῶν.

14. eite 'eigemosin, 'os di autou pempomenois eis ekdikeisin kakopoion, epainon de agathopoion.

יד. וְאִם-לַשָּׂרִים כַּאֲשֶׁר הֵם שְׁלוּחָיו לָתֵת נְקָמָה בְּפֹעֲלֵי אָוֶן וְכָבוֹד לְעֹשֵׂי טוֹב:

14. Ve•eem - la•sa•rim ka•a•sher hem sh`loo•chav la•tet n`ka•ma be•fo•a•ley aven ve•cha•vod le•o•sey tov.

---

15. For so is the will of God, that with well doing ye may put to silence the ignorance of foolish men:

15. Ὅτι οὕτως ἐστὶν τὸ θέλημα τοῦ θεοῦ, ἀγαθοποιοῦντας φιμοῦν τὴν τῶν ἀφρόνων ἀνθρώπων ἀγνωσίαν·

15. 'Oti 'outos estin to theleima tou theou, agathopoiountas phimoun tein ton aphronon anthropon agnosian.

טו. כִּי כֵן חָפֵץ אֱלֹהִים בַּעֲשׂוֹתְכֶם טוֹב לָשִׂים מַחְסוֹם לְפִי הַסְּכָלִים אֵין תְּבוּנָה בָּם:

15. Ki chen cha•fetz Elohim ba•a•sht•chem tov la•sim mach•som le•fi has•cha•lim eyn te•voo•na bam.

---

1 Peter 2

16. As free, and not using your liberty for a cloke of maliciousness, but as the servants of God.

16. ὡς ἐλεύθεροι, καὶ μὴ ὡς ἐπικάλυμμα ἔχοντες τῆς κακίας τὴν ἐλευθερίαν, ἀλλ᾽ ὡς δοῦλοι θεοῦ.

16. 'os eleutheroi, kai mei 'os epikalumma echontes teis kakias tein eleutherian, all 'os douloi theou.

טז. וֶהְיוּ כִבְנֵי חוֹרִים אַךְ לֹא לָשִׁית חֻפְשַׁתְכֶם כְּמִכְסֶה עַל־פְּנֵי מַעֲשִׂים רָעִים כִּי אִם־כְּעַבְדֵי אֵל:

16. Ve•he•yoo chiv•ney cho•rim ach lo la•sheet choof•shat•chem ke•mich•se al - p`ney ma•a•sim ra•eem ki eem - ke•av•dey El.

---

17. Honour all men. Love the brotherhood. Fear God. Honour the king.

17. Πάντας τιμήσατε. Τὴν ἀδελφότητα ἀγαπήσατε. Τὸν θεὸν φοβεῖσθε. Τὸν βασιλέα τιμᾶτε.

17. Pantas timeisate. Tein adelphoteita agapeisate. Ton theon phobeisthe. Ton basilea timate.

יז. כַּבְּדוּ כָל־אִישׁ כִּכְבוֹדוֹ אֶהֱבוּ אֶת־אֲחֵיכֶם יְראוּ אֶת־הָאֱלֹהִים וְהָבוּ כָבוֹד לַמֶּלֶךְ:

17. Kab•doo chol - eesh kich•vo•do e•he•voo et - a•chey•chem yir•oo et - ha•Elohim ve•ha•voo cha•vod la•me•lech.

---

18. Servants, be subject to your masters with all fear; not only to the good and gentle, but also to the froward.

18. Οἱ οἰκέται, ὑποτασσόμενοι ἐν παντὶ φόβῳ τοῖς δεσπόταις, οὐ μόνον τοῖς ἀγαθοῖς καὶ ἐπιεικέσιν, ἀλλὰ καὶ τοῖς σκολιοῖς.

18. 'Oi oiketai, 'upotassomenoi en panti phobo tois despotais, ou monon tois agathois kai epieikesin, alla kai tois skoliois.

יח. וַעֲבָדִים בָּכֶם הִכָּנְעוּ לִפְנֵי אֲדֹנֵיכֶם בְּכָל-יִרְאָה לֹא לְבַד לִפְנֵי יְשָׁרִים וְטוֹבִים כִּי אִם-גַּם-לִפְנֵי נְלוֹזִים:

18. Va•a•va•dim ba•chem hi•kan•oo lif•ney ado•ney•chem be•chol - yir•ah lo le•vad lif•ney ye•sha•rim ve•to•vim ki eem - gam - lif•ney n`lo•zim.

1 Peter 2

19. For this is thankworthy, if a man for conscience toward God endure grief, suffering wrongfully.

19. Τοῦτο γὰρ χάρις, εἰ διὰ συνείδησιν θεοῦ ὑποφέρει τις λύπας, πάσχων ἀδίκως.

19. Touto gar charis, ei dya suneideisin theou 'upopherei tis lupas, paschon adikos.

יט. כִּי בְזֹאת יְאֻשַׁר אָדָם אִם-יִשָּׂא מַכְאֹב וְיֵעָנֶה חִנָּם רַק לִהְיוֹת לִבּוֹ תָמִים עִם-אֱלֹהָיו:

19. Ki ve•zot ye•oo•shar adam eem - yi•sa mach•ov viy•oo•ne chi•nam rak li•hee•yot li•bo ta•mim eem - Elohav.

20. For what glory is it, if, when ye be buffeted for your faults, ye shall take it patiently? But if, when ye do well, and suffer for it, ye take it patiently, this is acceptable with God.

20. Ποῖον γὰρ κλέος, εἰ ἁμαρτάνοντες καὶ κολαφιζόμενοι ὑπομενεῖτε; Ἀλλ᾽ εἰ ἀγαθοποιοῦντες καὶ πάσχοντες ὑπομενεῖτε, τοῦτο χάρις παρὰ θεῷ.

20. Poion gar kleos, ei 'amartanontes kai kolaphizomenoi 'upomeneite? All ei agathopoiountes kai paschontes 'upomeneite, touto charis para theo.

כ. כִּי מַה-תִּפְאַרְתְּכֶם אִם תַּחֲרִישׁוּ כַּאֲשֶׁר תֻּכּוּ בְּאַשְׁמוֹתֵיכֶם רַק אִם-תְּעֻנּוּ עֵקֶב מַעֲשִׂים טוֹבִים וְהֶחֱרַשׁ תַּחֲרִשׁוּן זֹאת תִּהְיֶה לָכֶם לִתְהִלָּה מֵאֵת הָאֱלֹהִים

20. Ki ma - tif•ar•te•chem eem ta•cha•ri•shoo ka•a•sher too•koo ve•ash•mo•tey•chem rak eem - te•oo•noo e•kev ma•a•sim to•vim ve•ha•cha•resh ta•cha•ri•shoon zot ti•hi•ye la•chem lit•hi•la me•et ha•Elohim.

1 Peter 2

21. For even hereunto were ye called: because Christ also suffered for us, leaving us an example, that ye should follow his steps:

21. Εἰς τοῦτο γὰρ ἐκλήθητε, ὅτι καὶ χριστὸς ἔπαθεν ὑπὲρ ἡμῶν, ὑμῖν ὑπολιμπάνων ὑπογραμμόν, ἵνα ἐπακολουθήσητε τοῖς ἴχνεσιν αὐτοῦ·

21. Eis touto gar ekleitheite, 'oti kai christos epathen 'uper 'eimon, 'umin 'upolimpanon 'upogrammon, 'ina epakoloutheiseite tois ichnesin autou.

כא. כִּי הֲלֹא לָזֹאת נִקְרֵאתֶם וְאַף גַּם-הַמָּשִׁיחַ נִדְכָּה בִּגְלַלְכֶם וַיְהִי לָכֶם לְמוֹפֵת לָלֶכֶת בְּעִקְּבוֹתָיו:

21. Ki ha•lo la•zot nik•re•tem ve•af gam - ha•Ma•shi•ach nid•ka big•lal•chem vay•hi la•chem le•mo•fet la•le•chet be•eek•vo•tav.

22. Who did no sin, neither was guile found in his mouth:

22. ὃς ἁμαρτίαν οὐκ ἐποίησεν, οὐδὲ εὑρέθη δόλος ἐν τῷ στόματι αὐτοῦ·

22. 'os 'amartian ouk epoieisen, oude 'eurethei dolos en to stomati autou.

כב. אֲשֶׁר לֹא-חָמָס עָשָׂה וְלֹא מִרְמָה בְּפִיו:

22. Asher lo - cha•mas asa ve•lo mir•ma be•fiv.

23. Who, when he was reviled, reviled not again; when he suffered, he threatened not; but committed himself to him that judgeth righteously:

23. ὃς λοιδορούμενος οὐκ ἀντελοιδόρει, πάσχων οὐκ ἠπείλει, παρεδίδου δὲ τῷ κρίνοντι δικαίως·

23. 'os loidoroumenos ouk anteloidorei, paschon ouk eipeilei, paredidou de to krinonti dikaios.

כג. אֲשֶׁר חֵרְפוּהוּ חוֹרְפָיו וְלֹא הֵשִׁיב חֶרְפָּתָם אֶל-חֵיקָם נֶעֱנֶה וְלֹא יִפְתַּח-פִּיו כִּי אִם-הַפְקִיד מִשְׁפָּטוֹ לְשֹׁפֵט צֶדֶק

23. Asher cher•foo•hoo chor•fav ve•lo he•shiv cher•pa•tam el - chey•kam na•a•ne ve•lo yif•tach - piv ki eem - hif•kid mish•pa•to le•sho•fet tze•dek.

---

1 Peter 2

24. Who his own self bare our sins in his own body on the tree, that we, being dead to sins, should live unto righteousness: by whose stripes ye were healed.

24. ὃς τὰς ἁμαρτίας ἡμῶν αὐτὸς ἀνήνεγκεν ἐν τῷ σώματι αὐτοῦ ἐπὶ τὸ ξύλον, ἵνα, ταῖς ἁμαρτίαις ἀπογενόμενοι, τῇ δικαιοσύνῃ ζήσωμεν· οὗ τῷ μώλωπι αὐτοῦ ἰάθητε.

24. 'os tas 'amartias 'eimon autos aneinegken en to somati autou epi to xulon, 'ina, tais 'amartiais apogenomenoi, tei dikaiosunei zeisomen. 'ou to molopi autou iatheite.

כד. וְהוּא נָשָׂא אֶת-חַטֹּאתֵינוּ בִּבְשָׂרוֹ עַל-הָעֵץ לַעֲבוּר נָמוּת לַחֲטָאָה וְנִחְיֶה לִצְדָקָה וַאֲשֶׁר בַּחֲבֻרָתוֹ נִרְפָּא לָכֶם

24. Ve•hoo na•sa et - cha•to•tey•noo biv•sa•ro al - ha•etz le•va•a•voor na•moot la•cha•ta•ah ve•nich•ye litz•da•ka va•a•sher ba•cha•voo•ra•to nir•pa la•chem.

Rabbinic Jewish Commentary
by whose stripes ye were healed; the passage referred to is in Isa.53:5 which is a prophecy of the Messiah, as is acknowledged by the Jews (g), who say (h),

"This is the King Messiah, who was in the generation of the ungodly, as it is said, Isa.53:5 "and with his stripes we are healed"; and for this cause God saved him, that he might save Israel, and rejoice with them in the resurrection of the dead.

See Psa.103:3 on which latter text a learned Jew (i) has this note, "This interpreters explain לשון סליחה, "as expressive of forgiveness"; and the Jews say, there is no healing of diseases but it signifies forgiveness (k): it is an uncommon way of healing by the stripes of another. Some think the apostle alludes to the stripes which servants receive from their masters, to whom he was now speaking; and in order to encourage them to bear them patiently, observes, that Messiah himself suffered stripes, and that they had healing for their diseases and wounds, by means of his stripes, or through his being wounded and bruised for them.

(g) Zohar in Exod. fol. 85. 2. Midrash Ruth, fol. 33. 2. Yalkut Simeoni, par. 2. fol. 53. 3. & 90. 1. (h) R. Moses Haddarsan apud Galatin. de Areanis Cathol. Verit. l. 6. c. 2. (i) R. Sol. Urbin Ohel Moed, fol. 64. 1. (k) Yalkut Simeoni, par. 2. fol. 43. 1.

---

1 Peter 2

25. For ye were as sheep going astray; but are now returned unto the Shepherd and Bishop of your souls.

25. ῏Ητε γὰρ ὡς πρόβατα πλανώμενα· ἀλλ᾽ ἐπεστράφητε νῦν ἐπὶ τὸν ποιμένα καὶ ἐπίσκοπον τῶν ψυχῶν ὑμῶν.

25. Eite gar 'os probata planomena. all epestrapheite nun epi ton poimena kai episkopon ton psuchon 'umon.

:כה. כִּי צֹאן אֹבְדוֹת הֱיִיתֶם וַתָּשֻׁבוּ כַיּוֹם אֶל-הָרֹעֶה הַמַּשְׁגִּיחַ אֶל-נַפְשֹׁתֵיכֶם

25. Ki tzon ov•dot he•yi•tem va•ta•shoo•voo cha•yom el - ha•ro•eh ha•mash•gi•ach el - naf•sho•tey•chem.

Rabbinic Jewish Commentary
Philo the Jew (l) observes, that "to be a shepherd is so good a work, that it is not only a title given to kings and wise men, and souls perfectly purified, but to God the governor of all---who, as a Shepherd and King, leads according to justice and Torah, setting over them his right Logos, "the first begotten Son", who has taken the care of this holy flock, as does the deputy of a great king.

(l) De Agricultura, p. 194, 195.

(1Peter Chapter 2 End)

1 Peter, Chapter 3

1. Likewise, ye wives, be in subjection to your own husbands; that, if any obey not the word, they also may without the word be won by the conversation of the wives;

1. Ὁμοίως, αἱ γυναῖκες, ὑποτασσόμεναι τοῖς ἰδίοις ἀνδράσιν, ἵνα, καὶ εἴ τινες ἀπειθοῦσιν τῷ λόγῳ, διὰ τῆς τῶν γυναικῶν ἀναστροφῆς ἄνευ λόγου κερδηθήσονται,

1. 'Omoios, 'ai gunaikes, 'upotassomenai tois idiois andrasin, 'ina, kai ei tines apeithousin to logo, dya teis ton gunaikon anastropheis aneu logou kerdeitheisontai,

א. וְכֵן גַּם-הַנָּשִׁים הַכְּנַעֲנָה לִפְנֵי בַעֲלֵיכֶן וְאִם-יֵשׁ אֲנָשִׁים מְמָאֲנִים לִשְׁמֹעַ הַבְּשׂוֹרָה אַתֶּן בְּעַנְוַת דַּרְכְּכֶן תִּקְנֶינָה:אֹתָם לַיהֹוָה בְּאֵין-אֹמֶר וּדְבָרִים

1. Ve•chen gam - ha•na•shim hi•ka•na•a•na lif•ney va•a•ley•chen ve•eem - yesh a•na•shim me•ma•anim lish•mo•a ha•b`so•hra aten be•an•vat dar•ke•chen tik•nei•na o•tam la`Adonai be•eyn - o•mer ood•va•rim.

---

2. While they behold your chaste conversation coupled with fear.

2. ἐποπτεύσαντες τὴν ἐν φόβῳ ἁγνὴν ἀναστροφὴν ὑμῶν.

2. epopteusantes tein en phobo 'agnein anastrophein 'umon.

ב. כַּאֲשֶׁר יֶחֱזוּ כִּי בְיִרְאָה וּבְתֹם דַּרְכְּכֶן:

2. Ka•a•sher ye•che•zoo ki ve•yir•ah oov•tom dar•ke•chen.

---

3. Whose adorning let it not be that outward adorning of plaiting the hair, and of wearing of gold, or of putting on of apparel;

3. Ὧν ἔστω οὐχ ὁ ἔξωθεν ἐμπλοκῆς τριχῶν, καὶ περιθέσεως χρυσίων, ἢ ἐνδύσεως ἱματίων κόσμος·

3. 'On esto ouch 'o exothen emplokeis trichon, kai peritheseos chrusion, ei enduseos 'imation kosmos.

ג. וּפְאֵרְכֶן לֹא יִהְיֶה פְּאֵר חִיצוֹן בְּמַחְלְפוֹת רֹאשׁ וַעֲדִי זָהָב אוֹ בִגְדֵי חֲמֻדוֹת:

3. Oof•er•chen lo yi•hee•ye fe•er chi•tzon be•mach•la•fot rosh va•a•di za•hav oh vig•dey cha•moo•dot.

Rabbinic Jewish Commentary

There were women among the Jews, whose business it was to plait women's hair; Mary Magdalene is thought to have her name from thence, and that to be her business. The Jews often speak of one Miriam or Mary, by whom they seem to mean the mother of our Lord, who, they say (m) was, "a plaiter of women's hair"

The Jewish women used to wear a crown of gold on their head, in the form of the city of Jerusalem, called a golden city (n); and which they wore, after its destruction, in memory of it; but with those they might not go out on a sabbath day. R. Akibah, it is said (o), made a golden city for his wife, and the wife of Rabban Gamaliel envied her, for it seems this was reckoned a grand dress. Not that the sense is, that every thing of this kind is forbidden, but when used to excess and extravagance; otherwise the daughters of Abraham and Sarah were decked with ear rings, bracelets, and jewels of gold.

(m) T. Bab. Sabbat, fol. 104. 2. Chagiga, fol. 4. 2. & Sanhedrin, fol. 67. 1. (n) Misn. Sabbat, c. 6. sect. 1. (o) T. Hieros. Sabbat, fol. 7. 4.

---

4. But let it be the hidden man of the heart, in that which is not corruptible, even the ornament of a meek and quiet spirit, which is in the sight of God of great price.

4. ἀλλ᾽ ὁ κρυπτὸς τῆς καρδίας ἄνθρωπος, ἐν τῷ ἀφθάρτῳ τοῦ πραέος καὶ ἡσυχίου πνεύματος, ὅ ἐστιν ἐνώπιον τοῦ θεοῦ πολυτελές.

4. all 'o kruptos teis kardias anthropos, en to aphtharto tou praeos kai 'eisuchiou pneumatos, 'o estin enopion tou theou poluteles.

ד. כִּי אִם-הָאָדָם הַפְּנִימִי בְּסֵתֶר הַלֵּב בְּרוּחַ עֲנָוָה וְהַשְׁקֵט אֲשֶׁר אֵין לוֹ כִלָּיוֹן וְהוּא יָקָר בְּעֵינֵי הָאֱלֹהִים:

4. Ki eem - ha•a•dam ha•p`ni•mi be•se•ter ha•lev be•roo•ach ana•va ve•hash•ket asher eyn lo chi•la•yon ve•hoo ya•kar be•ei•ney ha•Elohim.

1 Peter 3

5. For after this manner in the old time the holy women also, who trusted in God, adorned themselves, being in subjection unto their own husbands:

5. Οὕτως γάρ ποτε καὶ αἱ ἅγιαι γυναῖκες αἱ ἐλπίζουσαι ἐπὶ θεὸν ἐκόσμουν ἑαυτάς, ὑποτασσόμεναι τοῖς ἰδίοις ἀνδράσιν·

5. 'Outos gar pote kai 'ai 'agyai gunaikes 'ai elpizousai epi theon ekosmoun 'eautas, 'upotassomenai tois idiois andrasin.

ה. כִּי-כֵן הָיָה לְפָנִים פְּאֵר הַנָּשִׁים הַקְּדוֹשׁוֹת אֲשֶׁר שָׂמוּ תוֹחַלְתָּן בֵּאלֹהִים וְלִפְנֵי בַעֲלֵיהֶן נִכְנָעוּ:

5. Ki - chen ha•ya le•fa•nim pe•er ha•na•shim hak•do•shot asher sa•moo to•chal•tan be•Elohim ve•lif•ney va•a•ley•hen nich•na•oo.

---

6. Even as Sara obeyed Abraham, calling him lord: whose daughters ye are, as long as ye do well, and are not afraid with any amazement.

6. ὡς Σάρρα ὑπήκουσεν τῷ Ἀβραάμ, κύριον αὐτὸν καλοῦσα, ἧς ἐγενήθητε τέκνα, ἀγαθοποιοῦσαι καὶ μὴ φοβούμεναι μηδεμίαν πτόησιν.

6. 'os Sarra 'upeikousen to Abra'am, kurion auton kalousa, 'eis egeneitheite tekna, agathopoiousai kai mei phoboumenai meidemian ptoeisin.

ו. כְּמוֹ שָׂרָה אֲשֶׁר שָׁמְעָה בְּקוֹל אַבְרָהָם וְקָרְאָה-לוֹ אֲדֹנִי וְאַתֶּן לִבָנוֹת לָהּ אִם טוֹב תַּעֲשֶׂינָה וְלֹא יָבֹא בְתוֹכְכֶן:מֹרֶךְ לֵב מִפָּחַד

6. K`mo Sa•ra asher sham•ah ve•kol Avraham ve•kar•ah - lo a•do•ni ve•a•ten le•va•not la eem tov ta•a•sei•na ve•lo ya•vo ve•to•cha•chen mo•rech lev mi•pa•chad.

Rabbinic Jewish Commentary

The Jews use this instance to the same purpose the apostle does, saying (p), "The wife ought to take care of the family, to educate her children, to serve and minister to her husband in all things, "calling him her own lord"; which is what we learn from the example of Sarah, who called Abraham her lord, saying, "my lord is old".

(p) Sepher Musar apud Drus. de Quaesitis, Ep. 54. & in loc.

1 Peter 3

7. Likewise, ye husbands, dwell with them according to knowledge, giving honour unto the wife, as unto the weaker vessel, and as being heirs together of the grace of life; that your prayers be not hindered.

7. Οἱ ἄνδρες ὁμοίως, συνοικοῦντες κατὰ γνῶσιν, ὡς ἀσθενεστέρῳ σκεύει τῷ γυναικείῳ ἀπονέμοντες τιμήν, ὡς καὶ συγκληρονόμοι χάριτος ζωῆς, εἰς τὸ μὴ ἐγκόπτεσθαι τὰς προσευχὰς ὑμῶν.

7. 'Oi andres 'omoios, sunoikountes kata gnosin, 'os asthenestero skeuei to gunaikeio aponemontes timein, 'os kai sugkleironomoi charitos zoeis, eis to mei egkoptesthai tas proseuchas 'umon.

ז. וְכֵן אַתֶּם הָאֲנָשִׁים רְאוּ לָשֶׁבֶת עִם-נְשֵׁיכֶם בְּהַשְׂכֵּל תְּנוּ כָבוֹד לְאִשָּׁה כִּי-כְלִי רַךְ הִיא מִכֶּם וְגַם חֲבֶרְתְּכֶם:בְּמַתְּנַת הַחֶסֶד וְהַחַיִּים וּבְכֵן לֹא תִמָּנַע תְּפִלָּה מִבָּתֵּיכֶם

7. Ve•chen atem ha•a•na•shim r`oo la•she•vet eem - n`shey•chem be•has•kel t`noo cha•vod le•ee•sha ki - che•li rach hee mi•kem ve•gam cha•ver•te•chem be•mat•nat ha•che•sed ve•ha•cha•yim oov•chen lo ti•ma•na te•fi•la mi•ba•tey•chem.

Rabbinic Jewish Commentary
The Jews (q) say,

"Let a man always take care בכבוד אשתו, "of the glory of his wife"; for there is no blessing found in a man's house, but for the sake of his wife, as it is said, Gen.12:16 "and he entreated Abraham well for her sake": and Rabba used to say to the citizens, אוקירו לנשייכו, "honour your wives", that ye may be rich.

And indeed this is what they promised in their marriage contract, which runs thus (r):

"Be thou unto me for a wife, according to the law of Moses and Israel, and I, by the word of heaven, or God, will worship, ואוקיר, "and honour", and nourish, and take care of thee, according to the custom of the Jews, who worship, and "honour", and nourish, and take care of their wives.

It is a saying of the Jews (s),

"If thy wife be short of stature, bow thyself, and whisper to her. The meaning of the proverb is, that he ought to suit himself to her capacity and weakness.

(q) T. Bab. Bava Metzia, fol. 59. 1. & Sepher Musar apud Drusium in loc. (r) Apud. Buxtorf. Chald. Gram. p. 389. (s) T. Bab. Bava Metzia, fol. 59. 1.

1 Peter 3

8. Finally, be ye all of one mind, having compassion one of another, love as brethren, be pitiful, be courteous:

8. Τὸ δὲ τέλος, πάντες ὁμόφρονες, συμπαθεῖς, φιλάδελφοι, εὔσπλαγχνοι, φιλόφρονες·

8. To de telos, pantes 'omophrones, sumpatheis, philadelphoi, eusplagchnoi, philophrones.

ח. סוֹף דָּבָר הֱיוּ כֻלְּכֶם לְאַנְשֵׁי לֵב אֶחָד אַנְשֵׁי חֶמְלָה אֹהֲבֵי אַחֲוָה אַנְשֵׁי רַחֲמִים וְשִׁפְלֵי רוּחַ:

8. Sof da•var he•yoo chool•chem le•an•shey lev e•chad an•shey chem•la o•ha•vey a•cha•va an•shey ra•cha•mim ve•shif•ley roo•ach.

9. Not rendering evil for evil, or railing for railing: but contrariwise blessing; knowing that ye are thereunto called, that ye should inherit a blessing.

9. μὴ ἀποδιδόντες κακὸν ἀντὶ κακοῦ, ἢ λοιδορίαν ἀντὶ λοιδορίας· τοὐναντίον δὲ εὐλογοῦντες, εἰδότες ὅτι εἰς τοῦτο ἐκλήθητε, ἵνα εὐλογίαν κληρονομήσητε.

9. mei apodidontes kakon anti kakou, ei loidorian anti loidorias. tounantion de eulogountes, eidotes 'oti eis touto ekleitheite, 'ina eulogian kleironomeiseite.

ט. לֹא תִגְמְלוּ לְאִישׁ רָעָה תַּחַת רָעָה אוֹ קְלָלָה תַּחַת קְלָלָה כִּי אִם-בְּרָכָה כִּי לָזֹאת נִקְרֵאתֶם לְמַעַן תִּירְשׁוּ אֶת-הַבְּרָכָה:

9. Lo tig•me•loo le•eesh ra•ah ta•chat ra•ah oh k`la•la ta•chat k`la•la ki eem - b`ra•cha ki la•zot nik•re•tem le•ma•an tir•shoo et - ha•b`ra•cha.

10. For he that will love life, and see good days, let him refrain his tongue from evil, and his lips that they speak no guile:

10. Ὁ γὰρ θέλων ζωὴν ἀγαπᾷν, καὶ ἰδεῖν ἡμέρας ἀγαθάς, παυσάτω τὴν γλῶσσαν αὐτοῦ ἀπὸ κακοῦ, καὶ χείλη αὐτοῦ τοῦ μὴ λαλῆσαι δόλον·

10. 'O gar thelon zoein agapan, kai idein 'eimeras agathas, pausato tein glossan autou apo kakou, kai cheilei autou tou mei laleisai dolon.

י. מִי-הָאִישׁ הֶחָפֵץ חַיִּים וְלֹרְאוֹת יָמִים טוֹבִים יְצֹר לְשׁוֹנוֹ מֵרָע וּשְׂפָתָיו מִדַּבֵּר מִרְמָה:

10. Mee - ha•eesh he•cha•fetz cha•yim ve•lir•ot ya•mim to•vim yi•tzor le•sho•no me•ra oos•fa•tav mi•da•ber mir•ma.

Rabbinic Jewish Commentary
The Jewish interpreters (u) understand by life and good days, in the psalm, such as are both in this world, and in that which is to come.

(u) Kimchi in Psal. xxxiv. 17.

---

11. Let him eschew evil, and do good; let him seek peace, and ensue it.

11. ἐκκλινάτω ἀπὸ κακοῦ, καὶ ποιησάτω ἀγαθόν· ζητησάτω εἰρήνην, καὶ διωξάτω αὐτήν.

11. ekklinato apo kakou, kai poieisato agathon. zeiteisato eireinein, kai dioxato autein.

יא. סוּר מֵרָע וַעֲשֵׂה-טוֹב יְבַקֵּשׁ שָׁלוֹם וְיִרְדְּפֵהוּ:

11. Ya•soor me•ra ve•ya•a•se - tov ye•va•kesh sha•lom ve•yir•de•fe•hoo.

Rabbinic Jewish Commentary
The Jewish interpreters (w) on the psalm from whence these words are taken observe, that in the first of these clauses are contained all the negative precepts, whose number with them is three hundred, sixty, and five; and in the latter of them, all the affirmative precepts, which amount to two hundred and forty eight

The note of one of the Jewish commentators (x) on this passage is, "seek peace", in thine own place; "and pursue it", in another place.

(w) Aben Ezra & Kimchi in Psal. xxxiv. 14. (x) Jarchi.

1 Peter 3

12. For the eyes of the Lord are over the righteous, and his ears are open unto their prayers: but the face of the Lord is against them that do evil.

12. Ὅτι ὀφθαλμοὶ κυρίου ἐπὶ δικαίους, καὶ ὦτα αὐτοῦ εἰς δέησιν αὐτῶν· πρόσωπον δὲ κυρίου ἐπὶ ποιοῦντας κακά.

12. 'Oti ophthalmoi kuriou epi dikaious, kai ota autou eis deeisin auton. prosopon de kuriou epi poiountas kaka.

יב. כִּי עֵינֵי יְהוָה אֶל־צַדִּיקִים וְאָזְנָיו אֶל־שַׁוְעָתָם פְּנֵי יְהוָה בְּעֹשֵׂי רָע:

12. Ki ey•ney Adonai el - tza•di•kim ve•oz•nav el - shav•a•tam p`ney Adonai be•o•sey ra.

Rabbinic Jewish Commentary

It is added in the psalm, "to cut off the remembrance of them from the earth": by "the face of the Lord" is meant, as the Jewish writers (y) interpret it, the anger of YHVH; it intends, not his kind, pleasant, and loving countenance, but his angry one with the former he beholds the upright, and with it he looks upon his righteous ones; but the latter is upon and against the wicked, and is dreadful and intolerable, and the consequence of it is everlasting destruction from the presence of YHVH, and from the glory of his power.

(y) Jarchi & Menachem apud ib. & Aben Ezra in loc.

13. And who is he that will harm you, if ye be followers of that which is good?

13. Καὶ τίς ὁ κακώσων ὑμᾶς, ἐὰν τοῦ ἀγαθοῦ μιμηταὶ γένησθε;

13. Kai tis 'o kakoson 'umas, ean tou agathou mimeitai geneisthe?

יג. וּמִי יַעֲשֶׂה עִמָּכֶם רָע אִם־תִּרְדְּפוּ לַעֲשׂוֹת טוֹב:

13. Oo•mi ya•a•se ee•ma•chem ra eem - tir•de•foo la•a•sot tov?

1 Peter 3

14. But and if ye suffer for righteousness' sake, happy are ye: and be not afraid of their terror, neither be troubled;

14. Ἀλλ' εἰ καὶ πάσχοιτε διὰ δικαιοσύνην, μακάριοι· τὸν δὲ φόβον αὐτῶν μὴ φοβηθῆτε, μηδὲ ταραχθῆτε·

14. All ei kai paschoite dya dikaiosunein, makarioi. ton de phobon auton mei phobeitheite, meide tarachtheite.

יד: אֶפֶס אִם-גַּם-תְּעֻנּוּ עֵקֶב צְדָקָה אַשְׁרֵיכֶם אַךְ אֶת-מוֹרָאָם לֹא תִירְאוּ וְלֹא תַעֲרוֹצוּ

14. E•fes eem - gam - te•oo•noo e•kev tze•da•ka ash•rey•chem ach et - mo•ra•am lo tir•oo ve•lo ta•a•ro•tzoo.

---

15. But sanctify the Lord God in your hearts: and be ready always to give an answer to every man that asketh you a reason of the hope that is in you with meekness and fear:

15. κύριον δὲ τὸν θεὸν ἁγιάσατε ἐν ταῖς καρδίαις ὑμῶν· ἕτοιμοι δὲ ἀεὶ πρὸς ἀπολογίαν παντὶ τῷ αἰτοῦντι ὑμᾶς λόγον περὶ τῆς ἐν ὑμῖν ἐλπίδος, μετὰ πραΰτητος καὶ φόβου·

15. kurion de ton theon 'agyasate en tais kardiais 'umon. 'etoimoi de aei pros apologian panti to aitounti 'umas logon peri teis en 'umin elpidos, meta prauteitos kai phobou.

טו. אֶת-יְהֹוָה אֱלֹהִים אֹתוֹ תַקְדִּישׁוּ בִּלְבַבְכֶם וּבַעֲנָוָה וְיִרְאָה הֱיוּ נְכֹנִים תָּמִיד לָתֵת מַעֲנֶה לְכָל-הַדֹּרֵשׁ מִכֶּם:מַה יְסוֹד תִּקְוַתְכֶם

15. Et - Adonai Elohim o•to tak•di•shoo bil•vav•chem oo•va•ana•va ve•yir•ah he•yoo n`cho•nim ta•mid la•tet ma•a•ne le•chol - ha•do•resh mi•kem ma ye•sod tik•vat•chem.

Rabbinic Jewish Commentary
Agreeably to this is the advice of R. Eleazar (z),

"Be diligent to learn the Torah, and know what thou shouldest answer to an Epicure, or heretic: says R. Jochanan (a),

289

"In every place where the Sadducees object, תשובתן בצידן their answer is at their side,

Or ready; that is, in the same Scriptures on which they form their objections,

(z) Pirke Abot, c. 2. sect. 14. (a) T. Bab. Sanhedrin, fol. 38. 2.

1 Peter 3

16. Having a good conscience; that, whereas they speak evil of you, as of evildoers, they may be ashamed that falsely accuse your good conversation in Christ.

16. συνείδησιν ἔχοντες ἀγαθήν, ἵνα, ἐν ᾧ καταλαλοῦσιν ὑμῶν ὡς κακοποιῶν, καταισχυνθῶσιν οἱ ἐπηρεάζοντες ὑμῶν τὴν ἀγαθὴν ἐν χριστῷ ἀναστροφήν.

16. suneideisin echontes agathein, 'ina, en 'o katalalousin 'umon 'os kakopoion, kataischunthosin 'oi epeireazontes 'umon tein agathein en christo anastrophein.

טז. וברוח נכון אשר בקרבכם יבושו הדברים סרה על-דרככם הטובה במשיח וְהַמַּלְשִׁינִים אֶתְכֶם כְּפֹעֲלֵי אָוֶן:

16. Oov•roo•ach na•chon asher be•kir•be•chem ye•vo•shoo ha•dov•rim sa•ra al - dar•ke•chem ha•to•va ba•Ma•shi•ach ve•ha•mal•shi•nim et•chem ke•fo•a•ley aven.

---

17. For it is better, if the will of God be so, that ye suffer for well doing, than for evil doing.

17. Κρεῖττον γὰρ ἀγαθοποιοῦντας, εἰ θέλοι τὸ θέλημα τοῦ θεοῦ, πάσχειν, ἢ κακοποιοῦντας.

17. Kreitton gar agathopoiountas, ei theloi to theleima tou theou, paschein, ei kakopoiountas.

יז. כִּי טוֹב לָכֶם לְהִתְעַנּוֹת אִם כֵּן רָצָה הָאֱלֹהִים עֵקֶב עֲשׂוֹת טוֹב מֵאֲשֶׁר תִּתְעַנּוּ עֵקֶב עֲשׂוֹת רָע:

17. Ki tov la•chem le•hit•a•not eem ken ra•tza ha•Elohim e•kev asot tov me•a•sher tit•a•noo e•kev asot ra.

---

1 Peter 3

18. For Christ also hath once suffered for sins, the just for the unjust, that he might bring us to God, being put to death in the flesh, but quickened by the Spirit:

18. Ὅτι καὶ χριστὸς ἅπαξ περὶ ἁμαρτιῶν ἔπαθεν, δίκαιος ὑπὲρ ἀδίκων, ἵνα ὑμᾶς προσαγάγῃ τῷ θεῷ, θανατωθεὶς μὲν σαρκί, ζῳοποιηθεὶς δὲ πνεύματι,

18. 'Oti kai christos 'apax peri 'amartion epathen, dikaios 'uper adikon, 'ina 'umas prosagagei to theo, thanatotheis men sarki, zoopoieitheis de pneumati,

יח. כִּי גַם-הַמָּשִׁיחַ עֻנָּה פַּעַם אַחַת בְּחַטֹּאתֵינוּ אִישׁ צַדִּיק בְּעַד אֲנָשִׁים חַטָּאִים וַיְבִיאֵנוּ עַד-הָאֱלֹהִים אַחֲרֵי־אֲשֶׁר הוּמַת בִּשָׂרוֹ וַיְחִי בָרוּחַ

18. Ki gam - ha•Ma•shi•ach oo•na pa•am a•chat be•cha•to•tey•noo eesh tza•dik be•ad a•na•shim cha•ta•eem vay•vi•e•noo ad - ha•Elohim a•cha•rey asher hoo•mat be•sa•ro vay•chi va•Roo•ach.

---

19. By which also he went and preached unto the spirits in prison;

19. ἐν ᾧ καὶ τοῖς ἐν φυλακῇ πνεύμασιν πορευθεὶς ἐκήρυξεν,

19. en 'o kai tois en phulakei pneumasin poreutheis ekeiruxen,

יט. וַיַּעֲבֹר וַיִּקְרָא אֶת-הַקְּרִיאָה גַּם אֶל-הָרוּחוֹת אֲשֶׁר בַּמִּשְׁמָר:

19. Va•ya•a•vor va•yik•ra et - hak•ri•ah gam el - ha•roo•chot asher ba•mish•mar.

---

20. Which sometime were disobedient, when once the longsuffering of God waited in the days of Noah, while the ark was a preparing, wherein few, that is, eight souls were saved by water.

20. ἀπειθήσασίν ποτε, ὅτε ἀπεξεδέχετο ἡ τοῦ θεοῦ μακροθυμία ἐν ἡμέραις Νῶε, κατασκευαζομένης κιβωτοῦ, εἰς ἣν ὀλίγαι, τοῦτ᾽ ἔστιν ὀκτὼ ψυχαί, διεσώθησαν δι᾽ ὕδατος·

20. apeitheisasin pote, 'ote apexedecheto 'ei tou theou makrothumia en 'eimerais Noe, kataskeuazomeneis kibotou, eis 'ein oligai, tout estin okto psuchai, diesotheisan di 'udatos.

כ. הֲלֹא הֵם אֲשֶׁר לֹא הֶאֱמִינוּ לְפָנִים כַּאֲשֶׁר חִכָּה אֱלֹהִים אֲלֵיהֶם בְּאֹרֶךְ אַפּוֹ בִּימֵי נֹחַ עַד-אֲשֶׁר נֶעֶשְׂתָה הַתֵּבָה:וַאֲנָשִׁים מְעַטִּים שְׁמֹנֶה נְפָשׁוֹת נִמְלְטוּ בָה מִן-הַמָּיִם

20. Ha•lo hem asher lo he•e•mi•noo le•fa•nim ka•a•sher chi•ka Elohim aley•hem be•o•rech apo bi•mey no•ach ad - asher ne•es•ta ha•te•va va•a•na•shim me•a•tim sh`mo•ne n`fa•shot nim•le•too va min - ha•ma•yim.

Rabbinic Jewish Commentary

The Syriac version connects with this clause, reading it thus, "who of old were disobedient in the days of Noah."

while the ark was preparing; by Noah, according to the directions which God gave him, Gen.6:14 and which, as R. Tanchuma says (b), was fifty two years a building; others say (c) an hundred years; but Jarchi says (d) it was an hundred and twenty; and which seems most likely, that being the term of time in which God's longsuffering waited on them; during which time Noah was preaching to them, and building the ark.

wherein few, that is, eight souls, were saved by water; the eight persons were, Noah, and his wife, and his three sons, Shem, Ham, and Japhet, and their three wives. It is a common tradition with the Jews (e), that besides these, Og, king of Bashan, escaped the flood; and who, they say, is the same that escaped, and told Abraham of Lot's being carried captive by the kings (f); the manner of his escape at the flood they relate thus (g), "Og came, who was delivered from the men that died at the flood; and he rode upon the ark, and he had a covering upon his head, and was fed with the food of Noah; but not for his worthiness was he delivered, but that the inhabitants of the world might see the power of YHVH.

And elsewhere (h), after this manner, citing those words, "and Noah only remained alive, and they that were with him in the ark", Gen.7:23 they add, "except Og, king of Bashan, who sat on a certain piece of wood which belonged to the scaffolding of the ark, and he swore to Noah, and his sons, that he would be their servant for ever. What did Noah do? he bored an hole in the ark, and every day reached out food to him, and he remained alive, according to what is said, Deu.3:11 "only Og, king of Bashan". But this is all a mere fiction; and equally fabulous is the account the Arabians give, who say (i) that eighty persons, together with Noah, were taken into the ark, among whom was Jorham, their father; for there were no more than eight persons saved; and this is the apostle's sense; and agreeably the Syriac version renders it, "and eight souls" בלחוד, "only entered into it, and were saved by water"; and we are told by some of the eastern writers (k), that when these eight went out of the ark, they built a city, which they called Themanin, which, in the Arabic language, signifies "eight", according to their number.

(b) In Pirke Eliezer, c. 23. (c) Elmacin. Hist. apud Hottinger. Smegma Orient. l. 1. c. 8. p. 249. (d) In Gen. vi. 15. (e) Targum Jon. in Deut. iii. 11. T. Bab. Nidda, fol. 61. 1. (f) Bereshit Rabba, sect. 42. fol. 37. 2. Targum Jon. & Jarchi in Gen. xiv. 13. (g) Targum Jon. in Gen. xiv. 13. (h) Pirke Eliezer, c. 23. (i) Pocock. Specim. Hist. Arab. p. 38. (k) Eutychii Annal. p. 43. Elmacin. Hist. l. 1. c. 1. p. 12. Patricides, p. 10. Apud Hottinger, Smegma Orient. l. 1. c. 8. p. 251, 252.

---

21. The like figure whereunto even baptism doth also now save us (not the putting away of the filth of the flesh, but the answer of a good conscience toward God,) by the resurrection of Jesus Christ:

21. ὃ ἀντίτυπον νῦν καὶ ἡμᾶς σῴζει βάπτισμα, οὐ σαρκὸς ἀπόθεσις ῥύπου, ἀλλὰ συνειδήσεως ἀγαθῆς ἐπερώτημα εἰς θεόν, δι᾽ ἀναστάσεως Ἰησοῦ χριστοῦ,

21. 'o antitupon nun kai 'eimas sozei baptisma, ou sarkos apothesis 'rupou, alla suneideiseos agatheis eperoteima eis theon, di anastaseos Yeisou christou,

כא. וַיְהִי לְמוֹפֵת לִטְבִילָתֵנוּ בְּמַיִם אֲשֶׁר תּוֹשִׁיעַ לָנוּ גַּם-הַיּוֹם לֹא לִרְחֹץ אֶת-צוֹאַת הַבָּשָׂר כִּי אִם-לְזַכּוֹת אֶת-לִבֵּנוּ בְּרוּחַ נָכוֹן לִפְנֵי הָאֱלֹהִים עַל-יְדֵי תְּקוּמַת יֵשׁוּעַ הַמָּשִׁיחַ

21. Vay•hi le•mo•fet lit•vi•la•te•noo ve•ma•yim asher to•shi•a la•noo gam - ha•yom lo lir•chotz et - tzo•at ha•ba•sar ki eem - le•za•kot et - li•be•noo be•roo•ach na•chon lif•ney ha•Elohim al - ye•dey te•koo•mat Yeshua ha•Ma•shi•ach.

Rabbinic Jewish Commentary

The Vulgate Latin renders it, "the interrogation of a good conscience"; referring, it may be, to the interrogations that used to be put to those who desired baptism.

The Ethiopic version renders it, "confession of God"; and to this the Syriac version agrees, rendering it, "confessing God with a pure conscience".

1 Peter 3

22. Who is gone into heaven, and is on the right hand of God; angels and authorities and powers being made subject unto him.

22. ὅς ἐστιν ἐν δεξιᾷ τοῦ θεοῦ, πορευθεὶς εἰς οὐρανόν, ὑποταγέντων αὐτῷ ἀγγέλων καὶ ἐξουσιῶν καὶ δυνάμεων.

22. 'os estin en dexya tou theou, poreutheis eis ouranon, 'upotagenton auto angelon kai exousion kai dunameon.

כב. אֲשֶׁר עָלָה הַשָּׁמַיְמָה וַיֵּשֶׁב לִימִין הָאֱלֹהִים וּמַלְאָכִים שָׂרֵי צָבָא וְגִבֹּרֵי כֹּחַ שָׁת אֱלֹהִים תַּחַת יָדוֹ:

22. Asher ala ha•sha•mai•ma va•ye•shev li•y`min ha•Elohim oo•mal•a•chim sa•rey tza•va ve•gi•bo•rey cho•ach shat Elohim ta•chat ya•do.

(1Peter Chapter 3 End)

1 Peter, Chapter 4

1. Forasmuch then as Christ hath suffered for us in the flesh, arm yourselves likewise with the same mind: for he that hath suffered in the flesh hath ceased from sin;

1. Χριστοῦ οὖν παθόντος ὑπὲρ ἡμῶν σαρκί, καὶ ὑμεῖς τὴν αὐτὴν ἔννοιαν ὁπλίσασθε· ὅτι ὁ παθὼν ἐν σαρκί, πέπαυται ἁμαρτίας·

1. Christou oun pathontos 'uper 'eimon sarki, kai 'umeis tein autein ennoyan 'oplisasthe. 'oti 'o pathon en sarki, pepautai 'amartias.

א. וְעַתָּה אַחֲרֵי אֲשֶׁר עֻנָּה הַמָּשִׁיחַ בַּעֲדֵנוּ בַּבָּשָׂר הִתְאָזְרוּ עֹז רוּחַ כָּמוֹהוּ גַּם-אַתֶּם כִּי הַמֻּכֶּה וְהַמְעֻנֶּה בִּבְשָׂרוֹ: יֶחְדַּל מֵחֲטוֹא

1. Ve•a•ta a•cha•rey asher oo•na ha•Ma•shi•ach ba•a•de•noo ba•ba•sar hit•az•roo oz roo•ach ka•mo•hoo gam - atem ki ha•moo•ke ve•ham•oo•ne viv•sa•ro yech•dal me•cha•to.

---

2. That he no longer should live the rest of his time in the flesh to the lusts of men, but to the will of God.

2. εἰς τὸ μηκέτι ἀνθρώπων ἐπιθυμίαις, ἀλλὰ θελήματι θεοῦ τὸν ἐπίλοιπον ἐν σαρκὶ βιῶσαι χρόνον.

2. eis to meiketi anthropon epithumiais, alla theleimati theou ton epiloipon en sarki biosai chronon.

ב: וְלֹא תָתוּרוּ אַחֲרֵי תַאֲוַת בָּשָׂר וָדָם כָּל-יְמֵי חַיֵּיכֶם עַל-הָאֲדָמָה כִּי אִם-אַחֲרֵי חֵפֶץ אֱלֹהִים

2. Ve•lo ta•too•roo a•cha•rey ta•a•vat ba•sar va•dam kol - ye•mey cha•yey•chem al - ha•a•da•ma ki eem - a•cha•rey che•fetz Elohim.

Rabbinic Jewish Commentary

The Arabic version reads, "that ye no longer should live". The phrase, "his time in the flesh", means the present time of life, in the body, and is the same with those phrases, in the days of his flesh, to abide in the flesh, and be at home in the body.

3. For the time past of our life may suffice us to have wrought the will of the Gentiles, when we walked in lasciviousness, lusts, excess of wine, revellings, banquetings, and abominable idolatries:

3. Ἀρκετὸς γὰρ ἡμῖν ὁ παρεληλυθὼς χρόνος τοῦ βίου τὸ θέλημα τῶν ἐθνῶν κατεργάσασθαι, πεπορευμένους ἐν ἀσελγείαις, ἐπιθυμίαις, οἰνοφλυγίαις, κώμοις, πότοις, καὶ ἀθεμίτοις εἰδωλολατρείαις·

3. Arketos gar 'eimin 'o pareleiluthos chronos tou biou to theleima ton ethnon katergasasthai, peporeumenous en aselgeiais, epithumiais, oinophlugiais, komois, potois, kai athemitois eidololatreiais.

ג. כִּי רַב לָנוּ אֲשֶׁר עָשִׂינוּ כְּחֵפֶץ הַגּוֹיִם בַּיָּמִים עָבְרוּ עָלֵינוּ בְּלֶכְתֵּנוּ עִמָּהֶם בְּאָרְחוֹת זִמָּה וַעֲגָבִים בְּבָתֵּי זוֹלְלִים וְסֹבְאִים וְהִלּוּלִים וּבְגִלּוּלֵי הָאֱלִילִים׃

3. Ki rav la•noo asher asi•noo ke•che•fetz ha•go•yim ba•ya•mim av•roo aley•noo be•lech•te•noo ee•ma•hem be•or•chot zi•ma va•a•ga•vim be•va•tey zo•le•lim ve•sov•eem ve•hi•loo•lim oov•gi•loo•ley ha•e•li•lim.

---

4. Wherein they think it strange that ye run not with them to the same excess of riot, speaking evil of you:

4. ἐν ᾧ ξενίζονται, μὴ συντρεχόντων ὑμῶν εἰς τὴν αὐτὴν τῆς ἀσωτίας ἀνάχυσιν, βλασφημοῦντες·

4. en 'o xenizontai, mei suntrechonton 'umon eis tein autein teis asotias anachusin, blaspheimountes.

ד. וְכַיּוֹם יָנִיעוּ רֹאשׁ וְיַלְעִיבוּ בָכֶם כִּי לֹא-תָרוּצוּ עוֹד עִמָּהֶם לְשֶׁטֶף זִמָּתָם:

4. Ve•cha•yom ya•ni•oo rosh ve•yal•ee•voo va•chem ki lo - ta•roo•tzoo od ee•ma•hem le•she•tef zi•ma•tam.

---

5. Who shall give account to him that is ready to judge the quick and the dead.

5. οἳ ἀποδώσουσιν λόγον τῷ ἑτοίμως ἔχοντι κρῖναι ζῶντας καὶ νεκρούς.

5. 'oi apodosousin logon to 'etoimos echonti krinai zontas kai nekrous.

:ה. הָעֲתִידִים לָתֵת דִּין וְחֶשְׁבּוֹן לִפְנֵי הֶעָתִיד לָבוֹא לִשְׁפֹּט אֶת-הַחַיִּים וְאֶת-הַמֵּתִים

5. Ha•a•ti•dim la•tet din ve•chesh•bon lif•ney he•a•tid la•vo lish•pot et - ha•cha•yim ve•et - ha•me•tim.

1 Peter 4

6. For for this cause was the gospel preached also to them that are dead, that they might be judged according to men in the flesh, but live according to God in the spirit.

6. Εἰς τοῦτο γὰρ καὶ νεκροῖς εὐηγγελίσθη, ἵνα κριθῶσιν μὲν κατὰ ἀνθρώπους σαρκί, ζῶσιν δὲ κατὰ θεὸν πνεύματι.

6. Eis touto gar kai nekrois eueingelisthei, 'ina krithosin men kata anthropous sarki, zosin de kata theon pneumati.

ו. כִּי עַל-כֵּן הָיְתָה קְרִיאַת הַבְּשֹׂרָה גַּם אֶל-הַמֵּתִים לְמַעַן יִשָּׁפְטוּ בַבָּשָׂר כִּבְנֵי אָדָם וְיִחְיוּ בְּחַיֵּי רוּחַ כֵּאלֹהִים:

6. Ki al - ken hai•ta k`ri•at ha•b`so•hra gam el - ha•me•tim le•ma•an yi•shaf•too va•ba•sar kiv•ney adam ve•yich•yoo ve•cha•yey roo•ach ke•Elohim.

7. But the end of all things is at hand: be ye therefore sober, and watch unto prayer.

7. Πάντων δὲ τὸ τέλος ἤγγικεν· σωφρονήσατε οὖν καὶ νήψατε εἰς τὰς προσευχάς·

7. Panton de to telos eingiken. sophroneisate oun kai neipsate eis tas proseuchas.

:ז. הִנֵּה קֵץ כָּל-דָּבָר קָרוֹב עַל-כֵּן הַשְׂכִּילוּ וְהִתְעוֹרְרוּ בִתְפִלָּה

7. Hee•ne ketz kol - da•var ka•rov al - ken has•ki•loo ve•hit•o•re•roo vit•fi•la.

Rabbinic Jewish Commentary

Very rightly does the apostle join the above exhortation with this, since a man that is not sober is neither fit to watch nor pray; and a drunken man, according to the Jewish canons, might not pray (l):

"One that is a drinker, or in drink, let him not pray, or if he prays, his prayer is deprecations; a drunken man, let him not pray, and if he prays his prayer is blasphemies."

Or, as it is elsewhere (m) expressed,

"Let not a drunken man pray, because he has no intention; and if he prays, his prayer is an abomination, therefore let him return and, pray when he is clear of his drunkenness: let no one in drink pray, and if he prays, his prayer is prayer (unless the word תפלה should rather be rendered "folly", as it may); who is a drunken man? he that cannot speak before a king; a man in drink can speak before a king, and not be confounded; even though he drinks but a fourth part, or a quarter of wine, let him not pray until his wine is departed from him."

(l) T. Hieros. Terumot, fol. 40. 4. (m) Maimon. Hilch Tephilla, c. 4. sect. 17.

---

8. And above all things have fervent charity among yourselves: for charity shall cover the multitude of sins.

8. πρὸ πάντων δὲ τὴν εἰς ἑαυτοὺς ἀγάπην ἐκτενῆ ἔχοντες, ὅτι ἀγάπη καλύψει πλῆθος ἁμαρτιῶν·

8. pro panton de tein eis 'eautous agapein ektenei echontes, 'oti agapei kalupsei pleithos 'amartion.

ח. אַךְ בְּרֹאשׁ כָּל־דָּבָר אֱהֶבוּ אִישׁ אֶת־רֵעֵהוּ בְּאַהֲבָה רַבָּה כִּי אַהֲבָה תְּכַסֶּה עַל־פְּשָׁעִים רַבִּים:

8. Ach be•rosh kol - da•var e•he•voo eesh et - re•e•hoo be•a•ha•va ra•ba ki a•ha•va te•cha•se al - pe•sha•eem ra•bim.

---

9. Use hospitality one to another without grudging.

9. φιλόξενοι εἰς ἀλλήλους ἄνευ γογγυσμῶν·

9. philoxenoi eis alleilous aneu gongusmon.

ט. שִׁמְרוּ אַהֲבַת אַחִים בְּקִרְבְּכֶם וְלֹא תִתְעָרֵב תְּלוּנָה בָּהּ:

9. Shim•roo a•ha•vat a•chim be•kir•be•chem ve•lo tit•a•rev t`loo•na ba.

---

1 Peter 4

10. As every man hath received the gift, even so minister the same one to another, as good stewards of the manifold grace of God.

10. ἕκαστος καθὼς ἔλαβεν χάρισμα, εἰς ἑαυτοὺς αὐτὸ διακονοῦντες, ὡς καλοὶ οἰκονόμοι ποικίλης χάριτος θεοῦ·

10. 'ekastos kathos elaben charisma, eis 'eautous auto dyakonountes, 'os kaloi oikonomoi poikileis charitos theou.

י. אִישׁ אִישׁ מִכֶּם כַּמַּתָּן אֲשֶׁר תַּשִּׂיג יָדוֹ כֵּן תְּפַזְּרוּ אִישׁ לְרֵעֵהוּ כִּפְקִידִים נֶאֱמָנִים עַל-חַסְדֵי אֱלֹהִים הָרַבִּים:

10. Eesh eesh mi•kem ka•ma•tan asher ta•sig ya•do ken te•faz•roo eesh le•re•e•hoo kif•ki•dim ne•e•ma•nim al - chas•dey Elohim ha•ra•bim.

---

11. If any man speak, let him speak as the oracles of God; if any man minister, let him do it as of the ability which God giveth: that God in all things may be glorified through Jesus Christ, to whom be praise and dominion for ever and ever. Amen.

11. εἴ τις λαλεῖ, ὡς λόγια θεοῦ· εἴ τις διακονεῖ, ὡς ἐξ ἰσχύος ὡς χορηγεῖ ὁ θεός· ἵνα ἐν πᾶσιν δοξάζηται ὁ θεὸς διὰ Ἰησοῦ χριστοῦ, ᾧ ἐστὶν ἡ δόξα καὶ τὸ κράτος εἰς τοὺς αἰῶνας τῶν αἰώνων. Ἀμήν.

11. ei tis lalei, 'os logya theou. ei tis dyakonei, 'os ex ischuos 'os choreigei 'o theos. 'ina en pasin doxazeitai 'o theos dya Yeisou christou, 'o estin 'ei doxa kai to kratos eis tous aionas ton aionon. Amein.

יא. כִּי יְדַבֵּר אִישׁ בְּקָהָל יְהִי דְבָרוֹ כִּדְבַר אֱלֹהִים וְהַמְשָׁרֵת יְמַלֵּא פְקֻדָּתוֹ כְּיַד אֱלֹהִים הַטּוֹבָה עָלָיו לְמַעַן יְכֻבַּד: שֵׁם אֱלֹהִים בַּכֹּל עַל-יְדֵי יֵשׁוּעַ הַמָּשִׁיחַ אֲשֶׁר לוֹ הַכָּבוֹד וְהַמֶּמְשָׁלָה לְעוֹלָם וָעֶד אָמֵן

11. Ki ye•da•ber eesh be•ka•hal ye•hee de•va•ro ki•d`var Elohim ve•ham•sha•ret ye•ma•le f`koo•da•to ke•yad Elohim ha•to•va alav le•ma•an yi•ka•ved shem Elohim ba•kol al - ye•dey Yeshua ha•Ma•shi•ach asher lo ha•ka•vod ve•ha•mem•sha•la le•o•lam va•ed Amen.

---

1 Peter 4

12. Beloved, think it not strange concerning the fiery trial which is to try you, as though some strange thing happened unto you:

12. Ἀγαπητοί, μὴ ξενίζεσθε τῇ ἐν ὑμῖν πυρώσει πρὸς πειρασμὸν ὑμῖν γινομένῃ, ὡς ξένου ὑμῖν συμβαίνοντος·

12. Agapeitoi, mei xenizesthe tei en 'umin purosei pros peirasmon 'umin ginomenei, 'os xenou 'umin sumbainontos.

יב. אַל-תִּתְפַּלְאוּ יְדִידִים כִּי תָבוֹאוּ לְהִבָּחֵן בְּכוּר עֹנִי כְּמוֹ אִם-קָרָה אֶתְכֶם דָּבָר זָר:

12. Al - tit•pal•oo ye•di•dim ki ta•vo•oo le•hi•ba•chen be•choor o•ni k`mo eem - ka•ra et•chem da•var zar.

---

13. But rejoice, inasmuch as ye are partakers of Christ's sufferings; that, when his glory shall be revealed, ye may be glad also with exceeding joy.

13. ἀλλὰ καθὸ κοινωνεῖτε τοῖς τοῦ χριστοῦ παθήμασιν, χαίρετε, ἵνα καὶ ἐν τῇ ἀποκαλύψει τῆς δόξης αὐτοῦ χαρῆτε ἀγαλλιώμενοι.

13. alla katho koinoneite tois tou christou patheimasin, chairete, 'ina kai en tei apokalupsei teis doxeis autou chareite agalliomenoi.

יג. אַךְ תָּשִׂישׂוּ בַּאֲשֶׁר חֲבֵרִים אַתֶּם לְחֶבְלֵי הַמָּשִׁיחַ וְכֵן תָּשִׂישׂוּ וְתַעַלְצוּ בְּהִגָּלוֹת נִגְלוֹת כְּבוֹדוֹ:

13. Ach ta•si•soo ba•a•sher cha•ve•rim atem le•chev•ley ha•Ma•shi•ach ve•chen ta•si•soo ve•ta•al•tzoo be•hi•ga•lot nig•lot k`vo•do.

1 Peter 4

14. If ye be reproached for the name of Christ, happy are ye; for the spirit of glory and of God resteth upon you: on their part he is evil spoken of, but on your part he is glorified.

14. Εἰ ὀνειδίζεσθε ἐν ὀνόματι χριστοῦ, μακάριοι· ὅτι τὸ τῆς δόξης καὶ τὸ τοῦ θεοῦ πνεῦμα ἐφ᾽ ὑμᾶς ἀναπαύεται· κατὰ μὲν αὐτοὺς βλασφημεῖται, κατὰ δὲ ὑμᾶς δοξάζεται.

14. Ei oneidizesthe en onomati christou, makarioi. 'oti to teis doxeis kai to tou theou pneuma eph 'umas anapauetai. kata men autous blaspheimeitai, kata de 'umas doxazetai.

יד. אַשְׁרֵיכֶם אִם יְחָרְפוּ אֶתְכֶם בַּעֲבוּר שֵׁם הַמָּשִׁיחַ כִּי נָחָה עֲלֵיכֶם רוּחַ הַכָּבוֹד וְרוּחַ אֱלֹהִים אֶצְלָם מְנֹאָץ הוּא:וְאֶצְלְכֶם נִכְבָּד

14. Ash•rey•chem eem ye•char•foo et•chem ba•a•voor shem ha•Ma•shi•ach ki na•cha aley•chem roo•ach ha•ka•vod ve•Roo•ach Elohim etz•lam me•no•atz hoo ve•etz•le•chem nich•bad.

Rabbinic Jewish Commentary

The Jews have a saying (n), that the Holy Spirit does not dwell on any, but on him that has a cheerful heart

(n) T. Hieros. Succa, fol. 55. 1.

---

15. But let none of you suffer as a murderer, or as a thief, or as an evildoer, or as a busybody in other men's matters.

15. Μὴ γάρ τις ὑμῶν πασχέτω ὡς φονεύς, ἢ κλέπτης, ἢ κακοποιός, ἢ ὡς ἀλλοτριοεπίσκοπος·

15. Mei gar tis 'umon paschetō 'os phoneus, ei klepteis, ei kakopoios, ei 'os allotrioepiskopos.

טו. וְלֹא יִוָּסֵר אִישׁ מִכֶּם כְּרֹצֵחַ אוֹ-כְגַנָּב אוֹ-כְפֹעֵל אָוֶן אוֹ-כִמְרַגֵּל בִּפְקֻדַת אֲחֵרִים:

15. Ve•lo yi•va•ser eesh mi•kem ke•ro•tze•ach oh - che•ga•nav oh - che•fo•el aven oh - chim•ra•gel bif•koo•dat a•che•rim.

16. Yet if any man suffer as a Christian, let him not be ashamed; but let him glorify God on this behalf.

16. εἰ δὲ ὡς Χριστιανός, μὴ αἰσχυνέσθω, δοξαζέτω δὲ τὸν θεὸν ἐν τῷ μέρει τούτῳ.

16. ei de 'os Christyanos, mei aischunestho, doxazeto de ton theon en to merei touto.

טז. אֲבָל אִם-יְעֻנֶּה בַּאֲשֶׁר שֵׁם הַמָּשִׁיחַ נִקְרָא עָלָיו אַל-יֵבוֹשׁ כִּי אִם-יוֹדֶה אֶת-אֱלֹהִים בַּשֵּׁם הַזֶּה:

16. Aval eem - ye•oo•ne ba•a•sher shem ha•Ma•shi•ach nik•ra alav al - ye•vosh ki eem - yo•de et - Elohim ba•shem ha•ze.

---

1 Peter 4

17. For the time is come that judgment must begin at the house of God: and if it first begin at us, what shall the end be of them that obey not the gospel of God?

17. Ὅτι ὁ καιρὸς τοῦ ἄρξασθαι τὸ κρίμα ἀπὸ τοῦ οἴκου τοῦ θεοῦ· εἰ δὲ πρῶτον ἀφ᾽ ἡμῶν, τί τὸ τέλος τῶν ἀπειθούντων τῷ τοῦ θεοῦ εὐαγγελίῳ;

17. 'Oti 'o kairos tou arxasthai to krima apo tou oikou tou theou. ei de proton aph 'eimon, ti to telos ton apeithounton to tou theou euangelio?

יז. כִּי בָא הַיּוֹם לְהָחֵל מִשְׁפָּט מִבֵּית אֱלֹהִים וְאִם-בָּנוּ הֵחֵל מָה-אֵפוֹא תִהְיֶה אַחֲרִית הַמַּמְרִים אֶת-בְּשֹׂרַת:אֱלֹהִים

17. Ki va ha•yom le•ha•chel mish•pat mi•beit Elohim ve•eem - ba•noo he`chel ma - e•fo ti•hi•ye acha•rit ha•mam•rim et - be•so•rat Elohim.

Rabbinic Jewish Commentary

The Jews have various phrases, and frequent expressions in their writings, which resemble these, and serve to illustrate them. When Noah told the old world of the flood, and called upon them to repent, they are represented as saying to him (o),

"Where does punishment begin? מן ביתיה, "at the house" of that man does it "begin?" when Methuselah died, they said unto him, does not punishment begin at the house of that man?"

And elsewhere (p), says R. Jonathan,

"Punishment does not come into the world, but in the time that the wicked are in the world; and it does not begin (i.e. at them) אלא מן הצדיקים תחלה, but it begins at the righteous;"

And again (q).

"When God executes judgment on the righteous, he is praised; for if he executes this on them, how much more on the ungodly?" See Isa.10:11.

(o) Midrash Kohelet, fol. 79. 4. (p) T. Bab. Bava Kama, fol. 60. 1. Caphtor, fol. 70. 2. (q) Jarchi in Numb. 179. apud Grotium in loc.

---

1 Peter 4

18. And if the righteous scarcely be saved, where shall the ungodly and the sinner appear?

18. Καὶ εἰ ὁ δίκαιος μόλις σῴζεται, ὁ ἀσεβὴς καὶ ἁμαρτωλὸς ποῦ φανεῖται;

18. Kai ei 'o dikaios molis sozetai, 'o asebeis kai 'amartolos pou phaneitai?

יח. וְאִם לַצַּדִּיק קָשֶׁה לְהִנָּצֵל אֵל-מִי יִפְנֶה רָשָׁע וְחֹטֵא:

18. Ve•eem la•tza•dik ka•she le•hi•na•tzel el - mee yif•ne ra•sha ve•cho•te.

---

19. Wherefore let them that suffer according to the will of God commit the keeping of their souls to him in well doing, as unto a faithful Creator.

19. Ὥστε καὶ οἱ πάσχοντες κατὰ τὸ θέλημα τοῦ θεοῦ, ὡς πιστῷ κτίστῃ παρατιθέσθωσαν τὰς ψυχὰς αὐτῶν ἐν ἀγαθοποιΐᾳ.

19. 'Oste kai 'oi paschontes kata to theleima tou theou, 'os pisto ktistei paratithesthosan tas psuchas auton en agathopoi'ia.

יט. עַל־כֵּן הַמְעֻנִּים כִּרְצוֹן אֱלֹהִים יוֹסִיפוּ לְהֵיטִיב וְיַפְקִידוּ אֶת־נַפְשָׁם בְּיַד יוֹצְרָם כִּי נֶאֱמָן הוּא:

19. Al - ken ha•me•oo•nim kir•tzon Elohim yo•si•foo le•hey•tiv ve•yaf•ki•doo et - naf•sham be•yad yotz•ram ki ne•e•man hoo.

(1Peter Chapter 4 End)

1 Peter, Chapter 5

1. The elders which are among you I exhort, who am also an elder, and a witness of the sufferings of Christ, and also a partaker of the glory that shall be revealed:

1. Πρεσβυτέρους τοὺς ἐν ὑμῖν παρακαλῶ ὁ συμπρεσβύτερος καὶ μάρτυς τῶν τοῦ χριστοῦ παθημάτων, ὁ καὶ τῆς μελλούσης ἀποκαλύπτεσθαι δόξης κοινωνός·

1. Presbuterous tous en 'umin parakalo 'o sumpresbuteros kai martus ton tou christou patheimaton, 'o kai teis mellouseis apokaluptesthai doxeis koinonos.

א. וְאֶל-הַזְּקֵנִים בָּכֶם אֲנִי הַזָּקֵן כְּחָבֵר לָהֶם וְעֵד לְחֶבְלֵי הַמָּשִׁיחַ וַאֲשֶׁר נָכוֹן לִי חֵלֶק בַּכָּבוֹד הֶעָתִיד לְהִגָּלוֹת:אֶקְרָא וַאֲצַוֶּה לֵאמֹר

1. Ve•el - haz`ke•nim ba•chem ani ha•za•ken ke•cha•ver la•hem ve•ed le•chev•ley ha•Ma•shi•ach va•a•sher na•chon li che•lek ba•ka•vod he•a•tid le•hi•ga•lot ek•ra va•a•tza•ve le•mor.

---

2. Feed the flock of God which is among you, taking the oversight thereof, not by constraint, but willingly; not for filthy lucre, but of a ready mind;

2. ποιμάνατε τὸ ἐν ὑμῖν ποίμνιον τοῦ θεοῦ, ἐπισκοποῦντες μὴ ἀναγκαστῶς, ἀλλ᾽ ἑκουσίως· μηδὲ αἰσχροκερδῶς, ἀλλὰ προθύμως·

2. poimanate to en 'umin poimnion tou theou, episkopountes mei anagkastos, all 'ekousios. meide aischrokerdos, alla prothumos.

ב. רְעוּ אֶת-עֵדֶר הָאֱלֹהִים הַנִּמְצָא אִתְּכֶם הַשְׁגִּיחוּ אֲלֵיהֶם לֹא בְאֹנֶס כִּי אִם-בְּרוּחַ נְדִיבָה בְּנֶפֶשׁ חֲפֵצָה וְלֹא:לְמַעַן בֶּצַע בָּצַע

2. R`oo et - eder ha•Elohim ha•nim•tza eet•chem hash•gi•choo aley•hem lo ve•o•nes ki eem - be•roo•ach n`di•va be•ne•fesh cha•fe•tza ve•lo le•ma•an be•tzo•a ba•tza.

Rabbinic Jewish Commentary

The Syriac version renders it, which "Is delivered unto you"; which was committed to their care, and they were made overseers of, and stood in a special relation to; wherefore it was incumbent on them to regard them, so as they did not, and were not obliged to regard, any other distinct flock: by "the flock of God"; or, "of Messiah", as some copies read, is meant, not the whole world, which Philo the Jew (r) calls the greatest and most perfect, του οντος θεου ποιμην, "flock of the true God."

The Arabic version renders it, "watching, not forced watches, but willing ones". This contrast of phrases seems to be Jewish, or Rabbinical (s); it is a tradition of the Rabbis;

"Blood which is defiled, and they sprinkle it ignorantly, it is accepted; presumptuously, not accepted; of what things are these said? of a private person; but of a congregation, whether ignorantly or presumptuously, it is accepted; and of a stranger, whether ignorantly or presumptuously, בין באונס בין ברצון, "whether by constraint or willingly", it is not accepted.

(r) De Agricultura, p. 195. (s) T. Bab. Menachot, fol. 25. 1. Vid. T. Bab. Avoda Zara, fol. 54. 1. & Maimon. Hilch. Issure Mizbeach, c. 4. sect. 5, 6.

---

3. Neither as being lords over God's heritage, but being ensamples to the flock.

3. μηδὲ ὡς κατακυριεύοντες τῶν κλήρων, ἀλλὰ τύποι γινόμενοι τοῦ ποιμνίου.

3. meide 'os katakurieuontes ton kleiron, alla tupoi ginomenoi tou poimniou.

ג: לֹא לְהִשְׂתָּרֵר עַל-נַחֲלַת יְהֹוָה כִּי אִם-לִהְיוֹת לְמוֹפֵת לַצֹּאן

3. Lo le•his•ta•rer al - na•cha•lat Adonai ki eem - li•hee•yot le•mo•fet la•tzon.

---

4. And when the chief Shepherd shall appear, ye shall receive a crown of glory that fadeth not away.

4. Καὶ φανερωθέντος τοῦ ἀρχιποίμενος, κομιεῖσθε τὸν ἀμαράντινον τῆς δόξης στέφανον.

4. Kai phanerothentos tou archipoimenos, komieisthe ton amarantinon teis doxeis stephanon.

ד. וְכַאֲשֶׁר יוֹפִיעַ אַבִּיר הָרֹעִים אָז תִּשְׂאוּ עֲטֶרֶת תִּפְאֶרֶת אֲשֶׁר לֹא תִבּוֹל:

4. Ve•cha•a•sher yo•fi•a abir ha•ro•eem az tis•oo ate•ret tif•e•ret asher lo ti•bol.

Rabbinic Jewish Commentary

Aben Ezra says (s), it was customary for the shepherd to have under him רועים קטנים, "little shepherds": the same perhaps with the hirelings, whose own the sheep are not, Joh.10:12 who are retained, or removed, according to their behaviour; these, in the Talmudic language, are called ברזלי (t), or כרזלי; though, according to Guido (u), the word, pronounced in the latter way, signifies a "chief shepherd", who takes care of men, and has other shepherds, servants under him; and such an one used to be called הרועה הגדול, "the great", or "chief shepherd";

So Maimonides (w) says, it was the custom of shepherds to have servants under them, to whom they committed the flocks to keep; so that when הרועה הגדול, "the chief shepherd", delivered to other shepherds what was under his care, these came in his room; and if there was any loss, the second shepherd, who was under the "chief shepherd", was obliged to make good the loss, and not the first shepherd, who was the chief shepherd; and to the same purpose says another of their commentators (x); it is the custom of הרועה הגדול, "the chief shepherd", to deliver (the flock) to the little shepherd that is under him; wherefore the shepherd that is under him is obliged to make good any loss: now, such a shepherd is Christ; he has others under him, whom he employs in feeding his sheep, and who are accountable to him, and must give up their account when he appears: at present he is out of the bodily sight of men, being received up to heaven, where he will be retained till the time of the restitution of all things; and then he will appear a second time in great glory, in his own, and in his Father's.

(s) Comment. in Zech. xi. 8. (t) T. Bab. Bava Kama, fol. 56. 2. (u) Dictionar. Syr. Chald. p. 102. (w) In Misn. Bava Kama, c. 6. sect. 2. (x) Bartenora in Misn. Bava Kama, c. 6. sect. 2.

---

1 Peter 5

5. Likewise, ye younger, submit yourselves unto the elder. Yea, all of you be subject one to another, and be clothed with humility: for God resisteth the proud, and giveth grace to the humble.

5. Ὁμοίως, νεώτεροι, ὑποτάγητε πρεσβυτέροις· πάντες δὲ ἀλλήλοις ὑποτασσόμενοι, τὴν ταπεινοφροσύνην ἐγκομβώσασθε· ὅτι ὁ θεὸς ὑπερηφάνοις ἀντιτάσσεται, ταπεινοῖς δὲ δίδωσιν χάριν.

5. 'Omoios, neoteroi, 'upotageite presbuterois. pantes de alleilois 'upotassomenoi, tein tapeinophrosunein egkombosasthe. 'oti 'o theos 'upereiphanois antitassetai, tapeinois de didosin charin.

ה. וְכֵן הַנְּעָרִים בָּכֶם הִכָּנְעוּ לִפְנֵי הַזְּקֵנִים וְכֻלְּכֶם הִתְאַזְּרוּ עֹז הָעֲנָוָה וְעִזְרוּ אִישׁ לְאָחִיו כִּי בֵית גֵּאִים יִסַּח:אֱלֹהִים וְלָעֲנָוִים יִתֶּן-חֵן

5. Ve•chen ha•ne•arim ba•chem hi•kan•oo lif•ney haz`ke•nim ve•chool•chem hit•az•roo oz ha•a•na•va ve•eez•roo eesh le•a•chiv ki veit ge•eem yi•sach Elohim ve•la•a•na•vim yi•ten - chen.

Rabbinic Jewish Commentary

The phrase seems to be Jewish, and is to be met with in the writings of the Jews. It is said (a),

"He that has fear, ונתלבש בענוה, "and is clothed with humility"; humility is the most excellent, and is comprehended in all, as it is said, Pro.22:4. He who has the fear of God is worthy of humility, and everyone that hath humility is worthy of kindness or holiness."

And it is a saying of R. Meir (b),

"He that loves God loves men; he that makes God glad makes men glad; and it (the law) מלבשתו ענוה, "clothes him with humility and fear"."

(a) Zohar in Numb. fol. 60. 3. (b) Pirke Abot, c. 6. sect. 1.

---

1 Peter 5

6. Humble yourselves therefore under the mighty hand of God, that he may exalt you in due time:

6. Ταπεινώθητε οὖν ὑπὸ τὴν κραταιὰν χεῖρα τοῦ θεοῦ, ἵνα ὑμᾶς ὑψώσῃ ἐν καιρῷ,

6. Tapeinotheite oun 'upo tein kratayan cheira tou theou, 'ina 'umas 'upsosei en kairo,

:ו. הַשְׁפִּילוּ נַפְשְׁכֶם תַּחַת יַד-אֵל שַׁדָּי וְהוּא יְרוֹמֵם אֶתְכֶם בְּעִתּוֹ

6. Hash•pi•loo naf•she•chem ta•chat yad - El Sha•dai ve•hoo ye•ro•mem et•chem be•ee•to.

---

1 Peter 5

7. Casting all your care upon him; for he careth for you.

7. πᾶσαν τὴν μέριμναν ὑμῶν ἐπιρρίψαντες ἐπ' αὐτόν, ὅτι αὐτῷ μέλει περὶ ὑμῶν.

7. pasan tein merimnan 'umon epirripsantes ep auton, 'oti auto melei peri 'umon.

:ז. וְכָל־יְהָבְכֶם הַשְׁלִיכוּ עָלָיו וְהוּא יִדְאַג לָכֶם

7. Ve•chol - ye•hav•chem hash•li•choo alav ve•hoo yid•ag la•chem.

---

8. Be sober, be vigilant; because your adversary the devil, as a roaring lion, walketh about, seeking whom he may devour:

8. Νήψατε, γρηγορήσατε· ὁ ἀντίδικος ὑμῶν διάβολος, ὡς λέων ὠρυόμενος, περιπατεῖ ζητῶν τίνα καταπίῃ·

8. Neipsate, greigoreisate. 'o antidikos 'umon dyabolos, 'os leon oruomenos, peripatei zeiton tina katapiei.

ח. הִתְעוֹרְרוּ הִשָּׁמְרוּ לָכֶם מְאֹד כִּי הַשָּׂטָן הַצֹּרֵר אֶתְכֶם יָתוּר כָּאֲרִי נֹהֵם וִישַׁחֵר אֶל־אֲשֶׁר יְבַלֵּעַ:

8. Hit•o•re•roo hi•sham•roo la•chem me•od ki ha•Satan ha•tzo•rer et•chem ya•toor ka•a•ri no•hem viy•sha•cher el - asher ye•va•le•a.

Rabbinic Jewish Commentary

The Jews (c) have adopted this word into their language, and explain it by בעל דין, "a law adversary", or one that has a suit of law depending against another. Satan accuses men of the breach of the Torah, and pleads that justice might take place, and punishment be inflicted, and which he pursues with great violence and diligence.

So the young lions in Psa.104:21 are, by the Cabalistic Jews (d), understood of devils; to which, for the above reasons, they may be truly compared: This is the end of his walking about: and the like is expressed in the Targum on Job.1:7

"And Satan answered before YHVH, and said, from going about in the earth למבדק בעובדי, "to search into the works" of the children of men, and from walking in it."

(c) Yalkut Simeoni, par. 2. fol. 41. 4. Bereshit Rabba, sect. 82. fol. 41. 4. & Jarchi & Aruch in Mattanot Cehuna in ib. (d) Lex. Cabal. p. 231, 417.

1 Peter 5

9. Whom resist stedfast in the faith, knowing that the same afflictions are accomplished in your brethren that are in the world.

9. ᾧ ἀντίστητε στερεοὶ τῇ πίστει, εἰδότες τὰ αὐτὰ τῶν παθημάτων τῇ ἐν κόσμῳ ὑμῶν ἀδελφότητι ἐπιτελεῖσθαι.

9. 'o antisteite stereoi tei pistei, eidotes ta auta ton patheimaton tei en kosmo 'umon adelphoteiti epiteleisthai.

ט. אַךְ בָּאֱמוּנָה תַעַמְדוּ נֶגְדּוֹ כְגִבֹּרִים וְתֵדְעוּן כִּי צָרוֹת כָּאֵלֶּה עָבְרוּ גַּם עַל־אֲחֵיכֶם אֲשֶׁר בָּאָרֶץ הֵמָּה:

9. Ach ba•e•moo•na ta•am•doo neg•do che•gi•bo•rim ve•ted•oon ki tza•rot ka•e•le av•roo gam al - a•chey•chem asher ba•a•retz he•ma.

10. But the God of all grace, who hath called us unto his eternal glory by Christ Jesus, after that ye have suffered a while, make you perfect, stablish, strengthen, settle you.

10. Ὁ δὲ θεὸς πάσης χάριτος, ὁ καλέσας ὑμᾶς εἰς τὴν αἰώνιον αὐτοῦ δόξαν ἐν χριστῷ Ἰησοῦ, ὀλίγον παθόντας αὐτὸς καταρτίσαι ὑμᾶς, στηρίξει, σθενώσει, θεμελιώσει.

10. 'O de theos paseis charitos, 'o kalesas 'umas eis tein aionion autou doxan en christo Yeisou, oligon pathontas autos katartisai 'umas, steirixei, sthenosei, themeliosei.

י. וְאַחֲרֵי אֲשֶׁר עֻנֵּיתֶם לְיָמִים מְעַטִּים יִתֵּן לָכֶם לֵב שָׁלֵם מֵאֵת אֱלֹהֵי הַחֶסֶד אֲשֶׁר קָרָא אֶתְכֶם לִכְבוֹדוֹ עַד־עוֹלָמֵי עַד בַּמָּשִׁיחַ יֵשׁוּעַ וִיחַזֵּק וִיאַמֵּץ וִיכוֹנֵן אֶתְכֶם לָנֶצַח

10. Ve•a•cha•rey asher oo•ney•tem le•ya•mim me•a•tim yi•na•ten la•chem lev sha•lem me•et Elohey ha•che•sed asher ka•ra et•chem lich•vo•do ad - ol•mey ad ba•Ma•shi•ach Yeshua vi•cha•zek vi•a•metz vi•cho•nen et•chem la•ne•tzach.

1 Peter 5

11. To him be glory and dominion for ever and ever. Amen.

11. Αὐτῷ ἡ δόξα καὶ τὸ κράτος εἰς τοὺς αἰῶνας τῶν αἰώνων. Ἀμήν.

11. Auto 'ei doxa kai to kratos eis tous aionas ton aionon. Amein.

יא. וְלוֹ הַכָּבוֹד וְהַמֶּמְשָׁלָה עַד-עוֹלְמֵי עוֹלָמִים אָמֵן:

11. Ve•lo ha•ka•vod ve•ha•mem•sha•la ad - ol•mey o•la•mim Amen.

12. By Silvanus, a faithful brother unto you, as I suppose, I have written briefly, exhorting, and testifying that this is the true grace of God wherein ye stand.

12. Διὰ Σιλουανοῦ ὑμῖν τοῦ πιστοῦ ἀδελφοῦ, ὡς λογίζομαι, δι' ὀλίγων ἔγραψα, παρακαλῶν καὶ ἐπιμαρτυρῶν ταύτην εἶναι ἀληθῆ χάριν τοῦ θεοῦ εἰς ἣν ἑστήκατε.

12. Dya Silouanou 'umin tou pistou adelphou, 'os logizomai, di oligon egrapsa, parakalon kai epimarturon tautein einai aleithei charin tou theou eis 'ein 'esteikate.

יב. אֶת-הַדְּבָרִים הַמְּעַטִים הָאֵלֶּה כָּתַבְתִּי אֲלֵיכֶם בְּיַד-סִלְוָנוֹס אֲחִיכֶם הַנֶּאֱמָן לְהַזְהִיר אֶתְכֶם לְפִי חַוֹּת דַעְתִּי:וּלְהָעִיד לָכֶם כִּי חֶסֶד אֱלֹהִים הוּא חֶסֶד אֱמֶת עִמְדוּ בּוֹ הָכֵן

12. Et - ha•d`va•rim ha•me•a•tim ha•e•le ka•tav•ti aley•chem be•yad - Sil•vanos a•chi•chem ha•ne•e•man le•haz•hir et•chem le•fi cha•vot da•a•ti ool•ha•eed la•chem ki che•sed Elohim hoo che•sed emet eem•doo bo ha•chen.

13. The church that is at Babylon, elected together with you, saluteth you; and so doth Marcus my son.

13. Ἀσπάζεται ὑμᾶς ἡ ἐν Βαβυλῶνι συνεκλεκτή, καὶ Μάρκος ὁ υἱός μου.

13. Aspazetai 'umas 'ei en Babuloni suneklektei, kai Markos 'o 'wios mou.

יג: עֲדַת בָּבֶל הַנִּבְחָרָה כְּמוֹכֶם שֹׁאֶלֶת לְשָׁלוֹם לָכֶם וְכֵן גַּם-מַרְקוֹס בְּנִי

13. Adat Bavel ha•niv•cha•ra ke•mo•chem sho•e•let le•sha•lom la•chem ve•chen gam - Markos b`ni.

Rabbinic Jewish Commentary

The Vulgate Latin, Syriac, and Arabic versions, supply the word "church", as we do. Some, by "Babylon", understand Rome, which is so called, in a figurative sense, in the book of the Revelations: this is an ancient opinion; so Papias understood it, as (e) Eusebius relates; but that Peter was at Rome, when he wrote this epistle, cannot be proved, nor any reason be given why the proper name of the place should be concealed, and a figurative one expressed. It is best therefore to understand it literally, of Babylon in Assyria, the metropolis of the dispersion of the Jews, and the centre of it, to whom the apostle wrote; and where, as the minister of the circumcision, he may be thought to reside, here being a number of persons converted and formed into a Gospel church state, whereby was fulfilled the prophecy in Psa.87:4 perhaps this church might consist chiefly of Jews, which might be the reason of the apostle's being here, since there were great numbers which continued here, from the time of the captivity, who returned not with Ezra; and these are said by the Jews (f) to be of the purest blood: many of the Jewish Rabbis lived here; they had three famous universities in this country, and here their Talmud was written, called from hence (g) Babylonian.

This seems to be Mark the evangelist, who was called John Mark, was Barnabas's sister's son, and his mother's name was Mary. He is said (h) to be the interpreter of Peter, and to have wrote his Gospel from what he heard from him; and who approved of it, and confirmed it, and indeed it is said to be his.

(e) Eccl. Hist. l. 2. c. 15. (f) T. Bab. Kiddushin, fol. 69. 2. & 71. 2. & Gloss. in ib. (g) T. Bab. Sanhedrin, fol. 24. 1. (h) Papias apud Euseb. Hist. Eccl. l. 3. c. 39. Tertullian. adv. Marcion, l. 4. c. 5. Hieron. Catalog. Script. Eccl. sect. 2. 18.

14. Greet ye one another with a kiss of charity. Peace be with you all that are in Christ Jesus. Amen.

14. Ἀσπάσασθε ἀλλήλους ἐν φιλήματι ἀγάπης. Εἰρήνη ὑμῖν πᾶσιν τοῖς ἐν χριστῷ Ἰησοῦ. Ἀμήν.

14. Aspasasthe alleilous en phileimati agapeis. Eireinei 'umin pasin tois en christo Yeisou. Amein.

יד. שַׁאֲלוּ אִישׁ לְרֵעֵהוּ לְשָׁלוֹם בִּנְשִׁיקַת אַהֲבָה שָׁלוֹם לְכֻלְּכֶם אֲשֶׁר בַּמָּשִׁיחַ יֵשׁוּעַ אָמֵן:

14. Sha•a•loo eesh le•re•e•hoo le•sha•lom bin•shi•kat a•ha•va sha•lom le•chool•chem asher ba•Ma•shi•ach Yeshua Amen.

Rabbinic Jewish Commentary
Such a love the Jews call, as the apostle does here, נשיקה דרחימו, "a kiss of love" (i); for as Philo the Jew (k) observes, a kiss and love differ, the one may be without the other, a mere compliment, a show of friendship, and not arise from sincere love.

(i) Zohar in Exod. fol. 60. 3, 4. (k) Quis rerum divin. Haeres. p. 486, 487.

(1 Peter Chapter 5 End)

THE SECOND EPISTLE GENERAL OF PETER

2 Peter, Chapter 1

1. Simon Peter, a servant and an apostle of Jesus Christ, to them that have obtained like precious faith with us through the righteousness of God and our Saviour Jesus Christ:

1. Συμεὼν Πέτρος, δοῦλος καὶ ἀπόστολος Ἰησοῦ χριστοῦ, τοῖς ἰσότιμον ἡμῖν λαχοῦσιν πίστιν ἐν δικαιοσύνῃ τοῦ θεοῦ ἡμῶν καὶ σωτῆρος Ἰησοῦ χριστοῦ·

1. Sumeon Petros, doulos kai apostolos Yeisou christou, tois isotimon 'eimin lachousin pistin en dikaiosunei tou theou 'eimon kai soteiros Yeisou christou.

א. שִׁמְעוֹן פֶּטְרוֹס עֶבֶד יֵשׁוּעַ הַמָּשִׁיחַ וּשְׁלִיחוֹ אֶל-אֲשֶׁר נֹאחֲזוּ עִמָּנוּ בָּאֱמוּנָה הַיְקָרָה וּבְצִדְקַת אֱלֹהֵינוּ וּמוֹשִׁיעֵנוּ:יֵשׁוּעַ הַמָּשִׁיחַ

1. Shimon Petros eved Yeshua ha•Ma•shi•ach oosh•li•cho el - asher no•cha•zoo ee•ma•noo ba•e•moo•na hai•ka•ra oov•tzid•kat Elohey•noo oo•Mo•shi•e•noo Yeshua ha•Ma•shi•ach.

---

2. Grace and peace be multiplied unto you through the knowledge of God, and of Jesus our Lord,

2. χάρις ὑμῖν καὶ εἰρήνη πληθυνθείη ἐν ἐπιγνώσει τοῦ θεοῦ, καὶ Ἰησοῦ τοῦ κυρίου ἡμῶν·

2. charis 'umin kai eireinei pleithuntheiei en epignosei tou theou, kai Yeisou tou kuriou 'eimon.

ב. חֶסֶד לָכֶם וְשָׁלוֹם רָב בְּדַעַת אֱלֹהִים וְיֵשׁוּעַ אֲדֹנֵינוּ:

2. Che•sed la•chem ve•sha•lom rav be•da•at Elohim ve•Yeshua Ado•ney•noo.

3. According as his divine power hath given unto us all things that pertain unto life and godliness, through the knowledge of him that hath called us to glory and virtue:

3. Ὡς πάντα ἡμῖν τῆς θείας δυνάμεως αὐτοῦ τὰ πρὸς ζωὴν καὶ εὐσέβειαν δεδωρημένης, διὰ τῆς ἐπιγνώσεως τοῦ καλέσαντος ἡμᾶς διὰ δόξης καὶ ἀρετῆς·

3. 'Os panta 'eimin teis theias dunameos autou ta pros zoein kai eusebeyan dedoreimeneis, dya teis epignoseos tou kalesantos 'eimas dya doxeis kai areteis.

ג. כַּאֲשֶׁר נָתַן לָנוּ יְהוָה בִּגְבוּרָתוֹ כָּל־מִשְׁעַן הַחַיִּים וְיִרְאַת שָׁמַיִם עַל־יְדֵי דַעַת הַקֹּרֵא אֹתָנוּ בְּעֹז צִדְקָתוֹ:

3. Ka•a•sher na•tan la•noo Adonai big•voo•ra•to kol - mish•an ha•cha•yim ve•yir•at sha•ma•yim al - ye•dey da•at ha•ko•re o•ta•noo be•oz tzid•ka•to.

2 Peter 1

4. Whereby are given unto us exceeding great and precious promises: that by these ye might be partakers of the divine nature, having escaped the corruption that is in the world through lust.

4. δι' ὧν τὰ τίμια ἡμῖν καὶ μέγιστα ἐπαγγέλματα δεδώρηται, ἵνα διὰ τούτων γένησθε θείας κοινωνοὶ φύσεως, ἀποφυγόντες τῆς ἐν κόσμῳ ἐν ἐπιθυμίᾳ φθορᾶς.

4. di 'on ta timya 'eimin kai megista epangelmata dedoreitai, 'ina dya touton geneisthe theias koinonoi phuseos, apophugontes teis en kosmo en epithumia phthoras.

ד. וְעַל־יָדָם נָתַן לָנוּ הַבְטָחוֹת גְּדֹלוֹת יְקָרוֹת עַד־מְאֹד לְהַנְחִיל לָכֶם חֵלֶק מִטֶּבַע אֱלוֹהַּ אַחֲרֵי אֲשֶׁר נִצַּלְתֶּם מִשַּׁחַת וְתַאֲוֹת הָעוֹלָם:

4. Ve•al - ya•dam na•tan la•noo hav•ta•chot ge•do•lot ye•ka•rot ad - me•od le•han•chil la•chem che•lek mi•te•va Eloha a•cha•rey asher ni•tzal•tem mi•sha•chat ve•ta•a•vot ha•o•lam.

5. And beside this, giving all diligence, add to your faith virtue; and to virtue knowledge;

5. Καὶ αὐτὸ τοῦτο δέ, σπουδὴν πᾶσαν παρεισενέγκαντες, ἐπιχορηγήσατε ἐν τῇ πίστει ὑμῶν τὴν ἀρετήν, ἐν δὲ τῇ ἀρετῇ τὴν γνῶσιν,

5. Kai auto touto de, spoudein pasan pareisenegkantes, epichoreigeisate en tei pistei 'umon tein aretein, en de tei aretei tein gnosin,

ה. בַּעֲבוּר זֹאת הִתְאַמְּצוּ בְּכָל-מְאֹדְכֶם לְהוֹסִיף אֶל-אֱמוּנַתְכֶם צְדָקָה וְאֶל-צְדָקָה דָּעַת:

5. Ba•a•voor zot hit•am•tzoo ve•chol - me•od•chem le•ho•sif el - emoo•nat•chem tze•da•ka ve•el - tze•da•ka da•at.

---

2 Peter 1

6. And to knowledge temperance; and to temperance patience; and to patience godliness;

6. ἐν δὲ τῇ γνώσει τὴν ἐγκράτειαν, ἐν δὲ τῇ ἐγκρατείᾳ τὴν ὑπομονήν, ἐν δὲ τῇ ὑπομονῇ τὴν εὐσέβειαν,

6. en de tei gnosei tein egkrateyan, en de tei egkrateia tein 'upomonein, en de tei 'upomonei tein eusebeyan,

ו. וְאֶל-דַּעַת מַעְצָר לָרוּחַ וְאֶל-מַעְצָר לָרוּחַ כֹּחַ הַסַּבָּל וְאֶל-כֹּחַ הַסַּבָּל יִרְאַת אֱלֹהִים:

6. Ve•el - da•at ma•a•tzar le•roo•ach ve•el - ma•a•tzar le•roo•ach ko•ach ha•sa•bal ve•el - ko•ach ha•sa•bal yir•at Elohim.

---

7. And to godliness brotherly kindness; and to brotherly kindness charity.

7. ἐν δὲ τῇ εὐσεβείᾳ τὴν φιλαδελφίαν, ἐν δὲ τῇ φιλαδελφίᾳ τὴν ἀγάπην.

7. en de tei eusebeia tein philadelphian, en de tei philadelphia tein agapein.

וְאֶל-יִרְאַת אֱלֹהִים אַחֲוָה וְאֶל-אַחֲוָה אַהֲבָה :ז.

7. Ve•el - yir•at Elohim a•cha•va ve•el - a•cha•va a•ha•va.

---

2 Peter 1

8. For if these things be in you, and abound, they make you that ye shall neither be barren nor unfruitful in the knowledge of our Lord Jesus Christ.

8. Ταῦτα γὰρ ὑμῖν ὑπάρχοντα καὶ πλεονάζοντα, οὐκ ἀργοὺς οὐδὲ ἀκάρπους καθίστησιν εἰς τὴν τοῦ κυρίου ἡμῶν Ἰησοῦ χριστοῦ ἐπίγνωσιν.

8. Tauta gar 'umin 'uparchonta kai pleonazonta, ouk argous oude akarpous kathisteisin eis tein tou kuriou 'eimon Yeisou christou epignosin.

ח. כִּי אִם-אֵלֶּה תִּהְיֶינָה בָכֶם כְּדֵי הַמִּדָּה אוֹ יֶתֶר עַל-הַמִּדָּה לֹא תוּכְלוּ לָשֶׁבֶת בַּעֲצַלְתַּיִם מִבְּלִי עֲשׂוֹת פְּרִי בְגַן:הַדַעַת לְיֵשׁוּעַ הַמָּשִׁיחַ אֲדֹנֵינוּ

8. Ki eem - ele ti•hi•ye•na va•chem ke•dey ha•mi•da oh ye•ter al - ha•mi•da lo tooch•loo la•she•vet ba•a•tzal•ta•yim mi•b`li asot p`ri be•gan ha•da•at le•Yeshua ha•Ma•shi•ach Ado•ney•noo.

---

9. But he that lacketh these things is blind, and cannot see afar off, and hath forgotten that he was purged from his old sins.

9. ᾧ γὰρ μὴ πάρεστιν ταῦτα, τυφλός ἐστιν, μυωπάζων, λήθην λαβὼν τοῦ καθαρισμοῦ τῶν πάλαι αὐτοῦ ἁμαρτιῶν.

9. ' gar mei parestin tauta, tuphlos estin, muopazon, leithein labon tou katharismou ton palai autou 'amartion.

ט. כִּי הָאִישׁ אֲשֶׁר אֵלֶּה אֵין-לוֹ הוּא עִוֵּר אוֹ עֹצֵם עֵינָיו מֵרְאוֹת וְשֹׁכֵחַ אֶת-טָהֳרָתוֹ מֵחֲטָאָיו הָרִאשֹׁנִים:

9. Ki ha•eesh asher ele eyn - lo hoo ee•ver oh o•tzem ey•nav mer•ot ve•sho•che•ach et - ta•ho•ra•to me•cha•ta•av ha•ri•sho•nim.

10. Wherefore the rather, brethren, give diligence to make your calling and election sure: for if ye do these things, ye shall never fall:

10. Διὸ μᾶλλον, ἀδελφοί, σπουδάσατε βεβαίαν ὑμῶν τὴν κλῆσιν καὶ ἐκλογὴν ποιεῖσθαι· ταῦτα γὰρ ποιοῦντες οὐ μὴ πταίσητέ ποτε·

10. Dio mallon, adelphoi, spoudasate bebaian 'umon tein kleisin kai eklogein poieisthai. Tauta gar poiountes ou mei ptaiseite pote.

י. וְעַל-כֵּן אַחַי עֲשׂוּ כָל-אֲשֶׁר בְּכֹחֲכֶם לְקַיֵּם כִּי נִקְרֵאתֶם וְנִבְחַרְתֶּם אֶל-נָכוֹן וְאִם כֵּן תַּעֲשׂוּ לֹא תִכָּשְׁלוּ לָנֶצַח:

10. Ve•al - ken a•chai a•soo chol - asher be•cho•cha•chem le•ka•yem ki nik•re•tem ve•niv•char•tem el - na•chon ve•eem ken ta•a•soo lo ti•kash•loo la•ne•tzach.

---

2 Peter 1

11. For so an entrance shall be ministered unto you abundantly into the everlasting kingdom of our Lord and Saviour Jesus Christ.

11. οὕτως γὰρ πλουσίως ἐπιχορηγηθήσεται ὑμῖν ἡ εἴσοδος εἰς τὴν αἰώνιον βασιλείαν τοῦ κυρίου ἡμῶν καὶ σωτῆρος Ἰησοῦ χριστοῦ.

11. 'outos gar plousios epichoreigeitheisetai 'umin 'ei eisodos eis tein aionion basileian tou kuriou 'eimon kai soteiros Yeisou christou.

יא. כִּי בָזֶה יִפָּתַח לָכֶם הַשַּׁעַר לְמַלְכוּת עוֹלָם אֲשֶׁר לַאֲדֹנֵינוּ מוֹשִׁיעֵנוּ יֵשׁוּעַ הַמָּשִׁיחַ:

11. Ki va•ze yi•pa•tach la•chem ha•sha•ar le•mal•choot o•lam asher la•Ado•ney•noo Mo•shi•e•noo Yeshua ha•Ma•shi•ach.

---

12. Wherefore I will not be negligent to put you always in remembrance of these things, though ye know them, and be established in the present truth.

12. Διὸ οὐκ ἀμελήσω ἀεὶ ὑμᾶς ὑπομιμνήσκειν περὶ τούτων, καίπερ εἰδότας, καὶ ἐστηριγμένους ἐν τῇ παρούσῃ ἀληθείᾳ.

12. Dio ouk ameleiso aei 'umas 'upomimneiskein peri touton, kaiper eidotas, kai esteirigmenous en tei parousei aleitheia.

יב. עַל־כֵּן לֹא אֶרֶף מֵהַזְכִּירְכֶם תָּמִיד עַל־אֵלֶּה אַף כִּי־יְדַעְתֶּם אֶת־הָאֱמֶת בַּאֲשֶׁר הִיא וּבָהּ אַתֶּם מְיֻסָּדִים:

12. Al - ken lo eref me•haz•kir•chem ta•mid al - ele af ki - ye•da•a•tem et - ha•e•met ba•a•sher hee oo•va atem me•yoo•sa•dim.

---

2 Peter 1

13. Yea, I think it meet, as long as I am in this tabernacle, to stir you up by putting you in remembrance;

13. Δίκαιον δὲ ἡγοῦμαι, ἐφ᾽ ὅσον εἰμὶ ἐν τούτῳ τῷ σκηνώματι, διεγείρειν ὑμᾶς ἐν ὑπομνήσει·

13. Dikaion de 'eigoumai, eph 'oson eimi en touto to skeinomati, diegeirein 'umas en 'upomneisei.

יג. וְרָחַשׁ לִבִּי דָּבָר טוֹב לְהַעֲלוֹת עַל־רוּחֲכֶם וּלְהָעִיר אֶתְכֶם כָּל־יְמֵי שִׁבְתִּי בְּאָהֳלִי הַזֶּה:

13. Ve•ra•chash li•bi da•var tov le•ha•a•lot al - roo•cha•chem ool•ha•eer et•chem kol - ye•mey shiv•ti ve•o•ho•li ha•ze.

---

14. Knowing that shortly I must put off this my tabernacle, even as our Lord Jesus Christ hath shewed me.

14. εἰδὼς ὅτι ταχινή ἐστιν ἡ ἀπόθεσις τοῦ σκηνώματός μου, καθὼς καὶ ὁ κύριος ἡμῶν Ἰησοῦς χριστὸς ἐδήλωσέν μοι.

14. eidos 'oti tachinei estin 'ei apothesis tou skeinomatos mou, kathos kai 'o kurios 'eimon Yeisous christos edeilosen moi.

יד. כִּי יֹדֵעַ אֲנִי כִּי חִישׁ יֵעָתֵק אָהֳלִי כַּאֲשֶׁר גַּם־יֵשׁוּעַ הַמָּשִׁיחַ אֲדֹנֵינוּ גִּלָּה אֶת־אָזְנִי:

14. Ki yo•de•a ani ki chish ye•e•tak o•ho•li ka•a•sher gam - Yeshua ha•Ma•shi•ach Ado•ney•noo gila et - oz•ni.

---

15. Moreover I will endeavour that ye may be able after my decease to have these things always in remembrance.

15. Σπουδάσω δὲ καὶ ἑκάστοτε ἔχειν ὑμᾶς μετὰ τὴν ἐμὴν ἔξοδον τὴν τούτων μνήμην ποιεῖσθαι.

15. Spoudaso de kai 'ekastote echein 'umas meta tein emein exodon tein touton mneimein poieisthai.

טו. וְהִנְנִי עָמֵל כַּיוֹם לְבִלְתִּי יָמוּשׁ מִכֶּם זִכְרוֹן הַדְּבָרִים הָהֵם גַּם-אַחֲרֵי חֲלִיפָתִי:

15. Ve•hi•ne•ni amel ka•yom le•vil•ti ya•moosh mi•kem zich•ron ha•d`va•rim ha•hem gam - a•cha•rey cha•li•fa•ti.

2 Peter 1

16. For we have not followed cunningly devised fables, when we made known unto you the power and coming of our Lord Jesus Christ, but were eyewitnesses of his majesty.

16. Οὐ γὰρ σεσοφισμένοις μύθοις ἐξακολουθήσαντες ἐγνωρίσαμεν ὑμῖν τὴν τοῦ κυρίου ἡμῶν Ἰησοῦ χριστοῦ δύναμιν καὶ παρουσίαν, ἀλλ᾽ ἐπόπται γενηθέντες τῆς ἐκείνου μεγαλειότητος.

16. Ou gar sesophismenois muthois exakoloutheisantes egnorisamen 'umin tein tou kuriou 'eimon Yeisou christou dunamin kai parousian, all epoptai geneithentes teis ekeinou megaleioteitos.

טז. כִּי לֹא אַחֲרֵי מִשְׁלֵי שָׁוְא וּמַדּוּחִים הָלַכְנוּ כַּאֲשֶׁר הוֹדַעֲנוּכֶם אֶת-גְּבוּרוֹת אֲדֹנֵינוּ יֵשׁוּעַ הַמָּשִׁיחַ וּבֹאוֹ כִּי אִם-עֵינֵינוּ הָיוּ רֹאוֹת אֶת-הוֹד פָּנָיו:

16. Ki lo a•cha•rey mish•ley shav oo•ma•doo•chim ha•lach•noo ka•a•sher ho•da•a•noo•chem et - g`voo•rot Ado•ney•noo Yeshua ha•Ma•shi•ach oo•voo ki eem - ey•ney•noo ha•yoo ro•ot et - hod pa•nav.

17. For he received from God the Father honour and glory, when there came such a voice to him from the excellent glory, This is my beloved Son, in whom I am well pleased.

17. Λαβὼν γὰρ παρὰ θεοῦ πατρὸς τιμὴν καὶ δόξαν, φωνῆς ἐνεχθείσης αὐτῷ τοιᾶσδε ὑπὸ τῆς μεγαλοπρεποῦς δόξης, Οὗτός ἐστιν ὁ υἱός μου ὁ ἀγαπητός, εἰς ὃν ἐγὼ εὐδόκησα·

17. Labon gar para theou patros timein kai doxan, phoneis enechtheiseis auto toyasde 'upo teis megaloprepous doxeis, 'Outos estin 'o 'wios mou 'o agapeitos, eis 'on ego eudokeisa.

יז. כַּאֲשֶׁר נָשָׂא כָבוֹד וָעֹז מֵאֵת הָאֱלֹהִים הָאָב כְּבֹא אֵלָיו קוֹל מֵהֲדַר גְּאוֹנוֹ לֵאמֹר זֶה בְּנִי יְדִידִי אֲשֶׁר בּוֹ רָצְתָה־נַפְשִׁי׃

17. Ka•a•sher na•sa cha•vod va•oz me•et ha•Elohim ha•Av ke•vo elav kol me•ha•dar ge•o•no le•mor ze B`ni ye•di•di asher bo ratz•ta naf•shi.

Rabbinic Jewish Commentary
when there came such a voice to him from the excellent glory; from the bright cloud which overshadowed Jesus, Moses, and Elijah and was a symbol of the glory and presence of God, as the cloud in the tabernacle and temple were, Exo.40:35, or from heaven, the habitation of the holiness and glory of God, and where he displays the glory of his being and perfections; or from himself, who is the God and Father of glory, and is glorious in himself, in all his attributes and works.

So כבוד, "glory", with the Cabalistic Jews, signifies the Shechinah, or divine presence (d); and every number in the Cabalistic tree is called by the name of "glory"; the second number, which is "wisdom", is called "the first glory"; and the third number, "understanding", is called כבוד עליון, "the supreme", or "chief glory" (e): so the first path, which is the supreme crown, is sometimes called the first glory, as the Father is here the most excellent glory; and the second path, which is the understanding enlightening, the second glory (f).

(d) Guido. Dictionar. Syr. Chald. p. 92. (e) Lex. Cabalist. p. 464. (f) Sepher Jetzirah, p. 1. 4.

---

18. And this voice which came from heaven we heard, when we were with him in the holy mount.

18. καὶ ταύτην τὴν φωνὴν ἡμεῖς ἠκούσαμεν ἐξ οὐρανοῦ ἐνεχθεῖσαν, σὺν αὐτῷ ὄντες ἐν τῷ ὄρει τῷ ἁγίῳ.

18. kai tautein tein phonein 'eimeis eikousamen ex ouranou enechtheisan, sun auto ontes en to orei to 'agio.

יח. וְאֶת־הַקּוֹל הַהוּא שְׁמַעְנוּ בְאָזְנֵינוּ יֹצֵא מִן־הַשָּׁמַיִם בִּהְיוֹתֵנוּ עִמּוֹ בְּהַר הַקֹּדֶשׁ׃

18. Ve•et - ha•kol ha•hoo sha•ma•a•noo ve•oz•ney•noo yo•tze min - ha•sha•ma•yim bi•hi•yo•te•noo ee•mo be•har ha•ko•desh.

2 Peter 1

19. We have also a more sure word of prophecy; whereunto ye do well that ye take heed, as unto a light that shineth in a dark place, until the day dawn, and the day star arise in your hearts:

19. Καὶ ἔχομεν βεβαιότερον τὸν προφητικὸν λόγον, ᾧ καλῶς ποιεῖτε προσέχοντες, ὡς λύχνῳ φαίνοντι ἐν αὐχμηρῷ τόπῳ, ἕως οὗ ἡμέρα διαυγάσῃ, καὶ φωσφόρος ἀνατείλῃ ἐν ταῖς καρδίαις ὑμῶν·

19. Kai echomen bebaioteron ton propheitikon logon, 'o kalos poieite prosechontes, 'os luchno phainonti en auchmeiro topo, 'eos 'ou 'eimera dyaugasei, kai phosphoros anateilei en tais kardiais 'umon.

יט. וּדְבַר הַנְּבוּאָה בָּרוּר לָנוּ כַּיּוֹם פִּי שְׁנַיִם וְאַתֶּם תֵּיטִיבוּ לָשִׁית אֵלָיו לֵב כְּמוֹ אֶל־לַפִּיד בֹּעֵר בְּמַחֲשַׁכִּים עַד אֲשֶׁר־יִבָּקַע הַשַּׁחַר וְאוֹר הַיּוֹם יִזְרַח בִּלְבַבְכֶם

19. Oo•d`var ha•n`voo•ah ba•roor la•noo ka•yom pi sh`na•yim ve•a•tem tey•ti•voo la•sheet elav lev k`mo el - la•pid bo•er be•ma•cha•sha•kim ad asher yi•ba•ka ha•sha•char ve•or ha•yom yiz•rach bil•vav•chem.

20. Knowing this first, that no prophecy of the scripture is of any private interpretation.

20. τοῦτο πρῶτον γινώσκοντες, ὅτι πᾶσα προφητεία γραφῆς ἰδίας ἐπιλύσεως οὐ γίνεται.

20. touto proton ginoskontes, 'oti pasa propheiteia grapheis idias epiluseos ou ginetai.

כ. וְזֹאת יָדֹעַ תֵּדְעוּן מֵרֹאשׁ כִּי נְבוּאַת כִּתְבֵי הַקֹּדֶשׁ אֵינֶנָּה תְלוּיָה בְּפִתְרוֹן הַפֹּתֵר אֹתָהּ לִרְצוֹנוֹ:

20. Ve•zot ya•doa ted•oon me•rosh ki n`voo•at kit•vey ha•ko•desh ey•ne•na t`loo•ya be•fit•ron ha•po•ter o•ta lir•tzo•no.

2 Peter 1

21. For the prophecy came not in old time by the will of man: but holy men of God spake as they were moved by the Holy Ghost.

21. Οὐ γὰρ θελήματι ἀνθρώπου ἠνέχθη ποτὲ προφητεία, ἀλλ᾽ ὑπὸ πνεύματος ἁγίου φερόμενοι ἐλάλησαν ἅγιοι θεοῦ ἄνθρωποι.

21. Ou gar theleimati anthropou einechthei pote propheiteia, all 'upo pneumatos 'agiou pheromenoi elaleisan 'agioi theou anthropoi.

כא. כִּי מֵעוֹלָם לֹא-יָצְאָה נְבוּאָה מִפִּי אִישׁ לִרְצוֹנוֹ כִּי אִם-אַנְשֵׁי אֱלֹהִים הַקְּדוֹשִׁים הִבִּיעוּ מִן-הָאֱלֹהִים כַּאֲשֶׁר:נְתָנָם רוּחַ הַקֹּדֶשׁ לְהַבִּיעַ

21. Ki me•o•lam lo - yatz•ah n`voo•ah mi•pi eesh lir•tzo•no ki eem - an•shey Elohim ha•k`do•shim hi•bi•oo min - ha•Elohim ka•a•sher n`ta•nam Roo•ach ha•Ko•desh le•ha•bi•a.

Rabbinic Jewish Commentary

The whole Hebrew Scripture, all the prophetic writings; so the Jews call the Scriptures הנבואה, "the prophecy" (g), by way of eminence, and from the subject matter of the sacred word.

R. Sangari says,

"That the speech of the prophets, when the Holy Spirit clothed them, in all their words was directed by a divine influence, and the prophet could not speak in the choice of his own words."

(g) R. Eliahu in Adderet apud Trigland. de Sect Karaeorum, c. 10. p. 153.

(2Peter Chapter 1 End)

2 Peter, Chapter 2

1. But there were false prophets also among the people, even as there shall be false teachers among you, who privily shall bring in damnable heresies, even denying the Lord that bought them, and bring upon themselves swift destruction.

1. Ἐγένοντο δὲ καὶ ψευδοπροφῆται ἐν τῷ λαῷ, ὡς καὶ ἐν ὑμῖν ἔσονται ψευδοδιδάσκαλοι, οἵτινες παρεισάξουσιν αἱρέσεις ἀπωλείας, καὶ τὸν ἀγοράσαντα αὐτοὺς δεσπότην ἀρνούμενοι, ἐπάγοντες ἑαυτοῖς ταχινὴν ἀπώλειαν.

1. Egenonto de kai pseudopropheitai en to lao, 'os kai en 'umin esontai pseudodidaskaloi, 'oitines pareisaxousin 'aireseis apoleias, kai ton agorasanta autous despotein arnoumenoi, epagontes 'eautois tachinein apoleyan.

א. וְגַם־נְבִיאֵי שֶׁקֶר הָיוּ בָעָם כַּאֲשֶׁר יִהְיוּ מוֹרִים מַתְעִים גַּם־בָּכֶם אֲשֶׁר יַגִּדוּ גְדוּדִים מַשְׁחִיתִים יְכַחֲשׁוּ בַּאֲדֹנָם:אֲשֶׁר קָנָם וְיָבִיאוּ שׂוֹאַת פִּתְאֹם עַל־נַפְשָׁם

1. Ve•gam - n`vi•ey she•ker ha•yoo va•am ka•a•sher yi•hee•yoo mo•rim mat•eem gam - ba•chem asher ya•go•doo g`doo•dim mash•chi•tim ye•cha•cha•shoo va•a•do•nam asher ka•nam ve•ya•vi•oo sho•at pit•om al - naf•sham.

---

2. And many shall follow their pernicious ways; by reason of whom the way of truth shall be evil spoken of.

2. Καὶ πολλοὶ ἐξακολουθήσουσιν αὐτῶν ταῖς ἀσελγείαις, δι' οὓς ἡ ὁδὸς τῆς ἀληθείας βλασφημηθήσεται.

2. Kai polloi exakoloutheisousin auton tais aselgeiais, di 'ous 'ei 'odos teis aleitheias blaspheimeitheisetai.

ב. וּמִפְּנֵי רֹעַ מַעַלְלֵיהֶם רַבִּים יִמְשְׁכוּ אַחֲרֵיהֶם וּבַעֲבוּרָם דֶּרֶךְ הָאֱמֶת יְחֻלָּל:

2. Oo•mip•ney ro•a ma•a•le•ley•hem ra•bim yi•mash•choo a•cha•rey•hem oo•va•a•voo•ram de•rech ha•e•met ye•choo•lal.

---

3. And through covetousness shall they with feigned words make merchandise of you: whose judgment now of a long time lingereth not, and their damnation slumbereth not.

3. Καὶ ἐν πλεονεξίᾳ πλαστοῖς λόγοις ὑμᾶς ἐμπορεύσονται· οἷς τὸ κρίμα ἔκπαλαι οὐκ ἀργεῖ, καὶ ἡ ἀπώλεια αὐτῶν οὐ νυστάξει.

3. Kai en pleonexia plastois logois 'umas emporeusontai. 'ois to krima ekpalai ouk argei, kai 'ei apoleya auton ou nustaxei.

ג. וְלִבְצֹעַ בֶּצַע בְּמַשְׂאוֹת שָׁוְא יַעֲשׂוּ אֶתְכֶם לְמִסְחָר לָהֶם אֲשֶׁר מִשְׁפָּטָם הוּכַן מֵאָז לֹא יְאַחֵר בֹּאוֹ וְאֵידָם לֹא יָנוּם:וְלֹא יִישָׁן

3. Ve•liv•tzo•a be•tza be•mas•ot shav ya•a•soo et•chem le•mis•char la•hem asher mish•pa•tam hoo•chan me•az lo ye•a•cher bo•oo ve•ey•dam lo ya•noom ve•lo yi•shan.

2 Peter 2

4. For if God spared not the angels that sinned, but cast them down to hell, and delivered them into chains of darkness, to be reserved unto judgment;

4. Εἰ γὰρ ὁ θεὸς ἀγγέλων ἁμαρτησάντων οὐκ ἐφείσατο, ἀλλὰ σειραῖς ζόφου ταρταρώσας παρέδωκεν εἰς κρίσιν τηρουμένους·

4. Ei gar 'o theos angelon 'amarteisanton ouk epheisato, alla seirais zophou tartarosas paredoken eis krisin teiroumenous.

ד. הֵן אֱלֹהִים לֹא חָס עַל-הַמַּלְאָכִים הַחַטָּאִים אֲשֶׁר הוֹרִידָם לִבְאֵר שַׁחַת וַיַּסְגִּירֵם בְּמִשְׁמָר וּבָאֹפֶל עַד-יוֹם הַמִּשְׁפָּט:

4. Hen Elohim lo chas al - ha•mal•a•chim ha•cha•ta•eem asher ho•ri•dam liv•er sha•chat va•yas•gi•rem ba•mish•mar oo•va•o•fel ad - yom ha•mish•pat.

Rabbinic Jewish Commentary

The Jews give an adobted pagan account of the dejection, fall, and punishment of the angels, in a manner pretty much like this of Peter's, whom they speak of under different names; so of the serpent that deceived Adam and Eve, whom they call Samael, and because of that sin of his, they say (k) that YHVH,

"Cast down Samael and his company from the place of their holiness, out of heaven;"

And of Aza and Azael, angels, who, they say, sinned by lusting after the daughters of men, they frequently affirm, that God cast them down from their holiness (l), and that he אפיל לון לתתא, "cast them down below in chains" (m); and that God cast them down from their holiness from above; and when they descended, they were rolled in the air--and he brought them to the mountains of darkness, which are called the mountains of the east, and bound them "in chains" of iron, and the chains were sunk into the midst of the great deep (n): and elsewhere they say (o), that God cast them down from their holy degree, out of heaven--from their holy place out of heaven--and bound them in "chains" of iron, in the mountains of "darkness".

(k) Sepher Bahir in Zohar in Gen. fol. 27. 3. (l) Zohar in Gen. fol. 25. 3. (m) Ib. fol. 32. 3. (n) Midrash Ruth in Zohar in Gen. fol. 45. 1. 2. vid. fol. 77. 3. (o) Zohar in Numb. fol. 84. 1. vid. Tzeror Hammor, fol. 6. 4. & 9. 4. & Raziel, fol. 14. 2. & 18. 2.

---

2 Peter 2

5. And spared not the old world, but saved Noah the eighth person, a preacher of righteousness, bringing in the flood upon the world of the ungodly;

5. καὶ ἀρχαίου κόσμου οὐκ ἐφείσατο, ἀλλὰ ὄγδοον Νῶε δικαιοσύνης κήρυκα ἐφύλαξεν, κατακλυσμὸν κόσμῳ ἀσεβῶν ἐπάξας·

5. kai archaiou kosmou ouk epheisato, alla ogdoon Noe dikaiosuneis keiruka ephulaxen, kataklusmon kosmo asebon epaxas.

ה. וְכֵן לֹא חָס עַל-דֹרוֹת קְדוּמִים מַשְׁחִיתֵי דַרְכָּם עַל-הָאָרֶץ אֲשֶׁר מָחָה אֹתָם בְּמֵי הַמַּבּוּל וַיְמַלֵּט רַק אֶת-נֹחַ:הַקֹּרֵא בְצֶדֶק הוּא וְשִׁבְעָה נְפָשׁוֹת עִמּוֹ

5. Ve•chen lo chas al - do•rot ke•doo•mim mash•chi•tey dar•kam al - ha•a•retz asher ma•cha o•tam be•mey ha•ma•bool vay•ma•let rak et - No•ach ha•ko•re ve•tze•dek hoo ve•she•va n`fa•shot ee•mo.

Rabbinic Jewish Commentary

but saved Noah the eighth person; not the eighth from Adam, as Enoch is said to be the seventh from him, Jud.1:14 for he was the tenth; nor is it to be read with the following clause, "the eighth preacher of righteousness";

but he was the eighth person, or one of the eight persons, saved from the flood; see 1Pe.3:20 hence the Ethiopic version, rather as a paraphrase than a version, renders it, "but caused to remain seven souls with Noah; whom he saved"; Hottinger (p) and Dr. Hammond (q) observe, from the Arabic writers, that the mountain on which the ark rested, and a town near it, were called Themenim; that is, "the eight", from the number of persons then and there saved.

The Jews (r) say that Noah was a prophet; and they represent him also, as a preacher, and even tell us the very words he used in his exhortations to the old world (s), saying,

"Be ye turned from your evil ways and works, lest the waters of the flood come upon you, and cut off all the seed of the children of men."

bringing in the flood upon the world of the ungodly; or "the ungodly of the world", as רשעי ארעא "the ungodly of the earth" (t); see Psa.75:8 though here it indeed means a whole world of wicked men, all but a very few, which were destroyed by the flood. This expresses both the wickedness of the men of that generation, the imagination of the thoughts of whose heart were evil continually; and whose lives were filled up with uncleanness, violence, rapine, oppression, injustice, and corruption, of all sorts; and likewise the large numbers of them, there was a whole world of them; and yet this did not secure them from the wrath of God.

It is the general notion of the Jews (u), that

"The generation of the flood shall have no part in the world to come, nor shall they stand in judgment."

(p) Smegma Orientale, p. 251, 252. (q) In loc. (r) Aben Ezra in Gen. viii. 21. (s) Pirke Eliezer, c. 22. (t) Targum in Psal. xlvi. 8. (u) Misna Sanhedrin, c. 11. sect. 3. Vajikra Rabba, sect. 4. fol. 149. 1. Yalkut Simeoni, par. 2. fol. 89. 2.

---

6. And turning the cities of Sodom and Gomorrha into ashes condemned them with an overthrow, making them an ensample unto those that after should live ungodly;

6. καὶ πόλεις Σοδόμων καὶ Γομόρρας τεφρώσας καταστροφῇ κατέκρινεν, ὑπόδειγμα μελλόντων ἀσεβεῖν τεθεικώς·

6. kai poleis Sodomon kai Gomorras tephrosas katastrophei katekrinen, 'upodeigma mellonton asebein tetheikos.

ו. וְאֶת-עָרֵי סְדֹם וַעֲמֹרָה שָׂחֵת עַד אֲשֶׁר הָיוּ לְאֵפֶר וְאֶת-הָאֲשֵׁמִים שָׂת לְמַהְפֵּכָה לִהְיוֹת לְאוֹת לְזֵדִים הַבָּאִים:אַחֲרֵיהֶם

6. Ve•et - arey S`dom va•A•mo•ra shi•chet ad asher ha•yoo le•e•fer ve•et - ha•a•she•mim shat le•ma•ha•pe•cha li•hee•yot le•ot le•ze•dim ha•ba•eem a•cha•rey•hem.

Rabbinic Jewish Commentary

By raining brimstone and fire upon them from heaven, Gen.19:24 which soon reduced them to ashes, with Admah and Zeboiim, Deu.29:25, cities delightfully situated, which were as the garden of God, and the land of Egypt, together with the inhabitants of them; and after they had received a signal mercy, in being rescued by Abraham from the kings who had carried them captive; and though Abraham, the friend of God, interceded for them, and righteous Lot dwelt among them. The first of these cities is in the Hebrew language called Sedom; Philo the Jew (w) calls it Sodoma, as in Rom.9:29 and in the Septuagint on Gen.13:10 here it is said to be a city, and Josephus (x) always calls it the city of the Sodomites, but in Mat.10:15 we read of the land of Sodom; and so Philo (y) the Jew speaks of χωρα, the region or country of the Sodomites; here the word is of the plural number, as in Mat.10:15 as it is also in the Septuagint in Gen.10:19 and in Philo the Jew (z), and so is Gomorrah in some copies of this, place, as in Mat.10:15. Solinus, the historian, gives an account of these cities, in agreement with this;

"A good way off of Jerusalem (he says (a)) is opened a sorrowful gulf, which the black ground, "in cinerem soluta", "reduced to ashes", shows it to be touched by heaven; there were two towns, or cities, the one called Sodom, and the other Gomorrah; where an apple is produced, which, although it has an appearance of ripeness, cannot be eaten; for the outward skin that encompasses it only contains a sort of soot, or embers within, which, ever so lightly squeezed, evaporates into smoke and dust;"
and so the author of the book of Wisdom 10:7 speaking of the five cities, on which fire fell, says,

"Of whose wickedness, even to this day, the waste land that smoketh is a testimony; and plants bearing fruit, that never come to ripeness."
Philo the Jew (b) says, that

"There are showed to this day in Syria monuments of this unspeakable destruction that happened; as ruins, ashes, sulphur, smoke, and a weak flame, breaking forth as of a fire burning:"

The Jews say (c) the same of the men of Sodom and Gomorrah as of the old world;

"The men of Sodom have no part in the world to come, as is said Gen.13:13 "but the men of Sodom were wicked, and sinners before the Lord exceedingly"; wicked in this world, and sinners in the world to come;"

(w) De Temulentia, p. 272. (x) Antiqu. l. 1. c. 8. sect. 3. c. 11. sect. 3. (y) De Abrahamo, p. 381. (z) De Temulentia, p. 272. (a) Polyhistor. c. 48. (b) De Vifa Mosis, l. 2. p. 662. (c) Misn. Sanhedrin, c. 11. sect. 3. Vajikra Rabba, sect. 4. fol. 149. 1.

2 Peter 2

7. And delivered just Lot, vexed with the filthy conversation of the wicked:

7. καὶ δίκαιον Λώτ, καταπονούμενον ὑπὸ τῆς τῶν ἀθέσμων ἐν ἀσελγείᾳ ἀναστροφῆς, ἐρρύσατο·

7. kai dikaion Lot, kataponoumenon 'upo teis ton athesmon en aselgeia anastropheis, errusato.

ז: וַיַּצֵּל אֶת-לוֹט הַצַּדִּיק אֲשֶׁר הִתְעַצֵּב אֶל-לִבּוֹ בִּרְאֹתוֹ מַעֲשֵׂה תַעְתֻּעִים בְּקֶרֶב בְּנֵי בְלִיָּעַל

7. Va•ya•tzel et - Lot ha•tza•dik asher hit•a•tzev el - li•bo bir•o•to ma•a•se ta•a•too•eem be•ke•rev b`ney ve•li•yaal.

Rabbinic Jewish Commentary

The Jews are very injurious to this good man's character, and give a very different one of him from this of the apostle's; they call him a wicked man, a perfect wicked man, as wicked as the inhabitants of Sodom (d); and say, that because they abounded in sin, therefore Lot chose to dwell among them (e); and affirm (f), that all the time he was with Abraham, God did not join himself to him, and did not commune with Abraham on his account; but, when he was separated from him, did; they call him the evil imagination, and the old serpent that was accursed, and cursed Lot (g); but Philo the Jew (h) speaks better of him, and says that he did not embrace and delight in the iniquities of the inhabitants, though he did not arrive to the perfection of wisdom; and the author of the book of Wisdom calls him the "righteous man",

"When the ungodly perished, she delivered the righteous man, who fled from the fire which fell down upon the five cities." (Wisdom 10:6)

(d) Tzeror Hammot, fol. 14. 4. & 16. 4. & 20. 2. (e) Jarchi in Gen. xiii. 10. (f) Zohar in Gen. fol. 57. 2. Jarchi in Gen. xiii. 13. (g) Zohar in Gen. fol. 56. 1, 2. Tzeror Hammor, fol. 7. 3. & 14. 3. & 20. 2. Bereshit Rabba, sect. 44. fol. 39. 1. (h) De Vita Mosis, l. 2. p. 662.

2 Peter 2

8. (For that righteous man dwelling among them, in seeing and hearing, vexed his righteous soul from day to day with their unlawful deeds;)

8. βλέμματι γὰρ καὶ ἀκοῇ ὁ δίκαιος, ἐγκατοικῶν ἐν αὐτοῖς, ἡμέραν ἐξ ἡμέρας ψυχὴν δικαίαν ἀνόμοις ἔργοις ἐβασάνιζεν·

8. blemmati gar kai akoei 'o dikaios, egkatoikon en autois, 'eimeran ex 'eimeras psuchein dikaian anomois ergois ebasanizen.

ח. כִּי הַצַּדִּיק הַזֶּה אֲשֶׁר יָשַׁב בְּתוֹכָם דָּאֲבָה עָלָיו נַפְשׁוֹ הַיְשָׁרָה בִּרְאֹתוֹ יוֹם יוֹם וּבְשָׁמְעוֹ רֹעַ מַעֲלֲלֵיהֶם:

8. Ki ha•tza•dik ha•ze asher ya•shav be•to•cham da•a•va alav naf•sho ha•y`sha•ra bir•o•to yom yom oov•shom•oh ro•a ma•a•la•ley•hem.

Rabbinic Jewish Commentary
Which is sometimes the lot of good men, to their great sorrow and grief, Psa.120:5. Upon mentioning those words in Gen.13:12 "and pitched his tent towards Sodom", but the men of Sodom were wicked, &c. says R. Eleazar (i);
"He is a righteous man that dwells between two wicked men, and does not learn their works;"

And such an one was Lot, whatever they are elsewhere pleased to say of him: "in seeing and hearing"; the Vulgate Latin version reads this in connection with the word "righteous", thus, "in seeing and hearing he was righteous"

(i) T. Bab. Yoma, fol. 38. 2.

2 Peter 2

9. The Lord knoweth how to deliver the godly out of temptations, and to reserve the unjust unto the day of judgment to be punished:

9. οἶδεν κύριος εὐσεβεῖς ἐκ πειρασμοῦ ῥύεσθαι, ἀδίκους δὲ εἰς ἡμέραν κρίσεως κολαζομένους τηρεῖν·

9. oiden kurios eusebeis ek peirasmou 'ruesthai, adikous de eis 'eimeran kriseos kolazomenous teirein.

ט. כִּי יֹדֵעַ יְהוָה לְהַצִּיל אֶת-יְרֵאָיו מִכּוּר צָרְפָם וְלַחֲשֹׁךְ אֶת-הָרְשָׁעִים לְעֵת מִשְׁפָּט לְהָשִׁיב עֲלֵיהֶם אֶת-אוֹנָם:

9. Ki yo•de•a Adonai le•ha•tzil et - ye•re•av mi•koor tzor•fam ve•la•cha•soch et - har•sha•eem le•et mish•pat le•ha•shiv aley•hem et - o•nam.

Rabbinic Jewish Commentary
This phrase, "The day of judgment", is used in Judith and is a Jewish one.

"Woe to the nations that rise up against my kindred! the Lord Almighty will take vengeance of them in the day of judgment, in putting fire and worms in their flesh; and they shall feel them, and weep for ever."
(Judith 16:17)

---

10. But chiefly them that walk after the flesh in the lust of uncleanness, and despise government. Presumptuous are they, selfwilled, they are not afraid to speak evil of dignities.

10. μάλιστα δὲ τοὺς ὀπίσω σαρκὸς ἐν ἐπιθυμίᾳ μιασμοῦ πορευομένους, καὶ κυριότητος καταφρονοῦντας. Τολμηταί, αὐθάδεις, δόξας οὐ τρέμουσιν βλασφημοῦντες·

10. malista de tous opiso sarkos en epithumia myasmou poreuomenous, kai kurioteitos kataphronountas. Tolmeitai, authadeis, doxas ou tremousin blaspheimountes.

י. וּבְרֹאשָׁם הֵם הַמְבַקְשִׁים תַּעֲנוּגֵי בְשָׂרִים בְּזִמָּה וַעֲגָבִים בּוֹזֵי מֶמְשָׁלָה עַזֵּי פָנִים וּקְשֵׁי עֹרֶף אֲשֶׁר לֹא יָחִילוּ:מִפְּנֵי אַדִּירִים לְדַבֵּר עֲלֵיהֶם עָתָק

10. Oov•ro•sham hem ha•m`vak•shim ta•a•noo•gey ve•sa•rim be•zi•ma va•a•ga•vim bo•zey mem•sha•la a•zey fa•nim ook•shey o•ref asher lo ya•chi•loo mip•ney adi•rim le•da•ber aley•hem atak.

2 Peter 2

11. Whereas angels, which are greater in power and might, bring not railing accusation against them before the Lord.

11. ὅπου ἄγγελοι, ἰσχύϊ καὶ δυνάμει μείζονες ὄντες, οὐ φέρουσιν κατ᾽ αὐτῶν παρὰ κυρίῳ βλάσφημον κρίσιν.

11. 'opou angeloi, ischui kai dunamei meizones ontes, ou pherousin kat auton para kurio blaspheimon krisin.

יא. אַף כִּי מַלְאָכִים גְּדֹלִים מֵהֶם בְּעֹז וָכֹחַ לֹא יָבִיעוּן עָתָק עֲלֵיהֶם לִפְנֵי יְהוָֹה בַּמִּשְׁפָּט:

11. Af ki mal•a•chim ge•do•lim me•hem be•oz va•cho•ach lo ya•bi•oon atak aley•hem lif•ney Adonai ba•mish•pat.

12. But these, as natural brute beasts, made to be taken and destroyed, speak evil of the things that they understand not; and shall utterly perish in their own corruption;

12. Οὗτοι δέ, ὡς ἄλογα ζῷα φυσικὰ γεγενημένα εἰς ἅλωσιν καὶ φθοράν, ἐν οἷς ἀγνοοῦσιν βλασφημοῦντες, ἐν τῇ φθορᾷ αὐτῶ καταφθαρήσονται,

12. 'Outoi de, 'os aloga zoa phusika gegeneimena eis 'alosin kai phthoran, en 'ois agnoousin blaspheimountes, en tei phthora auton kataphthareisontai,

יב. אַךְ בֹּעֲרִים אֵלֶּה יֵחָרְפוּן וְלֹא יֵדְעוּן מָה כִּבְהֵמוֹת אֵין הָבִין הַנּוֹצָרִים לְפִי חֻקָּם יִלָּכְדוּ וְיוּבָלוּ אֶל-טֶבַח כֵּן יִתַּפְּשׂוּ בִשְׁחִיתוֹתָם וְיֹאבֵדוּ:

12. Ach bo•a•rim ele ye•char•foon ve•lo yed•oon ma kiv•he•mot eyn ha•vin ha•no•tza•rim le•fi choo•kam yi•lach•doo ve•yoo•va•loo el - te•vach ken yi•taf•soo vish•chi•to•tam ve•yo•ve•doo.

13. And shall receive the reward of unrighteousness, as they that count it pleasure to riot in the day time. Spots they are and blemishes, sporting themselves with their own deceivings while they feast with you;

13. κομιούμενοι μισθὸν ἀδικίας, ἡδονὴν ἡγούμενοι τὴν ἐν ἡμέρᾳ τρυφήν, σπίλοι καὶ μῶμοι, ἐντρυφῶντες ἐν ταῖς ἀπάταις αὐτῶν συνευωχούμενοι ὑμῖν,

13. komioumenoi misthon adikias, 'eidonein 'eigoumenoi tein en 'eimera truphein, spiloi kai momoi, entruphontes en tais apatais auton suneuochoumenoi 'umin,

יג. זֶה גְמוּל לָהֶם כִּפְרִי מַעַלְלֵיהֶם הֲלֹא הֵם הַמִּתְעַנְּגִים עַל־מִרְזַח סְרוּחִים לְאוֹר הַיּוֹם וְהַמְגֹאָלִים בַּחֲבַרְבֻּרוֹת: וּמוּמִים וּבְמִשְׁתֵּה אֲהָבִים יִתְעַלְּסוּ כַּאֲשֶׁר יָחֹגּוּ עִמָּכֶם

13. Ze g`mool la•hem kif•ri ma•a•la•ley•hem ha•lo hem ha•mit•an•gim al - mir•zach s`roo•chim le•or ha•yom ve•ham•go•a•lim ba•cha•var•boo•rot oo•moo•mim oov•mish•te a•ha•vim yit•al•soo ka•a•sher ya•cho•goo ee•ma•chem.

---

2 Peter 2

14. Having eyes full of adultery, and that cannot cease from sin; beguiling unstable souls: an heart they have exercised with covetous practices; cursed children:

14. ὀφθαλμοὺς ἔχοντες μεστοὺς μοιχαλίδος καὶ ἀκαταπαύστους ἁμαρτίας, δελεάζοντες ψυχὰς ἀστηρίκτους, καρδίαν γεγυμνασμένην πλεονεξίας ἔχοντες, κατάρας τέκνα·

14. ophthalmous echontes mestous moichalidos kai akatapaustous 'amartias, deleazontes psuchas asteiriktous, kardian gegumnasmenein pleonexias echontes, kataras tekna.

יד. עֵינַיִם לָהֶם מְלֵאוֹת נֹאֲפִים מֵחֲטוֹא לֹא יִשְׂבָּעוּן נַפְשׁוֹת פְּתָאִים יְצֹדְדוּ וְאַחֲרֵי בִצְעָם לִבָּם הֹלֵךְ בָּנִים מְקֻלָּלִים:

14. Ey•na•yim la•hem me•le•ot ni•oo•fim me•cha•to lo yis•ba•oon naf•shot pe•ta•eem ye•tzo•de•doo ve•a•cha•rey vitz•am li•bam ho•lech ba•nim me•koo•la•lim.

Rabbinic Jewish Commentary

For the seventh command is not only violated by unclean actions, and obscene words, but also by unchaste looks: and so the Jews explain (k) that precept,

""Thou shalt not commit adultery", Exo.20:14; you shall not go after your hearts, nor after "your eyes"; says R. Levi, the heart and the "eye" are sin's two brokers."

Hence we read (l) of נואף בעיניו, "one that commits adultery with his eyes"; compare Job.31:1. Some read the words, "having eyes full of the adulteress": that is, having a lewd and infamous woman always in mind and sight, continually looking at her and lusting after her.

(k) T. Hieros. Beracot, fol. 3. 3. (l) Vajikra Rabba, sect. 23. fol. 165. 1. Vid. A. Gell. Noct. Attic. l. 3. c. 5.

---

2 Peter 2

15. Which have forsaken the right way, and are gone astray, following the way of Balaam the son of Bosor, who loved the wages of unrighteousness;

15. καταλιπόντες εὐθεῖαν ὁδὸν ἐπλανήθησαν, ἐξακολουθήσαντες τῇ ὁδῷ τοῦ Βαλαὰμ τοῦ Βοσόρ, ὃς μισθὸν ἀδικίας ἠγάπησεν,

15. katalipontes eutheian 'odon eplaneitheisan, exakoloutheisantes tei 'odo tou Bala'am tou Bosor, 'os misthon adikias eigapeisen,

טו. עָזְבוּ אֹרַח יְשָׁרָה וַיִּתְעוּ וַיֵּלְכוּ בְדֶרֶךְ בִּלְעָם בֶּן-בְּעוֹר אֲשֶׁר חָמַד שַׁלְמֹנִים עֵקֶב עַוְלָתָה:

15. Az•voo o•rach ye•sha•ra va•yit•oo va•yel•choo ve•de•rech Bilam ben - be•or asher cha•mad shal•mo•nim e•kev av•la•ta.

---

16. But was rebuked for his iniquity: the dumb ass speaking with man's voice forbad the madness of the prophet.

16. ἔλεγξιν δὲ ἔσχεν ἰδίας παρανομίας· ὑποζύγιον ἄφωνον, ἐν ἀνθρώπου φωνῇ φθεγξάμενον, ἐκώλυσεν τὴν τοῦ προφήτου παραφρονίαν.

16. elegxin de eschen idias paranomias. 'upozugion aphonon, en anthropou phonei phthegxamenon, ekolusen tein tou propheitou paraphronian.

טז. אַךְ הוֹכַח בְּתוֹכָחָה עֵקֶב פִּשְׁעוֹ וְאָתוֹן נֶאֱלָמָה דִּבְּרָה בְּקוֹל אָדָם בְּאָזְנֵי הַנָּבִיא לַחְשֹׂךְ אֶת-מְשׁוּגָתוֹ:

16. Ach hoo•chach be•to•cha•cha e•kev pish•oh ve•a•ton ne•e•la•ma dib•ra ve•kol adam be•oz•ney ha•na•vee lach•soch et - me•shoo•ga•to.

Rabbinic Jewish Commentary

speaking with man's voice; which was supernatural and miraculous, for it was God that opened the mouth of the ass: the mouth of that ass is said, by the Jews (m), to be one of the ten things created between the two evenings on the sixth day of the creation; that is, as the gloss on it says, concerning which it was decreed, that its mouth should be opened to speak what this ass said; and the occasion of it may be seen in Num.22:22. Lactantius (n) observes, that there are two stars in the constellation of Cancer, which the Greeks call the "asses"; and which, the poets feign, are those that carried Liberus over a river, when he could not pass it; to one of which he gave this for a reward, "ut humana voce loqueretur", "that it should speak with man's voice"; a fable, no doubt, hatched from the sacred history, and said in imitation of this ass.

And so Balaam, though a diviner and soothsayer, is called by the Jewish writers (o); who, they say, was first a prophet, and then a soothsayer, from whom Jerom (p) seems to have received the tradition; who says, that he was first a holy man, and a prophet of God, and afterwards, through disobedience, and a desire of gifts, was called a diviner; for his eyes were opened, and he saw the vision of the Almighty; and the Spirit of God came upon him, and he prophesied many things concerning Israel, and the Messiah, and others, Num.24:4. His madness lay in going with the messengers of Balak, Num.22:21, in order to curse Israel, contrary to the will of God, Num.22:12; and it is madness in any to oppose God in his counsels, purposes, providences, and precepts; and every sin, which is an act of hostility against God, has madness in it; and this of Balaam's was forbid by his ass, and he was convinced of it. Very appropriately is mention made of this dumb ass, when the persons here spoken of were as natural brute beasts, and worse than them.

(m) Pirke Abot, c. 5. sect. 6. & Jarchi in ib. Sepher Cosri, par. 2. p. 254. (n) De falsa Religione, l. 1. c. 21. (o) Pesikta, Ilmedenu & Gerundensis apud Drus in loc. T. Bab Sanhedrin fol. 106. 1. Aben Ezra in Numb. xxxii. 28. (p) Tradition. Heb. in Genes. fol. 69. D.

17. These are wells without water, clouds that are carried with a tempest; to whom the mist of darkness is reserved for ever.

17. Οὗτοί εἰσιν πηγαὶ ἄνυδροι, νεφέλαι ὑπὸ λαίλαπος ἐλαυνόμεναι, οἷς ὁ ζόφος τοῦ σκότους εἰς αἰῶνα τετήρηται.

17. 'Outoi eisin peigai anudroi, nephelai 'upo lailapos elaunomenai, 'ois 'o zophos tou skotous eis aiona teteireitai.

יז. בְּאֵרוֹת הֵם בְּאֵין מַיִם נְשִׂיאִים נֶהְדָּפִים בְּרוּחַ וְאֵין גֶּשֶׁם וְחֹשֶׁךְ אֲפֵלָה צָפוּן לָהֶם לְעוֹלָם:

17. Be•e•rot hem be•eyn ma•yim n`si•eem ne•he•da•fim be•roo•ach ve•eyn ga•shem ve•cho•shech a•fe•la tza•foon la•hem le•o•lam.

---

2 Peter 2

18. For when they speak great swelling words of vanity, they allure through the lusts of the flesh, through much wantonness, those that were clean escaped from them who live in error.

18. Ὑπέρογκα γὰρ ματαιότητος φθεγγόμενοι, δελεάζουσιν ἐν ἐπιθυμίαις σαρκός, ἀσελγείαις, τοὺς ὄντως ἀποφυγόντας τοὺς ἐν πλάνῃ ἀναστρεφομένους,

18. 'Uperogka gar mataioteitos phthengomenoi, deleazousin en epithumiais sarkos, aselgeiais, tous ontos apophugontas tous en planei anastrephomenous,

יח. כִּי שָׁוְא יְדַבְּרוּ בִּלְשׁוֹן מְדַבֶּרֶת גְּדֹלוֹת וּבִתְשׁוּקַת חַיֵּי בְשָׂרִים יָצוּדוּ בְרֶשֶׁת עָרְמָתָם אֶת-הַמְמַלְּטִים מִן-תֹּעֵי דָרֶךְ:

18. Ki shav ye•dab•roo be•la•shon me•da•be•ret ge•do•lot oo•vit•shoo•kat cha•yey ve•sa•rim ya•tzoo•doo ve•re•shet or•ma•tam et - ha•me•mal•tim min - to•ey da•rech.

---

19. While they promise them liberty, they themselves are the servants of corruption: for of whom a man is overcome, of the same is he brought in bondage.

19. ἐλευθερίαν αὐτοῖς ἐπαγγελλόμενοι, αὐτοὶ δοῦλοι ὑπάρχοντες τῆς φθορᾶς· ᾧ γάρ τις ἥττηται, τούτῳ καὶ δεδούλωται.

19. eleutherian autois epangellomenoi, autoi douloi 'uparchontes teis phthoras. 'o gar tis 'eitteitai, touto kai dedoulotai.

יט. דְּרוֹר יִקְרְאוּ לָהֶם וְהֵם בְּנַפְשָׁם עֲבָדִים לַמַּשְׁחִית כִּי לְמִי אֲשֶׁר יִכָּבֵשׁ-אִישׁ גַּם-עֶבֶד הוּא לוֹ:

19. D`ror yik•re•oo la•hem ve•hem be•naf•sham a•va•dim la•mash•chit ki le•mi asher yi•ka•vesh - eesh gam - eved hoo lo.

---

2 Peter 2

20. For if after they have escaped the pollutions of the world through the knowledge of the Lord and Saviour Jesus Christ, they are again entangled therein, and overcome, the latter end is worse with them than the beginning.

20. Εἰ γὰρ ἀποφυγόντες τὰ μιάσματα τοῦ κόσμου ἐν ἐπιγνώσει τοῦ κυρίου καὶ σωτῆρος Ἰησοῦ χριστοῦ, τούτοις δὲ πάλιν ἐμπλακέντες ἡττῶνται, γέγονεν αὐτοῖς τὰ ἔσχατα χείρονα τῶν πρώτων.

20. Ei gar apophugontes ta myasmata tou kosmou en epignosei tou kuriou kai soteiros Yeisou christou, toutois de palin emplakentes 'eittontai, gegonen autois ta eschata cheirona ton proton.

כ. וְאֵלֶּה אֲשֶׁר נִמְלְטוּ מִתּוֹעֲבוֹת הָאָרֶץ בְּדַעַת אֶת-אֲדֹנֵינוּ וּמוֹשִׁיעֵנוּ יֵשׁוּעַ הַמָּשִׁיחַ אִם-יָשׁוּבוּ יִשְׁקְעוּ בַתּוֹעֲבוֹת:הָאֵלֶּה יִכָּבְשׁוּ תַּחַת יָדָן וְאַחֲרִיתָם רָעָה מֵרֵאשִׁיתָם

20. Ve•e•le asher nim•le•too mi•to•a•vot ha•a•retz be•da•at et - Ado•ney•noo oo•Mo•shi•e•noo Yeshua ha•Ma•shi•ach eem - ya•shoo•voo yish•ke•oo va•to•e•vot ha•e•le yi•kav•shoo ta•chat ya•dan ve•a•cha•ri•tam ra•ah me•re•shi•tam.

Rabbinic Jewish Commentary

The sins of it, the governing vices of it, which the men of the world are addicted to, and immersed in; for the whole world lies in wickedness, and which are of a defiling nature: the phrase is Rabbinical; it is said (q),

"He that studies not in the Torah in this world, but is defiled בטנופי עלמא, "with the pollutions of the world", what is written of him? and they took him, and cast him without."

(q) Zohar in Gen. fol. 104. 3. Vid. Bechinot Olam, p. 178.

21. For it had been better for them not to have known the way of righteousness, than, after they have known it, to turn from the holy commandment delivered unto them.

21. Κρεῖττον γὰρ ἦν αὐτοῖς μὴ ἐπεγνωκέναι τὴν ὁδὸν τῆς δικαιοσύνης, ἢ ἐπιγνοῦσιν ἐπιστρέψαι ἐκ τῆς παραδοθείσης αὐτοῖς ἁγίας ἐντολῆς.

21. Kreitton gar ein autois mei epegnokenai tein 'odon teis dikaiosuneis, ei epignousin epistrepsai ek teis paradotheiseis autois 'agias entoleis.

כא. טוֹב לָהֶם לֹא לָדַעַת מַעְגְּלֵי צֶדֶק מֵאֲשֶׁר יֵדָעוּן וְסוּר מִמִּצְוָה הַקְּדֹשָׁה הַנְּתוּנָה לָהֶם:

21. Tov la•hem lo la•da•at ma•ag•ley tze•dek me•a•sher yed•oon ve•soor mi•mitz•va ha•k`do•sha ha•ne•too•na la•hem.

---

2 Peter 2

22. But it is happened unto them according to the true proverb, The dog is turned to his own vomit again; and the sow that was washed to her wallowing in the mire.

22. Συμβέβηκεν δὲ αὐτοῖς τὸ τῆς ἀληθοῦς παροιμίας, Κύων ἐπιστρέψας ἐπὶ τὸ ἴδιον ἐξέραμα, καὶ ὗς λουσαμένη εἰς κύλισμα βορβόρου.

22. Sumbebeiken de autois to teis aleithous paroimias, Kuon epistrepsas epi to idion exerama, kai 'us lousamenei eis kulisma borborou.

כב. וַיֵּאָמֵן עֲלֵיהֶם הַמָּשָׁל אֶל-נָכוֹן כֶּלֶב שָׁב עַל-קֵאוֹ וַחֲזִיר עֹלֶה מִן-הָרַחְצָה לְהִתְגֹּלֵל בָּרֶפֶשׁ:

22. Va•ye•a•men aley•hem ha•ma•shal el - na•chon ke•lev shav al - keo va•cha•zir o•le min - ha•rach•tza le•hit•go•lel ba•ra•fesh.

Rabbinic Jewish Commentary

In the Hebrew language, a "sow" is called חזיר, from the root חזר, which signifies to "return", because that creature, as soon as it is out of the mire and dirt, and is washed from its filthiness, naturally returns to it again: so such apostates return to what they were before, to their former principles and practices: in this manner the Jews explain the proverb,

"Tobiah returns to Tobiah, as it is said, Pro.26:11; as a dog returneth to his vomit (r)."

(r) Vajikra Rabba, sect. 16. fol. 158. 4.

(2Peter Chapter 2 End)

2 Peter, Chapter 3

1. This second epistle, beloved, I now write unto you; in both which I stir up your pure minds by way of remembrance:

1. Ταύτην ἤδη, ἀγαπητοί, δευτέραν ὑμῖν γράφω ἐπιστολήν, ἐν αἷς διεγείρω ὑμῶν ἐν ὑπομνήσει τὴν εἰλικρινῆ διάνοιαν,

1. Tautein eidei, agapeitoi, deuteran 'umin grapho epistolein, en 'ais diegeiro 'umon en 'upomneisei tein eilikrinei dyanoyan,

א. זֹאת הִיא הָאִגֶּרֶת הַשֵּׁנִית יְדִידִים אֲשֶׁר אֲנִי כֹתֵב לָכֶם עַתָּה וּבִשְׁתֵּיהֶן בָּאתִי כְמַזְכִּיר לְעוֹרֵר אֶת-לִבְּכֶם הַטּוֹב:

1. Zot hee ha•ee•ge•ret ha•she•nit ye•di•dim asher ani cho•tev la•chem ata oo•vish•tey•hen ba•ti che•maz•kir le•o•rer et - lib•chem ha•tov.

---

2. That ye may be mindful of the words which were spoken before by the holy prophets, and of the commandment of us the apostles of the Lord and Saviour:

2. μνησθῆναι τῶν προειρημένων ῥημάτων ὑπὸ τῶν ἁγίων προφητῶν, καὶ τῆς τῶν ἀποστόλων ὑμῶν ἐντολῆς τοῦ κυρίου καὶ σωτῆρος·

2. mneistheinai ton proeireimenon 'reimaton 'upo ton 'agion propheiton, kai teis ton apostolon 'umon entoleis tou kuriou kai soteiros.

ב. לְמַעַן תִּזְכְּרוּ אֶת-הַדְּבָרִים אֲשֶׁר נֶאֶמְרוּ מִקֶּדֶם בְּיַד הַנְּבִיאִים הַקְּדוֹשִׁים וְאֶת-מִצְוֹת אֲדֹנֵינוּ וּמוֹשִׁיעֵנוּ עַל-יְדֵי שְׁלִיחֵיכֶם:

2. Le•ma•an tiz•ke•roo et - ha•d`va•rim asher ne•em•roo mi•ke•dem be•yad ha•n`vi•eem ha•k`do•shim ve•et - mitz•vot Ado•ney•noo oo•Mo•shi•e•noo al - ye•dey sh`li•chey•chem.

---

3. Knowing this first, that there shall come in the last days scoffers, walking after their own lusts,

3. τοῦτο πρῶτον γινώσκοντες, ὅτι ἐλεύσονται ἐπ' ἐσχάτου τῶν ἡμερῶν ἐμπαῖκται, κατὰ τὰς ἰδίας ἐπιθυμίας αὐτῶν πορευόμενοι,

3. touto proton ginoskontes, 'oti eleusontai ep eschatou ton 'eimeron empaiktai, kata tas idias epithumias auton poreuomenoi,

ג. אַךְ דְּעוּ לָכֶם מֵרֹאשׁ כִּי בְּאַחֲרִית הַיָּמִים יָבֹאוּ לֵצִים הַזֹּנִים אַחֲרֵי תַאֲוָתָם וְיִתְלוֹצְצוּ לֵאמֹר:

3. Ach de•oo la•chem me•rosh ki ve•a•cha•rit ha•ya•mim ya•vo•oo le•tzim ha•zo•nim a•cha•rey ta•a•va•tam ve•yit•lo•tze•tzoo le•mor.

Rabbinic Jewish Commentary
For it is a rule with the Jews (s), that wherever the last days are mentioned, the days of the Messiah are intended; when the prophets foretold such scoffers should come; or in the last days of the Jewish state, both civil and religious, called "the ends of the world", 1Co.10:11; a little before the destruction of Jerusalem, when iniquity greatly abounded, Mat.24:11; or "in the last of the days"; as the words may be rendered; and so answer to באחרית הימים, in Isa.2:2, and may regard the latter part of the last times; the times of the apostles were the last days, 1Jn.2:18.

(s) Kimchi in Isa. ii. 2.

---

2 Peter 3

4. And saying, Where is the promise of his coming? for since the fathers fell asleep, all things continue as they were from the beginning of the creation.

4. καὶ λέγοντες, Ποῦ ἐστιν ἡ ἐπαγγελία τῆς παρουσίας αὐτοῦ; Ἀφ᾽ ἧς γὰρ οἱ πατέρες ἐκοιμήθησαν, πάντα οὕτως διαμένει ἀπ᾽ ἀρχῆς κτίσεως.

4. kai legontes, Pou estin 'ei epangelia teis parousias autou? Aph 'eis gar 'oi pateres ekoimeitheisan, panta 'outos dyamenei ap archeis ktiseos.

ד: אַיֵּה הַבְטָחַת בֹּאוֹ כִּי מֵאָז שָׁכְבוּ הָאָבוֹת נִשְׁאַר כָּל-דָּבָר עַל-חָקוֹ כְּמוֹ מֵרֵאשִׁית הַבְּרִיאָה
4. A•ye hav•ta•chat bo•oo ki me•az shach•voo ha•a•vot nish•ar kol - da•var al - choo•ko k`mo me•re•sheet hab•ri•ah.

5. For this they willingly are ignorant of, that by the word of God the heavens were of old, and the earth standing out of the water and in the water:

5. Λανθάνει γὰρ αὐτοὺς τοῦτο θέλοντας, ὅτι οὐρανοὶ ἦσαν ἔκπαλαι, καὶ γῆ ἐξ ὕδατος καὶ δι' ὕδατος συνεστῶσα, τῷ τοῦ Θεοῦ λόγῳ,

5. Lanthanei gar autous touto thelontas, 'oti ouranoi eisan ekpalai, kai gei ex 'udatos kai di 'udatos sunestosa, to tou theou logo,

ה. וְנֶעְלָם מֵעֵינֵיהֶם כְּאַוַּת נַפְשָׁם כִּי הַשָּׁמַיִם נַעֲשׂוּ מִקֶּדֶם וְעַל-יְדֵי הַמַּיִם נִבְרְאָה הָאָרֶץ מִן-הַמַּיִם בִּדְבַר:אֱלֹהִים

5. Ve•ne•e•lam me•ey•ne•hem ke•a•vat naf•sham ki ha•sha•ma•yim na•a•soo mi•ke•dem ve•al - ye•dey ha•ma•yim niv•re•ah ha•a•retz min - ha•ma•yim bid•var Elohim.

Rabbinic Jewish Commentary

That is, "by the Word of God"; for this phrase, in the original text, is placed after this clause, and last of all; and refers not only to the being of the heavens of old, but to the rise, standing, and subsistence of the earth, which is here particularly described for the sake of the deluge, the apostle afterwards mentions: and it is said to be "standing out of the water", or "consisting out of it"; it consists of it as a part; the globe of the earth is terraqueous, partly land and partly water; and even the dry land itself has its rise and spring out of water; the first matter that was created is called the deep, and waters in which darkness was, and upon which the Spirit of God moved, Gen.1:2; agreeably to which Thales the Milesian asserted (t), that water was the principle of all things; and the Ethiopic version here renders the words thus, "and the Word of God created also the earth out of water, and confirmed it": the account the Jews give of the first formation of the world is this (u);

"At first the world was מים במים, "water in water"; what is the sense (of that passage Gen.1:2;) "and the Spirit of God moved upon the face of the waters?" he returned, and made it snow; he casteth forth his ice like morsels, Psa.147:17; he returned and made it earth; "for to the snow he saith, Be thou earth", Job.37:6, and the earth stood upon the waters; "to him that stretched out the earth above the waters", Psa.136:6;"

(t) Vid. Laert. l. i. in Vit. Thaletis. (u) T. Hieros. Chagiga, fol. 77. 1.

6. Whereby the world that then was, being overflowed with water, perished:

6. δι᾽ ὧν ὁ τότε κόσμος ὕδατι κατακλυσθεὶς ἀπώλετο·

6. di 'on 'o tote kosmos 'udati kataklustheis apoleto.

ו. וּבַמַּיִם אָז אָבְדָה הָאָרֶץ הַהִיא בַּעֲבוּר שׁוֹט שׁוֹטֵף עָלֶיהָ:

6. Oo•va•ma•yim az av•da ha•a•retz ha•hee ba•a•vor shot sho•tef a•le•ha.

2 Peter 3

7. But the heavens and the earth, which are now, by the same word are kept in store, reserved unto fire against the day of judgment and perdition of ungodly men.

7. οἱ δὲ νῦν οὐρανοὶ καὶ ἡ γῆ τῷ αὐτοῦ λόγῳ τεθησαυρισμένοι εἰσίν, πυρὶ τηρούμενοι εἰς ἡμέραν κρίσεως καὶ ἀπωλείας τῶν ἀσεβῶν ἀνθρώπων.

7. 'oi de nun ouranoi kai 'ei gei to autou logo tetheisaurismenoi eisin, puri teiroumenoi eis 'eimeran kriseos kai apoleias ton asebon anthropon.

ז. הַשָּׁמַיִם וְהָאָרֶץ אֲשֶׁר לְפָנֵינוּ הַיּוֹם הוּכְנוּ בִדְבָרוֹ לְמַאֲכֹלֶת אֵשׁ וּשְׁמֻרִים הֵם לְיוֹם הַמִּשְׁפָּט בַּאֲבֹד רְשָׁעִים:

7. Ha•sha•ma•yim ve•ha•a•retz asher le•fa•ney•noo ha•yom hoo•cha•noo vid•va•ro le•ma•a•cho•let esh oosh•moo•rim hem le•yom ha•mish•pat ba•a•vod r`sha•eem.

Rabbinic Jewish Commentary

Josephus (w) relates, that Adam foretold that there would be a destruction of all things, once by the force of fire, and once by the power and multitude of water; and it is certain the Jews had knowledge of the destruction of the earth by fire, as by water: they say (x),

"That when the Torah was given to Israel, his (God's) voice went from one end of the world to the other, and trembling laid hold on all the nations of the world in their temples, and they said a song, as it is said, Psa.29:9, "and in his temple doth everyone speak of his glory": all of them gathered together to wicked Balaam, and said to him, what is the voice of the multitude which we hear, perhaps a flood is coming upon the world? he said unto them, "YHVH sitteth upon the flood, yea, YHVH sitteth King for ever", Psa.29:10. Thus hath YHVH swore, that he will not bring a flood upon the world; they replied to him, a flood of water he will not bring, but מבול של אש, "a flood of fire" he will bring, as it is said, Isa.66:16, "for by fire will YHVH plead","

Or judge: and hence they speak (y) of the wicked being judged with two sorts of, judgments, by water, and by fire: and, according to our apostle, the heavens and earth are kept and reserved to fire which could also be an allusion to the Temple built to represent creation.

(w) Antiqu. Jud. l. 1. c. 2. sect. 3. (x) T. Bab. Zebachim, fol. 116. 1. (y) Zohar in Gen. fol. 50. 4. & 51. 1.

2 Peter 3

8. But, beloved, be not ignorant of this one thing, that one day is with the Lord as a thousand years, and a thousand years as one day.

8. Ἐν δὲ τοῦτο μὴ λανθανέτω ὑμᾶς, ἀγαπητοί, ὅτι μία ἡμέρα παρὰ κυρίῳ ὡς χίλια ἔτη, καὶ χίλια ἔτη ὡς ἡμέρα μία.

8. 'En de touto mei lanthaneto 'umas, agapeitoi, 'oti mia 'eimera para kurio 'os chilya etei, kai chilya etei 'os 'eimera mia.

ח. אַךְ אַל-תִּשְׁכְּחוּ יְדִידִים זֹאת אֶחָת כִּי יוֹם אֶחָד בְּעֵינֵי יְהֹוָה כְּאֶלֶף שָׁנִים וְאֶלֶף שָׁנִים כְּיוֹם אֶחָד:

8. Ach al - tish•ke•choo ye•di•dim zot e•chat ki yom e•chad be•ei•ney Adonai ke•e•lef sha•nim ve•e•lef sha•nim ke•yom e•chad.

Rabbinic Jewish Commentary

Referring either to Psa.90:4; or to a common saying among the Jews, founded on the same passage, יומו של הק בה אלף שנים, "the day of the holy blessed God is a thousand years." (z)

For though such a number of years is very considerable among men, ye not "with God", as the Arabic and Ethiopic versions read, with whom a thousand years, and even eternity itself, is but as a day, Isa.43:13. Unless this phrase should be thought to refer, as it is by some, to the day of judgment, and be expressive of the duration of that: it is certain that the

Jews interpreted days of millenniums, and reckoned millenniums by days, and used this phrase in confirmation of it. Thus they say (a),

"In the time to come, which is in the last days, on the sixth day, which is the sixth millennium, when the Messiah comes, for the day of the holy blessed God is a thousand years."

And a little after,
""YHVH hath created a new thing in the earth, a woman shall compass a man". This is in the time of the Messiah which is in the sixth day."

And elsewhere (b),
"The sixth degree is called the sixth day, the day of the holy blessed God is a thousand years. And in that day the King Messiah shall come, and it shall be called the feast of gathering, for the holy blessed God will gather in it the captivity of his people."

So they call the sabbath, or seventh day, the seventh millennium, and interpret (c).
""The song for the sabbath day", Psa.92:1 title, for the seventh millennium, for one day of the holy blessed God is a thousand years."

To which agrees the tradition of Elias, which runs thus (d);
"It is the tradition of the house of Elias, that the world shall be six thousand years, two thousand years void (of the law), two thousand years the Torah, and two thousand years the days of the Messiah;"

For they suppose that the six days of the creation were expressive of the six thousand years in which the world will stand; and that the seventh day prefigures the last millennium, in which will be the day of judgment, and the world to come; for

"The six days of the creation (they say (e)) is a sign or intimation of these things: on the sixth day man was created; and on the seventh his work was finished; so the kings of the nations of the world (continue) five millenniums, answering to the five days, in which were created the fowls, and the creeping things of the waters, and other things; and the enjoyment of their kingdom is a little in the sixth, answerable to the creation of the beasts, and living creatures created at this time in the beginning of it; and the kingdom of the house of David is in the sixth millennium, answerable to the creation of man, who knew his Creator, and ruled over them all; and in the end of that millennium will be the day of judgment, answerable to man, who was judged in the end of it; and the seventh is the sabbath, and it is the beginning of the world to come."

(z) Bereshit Rabba, sect. 8. fol. 7. 3. Vajikra Rabba, sect. 19. fol. 160. 2. Bemidbar Rabba, sect. 14. fol. 216. 1. Shirhashirim Rabba, fol. 20. 1. Zohar in Exod. fol. 60. 1. Tzeror Hammor, fol. 157. 1. & Nishmet Chayim Orat. 1. c. 5. fol. 12. 1. (a) Zohar in Gen. fol. 13. 4. (b) Ib. fol. 16. 1. (c) Bartenora in Misn. Tamid, c. 7. sect. 4. (d) T. Bab. Sanhedrin, fol. 97. 1. & Avoda Zara, fol. 9. 1. (e) Ceseph Misna in Maimon. Hilchot Teshuva, c. 9. sect. 2.

---

2 Peter 3

9. The Lord is not slack concerning his promise, as some men count slackness; but is longsuffering to us-ward, not willing that any should perish, but that all should come to repentance.

9. Οὐ βραδύνει ὁ κύριος τῆς ἐπαγγελίας, ὥς τινες βραδυτῆτα ἡγοῦνται· ἀλλὰ μακροθυμεῖ εἰς ἡμᾶς, μὴ βουλόμενός τινας ἀπολέσθαι, ἀλλὰ πάντας εἰς μετάνοιαν χωρῆσαι.

9. Ou bradunei 'o kurios teis epangelias, 'os tines braduteita 'eigountai. alla makrothumei eis 'eimas, mei boulomenos tinas apolesthai, alla pantas eis metanoyan choreisai.

ט. וְלֹא יְאַחֵר יְהוָה לְמַלֹּאת אֶת אֲשֶׁר דִּבֶּר נֶגֶד הַחֹשְׁבִים כִּי עָבַר הַמּוֹעֵד כִּי אִם-מַאֲרִיךְ לָנוּ אַף אַחֲרֵי אֲשֶׁר לֹא:יַחְפֹּץ בָּאֲבֹד אִישׁ כִּי אִם-בְּהָבִיא כָל-אָדָם אֶת-לִבּוֹ לִתְשׁוּבָה

9. Ve•lo ye•a•cher Adonai le•ma•lot et asher di•ber ne•ged ha•chosh•vim ki avar ha•mo•ed ki eem - ma•a•rich la•noo af a•cha•rey asher lo yach•potz ba•a•vod eesh ki eem - be•ha•vi chol - adam et - li•bo lit•shoo•va.

Rabbinic Jewish Commentary

The Alexandrian copy reads, "for you", or your sakes; and so the Vulgate Latin, Syriac, and Ethiopic versions. A passage somewhat like to this is met with in a book of the Jews (f), esteemed by them very ancient. "God prolongs or defers his anger with men; and one day, which is a thousand years, is fixed, besides the seventy years he delivered to David the king.--And he does not judge man by his evil works which he continually does, for if so, the world would not stand; but the holy blessed God defers his anger with the righteous, and the wicked, that they may return, by perfect repentance, and be established in this world, and in the world to come."

And it is an observation of theirs (g), that when God is said to be "longsuffering", it is not written ארך אף, but ארך אפים, intimating, that he is longsuffering both to the righteous and the wicked; but then he bears with the latter, for the sake of the former

(f) Zohar in Gen. fol. 83. 3. (g) T. Hieros, Taanioth, fol. 65. 2. T. Bab. Bava Kama, fol. 50. 2.

2 Peter 3

10. But the day of the Lord will come as a thief in the night; in the which the heavens shall pass away with a great noise, and the elements shall melt with fervent heat, the earth also and the works that are therein shall be burned up.

10. Ἥξει δὲ ἡ ἡμέρα κυρίου ὡς κλέπτης ἐν νυκτί, ἐν ᾗ οἱ οὐρανοὶ ῥοιζηδὸν παρελεύσονται, στοιχεῖα δὲ καυσούμενα λυθήσονται, καὶ γῆ καὶ τὰ ἐν αὐτῇ ἔργα κατακαήσεται.

10. 'Eixei de 'ei 'eimera kuriou 'os klepteis en nukti, en 'oi ouranoi 'roizeidon pareleusontai, stoicheia de kausoumena lutheisontai, kai gei kai ta en autei erga katakaeisetai.

י. אַךְ יוֹם יְהֹוָה כְּגַנָּב יָבֹא בַּלָּיְלָה אָז יַחְלְפוּ הַשָּׁמַיִם בְּרַעַשׁ גָּדוֹל הַיְסֹדוֹת יִמַּסּוּ מִפְּנֵי הָאֵשׁ וְהָאָרֶץ וְהַמַּעֲשִׂים:אֲשֶׁר בָּהּ יַעֲלוּ בְלַהַב

10. Ach yom Adonai ke•ga•nav ya•vo ba•lai•la az yach•le•foo ha•sha•ma•yim be•ra•ash ga•dol hay•so•dot yi•ma•soo mip•ney ha•esh ve•ha•a•retz ve•ha•ma•a•sim asher ba ya•a•loo ve•la•hav.

Rabbinic Jewish Commentary
and the elements shall melt with fervent heat: not what are commonly called the four elements, earth, air, tire, and water, the first principles of all things: the ancient philosophers distinguished between principles and elements; principles, they say (h), are neither generated, nor corrupted; τα τε στοιχεια κατα την εκπυρωσιν φθειρεσθαι, "but the elements will be corrupted, or destroyed by the conflagration."

and the works that are therein shall be burnt up; This general conflagration was not only known to the Jews, but to the Heathens, to the poets, and Platonist and Stoic philosophers, who frequently (i) speak of it in plain terms. Some are of opinion that these words refer to the destruction of Jerusalem; and so the passing away of the heavens may design the removal of their assembly state and ordinances, Heb.12:26, and the melting of the elements the ceasing of the ceremonial Torah, called the elements of the world, Gal.4:3, and the burning of the earth the destruction of the land of Judea, expressed in such a manner in Deu.29:23, and particularly of the temple, and the curious works in that, which were all burnt up and destroyed by fire, though Titus endeavoured to prevent it, but could not (k): which sense may be included, inasmuch as there was a promise of Yeshua's coming to destroy the Jewish nation, and was expected.

(h) Diog. Laert. l. 7. in Vita Zenonis. (i) Vid. Diog. Laert ib. & l. 9. in Vita Heraclit. & Hesych. de Philos. p. 36. Arrian. Epict. l. 3. c. 13. Phurut. de Natura Deorum, p. 39. Ovid. Metamorph, fab. 7. Min. Felix, p. 37. & Justin. Martyr. Apol. 2. p. 66. (k) Vid. Joseph. de Bello Jud. l. 3. c. 9, 10. & l. 7. c. 14, 16.

2 Peter 3

11. Seeing then that all these things shall be dissolved, what manner of persons ought ye to be in all holy conversation and godliness,

11. Τούτων οὖν πάντων λυομένων, ποταποὺς δεῖ ὑπάρχειν ὑμᾶς ἐν ἁγίαις ἀναστροφαῖς καὶ εὐσεβείαις,

11. Touton oun panton luomenon, potapous dei 'uparchein 'umas en 'agiais anastrophais kai eusebeiais,

יא. וְעַתָּה אִם נְמֹגִים כָּל־אֵלֶּה עַד־כַּמָּה עֲלֵיכֶם לְהִזָּהֵר לְהִתְהַלֵּךְ בַּקֹּדֶשׁ וּבְיִרְאַת אֱלֹהִים:
11. Ve•a•ta eem n`mo•gim kol - ele ad - ka•ma aley•chem le•hi•za•her le•hit•ha•lech ba•ko•desh oov•yir•at Elohim.

12. Looking for and hasting unto the coming of the day of God, wherein the heavens being on fire shall be dissolved, and the elements shall melt with fervent heat?

12. προσδοκῶντας καὶ σπεύδοντας τὴν παρουσίαν τῆς τοῦ θεοῦ ἡμέρας, δι' ἣν οὐρανοὶ πυρούμενοι λυθήσονται, καὶ στοιχεῖα καυσούμενα τήκεται;

12. prosdokontas kai speudontas tein parousian teis tou theou 'eimeras, di 'ein ouranoi puroumenoi lutheisontai, kai stoicheia kausoumena teiketai?

יב. וּלְחַכּוֹת וּלְצַפּוֹת לְבֹא יוֹם הָאֱלֹהִים אֲשֶׁר יְלַהֵט אֶת-הַשָּׁמַיִם וְיַמְסֵם וְהַיְסֹדוֹת נְמֹגִים בְּאֵשׁ כֻּלָּם:

12. Ool•cha•kot ool•tza•pot le•vo yom ha•Elohim asher ye•la•het et - ha•sha•ma•yim ve•yam•sem ve•hay•so•dot n`mo•gim ba•esh koo•lam?

Rabbinic Jewish Commentary
There seems to be some reference to the prayers of the Jews for the Messiah's coming, which they desire may be במהירה, "in haste"; which will show that they are in haste for the coming of this day; and all which things God will hasten, though it will be in his own time.

2 Peter 3

13. Nevertheless we, according to his promise, look for new heavens and a new earth, wherein dwelleth righteousness.

13. Καινοὺς δὲ οὐρανοὺς καὶ γῆν καινὴν κατὰ τὸ ἐπάγγελμα αὐτοῦ προσδοκῶμεν, ἐν οἷς δικαιοσύνη κατοικεῖ.

13. Kainous de ouranous kai gein kainein kata to epangelma autou prosdokomen, en 'ois dikaiosunei katoikei.

יג. וַאֲנַחְנוּ כְּפִי אֲשֶׁר-דִּבֶּר-לָנוּ מְחַכִּים לְשָׁמַיִם חֲדָשִׁים וְאֶרֶץ חֲדָשָׁה אֲשֶׁר-צֶדֶק יָלִין בָּם:

13. Va•a•nach•noo ke•fi asher - di•ber - la•noo me•cha•kim le•sha•ma•yim cha•da•shim ve•e•retz cha•da•sha asher - tze•dek ya•lin bam.

Rabbinic Jewish Commentary
None but righteous persons can look for these new heavens and earth, for to these only are they promised, and such only shall dwell in them; so the Targum on Jer.23:23 paraphrases the words,

"I God have created the world from the beginning, saith YHVH, I God will "renew the world for the righteous":"

And this will be, the Jews say, for the space of a thousand years;

"It is a tradition (they say (l)) of the house of Elias, that the righteous, whom the holy blessed God will raise from the dead shall not return to their dust, as is said, Isa.4:3, and it shall come to pass, as the Holy One continues for ever, so they shall continue for ever; and if you should say those years (some editions read, "those thousand years", and so the gloss upon the place) in which the holy blessed God "renews the world": as it is said Isa.2:11, and the Lord alone; what shall they do? the holy blessed God will make them wings as eagles, and they shall fly upon the face of the waters:"

And this renovation of the heavens and the earth, they say, will be in the seventh millennium;

"In the seventh thousand year (they assert (m)) there will be found new heavens and a new earth."

(l) T. Bab. Sanhedrin, fol. 92. 1, 2. Ed. Coch. p. 317. (m) Zohar in Gen. fol. 35. 3.

2 Peter 3

14. Wherefore, beloved, seeing that ye look for such things, be diligent that ye may be found of him in peace, without spot, and blameless.

14. Διό, ἀγαπητοί, ταῦτα προσδοκῶντες, σπουδάσατε ἄσπιλοι καὶ ἀμώμητοι αὐτῷ εὑρεθῆναι ἐν εἰρήνῃ.

14. Dio, agapeitoi, tauta prosdokontes, spoudasate aspiloi kai amomeitoi auto 'euretheinai en eireinei.

יד. עַל־כֵּן יְדִידִים בַּאֲשֶׁר אַתֶּם מְחַכִּים לָאֵלֶּה שְׁקְדוּ לְהִמָּצֵא לְפָנָיו זַכִּים וּתְמִימִים בְּשָׁלוֹם:

14. Al - ken ye•di•dim ba•a•sher atem me•cha•kim la•e•le shik•doo le•hi•ma•tze le•fa•nav za•kim oot•mi•mim be•sha•lom.

15. And account that the longsuffering of our Lord is salvation; even as our beloved brother Paul also according to the wisdom given unto him hath written unto you;

15. Καὶ τὴν τοῦ κυρίου ἡμῶν μακροθυμίαν σωτηρίαν ἡγεῖσθε, καθὼς καὶ ὁ ἀγαπητὸς ἡμῶν ἀδελφὸς Παῦλος κατὰ τὴν αὐτῷ δοθεῖσαν σοφίαν ἔγραψεν ὑμῖν·

15. Kai tein tou kuriou 'eimon makrothumian soteirian 'eigeisthe, kathos kai 'o agapeitos 'eimon adelphos Paulos kata tein auto dotheisan sophian egrapsen 'umin.

טו. וְאֶת-אֹרֶךְ רוּחַ אֲדֹנֵינוּ תַּחְשְׁבוּ לִתְשׁוּעָה כַּאֲשֶׁר כָּתַב אֲלֵיכֶם גַּם-פּוֹלוֹס אָחִינוּ יְדִידֵנוּ כְּפִי חָכְמָתוֹ הַנְּתוּנָה לוֹ:

15. Ve•et - o•rech roo•ach Ado•ney•noo tach•she•voo lit•shoo•ah ka•a•sher ka•tav aley•chem gam - Polos achi•noo ye•di•de•noo ke•fi choch•ma•to ha•ne•too•na lo.

---

2 Peter 3

16. As also in all his epistles, speaking in them of these things; in which are some things hard to be understood, which they that are unlearned and unstable wrest, as they do also the other scriptures, unto their own destruction.

16. ὡς καὶ ἐν πάσαις ταῖς ἐπιστολαῖς, λαλῶν ἐν αὐταῖς περὶ τούτων· ἐν οἷς ἐστιν δυσνόητά τινα, ἃ οἱ ἀμαθεῖς καὶ ἀστήρικτοι στρεβλοῦσιν, ὡς καὶ τὰς λοιπὰς γραφάς, πρὸς τὴν ἰδίαν αὐτῶν ἀπώλειαν.

16. 'os kai en pasais tais epistolais, lalon en autais peri touton. en 'ois estin dusnoeita tina, 'a 'oi amatheis kai asteiriktoi streblousin, 'os kai tas loipas graphas, pros tein idian auton apoleyan.

טז. וְכֵן כָּתַב בְּכָל-אִגְּרוֹתָיו בְּדַבְּרוֹ שָׁם עַל-אֵלֶּה וּבָהֵן יֵשׁ דְּבָרִים קָשִׁים מֵהָבִין אֲשֶׁר בֹּעֲרִים וּפֹחֲזִים יְסַלְּפוּם:כַּאֲשֶׁר גַּם-יַעֲשׂוּ בְּיֶתֶר הַסְּפָרִים לְהַשְׁחִית נַפְשָׁם

16. Ve•chen ka•tav be•chol - eeg•ro•tav be•dab•ro sham al - ele oo•va•hen yesh d`va•rim ka•shim me•ha•vin asher bo•a•rim oo•fo•cha•zim ye•sal•foom ka•a•sher gam - ya•a•soo be•ye•ter has•fa•rim le•hash•chit naf•sham.

Rabbinic Jewish Commentary

in which are some things hard to be understood. The phrase, "in which", refers either to the epistles, or the things spoken in them. The Alexandrian manuscript, and three of Robert Stephens's copies, read εν αις, "in which" epistles, but the generality of copies read εν οις, "in", or "among which things", spoken of in them, concerning the subject here treated of, the coming judgment upon the Temple and the nation.

17. Ye therefore, beloved, seeing ye know these things before, beware lest ye also, being led away with the error of the wicked, fall from your own stedfastness.

17. Ὑμεῖς οὖν, ἀγαπητοί, προγινώσκοντες φυλάσσεσθε, ἵνα μή, τῇ τῶν ἀθέσμων πλάνῃ συναπαχθέντες, ἐκπέσητε τοῦ ἰδίου στηριγμοῦ.

17. 'Umeis oun, agapeitoi, proginoskontes phulassesthe, 'ina mei, tei ton athesmon planei sunapachthentes, ekpeseite tou idiou steirigmou.

יז. וְאַתֶּם יְדִידִים אֲחֲרֵי אֲשֶׁר יְדַעְתֶּם כָּל-זֹאת מֵרֹאשׁ הִשָּׁמְרוּ לָכֶם פֶּן-תָּתוּרוּ אַחֲרֵי תַעְתֻעֵי בְנֵי-בְלִיַּעַל וּנְפַלְתֶּם:מִמַּצַּבְכֶם הַנֶּאֱמָן

17. Ve•a•tem ye•di•dim a•cha•rey asher ye•da•a•tem kol - zot me•rosh hi•sham•roo la•chem pen - ta•too•roo a•cha•rey ta•a•too•ey v`ney - ve•li•ya•al oon•fal•tem mi•ma•tzav•chem ha•ne•e•man.

---

2 Peter 3

18. But grow in grace, and in the knowledge of our Lord and Saviour Jesus Christ. To him be glory both now and for ever. Amen.

18. Αὐξάνετε δὲ ἐν χάριτι καὶ γνώσει τοῦ κυρίου ἡμῶν καὶ σωτῆρος Ἰησοῦ χριστοῦ. Αὐτῷ ἡ δόξα καὶ νῦν καὶ εἰς ἡμέραν αἰῶνος. Ἀμήν.

18. Auxanete de en chariti kai gnosei tou kuriou 'eimon kai soteiros Yeisou christou. Auto 'ei doxa kai nun kai eis 'eimeran aionos. Amein.

יח. אַךְ תִּגְדְּלוּ הָלוֹךְ וְגָדוֹל בְּחֶסֶד וּבְדַעַת אֲדֹנֵינוּ וּמוֹשִׁיעֵינוּ יֵשׁוּעַ הַמָּשִׁיחַ אֲשֶׁר-לוֹ הַכָּבוֹד מֵעַתָּה וְעַד-עוֹלָם:אָמֵן

18. Ach tig•de•loo ha•loch ve•ga•dol be•che•sed oov•da•at Ado•ney•noo oo•Mo•shi•ey•noo Yeshua ha•Ma•shi•ach asher - lo ha•ka•vod me•a•ta ve•ad - o•lam Amen.

(2Peter Chapter 3 End)

THE FIRST EPISTLE GENERAL OF JOHN

1 John, Chapter 1

1. That which was from the beginning, which we have heard, which we have seen with our eyes, which we have looked upon, and our hands have handled, of the Word of life;

1. Ὃ ἦν ἀπ' ἀρχῆς, ὃ ἀκηκόαμεν, ὃ ἑωράκαμεν τοῖς ὀφθαλμοῖς ἡμῶν, ὃ ἐθεασάμεθα, καὶ αἱ χεῖρες ἡμῶν ἐψηλάφησαν περὶ τοῦ λόγου τῆς ζωῆς.

1. 'O ein ap archeis, 'o akeikoamen, 'o 'eorakamen tois ophthalmois 'eimon, 'o etheasametha, kai 'ai cheires 'eimon epseilapheisan peri tou logou teis zoeis.

א. הִנֵּה אֲנַחְנוּ מַגִּידִים לָכֶם אֶת-דְּבַר הַחַיִּים הוּא אֲשֶׁר הָיָה מֵרֵאשִׁית אֲשֶׁר שָׁמַעְנוּ בְּאָזְנֵינוּ רָאִינוּ בְעֵינֵינוּ אֲשֶׁר הִבַּטְנוּ וַאֲשֶׁר יָדֵינוּ מִשְׁשׁוּ מְקוֹרוֹ:

1. Hee•ne a•nach•noo ma•gi•dim la•chem et - de•var ha•cha•yim hoo asher ha•ya me•re•sheet asher sha•ma•a•noo ve•oz•ney•noo ra•ee•noo ve•ey•ney•noo asher hi•bat•noo va•a•sher ya•dey•noo mi•sha•shoo me•ko•ro.

Rabbinic Jewish Commentary

The phrase, מימרא דיי, "The Word of YHVH", (Word of Life), so frequently used by the Targumists, is well known: and it is to be observed, that the same things which John here says of the word, they say likewise, as will be observed on the several clauses; from whence it is more likely, that John should take this phrase, since the paraphrases of Onkelos and Jonathan ben Uzziel were written before his time, than that he should borrow it from the writings of Plato, or his followers, as some have thought; with whose philosophy, Ebion and Cerinthus are said to be acquainted; wherefore John, the more easily to gain upon them, uses this phrase, when that of the Son of God would have been disagreeable to them: that there is some likeness between the Evangelist John and Plato in their sentiments concerning the word, will not be denied. Amelius (f), a Platonic philosopher, who lived after the times of John, manifestly refers to these words of his, in agreement with his master's doctrine: his words are these,

"And this was truly "Logos", or the word, by whom always existing, the things that are made, were made, as also Heraclitus thought; and who, likewise that Barbarian (meaning the Evangelist John) reckons was in the order and dignity of the beginning, constituted with God, and was God, by whom all things are entirely made; in whom, whatsoever is made, lives, and has life, and being; and who entered into bodies, and was clothed with flesh, and appeared a man; so notwithstanding, that he showed forth the majesty of his nature; and after his dissolution, he was again deified, and was God, as he was before he descended into a body, flesh and man.

Philo the Jew often calls the Logos, or Word, the eternal Word, the most ancient Word, and more ancient than any thing that is made (p). The eternity of the Messiah is acknowledged by the ancient Jews: Mic.5:2 is a full proof of it; which by them (q) is thus paraphrased,

"Out of thee, before me, shall come forth the Messiah, that he may exercise dominion over Israel; whose name is said from eternity, from the days of old.

Jarchi upon it only mentions Psa.72:17 which is rendered by the Targum on the place, before the sun his name was prepared; it may be translated, "before the sun his name was Yinnon"; that is, the Son, namely the Son of God; and Aben Ezra interprets it, יקרא בן, "he shall be called the son"; and to this agrees what the Talmudisis say (r), that the name of the Messiah was before the world was created; in proof of which they produce the same passage.

And as John here speaks of the word, as a distinct person from God the Father, so do the Targums, or Chaldee paraphrases;

Psa.110:1 "YHVH said to my Lord", is rendered, "YHVH said to his Word"; where he is manifestly distinguished from Yehovah, that speaks to him; and in Hos.1:7 YHVH promises to "have mercy on the house of Judah", and "save them by YHVH their God". The Targum is, "I will redeem them by the Word of the YHVH their God"; where the Word of YHVH, who is spoken of as a Redeemer and Saviour, is distinguished from the Lord, who promises to save by him. This distinction of Yehovah and his word, may be observed in multitudes of places, in the Chaldee paraphrases, and in the writings of Philo the Jew; and this phrase, of "the Word" being "with God", is in the Targums expressed by, מימר מן קדם, "the Word from before YHVH", or "which is before YHVH": being always in his presence, and the angel of it; so Onkelos paraphrases Gen.31:22 "and the Word from before YHVH, came to Laban", &c. and Exo.20:19 thus, "and let not the Word from before YHVH speak with us, lest we die"; for so it is read in the King of Spain's Bible; and wisdom, which is the same with the word of God, is said to be by him, or with him, in Pro.8:1 agreeably to which John here speaks.

So the Jews often use the word of the Lord for Jehovah, and call him God. Thus the words in Gen.28:20 are paraphrased by Onkelos,

"If "The Word of YHVH" will be my help, and will keep me, &c. then "The Word of YHVH" shall be, לי לאלהא, "my God":

Again, Lev.26:12 is paraphrased, by the Targum ascribed to Jonathan Ben Uzziel, thus,

"I will cause the glory of my Shekinah to dwell among you, and my Word shall "be your God", the Redeemer;

Once more, Deu.26:17 is rendered by the Jerusalem Targum after this manner,

"Ye have made "The Word of YHVH" king over you this day, that he may be your God:

And this is frequent with Philo the Jew, who says, the name of God is His Word, and calls him, my YHVH, the divine Word; and affirms, that the most ancient Word is God (s).

(f) Apud Euseb. Prepar. Evangel. l. 11. c. 19. (g) Stromat. l. 1. p. 274. (h) Ib. p. 303. (i) Ib. Paedagog. l. 2. c. 1. p. 150. (k) Valer. Maxim. l. 8. c. 7. (l) Apuleius de dogmate Platonis, l. 1. in principio. (m) Apud. Euseb. Prepar. Evangel. l. 13. c. 12. (n) Hesych. Miles. de Philosophis. p. 50. (o) Prepar. Evangel. l. 11. c. 9. (p) De Leg. Alleg. l. 2. p. 93. de Plant. Noe, p. 217. de Migrat. Abraham, p. 389. de Profugis, p. 466. quis. rer. divin. Haeres. p. 509. (q) Targum Jon. in loc. (r) T. Bab. Pesachim, fol. 54. 1. & Nedarim, fol. 39. 2. Pirke Eliezer, c. 3. (s) De Allegor. l. 2. p. 99, 101. & de Somniis, p. 599.

---

2. (For the life was manifested, and we have seen it, and bear witness, and shew unto you that eternal life, which was with the Father, and was manifested unto us;)

2. Καὶ ἡ ζωὴ ἐφανερώθη, καὶ ἑωράκαμεν, καὶ μαρτυροῦμεν, καὶ ἀπαγγέλλομεν ὑμῖν τὴν ζωὴν τὴν αἰώνιον, ἥτις ἦν πρὸς τὸν πατέρα, καὶ ἐφανερώθη ἡμῖν.

2. Kai 'ei zoei ephanerothei, kai 'eorakamen, kai marturoumen, kai apangellomen 'umin tein zoein tein aionion, 'eitis ein pros ton patera, kai ephanerothei 'eimin.

ב. הוּא מְקוֹר הַחַיִּים אֲשֶׁר נִגְלָה לָנוּ וַנִּרְאֵהוּ וַנָּעִיד וַנַגִּיד לָכֶם כִּי זֶה הוּא מְקוֹר חַיֵּי עוֹלָם אֲשֶׁר הָיָה עִם-הָאָב:וַאֲשֶׁר נִגָּה לָנוּ

2. Hoo me•kor ha•cha•yim asher nig•la la•noo va•nir•e•hoo va•na•eed va•na•gid la•chem ki ze hoo me•kor cha•yey o•lam asher ha•ya eem - ha•Av va•a•sher ni•ga la•noo.

1 John 1

3. That which we have seen and heard declare we unto you, that ye also may have fellowship with us: and truly our fellowship is with the Father, and with his Son Jesus Christ.

3. Ὃ ἑωράκαμεν καὶ ἀκηκόαμεν, ἀπαγγέλλομεν ὑμῖν, ἵνα καὶ ὑμεῖς κοινωνίαν ἔχητε μεθ᾽ ἡμῶν· καὶ ἡ κοινωνία δὲ ἡ ἡμετέρα μετὰ τοῦ πατρὸς καὶ μετὰ τοῦ υἱοῦ αὐτοῦ Ἰησοῦ χριστοῦ·

3. 'O 'eorakamen kai akeikoamen, apangellomen 'umin, 'ina kai 'umeis koinonian echeite meth 'eimon. kai 'ei koinonia de 'ei 'eimetera meta tou patros kai meta tou 'wiou autou Yeisou christou.

ג. כִּי אֶת-אֲשֶׁר רָאִינוּ וְשָׁמַעְנוּ נַגִּיד לָכֶם לְמַעַן תִּדְבְּקוּ בָנוּ גַם-אַתֶּם כִּי הֲלֹא דְבֵקִים אֲנַחְנוּ בָאָב וּבִבְנוֹ יֵשׁוּעַ:הַמָּשִׁיחַ

3. Ki et - asher ra•ee•noo ve•sha•ma•a•noo na•gid la•chem le•ma•an tid•be•koo va•noo gam - atem ki ha•lo d`ve•kim a•nach•noo va•Av oo•vi•V`no Yeshua ha•Ma•shi•ach.

---

4. And these things write we unto you, that your joy may be full.

4. καὶ ταῦτα γράφομεν ὑμῖν, ἵνα ἡ χαρὰ ἡμῶν ᾖ πεπληρωμένη.

4. kai tauta graphomen 'umin, 'ina 'ei chara 'eimon ei pepleiromenei.

ד. וַאֲנַחְנוּ כֹּתְבִים לָכֶם כַּדְּבָרִים הָאֵלֶּה לְמַלֹּאת אֶת-לִבְּכֶם שִׂמְחָה.:

4. Va•a•nach•noo chot•vim la•chem ka•d`va•rim ha•e•le le•ma•lot et - lib•chem sim•cha.

---

1 John 1

5. This then is the message which we have heard of him, and declare unto you, that God is light, and in him is no darkness at all.

5. Καὶ ἔστιν αὕτη ἡ ἀγγελία ἣν ἀκηκόαμεν ἀπ᾽ αὐτοῦ καὶ ἀναγγέλλομεν ὑμῖν, ὅτι ὁ θεὸς φῶς ἐστίν, καὶ σκοτία ἐν αὐτῷ οὐκ ἔστιν οὐδεμία.

5. Kai estin 'autei 'ei angelia 'ein akeikoamen ap autou kai anangellomen 'umin, 'oti 'o theos phos estin, kai skotia en auto ouk estin oudemia.

ה. וְזֹאת הִיא מַלְאֲכוּת-יָהּ אֲשֶׁר שָׁמַעְנוּ מִמֶּנּוּ לְהַגִּיד לָכֶם כִּי אֱלֹהִים אוֹר הוּא וְכָל-חֹשֶׁךְ אֵין בּוֹ:

5. Ve•zot hee mal•a•choot - Ya asher sha•ma•a•noo mi•me•noo le•ha•gid la•chem ki Elohim or hoo ve•chol - cho•shech eyn bo.

Rabbinic Jewish Commentary
It is usual with the Cabalistic Jews (e), to call the supreme Being אור, "light" the most simple light, hidden light, and infinite light, with respect to his nature, glory, and majesty, and with regard also to his grace and mercy, justice and judgment; though, as R. Sangart says (f), this is to be understood of him figuratively.

(e) Lex. Cabalist, p. 63, 64. (f) Sepher Cosri, par. 2. sect. 2. fol. 61. 2.

---

6. If we say that we have fellowship with him, and walk in darkness, we lie, and do not the truth:

6. Ἐὰν εἴπωμεν ὅτι κοινωνίαν ἔχομεν μετ᾽ αὐτοῦ, καὶ ἐν τῷ σκότει περιπατῶμεν, ψευδόμεθα, καὶ οὐ ποιοῦμεν τὴν ἀλήθειαν·

6. Ean eipomen 'oti koinonian echomen met autou, kai en to skotei peripatomen, pseudometha, kai ou poioumen tein aleitheyan.

ו. אִם-נֹאמַר כִּי דְבֵקִים אֲנַחְנוּ בּוֹ וּבַחֲשֵׁכָה נִתְהַלָּךְ כָּזָב הוּא בְּפִינוּ וֶאֱמֶת לֹא פָעֳלָנוּ:

6. Eem - no•mar ki d`ve•kim a•nach•noo vo oo•va•cha•she•cha nit•ha•lach ka•zav hoo ve•fi•noo ve•e•met lo fa•al•noo.

1 John 1

7. But if we walk in the light, as he is in the light, we have fellowship one with another, and the blood of Jesus Christ his Son cleanseth us from all sin.

7. ἐὰν δὲ ἐν τῷ φωτὶ περιπατῶμεν, ὡς αὐτός ἐστιν ἐν τῷ φωτί, κοινωνίαν ἔχομεν μετ᾽ ἀλλήλων, καὶ τὸ αἷμα Ἰησοῦ χριστοῦ τοῦ υἱοῦ αὐτοῦ καθαρίζει ἡμᾶς ἀπὸ πάσης ἁμαρτίας.

7. ean de en to photi peripatomen, 'os autos estin en to photi, koinonian echomen met alleilon, kai to 'aima Yeisou christou tou 'wiou autou katharizei 'eimas apo paseis 'amartias.

ז. אַךְ אִם-בָּאוֹר נִתְהַלֵּךְ כַּאֲשֶׁר הוּא בָּאוֹר הִנֵּהוּ אָז חֲבֵרֵנוּ יַחְדָּו וְדַם-בְּנוֹ יֵשׁוּעַ הַמָּשִׁיחַ יְטַהֲרֵנוּ מִכָּל-עָוֹן:

7. Ach eem - ba•or nit•ha•lech ka•a•sher hoo ba•or hi•ne•hoo az choo•bar•noo yach•dav ve•dam - B`no Yeshua ha•Ma•shi•ach ye•ta•ha•re•noo mi•kol - a•von.

Rabbinic Jewish Commentary

The Arabic and Ethiopic versions render it, "from all our sins";

The Jews say (g), that,

"It atoned for all the transgressions of the Torah, whether small or great, sins of presumption, or of ignorance, known, or not known, which were against an affirmative or negative command, which deserved cutting off (by the hand of God), or death by the sanhedrim."

(g) Misn. Shebuot, c. 1. sect. 6.

8. If we say that we have no sin, we deceive ourselves, and the truth is not in us.

8. Ἐὰν εἴπωμεν ὅτι ἁμαρτίαν οὐκ ἔχομεν, ἑαυτοὺς πλανῶμεν, καὶ ἡ ἀλήθεια οὐκ ἔστιν ἐν ἡμῖν.

8. Ean eipomen 'oti 'amartian ouk echomen, 'eautous planomen, kai 'ei aleitheya ouk estin en 'eimin.

ח. אִם-נֹאמַר כִּי אֵין-בָּנוּ עָוֹן מַתְעִים אֲנַחְנוּ אֶת-נַפְשֹׁתֵינוּ וֶאֱמֶת בְּקִרְבֵּנוּ נֶעְדָּרֶת:

8. Eem - no•mar ki eyn - ba•noo a•von mat•eem a•nach•noo et - naf•sho•tey•noo ve•e•met be•kir•be•noo ne•e•da•ret.

1 John 1

9. If we confess our sins, he is faithful and just to forgive us our sins, and to cleanse us from all unrighteousness.

9. Ἐὰν ὁμολογῶμεν τὰς ἁμαρτίας ἡμῶν, πιστός ἐστιν καὶ δίκαιος ἵνα ἀφῇ ἡμῖν τὰς ἁμαρτίας, καὶ καθαρίσῃ ἡμᾶς ἀπὸ πάσης ἀδικίας.

9. Ean 'omologomen tas 'amartias 'eimon, pistos estin kai dikaios 'ina aphei 'eimin tas 'amartias, kai katharisei 'eimas apo paseis adikias.

ט. אִם-נִתְוַדֶּה אֶת-חַטֹּאתֵינוּ נֶאֱמָן הוּא וְצַדִּיק לִסְלֹחַ לָנוּ אֶת-חַטֹּאתֵינוּ וּלְטַהֵר אֶת-נַפְשֵׁנוּ מִכָּל-עָוֹן:

9. Eem - nit•va•de et - cha•to•tey•noo ne•e•man hoo ve•tza•dik lis•loach la•noo et - cha•to•tey•noo ool•ta•her et - naf•she•noo mi•kol - a•von.

Rabbinic Jewish Commentary

The Hebrew word צדיק, "righteous" which sometimes carries in it the notion and idea of mercy and beneficence; hence mercy to the poor is sometimes expressed by righteousness; and the righteous acts of God intend his mercies and benefits unto men; Dan.4:27; and so forgiveness of sin springs from the tender mercies of our God, and is both an act of justice and of mercy; of justice, with respect to the blood of Christ, and of pure grace and mercy to the pardoned sinner.

10. If we say that we have not sinned, we make him a liar, and his word is not in us.

10. Ἐὰν εἴπωμεν ὅτι οὐχ ἡμαρτήκαμεν, ψεύστην ποιοῦμεν αὐτόν, καὶ ὁ λόγος αὐτοῦ οὐκ ἔστιν ἐν ἡμῖν.

10. Ean eipomen 'oti ouch 'eimarteikamen, pseustein poioumen auton, kai 'o logos autou ouk estin en 'eimin.

י. וְאִם-נֹאמַר כִּי לֹא חָטָאנוּ שַׂמְנוּ אֹתוֹ לִמְכַזֵּב וּדְבָרוֹ בְּקִרְבֵּנוּ אָיִן:

10. Ve•eem - no•mar ki lo cha•ta•noo sam•noo o•to lim•cha•zev ood•va•ro ve•kir•be•noo a•yin.

Rabbinic Jewish Commentary
The apostle has regard either to the Gnostics, a set of heretics of this age, who fancied themselves pure, spiritual, and perfect, even in the midst of all their impurities, and notwithstanding their vicious lives; or to judaizing believers, and it may be to the Jews themselves, who entertained such sort of notions as these of being perfect and without sin (h).

(h) Vid. T. Bab. Temura, fol. 15. 2. & Bava Kama, fol. 80. 1. T. Hieros. Sota, fol. 24. 1. &. Chagiga, fol. 77. 4.

(1John Chapter 1 End)

1 John, Chapter 2

1. My little children, these things write I unto you, that ye sin not. And if any man sin, we have an advocate with the Father, Jesus Christ the righteous:

1. Τεκνία μου, ταῦτα γράφω ὑμῖν, ἵνα μὴ ἁμάρτητε. Καὶ ἐάν τις ἁμάρτῃ, παράκλητον ἔχομεν πρὸς τὸν πατέρα, Ἰησοῦν χριστὸν δίκαιον·

1. Teknia mou, tauta grapho 'umin, 'ina mei 'amarteite. Kai ean tis 'amartei, parakleiton echomen pros ton patera, Yeisoun christon dikaion.

א. הִנְנִי כֹתֵב אֲלֵיכֶם יְלָדַי כַּדְּבָרִים הָאֵלֶּה לְבִלְתִּי תֶחֱטָאוּ וְאִם-יֶחֱטָא אִישׁ יֵשׁ עָלָיו מַלְאָךְ מֵלִיץ לִפְנֵי אָבִינוּ: הוּא יֵשׁוּעַ הַמָּשִׁיחַ הַצַּדִּיק

1. Hi•ne•ni cho•tev aley•chem ye•la•dai ka•d`va•rim ha•e•le le•vil•ti te•che•ta•oo ve•eem - ye•che•ta eesh yesh alav mal•ach me•litz lif•ney Avi•noo hoo Yeshua ha•Ma•shi•ach ha•tza•dik.

Rabbinic Jewish Commentary
The Jews (i) have adopted the word in the text into their language, but have applied it to a different purpose, to alms deeds, repentance, and good works. Much more agreeably Philo the Jew (k) speaks of the son of perfect virtue, παρακλητῳ, "as an advocate" for the forgiveness of sins, and for a supply of everlasting good things.

(i) Pirke Abot, c. 4. sect. 11. T. Bab. Sabbat, fol. 32. 1. T. Bab. Bava Bathra, fol. 10. 1. (k) De Vita Mosis, l. iii. p. 673.

---

2. And he is the propitiation for our sins: and not for ours only, but also for the sins of the whole world.

2. καὶ αὐτὸς ἱλασμός ἐστιν περὶ τῶν ἁμαρτιῶν ἡμῶν· οὐ περὶ τῶν ἡμετέρων δὲ μόνον, ἀλλὰ καὶ περὶ ὅλου τοῦ κόσμου.

2. kai autos 'ilasmos estin peri ton 'amartion 'eimon. ou peri ton 'eimeteron de monon, alla kai peri 'olou tou kosmou.

ב. וְהוּא כֹפֶר עַל-חַטֹּאתֵינוּ וְלֹא לְבַד עַל-חַטֹּאתֵינוּ כִּי אִם-גַּם עַל-כָּל-הָאָרֶץ:

2. Ve•hoo cho•fer al - cha•to•tey•noo ve•lo le•vad al - cha•to•tey•noo ki eem - gam al - kol - ha•a•retz.

Rabbinic Jewish Commentary

but also for the sins of the whole world; the Syriac version renders it, "not for us only, but also for the whole world"; that is, not for the Jews only, for John was a Jew, and so were those he wrote unto, but for the Nations also. Nothing is more common in Jewish writings than to call the Gentiles עלמא, "the world"; and כל העולם, "the whole world"; and אומות העולם, "the nations of the world" (l); and the word "world" is so used in Scripture; and stands opposed to a notion the Jews have of the Gentiles, that אין להן כפרה, "there is no propitiation for them" (m): and it is easy to observe, that when this phrase is not used of the Gentiles, it is to be understood in a limited and restrained sense; as when they say (n),

"It happened to a certain high priest, that when he went out of the sanctuary, כולי עלמא, "the whole world" went after him;"

which could only design the people in the temple. And elsewhere (o) it is said,

"The "whole world" has left the Mishna, and gone after the "Gemara";"

Which at most can only intend the Jews; and indeed only a majority of their doctors, who were conversant with these writings: and in another place (p),

"The whole world" fell on their faces, but Raf did not fall on his face;" where it means no more than the congregation. Once more, it is said (q), when

"R. Simeon ben Gamaliel entered (the synagogue), כולי עלמא, "the whole world" stood up before him;"

That is, the people in the synagogue: to which may be added (r),

"When a great man makes a mourning, כולי עלמא, "the whole world" come to honour him;"

i.e. a great number of persons attend the funeral pomp: and so these phrases, כולי עלמא לא פליגי, "the whole world" is not divided, or does not dissent (s); כולי עלמא סברי, "the whole world" are of opinion (t), are frequently met with in the Talmud, by which, an agreement among the Rabbins, in certain points, is designed; yea, sometimes the phrase, "all the men of the world" (u), only intend the inhabitants of a city where a synagogue was, and, at most, only the Jews: and so this phrase, "all the world", or "the whole world", in Scripture, unless when it signifies the whole universe, or the habitable earth, is always used in a limited sense, either for the Roman empire.

In what sense Messiah is a propitiation. The Jews have no notion of the Messiah as a propitiation or atonement; sometimes they say (w) repentance atones for all sin; sometimes the death of the righteous (x); sometimes incense (y); sometimes the priests' garments (z); sometimes it is the day of atonement (a); and indeed they are in the utmost puzzle about atonement; and they even confess in their prayers (b), that they have now neither altar nor priest to atone for them.

(l) Jarchi in Isa. liii. 5. (m) T. Hieros. Nazir, fol. 57. 3. Vid. T. Bab. Succa, fol. 55. 2. (n) T. Bab. Yoma, fol. 71. 2. (o) T. Bab. Bava Metzia, fol. 33. 2. (p) T. Bab. Megilla, fol. 22. 2. (q) T. Bab. Horayot, fol. 13. 2. (r) Piske Toseph. Megilla, art. 104. (s) T. Bab. Cetubot, fol. 90. 2. & Kiddushin, fol. 47. 2. & 49. 1. & 65. 2. & Gittin, fol. 8. 1. & 60. 2. (t) T. Bab. Kiddushin, fol. 48. 1. (u) Maimon. Hilch. Tephilla, c. 11. sect. 16. (w) Zohar in Lev. fol. 29. 1. (x) Ib. fol. 24. 1. T. Hieros. Yoma, fol. 38. 2. (y) T. Bab. Zebachim, fol. 88. 2. & Erachin, fol. 16. 1. (z) T. Bab. Zebachim, ib. T. Hieros. Yoma, fol. 44. 2. (a) T. Bab. Yoma, fol. 87. 1. & T. Hieros. Yoma, fol. 45. 2, 3. (b) Seder Tephillot, fol. 41. 1. Ed. Amsterd.

---

1 John 2

3. And hereby we do know that we know him, if we keep his commandments.

3. Καὶ ἐν τούτῳ γινώσκομεν ὅτι ἐγνώκαμεν αὐτόν, ἐὰν τὰς ἐντολὰς αὐτοῦ τηρῶμεν.

3. Kai en touto ginoskomen 'oti egnokamen auton, ean tas entolas autou teiromen.

‏ג: וּבָזֹאת נַכִּיר כִּי יָדַעְנוּ אֹתוֹ אִם-נִשְׁמֹר אֶת-מִצְוֹתָיו‎

3. Oo•va•zot na•kir ki ya•da•a•noo o•to eem - nish•mor et - mitz•vo•tav.

4. He that saith, I know him, and keepeth not his commandments, is a liar, and the truth is not in him.

4. Ὁ λέγων, Ἔγνωκα αὐτόν, καὶ τὰς ἐντολὰς αὐτοῦ μὴ τηρῶν, ψεύστης ἐστίν, καὶ ἐν τούτῳ ἡ ἀλήθεια οὐκ ἔστιν·

4. 'O legon, Egnoka auton, kai tas entolas autou mei teiron, pseusteis estin, kai en touto 'ei aleitheya ouk estin.

ד: הָאֹמֵר יָדַעְתִּי אֹתוֹ וְאֶת־מִצְוֹתָיו לֹא יִשְׁמֹר כֹּזֵב הוּא וְאֵין אֱמֶת בּוֹ

4. Ha•o•mer ya•da•a•ti o•to ve•et - mitz•vo•tav lo yish•mor ko•zev hoo ve•eyn emet bo.

1 John 2

5. But whoso keepeth his word, in him verily is the love of God perfected: hereby know we that we are in him.

5. ὃς δ' ἂν τηρῇ αὐτοῦ τὸν λόγον, ἀληθῶς ἐν τούτῳ ἡ ἀγάπη τοῦ θεοῦ τετελείωται. Ἐν τούτῳ γινώσκομεν ὅτι ἐν αὐτῷ ἐσμέν·

5. 'os d an teirei autou ton logon, aleithos en touto 'ei agapei tou theou teteleiotai. En touto ginoskomen 'oti en auto esmen.

ה: אַךְ הַשֹּׁמֵר אֶת־דְּבָרוֹ אַהֲבַת אֱלֹהִים כְּלוּלָה בוֹ בֶּאֱמֶת וּבָזֹאת נַכִּיר כִּי־בוֹ נִתְלוֹנָן

5. Ach ha•sho•mer et - de•va•ro a•ha•vat Elohim ke•loo•la vo be•e•met oo•va•zot na•kir ki - vo nit•lo•nan.

6. He that saith he abideth in him ought himself also so to walk, even as he walked.

6. ὁ λέγων ἐν αὐτῷ μένειν ὀφείλει, καθὼς ἐκεῖνος περιεπάτησεν, καὶ αὐτὸς οὕτως περιπατεῖν.

6. 'o legon en auto menein opheilei, kathos ekeinos periepateisen, kai autos 'outos peripatein.

ו: הָאֹמֵר כִּי הוּא מִתְלוֹנֵן בּוֹ יֶשׁ־לוֹ לָלֶכֶת גַּם־בְּעִקְּבוֹתָיו

6. Ha•o•mer ki hoo mit•lo•nen bo yesh - lo la•le•chet gam - be•eek•vo•tav.

---

1 John 2

7. Brethren, I write no new commandment unto you, but an old commandment which ye had from the beginning. The old commandment is the word which ye have heard from the beginning.

7. Ἀδελφοί, οὐκ ἐντολὴν καινὴν γράφω ὑμῖν, ἀλλ᾽ ἐντολὴν παλαιάν, ἣν εἴχετε ἀπ᾽ ἀρχῆς· ἡ ἐντολὴ ἡ παλαιά ἐστιν ὁ λόγος ὃν ἠκούσατε ἀπ᾽ ἀρχῆς.

7. Adelphoi, ouk entolein kainein grapho 'umin, all entolein palayan, 'ein eichete ap archeis. 'ei entolei 'ei palaya estin 'o logos 'on eikousate ap archeis.

ז. אַחַי לֹא מִצְוָה חֲדָשָׁה אֲנִי-כֹתֵב אֲלֵיכֶם מִצְוָה יְשָׁנָה הִיא אֲשֶׁר הָיְתָה לָכֶם מִקֶּדֶם וְהַמִּצְוָה הַיְשָׁנָה הִיא:הַתּוֹרָה אֲשֶׁר שְׁמַעְתֶּם מִקֶּדֶם

7. A•chai lo mitz•va cha•da•sha ani - cho•tev aley•chem mitz•va ye•sha•na hee asher hai•ta la•chem mi•ke•dem ve•ha•mitz•va hai•sha•na hee ha`Torah asher sh`ma•a•tem mi•ke•dem.

---

8. Again, a new commandment I write unto you, which thing is true in him and in you: because the darkness is past, and the true light now shineth.

8. Πάλιν ἐντολὴν καινὴν γράφω ὑμῖν, ὅ ἐστιν ἀληθὲς ἐν αὐτῷ καὶ ἐν ὑμῖν· ὅτι ἡ σκοτία παράγεται, καὶ τὸ φῶς τὸ ἀληθινὸν ἤδη φαίνει.

8. Palin entolein kainein grapho 'umin, 'o estin aleithes en auto kai en 'umin. 'oti 'ei scotia paragetai, kai to phos to aleithinon eidei phainei.

ח. וְהִנְנִי מוֹסִיף וְכֹתֵב לָכֶם מִצְוָה חֲדָשָׁה וְנֶאֱמֶנֶת הִיא גַם-בּוֹ גַם-בָּכֶם כִּי הַחֹשֶׁךְ עָבַר וְאוֹר אֱמֶת זוֹרֵחַ:

8. Ve•hi•ne•ni mo•sif ve•cho•tev la•chem mitz•va cha•da•sha ve•ne•e•me•net hee gam - bo gam - ba•chem ki ha•cho•shech avar ve•or emet zo•re•ach.

Rabbinic Jewish Commentary

The Jews (c) expect תורה חדשה, "a new Torah" to be given them by the bands of the Messiah; and a new one he has given, even the new commandment of love, and which is the fulfilling of the Torah.

(c) Yalkut Simconi, par. 2. fol. 461.

---

1 John 2

9. He that saith he is in the light, and hateth his brother, is in darkness even until now.

9. Ὁ λέγων ἐν τῷ φωτὶ εἶναι καὶ τὸν ἀδελφὸν αὐτοῦ μισῶν, ἐν τῇ σκοτίᾳ ἐστὶν ἕως ἄρτι.

9. 'O legon en to photi einai kai ton adelphon autou mison, en tei skotia estin 'eos arti.

ט. הָאֹמֵר כִּי-בָאוֹר הִנֵּהוּ וְשֹׂנֵא אֶת-אָחִיו הוּא עוֹדֶנּוּ בַּחֲשֵׁכָה:

9. Ha•o•mer ki - va•or hi•ne•hoo ve•so•ne et - a•chiv hoo o•de•noo ba•cha•she•cha.

Rabbinic Jewish Commentary

This seems to be very much levelled against the Jews, who make hatred of the brother in some cases lawful: for they say (d),

"If one man observes sin in another, and reproves him for it, and he does not receive his reproof, מותר לשנאותו, "it is lawful to hate him";"

(d) Moses Kotsensis Mitzvot Tora, pr. neg. 5.

---

10. He that loveth his brother abideth in the light, and there is none occasion of stumbling in him.

10. Ὁ ἀγαπῶν τὸν ἀδελφὸν αὐτοῦ ἐν τῷ φωτὶ μένει, καὶ σκάνδαλον ἐν αὐτῷ οὐκ ἔστιν.

10. 'O agapon ton adelphon autou en to photi menei, kai skandalon en auto ouk estin.

:י. הָאֹהֵב אֶת-אָחִיו הוּא שֹׁכֵן בָּאוֹר וְאֵין לוֹ מִכְשׁוֹל

10. Ha•o•hev et - a•chiv hoo sho•chen ba•or ve•eyn lo mich•shol.

1 John 2

11. But he that hateth his brother is in darkness, and walketh in darkness, and knoweth not whither he goeth, because that darkness hath blinded his eyes.

11. Ὁ δὲ μισῶν τὸν ἀδελφὸν αὐτοῦ ἐν τῇ σκοτίᾳ ἐστίν, καὶ ἐν τῇ σκοτίᾳ περιπατεῖ, καὶ οὐκ οἶδεν ποῦ ὑπάγει, ὅτι ἡ σκοτία ἐτύφλωσεν τοὺς ὀφθαλμοὺς αὐτοῦ.

11. 'O de mison ton adelphon autou en tei skotia estin, kai en tei skotia peripatei, kai ouk oiden pou 'upagei, 'oti 'ei skotia etuphlosen tous ophthalmous autou.

:יא. וְהַשֹּׂנֵא הוּא יֹשֵׁב חֹשֶׁךְ וּבַחֹשֶׁךְ יֵלֵךְ וְלֹא-יֵדַע אָנָה הוּא הֹלֵךְ כִּי הַחֹשֶׁךְ עִוֵּר אֶת-עֵינָיו

11. Ve•ha•so•ne hoo Yo•shev cho•shech oo•va•cho•shech ye•lech ve•lo - ye•da ana hoo ho•lech ki ha•cho•shech ee•ver et - ey•nav.

Rabbinic Jewish Commentary
The Jews were used to call the evil messengers by this name; for so they say (i),

"The destroying angels are called, חשך ואפלה, "darkness, and thick darkness"."

(i) Raya Mehimna in Zohar in Lev. fol. 37. 2.

---

12. I write unto you, little children, because your sins are forgiven you for his name's sake.

12. Γράφω ὑμῖν, τεκνία, ὅτι ἀφέωνται ὑμῖν αἱ ἁμαρτίαι διὰ τὸ ὄνομα αὐτοῦ.

12. Grapho 'umin, teknia, 'oti apheontai 'umin 'ai 'amartiai dya to onoma autou.

יב. הִנְנִי כֹתֵב אֲלֵיכֶם יְלָדִים כִּי-נִסְלְחוּ לָכֶם חַטֹּאתֵיכֶם בַּעֲבוּר שְׁמוֹ:

12. Hi•ne•ni cho•tev aley•chem ye•la•dim ki - nis•le•choo la•chem cha•to•tey•chem ba•a•voor sh`mo.

Rabbinic Jewish Commentary
It may be, they may be called here "little children", with a view to their interest in this blessing of grace. So the Jews say (f), that Saul was called ""the son of one year in his reign"; 1Sa.13:1; because all his iniquities were forgiven him, כתינוק "as a sucking child" of a year old."

(f) T. Hieros. Biccurim, fol. 65. 4.

---

1 John 2

13. I write unto you, fathers, because ye have known him that is from the beginning. I write unto you, young men, because ye have overcome the wicked one. I write unto you, little children, because ye have known the Father.

13. Γράφω ὑμῖν, πατέρες, ὅτι ἐγνώκατε τὸν ἀπ᾽ ἀρχῆς. Γράφω ὑμῖν, νεανίσκοι, ὅτι νενικήκατε τὸν πονηρόν. Γράφω ὑμῖν, παιδία, ὅτι ἐγνώκατε τὸν πατέρα.

13. Grapho 'umin, pateres, 'oti egnokate ton ap archeis. Grapho 'umin, neaniskoi, 'oti nenikeikate ton poneiron. Grapho 'umin, paidia, 'oti egnokate ton patera.

יג. כֹּתֵב אֲנִי אֲלֵיכֶם אָבוֹת כִּי-יְדַעְתֶּם אֹתוֹ אֲשֶׁר מוֹצָאֹתָיו מִקֶּדֶם כֹּתֵב אֲנִי אֲלֵיכֶם בַּחוּרִים כִּי-גְבַרְתֶּם עַל-הָרָע: כָּתַבְתִּי אֲלֵיכֶם יְלָדִים כִּי יְדַעְתֶּם אֶת-הָאָב

13. Ko•tev ani aley•chem avot ki - ye•da•a•tem o•to asher mo•tza•o•tav mi•ke•dem ko•tev ani aley•chem ba•choo•rim ki - g`var•tem al - ha•ra ka•tav•ti aley•chem ye•la•dim ki ye•da•a•tem et - ha•Av.

Rabbinic Jewish Commentary
The Jews used to call their men of wisdom, and knowledge, and understanding, אבות, "Abot", "fathers". Hence there is a whole treatise in the Misna called Pirke Abot, which contains the apophthegms, wise sayings, and sentences of their fathers, or wise men. Now the apostle writes the new commandment of love, and urges it on these.

1 John 2

14. I have written unto you, fathers, because ye have known him that is from the beginning. I have written unto you, young men, because ye are strong, and the word of God abideth in you, and ye have overcome the wicked one.

14. Ἔγραψα ὑμῖν, πατέρες, ὅτι ἐγνώκατε τὸν ἀπ᾽ ἀρχῆς. Ἔγραψα ὑμῖν, νεανίσκοι, ὅτι ἰσχυροί ἐστε, καὶ ὁ λόγος τοῦ θεοῦ ἐν ὑμῖν μένει, καὶ νενικήκατε τὸν πονηρόν.

14. Egrapsa 'umin, pateres, 'oti egnokate ton ap archeis. Egrapsa 'umin, neaniskoi, 'oti ischuroi este, kai 'o logos tou theou en 'umin menei, kai nenikeikate ton poneiron.

יד. כָּתַבְתִּי אֲלֵיכֶם אָבוֹת כִּי-יְדַעְתֶּם אֹתוֹ אֲשֶׁר מוֹצָאֹתָיו מִקֶּדֶם כָּתַבְתִּי אֲלֵיכֶם בַּחוּרִים כִּי-בְּנֵי חַיִל אַתֶּם וּדְבַר-אֱלֹהִים שֹׁכֵן בְּקִרְבְּכֶם וּגְבַרְתֶּם עַל-הָרָע

14. Ka•tav•ti aley•chem avot ki - ye•da•a•tem o•to asher mo•tza•o•tav mi•ke•dem ka•tav•ti aley•chem ba•choo•rim ki - v`ney cha•yil atem oo•d`var Elohim sho•chen be•kir•be•chem oog•var•tem al - ha•ra.

---

15. Love not the world, neither the things that are in the world. If any man love the world, the love of the Father is not in him.

15. Μὴ ἀγαπᾶτε τὸν κόσμον, μηδὲ τὰ ἐν τῷ κόσμῳ. Ἐάν τις ἀγαπᾷ τὸν κόσμον, οὐκ ἔστιν ἡ ἀγάπη τοῦ πατρὸς ἐν αὐτῷ.

15. Mei agapate ton kosmon, meide ta en to kosmo. Ean tis agapa ton kosmon, ouk estin 'ei agapei tou patros en auto.

טו. לֹא תֶאֱהָבוּן אֶת-הָעוֹלָם וְלֹא אֶת-אֲשֶׁר לָעוֹלָם אִישׁ כִּי-יֶאֱהַב אֶת-הָעוֹלָם אֵין בְּקִרְבּוֹ אַהֲבַת הָאָב:

15. Lo te•e•ha•voon et - ha•o•lam ve•lo et - asher la•o•lam eesh ki - ye•e•hav et - ha•o•lam eyn be•kir•bo a•ha•vat ha•Av.

Rabbinic Jewish Commentary

This is the character of worldly men; so the Jews call such, אהבי העולם הזה, "such that love world" (g).

(g) Kimchi in Psal. xlix. 9. Ben Melech in ib. ver. 14.

16. For all that is in the world, the lust of the flesh, and the lust of the eyes, and the pride of life, is not of the Father, but is of the world.

16. Ὅτι πᾶν τὸ ἐν τῷ κόσμῳ, ἡ ἐπιθυμία τῆς σαρκός, καὶ ἡ ἐπιθυμία τῶν ὀφθαλμῶν, καὶ ἡ ἀλαζονεία τοῦ βίου, οὐκ ἔστιν ἐκ τοῦ πατρός, ἀλλ᾽ ἐκ τοῦ κόσμου ἐστίν.

16. 'Oti pan to en to kosmo, 'ei epithumia teis sarkos, kai 'ei epithumia ton ophthalmon, kai 'ei alazoneia tou biou, ouk estin ek tou patros, all ek tou kosmou estin.

טז. כִּי כָל־אֲשֶׁר בָּעוֹלָם חֶמְדַּת הַבָּשָׂר תַּאֲוַת הָעֵינַיִם וּגְאוֹן שָׁוְא אֲשֶׁר בְּחַיֵּי אָדָם אֵינָם מִן־הָאָב כִּי אִם־מִן־הָעוֹלָם:

16. Ki chol - asher ba•o•lam chem•dat ha•ba•sar ta•a•vat ha•ey•na•yim oog•on shav asher be•cha•yey adam ey•nam min - ha•Av ki eem - min - ha•o•lam.

---

1 John 2

17. And the world passeth away, and the lust thereof: but he that doeth the will of God abideth for ever.

17. Καὶ ὁ κόσμος παράγεται, καὶ ἡ ἐπιθυμία αὐτοῦ· ὁ δὲ ποιῶν τὸ θέλημα τοῦ θεοῦ μένει εἰς τὸν αἰῶνα.

17. Kai 'o kosmos paragetai, kai 'ei epithumia autou. 'o de poion to theleima tou theou menei eis ton aiona.

יז. וְהָעוֹלָם הַזֶּה כָּלִיל יַחֲלֹף עִם־תַּאֲוָתוֹ וְהָעֹשֶׂה רְצוֹן הָאֱלֹהִים יִשְׁכֹּן לָנֶצַח:

17. Ve•ha•olam ha•ze ka•lil ya•cha•lof eem - ta•a•va•to ve•ha•o•se r`tzon ha•Elohim yish•kon la•ne•tzach.

---

18. Little children, it is the last time: and as ye have heard that antichrist shall come, even now are there many antichrists; whereby we know that it is the last time.

18. Παιδία, ἐσχάτη ὥρα ἐστίν· καὶ καθὼς ἠκούσατε ὅτι ὁ ἀντίχριστος ἔρχεται, καὶ νῦν ἀντίχριστοι πολλοὶ γεγόνασιν· ὅθεν γινώσκομεν ὅτι ἐσχάτη ὥρα ἐστίν.

18. Paidia, eschatei 'ora estin. kai kathos eikousate 'oti 'o antichristos erchetai, kai nun antichristoi polloi gegonasin. 'othen ginoskomen 'oti eschatei 'ora estin.

יח. יְלָדַי הִנֵּה עֵת הַקֵּץ בָּאָה וְאַתֶּם שְׁמַעְתֶּם כִּי יָבֹא שׂוֹטֵן הַמָּשִׁיחַ וְאַחֲרֵי אֲשֶׁר רַבִּים עַתָּה שֹׂטְנֵי הַמָּשִׁיחַ נֵדַע:בָּזֹאת כִּי עֵת הַקֵּץ הִיא

18. Ye•la•dai hee•ne et ha•ketz ba•ah ve•a•tem sh`ma•a•tem ki ya•vo so•ten ha•Ma•shi•ach ve•a•cha•rey asher ra•bim ata sot•ney ha•Ma•shi•ach ne•da ba•zot ki et ha•ketz hee.

Rabbinic Jewish Commentary

The Syriac and Ethiopic versions read, "false Messiahs"; that set up for Messiahs, whom Christ foretold should arise before the destruction of Jerusalem, Mat.24:24.

The apostle might well say there were many, since in his time were the followers of Simon Magus, the Menandrians, Saturnilians, Basilidians, Nicolaites, Gnostics, Carpocratians, Cerinthians, Ebionites, and Nazarenes, as reckoned up by Epiphanius. And hence we learn, that antichrist is not one single individual, but many; antichrist in the former clause is explained by antichrists in this.

---

1 John 2

19. They went out from us, but they were not of us; for if they had been of us, they would no doubt have continued with us: but they went out, that they might be made manifest that they were not all of us.

19. Ἐξ ἡμῶν ἐξῆλθον, ἀλλ' οὐκ ἦσαν ἐξ ἡμῶν· εἰ γὰρ ἦσαν ἐξ ἡμῶν, μεμενήκεισαν ἂν μεθ' ἡμῶν· ἀλλ' ἵνα φανερωθῶσιν ὅτι οὐκ εἰσὶν πάντες ἐξ ἡμῶν.

19. Ex 'eimon exeilthon, all ouk eisan ex 'eimon. ei gar eisan ex 'eimon, memeneikeisan an meth 'eimon. all 'ina phanerothosin 'oti ouk eisin pantes ex 'eimon.

יט. וְהֵם יָצְאוּ מֵאִתָּנוּ אֶפֶס לֹא-מִשֶּׁלָּנוּ הָיוּ כִּי לוּ הָיוּ מִשֶּׁלָּנוּ אָז נִשְׁאֲרוּ עִמָּנוּ אַךְ יָצְאוּ לַבַעֲבוּר יִוָּדַע כִּי לֹא כֻלָּם:מִשֶּׁלָּנוּ הֵם

19. Ve•hem yatz•oo me•ee•ta•noo e•fes lo - mi•she•la•noo ha•yoo ki loo ha•yoo mi•she•la•noo az nish•a•roo ee•ma•noo ach yatz•oo le•va•a•voor yi•va•da ki lo choo•lam mi•she•la•noo hem.

---

1 John 2

20. But ye have an unction from the Holy One, and ye know all things.

20. Καὶ ὑμεῖς χρίσμα ἔχετε ἀπὸ τοῦ ἁγίου, καὶ οἴδατε πάντα.

20. Kai 'umeis chrisma echete apo tou 'agiou, kai oidate panta.

כ: אֲבָל אַתֶּם שֶׁמֶן מִשְׁחַת הַקֹּדֶשׁ עֲלֵיכֶם וְאֶת-כֹּל יְדַעְתֶּם

20. Aval atem she•men mish•chat ha•Ko•desh aley•chem ve•et - kol ye•da•a•tem.

Rabbinic Jewish Commentary

The grace of the Spirit is called a chrism, or an ointment, or an anointing, in allusion to the anointing oil under the law; of which anointing oil the Jews say (h), that it continues all of it, לעתיד לבוא, "to time to come", (i.e. to the times of the Messiah,) as it is said, Exo 30:31. Now this these saints had, "from the Holy One"; or that Holy One.

(h) T. Hieros. Horayot, fol. 47. 3.

---

21. I have not written unto you because ye know not the truth, but because ye know it, and that no lie is of the truth.

21. Οὐκ ἔγραψα ὑμῖν, ὅτι οὐκ οἴδατε τὴν ἀλήθειαν, ἀλλ᾽ ὅτι οἴδατε αὐτήν, καὶ ὅτι πᾶν ψεῦδος ἐκ τῆς ἀληθείας οὐκ ἔστιν.

21. Ouk egrapsa 'umin, 'oti ouk oidate tein aleitheyan, all 'oti oidate autein, kai 'oti pan pseudos ek teis aleitheias ouk estin.

כא. לֹא כָתַבְתִּי אֲלֵיכֶם עַל כִּי לֹא-יְדַעְתֶּם אֶת-הָאֱמֶת כִּי יְדַעְתֶּם אֹתָהּ וְכִי כָּל-שֶׁקֶר אֵינֶנּוּ יְלִיד הָאֱמֶת:

21. Lo cha•tav•ti aley•chem al ki lo - ye•da•a•tem et - ha•e•met ki ye•da•a•tem o•ta ve•chi chol - she•ker ey•ne•noo ye•lid ha•e•met.

1 John 2

22. Who is a liar but he that denieth that Jesus is the Christ? He is antichrist, that denieth the Father and the Son.

22. Τίς ἐστιν ὁ ψεύστης, εἰ μὴ ὁ ἀρνούμενος ὅτι Ἰησοῦς οὐκ ἔστιν ὁ χριστός; Οὗτός ἐστιν ὁ ἀντίχριστος, ὁ ἀρνούμενος τὸν πατέρα καὶ τὸν υἱόν.

22. Tis estin 'o pseusteis, ei mei 'o arnoumenos 'oti Yeisous ouk estin 'o christos? 'Outos estin 'o antichristos, 'o arnoumenos ton patera kai ton 'wion.

כב. מִי הוּא הַכֹּזֵב בִּלְתִּי הַמְכַחֵשׁ בְּיֵשׁוּעַ לֵאמֹר כִּי לֹא הַמָּשִׁיחַ הוּא זֶה הוּא שׂוֹטֵן הַמָּשִׁיחַ הַמְכַחֵשׁ בָּאָב וּבַבֵּן:

22. Mee hoo ha•ko•zev bil•tee ham•cha•chesh be•Yeshua le•mor ki lo ha•Ma•shi•ach hoo ze hoo so•ten ha•Ma•shi•ach ham•cha•chesh ba•Av oo•va•Ben.

---

1 John 2

23. Whosoever denieth the Son, the same hath not the Father: (but) he that acknowledgeth the Son hath the Father also.

23. Πᾶς ὁ ἀρνούμενος τὸν υἱὸν οὐδὲ τὸν πατέρα ἔχει.

23. Pas 'o arnoumenos ton 'wion oude ton patera echei.

כג. כָּל-הַמְכַחֵשׁ בַּבֵּן גַּם-הָאָב אֵין-לוֹ וְהַנֹּתֵן תּוֹדָה לַבֵּן לוֹ גַּם-הָאָב:

23. Kol - ham•cha•chesh ba•Ben gam - ha•Av eyn - lo ve•ha•no•ten to•da la•Ben lo gam - ha•Av.

---

24. Let that therefore abide in you, which ye have heard from the beginning. If that which ye have heard from the beginning shall remain in you, ye also shall continue in the Son, and in the Father.

24. Ὑμεῖς οὖν ὃ ἠκούσατε ἀπ' ἀρχῆς, ἐν ὑμῖν μενέτω. Ἐὰν ἐν ὑμῖν μείνῃ ὃ ἀπ' ἀρχῆς ἠκούσατε, καὶ ὑμεῖς ἐν τῷ υἱῷ καὶ ἐν τῷ πατρὶ μενεῖτε.

24. 'Umeis oun 'o eikousate ap archeis, en 'umin meneto. Ean en 'umin meinei 'o ap archeis eikousate, kai 'umeis en to 'wio kai en to patri meneite.

כד. וְאַתֶּם שִׁמְרוּ בִלְבַבְכֶם אֶת-הַדָּבָר אֲשֶׁר שְׁמַעְתֶּם מֵרֹאשׁ כִּי אִם-תִּשְׁמְרוּ אֶת-הַדָּבָר אֲשֶׁר שְׁמַעְתֶּם מֵרֹאשׁ:תִּתְלוֹנְנוּ גַּם-בַּבֵּן גַּם-בָּאָב

24. Ve•a•tem shim•roo vil•vav•chem et - ha•da•var asher sh`ma•a•tem me•rosh ki eem - tish•me•roo et - ha•da•var asher sh`ma•a•tem me•rosh tit•lo•ne•noo gam - ba•Ben gam - ba•Av.

1 John 2

25. And this is the promise that he hath promised us, even eternal life.

25. Καὶ αὕτη ἐστὶν ἡ ἐπαγγελία ἣν αὐτὸς ἐπηγγείλατο ἡμῖν, τὴν ζωὴν τὴν αἰώνιον.

25. Kai 'autei estin 'ei epangelia 'ein autos epeingeilato 'eimin, tein zoein tein aionion.

כה. וְאֵת אֲשֶׁר דִּבֶּר לָתֶת-לָנוּ הוּא חַיֵּי עוֹלָם:

25. Ve•et asher di•ber la•tet - la•noo hoo cha•yey o•lam.

26. These things have I written unto you concerning them that seduce you.

26. Ταῦτα ἔγραψα ὑμῖν περὶ τῶν πλανώντων ὑμᾶς.

26. Tauta egrapsa 'umin peri ton planonton 'umas.

כו. כָּזֹאת כָּתַבְתִּי אֲלֵיכֶם מִפְּנֵי הַחֲפֵצִים לְהַתְעוֹת אֶתְכֶם:

26. Ka•zot ka•tav•ti aley•chem mip•ney ha•cha•fe•tzim le•hat•ot et•chem.

27. But the anointing which ye have received of him abideth in you, and ye need not that any man teach you: but as the same anointing teacheth you of all things, and is truth, and is no lie, and even as it hath taught you, ye shall abide in him.

27. Καὶ ὑμεῖς, τὸ χρίσμα ὃ ἐλάβετε ἀπ᾽ αὐτοῦ ἐν ὑμῖν μένει, καὶ οὐ χρείαν ἔχετε ἵνα τις διδάσκῃ ὑμᾶς· ἀλλ᾽ ὡς τὸ αὐτὸ χρίσμα διδάσκει ὑμᾶς περὶ πάντων, καὶ ἀληθές ἐστιν, καὶ οὐκ ἔστιν ψεῦδος, καὶ καθὼς ἐδίδαξεν ὑμᾶς, μενεῖτε ἐν αὐτῷ.

27. Kai 'umeis, to chrisma 'o elabete ap autou en 'umin menei, kai ou chreian echete 'ina tis didaskei 'umas. all 'os to auto chrisma didaskei 'umas peri panton, kai aleithes estin, kai ouk estin pseudos, kai kathos edidaxen 'umas, meneite en auto.

כז. וְהִנֵּה הַמִּשְׁחָה אֲשֶׁר נִמְשַׁחְתֶּם מִיָּדוֹ נִשְׁאֶרֶת עֲלֵיכֶם וְאֵין מַחְסוֹר לָכֶם לְאַחַד הָאֲנָשִׁים לְלַמֶּדְכֶם דָּבָר כִּי־הַמִּשְׁחָה הַהִיא תּוֹרֶה אֶתְכֶם כָּל־דְּבַר אֱמֶת וּבָהּ אֵין שֶׁקֶר: וְכַאֲשֶׁר תּוֹרֶה אֶתְכֶם כֵּן בּוֹ תִּתְלוֹנָנוּ

27. Ve•hee•ne ha•mish•cha asher nim•shach•tem mi•ya•do nish•e•ret aley•chem ve•eyn mach•sor la•chem le•a•chad ha•a•na•shim le•lam•de•chem da•var ki ha•mish•cha ha•hee to•re et•chem kol - de•var emet oo•va eyn she•ker ve•cha•a•sher to•re et•chem ken bo tit•lo•na•noo.

Rabbinic Jewish Commentary
So the second "Sephira", or number in the Jews' Cabalistic tree, which is wisdom, has for one of its surnames, the fountain of the oil of unction (i).

(i) Cabala Denudata, par. 2. p. 8.

---

28. And now, little children, abide in him; that, when he shall appear, we may have confidence, and not be ashamed before him at his coming.

28. Καὶ νῦν, τεκνία, μένετε ἐν αὐτῷ· ἵνα ὅταν φανερωθῇ, ἔχωμεν παρρησίαν, καὶ μὴ αἰσχυνθῶμεν ἀπ᾽ αὐτοῦ ἐν τῇ παρουσίᾳ αὐτοῦ.

28. Kai nun, teknia, menete en auto. 'ina 'otan phanerothei, echomen parreisian, kai mei aischunthomen ap autou en tei parousia autou.

כח. וְעַתָּה יְלָדַי הִתְלוֹנְנוּ בְצִלּוֹ לְמַעַן נָגִילָה בְהִגָּלוֹתוֹ וְלֹא־נֵבוֹשׁ מִלְּפָנָיו בְּיוֹם בֹּאוֹ:

28. Ve•a•ta ye•la•dai hit•lo•ne•noo ve•tzi•lo le•ma•an na•gi•la ve•hi•ga•lo•to ve•lo - ne•vosh mil•fa•nav be•yom bo•oo.

---

29. If ye know that he is righteous, ye know that every one that doeth righteousness is born of him.

29. Ἐὰν εἰδῆτε ὅτι δίκαιός ἐστιν, γινώσκετε ὅτι πᾶς ὁ ποιῶν τὴν δικαιοσύνην ἐξ αὐτοῦ γεγέννηται.

29. Ean eideite 'oti dikaios estin, ginoskete 'oti pas 'o poion tein dikaiosunein ex autou gegenneitai.

כט. אִם-יְדַעְתֶּם כִּי-צַדִּיק הוּא הֲלֹא תֵדְעוּן כִּי גַם כָּל-פֹּעֵל צֶדֶק נוֹלַד מִמֶּנּוּ:

29. Eem - ye•da•a•tem ki - tza•dik hoo ha•lo ted•oon ki gam kol - po•el tze•dek no•lad mi•me•noo.

(1John Chapter 2 End)

1 John, Chapter 3

1. Behold, what manner of love the Father hath bestowed upon us, that we should be called the sons of God: therefore the world knoweth us not, because it knew him not.

1. Ἴδετε ποταπὴν ἀγάπην δέδωκεν ἡμῖν ὁ πατήρ, ἵνα τέκνα θεοῦ κληθῶμεν. Διὰ τοῦτο ὁ κόσμος οὐ γινώσκει ὑμᾶς, ὅτι οὐκ ἔγνω αὐτόν.

1. Ydete potapein agapein dedoken 'eimin 'o pateir, 'ina tekna theou kleithomen. Dya touto 'o kosmos ou ginoskei 'umas, 'oti ouk egno auton.

א. רְאוּ מַה-נִּפְלָאָה אַהֲבַת הָאָב אֲשֶׁר נָתַן לָנוּ לְהִקָּרֵא וְנִהְיֶה בְּנֵי אֱלֹהִים וּבַעֲבוּר זֹאת לֹא יָדַע אֹתָנוּ הָעוֹלָם כִּי:גַם-אֹתוֹ לֹא יָדָע

1. R`oo ma - nif•la•ah a•ha•vat ha•Av asher na•tan la•noo le•hi•ka•re ve•ni•hi•ye v`ney Elohim oo•va•a•voor zot lo ya•da o•ta•noo ha•o•lam ki gam - o•to lo ya•da.

---

2. Beloved, now are we the sons of God, and it doth not yet appear what we shall be: but we know that, when he shall appear, we shall be like him; for we shall see him as he is.

2. Ἀγαπητοί, νῦν τέκνα θεοῦ ἐσμέν, καὶ οὔπω ἐφανερώθη τί ἐσόμεθα· οἴδαμεν δὲ ὅτι ἐὰν φανερωθῇ, ὅμοιοι αὐτῷ ἐσόμεθα, ὅτι ὀψόμεθα αὐτὸν καθώς ἐστιν.

2. Agapeitoi, nun tekna theou esmen, kai oupo ephanerothei ti esometha. oidamen de 'oti ean phanerothei, 'omoioi auto esometha, 'oti opsometha auton kathos estin.

ב. וְעַתָּה יְדִידִים בָּנִים אֲנַחְנוּ לֵאלֹהִים וְעַד-כֹּה לֹא נוֹדַע מַה-נִּהְיֶה בְּאַחֲרִיתֵנוּ אַךְ יָדַעְנוּ כִּי נִשְׁוֶה-לוֹ לְעֵת:יִגָּלֶה כִּי נִרְאֵהוּ אָז כַּאֲשֶׁר הוּא

2. Ve•a•ta ye•di•dim ba•nim a•nach•noo le•Elohim ve•ad - ko lo no•da ma - ni•hee•ye ve•a•cha•ri•te•noo ach ya•da•a•noo ki nish•ve - lo le•et yi•ga•le ki nir•e•hoo az ka•a•sher hoo.

Rabbinic Jewish Commentary

Philo the Jew observes (k), that Israel may be interpreted one that sees God; but adds, ουχ οιος εστιν ο θεος, "not what God is", for this is

377

impossible: it is indeed impossible to see him essentially as he is, or so as to comprehend his nature, being, and perfections.

(k) De Praemiis. & Paenis, p. 917.

---

1 John 3

3. And every man that hath this hope in him purifieth himself, even as he is pure.

3. Καὶ πᾶς ὁ ἔχων τὴν ἐλπίδα ταύτην ἐπ᾽ αὐτῷ ἁγνίζει ἑαυτόν, καθὼς ἐκεῖνος ἁγνός ἐστιν.

3. Kai pas 'o echon tein elpida tautein ep auto 'agnizei 'eauton, kathos ekeinos 'agnos estin.

ג. וְכָל-הַשָּׂם מִבְטָחוֹ בוֹ יְטַהֵר אֶת-נַפְשׁוֹ כַּאֲשֶׁר גַּם הוּא טָהוֹר:

3. Ve•chol - ha•sam miv•ta•cho vo ye•ta•her et - naf•sho ka•a•sher gam hoo ta•hor.

---

4. Whosoever committeth sin transgresseth also the law: for sin is the transgression of the law.

4. Πᾶς ὁ ποιῶν τὴν ἁμαρτίαν, καὶ τὴν ἀνομίαν ποιεῖ· καὶ ἡ ἁμαρτία ἐστὶν ἡ ἀνομία.

4. Pas 'o poion tein 'amartian, kai tein anomian poiei. kai 'ei 'amartia estin 'ei anomia.

ד. כָּל-הַחֹטֵא מַמְרֶה הוּא בַתּוֹרָה כִּי הַחֵטְא מְרִי הוּא בַתּוֹרָה:

4. Kol - ha•cho•te mam•re hoo va•Torah ki ha•chet me•ri hoo va•Torah.

---

5. And ye know that he was manifested to take away our sins; and in him is no sin.

378

5. Καὶ οἴδατε ὅτι ἐκεῖνος ἐφανερώθη, ἵνα τὰς ἁμαρτίας ἡμῶν ἄρῃ· καὶ ἁμαρτία ἐν αὐτῷ οὐκ ἔστιν.

5. Kai oidate 'oti ekeinos ephanerothei, 'ina tas 'amartias 'eimon arei. kai 'amartia en auto ouk estin.

ה. וְאַתֶּם יְדַעְתֶּם כִּי הוּא בָא לָשֵׂאת אֶת־חַטֹּאתֵינוּ וְחֵטְא לֹא הָיָה בוֹ:

5. Ve•a•tem ye•da•a•tem ki hoo va la•set et - cha•to•tey•noo ve•chet lo ha•ya vo.

Rabbinic Jewish Commentary

The Jews (l) speak of a man after the image of God, and who is the mystery, of the name Yehovah; and in that man, they say, there is no sin, neither shall death rule over him; and this is that which is said, Psa.5:4; neither shall evil dwell with thee.

(l) Sepher Tikkunim, fol. 112. 1. apud Rittangel, de ver. Rel. Christ, p. 68.

1 John 3

6. Whosoever abideth in him sinneth not: whosoever sinneth hath not seen him, neither known him.

6. Πᾶς ὁ ἐν αὐτῷ μένων οὐχ ἁμαρτάνει· πᾶς ὁ ἁμαρτάνων οὐχ ἑώρακεν αὐτόν, οὐδὲ ἔγνωκεν αὐτόν.

6. Pas 'o en auto menon ouch 'amartanei. pas 'o 'amartanon ouch 'eoraken auton, oude egnoken auton.

ו. כָּל־הַמִּתְלוֹנֵן בּוֹ לֹא יֶחֱטָא וְכָל־חֹטֵא לֹא רָאָהוּ וְלֹא יְדָעוֹ:

6. Kol - ha•mit•lo•nen bo lo ye•che•ta ve•chol - cho•te lo ra•a•hoo ve•lo ye•da•o.

7. Little children, let no man deceive you: he that doeth righteousness is righteous, even as he is righteous.

7. Τεκνία, μηδεὶς πλανάτω ὑμᾶς· ὁ ποιῶν τὴν δικαιοσύνην δίκαιός ἐστιν, καθὼς ἐκεῖνος δίκαιός ἐστιν·

7. Teknia, meideis planato 'umas. 'o poion tein dikaiosunein dikaios estin, kathos ekeinos dikaios estin.

ז. יְלָדַי אַל-יַתְעֶה אֶתְכֶם אִישׁ מִי הוּא פֹעֵל צֶדֶק צַדִּיק הוּא כַּאֲשֶׁר גַּם-הוּא צַדִּיק:

7. Ye•la•dai al - yat•eh et•chem eesh mee hoo fo•el tze•dek tza•dik hoo ka•a•sher gam - hoo tza•dik.

---

1 John 3

8. He that committeth sin is of the devil; for the devil sinneth from the beginning. For this purpose the Son of God was manifested, that he might destroy the works of the devil.

8. ὁ ποιῶν τὴν ἁμαρτίαν ἐκ τοῦ διαβόλου ἐστίν, ὅτι ἀπ' ἀρχῆς ὁ διάβολος ἁμαρτάνει. Εἰς τοῦτο ἐφανερώθη ὁ υἱὸς τοῦ θεοῦ, ἵνα λύσῃ τὰ ἔργα τοῦ διαβόλου.

8. 'o poion tein 'amartian ek tou dyabolou estin, 'oti ap archeis 'o dyabolos 'amartanei. Eis touto ephanerothei 'o 'wios tou theou, 'ina lusei ta erga tou dyabolou.

ח. וּמִי הוּא פֹעֵל אָוֶן מִן-הַשָּׂטָן הוּא כִּי הַשָּׂטָן פֹּעֵל אָוֶן הוּא מִקֶּדֶם וּבַעֲבוּר זֹאת בָּא בֶן-הָאֱלֹהִים לַהֲרֹס פְּעֻלּוֹת הַשָּׂטָן:

8. Oo•mi hoo fo•el aven min - ha•Satan hoo ki ha•Satan po•el aven hoo mi•ke•dem oo•va•a•voor zot ba Ven - ha•Elohim la•ha•ros pe•oo•lot ha•Satan.

---

9. Whosoever is born of God doth not commit sin; for his seed remaineth in him: and he cannot sin, because he is born of God.

9. Πᾶς ὁ γεγεννημένος ἐκ τοῦ θεοῦ ἁμαρτίαν οὐ ποιεῖ, ὅτι σπέρμα αὐτοῦ ἐν αὐτῷ μένει· καὶ οὐ δύναται ἁμαρτάνειν, ὅτι ἐκ τοῦ θεοῦ γεγέννηται.

9. Pas 'o gegenneimenos ek tou theou 'amartian ou poiei, 'oti sperma autou en auto menei. Kai ou dunatai 'amartanein, 'oti ek tou theou gegenneitai.

ט. כָּל־הַנּוֹלָד מֵאֱלֹהִים לֹא יֶחֱטָא כִּי זַרְעוֹ נִשְׁאָר בְּתוֹכוֹ וְלֹא יוּכַל לַחֲטֹא אַחֲרֵי אֲשֶׁר נוֹלַד מֵאֱלֹהִים:

9. Kol - ha•no•lad me•Elohim lo ye•che•ta ki zar•oh nish•ar be•to•cho ve•lo yoo•chal la•cha•to a•cha•rey asher no•lad me•Elohim.

1 John 3

10. In this the children of God are manifest, and the children of the devil: whosoever doeth not righteousness is not of God, neither he that loveth not his brother.

10. Ἐν τούτῳ φανερά ἐστιν τὰ τέκνα τοῦ θεοῦ καὶ τὰ τέκνα τοῦ διαβόλου· πᾶς ὁ μὴ ποιῶν δικαιοσύνην οὐκ ἔστιν ἐκ τοῦ θεοῦ, καὶ ὁ μὴ ἀγαπῶν τὸν ἀδελφὸν αὐτοῦ.

10. En touto phanera estin ta tekna tou theou kai ta tekna tou dyabolou. pas 'o mei poion dikaiosunein ouk estin ek tou theou, kai 'o mei agapon ton adelphon autou.

י. בְּזֹאת יִוָּדְעוּ בְנֵי הָאֱלֹהִים וּבְנֵי הַשָּׂטָן כָּל־אִישׁ אֲשֶׁר צְדָקוֹת לֹא־יַעֲשֶׂה אֵינֶנּוּ מֵאֱלֹהִים - וְכֵן כָּל־אֲשֶׁר לֹא־יֶאֱהַב אֶת־אָחִיו:

10. Ba•zot yi•vad•oo v`ney ha•Elohim oov•ney ha•Satan kol - eesh asher tze•da•kot lo - ya•a•se ey•ne•noo me•Elohim ve•chen kol - asher lo - ye•e•hav et - a•chiv.

Rabbinic Jewish Commentary

The people of the nations of the world are called, בנוי, "the children of Samael", and the serpent, by the Jews (m), which are with them the names of the devil.

(m) Raya Mehimna in Zohar in Lev. fol. 34. 2.

---

11. For this is the message that ye heard from the beginning, that we should love one another.

11. Ὅτι αὕτη ἐστὶν ἡ ἀγγελία ἣν ἠκούσατε ἀπ' ἀρχῆς, ἵνα ἀγαπῶμεν ἀλλήλους·

11. 'Oti 'autei estin 'ei angelia 'ein eikousate ap archeis, 'ina agapomen alleilous.

יא. כִּי זֹאת הִיא הַפְּקֻדָּה אֲשֶׁר שְׁמַעְתֶּם מִקֶּדֶם לְאַהֲבָה אִישׁ אֶת-אָחִיו:

11. Ki zot hee hap•koo•da asher sh`ma•a•tem mi•ke•dem le•a•ha•va eesh et - a•chiv.

---

1 John 3

12. Not as Cain, who was of that wicked one, and slew his brother. And wherefore slew he him? Because his own works were evil, and his brother's righteous.

12. οὐ καθὼς Κάϊν ἐκ τοῦ πονηροῦ ἦν, καὶ ἔσφαξεν τὸν ἀδελφὸν αὐτοῦ. Καὶ χάριν τίνος ἔσφαξεν αὐτόν; Ὅτι τὰ ἔργα αὐτοῦ πονηρὰ ἦν, τὰ δὲ τοῦ ἀδελφοῦ αὐτοῦ δίκαια.

12. ou kathos Kain ek tou poneirou ein, kai esphaxen ton adelphon autou. Kai charin tinos esphaxen auton? 'Oti ta erga autou poneira ein, ta de tou adelphou autou dikaya.

יב. לֹא כְקַיִן הַבָּא מִמְּקוֹר הָרָע וַיַּהֲרֹג אֶת-אָחִיו וּמַדּוּעַ הֲרָגוֹ יַעַן כִּי-מַעֲשָׂיו הָיוּ רָעִים וּמַעֲשֵׂי אָחִיו יְשָׁרִים:

12. Lo che•Kayin ha•ba mim•kor ha•ra va•ya•ha•rog et - a•chiv oo•ma•doo•a ha•ra•go ya•an ki - ma•a•sav ha•yoo ra•eem oo•ma•a•sey a•chiv ye•sha•rim.

Rabbinic Jewish Commentary
So the Jews say of Cain (n), that

"He was of the side of the serpent and as the way of the serpent is to slay and to kill, so Cain immediately became a murderer."

And again,
"Because Cain came from the side of the angel of death, he slew his brother (o);"

Though they say that he afterwards repented, and became worthy of paradise (p).

And slew his brother; Gen.4:8. According to the tradition of the Jews (q) he struck a stone into his forehead, and killed him.

The Jews (r) relate the occasion of it after this manner;

"Cain said to Abel his brother, come, and let us go out into the open field; and when they were both out in the open field, Cain answered and said to Abel his brother, there is no judgment, nor Judge, nor another world; neither will a good reward be given to the righteous, nor vengeance be taken on the wicked; neither was the world created in mercy, nor is it governed in mercy; or why is thy offering kindly accepted, and mine is not kindly accepted? Abel answered and said to Cain, there is judgment, and there is a Judge, and there is another world; and there are gifts of a good reward to the righteous, and vengeance will be taken on the wicked; and the world was created in mercy, and in mercy it is governed, for according to the fruit of good works it is governed; because that my works are better than thine, my offering is kindly accepted, and thine is not kindly accepted; and they both strove together in the field, and Cain rose up against Abel his brother, and slew him."

Philo the Jew says (s), that in the contention or dispute between Cain and Abel, Abel attributed all things to God, and Cain ascribed everything to himself;

(n) Midrash Ruth in Zohar in Gen. fol. 42. 4. (o) Zohar in ib. fol. 43. 1. (p) Ib. fol. 41. 1, 2. (q) Targum Jon. in Gen. iv. 8. Pirke Eliezer, c. 21. (r) Targum Hieros. & Jon. in Gen. iv. 8. (s) Quod Det. Potior. p. 161.

---

1 John 3

13. Marvel not, my brethren, if the world hate you.

13. Μὴ θαυμάζετε, ἀδελφοί μου, εἰ μισεῖ ὑμᾶς ὁ κόσμος·

13. Mei thaumazete, adelphoi mou, ei misei 'umas 'o kosmos.

יג. אַל-תִּתְמְהוּ אֶחָי אִם הָעוֹלָם יִשְׂנָא אֶתְכֶם:

13. Al - tit•me•hoo e•chai eem ha•o•lam yis•na et•chem.

14. We know that we have passed from death unto life, because we love the brethren. He that loveth not his brother abideth in death.

14. ἡμεῖς οἴδαμεν ὅτι μεταβεβήκαμεν ἐκ τοῦ θανάτου εἰς τὴν ζωήν, ὅτι ἀγαπῶμεν τοὺς ἀδελφούς. Ὁ μὴ ἀγαπῶν τὸν ἀδελφόν, μένει ἐν τῷ θανάτῳ.

14. 'eimeis oidamen 'oti metabebeikamen ek tou thanatou eis tein zoein, 'oti agapomen tous adelphous. 'O mei agapon ton adelphon, menei en to thanato.

יד. הֵן יֹדְעִים אֲנַחְנוּ כִּי עָבַרְנוּ מִן-הַמָּוֶת אֶל-הַחַיִּים בַּאֲשֶׁר אָהַבְנוּ אֶת-אַחֵינוּ אִישׁ אֲשֶׁר לֹא יֶאֱהַב אֶת-אָחִיו:שֹׁכֵן מָוֶת הוּא

14. Hen yod•eem a•nach•noo ki avar•noo min - ha•ma•vet el - ha•cha•yim ba•a•sher a•hav•noo et - achey•noo eesh asher lo ye•e•hav et - a•chiv sho•chen ma•vet hoo.

1 John 3

15. Whosoever hateth his brother is a murderer: and ye know that no murderer hath eternal life abiding in him.

15. Πᾶς ὁ μισῶν τὸν ἀδελφὸν αὐτοῦ ἀνθρωποκτόνος ἐστίν· καὶ οἴδατε ὅτι πᾶς ἀνθρωποκτόνος οὐκ ἔχει ζωὴν αἰώνιον ἐν ἑαυτῷ μένουσαν.

15. Pas 'o mison ton adelphon autou anthropoktonos estin. kai oidate 'oti pas anthropoktonos ouk echei zoein aionion en 'eauto menousan.

טו. כָּל-הַשֹּׂנֵא אֶת-אָחִיו רֹצֵחַ הוּא וִידַעְתֶּם כִּי כָל-רֹצֵחַ אֵין לוֹ חֵלֶק בְּחַיֵּי עוֹלָם:

15. Kol - ha•so•ne et - a•chiv ro•tze•ach hoo viy•da•a•tem ki chol - ro•tze•ach eyn lo che•lek be•cha•yey o•lam.

16. Hereby perceive we the love of God, because he laid down his life for us: and we ought to lay down our lives for the brethren.

16. Ἐν τούτῳ ἐγνώκαμεν τὴν ἀγάπην, ὅτι ἐκεῖνος ὑπὲρ ἡμῶν τὴν ψυχὴν αὐτοῦ ἔθηκεν· καὶ ἡμεῖς ὀφείλομεν ὑπὲρ τῶν ἀδελφῶν τὰς ψυχὰς τιθέναι.

16. En touto egnokamen tein agapein, 'oti ekeinos 'uper 'eimon tein psuchein autou etheiken. kai 'eimeis opheilomen 'uper ton adelphon tas psuchas tithenai.

טז. בְּזֹאת נַשְׂכִּיל מָה הִיא אַהֲבָה כִּי הוּא נָתַן נַפְשׁוֹ תַּחַת נַפְשֵׁנוּ כֵּן גַּם-עָלֵינוּ לָתֵת נֶפֶשׁ תַּחַת נֶפֶשׁ אַחֵינוּ:

16. Ba•zot nas•kil ma hee a•ha•va ki hoo na•tan naf•sho ta•chat naf•she•noo ken gam - aley•noo la•tet ne•fesh ta•chat ne•fesh achey•noo.

---

1 John 3

17. But whoso hath this world's good, and seeth his brother have need, and shutteth up his bowels of compassion from him, how dwelleth the love of God in him?

17. Ὃς δ᾽ ἂν ἔχῃ τὸν βίον τοῦ κόσμου, καὶ θεωρῇ τὸν ἀδελφὸν αὐτοῦ χρείαν ἔχοντα, καὶ κλείσῃ τὰ σπλάγχνα αὐτοῦ ἀπ᾽ αὐτοῦ, πῶς ἡ ἀγάπη τοῦ θεοῦ μένει ἐν αὐτῷ;

17. 'Os d an echei ton bion tou kosmou, kai theorei ton adelphon autou chreian echonta, kai kleisei ta splagchna autou ap autou, pos 'ei agapei tou theou menei en auto?

יז. מִי הוּא אֲשֶׁר-לוֹ הוֹן בָּאָרֶץ וְרָאָה אֶת-אָחִיו בְּחֹסֶר כֹּל וְקָפַץ רַחֲמָיו מֵאִתּוֹ אֵיךְ תָּלִן-בּוֹ אַהֲבַת אֱלֹהִים:

17. Mee hoo asher - lo hon ba•a•retz ve•ra•ah et - a•chiv be•cho•ser kol ve•ka•fatz ra•cha•mav me•ee•to eych ta•len - bo a•ha•vat Elohim.

---

18. My little children, let us not love in word, neither in tongue; but in deed and in truth.

18. Τεκνία μου, μὴ ἀγαπῶμεν λόγῳ μηδὲ τῇ γλώσσῃ, ἀλλ᾽ ἐν ἔργῳ καὶ ἀληθείᾳ.

18. Teknia mou, mei agapomen logo meide tei glossei, all en ergo kai aleitheia.

:יח. יְלָדַי אַל-נֶאֱהַב בְּנִיב שְׂפָתַיִם וּבְמַעֲנֵה לָשׁוֹן כִּי אִם-בְּמַעֲשֵׂה יָד וּבְדֶרֶךְ אֱמֶת

18. Ye•la•dai al - ne•e•hav be•niv s`fa•ta•yim oov•ma•a•ne la•shon ki eem - be•ma•a•se yad oov•de•rech emet.

---

1 John 3

19. And hereby we know that we are of the truth, and shall assure our hearts before him.

19. Καὶ ἐν τούτῳ γινώσκομεν ὅτι ἐκ τῆς ἀληθείας ἐσμέν, καὶ ἔμπροσθεν αὐτοῦ πείσομεν τὰς καρδίας ἡμῶν,

19. Kai en touto ginoskomen 'oti ek teis aleitheias esmen, kai emprosthen autou peisomen tas kardias 'eimon,

:יט. וּבְזֹאת אֲנַחְנוּ מַכִּירִים כִּי מִמְּקוֹר אֱמֶת אֲנָחְנוּ וְלִקְרַאת פָּנָיו סָמוּךְ יִהְיֶה לִבֵּנוּ

19. Oo•va•zot a•nach•noo ma•ki•rim ki mim•kor emet a•nach•noo ve•lik•rat pa•nav sa•mooch yi•hee•ye li•be•noo.

---

20. For if our heart condemn us, God is greater than our heart, and knoweth all things.

20. ὅτι ἐὰν καταγινώσκῃ ἡμῶν ἡ καρδία, ὅτι μείζων ἐστὶν ὁ θεὸς τῆς καρδίας ἡμῶν, καὶ γινώσκει πάντα.

20. 'oti ean kataginoskei 'eimon 'ei kardia, 'oti meizon estin 'o theos teis kardias 'eimon, kai ginoskei panta.

:כ. אִם-לִבֵּנוּ יַרְשִׁיעַ אֹתָנוּ אֱלֹהִים גָּדוֹל מִלִּבֵּנוּ וּמֵבִין-כֹּל הוּא

20. Eem - li•be•noo yar•shi•a o•ta•noo Elohim ga•dol mi•li•be•noo oo•me•vin - kol hoo.

---

21. Beloved, if our heart condemn us not, then have we confidence toward God.

21. Ἀγαπητοί, ἐὰν ἡ καρδία ἡμῶν μὴ καταγινώσκῃ ἡμῶν, παρρησίαν ἔχομεν πρὸς τὸν θεόν,

21. Agapeitoi, ean 'ei kardia 'eimon mei kataginoskei 'eimon, parreisian echomen pros ton theon,

כא. אִם-לִבֵּנוּ יְדִידִים לֹא-יַרְשִׁיעַ אֹתָנוּ נָכוֹן לִבֵּנוּ לִפְנֵי אֱלֹהִים:

21. Eem - li•be•noo ye•di•dim lo - yar•shi•a o•ta•noo na•chon li•be•noo lif•ney Elohim.

---

1 John 3

22. And whatsoever we ask, we receive of him, because we keep his commandments, and do those things that are pleasing in his sight.

22. καὶ ὃ ἐὰν αἰτῶμεν, λαμβάνομεν παρ᾽ αὐτοῦ, ὅτι τὰς ἐντολὰς αὐτοῦ τηροῦμεν, καὶ τὰ ἀρεστὰ ἐνώπιον αὐτοῦ ποιοῦμεν.

22. kai 'o ean aitomen, lambanomen par autou, 'oti tas entolas autou teiroumen, kai ta aresta enopion autou poioumen.

כב. וְכָל-אֲשֶׁר נִשְׁאַל נִקַּח מִיָּדוֹ כִּי-נִשְׁמֹר אֶת-מִצְוֹתָיו וְאֶת-הַטּוֹב בְּעֵינָיו נַעֲשֶׂה:

22. Ve•chol - asher nish•al ni•kach mi•ya•do ki - nish•mor et - mitz•vo•tav ve•et - ha•tov be•ey•nav na•a•se.

---

23. And this is his commandment, That we should believe on the name of his Son Jesus Christ, and love one another, as he gave us commandment.

23. Καὶ αὕτη ἐστὶν ἡ ἐντολὴ αὐτοῦ, ἵνα πιστεύσωμεν τῷ ὀνόματι τοῦ υἱοῦ αὐτοῦ Ἰησοῦ χριστοῦ, καὶ ἀγαπῶμεν ἀλλήλους, καθὼς ἔδωκεν ἐντολήν.

23. Kai 'autei estin 'ei entolei autou, 'ina pisteusomen to onomati tou 'wiou autou Yeisou christou, kai agapomen alleilous, kathos edoken entolein.

כג. וְזֹאת הִיא מִצְוָתוֹ לְהַאֲמִין בְּשֵׁם יֵשׁוּעַ הַמָּשִׁיחַ בְּנוֹ וּלְאַהֲבָה אִישׁ אֶת-רֵעֵהוּ כַּאֲשֶׁר צִוָּנוּ:

23. Ve•zot hee mitz•va•to le•ha•a•min be•shem Yeshua ha•Ma•shi•ach B`no ool•a•ha•va eesh et - re•e•hoo ka•a•sher tzi•va•noo.

Rabbinic Jewish Commentary
The Hebrew words, תורה, and מצוה, both signify any teaching, and instruction in general; see Psa.19:7.

---

24. And he that keepeth his commandments dwelleth in him, and he in him. And hereby we know that he abideth in us, by the Spirit which he hath given us.

24. Καὶ ὁ τηρῶν τὰς ἐντολὰς αὐτοῦ ἐν αὐτῷ μένει, καὶ αὐτὸς ἐν αὐτῷ. Καὶ ἐν τούτῳ γινώσκομεν ὅτι μένει ἐν ἡμῖν, ἐκ τοῦ πνεύματος οὗ ἡμῖν ἔδωκεν.

24. Kai 'o teiron tas entolas autou en auto menei, kai autos en auto. Kai en touto ginoskomen 'oti menei en 'eimin, ek tou pneumatos 'ou 'eimin edoken.

כד. וְהַשֹּׁמֵר אֶת-מִצְוֹתָיו בּוֹ יִתְלוֹנָן וְהוּא גַם-כֵּן יִשְׁכָּן-בּוֹ וּבָזֹאת נַכִּיר כִּי-הוּא שֹׁכֵן בָּנוּ וּבָרוּחַ אֲשֶׁר-נָתַן לָנוּ:

24. Ve•ha•sho•mer et - mitz•vo•tav bo yit•lo•nan ve•hoo gam - ken yish•kon - bo oo•va•zot na•kir ki - hoo sho•chen ba•noo oo•va•Roo•ach asher - na•tan la•noo.

(1John Chapter 3 End)

1 John, Chapter 4

1. Beloved, believe not every spirit, but try the spirits whether they are of God: because many false prophets are gone out into the world.

1. Ἀγαπητοί, μὴ παντὶ πνεύματι πιστεύετε, ἀλλὰ δοκιμάζετε τὰ πνεύματα, εἰ ἐκ τοῦ θεοῦ ἐστιν· ὅτι πολλοὶ ψευδοπροφῆται ἐξεληλύθασιν εἰς τὸν κόσμον.

1. Agapeitoi, mei panti pneumati pisteuete, alla dokimazete ta pneumata, ei ek tou theou estin. 'oti polloi pseudopropheitai exeleiluthasin eis ton kosmon.

א. יְדִידִים אַל-תַּאֲמִינוּ לְכָל-רוּחַ כִּי אִם-בַּחֲנוּ אֶת-הָרוּחוֹת אִם-מֵאֱלֹהִים הֵם כִּי נְבִיאֵי שֶׁקֶר רַבִּים יָצְאוּ בָאָרֶץ:

1. Ye•di•dim al - ta•a•mi•noo le•chol - roo•ach ki eem - ba•cha•noo et - ha•roo•chot eem - me•Elohim hem ki n`vi•ey she•ker ra•bim yatz•oo va•a•retz.

---

2. Hereby know ye the Spirit of God: Every spirit that confesseth that Jesus Christ is come in the flesh is of God:

2. Ἐν τούτῳ γινώσκεται τὸ πνεῦμα τοῦ θεοῦ· πᾶν πνεῦμα ὃ ὁμολογεῖ Ἰησοῦν χριστὸν ἐν σαρκὶ ἐληλυθότα ἐκ τοῦ θεοῦ ἐστίν·

2. En touto ginosketai to pneuma tou theou. pan pneuma 'o 'omologei Yeisoun christon en sarki eleiluthota ek tou theou estin.

ב. בְּזֹאת תַּכִּירוּן אֶת-רוּחַ הָאֱלֹהִים כָּל-רוּחַ אֲשֶׁר מוֹדֶה כִּי-יֵשׁוּעַ הוּא הַמָּשִׁיחַ וּבָא בַבָּשָׂר מֵאֵת אֱלֹהִים הוּא:

2. Ba•zot ta•ki•roon et - Roo•ach ha•Elohim kol - roo•ach asher mo•de ki - Yeshua hoo ha•Ma•shi•ach oo•va va•ba•sar me•et Elohim hoo.

---

3. And every spirit that confesseth not that Jesus Christ is come in the flesh is not of God: and this is that spirit of antichrist, whereof ye have heard that it should come; and even now already is it in the world.

3. καὶ πᾶν πνεῦμα ὃ μὴ ὁμολογεῖ Ἰησοῦν χριστὸν ἐν σαρκὶ ἐληλυθότα, ἐκ τοῦ θεοῦ οὐκ ἔστιν· καὶ τοῦτό ἐστιν τὸ τοῦ ἀντιχρίστου, ὃ ἀκηκόατε ὅτι ἔρχεται, καὶ νῦν ἐν τῷ κόσμῳ ἐστὶν ἤδη.

3. kai pan pneuma 'o mei 'omologei Yeisoun christon en sarki eleiluthota, ek tou theou ouk estin. kai touto estin to tou antichristou, 'o akeikoate 'oti erchetai, kai nun en to kosmo estin eidei.

ג. וְכָל-רוּחַ אֲשֶׁר לֹא מוֹדֶה בְּיֵשׁוּעַ הַמָּשִׁיחַ הַבָּא בַּבָּשָׂר אֵינֶנּוּ מֵאֱלֹהִים וְהוּא רוּחַ שֹׂטֵן הַמָּשִׁיחַ אֲשֶׁר שְׁמַעְתֶּם:עָלָיו כִּי-יָבֹא וּכְבָר יֶשְׁנוֹ בָּאָרֶץ

3. Ve•chol - roo•ach asher lo mo•de be•Yeshua ha•Ma•shi•ach ha•ba va•ba•sar ey•ne•noo me•Elohim ve•hoo roo•ach so•ten ha•Ma•shi•ach asher sh`ma•a•tem alav ki - ya•vo ooch•var yesh•no ba•a•retz.

---

4. Ye are of God, little children, and have overcome them: because greater is he that is in you, than he that is in the world.

4. Ὑμεῖς ἐκ τοῦ θεοῦ ἐστέ, τεκνία, καὶ νενικήκατε αὐτούς· ὅτι μείζων ἐστὶν ὁ ἐν ὑμῖν ἢ ὁ ἐν τῷ κόσμῳ.

4. 'Umeis ek tou theou este, teknia, kai nenikeikate autous. 'oti meizon estin 'o en 'umin ei 'o en to kosmo.

ד. וְאַתֶּם יְלָדַי מֵאֵת אֱלֹהִים הִנְּכֶם וְאֶת-נְבִיאֵי שֶׁקֶר נִצַּחְתֶּם כִּי-גָדוֹל הוּא אֲשֶׁר אִתְּכֶם מֵאֲשֶׁר אִתָּם בָּאָרֶץ:

4. Ve•a•tem ye•la•dai me•et Elohim hin•chem ve•et - n`vi•ey she•ker ni•tzach•tem ki - ga•dol hoo asher eet•chem me•a•sher ee•tam ba•a•retz.

---

1 John 4

5. They are of the world: therefore speak they of the world, and the world heareth them.

5. Αὐτοὶ ἐκ τοῦ κόσμου εἰσίν· διὰ τοῦτο ἐκ τοῦ κόσμου λαλοῦσιν, καὶ ὁ κόσμος αὐτῶν ἀκούει.

5. Autoi ek tou kosmou eisin. dya touto ek tou kosmou lalousin, kai 'o kosmos auton akouei.

ה. הֵם מִן-הָאָרֶץ עַל-כֵּן עַל-הָאָרֶץ יְדַבֵּרוּן וְהָאָרֶץ תִּשְׁמַע אֲלֵיהֶם:

5. Hem min - ha•a•retz al - ken al - ha•a•retz ye•da•be•roon ve•ha•a•retz tish•ma aley•hem.

---

1 John 4

6. We are of God: he that knoweth God heareth us; he that is not of God heareth not us. Hereby know we the spirit of truth, and the spirit of error.

6. Ἡμεῖς ἐκ τοῦ θεοῦ ἐσμεν· ὁ γινώσκων τὸν θεόν, ἀκούει ἡμῶν· ὃς οὐκ ἔστιν ἐκ τοῦ θεοῦ, οὐκ ἀκούει ἡμῶν. Ἐκ τούτου γινώσκομεν τὸ πνεῦμα τῆς ἀληθείας καὶ τὸ πνεῦμα τῆς πλάνης.

6. 'Eimeis ek tou theou esmen. 'o ginoskon ton theon, akouei 'eimon. 'os ouk estin ek tou theou, ouk akouei 'eimon. Ek toutou ginoskomen to pneuma teis aleitheias kai to pneuma teis planeis.

ו. וַאֲנַחְנוּ מֵאֵת אֱלֹהִים וְהַיּוֹדֵעַ אֶת-אֱלֹהִים יִשְׁמַע אֵלֵינוּ וַאֲשֶׁר אֵינֶנּוּ מֵאֵת אֱלֹהִים לֹא יִשְׁמַע אֵלֵינוּ בָּזֹאת נַכִּיר:רוּחַ אֱמֶת וְרוּחַ תַּעְתֻּעִים

6. Va•a•nach•noo me•et Elohim ve•ha•yo•de•a et - Elohim yish•ma e•ley•noo va•a•sher ey•ne•noo me•et Elohim lo yish•ma e•ley•noo ba•zot na•kir roo•ach emet ve•roo•ach ta•a•too•eem.

---

7. Beloved, let us love one another: for love is of God; and every one that loveth is born of God, and knoweth God.

7. Ἀγαπητοί, ἀγαπῶμεν ἀλλήλους· ὅτι ἡ ἀγάπη ἐκ τοῦ θεοῦ ἐστιν, καὶ πᾶς ὁ ἀγαπῶν ἐκ τοῦ θεοῦ γεγέννηται, καὶ γινώσκει τὸν θεόν.

7. Agapeitoi, agapomen alleilous. 'oti 'ei agapei ek tou theou estin, kai pas 'o agapon ek tou theou gegenneitai, kai ginoskei ton theon.

ז. יְדִידִים נֶאֱהַב-נָא אִישׁ אֶת-רֵעֵהוּ כִּי הָאַהֲבָה מֵאֵת אֱלֹהִים הִיא וְכָל-אֲשֶׁר יֶאֱהַב נוֹלַד מֵאֱלֹהִים וְיֹדֵעַ אֶת:אֱלֹהִים

7. Ye•di•dim ne•e•hav - na eesh et - re•e•hoo ki ha•a•ha•va me•et Elohim hee ve•chol - asher ye•e•hav no•lad me•Elohim ve•yo•dea et - Elohim.

8. He that loveth not knoweth not God; for God is love.

8. Ὁ μὴ ἀγαπῶν οὐκ ἔγνω τὸν θεόν· ὅτι ὁ θεὸς ἀγάπη ἐστίν.

8. 'O mei agapon ouk egno ton theon. 'oti 'o theos agapei estin.

ח. וּמִי אֲשֶׁר לֹא יֶאֱהַב אֵינֶנּוּ יֹדֵעַ אֶת־אֱלֹהִים כִּי אֱלֹהִים הוּא אַהֲבָה:

8. Oo•mi asher lo ye•e•hav ey•ne•noo yo•de•a et - Elohim ki Elohim hoo a•ha•va.

Rabbinic Jewish Commentary
The Shekinah is, by the Cabalistic Jews (t), called אהבה, "love".

(t) Shirhashirim Rabba, fol. 15. 1. & Lex. Cabal. p. 43, 44.

---

1 John 4

9. In this was manifested the love of God toward us, because that God sent his only begotten Son into the world, that we might live through him.

9. Ἐν τούτῳ ἐφανερώθη ἡ ἀγάπη τοῦ θεοῦ ἐν ἡμῖν, ὅτι τὸν υἱὸν αὐτοῦ τὸν μονογενῆ ἀπέσταλκεν ὁ θεὸς εἰς τὸν κόσμον, ἵνα ζήσωμεν δι᾽ αὐτοῦ.

9. En touto ephanerothei 'ei agapei tou theou en 'eimin, 'oti ton 'wion autou ton monogenei apestalken 'o theos eis ton kosmon, 'ina zeisomen di autou.

ט. בְּזֹאת נִגְלְתָה אַהֲבַת אֱלֹהִים לָנוּ כִּי־שָׁלַח אֶת־בְּנוֹ יְחִידוֹ בָּאָרֶץ לְמַעַן נִחְיֶה בּוֹ:

9. Ba•zot nig•le•ta a•ha•vat Elohim la•noo ki - sha•lach et - B`no ye•chi•do va•a•retz le•ma•an nich•ye bo.

---

10. Herein is love, not that we loved God, but that he loved us, and sent his Son to be the propitiation for our sins.

10. Ἐν τούτῳ ἐστὶν ἡ ἀγάπη, οὐχ ὅτι ἡμεῖς ἠγαπήσαμεν τὸν θεόν, ἀλλ᾽ ὅτι αὐτὸς ἠγάπησεν ἡμᾶς, καὶ ἀπέστειλεν τὸν υἱὸν αὐτοῦ ἱλασμὸν περὶ τῶν ἁμαρτιῶν ἡμῶν.

10. En touto estin 'ei agapei, ouch 'oti 'eimeis eigapeisamen ton theon, all 'oti autos eigapeisen 'eimas, kai apesteilen ton 'wion autou 'ilasmon peri ton 'amartion 'eimon.

י. פֹּה הִיא אַהֲבָה מֹצֵאת לֹא כִּי אֲנַחְנוּ אָהַבְנוּ אֶת־אֱלֹהִים כִּי אִם־הוּא אָהַב אֹתָנוּ וַיִּשְׁלַח אֶת־בְּנוֹ לִהְיוֹת־לְכֹפֶר עַל־חַטֹּאתֵינוּ

10. Po hee a•ha•va mo•tzet lo chi a•nach•noo a•hav•noo et - Elohim ki eem - hoo ahav o•ta•noo va•yish•lach et - B`no li•hee•yot le•cho•fer al - cha•to•tey•noo.

Rabbinic Jewish Commentary
This phrase is expressive of the great love of Messiah to his people, and of his substitution in their room and stead; and so it is used among the Jews for a substitution in the room of others, לרוב אהבתו, "to express the greatness of love" (u).

(u) Misn. Negaim, c. 2. sect. 1. Maimon. & Bartenora in ib. Misn. Sanhedrin, c. 2. sect. 1. & Jarchi & Bartenora in ib. vid. T. Bab. Yoma, fol. 23. 1. & Succa, fol. 20. 1.

---

1 John 4

11. Beloved, if God so loved us, we ought also to love one another.

11. Ἀγαπητοί, εἰ οὕτως ὁ θεὸς ἠγάπησεν ἡμᾶς, καὶ ἡμεῖς ὀφείλομεν ἀλλήλους ἀγαπᾶν.

11. Agapeitoi, ei 'outos 'o theos eigapeisen 'eimas, kai 'eimeis opheilomen alleilous agapan.

יא. יְדִידִים אִם־כָּכָה אֹהֵב אֹתָנוּ הָאֱלֹהִים גַּם־עָלֵינוּ לֶאֱהֹב אִישׁ אֶת־רֵעֵהוּ:

11. Ye•di•dim eem - ka•cha o•hev o•ta•noo ha•Elohim gam - aley•noo le•e•hov eesh et - re•e•hoo.

---

12. No man hath seen God at any time. If we love one another, God dwelleth in us, and his love is perfected in us.

12. Θεὸν οὐδεὶς πώποτε τεθέαται· ἐὰν ἀγαπῶμεν ἀλλήλους, ὁ θεὸς ἐν ἡμῖν μένει, καὶ ἡ ἀγάπη αὐτοῦ τετελειωμένη ἐστὶν ἐν ἡμῖν.

12. Theon oudeis popote tetheatai. ean agapomen alleilous, 'o theos en 'eimin menei, kai 'ei agapei autou teteleiomenei estin en 'eimin.

יב. אֶת־אֱלֹהִים לֹא־רָאָה אִישׁ מֵעוֹלָם אִם־נֶאֱהַב אִישׁ אֶת־רֵעֵהוּ אֱלֹהִים יִשְׁכָּן־בָּנוּ וְהָיְתָה אַהֲבָתוֹ כְּלוּלָה׃ בְּתוֹכֵנוּ

12. Et - Elohim lo - ra•ah eesh me•o•lam eem - ne•e•hav eesh et - re•e•hoo Elohim yish•kon - ba•noo ve•hai•ta aha•va•to ke•loo•la ve•to•che•noo.

---

1 John 4

13. Hereby know we that we dwell in him, and he in us, because he hath given us of his Spirit.

13. Ἐν τούτῳ γινώσκομεν ὅτι ἐν αὐτῷ μένομεν καὶ αὐτὸς ἐν ἡμῖν, ὅτι ἐκ τοῦ πνεύματος αὐτοῦ δέδωκεν ἡμῖν.

13. En touto ginoskomen 'oti en auto menomen kai autos en 'eimin, 'oti ek tou pneumatos autou dedoken 'eimin.

יג. בָּזֹאת נֵדַע כִּי אָנוּ מִתְלוֹנְנִים בּוֹ וְהוּא בָנוּ כִּי־נָתַן מֵרוּחוֹ עָלֵינוּ:

13. Ba•zot ne•da ki a•noo mit•lo•ne•nim bo ve•hoo va•noo ki - na•tan me•Roo•cho aley•noo.

---

14. And we have seen and do testify that the Father sent the Son to be the Saviour of the world.

14. Καὶ ἡμεῖς τεθεάμεθα καὶ μαρτυροῦμεν ὅτι ὁ πατὴρ ἀπέσταλκεν τὸν υἱὸν σωτῆρα τοῦ κόσμου.

14. Kai 'eimeis tetheametha kai marturoumen 'oti 'o pateir apestalken ton 'wion soteira tou kosmou.

יד. וַאֲנַחְנוּ רָאִינוּ וַנָּעִידָה כִּי שָׁלַח הָאָב אֶת־הַבֵּן גֹּאֵל הָאָרֶץ:

14. Va•a•nach•noo ra•ee•noo va•na•ee•da ki sha•lach ha•Av et - ha•Ben Go•el ha•a•retz.

15. Whosoever shall confess that Jesus is the Son of God, God dwelleth in him, and he in God.

15. Ὃς ἂν ὁμολογήσῃ ὅτι Ἰησοῦς ἐστιν ὁ υἱὸς τοῦ θεοῦ, ὁ θεὸς ἐν αὐτῷ μένει, καὶ αὐτὸς ἐν τῷ θεῷ.

15. 'Os an 'omologeisei 'oti Yeisous estin 'o 'wios tou theou, 'o theos en auto menei, kai autos en to theo.

טו. מִי הוּא אֲשֶׁר מוֹדֶה כִּי יֵשׁוּעַ הוּא בֶּן-הָאֱלֹהִים אֱלֹהִים יִגְוֶה בְתוֹכוֹ וְהוּא בֵאלֹהִים:

15. Mee hoo asher mo•de ki Yeshua hoo Ben - ha•Elohim Elohim yin•ve ve•to•cho ve•hoo be•Elohim.

1 John 4

16. And we have known and believed the love that God hath to us. God is love; and he that dwelleth in love dwelleth in God, and God in him.

16. Καὶ ἡμεῖς ἐγνώκαμεν καὶ πεπιστεύκαμεν τὴν ἀγάπην ἣν ἔχει ὁ θεὸς ἐν ἡμῖν. Ὁ θεὸς ἀγάπη ἐστίν, καὶ ὁ μένων ἐν τῇ ἀγάπῃ, ἐν τῷ θεῷ μένει, καὶ ὁ θεὸς ἐν αὐτῷ μένει.

16. Kai 'eimeis egnokamen kai pepisteukamen tein agapein 'ein echei 'o theos en 'eimin. 'O theos agapei estin, kai 'o menon en tei agapei, en to theo menei, kai 'o theos en auto menei.

טז. וַאֲנַחְנוּ יָדַעְנוּ וַנִּבְטַח בְּאַהֲבַת אֱלֹהִים אֱלֹהִים הוּא אַהֲבָה וּמִי אֲשֶׁר יִגְוֶה בָּאַהֲבָה יִגְוֶה בֵאלֹהִים וֵאלֹהִים יִגְוֶה בּוֹ:

16. Va•a•nach•noo ya•da•a•noo va•niv•tach be•a•ha•vat Elohim Elohim hoo a•ha•va oo•mi asher yin•ve va•a•ha•va yin•ve ve•Elohim ve•Elohim yin•ve bo.

17. Herein is our love made perfect, that we may have boldness in the day of judgment: because as he is, so are we in this world.

17. Ἐν τούτῳ τετελείωται ἡ ἀγάπη μεθ᾽ ἡμῶν, ἵνα παρρησίαν ἔχωμεν ἐν τῇ ἡμέρᾳ τῆς κρίσεως, ὅτι καθὼς ἐκεῖνός ἐστιν, καὶ ἡμεῖς ἐσμεν ἐν τῷ κόσμῳ τούτῳ.

17. En touto teteleiotai 'ei agapei meth 'eimon, 'ina parreisian echomen en tei 'eimera teis kriseos, 'oti kathos ekeinos estin, kai 'eimeis esmen en to kosmo touto.

יז. בְּזֹאת כְּלוּלָה-בָּנוּ תַכְלִית אַהֲבָה בִּהְיוֹת לָנוּ בִטָּחוֹן לְיוֹם הַמִּשְׁפָּט כִּי גַם-אֲנַחְנוּ בָּאָרֶץ הַזֹּאת מְלֵאֵי אַהֲבָה:כָּמוֹהוּ

17. Ba•zot ke•loo•la - va•noo tach•lit a•ha•va bi•hee•yot la•noo vi•ta•chon le•yom ha•mish•pat ki gam - a•nach•noo ba•a•retz ha•zot me•le•ey a•ha•va ka•mo•hoo.

---

1 John 4

18. There is no fear in love; but perfect love casteth out fear: because fear hath torment. He that feareth is not made perfect in love.

18. Φόβος οὐκ ἔστιν ἐν τῇ ἀγάπῃ, ἀλλ᾽ ἡ τελεία ἀγάπη ἔξω βάλλει τὸν φόβον, ὅτι ὁ φόβος κόλασιν ἔχει· ὁ δὲ φοβούμενος οὐ τετελείωται ἐν τῇ ἀγάπῃ.

18. Phobos ouk estin en tei agapei, all 'ei teleia agapei exo ballei ton phobon, 'oti 'o phobos kolasin echei. 'o de phoboumenos ou teteleiotai en tei agapei.

יח. אֵין פַּחַד בָּאַהֲבָה אֲבָל אַהֲבָה שְׁלֵמָה תְגָרֵשׁ פַּחַד כִּי-הַפַּחַד הוּא פַּחַד מִפְּנֵי עֹנֶשׁ וְהַמְפַחֵד אֵינֶנּוּ שָׁלֵם:בְּאַהֲבָתוֹ

18. Eyn pa•chad ba•a•ha•va aval a•ha•va sh`le•ma te•ga•resh pa•chad ki - ha•pa•chad hoo pa•chad mip•ney o•nesh ve•ham•fa•ched ey•ne•noo sha•lem be•a•ha•va•to.

Rabbinic Jewish Commentary
The Jews have a saying (w),

"Worthy is his portion that rules over the place of fear, for lo, there is nothing that rules over the degree of "fear" but "love"."

(w) Zohar in Exod. fol. 87. 1.

19. We love him, because he first loved us.

19. Ἡμεῖς ἀγαπῶμεν αὐτόν, ὅτι αὐτὸς πρῶτος ἠγάπησεν ἡμᾶς.

19. 'Eimeis agapomen auton, 'oti autos protos eigapeisen 'eimas.

יט. אֲנַחְנוּ אֹהֲבִים אֹתוֹ כִּי הוּא אָהַב אֹתָנוּ מִקֶּדֶם:

19. A•nach•noo o•ha•vim o•to ki hoo ahav o•ta•noo mi•ke•dem.

---

1 John 4

20. If a man say, I love God, and hateth his brother, he is a liar: for he that loveth not his brother whom he hath seen, how can he love God whom he hath not seen?

20. Ἐάν τις εἴπῃ ὅτι Ἀγαπῶ τὸν θεόν, καὶ τὸν ἀδελφὸν αὐτοῦ μισῇ, ψεύστης ἐστίν· ὁ γὰρ μὴ ἀγαπῶν τὸν ἀδελφὸν αὐτοῦ ὃν ἑώρακεν, τὸν θεὸν ὃν οὐχ ἑώρακεν πῶς δύναται ἀγαπᾶν;

20. Ean tis eipei 'oti Agapo ton theon, kai ton adelphon autou misei, pseusteis estin. 'o gar mei agapon ton adelphon autou 'on 'eoraken, ton theon 'on ouch 'eoraken pos dunatai agapan?

כ. אִם-יֹאמַר אִישׁ אֶת-אֱלֹהִים אֲנִי אֹהֵב וְהוּא שֹׂנֵא אֶת-אָחִיו כֹּזֵב הוּא כִּי אִם-לֹא יֶאֱהַב אָחִיו אֲשֶׁר רֹאֵהוּ:אֵיכָכָה יוּכַל לֶאֱהֹב אֱלֹהִים אֲשֶׁר לֹא יִרְאֶנּוּ

20. Eem - yo•mar eesh et - Elohim ani o•hev ve•hoo so•ne et - a•chiv ko•zev hoo ki eem - lo ye•e•hav a•chiv asher ro•e•hoo ey•cha•cha yoo•chal le•e•hov Elohim asher lo yir•e•noo?

---

21. And this commandment have we from him, That he who loveth God love his brother also.

21. Καὶ ταύτην τὴν ἐντολὴν ἔχομεν ἀπ᾽ αὐτοῦ, ἵνα ὁ ἀγαπῶν τὸν θεόν, ἀγαπᾷ καὶ τὸν ἀδελφὸν αὐτοῦ.

21. Kai tautein tein entolein echomen ap autou, 'ina 'o agapon ton theon, agapa kai ton adelphon autou.

כא. וְזֹאת הַמִּצְוָה מֵאִתּוֹ בָּאָה אֵלֵינוּ כִּי הָאֹהֵב אֶת-אֱלֹהִים יֶאֱהַב גַּם-אֶת-אָחִיו:

21. Ve•zot ha•mitz•va me•ee•to va•ah e•ley•noo ki ha•o•hev et - Elohim ye•e•hav gam - et - a•chiv.

(1John Chapter 4 End)

1 John, Chapter 5

1. Whosoever believeth that Jesus is the Christ is born of God: and every one that loveth him that begat loveth him also that is begotten of him.

1. Πᾶς ὁ πιστεύων ὅτι Ἰησοῦς ἐστιν ὁ χριστός, ἐκ τοῦ θεοῦ γεγέννηται· καὶ πᾶς ὁ ἀγαπῶν τὸν γεννήσαντα ἀγαπᾷ καὶ τὸν γεγεννημένον ἐξ αὐτοῦ.

1. Pas 'o pisteuon 'oti Yeisous estin 'o christos, ek tou theou gegenneitai. kai pas 'o agapon ton genneisanta agapa kai ton gegenneimenon ex autou.

א. כָּל־הַמַּאֲמִין כִּי יֵשׁוּעַ הוּא הַמָּשִׁיחַ זֶה יֻלַּד מֵאֵת אֱלֹהִים וְהָאֹהֵב אֶת־מוֹלִידוֹ יֶאֱהַב גַּם אֶת־יְלִידָיו:

1. Kol - ha•ma•a•min ki Yeshua hoo ha•Ma•shi•ach ze yoo•lad met Elohim ve•ha•o•hev et - mo•li•do ye•e•hav gam et - ye•li•dav.

---

2. By this we know that we love the children of God, when we love God, and keep his commandments.

2. Ἐν τούτῳ γινώσκομεν ὅτι ἀγαπῶμεν τὰ τέκνα τοῦ θεοῦ, ὅταν τὸν θεὸν ἀγαπῶμεν, καὶ τὰς ἐντολὰς αὐτοῦ τηρῶμεν.

2. En touto ginoskomen 'oti agapomen ta tekna tou theou, 'otan ton theon agapomen, kai tas entolas autou teiromen.

ב. בְּזֹאת נֵדַע כִּי נֶאֱהַב אֶת־יַלְדֵי אֱלֹהִים אִם אֶת־אֱלֹהִים נֶאֱהַב וְאֶת־מִצְוֹתָיו נִשְׁמֹר:

2. Ba•zot ne•da ki ne•e•hav et - yil•dey Elohim eem et - Elohim ne•e•hav ve•et - mitz•vo•tav nish•mor.

---

3. For this is the love of God, that we keep his commandments: and his commandments are not grievous.

3. Αὕτη γάρ ἐστιν ἡ ἀγάπη τοῦ θεοῦ, ἵνα τὰς ἐντολὰς αὐτοῦ τηρῶμεν· καὶ αἱ ἐντολαὶ αὐτοῦ βαρεῖαι οὐκ εἰσίν.

3. 'Autei gar estin 'ei agapei tou theou, 'ina tas entolas autou teiromen. kai 'ai entolai autou bareiai ouk eisin.

:ג. כִּי זֹאת הִיא אַהֲבַת אֱלֹהִים לִשְׁמֹר אֶת-מִצְוֹתָיו וּמִצְוֹתָיו לֹא קָשׁוֹת הֵן מִנְּשֹׂא

3. Ki zot hee a•ha•vat Elohim lish•mor et - mitz•vo•tav oo•mitz•vo•tav lo ka•shot hen min•so.

1 John 5

4. For whatsoever is born of God overcometh the world: and this is the victory that overcometh the world, even our faith.

4. Ὅτι πᾶν τὸ γεγεννημένον ἐκ τοῦ θεοῦ νικᾷ τὸν κόσμον· καὶ αὕτη ἐστὶν ἡ νίκη ἡ νικήσασα τὸν κόσμον, ἡ πίστις ἡμῶν.

4. 'Oti pan to gegenneimenon ek tou theou nika ton kosmon. kai 'autei estin 'ei nikei 'ei nikeisasa ton kosmon, 'ei pistis 'eimon.

:ד. כִּי כָל-הַיִּלּוֹד מֵאֵת אֱלֹהִים יְנַצַּח אֶת-הָעוֹלָם וְהַנִּצָּחוֹן לְנַצֵּחַ אֶת-הָעוֹלָם בְּיַד אֱמוּנָתֵנוּ

4. Ki chol - ha•yi•lod me•et Elohim ye•na•tzach et - ha•o•lam ve•ha•ni•tza•chon le•na•tzach at - ha•o•lam be•yad emoo•na•te•noo.

5. Who is he that overcometh the world, but he that believeth that Jesus is the Son of God?

5. Τίς ἐστιν ὁ νικῶν τὸν κόσμον, εἰ μὴ ὁ πιστεύων ὅτι Ἰησοῦς ἐστιν ὁ υἱὸς τοῦ θεοῦ;

5. Tis estin 'o nikon ton kosmon, ei mei 'o pisteuon 'oti Yeisous estin 'o 'wios tou theou?

:ה. וּמִי הוּא הַמְנַצֵּחַ אֶת-הָעוֹלָם בִּלְתִּי רַק הַמַּאֲמִין כִּי יֵשׁוּעַ הוּא בֶן-הָאֱלֹהִים

5. Oo•mi hoo ham•na•tze`ach et - ha•o•lam bil•tee rak ha•ma•a•min ki Yeshua hoo Ben - ha•Elohim?

6. This is he that came by water and blood, even Jesus Christ; not by water only, but by water and blood. And it is the Spirit that beareth witness, because the Spirit is truth.

6. Οὗτός ἐστιν ὁ ἐλθὼν δι᾽ ὕδατος καὶ αἵματος, Ἰησοῦς χριστός· οὐκ ἐν τῷ ὕδατι μόνον, ἀλλ᾽ ἐν τῷ ὕδατι καὶ τῷ αἵματι. Καὶ τὸ πνεῦμά ἐστιν τὸ μαρτυροῦν, ὅτι τὸ πνεῦμά ἐστιν ἡ ἀλήθεια.

6. 'Outos estin 'o elthon di 'udatos kai 'aimatos, Yeisous christos. ouk en to 'udati monon, all en to 'udati kai to 'aimati. Kai to pneuma estin to marturoun, 'oti to pneuma estin 'ei aleitheya.

ו. וְזֶה הוּא יֵשׁוּעַ הַמָּשִׁיחַ אֲשֶׁר-בָּא אֵלֵינוּ בְּמַיִם וּבְדָם לֹא בְמַיִם לְבַד כִּי אִם-בְּמַיִם וּבְדָם וְהָרוּחַ הוּא מֵעִיד:עָלָיו כִּי הָרוּחַ אֱמֶת הוּא

6. Ve•ze hoo Yeshua ha•Ma•shi•ach asher - ba e•ley•noo be•ma•yim oov•dam lo ve•ma•yim le•vad ki eem - be•ma•yim oov•dam ve•ha•Roo•ach hoo me•eed alav ki ha•Roo•ach emet hoo.

---

1 John 5

7. For there are three that bear record in heaven, the Father, the Word, and the Holy Ghost: and these three are one.

7. Ὅτι τρεῖς εἰσιν οἱ μαρτυροῦντες,

7. 'Oti treis eisin 'oi marturountes,

ז. כִּי שְׁלֹשָׁה הַמְעִידִים בַּשָּׁמַיִם הָאָב וְהַדָּבָר וְרוּחַ הַקֹּדֶשׁ וּשְׁלָשְׁתָּם אֶחָד הֵמָּה:

7. Ki sh`lo•sha ham•ee•dim ba•sha•ma•yim ha•Av ve•ha•Da•var ve•Roo•ach ha•Ko•desh oosh•losh•tam e•chad he•ma.

Rabbinic Jewish Commentary
The genuineness of this text has been called in question by some, because it is lacking in the Syriac version, as it also is in the Arabic and Ethiopic versions; and because the old Latin interpreter has it not; and it is not to be found in many Greek manuscripts.

As to the old Latin interpreter, it is certain it is to be seen in many Latin manuscripts of an early date, and stands in the Vulgate Latin edition of the London Polyglot Bible: and the Latin translation, which bears the name of Jerom, has it.

And as to its being lacking in some Greek manuscripts, as the Alexandrian, and others, it need only be said, that it is to be found in many others; it is in an old British copy, and in the Complutensian edition, the compilers of which made use of various copies; and out of sixteen ancient copies of Robert Stephens's, nine of them had it: and as to its not being cited by some of the ancient fathers, this can be no sufficient proof of the spuriousness of it, since it might be in the original copy, though not in the copies used by them, through the carelessness or unfaithfulness of transcribers; or it might be in their copies, and yet not cited by them, they having Scriptures enough without it, to defend the doctrine of the Trinity, and the divinity of Yeshua: and yet, after all, certain it is, that it is cited by many of them; by Fulgentius (z), in the beginning of the "sixth" century, against the Arians, without any scruple or hesitation; and Jerom, as before observed, has it in his translation made in the latter end of the "fourth" century; and it is cited by Athanasius (a) about the year 350; and before him by Cyprian (b), in the middle, of the "third" century, about the year 250; and is referred to by Tertullian (c) about, the year 200; and which was within a "hundred" years, or little more, of the writing of the epistle. There never was any dispute about it till Erasmus left it out in the, first edition of his translation of the New Testament; and yet he himself, upon the credit of the old British copy before mentioned, put it into another edition of his translation.

This being a proper place, I shall insert the faith of the ancient Jews concerning the doctrine of the Trinity; and the rather, as it agrees with the apostle's doctrine in words and language, as well as in matter. They call the three Persons in the Godhead three degrees: they say (d),

"Yehovah, Elohenu (our God), Yehovah, Deu.6:4; these are the three degrees with respect to this sublime mystery, in the beginning Elohim, or God, created, Gen.1:1."

And these three, they say, though they are distinct, yet are one, as appears by what follows (e):

"Come see the mystery of the word; there are three degrees, and every degree is by itself, yet they are all one, and are bound together in one, and one is not separated from the other."

Again, it is said (f),

"This is the unity of Yehovah the first, Elohenu, Yehovah, lo, all of them are one, and therefore: called one; lo, the three names are as if they were one, and therefore are called one, and they are one; but by the revelation of the Holy Spirit it is made known, and they by the sight of the eye may be known, דתלתא אלין אחד, "that these three are one": and this is the mystery of the voice which is heard; the voice is one, and there are three things, fire, and Spirit, and water, and all of them are one in the mystery of the voice, and they are but one: so here, Yehovah, Elohenu, Yehovah, they are one, the three, גוונין, forms, modes, or things, which are one."

Once more (g),

"There are two, and one is joined unto them, and they are three; and when the three are one, he says to them, these are the two names which Israel heard, Yehovah, Yehovah, and Elohenu is joined unto them, and it is the seal of the ring of truth; and when they are joined as one, they are one in one unity."

And this they illustrate by the three names of the soul of man (h);

"The three powers are all of them one, the soul, spirit, and breath, they are joined as one, and they are one; and all is according to the mode of the sublime mystery," meaning the Trinity.

"Says R. Isaac (i) worthy are the righteous in this world, and in the world to come, for lo, the whole of them is holy, their body is holy, their soul is holy, their Spirit is holy, their breath is holy, holy are these three degrees "according to the form above".--Come see these three degrees cleave together as one, the soul, Spirit, and breath."

The three first Sephirot, or numbers, in the Cabalistic tree, intend the three divine Persons; the first is called the chief *crown*, and first glory, which essence no creature can comprehend (k), and designs the Father, Joh.1:18;

The second is called *wisdom*, and the intelligence illuminating, the crown of the creation, the brightness of equal unity, who is exalted above every head; and he is called, by the Cabalists, the second glory (l); see 1Co.1:24 Heb.1:3. This is the Son of God:

The third is called *understanding* sanctifying, and is the foundation of ancient wisdom, which is called the worker of faith; and he is the parent of faith, and from his power faith flows (m); and this is the Holy Spirit; see 1Pe.1:2. Now they say (n) that these three first numbers are intellectual, and are not מדות, "properties", or "attributes", as the other seven are.

R. Simeon ben Jochai says (o),
"Of the three superior numbers it is said, Psa.62:11, "God hath spoken

once, twice have I heard this"; one and two, lo the superior numbers of whom it is said, one, one, one, three ones, and this is the mystery of Psa.62:11."

Says R. Judah Levi (p),
"Behold the mystery of the numberer, the number, and the numbered; in the bosom of God it is one thing, in the bosom of man three; because he weighs with his understanding, and speaks with his mouth, and writes with his hand."

It was usual with the ancient Jews to introduce Yehovah speaking, or doing anything, in this form, I and my house of judgment; and it is a rule with them, that wherever it is said, "and Yehovah", he and his house or judgment are intended (q); and Jarchi frequently makes use of this phrase to explain texts where a plurality in the Godhead is intended, as Gen_1:26; and it is to be observed, that a house of judgment, or a sanhedrim, among the Jews, never consisted of less than three. They also had used to write the word "Yehovah" with three "Yods", in the form of a triangle,

י י י

as representing the three divine Persons: one of their more modern (r) writers has this observation on the blessing of the priest in Num.6:24, "These three verses begin with a "Yod", in reference to the three "Yods" which we write in the room of the name, (i.e. Yehovah,) for they have respect to the three superior things."

(z) Respons. contr. Arian. obj. 10. & de Trinitate, c. 4. (a) Contr. Arium, p. 109. (b) De Unitate Eccles. p. 255. & in Ep. 73. ad Jubajan, p. 184. (c) Contr. Praxeam, c. 25. (d) Zohar in Gen. fol. 1. 3. (e) Ib. in Lev. fol. 27. 2. (f) Ib. in Exod. fol. 18. 3, 4. (g) Ib. in Numb. fol. 67. 3. (h) Ib. in Exod. fol. 73. 4. (i) Ib. in Lev. fol. 29. 2. (k) Sepher Jetzira, Semit. 1. (l) Sepher Jetzira, Semit. 2. (m) Ib. Semit. 3. (n) R. Menachem apud Rittangel. in Jetzira, p. 193. (o) Tikkune Zohar apud ib. p. 64. (p) Apud ib. p. 38. (q) Zohar in Gen. fol. 48. 4. Jarchi in Gen. xix. 24. Vid. T. Bab. Beracot, fol. 6. 1. & Gloss. in ib. & Sanhedrin, fol. 3. 2. (r) R. Abraham Seba in Tzeror Hammor, fol. 113. 2.

---

8. And there are three that bear witness in earth, the spirit, and the water, and the blood: and these three agree in one.

8. τὸ πνεῦμα, καὶ τὸ ὕδωρ, καὶ τὸ αἷμα· καὶ οἱ τρεῖς εἰς τὸ ἕν εἰσιν.

8. to pneuma, kai to 'udor, kai to 'aima. kai 'oi treis eis to 'en eisin.

ח. וּשְׁלֹשָׁה הַמְּעִידִים בָּאָרֶץ הָרוּחַ וְהַמַּיִם וְהַדָּם וּשְׁלָשְׁתָּם אֵלֶּה לְדָבָר אֶחָד יְעִידוּן:

8. Oosh•lo•sha ham•ee•dim ba•a•retz ha•roo•ach ve•ha•ma•yim ve•ha•dam oosh•losh•tam ele le•da•var e•chad ye•ee•doon.

1 John 5

9. If we receive the witness of men, the witness of God is greater: for this is the witness of God which he hath testified of his Son.

9. Εἰ τὴν μαρτυρίαν τῶν ἀνθρώπων λαμβάνομεν, ἡ μαρτυρία τοῦ θεοῦ μείζων ἐστίν· ὅτι αὕτη ἐστὶν ἡ μαρτυρία τοῦ θεοῦ, ἣν μεμαρτύρηκεν περὶ τοῦ υἱοῦ αὐτοῦ.

9. Ei tein marturian ton anthropon lambanomen, 'ei marturia tou theou meizon estin. 'oti 'autei estin 'ei marturia tou theou, 'ein memartureiken peri tou 'wiou autou.

ט. אִם-עֵדוּת אֲנָשִׁים נְכוֹנָה בְעֵינֵינוּ עֵדוּת אֱלֹהִים גְּדֹלָה מִזֹּאת כִּי זֹאת הִיא עֵדוּת אֱלֹהִים אֲשֶׁר הֵעִיד עַל-בְּנוֹ:

9. Eem - e•doot a•na•shim n`cho•na ve•ey•ne•noo e•doot Elohim ge•do•la mi•zot ki zot hee e•doot Elohim asher he•eed al - B`no.

10. He that believeth on the Son of God hath the witness in himself: he that believeth not God hath made him a liar; because he believeth not the record that God gave of his Son.

10. Ὁ πιστεύων εἰς τὸν υἱὸν τοῦ θεοῦ ἔχει τὴν μαρτυρίαν ἐν αὐτῷ· ὁ μὴ πιστεύων τῷ θεῷ ψεύστην πεποίηκεν αὐτόν, ὅτι οὐ πεπίστευκεν εἰς τὴν μαρτυρίαν, ἣν μεμαρτύρηκεν ὁ θεὸς περὶ τοῦ υἱοῦ αὐτοῦ.

10. 'O pisteuon eis ton 'wion tou theou echei tein marturian en auto. 'o mei pisteuon to theo pseustein pepoieiken auton, 'oti ou pepisteuken eis tein marturian, 'ein memartureiken 'o theos peri tou 'wiou autou.

י. הַמַּאֲמִין בְּבֶן-הָאֱלֹהִים יֶשׁ-לוֹ עֵדוּת בְּנַפְשׁוֹ וַאֲשֶׁר לֹא יַאֲמִין לְדִבְרֵי הָאֱלֹהִים נֹתֵן אֹתוֹ - לְכֹזֵב יַעַן כִּי לֹא: הֶאֱמִין לָעֵדוּת אֲשֶׁר הֵעִיד אֱלֹהִים עַל-בְּנוֹ

10. Ha•ma•a•min be•Ven - ha•Elohim yesh - lo e•doot be•naf•sho va•a•sher lo ya•a•min le•div•rey ha•Elohim no•ten o•to le•cho•zev ya•an ki lo - he•e•min la•e•doot asher he•eed Elohim al - B`no.

---

11. And this is the record, that God hath given to us eternal life, and this life is in his Son.

11. Καὶ αὕτη ἐστὶν ἡ μαρτυρία, ὅτι ζωὴν αἰώνιον ἔδωκεν ἡμῖν ὁ θεός, καὶ αὕτη ἡ ζωὴ ἐν τῷ υἱῷ αὐτοῦ ἐστιν.

11. Kai 'autei estin 'ei marturia, 'oti zoein aionion edoken 'eimin 'o theos, kai 'autei 'ei zoei en to 'wio autou estin.

יא. וְזֹאת הִיא הָעֵדוּת כִּי חַיֵּי עוֹלָם נָתַן לָנוּ אֱלֹהִים וְחַיֵּי עוֹלָם אֵלֶּה בְּיַד בְּנוֹ:

11. Ve•zot hee ha•e•doot ki cha•yey o•lam na•tan la•noo Elohim ve•cha•yey o•lam ele be•yad B`no.

---

1 John 5

12. He that hath the Son hath life; and he that hath not the Son of God hath not life.

12. Ὁ ἔχων τὸν υἱὸν ἔχει τὴν ζωήν· ὁ μὴ ἔχων τὸν υἱὸν τοῦ θεοῦ τὴν ζωὴν οὐκ ἔχει.

12. 'O echon ton 'wion echei tein zoein. 'o mei echon ton 'wion tou theou tein zoein ouk echei.

יב. מִי אֲשֶׁר-לוֹ הַבֵּן יֶשׁ-לוֹ חַיִּים וּמִי אֲשֶׁר אֵין-לוֹ בֵּן-הָאֱלֹהִים אֵין-לוֹ חַיִּים:

12. Mee asher - lo ha•Ben yesh - lo cha•yim oo•mi asher eyn - lo Ben - ha•Elohim eyn – lo cha•yim.

---

13. These things have I written unto you that believe on the name of the Son of God; that ye may know that ye have eternal life, and that ye may believe on the name of the Son of God.

13. Ταῦτα ἔγραψα ὑμῖν τοῖς πιστεύουσιν εἰς τὸ ὄνομα τοῦ υἱοῦ τοῦ θεοῦ, ἵνα εἰδῆτε ὅτι ζωὴν αἰώνιον ἔχετε, καὶ ἵνα πιστεύητε εἰς τὸ ὄνομα τοῦ υἱοῦ τοῦ θεοῦ.

13. Tauta egrapsa 'umin tois pisteuousin eis to onoma tou 'wiou tou theou, 'ina eideite 'oti zoein aionion echete, kai 'ina pisteueite eis to onoma tou 'wiou tou theou.

יג. כָּזֹאת כָּתַבְתִּי אֲלֵיכֶם הַמַּאֲמִינִים בְּשֵׁם בֶּן-הָאֱלֹהִים לְמַעַן תֵּדְעוּן כִּי יֵשׁ לָכֶם חַיֵּי עוֹלָמִים וּלְמַעַן תַּאֲמִינוּ:בְּשֵׁם בֶּן-אֱלֹהִים

13. Ka•zot ka•tav•ti aley•chem ha•ma•a•mi•nim be•shem Ben - ha•Elohim le•ma•an ted•oon ki yesh la•chem cha•yey o•la•mim ool•ma•an ta•a•mi•noo be•shem Ben - Elohim.

---

1 John 5

14. And this is the confidence that we have in him, that, if we ask any thing according to his will, he heareth us:

14. Καὶ αὕτη ἐστὶν ἡ παρρησία ἣν ἔχομεν πρὸς αὐτόν, ὅτι ἐάν τι αἰτώμεθα κατὰ τὸ θέλημα αὐτοῦ, ἀκούει ἡμῶν·

14. Kai 'autei estin 'ei parreisia 'ein echomen pros auton, 'oti ean ti aitometha kata to theleima autou, akouei 'eimon.

:יד. וְכֵן בִּטְחוֹנֵנוּ בוֹ אִם-נִשְׁאַל מִמֶּנּוּ דָבָר כִּרְצוֹנוֹ יִשְׁמַע בְּקוֹלֵנוּ

14. Ve•chen bit•cho•ne•noo vo eem - nish•al mi•me•noo da•var kir•tzo•no yish•ma be•ko•le•noo.

Rabbinic Jewish Commentary

The Jews call תפלה עיוּן, "the consideration", or "attention of prayer" (s), which they explain thus;

"After a man has prayed, he judges in his heart that the holy blessed God will give him his reward, and will do everything needful for him, and will hear his prayer, because he has prayed with intention."

(s) T. Bab. Bava Bathra, fol. 164. 2.

15. And if we know that he hear us, whatsoever we ask, we know that we have the petitions that we desired of him.

15. καὶ ἐὰν οἴδαμεν ὅτι ἀκούει ἡμῶν, ὃ ἐὰν αἰτώμεθα, οἴδαμεν ὅτι ἔχομεν τὰ αἰτήματα ἃ ᾐτήκαμεν παρ' αὐτοῦ.

15. kai ean oidamen 'oti akouei 'eimon, 'o ean aitometha, oidamen 'oti echomen ta aiteimata 'a eiteikamen par autou.

טו. וְאַחֲרֵי אֲשֶׁר יָדַעְנוּ כִּי שֹׁמֵעַ הוּא בְּקוֹלֵנוּ לְכָל-אֲשֶׁר נִשְׁאָלֵהוּ נִבְטַח כִּי מִשְׁאֲלוֹת לִבֵּנוּ יִתֶּן-לָנוּ כַּאֲשֶׁר שָׁאַלְנוּ מִמֶּנּוּ:

15. Ve•a•cha•rey asher ya•da•a•noo ki sho•me•a hoo ve•ko•le•noo le•chol – asher nish•a•le•hoo niv•tach ki mish•a•lot li•be•noo yi•ten - la•noo ka•a•sher sha•al•noo mi•me•noo.

---

1 John 5

16. If any man see his brother sin a sin which is not unto death, he shall ask, and he shall give him life for them that sin not unto death. There is a sin unto death: I do not say that he shall pray for it.

16. Ἐάν τις ἴδῃ τὸν ἀδελφὸν αὐτοῦ ἁμαρτάνοντα ἁμαρτίαν μὴ πρὸς θάνατον, αἰτήσει, καὶ δώσει αὐτῷ ζωὴν τοῖς ἁμαρτάνουσιν μὴ πρὸς θάνατον. Ἔστιν ἁμαρτία πρὸς θάνατον· οὐ περὶ ἐκείνης λέγω ἵνα ἐρωτήσῃ.

16. Ean tis idei ton adelphon autou 'amartanonta 'amartian mei pros thanaton, aiteisei, kai dosei auto zoein tois 'amartanousin mei pros thanaton. Estin 'amartia pros thanaton. ou peri ekeineis lego 'ina eroteisei.

טז. אִישׁ כִּי-יִרְאֶה אֶת-אָחִיו חֹטֵא חֵטְא אֲשֶׁר אֵין בּוֹ מִשְׁפַּט-מָוֶת יַפְגִּיעַ וְיִנָּתֶן-לוֹ חַיִּים כָּל-אֲשֶׁר לֹא חָטְאוּ חֵטְא מָוֶת כִּי-יֵשׁ חֵטְא מָוֶת אֲשֶׁר אֵינֶנִּי אֹמֵר לְהַפְגִּיעַ בַּעֲדוֹ: עוֹד הוּא מֵאֵלֶּה

16. Eesh ki - yir•eh et - a•chiv cha•ta chet asher eyn bo mish•pat - ma•vet yaf•gi•a ve•yi•na•ten - lo cha•yim kol - od hoo me•e•le asher lo chat•oo chet ma•vet ki - yesh chet ma•vet asher ey•ne•ni o•mer le•haf•gia ba•a•do.

Rabbinic Jewish Commentary

Some think there is an allusion to one of the kinds of excommunication among the Jews, called "shammatha", the etymology of which, according to some Jewish writers, is שם מיתה, "there is death" (t).

(t) T. Bab. Moed Katon, fol. 17. 1.

---

1 John 5

17. All unrighteousness is sin: and there is a sin not unto death.

17. Πᾶσα ἀδικία ἁμαρτία ἐστίν· καὶ ἔστιν ἁμαρτία οὐ πρὸς θάνατον.

17. Pasa adikia 'amartia estin. kai estin 'amartia ou pros thanaton.

יז. כָּל־מַעֲשֶׂה אֲשֶׁר לֹא נָכוֹן חֵטְא הוּא וְיֶשׁ־חֵטְא אֵין מָוֶת בּוֹ:

17. Kol - ma•a•se asher lo na•chon chet hoo ve•yesh - chet eyn ma•vet bo.

---

18. We know that whosoever is born of God sinneth not; but he that is begotten of God keepeth himself, and that wicked one toucheth him not.

18. Οἴδαμεν ὅτι πᾶς ὁ γεγεννημένος ἐκ τοῦ θεοῦ οὐχ ἁμαρτάνει· ἀλλ' ὁ γεννηθεὶς ἐκ τοῦ θεοῦ τηρεῖ ἑαυτόν, καὶ ὁ πονηρὸς οὐχ ἅπτεται αὐτοῦ.

18. Oidamen 'oti pas 'o gegenneimenos ek tou theou ouch 'amartanei. all 'o genneitheis ek tou theou teirei 'eauton, kai 'o poneiros ouch 'aptetai autou.

יח. יָדַעְנוּ כִּי כָל־הַיִּלּוֹד מֵאֵת אֱלֹהִים לֹא יֶחֱטָא כִּי הַיִּלּוֹד מֵאֵת אֱלֹהִים יִשְׁמֹר אֶת־נַפְשׁוֹ וְהָרָע לֹא־יִגַּע בּוֹ:

18. Ya•da•a•noo ki chol - ha•yi•lod me•et Elohim lo ye•che•ta ki ha•yi•lod me•et Elohim yish•mor et - naf•sho ve•ha•ra lo - yi•ga bo.

19. And we know that we are of God, and the whole world lieth in wickedness.

19. Οἴδαμεν ὅτι ἐκ τοῦ θεοῦ ἐσμεν, καὶ ὁ κόσμος ὅλος ἐν τῷ πονηρῷ κεῖται.

19. Oidamen 'oti ek tou theou esmen, kai 'o kosmos 'olos en to poneiro keitai.

יט. יָדַעְנוּ כִּי מֵאֵת אֱלֹהִים אֲנַחְנוּ וְכָל־הָעוֹלָם בְּרָע הוּא:

19. Ya•da•a•noo ki me•et Elohim a•nach•noo ve•chol - ha•o•lam be•ra hoo.

Rabbinic Jewish Commentary
This is known, by sad experience, it is easy of observation;

"And cannot comprehend the things that are promised to the righteous in time to come: for this world is full of unrighteousness and infirmities."
(2 Esdras 4:27)

---

1 John 5

20. And we know that the Son of God is come, and hath given us an understanding, that we may know him that is true, and we are in him that is true, even in his Son Jesus Christ. This is the true God, and eternal life.

20. Οἴδαμεν δὲ ὅτι ὁ υἱὸς τοῦ θεοῦ ἥκει, καὶ δέδωκεν ἡμῖν διάνοιαν ἵνα γινώσκωμεν τὸν ἀληθινόν· καὶ ἐσμὲν ἐν τῷ ἀληθινῷ, ἐν τῷ υἱῷ αὐτοῦ Ἰησοῦ χριστῷ. Οὗτός ἐστιν ὁ ἀληθινὸς θεός, καὶ ζωὴ αἰώνιος.

20. Oidamen de 'oti 'o 'wios tou theou 'eikei, kai dedoken 'eimin dyanoyan 'ina ginoskomen ton aleithinon. kai esmen en to aleithino, en to 'wio autou Yeisou christo. 'Outos estin 'o aleithinos theos, kai zoei aionios.

כ. וְיָדַעְנוּ כִּי בֶן־הָאֱלֹהִים בָּא וַיִּתֶּן־לָנוּ לֵב לְהַשְׂכִּיל אֹתוֹ אֲשֶׁר הוּא אָמֵן וְלוֹ אֲנַחְנוּ אֲשֶׁר הוּא אָמֵן הוּא יֵשׁוּעַ הַמָּשִׁיחַ בְּנוֹ זֶה הוּא אֱלֹהֵי אָמֵן וְחַיֵּי־עַד

20. Ve•ya•da•a•noo ki Ven - ha•Elohim ba va•yi•ten - la•noo lev le•has•kil o•to asher hoo amen ve•lo a•nach•noo asher hoo amen hoo Yeshua ha•Ma•shi•ach B`no ze hoo Elohey amen ve•cha•yey - ad.

21. Little children, keep yourselves from idols. Amen.

21. Τεκνία, φυλάξατε ἑαυτὰ ἀπὸ τῶν εἰδώλων. Ἀμήν.

21. Teknia, phulaxate 'eauta apo ton eidolon. Amein.

כא. יְלָדַי הִשָּׁמְרוּ לָכֶם מִן-הָאֱלִילִים אָמֵן:

21. Ye•la•dai hi•sham•roo la•chem min - ha•e•li•lim Amen.

(1John Chapter 5 End)

THE SECOND EPISTLE OF JOHN

2 John, Chapter 1

1. The elder unto the elect lady and her children, whom I love in the truth; and not I only, but also all they that have known the truth;

1. Ὁ πρεσβύτερος ἐκλεκτῇ κυρίᾳ καὶ τοῖς τέκνοις αὐτῆς, οὓς ἐγὼ ἀγαπῶ ἐν ἀληθείᾳ, καὶ οὐκ ἐγὼ μόνος, ἀλλὰ καὶ πάντες οἱ ἐγνωκότες τὴν ἀλήθειαν,

1. 'O presbuteros eklektei kuria kai tois teknois auteis, 'ous ego agapo en aleitheia, kai ouk ego monos, alla kai pantes 'oi egnokotes tein aleitheyan,

א. הַזָּקֵן אֶל-בַּעֲלַת הַבַּיִת הַבְּחִירָה וְאֶל-בָּנֶיהָ אֲשֶׁר אֲנִי אֹהֵב בְּתָם-לֵב וְלֹא-אֲנִי לְבַדִּי כִּי אִם-גַּם כָּל-יֹדְעֵי הָאֱמֶת יֶאֱהָבוּם:

1. Ha•za•ken el - ba•a•lat ha•ba•yit hab•chi•ra ve•el - ba•ne•ha asher ani o•hev be•tom - lev ve•lo - ani le•va•di ki eem - gam kol - yod•ey ha•e•met ye•e•ha•voom.

---

2. For the truth's sake, which dwelleth in us, and shall be with us for ever.

2. διὰ τὴν ἀλήθειαν τὴν μένουσαν ἐν ἡμῖν, καὶ μεθ᾽ ἡμῶν ἔσται εἰς τὸν αἰῶνα·

2. dya tein aleitheyan tein menousan en 'eimin, kai meth 'eimon estai eis ton aiona.

ב. בַּעֲבוּר הָאֱמֶת אֲשֶׁר תִּשְׁכֹּן בְּתוֹכֵנוּ וְגַם-תִּשָּׁאֵר לְעוֹלָם:

2. Ba•a•voor ha•e•met asher tish•kon be•to•che•noo ve•gam - ti•sha•er le•o•lam.

---

3. Grace be with you, mercy, and peace, from God the Father, and from the Lord Jesus Christ, the Son of the Father, in truth and love.

3. ἔσται μεθ᾽ ἡμῶν χάρις, ἔλεος, εἰρήνη παρὰ θεοῦ πατρός, καὶ παρὰ κυρίου Ἰησοῦ χριστοῦ τοῦ υἱοῦ τοῦ πατρός, ἐν ἀληθείᾳ καὶ ἀγάπῃ.

3. estai meth 'eimon charis, eleos, eireinei para theou patros, kai para kuriou Yeisou christou tou 'wiou tou patros, en aleitheia kai agapei.

ג. חֶסֶד רַחֲמִים וְשָׁלוֹם יִתֵּן לָנוּ הָאֱלֹהִים הָאָב וְיֵשׁוּעַ הַמָּשִׁיחַ אֲדוֹנֵינוּ בֶּן-הָאָב מִמְּקוֹר הָאֱמֶת וְהָאַהֲבָה:

3. Che•sed ra•cha•mim ve•sha•lom yi•ten la•noo ha•Elohim ha•Av ve•Yeshua ha•Ma•shi•ach Ado•ney•noo Ben - ha•Av mim•kor ha•e•met ve•ha•a•ha•va.

---

2 John 1

4. I rejoiced greatly that I found of thy children walking in truth, as we have received a commandment from the Father.

4. Ἐχάρην λίαν ὅτι εὕρηκα ἐκ τῶν τέκνων σου περιπατοῦντας ἐν ἀληθείᾳ, καθὼς ἐντολὴν ἐλάβομεν παρὰ τοῦ πατρός.

4. Echarein lian 'oti 'eureika ek ton teknon sou peripatountas en aleitheia, kathos entolein elabomen para tou patros.

ד. שָׂמַחְתִּי עַד-מְאֹד כִּי-מָצָאתִי מִבָּנַיִךְ הֹלְכִים בְּדֶרֶךְ אֱמֶת כְּמִצְוֹת אָבִינוּ אֲשֶׁר קִבַּלְנוּ עָלֵינוּ:

4. Sa•mach•ti ad - me•od ki - ma•tza•ti mi•ba•na•yich hol•chim be•de•rech emet ke•mitz•vot Avi•noo asher ki•bal•noo aley•noo.

---

5. And now I beseech thee, lady, not as though I wrote a new commandment unto thee, but that which we had from the beginning, that we love one another.

5. Καὶ νῦν ἐρωτῶ σε, κυρία, οὐχ ὡς ἐντολὴν γράφων σοι καινήν, ἀλλὰ ἣν εἴχομεν ἀπ᾽ ἀρχῆς, ἵνα ἀγαπῶμεν ἀλλήλους.

5. Kai nun eroto se, kuria, ouch 'os entolein graphon soi kainein, alla 'ein eichomen ap archeis, 'ina agapomen alleilous.

ה. וַאֲנִי שֹׁאֵל כַּיּוֹם מִמֵּךְ בַּעֲלַת הַבַּיִת לֹא כְּכתֹב אֵלַיִךְ מִצְוָה חֲדָשָׁה כִּי אִם-כָּזֹאת אֲשֶׁר עָלֵינוּ מִקֶּדֶם כִּי נֶאֱהַב: אִישׁ אֶת-רֵעֵהוּ

5. Va•a•ni sho•el ka•yom mi•mech ba•a•lat ha•ba•yit lo kich•tov ela•yich mitz•va cha•da•sha ki eem - ka•zot asher aley•noo mi•ke•dem ki ne•e•hav eesh et - re•e•hoo.

---

2 John 1

6. And this is love, that we walk after his commandments. This is the commandment, That, as ye have heard from the beginning, ye should walk in it.

6. Καὶ αὕτη ἐστὶν ἡ ἀγάπη, ἵνα περιπατῶμεν κατὰ τὰς ἐντολὰς αὐτοῦ. Αὕτη ἐστὶν ἡ ἐντολή, καθὼς ἠκούσατε ἀπ᾽ ἀρχῆς, ἵνα ἐν αὐτῇ περιπατῆτε.

6. Kai 'autei estin 'ei agapei, 'ina peripatomen kata tas entolas autou. 'Autei estin 'ei entolei, kathos eikousate ap archeis, 'ina en autei peripateite.

ו. וְזֹאת הִיא אַהֲבָה כִּי נִשְׁמֹר אֶת-מִצְוֹתָיו וְהַמִּצְוָה הִיא אֲשֶׁר תִּשְׁמְרוּן לַעֲשׂתָהּ כַּאֲשֶׁר שְׁמַעְתֶּם מֵרֹאשׁ:

6. Ve•zot hee a•ha•va ki nish•mor et - mitz•vo•tav ve•ha•mitz•va hee asher tish•me•roon la•a•so•ta ka•a•sher sh`ma•a•tem me•rosh.

---

7. For many deceivers are entered into the world, who confess not that Jesus Christ is come in the flesh. This is a deceiver and an antichrist.

7. Ὅτι πολλοὶ πλάνοι εἰσῆλθον εἰς τὸν κόσμον, οἱ μὴ ὁμολογοῦντες Ἰησοῦν χριστὸν ἐρχόμενον ἐν σαρκί. Οὗτός ἐστιν ὁ πλάνος καὶ ὁ ἀντίχριστος.

7. 'Oti polloi planoi eiseilthon eis ton kosmon, 'oi mei 'omologountes Yeisoun christen erchomenon en sarki. 'Outos estin 'o planos kai 'o antichristos.

ז. כִּי מַתְעִים רַבִּים יָצְאוּ בָאָרֶץ אֲשֶׁר לֹא יוֹדוּ כִּי-יֵשׁוּעַ הַמָּשִׁיחַ הוּא הַבָּא בַּבָּשָׂר כָּזֶה הוּא מַתְעֶה וְשׂוֹטֵן: הַמָּשִׁיחַ

7. Ki mat•eem ra•bim yatz•oo va•a•retz asher lo yo•doo ki - Yeshua ha•Ma•shi•ach hoo ha•ba va•ba•sar cha•ze hoo mat•eh ve•so•ten ha•Ma•shi•ach.

---

2 John 1

8. Look to yourselves, that we lose not those things which we have wrought, but that we receive a full reward.

8. Βλέπετε ἑαυτούς, ἵνα μὴ ἀπολέσωμεν ἃ εἰργασάμεθα, ἀλλὰ μισθὸν πλήρη ἀπολάβωμεν.

8. Blepete 'eautous, 'ina mei apolesomen 'a eirgasametha, alla misthon pleirei apolabomen.

ח. הִשָּׁמְרוּ לָכֶם לְבִלְתִּי תְאַבְּדוּן אֶת אֲשֶׁר פָּעָלְנוּ רַק רְאוּ לְהַשִּׂיג מְלֹא שְׂכַרְכֶם:

8. Hi•sham•roo la•chem le•vil•ti te•ab•doon et asher pa•al•noo rak r`oo le•ha•sig me•lo s`char•chem.

Rabbinic Jewish Commentary

The Septuagint interpreters use the same words as here; and which is thus paraphrased by the Targumist,

"YHVH give thee a good recompence in this world for thy good work, and let thy reward be שלימא, "full", or "perfect", in the world to come."

And the Jews (g) often speak of a full reward, and an equal one, to be received hereafter.

(g) Targum on Eccl. i. 3. & ii. 11. & Midrash Kohelet, fol. 72. 4.

---

9. Whosoever transgresseth, and abideth not in the doctrine of Christ, hath not God. He that abideth in the doctrine of Christ, he hath both the Father and the Son.

9. Πᾶς ὁ παραβαίνων καὶ μὴ μένων ἐν τῇ διδαχῇ τοῦ χριστοῦ, θεὸν οὐκ ἔχει· ὁ μένων ἐν τῇ διδαχῇ τοῦ χριστοῦ, οὗτος καὶ τὸν πατέρα καὶ τὸν υἱὸν ἔχει.

9. Pas 'o parabainon kai mei menon en tei didachei tou christou, theon ouk echei. 'o menon en tei didachei tou christou, 'outos kai ton patera kai ton 'wion echei.

ט. כָּל־הָעֹבֵר תּוֹרַת הַמָּשִׁיחַ וְאֵינֶנּוּ חֹסֶה בָּהּ אֵין־לוֹ אֱלֹהִים וְהַחֹסֶה בְּתוֹרַת הַמָּשִׁיחַ יֶשׁ־לוֹ גַּם־הָאָב וְגַם־הַבֵּן:

9. Kol - ha•o•ver to•rat ha•Ma•shi•ach ve•ey•ne•noo cho•se ba eyn - lo Elohim ve•ha•cho•se ve•to•rat ha•Ma•shi•ach yesh - lo gam - ha•Av ve•gam - ha•Ben.

Rabbinic Jewish Commentary

Concerning his office, as the Mediator, surety, and messenger of the covenant, and as the prophet, priest, and King of his church; and concerning his incarnation, obedience, sufferings, death, resurrection from the dead, ascension to heaven, session at God's right hand, intercession for his people, and second coming to judgment; concerning peace and pardon by his blood, atonement by his sacrifice, justification by his righteousness, and complete salvation by him: this is תלמודו של מלך המשיח, "the doctrine of the King Messiah", or the Messiah's Talmud (h), to use the Jewish phrase, and which agrees with John's.

(h) Bereshit Rabba, sect. 98. fol. 85. 3.

---

10. If there come any unto you, and bring not this doctrine, receive him not into your house, neither bid him God speed:

10. Εἴ τις ἔρχεται πρὸς ὑμᾶς, καὶ ταύτην τὴν διδαχὴν οὐ φέρει, μὴ λαμβάνετε αὐτὸν εἰς οἰκίαν, καὶ χαίρειν αὐτῷ μὴ λέγετε·

10. Ei tis erchetai pros 'umas, kai tautein tein didachein ou pherei, mei lambanete auton eis oikian, kai chairein auto mei legete.

י. כִּי־יָבֹא אֲלֵיכֶם אִישׁ וְלֹא יָבִיא אֶת־הַתּוֹרָה הַזֹּאת לֹא תַאַסְפוּ אֹתוֹ הַבַּיְתָה וְלֹא תִשְׁאֲלוּ־לוֹ לְשָׁלוֹם:

10. Ki - ya•vo aley•chem eesh ve•lo ya•vi et - ha•torah ha•zot lo ta•as•foo o•to ha•bai•ta ve•lo tish•a•loo - lo le•sha•lom.

Rabbinic Jewish Commentary

The word used by the Jews was אישר, which signifies "happiness"; so it is said (i), what do they salute with? אישר, "God speed"; which was forbidden to say to one that was ploughing in the seventh year.

(i) T. Hieros. Sheviith, fol. 35. 2. Vid. Taanith. fol. 64. 2.

2 John 1

11. For he that biddeth him God speed is partaker of his evil deeds.

11. ὁ γὰρ λέγων αὐτῷ χαίρειν κοινωνεῖ τοῖς ἔργοις αὐτοῦ τοῖς πονηροῖς.

11. 'o gar legon auto chairein koinonei tois ergois autou tois poneirois.

יא. כִּי הַשֹּׁאֵל לְשָׁלוֹם לוֹ חָבֵר הוּא לוֹ בְּרֹעַ מַעֲשָׂיו:

11. Ki ha•sho•el le•sha•lom lo cha•ver hoo lo be•ro•a ma•a•sav.

12. Having many things to write unto you, I would not write with paper and ink: but I trust to come unto you, and speak face to face, that our joy may be full.

12. Πολλὰ ἔχων ὑμῖν γράφειν, οὐκ ἐβουλήθην διὰ χάρτου καὶ μέλανος· ἀλλὰ ἐλπίζω ἐλθεῖν πρὸς ὑμᾶς, καὶ στόμα πρὸς στόμα λαλῆσαι, ἵνα ἡ χαρὰ ἡμῶν ᾖ πεπληρωμένη.

12. Polla echon 'umin graphein, ouk ebouleithein dya chartou kai melanos. alla elpizo elthein pros 'umas, kai stoma pros stoma laleisai, 'ina 'ei chara 'eimon ei pepleiromenei.

יב. רַבּוֹת לִי לִכְתֹּב אֲלֵיכֶם וְאֵינֶנִּי חָפֵץ לִכְתֹּב בְּסֵפֶר וּבִדְיוֹ כִּי אֲקַוֶּה לָבֹא אֲלֵיכֶם וּלְדַבֵּר פֶּה אֶל־פֶּה לְמַלֹּאת:לִבְּכֶם שִׂמְחָה

12. Ra•bot li lich•tov aley•chem ve•ey•ne•ni cha•fetz lich•tov be•se•fer oo•vid•yo ki a•ka•ve la•vo aley•chem ool•da•ber pe el - pe le•ma•lot lib•chem sim•cha.

13. The children of thy elect sister greet thee. Amen.

13. Ἀσπάζεταί σε τὰ τέκνα τῆς ἀδελφῆς σου τῆς ἐκλεκτῆς. Ἀμήν.

13. Aspazetai se ta tekna teis adelpheis sou teis eklekteis. Amein.

יג. בְּנֵי אֲחוֹתֵךְ הַבְּחִירָה דֹּרְשִׁים לְשָׁלוֹם לָךְ אָמֵן:

13. B`ney a•cho•tech hab•chi•ra dor•shim le•sha•lom lach Amen.

(2John Chapter 1 End)

THE THIRD EPISTLE OF JOHN

3 John, Chapter 1

1. The elder unto the wellbeloved Gaius, whom I love in the truth.

1. Ὁ πρεσβύτερος Γαΐῳ τῷ ἀγαπητῷ, ὃν ἐγὼ ἀγαπῶ ἐν ἀληθείᾳ.

1. 'O presbuteros Gaio to agapeito, 'on ego agapo en aleitheia.

א. הַזָּקֵן אֶל-גָּיוֹס הַיָּקָר אֲשֶׁר אֲנִי אֹהֵב בְּתָם-לֵב:

1. Ha•za•ken el - Gayos ha•ya•kar asher ani o•hev be•tom - lev.

---

2. Beloved, I wish above all things that thou mayest prosper and be in health, even as thy soul prospereth.

2. Ἀγαπητέ, περὶ πάντων εὔχομαί σε εὐοδοῦσθαι καὶ ὑγιαίνειν, καθὼς εὐοδοῦταί σου ἡ ψυχή.

2. Agapeite, peri panton euchomai se euodousthai kai 'ugyainein, kathos euodoutai sou 'ei psuchei.

ב. כָּלְתָה נַפְשִׁי יְדִידִי כִּי תַצְלִיחַ בְּכָל-חֲפָצֶיךָ וְהָיִיתִי שָׁלֵם בַּגּוּף וּבַנֶּפֶשׁ וְאִישׁ מַצְלִיחַ:

2. Kal•ta naf•shi ye•di•di ki tatz•li•ach be•chol - cha•fa•tze•cha ve•ha•yi•ti sha•lem ba•goof oo•va•ne•fesh ve•eesh matz•li•ach.

---

3. For I rejoiced greatly, when the brethren came and testified of the truth that is in thee, even as thou walkest in the truth.

3. Ἐχάρην γὰρ λίαν, ἐρχομένων ἀδελφῶν καὶ μαρτυρούντων σου τῇ ἀληθείᾳ, καθὼς σὺ ἐν ἀληθείᾳ περιπατεῖς.

3. Echarein gar lian, erchomenon adelphon kai marturounton sou tei aleitheia, kathos su en aleitheia peripateis.

ג. כִּי שָׂמַחְתִּי מְאֹד כַּאֲשֶׁר בָּאוּ אַחִים וַיַּגִּידוּ עַל-אֲמִתֶּךָ כִּי בְדֶרֶךְ אֱמֶת אַתָּה הֹלֵךְ:

3. Ki sa•mach•ti me•od ka•a•sher ba•oo a•chim va•ya•gi•doo al - ami•te•cha ki ve•de•rech emet ata ho•lech.

---

3 John 1

4. I have no greater joy than to hear that my children walk in truth.

4. Μειζοτέραν τούτων οὐκ ἔχω χαράν, ἵνα ἀκούω τὰ ἐμὰ τέκνα ἐν ἀληθείᾳ περιπατοῦντα.

4. Meizoteran touton ouk echo charan, 'ina akouo ta ema tekna en aleitheia peripatounta.

ד. אֵין גְּדֹלָה מִשִּׂמְחָתִי כִּי אֶשְׁמַע עַל-בָּנַי אֲשֶׁר בְּדֶרֶךְ אֱמֶת יְהַלֵּכוּן:

4. Eyn ge•do•la mi•sim•cha•ti ki esh•ma al - ba•nai asher be•de•rech emet ye•ha•le•choon.

---

5. Beloved, thou doest faithfully whatsoever thou doest to the brethren, and to strangers;

5. Ἀγαπητέ, πιστὸν ποιεῖς ὃ ἐὰν ἐργάσῃ εἰς τοὺς ἀδελφοὺς καὶ εἰς τοὺς ξένους,

5. Agapeite, piston poieis 'o ean ergasei eis tous adelphous kai eis tous xenous,

ה. בֶּאֱמוּנָה מַעֲשֶׂיךָ יְדִידִי כָּל-אֲשֶׁר אַתָּה עֹשֶׂה עִם-הָאַחִים הָאֹרְחִים:

5. Be•e•moo•na ma•a•se•cha ye•di•di kol - asher ata o•se eem - ha•a•chim ha•or•chim.

---

6. Which have borne witness of thy charity before the church: whom if thou bring forward on their journey after a godly sort, thou shalt do well:

6. οἳ ἐμαρτύρησάν σου τῇ ἀγάπῃ ἐνώπιον ἐκκλησίας· οὓς καλῶς ποιήσεις προπέμψας ἀξίως τοῦ θεοῦ.

6. 'oi emartureisan sou tei agapei enopion ekkleisias. 'ous kalos poieiseis propempsas axios tou theou.

ו. אֲשֶׁר נָתְנוּ עֵדוּתָם עַל-אַהֲבָתְךָ בִּפְנֵי הַקָּהָל וְטוֹב תַּעֲשֶׂה כִּי תַעֲזֹר לָהֶם עַל-דַּרְכֵיהֶם לְרָצוֹן לִפְנֵי אֱלֹהִים:

6. Asher nat•noo e•doo•tam al - aha•vat•cha bif•ney ha•ka•hal ve•tov ta•a•se ki ta•a•zor la•hem al - dar•chey•hem le•ra•tzon lif•ney Elohim.

Rabbinic Jewish Commentary

whom if thou bring forward on their journey; the word here used signifies, to send on before, as in Act.15:3, and is used by the Septuagint in the same sense as here, and in the above places, in Gen.18:16; where it is said, that "Abraham went with them (The 3 YHVHs) to bring them on in the way", לשלחם, "to send them on", or "send them away"; dismiss them, take his leave of them in a friendly and honourable way. The Targums of Onkelos and Jonathan render it, לאלוואיהון, "to accompany them"; and so this Greek word, which seems to answer to the Hebrew phrase, signifies an honourable accompanying, leading forth, and taking leave of friends.

---

3 John 1

7. Because that for his name's sake they went forth, taking nothing of the Gentiles.

7. Ὑπὲρ γὰρ τοῦ ὀνόματος ἐξῆλθον μηδὲν λαμβάνοντες ἀπὸ τῶν ἐθνῶν.

7. 'Uper gar tou onomatos exeilthon meiden lambanontes apo ton ethnon.

ז. כִּי לְמַעַן שְׁמוֹ יָצְאוּ וְלֹא לָקְחוּ מִיַּד הַגּוֹיִם מְאוּמָה:

7. Ki le•ma•an sh`mo ya•tza•oo ve•lo lak•choo mi•yad ha•go•yim me•oo•ma.

---

8. We therefore ought to receive such, that we might be fellowhelpers to the truth.

8. Ἡμεῖς οὖν ὀφείλομεν ἀπολαμβάνειν τοὺς τοιούτους, ἵνα συνεργοὶ γινώμεθα τῇ ἀληθείᾳ.

8. 'Eimeis oun opheilomen apolambanein tous toioutous, 'ina sunergoi ginometha tei aleitheia.

ח: עַל-כֵּן מוּטָל עָלֵינוּ לְקַבֵּל פְּנֵיהֶם וְלִהְיוֹת עֹזְרִים לָאֱמֶת.

8. Al - ken moo•tal aley•noo le•ka•bel p`ney•hem ve•li•hi•yot oz•rim la•e•met.

---

3 John 1

9. I wrote unto the church: but Diotrephes, who loveth to have the preeminence among them, receiveth us not.

9. Ἔγραψα τῇ ἐκκλησίᾳ· ἀλλ᾽ ὁ φιλοπρωτεύων αὐτῶν Διοτρεφὴς οὐκ ἐπιδέχεται ἡμᾶς.

9. Egrapsa tei ekkleisia. all 'o philoproteuon auton Diotrepheis ouk epidechetai 'eimas.

ט: וַאֲנִי כָתַבְתִּי אֶל-הָעֵדָה אַךְ דִיוֹטְרִיפַס הֶחָפֵץ לִהְיוֹת לְרֹאשׁ לָהֶם לֹא קִבֵּל אֹתָנוּ.

9. Va•a•ni cha•tav•ti el - ha•e•da ach Diyot•rifas he•cha•fetz li•hee•yot le•rosh la•hem lo ki•bel o•ta•noo.

---

10. Wherefore, if I come, I will remember his deeds which he doeth, prating against us with malicious words: and not content therewith, neither doth he himself receive the brethren, and forbiddeth them that would, and casteth them out of the church.

10. Διὰ τοῦτο, ἐὰν ἔλθω, ὑπομνήσω αὐτοῦ τὰ ἔργα ἃ ποιεῖ, λόγοις πονηροῖς φλυαρῶν ἡμᾶς· καὶ μὴ ἀρκούμενος ἐπὶ τούτοις, οὔτε αὐτὸς ἐπιδέχεται τοὺς ἀδελφούς, καὶ τοὺς βουλομένους κωλύει, καὶ ἐκ τῆς ἐκκλησίας ἐκβάλλει.

10. Dya touto, ean eltho, 'upomneiso autou ta erga 'a poiei, logois poneirois phluaron 'eimas. Kai mei arkoumenos epi toutois, oute autos epidechetai tous adelphous, kai tous boulomenous koluei, kai ek teis ekkleisias ekballei.

י. עַל-כֵּן בְּבֹאִי אֶפְקֹד עָלָיו מַעֲשָׂיו אֲשֶׁר עָשָׂה כִּי דִבֶּר סָרָה עָלֵינוּ וְאֵין דַּי לוֹ בָזֹאת כִּי אַף-לֹא יֹאבֶה לְקַבֵּל אֶת-הָאַחִים וְאֶת-אֵלֶּה אֲשֶׁר יֹאבוּ יַעְצָר-בָּם וּמִתּוֹךְ הַקָּהָל יְגָרְשֵׁם

10. Al - ken be•vo•ee ef•kod alav ma•a•sav asher asa ki di•ber sa•ra aley•noo ve•eyn dai lo va•zot ki af - lo yo•ve le•ka•bel et - ha•a•chim ve•et - ele asher yo•voo ya•a•tzar - bam oo•mi•toch ha•ka•hal ye•gar•shem.

Rabbinic Jewish Commentary
The phrase seems to be taken from the Jews, who expressed their excommunication, or putting out of the synagogue, by a casting out, John 9:34.

---

3 John 1

11. Beloved, follow not that which is evil, but that which is good. He that doeth good is of God: but he that doeth evil hath not seen God.

11. Ἀγαπητέ, μὴ μιμοῦ τὸ κακόν, ἀλλὰ τὸ ἀγαθόν. Ὁ ἀγαθοποιῶν ἐκ τοῦ θεοῦ ἐστίν· ὁ κακοποιῶν οὐχ ἑώρακεν τὸν θεόν.

11. Agapeite, mei mimou to kakon, alla to agathon. 'O agathopoion ek tou theou estin. 'o kakopoion ouch 'eoraken ton theon.

יא. יְדִידִי אַל-תֵּלֵךְ בְּעִקְבוֹת הָרָעִים כִּי אִם-בְּעִקְבוֹת הַטּוֹבִים הָעֹשֶׂה טוֹב הוּא מֵאֵת אֱלֹהִים - וְהַפֹּעֵל רָע אֶת:אֱלֹהִים לֹא רָאָה

11. Ye•di•di al - te•lech be•eek•vot ha•ra•eem ki eem - be•eek•vot ha•to•vim ha•o•se tov hoo me•et Elohim ve•ha•po•el ra et - Elohim lo ra•ah.

---

12. Demetrius hath good report of all men, and of the truth itself: yea, and we also bear record; and ye know that our record is true.

12. Δημητρίῳ μεμαρτύρηται ὑπὸ πάντων, καὶ ὑπ᾽ αὐτῆς τῆς ἀληθείας· καὶ ἡμεῖς δὲ μαρτυροῦμεν, καὶ οἴδατε ὅτι ἡ μαρτυρία ἡμῶν ἀληθής ἐστιν.

12. Deimeitrio memartureitai 'upo panton, kai 'up auteis teis aleitheias. kai 'eimeis de marturoumen, kai oidate 'oti 'ei marturia 'eimon aleitheis estin.

יב. וְדִימֶטְרִיּוֹס יֶשׁ-לוֹ עֵדוּת מִכָּל-הָעֵדָה גַּם-מִפִּי הָאֱמֶת וְגַם-מִפִּינוּ וְיָדַעְתָּ כִּי עֵדוּתֵנוּ נֶאֱמָנָה:

12. Ve•Dimet•riyos yesh - lo e•doot mi•kol - ha•e•da gam - mi•pi ha•e•met ve•gam - mi•pi•noo ve•ya•da•a•ta ki e•doo•te•noo ne•e•ma•na.

---

13. I had many things to write, but I will not with ink and pen write unto thee:

13. Πολλὰ εἶχον γράφειν, ἀλλ᾽ οὐ θέλω διὰ μέλανος καὶ καλάμου σοι γράψαι·

13. Polla eichon graphein, all ou thelo dya melanos kai kalamou soi grapsai.

יג. רַבּוֹת לִי לִכְתֹּב אֵלֶיךָ אַךְ לֹא חָפַצְתִּי לִכְתֹּב בְּעֵט וּבִדְיוֹ:

13. Ra•bot li lich•tov e•le•cha ach lo cha•fatz•ti lich•tov be•et oo•vid•yo.

---

3 John 1

14. But I trust I shall shortly see thee, and we shall speak face to face. Peace be to thee. Our friends salute thee. Greet the friends by name.

14. ἐλπίζω δὲ εὐθέως ἰδεῖν σε, καὶ στόμα πρὸς στόμα λαλήσομεν. Εἰρήνη σοι. Ἀσπάζονταί σε οἱ φίλοι. Ἀσπάζου τοὺς φίλους κατ᾽ ὄνομα.

14. elpizo de eutheos idein se, kai stoma pros stoma laleisomen. Eireinei soi. Aspazontai se 'oi philoi. Aspazou tous philous kat onoma.

יד. אֲבָל אֲקַוֶּה לִרְאוֹתְךָ בִּמְהֵרָה וּפֶה אֶל-פֶּה נְדַבֵּרָה שָׁלוֹם לָךְ רֵעֵינוּ פֹּקְדִים לִשְׁלוֹמְךָ וְאֶת-רֵעֵינוּ אַתָּה תִפְקֹד:לְשָׁלוֹם לְאִישׁ אִישׁ בִּשְׁמוֹ:

14. Aval a•ka•ve lir•ot•cha vim•he•ra oo•fe el - pe n`da•be•ra sha•lom lach re•ey•noo pok•dim lish•lom•cha ve•et - re•ey•noo eet•cha tif•kod le•sha•lom le•eesh eesh bish•mo.

(3John Chapter 1 End)

THE GENERAL EPISTLE OF JUDE

Jude, Chapter 1

1. Jude, the servant of Jesus Christ, and brother of James, to them that are sanctified by God the Father, and preserved in Jesus Christ, and called:

1. Ἰούδας Ἰησοῦ χριστοῦ δοῦλος, ἀδελφὸς δὲ Ἰακώβου, τοῖς ἐν θεῷ πατρὶ ἡγιασμένοις, καὶ Ἰησοῦ χριστῷ τετηρημένοις, κλητοῖς·

1. Youdas Yeisou christou doulos, adelphos de Yakobou, tois en theo patri 'eigyasmenois, kai Yeisou christo teteireimenois, kleitois.

א. יְהוּדָה עֶבֶד יֵשׁוּעַ הַמָּשִׁיחַ וַאֲחִי יַעֲקֹב אֶל-הַמְקֹרָאִים בֵּאלֹהִים הָאָב וַאֲהוּבִים נְצוּרֵי יֵשׁוּעַ הַמָּשִׁיחַ:

1. Ye•hoo•da eved Yeshua ha•Ma•shi•ach va•a•chi Yaakov el - ham•ko•ra•eem be•Elohim ha•Av va•a•hoo•vim n`tzoo•rey Yeshua ha•Ma•shi•ach.

Rabbinic Jewish Commentary
The author of this epistle is the same who is elsewhere called Judas, Luk.6:16, who was one of the twelve apostles of Yeshua, whose name was also Lebbaeus, and whose surname was Thaddaeus, Mat.10:3, the name is the same with Judah, Gen.29:35, which comes from a word that signifies "to praise" or "confess"; and in the Rabbinical dialect is called יודא, "Yuda" (e), as here. He styles himself "the servant of Jesus Christ."

(e) Yalkut Simeoni, par. 2. fol. 50. 2.

---

2. Mercy unto you, and peace, and love, be multiplied.

2. ἔλεος ὑμῖν καὶ εἰρήνη καὶ ἀγάπη πληθυνθείη.

2. eleos 'umin kai eireinei kai agapei pleithuntheiei.

ב. חֶסֶד שָׁלוֹם וְאַהֲבָה יִרְבְּיוּן לָכֶם:

2. Che•sed sha•lom ve•a•ha•va yir•be•yoon la•chem.

3. Beloved, when I gave all diligence to write unto you of the common salvation, it was needful for me to write unto you, and exhort you that ye should earnestly contend for the faith which was once delivered unto the saints.

3. Ἀγαπητοί, πᾶσαν σπουδὴν ποιούμενος γράφειν ὑμῖν περὶ τῆς κοινῆς σωτηρίας, ἀνάγκην ἔσχον γράψαι ὑμῖν, παρακαλῶν ἐπαγωνίζεσθαι τῇ ἅπαξ παραδοθείσῃ τοῖς ἁγίοις πίστει.

3. Agapeitoi, pasan spoudein poioumenos graphein 'umin peri teis koineis soteirias, anagkein eschon grapsai 'umin, parakalon epagonizesthai tei 'apax paradotheisei tois 'agiois pistei.

ג. יְדִידִים כַּאֲשֶׁר חַשְׁתִּי לִכְתֹּב אֲלֵיכֶם לְפִי כָל־חֶפְצִי עַל־דְּבַר יְשׁוּעַת כֻּלָּנוּ הֱצִיקַתְנִי רוּחִי לְעוֹרֵר אֶתְכֶם:בְּמִכְתָּבִי לְהִלָּחֵם מִלְחֲמוֹת אֱמוּנָה אֲשֶׁר נִתְּנָה כָלִיל לַקְּדֹשִׁים

3. Ye•di•dim ka•a•sher chash•ti lich•tov aley•chem le•fi chol - chef•tzi al - de•var ye•shoo•at koo•la•noo he•tzi•kat•ni roo•chi le•o•rer et•chem be•mich•ta•vi le•hi•la•chem mil•cha•mot e•moo•na asher nit•na cha•lil la•k`do•shim.

Jude 1

4. For there are certain men crept in unawares, who were before of old ordained to this condemnation, ungodly men, turning the grace of our God into lasciviousness, and denying the only Lord God, and our Lord Jesus Christ.

4. Παρεισέδυσαν γάρ τινες ἄνθρωποι, οἱ πάλαι προγεγραμμένοι εἰς τοῦτο τὸ κρίμα, ἀσεβεῖς, τὴν τοῦ θεοῦ ἡμῶν χάριν μετατιθέντες εἰς ἀσέλγειαν, καὶ τὸν μόνον δεσπότην θεὸν καὶ κύριον ἡμῶν Ἰησοῦν χριστὸν ἀρνούμενοι.

4. Pareisedusan gar tines anthropoi, 'oi palai progegrammenoi eis touto to krima, asebeis, tein tou theou 'eimon charin metatithentes eis aselgeyan, kai ton monon despotein theon kai kurion 'eimon Yeisoun christon arnoumenoi.

ד. כִּי בָאוּ אֲנָשִׁים בְּהִתְגַּנְּבָם בְּתוֹכֵנוּ אֲשֶׁר נִקְבוּ מֵאָז לִנְפֹּל בִּידֵי הַמִּשְׁפָּט אַנְשֵׁי רֶשַׁע הַהֹפְכִים חֶסֶד אֱלֹהֵינוּ
לִדְבַר בְּלִיַּעַל וּבַאֲדֹנֵינוּ מֹשֵׁל יָחִיד יֵשׁוּעַ הַמָּשִׁיחַ יְכַחֲשׁוּ לֵאמֹר לֹא הוּא:

4. Ki va•oo a•na•shim be•hit•gan•vam be•to•che•noo asher nik•voo me•az lin•pol biy•dey ha•mish•pat an•shey re•sha ha•hof•chim che•sed Elohey•noo lid•var b`li•ya•al oo•va•Ado•ney•noo mo•shel ya•chid Yeshua ha•Ma•shi•ach ye•cha•cha•shoo le•mor lo hoo.

Jude 1

5. I will therefore put you in remembrance, though ye once knew this, how that the Lord, having saved the people out of the land of Egypt, afterward destroyed them that believed not.

5. Ὑπομνῆσαι δὲ ὑμᾶς βούλομαι, εἰδότας ὑμᾶς ἅπαξ τοῦτο, ὅτι ὁ κύριος, λαὸν ἐκ γῆς Αἰγύπτου σώσας, τὸ δεύτερον τοὺς μὴ πιστεύσαντας ἀπώλεσεν.

5. 'Upomneisai de 'umas boulomai, eidotas 'umas 'apax touto, 'oti 'o kurios, laon ek geis Aiguptou sosas, to deuteron tous mei pisteusantas apolesen.

ה. וַאֲנִי לְהַעֲלוֹת עַל-לִבְּכֶם חָפַצְתִּי אֶת-כָּל-אֲשֶׁר יְדַעְתֶּם מֵאָז כִּי אַחֲרֵי אֲשֶׁר גָּאַל יְהוָה אֶת-הָעָם מֵאֶרֶץ מִצְרַיִם הֶאֱבִיד אֹתָם אֲשֶׁר לֹא הֶאֱמִינוּ

5. Va•a•ni le•ha•a•lot al - lib•chem cha•fatz•ti et - kol - asher ye•da•a•tem me•az ki a•cha•rey asher ga•al Adonai et - ha•am me•e•retz Mitz•ra•yim he•e•vid o•tam asher lo he•e•mi•noo.

Rabbinic Jewish Commentary

The Alexandrian copy, and some others, the Vulgate Latin, and Ethiopic versions, instead of "the Lord", read "Jesus": and yet, though they were a special people, and notwithstanding this wonderful deliverance, and great salvation.

6. And the angels which kept not their first estate, but left their own habitation, he hath reserved in everlasting chains under darkness unto the judgment of the great day.

6. Ἀγγέλους τε τοὺς μὴ τηρήσαντας τὴν ἑαυτῶν ἀρχήν, ἀλλὰ ἀπολιπόντας τὸ ἴδιον οἰκητήριον, εἰς κρίσιν μεγάλης ἡμέρας δεσμοῖς ἀϊδίοις ὑπὸ ζόφον τετήρηκεν.

6. Angelous te tous mei teireisantas tein 'eauton archein, alla apolipontas to idion oikeiteirion, eis krisin megaleis 'eimeras desmois aidiois 'upo zophon teteireiken.

ו. וְאֶת-הַמַּלְאָכִים אֲשֶׁר לֹא-שָׁמְרוּ אֶת-מֶמְשַׁלְתָּם וְאֶת-מְעוֹנָם עָזְבוּ הִסְגִּירָם לְגֵיא צַלְמָוֶת אֲסוּרִים בְּמוֹסֵרוֹת:לְמִשְׁפַּט הַיּוֹם הַגָּדוֹל

6. Ve•et - ha•mal•a•chim asher lo - sham•roo et - mem•shal•tam ve•et - me•o•nam a•za•voo his•gi•ram le•gey tzal•ma•vet asoo•rim be•mo•se•rot le•mish•pat ha•yom ha•ga•dol.

Rabbinic Jewish Commentary

They were cast out of, is by the Jews frequently called the place of their holiness, or their holy place (g), The judgment of the great day is the same the Jews call יום דינא רבא, "the day of the great judgment" (h). This account shows the imprisoned state of the wicked.

(g) Yalkut Simeoni, par. 2. fol. 73. 1. Pirke Eliezer, c. 14, 22, 27. Zohar in Gen. fol. 28. 1. & Sepher Bahir in ib. fol. 27. 3. (h) Targum in Psal. l. 3.

Jude 1

7. Even as Sodom and Gomorrha, and the cities about them in like manner, giving themselves over to fornication, and going after strange flesh, are set forth for an example, suffering the vengeance of eternal fire.

7. Ὡς Σόδομα καὶ Γόμορρα, καὶ αἱ περὶ αὐτὰς πόλεις, τὸν ὅμοιον τούτοις τρόπον ἐκπορνεύσασαι, καὶ ἀπελθοῦσαι ὀπίσω σαρκὸς ἑτέρας, πρόκεινται δεῖγμα, πυρὸς αἰωνίου δίκην ὑπέχουσαι.

7. 'Os Sodoma kai Gomorra, kai 'ai peri autas poleis, ton 'omoion toutois tropon ekporneusasai, kai apelthousai opiso sarkos 'eteras, prokeintai deigma, puros aioniou dikein 'upechousai.

ז. כִּסְדֹם וַעֲמֹרָה וְהֶעָרִים מִסָּבִיב אֲשֶׁר זָנוּ בְדַרְכֵי זְנוּנֵיהֶם וְאֶל-בְּשַׂר זָרִים עָגְבוּ גַמְנוּ לְנִקְמַת אֵשׁ עוֹלָם לִהְיוֹת:לְאוֹת דֵּרָאוֹן לְכָל-בָּשָׂר

7. Ki•S`dom va•A•mo•ra ve•he•a•rim mi•sa•viv asher za•noo ve•dar•chey z`noo•ney•hem ve•el - be•sar za•rim a•ga•voo nim•noo le•nik•mat esh o•lam li•hee•yot le•ot de•ra•on le•chol - ba•sar.

Rabbinic Jewish Commentary
The Jews make this to be a sin of theirs, and so interpret Gen.6:2 (i).

suffering the vengeance of eternal fire; which may be understood of that fire, with which those cities, and the inhabitants of it, were consumed; which, Philo the (k) Jew says, burnt till his time, and must be burning when Jude wrote this epistle.

The Jews, who say (l), that "The men of Sodom have no part or portion in the world to come, and shall not see the world to come. "

And says R. Isaac,
"Sodom is judged בדינא דגיהנם, "with the judgment of Gehennim" (m).

(i) Pirke Eliezer, c. 22. Joseph. Antiqu. l. 1. c. 3. sect. 1. (k) De Abrahamo, p. 370. (l) T. Hieros. Sanhedrin, fol. 29. 3. (m) Zohar in Gen. fol. 71. 3.

Jude 1

8. Likewise also these filthy dreamers defile the flesh, despise dominion, and speak evil of dignities.

8. Ὁμοίως μέντοι καὶ οὗτοι ἐνυπνιαζόμενοι σάρκα μὲν μιαίνουσιν, κυριότητα δὲ ἀθετοῦσιν, δόξας δὲ βλασφημοῦσιν.

8. 'Omoios mentoi kai 'outoi enupnyazomenoi sarka men myainousin, kurioteita de athetousin, doxas de blaspheimousin.

ח. וּכְמוֹ-כֵן חֹלְמֵי הַחֲלֹמוֹת הָאֵלֶּה אֲשֶׁר יְטַמְּאוּ אֶת-הַבָּשָׂר יִבְזוּ שָׂרֵי מַעְלָה וְעַל-אַדִּירִים יַבִּיעוּ עָתָק:

8. Ooch•mo - chen chol•mey ha•cha•lo•mot ha•e•le asher ye•tam•oo et - ha•ba•sar yiv•zoo sa•rey ma•a•la ve•al - adi•rim ya•bi•oo atak.

Rabbinic Jewish Commentary
Which may be literally understood, either of the Jewish doctors, who pretended to be interpreters of dreams, as R. Akiba, R. Lazar, and others (n); or of the false teachers in the apostle's time, and of their filthy dreams, and nocturnal pollutions in them; which sense the Arabic and Ethiopic versions confirm; the former rendering the words thus, "so these retiring in the time of sleep, defile their own flesh"; and the latter thus, "and likewise these, who in their own sleep, pollute their own flesh"; as also of their pretensions to divine assistance and intelligence by dreams; and likewise

may be figuratively understood of them; for false doctrines are dreams, and the teachers of them dreamers, Jer.23:25.

(n) T. Hieros. Maaser Sheni, fol. 55. 2, 3.

Jude 1

9. Yet Michael the archangel, when contending with the devil he disputed about the body of Moses, durst not bring against him a railing accusation, but said, The Lord rebuke thee.

9. Ὁ δὲ Μιχαὴλ ὁ ἀρχάγγελος, ὅτε τῷ διαβόλῳ διακρινόμενος διελέγετο περὶ τοῦ Μωϋσέως σώματος, οὐκ ἐτόλμησεν κρίσιν ἐπενεγκεῖν βλασφημίας, ἀλλ᾽ εἶπεν, Ἐπιτιμήσαι σοι κύριος.

9. 'O de Michaeil 'o archangelos, 'ote to dyabolo dyakrinomenos dielegeto peri tou Mouseos somatos, ouk etolmeisen krisin epenegkein blaspheimias, all eipen, Epitimeisai soi kurios.

ט. וּמִיכָאֵל הַשַּׂר הַגָּדוֹל לַמַּלְאָכִים כַּאֲשֶׁר רָב עִם-הַשָּׂטָן בִּמְרִיבַת גְּוִיַּת מֹשֶׁה לֹא-הֵבִיא עָתָק עָלָיו בַּמִּשְׁפָּט רַק:אָמַר יִגְעַר יְהֹוָה בָּךְ

9. Oo•Michael ha•sar ha•ga•dol la•mal•a•chim ka•a•sher rav eem - ha•Satan bim•ri•vat ge•vi•yat Moshe lo - hi•bia atak alav ba•mish•pat rak amar yig•ar Adonai bach.

Rabbinic Jewish Commentary

So Philo the Jew (o) calls the most ancient Word, firstborn of God, the archangel; Uriel is called the archangel in this passage from the Apocrypha:

"And unto these things Uriel the archangel gave them answer, and said, Even when the number of seeds is filled in you: for he hath weighed the world in the balance." (2 Esdras 4:36)

Some have thought that he took it out of an apocryphal book, called "the Ascension of Moses", as Origen (p), which is not likely; others, that he had it by tradition, by which means the Apostle Paul came by the names of the Egyptian magicians Jannes and Jambres; and some passages are referred to in some of their writings (q), as having some traces of this dispute; but it is best of all to understand it of the Torah of Moses, which is sometimes called Moses himself, Joh.5:45; and so the body of Moses, or the body of his laws, the system of them; just as we call a system of laws, and of divinity, such an one's body of laws, and such an one's body of divinity: and this agrees with the language of the Jews, who say (r), of statutes, service, purification, &c. that they are גופי התורה, "the bodies of the Torah"; and so of Mishnic treatises, as those which concern the offerings of turtle doves, and the purification of menstruous women, that they are גופי, "the bodies" of the traditions (s), that is, the sum and substance of them: so the decalogue is said (t) to be "the body of the Shema", or "Hear, O Israel", Deu.6:4, so Clemens of Alexandria (u) says, that there are some who consider the body of the Scriptures, the words and names, as if they were, το σωμα του μωσεως, "the body of Moses" (w). Now the Torah of Moses was restored in the time of Joshua the high priest, by Ezra and Nehemiah. Joshua breaks some of these laws, and is charged by Satan as guilty, who contended and insisted upon it that he should suffer for it; so that this dispute or contention might be said to be about the body of Moses, that is, the body of Moses's Torah, which Joshua had broken.

(o) De Confus. Ling. p. 341. & quis. rer. divin. Haeres. p. 509. (p) περι αρχων, l. 3. c. 2. (q) Debarim Rabba, fol. 245. 3, 4. Abot R. Nathan, c. 12. fol. 4. 2, 3. Petirath Mosis, fol. 57. 1. &. c. (r) Misn. Chagiga, c. 1. sect. 8. (s) Pirke Abot, c. 3. sect. 18. (t) T. Hieros. Beracot, fol. 6. 2. (u) Stromat, l. 6. p. 680. (w) Vid. Chion. Disput. Theolog. par. 1. & 2. De Corpore Mosis, sub Praesidio Trigland. Lugd. Batav. 1697.

---

10. But these speak evil of those things which they know not: but what they know naturally, as brute beasts, in those things they corrupt themselves.

10. Οὗτοι δὲ ὅσα μὲν οὐκ οἴδασιν βλασφημοῦσιν· ὅσα δὲ φυσικῶς, ὡς τὰ ἄλογα ζῷα, ἐπίστανται, ἐν τούτοις φθείρονται.

10. 'Outoi de 'osa men ouk oidasin blaspheimousin. 'osa de phusikos, 'os ta aloga zoa, epistantai, en toutois phtheirontai.

י. אַךְ אֵלֶּה יֵחָרְפוּן וְלֹא יֵדְעוּן מָה וּמַה אֲשֶׁר יֵדְעוּן כְּחֹק־בְּהֵמוֹת אֵין תְּבוּנָה בָם יֵהָפֵךְ עֲלֵיהֶם לְמַשְׁחִית:

10. Ach ele ye•char•foon ve•lo yed•oon ma oo•ma asher yed•oon ke•chok - be•he•mot eyn te•voo•na vam ye•ha•fech aley•hem le•mash•chit.

Jude 1

11. Woe unto them! for they have gone in the way of Cain, and ran greedily after the error of Balaam for reward, and perished in the gainsaying of Core.

11. Οὐαὶ αὐτοῖς· ὅτι τῇ ὁδῷ τοῦ Κάϊν ἐπορεύθησαν, καὶ τῇ πλάνῃ τοῦ Βαλαὰμ μισθοῦ ἐξεχύθησαν, καὶ τῇ ἀντιλογίᾳ τοῦ Κόρε ἀπώλοντο.

11. Ouai autois. 'oti tei 'odo tou Kain eporeutheisan, kai tei planei tou Bala'am misthou exechutheisan, kai tei antilogia tou Kore apolonto.

יא. אוֹי לָהֶם כִּי-הָלְכוּ בְדֶרֶךְ קַיִן וְעֵקֶב שָׂכָר נִדְחוּ בְתַעְתֻּעֵי בִלְעָם וּכְמוֹ בְמֶרֶד קֹרַח יָרְדוּ לַאֲבַדּוֹן:

11. Oy la•hem ki - hal•choo ve•de•rech Ka•yin ve•e•kev sa•char nid•choo ve•ta•a•too•ey Vil•am ooch•mo ve•me•red ko•rach yar•doo la•a•va•don.

Rabbinic Jewish Commentary

Balaam is one of the four private persons, who, according to the Jews, shall have no part or portion in the world to come (w),

So the Jews (z) say of Korah and his company, that they shall never ascend, or rise up and stand in judgment, and that they shall have no part or portion in the world to come (a)

(w) Misn. Sanhedrin, c. 11. sect. 2. (z) Misn. Sanhedrin, ib. sect. 2. Yalkut Simeoni, par. 2. fol. 89. 3. Sanhed. ib. sect. 3. (a) T. Hieros. Sanhedrin, fol. 29. 3.

---

12. These are spots in your feasts of charity, when they feast with you, feeding themselves without fear: clouds they are without water, carried about of winds; trees whose fruit withereth, without fruit, twice dead, plucked up by the roots;

12. Οὗτοί εἰσιν ἐν ταῖς ἀγάπαις ὑμῶν σπιλάδες, συνευωχούμενοι, ἀφόβως ἑαυτοὺς ποιμαίνοντες· νεφέλαι ἄνυδροι, ὑπὸ ἀνέμων παραφερόμεναι· δένδρα φθινοπωρινά, ἄκαρπα, δὶς ἀποθανόντα, ἐκριζωθέντα·

12. 'Outoi eisin en tais agapais 'umon spilades, suneuochoumenoi, aphobos 'eautous poimainontes. nephelai anudroi, 'upo anemon parapheromenai. dendra phthinoporina, akarpa, dis apothanonta, ekrizothenta.

יב. צוּרֵי מִכְשׁל הֵם עַל-דַּרְכֵיכֶם יֹשְׁבִים אִתְּכֶם לְמִשְׁתֶּה אֹהֲבִים וְרֹעִים אֶת-נַפְשָׁם וְלֹא יֵדְעוּ בֹשֶׁת נְשִׂיאִים:נִדָּפִים בָּרוּחַ וְאֵין גֶּשֶׁם עֵצִים בְּשַׁלֶּכֶת וְאֵין פְּרִי וּמֵתִים מָוֶת מִשְׁנֶה מֵעָנָף וְעַד-שֹׁרֶשׁ

12. Tzoo•rey mich•shol hem al - dar•chey•chem yosh•vim eet•chem le•mish•te a•ha•vim ve•ro•eem et - naf•sham ve•lo yed•oo vo•shet n`si•eem ni•da•fim ba•roo•ach ve•eyn ge•shem etzim be•sha•le•chet ve•eyn p`ri oo•me•tim ma•vet mish•ne me•a•naf ve•ad - sho•resh.

Rabbinic Jewish Commentary

Or "love". The Jews speak סעודתיה דמהימנותא, "of a feast of faith" (b).

Homer calls (d) those διθανεις, "twice dead", that go to grave alive: or rather the sense is this, that they were dying because of sin by nature, as all men are, and again having made a profession of religion, were now become dead to that profession; and so were twice dead, once as they were born, and a second time as they had apostatized.

(b) Zohar in Exod. fol. 36. 3, 4. (d) Odyss. l. 12. lin. 22.

---

13. Raging waves of the sea, foaming out their own shame; wandering stars, to whom is reserved the blackness of darkness for ever.

13. κύματα ἄγρια θαλάσσης, ἐπαφρίζοντα τὰς ἑαυτῶν αἰσχύνας· ἀστέρες πλανῆται, οἷς ὁ ζόφος τοῦ σκότους εἰς αἰῶνα τετήρηται.

13. kumata agrya thalasseis, epaphrizonta tas 'eauton aischunas. asteres planeitai, 'ois 'o zophos tou skotous eis aiona teteireitai.

יג. גַּלִּים סֹעֲרִים בַּיָּם אֲשֶׁר יִגְרְשׁוּ רֶפֶשׁ בָּשְׁתָּם כּוֹכָבִים נְבֻכִים אֲשֶׁר-חֹשֶׁךְ אֲפֵלָה צָפוּן לָהֶם עֲדֵי-עַד:

13. Ga•lim so•a•rim ba•yam asher yig•re•shoo re•fesh bosh•tam ko•cha•vim n`voo•chim asher - cho•shech a•fe•la tza•foon la•hem adey - ad.

Rabbinic Jewish Commentary
The Jews represent as a place of darkness: the Egyptian darkness, they say, came from the darkness of Sheol, and in Sheol the wicked will be covered with darkness; the darkness which was upon the face of the deep, at the creation, they interpret of Sheol (e),

(e) Shemot Rabba, sect. 14. fol. 99. 3.

Jude 1

14. And Enoch also, the seventh from Adam, prophesied of these, saying, Behold, the Lord cometh with ten thousands of his saints,

14. Προεφήτευσεν δὲ καὶ τούτοις ἕβδομος ἀπὸ ᾿Αδὰμ ῾Ενώχ, λέγων, ᾿Ιδού, ἦλθεν κύριος ἐν ἁγίαις μυριάσιν αὐτοῦ,

14. Proepheiteusen de kai toutois 'ebdomos apo Adam 'Enoch, legon, Ydou, eilthen kurios en 'agiais muryasin autou,

:יד. וְעַל-אֵלֶּה נִבָּא שְׁבִיעִי לְאָדָם הוּא חֲנוֹךְ לֵאמֹר הִנֵּה בָא יְהוָֹה וְרִבְבוֹת קְדֹשָׁיו עִמּוֹ

14. Ve•al - ele ni•ba sh`vi•ee le•A•dam hoo Cha•noch le•mor hee•ne va Adonai ve•ri•ve•vot ke•do•shav ee•mo.

Rabbinic Jewish Commentary
This was Enoch the son of Jared; his name signifies one "instructed", or "trained up"; as he doubtless was by his father, in the true religion, in the nurture and admonition of YHVH; and was one that had much communion with God; he walked with him, Gen.5:18; he is said to be "the seventh from Adam"; not the seventh man from him that was born into the world, for there were no doubt thousands born before him; but he was, as the Jews express it (f), דור שביעי, "the seventh generation" from him; and they have an observation (g), that all sevenths are always beloved by God; the seventh in lands, and the seventh in generations; Adam, Seth, Enos, Cainan, Mahalaleel, Jared, Enoch, as it is written, Gen.5:24;

The Arabic writers (h) call him Edris the prophet; and the Jews say (i), that he was in a higher degree than Moses or Elias; they also call (k) him Metatron, the great scribe, a name which they sometimes give to the Messenger that went before the children of Israel in the wilderness: that Enoch wrote a prophecy, and left it behind him in writing, does not appear from hence, or elsewhere; the Jews, in some of their writings, do cite and make mention of the book of Enoch; and there is a fragment now which bears his name, but is a spurious piece, and has nothing like this prophecy in it; wherefore Jude took this not from a book called the "Apocalypse of Enoch", but from tradition; this prophecy being handed down from age to age; and was in full credit with the Jews, and therefore the apostle very appropriately produces it; or rather he had it by divine inspiration.

(f) Juchasin, fol. 5. 2. Ganz. Tzemach David, par. 1. fol. 5. 1. (g) Vajikra Rabba, sect. 29. fol. 170. 1. (h) Elmacinus, p. 10. apud Hottinger. Smegma Orient. p. 240. (i) Shalshelet Hakabala, fol. 1, 2. (k) Targum Jon. in Gen. v. 24. Tosephot in T. Bab. Yebamot, fol. 16. 2. Juchasin, fol. 5. 2.

Jude 1

15. To execute judgment upon all, and to convince all that are ungodly among them of all their ungodly deeds which they have ungodly committed, and of all their hard speeches which ungodly sinners have spoken against him.

15. ποιῆσαι κρίσιν κατὰ πάντων, καὶ ἐλέγξαι πάντας τοὺς ἀσεβεῖς αὐτῶν περὶ πάντων τῶν ἔργων ἀσεβείας αὐτῶν ὧν ἠσέβησαν, καὶ περὶ πάντων τῶν σκληρῶν ὧν ἐλάλησαν κατ᾽ αὐτοῦ ἁμαρτωλοὶ ἀσεβεῖς.

15. poieisai krisin kata panton, kai elegxai pantas tous asebeis auton peri panton ton ergon asebeias auton 'on eisebeisan, kai peri panton ton skleiron 'on elaleisan kat autou 'amartoloi asebeis.

טו. לַעֲשׂוֹת מִשְׁפָּט בַּכֹּל וּלְהוֹכִיחַ אֶת-בְּנֵי בְלִיַּעַל כֻּלָּם עַל-כָּל-אֲשֶׁר הִרְשִׁיעוּ לַעֲשׂוֹת וְעַל-כָּל-דִּבְרֵי עָתָק אֲשֶׁר דִּבְּרוּ-בוֹ הַחַטָּאִים בְּזָדוֹן

15. La•a•sot mish•pat ba•kol ool•ho•chi•ach et - b`ney ve•li•ya•al koo•lam al - kol – asher hir•shi•oo la•a•sot ve•al - kol - div•rey atak asher dib•roo - vo ha•cha•ta•eem be•za•don.

---

16. These are murmurers, complainers, walking after their own lusts; and their mouth speaketh great swelling words, having men's persons in admiration because of advantage.

16. Οὗτοί εἰσιν γογγυσταί, μεμψίμοιροι, κατὰ τὰς ἐπιθυμίας αὐτῶν πορευόμενοι, καὶ τὸ στόμα αὐτῶν λαλεῖ ὑπέρογκα, θαυμάζοντες πρόσωπα ὠφελείας χάριν.

16. 'Outoi eisin gongustai, mempsimoiroi, kata tas epithumias auton poreuomenoi, kai to stoma auton lalei 'uperogka, thaumazontes prosopa opheleias charin.

טז. אֵלֶּה הֵם רֹגְנִים מִתְלוֹנְנִים וְזֹנִים אַחֲרֵי תַאֲוָתָם אֲשֶׁר פִּיהֶם יְדַבֵּר גְּדֹלוֹת וְנֹשְׂאִים פָּנִים בְּעַד בֶּצַע כָּסֶף:

16. Ele hem rog•nim mit•lo•ne•nim ve•zo•nim a•cha•rey ta•a•va•tam asher pi•hem ye•da•ber ge•do•lot ve•nos•eem pa•nim be•ad be•tza ka•sef.

---

17. But, beloved, remember ye the words which were spoken before of the apostles of our Lord Jesus Christ;

17. Ὑμεῖς δέ, ἀγαπητοί, μνήσθητε τῶν ῥημάτων τῶν προειρημένων ὑπὸ τῶν ἀποστόλων τοῦ κυρίου ἡμῶν Ἰησοῦ χριστοῦ·

17. 'Umeis de, agapeitoi, mneistheite ton 'reimaton ton proeireimenon 'upo ton apostolon tou kuriou 'eimon Yeisou christou.

יז. אַךְ אַתֶּם יְדִידִים זִכְרוּ אֶת-הַדְּבָרִים אֲשֶׁר נֶאֶמְרוּ מִקֶּדֶם בְּיַד שְׁלִיחֵי אֲדֹנֵינוּ יֵשׁוּעַ הַמָּשִׁיחַ:

17. Ach atem ye•di•dim zich•roo et - ha•d`va•rim asher ne•em•roo mi•ke•dem be•yad sh`li•chey Ado•ney•noo Yeshua ha•Ma•shi•ach.

---

18. How that they told you there should be mockers in the last time, who should walk after their own ungodly lusts.

18. ὅτι ἔλεγον ὑμῖν, ὅτι ἐν ἐσχάτῳ χρόνῳ ἔσονται ἐμπαῖκται, κατὰ τὰς ἑαυτῶν ἐπιθυμίας πορευόμενοι τῶν ἀσεβειῶν.

18. 'oti elegon 'umin, 'oti en eschato chrono esontai empaiktai, kata tas 'eauton epithumias poreuomenoi ton asebeion.

יח. אֵת אֲשֶׁר הִגִּידוּ לָכֶם כִּי בְאַחֲרִית הַיָּמִים יָקוּמוּ לֵצִים רֹדְפֵי תַאֲוָה לְפִי שְׁרִירוּת לִבָּם הָרָע:

18. Et asher hi•gi•doo la•chem ki ve•a•cha•rit ha•ya•mim ya•koo•moo le•tzim rod•fey ta•a•va le•fi sh`ri•root li•bam ha•ra.

Jude 1

19. These be they who separate themselves, sensual, having not the Spirit.

19. Οὗτοί εἰσιν οἱ ἀποδιορίζοντες, ψυχικοί, πνεῦμα μὴ ἔχοντες.

19. 'Outoi eisin 'oi apodiorizontes, psuchikoi, pneuma mei echontes.

יט: הֲלֹא הֵם הַמִּתְגֹּדְדִים לִגְדוּדִים בַּעֲלֵי-נֶפֶשׁ וְרוּחַ אֵין בָּהֶם

19. Ha•lo hem ha•mit•go•de•dim lig•doo•dim ba•a•ley - ne•fesh ve•Roo•ach eyn ba•hem.

---

20. But ye, beloved, building up yourselves on your most holy faith, praying in the Holy Ghost,

20. Ὑμεῖς δέ, ἀγαπητοί, τῇ ἁγιωτάτῃ ὑμῶν πίστει ἐποικοδομοῦντες ἑαυτούς, ἐν πνεύματι ἁγίῳ προσευχόμενοι,

20. 'Umeis de, agapeitoi, tei 'agiotatei 'umon pistei epoikodomountes 'eautous, en pneumatic 'agio proseuchomenoi,

כ. וְאַתֶּם יְדִידִים הָשִׁיבוּ נַפְשְׁכֶם בָּאֱמוּנָה אֲשֶׁר הִיא לָכֶם קֹדֶשׁ קֳדָשִׁים וְחַלּוּ פְנֵי-אֵל בְּרוּחַ הַקֹּדֶשׁ:

20. Ve•a•tem ye•di•dim ha•shi•voo naf•she•chem ba•e•moo•na asher hee la•chem ko•desh ko•da•shim ve•cha•loo f`ney - El be•Roo•ach ha•Ko•desh.

Rabbinic Jewish Commentary

This phrase, מהימנותא קדישא, "holy faith", is in use with the Jews (k)

(k) Zohar in Gen. fol. 47. 4.

---

21. Keep yourselves in the love of God, looking for the mercy of our Lord Jesus Christ unto eternal life.

21. ἑαυτοὺς ἐν ἀγάπῃ θεοῦ τηρήσατε, προσδεχόμενοι τὸ ἔλεος τοῦ κυρίου ἡμῶν Ἰησοῦ χριστοῦ εἰς ζωὴν αἰώνιον.

21. 'eautous en agapei theou teireisate, prosdechomenoi to eleos tou kuriou 'eimon Yeisou christou eis zoein aionion.

כא. וּשְׁמַרְתֶּם אֶת־נַפְשֹׁתֵיכֶם בְּאַהֲבַת אֱלֹהִים וּלְחַסְדֵי יֵשׁוּעַ הַמָּשִׁיחַ אֲדֹנֵינוּ חַכֵּה תְחַכּוּ לְחַיֵּי עוֹלָם:

21. Oosh•mar•tem et - naf•sho•tey•chem be•a•ha•vat Elohim ool•chas•dey Yeshua ha•Ma•shi•ach Ado•ney•noo cha•ke te•cha•koo le•cha•yey o•lam.

---

22. And of some have compassion, making a difference:

22. Καὶ οὓς μὲν ἐλεεῖτε διακρινόμενοι·

22. Kai 'ous men eleeite dyakrinomenoi.

כב. וְאֶת־אֵלֶּה הַמִּתְגּוֹדְדִים יַסֵּר תְּיַסְּרוּן אֹתָם בְּחֶמְלָה:

22. Ve•et - ele ha•mit•go•de•dim ya•sor te•yas•roon o•tam be•chem•la.

---

23. And others save with fear, pulling them out of the fire; hating even the garment spotted by the flesh.

23. οὓς δὲ ἐν φόβῳ σῴζετε, ἐκ πυρὸς ἁρπάζοντες, μισοῦντες καὶ τὸν ἀπὸ τῆς σαρκὸς ἐσπιλωμένον χιτῶνα.

23. 'ous de en phobo sozete, ek puros 'arpazontes, misountes kai ton apo teis sarkos espilomenon chitona.

כג. וְיֵשׁ מֵהֶם אֲשֶׁר תּוֹשִׁיעוּן וְהִצַּלְתֶּם אֹתָם כְּאוּד מִשְּׂרֵפָה וְיֵשׁ מֵהֶם אֲשֶׁר עֲלֵיהֶם תָּחוּסוּ בִּרְעָדָה וְשַׁקֵּץ תְּשַׁקְּצוּ:אֶת־הַבֶּגֶד הַמְגֹאָל מִזּוֹב הַבָּשָׂר

23. Ve•yesh me•hem asher to•shi•oon ve•ha•tzi•loo o•tam ke•ood mis•re•fa ve•yesh me•hem asher aley•hem ta•cho•soo vir•a•da ve•sha•ketz te•shak•tzoo et - ha•be•ged ham•go•al mi•zov ha•ba•sar.

Rabbinic Jewish Commentary

The allusion is not to garments defiled by profluvious persons, or menstruous women, as some think, but to garments spotted with nocturnal pollutions, or through unnatural lusts, which these persons were addicted to (l). It was reckoned very dishonourable for religious persons, in the time of divine service, or on a sabbath day, to have on a garment spotted with any thing; if a priest's garments were spotted, and he performed service in them, that service was not right (m); and if a disciple of a wise man had any grease on his garments (on a sabbath day), he was guilty of death (n).

(l) Vid. Sueton. in Vita Neronis, c. 28. (m) T. Bab. Pesachim, fol. 65. 2. & Zebachim, fol. 18. 2. & Piske Tosephot in Yoma, art. 9. & Maimon. Cele Hamikdash, c. 8. sect. 4. (n) T. Bab. Sabbat, fol. 114. 1.

---

24. Now unto him that is able to keep you from falling, and to present you faultless before the presence of his glory with exceeding joy,

24. Τῷ δὲ δυναμένῳ φυλάξαι αὐτοὺς ἀπταίστους, καὶ στῆσαι κατενώπιον τῆς δόξης αὐτοῦ ἀμώμους ἐν ἀγαλλιάσει,

24. To de dunameno phulaxai autous aptaistous, kai steisai katenopion teis doxeis autou amomous en agallyasei,

כד. וְהוּא אֲשֶׁר בְּיָדוֹ לִשְׁמָרְכֶם מִמּוֹקֵשׁ וְלַהֲקִימְכֶם תְּמִימִים לִפְנֵי כְבוֹדוֹ בְּשָׂשׂוֹן רָב:

24. Ve•hoo asher be•ya•do lish•mor•chem mi•mo•kesh ve•la•ha•kim•chem t`mi•mim lif•ney che•vo•do be•sa•son rav.

---

25. To the only wise God our Saviour, be glory and majesty, dominion and power, both now and ever. Amen.

25. μόνῳ σοφῷ θεῷ σωτῆρι ἡμῶν, δόξα καὶ μεγαλωσύνη, κράτος καὶ ἐξουσία, καὶ νῦν καὶ εἰς πάντας τοὺς αἰῶνας. Ἀμήν.

25. mono sopho theo soteiri 'eimon, doxa kai megalosunei, kratos kai exousia, kai nun kai eis pantas tous aionas. Amein.

כה. אֱלֹהִים הֶחָכָם לְבַדּוֹ הַגֹּאֵל אֹתָנוּ לוֹ הַכָּבוֹד וְהַגְּדֻלָּה וְהַמֶּמְשָׁלָה וְהַגְּבוּרָה מֵעוֹלָם וְעַד-עַתָּה וְעַד-עוֹלְמֵי-עוֹלָמִים אָמֵן

25. Elo•him he•cha•cham le•va•do ha•Go•el o•ta•noo lo ha•ka•vod ve•hag•doo•la ve•ha•mem•sha•la ve•hag•voo•ra me•o•lam ve•ad - ata ve•ad - ol•mey o•la•mim Amen

End of Epistles

JEWISH INTERTESTAMENTAL AND EARLY RABBINIC LITERATURE: BIBLIOGRAPHY

Berenbaum, Michael and Fred Skolnik. *Encyclopaedia Judaica.* 2d ed.; 22 vols.;
Detroit: Macmillan Reference USA and Keter, 2007. Also available electronically from Gale Virtual Reference Library. A fine substantial update of the original and still useful 16 volume *Encyclopaedia Judaica* (Jerusalem: Keter, 1972), which originally received several annual yearbooks and two update volumes (1982, 1994) and was issued on CD-ROM in 1997. Both editions were preceded by an incomplete 10-volume German set entitled *Encyclopaedia Judaica: das Judentum in Geschichte und Gegenwart* (Berlin:) Eschkol, 1928–34), which only covered articles beginning with the letters A–L but often contained longer treatments than the 1972 version. [*EncJud*]

Collins, John J. and Daniel C. Harlow, eds. *The Eerdmans Dictionary of Early Judaism.*
Grand Rapids/Cambridge: Eerdmans, 2010. Brief survey articles introduce "Early Judaism" (pp. 1–290) followed by dictionary entries on more specific matters (pp. 291–1360). Quite helpful. [*EDEJ*]

Evans, Craig A. and Stanley E. Porter, eds. *Dictionary of New Testament Background.*
Downers Grove/Leicester: InterVarsity, 2000. Helpful articles with good bibliography. [*DNTB*]

Freedman, David Noel, ed. *The Anchor Bible Dictionary.* 6 vols. New York:
Doubleday, 1992. Includes useful introductory articles on much intertestamental literature. Also on CD-ROM. [*ABD*]

Neusner, Jacob and Alan J. Avery-Peck, eds. *Encyclopaedia of Midrash: Biblical Interpretation in Formative Judaism.* 2 vols. Leiden: Brill, 2005.

---

* David Chapman is associate professor of New Testament and Archaeology at Covenant Theological Seminary, 12330 Conway Road, St. Louis, MO 63141. Andreas Köstenberger is research professor of New Testament and Biblical Theology at Southeastern Baptist Theological Seminary, 120 S. Wingate St., Wake Forest, NC 27587.

1 *JETS* 43 (2000): 577–618. Appreciation is again expressed to friends at Tyndale House and to the university and seminary libraries in Cambridge, Tübingen, and St. Louis.

Neusner, Jacob, Alan J. Avery-Peck, and William Scott Green, eds. *The Encyclopedia of Judaism.* 5 vols. New York: Continuum/Leiden: Brill, 1999–2003. 3 initial volumes plus 2 supplement volumes. Some articles with bibliography.

Neusner, Jacob and William Scott Green, eds. *Dictionary of Judaism in the Biblical Period: 450 B.C.E. to 600 C.E.* 2 vols. New York: Macmillan, 1996; repr. Peabody, MA: Hendrickson, 1999. Relatively short articles with no bibliography.

Singer, Isidore et al., eds. *The Jewish Encyclopedia.* 12 vols. New York/London: Funk & Wagnalls, 1901–1906. Older than *EncJud* but often has fuller articles. Available online at http://www.jewishencyclopedia.com and scanned images at http://archive.org. [*JE*]

Werblowsky, R. J. Zwi and Geoffrey Wigoder, eds. *The Oxford Dictionary of the Jewish Religion.* Oxford: OUP, 1997. Competent (but very concise) articles with limited bibliography. [*ODJR*]

1.2 Works Containing Surveys of Jewish Literature

Davies, W. D., Louis Finkelstein, John Sturdy, William Horbury, and Steven T. Katz, eds. *Cambridge History of Judaism.* 4 vols. Cambridge: CUP, 1984–2006. [*CHJ*]

Evans, Craig A. *Ancient Texts for New Testament Studies: A Guide to the Background Literature.* Peabody, MA: Hendrickson, 2005. Update of his *Noncanonical Writings and New Testament Interpretation* (1992).

Grabbe, Lester L. *A History of the Jews and Judaism in the Second Temple Period.* 4 vols. London/New York: T & T Clark, 2004–. Emphasis on discussing sources, with a tendency toward some skepticism and late dating.

Haase, Wolfgang, ed. *Aufstieg und Niedergang der Römischen Welt* II.19.1–2, II.20.1–2, and II.21.1–2. Berlin: de Gruyter, 1979–1987. [*ANRW*]

Helyer, Larry R. *Exploring Jewish Literature of the Second Temple Period: A Guide for New Testament Students.* Downers Grove: InterVarsity, 2002.

Kraft, Robert A. and George W. E. Nickelsburg, eds. *Early Judaism and Its Modern Interpreters.* Philadelphia: Fortress/Atlanta: Scholars, 1986.

McNamara, Martin. *Intertestamental Literature*. Wilmington, DE: Michael Glazier, 1983.

Mulder, Martin Jan, ed. *Mikra: Text, Translation, Reading and Interpretation of the Hebrew Bible in Ancient Judaism and Early Christianity*. CRINT 2.1. Assen/ Maastricht: Van Gorcum, 1988; Philadelphia: Fortress, 1988. Very helpful, especially on LXX, Targums, and other versions of the OT. [*Mikra*]

Neusner, Jacob, ed. *Judaism in Late Antiquity, Vol. 1: The Literary and Archaeological Sources*. Handbuch der Orientalistik 1.16; Leiden: Brill, 1995. [*JLA*]

Nickelsburg, George W. E. *Jewish Literature Between the Bible and the Mishnah*. 2d ed. Philadelphia: Fortress, 2005. Principally discusses DSS, Apocrypha, and Pseudepigrapha. With CD-ROM of entire book, plus images and a study guide. [Nickelsburg, *Jewish Literature*]

Sæbø, Magne, ed. *Hebrew Bible, Old Testament: The History of its Interpretation: Vol. 1 From the beginnings to the Middle Ages (until 1300)*. Part 1: Antiquity. Göttingen: Vandenhoeck & Ruprecht, 1996.

Schürer, Emil. *The History of the Jewish People in the Age of Jesus Christ (175 B.C.– A.D. 135)*. Ed. Geza Vermes et al. Rev. English ed. 3 vols. in 4. Edinburgh: T & T Clark, 1973–1987. For decades the standard work in the field (not to be confused with Hendrickson's reprinted translation of the original German edition, which is now out of date). [*HJPAJC*]

Stemberger, Günter. *Introduction to the Talmud and Midrash*. Fine work; see full bibliography under Rabbinic Literature. [Stemberger, *Introduction*]

Stone, Michael E., ed. *Jewish Writings of the Second Temple Period*. CRINT 2.2. Assen: Van Gorcum; Philadelphia: Fortress, 1984. See further CRINT volumes under Rabbinic Literature below. [*JWSTP*]

VanderKam, James C. *An Introduction to Early Judaism*. Grand Rapids: Eerdmans, 2001. Esp. pp. 53–173. 1.3 Sourcebooks

Barrett, C. K. *The New Testament Background: Writings from Ancient Greece and the Roman Empire that Illuminate Christian Origins*. San Francisco: Harper, 1987. A more recent edition (with different subtitle) of this classic sourcebook.

Chilton, Bruce D., gen. ed. *A Comparative Handbook to the Gospel of Mark: Comparisons with Pseudepigrapha, the Qumran Scrolls, and Rabbinic Literature*. The New Testament Gospels in their Judaic Contexts 1. Leiden: Brill, 2009. After each pericope in Mark, an extensive array of comparable Jewish sources are quoted and followed by a very brief commentary on those sources. De Lange, Nicholas. *Apocrypha: Jewish Literature of the Hellenistic Age.* New York: Viking, 1978. Excerpts Apocrypha and Pseudepigrapha writings in thematic categories.

Elwell, Walter A. and Robert W. Yarbrough, eds. *Readings from the First-Century World: Primary Sources for New Testament Study.* Encountering Biblical Studies. Grand Rapids: Baker, 1998. Intended for college students. First part topical, second part quotes illuminating Jewish and Graeco-Roman sources in NT canonical order.

Feldman, Louis H. and Meyer Reinhold. *Jewish Life and Thought among Greeks and Romans: Primary Readings.* Minneapolis: Augsburg Fortress, 1996; Edinburgh: T & T Clark, 1996. A fine collection covering a broad array of key topics.

Fitzmyer, Joseph A. and Daniel J. Harrington. *A Manual of Palestinian Aramaic Texts (second century B.C.–second century A.D.).* BibOr 34. Rome: Biblical Institute Press, 1978. Highly significant collection of texts with translations and introduction (includes many Qumran documents).

Ginzberg, Louis. *The Legends of the Jews.* 7 vols. Jewish Publication Society of America, 1909–1938; repr. Baltimore: Johns Hopkins, 1998. Puts in narrative form the various rabbinic and apocryphal stories about OT heroes. Vols. 5–6 notes; vol. 7 index. Currently available online at several sites, though often without the vital endnotes and index volumes (see http://archive.org).

Hayward, C. T. R. *The Jewish Temple: A non-biblical sourcebook.* London/New York: Routledge, 1996.

Instone-Brewer, David. *Traditions of the Rabbis from the Era of the New Testament.* Grand Rapid: Eerdmans, 2004–. Following the order of Mishnah, excerpts selections from the Mishnah and the Tosefta that likely predate the year 70; provides text, translation, and brief commentary. [*TRENT*]

Nadich, Judah. *The Legends of the Rabbis.* 2 vols. London: Jason Aronson, 1994. Puts in narrative form the various rabbinic stories about early rabbis (Neusner's *Rabbinic Traditions about the Pharisees* is to be preferred for academic use).

Neusner, Jacob. *The Rabbinic Traditions about the Pharisees before 70.* 3 vols. Leiden: Brill, 1971. An enormously helpful source book with commentary
and summary analysis (reprints from University of South Florida and Wipf & Stock).
Runesson, Anders, Donald D. Binder, and Birger Olsson. *The Ancient Synagogue
from its Origin to 200 C.E.: A Source Book.* Leiden: Brill, 2008; paperback Brill, 2010. Ancient literary sources, inscriptions and archaeological remains for both the land of Israel and the diaspora. Also includes a chapter on Jewish temples outside Jerusalem (e.g. Leontopolis).
Schiffman, Lawrence H. *Texts and Traditions: A Source Reader for the Study of Second Temple and Rabbinic Judaism.* Hoboken: Ktav, 1998. Complements his
history of early Judaism.
Williams, Margaret H, ed. *The Jews among the Greeks and Romans: A Diasporan
Sourcebook.* Baltimore: Johns Hopkins, 1998; London: Duckworth, 1998.
1.4 Bibliography Anderson, Norman Elliott. *Tools for Bibliographical and Backgrounds Research on the New Testament.* 2d ed. South Hamilton, MA: Gordon-Conwell Theological Seminary, 1987.
Delling, Gerhard. *Bibliographie zur Jüdisch-Hellenistischen und Intertestamentarischen Literatur 1900–1965.* TU 106. Berlin: Akademie, 1969.
Noll, Stephen F. *The Intertestamental Period: A Study Guide.* Inter-Varsity Christian Fellowship of the United States of America, 1985.
1.5 General Computer Programs and English-based Websites (current at time of writing)
Dinur Center for Research in Jewish History of the Hebrew University in Jerusalem (useful web links under "Second Temple and Talmudic Era"): http://jewishhistory.huji.ac.il/links/texts.htm.
Early Jewish Writings by Peter Kirby (links to older translations and introductions
to Apocrypha, Pseudepigrapha, Philo and Josephus; currently many broken links but still useful): http://www.earlyjewishwritings.com.
4 Enoch: The Online Encyclopedia of Second Temple Judaism and Christian Origins by the Enoch Seminar (edited wiki that is still in process):
http://www.4enoch.org.
HebrewBooks.org (classical Hebrew books for free download; website in Hebrew): http://www.hebrewbooks.org.
Internet Sacred Text Archive (older English translations of Jewish literature; primarily rabbinic works): http://www.sacred-texts.com/jud/index.htm.

The Judaic Classics Deluxe Edition: CD-ROM from Davka Software available for
Windows or Mac (see below under Rabbinic Literature).
New Testament Gateway (Judaica page): http://www.ntgateway.com/toolsandresources/ judaica.
Paleojudaica by James R. Davila: http://paleojudaica.blogspot.com.
Princeton University Library Jewish Studies Resources: http://www.princeton.edu/~pressman/jewsub.htm.
Resource Pages for Biblical Studies by Torrey Seland: http://torreys.org/bible.
Second Temple Synagogues by Donald Binder (includes links to introductions,
texts, and photos of early Jewish literature): http://www.pohick.org/sts.
Thesaurus Linguae Graecae (searchable database of ancient Greek literature
available on CD-ROM or via internet subscription; includes Philo, Josephus,
Greek Apocrypha and Pseudepigrapha). Website at http://www.tlg.uci.edu.
Tyndale House (helpful links for Biblical Studies): http://www.tyndale.cam.ac.uk/index.php?page=weblinks.
Virtual Religion Index: http://virtualreligion.net/vri/judaic.html (note links to
Biblical Studies and to Jewish Studies).

2. Old Testament Versions 2.1 Greek Versions 2.1.1 Septuagint

The term "Septuagint" is properly attributed only to the Old Greek
Pentateuch (translated c. 3d cent. BC), but common parlance labels the whole Old
Greek OT and Apocrypha as Septuagint (LXX). It represents the earliest extant
Jewish Greek translation of the OT. However, since the major LXX manuscripts
are Christian, the possibility exists of Christian tampering with the text at some
junctures. While earlier studies frequently focused on the LXX as a textual witness
to its Hebrew *Vorlage*, a significant trend now also views its renderings of
the OT as representing traditional Jewish interpretation. The individual
biblical books vary in their translation style, indicating a plurality of
translators and dates of translation.
Some biblical books differ significantly from the MT (e.g. Jeremiah, Samuel), and

others exist in double recensions (e.g. Judges, Esther, Tobit, Daniel). The LXX also provides a major witness to all the Apocrypha except 4 Ezra [= 2 Esdras] (including also 3–4 Maccabees and Odes, which are not in the traditional English Apocrypha). *Bibliographies*: Dogniez, Cécile. *Bibliography of the Septuagint (1970–1993).* VTSup 60. Leiden: Brill, 1995. Brock, Sebastian P., Charles T. Fritsch, and Sidney Jellicoe. *A Classified Bibliography of the Septuagint.* ALGHJ 6. Leiden: Brill, 1973. *See also*: bibliographic updates in *The Bulletin of the International Organization for Septuagint and Cognate Studies* (webpage at http://ccat.sas.upenn.edu/ioscs); also note the Septuagint Online webpage at http://www.kalvesmaki.com/LXX and the bibliography to the Septuaginta Deutsch at http://www.septuagintaforschung.de/files/WUNT-219-Bibilographie.pdf. *Critical and Diplomatic Texts*: *Septuaginta: Vetus Testamentum Graecum Auctoritate Academiae Scientiarum Gottingensis editum.* 16 vols. Göttingen: Vandenhoeck & Ruprecht, 1931–. The standard scholarly critical edition, but incomplete. Known as the "Göttingen edition." Some volumes are divided into separate "parts." Barthélemy, Dominique. *Les Devanciers D'Aquila: Première Publication Intégrale du Texte des Fragments du Dodécaprophéton.* VTSup 10. Leiden: Brill, 1963. Greek Minor Prophets scroll from Naal ever (8HevXIIgr). Also see DJD 8, and Lifshitz in *IEJ* 12 (1962) 201–207 and in *Yedio☐ t* 26 (1962) 183–90. Brooke, Alan England, Norman McLean, and Henry St. John Thackeray, eds. *The Old Testament in Greek.* London: Cambridge University Press, 1906–1940. Text of Codex Vaticanus with extensive apparatus. Since the Göttingen edition is incomplete, this still provides the best critical apparatus for the Former Prophets and Chronicles. Available online at http://archive.org. *Handbook Text*: Rahlfs, Alfred and Robert Hanhart, eds. *Septuaginta.* Rev. ed. 2 vols. in 1. Stuttgart: Deutsche Bibelgesellschaft, 2006. An eclectic text, but without adequate critical apparatus to evaluate editorial decisions (with a "moderate revision" from Rahlfs's 1935 edition). Rahlfs's original text is frequently found in Bible software (e.g. Accordance, BibleWorks, etc.) and online. *Text and Translation*: Brenton, Lancelot C. L. *The Septuagint with Apocrypha: Greek and English.* London:

Samuel Bagster & Sons, 1851; repr. Peabody, MA: Hendrickson, 1992. Now dated in comparison to the NETS translation (see below), but has the advantage of a facing Greek text. Digitized pages available free online at http://www.archive.org and at http://www.ccel.org /ccel/brenton/lxx.html and English text of Brenton at http://www.ecclesia.org/truth/septuagint-hyperlinked.html.

Translation:
Pietersma, Albert and Benjamin G. Wright, eds. *A New English Translation of the Septuagint.* Oxford/New York: Oxford University Press, 2007. Fine translation by a team of Septuagint scholars. Abbreviated NETS. Available for some Bible software, and free online access at http://ccat.sas.upenn.edu /nets/edition.

Concordance:
Hatch, Edwin and Henry A. Redpath. *A Concordance to the Septuagint and the Other Greek Versions of the Old Testament.* 3 vols. Oxford: Clarendon, 1897–1906. Available online at http://archive.org. "Second edition" (Grand Rapids: Baker, 1998) contains a Hebrew-Greek reverse index by Muraoka.
A number of volumes have been released in the Computer Bible Series (series editors J. Arthur Baird, David Noel Freedman, and Watson E. Mills) published by Biblical Research Associates or by Edwin Mellen Press. These have been produced by J. David Thompson and are entitled similar to *A Critical Concordance to the Septuagint Genesis* or to *A Critical Concordance to the Apocrypha: 1 Maccabees.* Each provides book-by-book concordances of the LXX with a number of statistical aides.
Many computer programs also contain tagged Septuagint texts (e.g. BibleWorks, Accordance).

Lexicons:
Chamberlain, Gary Alan. *The Greek of the Septuagint: A Supplemental Lexicon.* Peabody, MA: Hendrickson, 2011. Includes all words not in BDAG, and otherwise only supplements BDAG on words when Septuagintal Greek meanings differ from standard NT definitions (thus this book by itself does not include all LXX vocabulary).
Lust, Johan, Erik Eynikel, and Katrin Hauspie. *A Greek-English Lexicon of the Septuagint.* Rev. ed. Stuttgart: Deutsche Bibelgesellschaft, 2003. First edition

issued in two volumes (1992, 1996). Helpful glosses of all LXX vocabulary.

Muraoka, T. *A Greek-English Lexicon of the Septuagint.* Louvain: Peeters, 2009. Now complete, whereas previous iterations just focused on the Twelve Prophets (1993) or the Twelve Prophets and the Pentateuch (2002). A fine work by a careful lexicographer; should be consulted regularly.

Muraoka, T. *A Greek-Hebrew-Aramaic Two-way Index to the Septuagint.* Louvain: Peeters, 2010. Allows one to see what Greek words are used to translate the Hebrew/Aramaic OT, and vice versa. Previous parts of this tool were published in his earlier LXX lexicons (1993 and 2002) and in the Baker edition of Hatch's LXX concordance; but with the publication of his 2009 lexicon, this is now a stand-alone document.

Rehkopf, Friedrich. *Septuaginta-Vokabular.* Göttingen: Vandenhoeck & Ruprecht, 1989. Provides a single German gloss for each Greek word. For each entry he lists some LXX texts and compares with word count usage in the NT.

Taylor, Bernard A. *Analytical Lexicon to the Septuagint: Expanded edition.* Peabody, MA: Hendrickson; Stuttgart: Deutsche Bibelgesellschaft, 2009. Revision of his 1994 Zondervan edition, listing every word form found in Rahlfs's edition and employing glosses from the Lust/Eynikel/Hauspie lexicon; especially helpful for difficult parsings.

Grammars:

Conybeare, F. C. and St. George Stock. *Grammar of Septuagint Greek.* Boston: Ginn & Co., 1905; repr. Peabody, MA: Hendrickson, 1995. Introductory, but with section on syntax not in Thackeray (or in the German grammar by Helbing). Available online at http://archive.org and at http://www.ccel.org/c/conybeare /greekgrammar.

Thackeray, Henry St. John. *A Grammar of the Old Testament in Greek*, Vol. 1: Introduction, Orthography and Accidence. Cambridge: CUP, 1909; repr. Hildesheim: Olms, 1987. Available online at http://archive.org.

Introductions:

Dines, Jennifer M. *The Septuagint.* Understanding the Bible and its World. London: T & T Clark, 2004. Good short survey, especially helpful for first exposure to LXX studies.

Fernández Marcos, Natalio. *The Septuagint in Context: Introduction to the Greek Versions of the Bible.* Trans. Wilfred G. E. Watson from 2d Spanish ed.

Atlanta: Society of Biblical Literature, 2009. Useful introduction from standpoint of Spanish scholarship (previous English edition published by Leiden: Brill, 2000).

Harl, Marguerite, Gilles Dorival, and Olivier Munnich. *La Bible Grecque des Septante: Du judaïsme hellénistique au christianisme ancient.* Initiations au christianisme ancien; Paris: Cerf, 1988. Introduction by important French scholars.

Jellicoe, Sidney. *The Septuagint and Modern Study.* Oxford: Clarendon, 1968; repr. Winona Lake: Eisenbrauns, 1993. Assumes the earlier *Introduction* by Swete.

Jobes, Karen H. and Moisés Silva. *Invitation to the Septuagint.* Grand Rapids: Baker, 2000. Fine volume providing overall orientation to Septuagint study.

Siegert, Folker. *Zwischen Hebräischer Bibel und Altem Testament: Eine Einführung in die Septuaginta.* Münsteraner Judaistische Studien 9. Münster: LIT, 2001. Additional volume provides index and "Wirkungsgeschichte" of the LXX in antiquity (see *Register zur "Einführung in die Septuaginta"*; Münster: LIT, 2003).

Swete, Henry Barclay. *An Introduction to the Old Testament in Greek.* Rev. Richard Rusden Ottley. Cambridge: CUP, 1914; repr. Peabody, MA: Hendrickson, 1989. Classic textbook available online at http://archive.org and at http://www.ccel.org/s/ swete/greekot.

Also see *HJPAJC* 3.1:474–493; *Mikra* 161–88; *CHJ* 2:534–562; *ABD* 5:1093–1104. *Commentaries:*

Harl, Marguerite, et al. *La Bible d'Alexandrie.* 17+ vols. Paris: Cerf, 1986– . Focuses on how the LXX would have been read by Greek speakers in Jewish and Christian antiquity.

Septuagint Commentary Series. Leiden: Brill, 2005–. Edited by S. E. Porter, R. Hess, and J. Jarick.

Wevers, John William. *Notes on the Greek Text of Genesis.* SBLSCS 35. Atlanta: Scholars, 1993. Discusses textual and philological issues. Wevers has produced similar volumes for the rest of the Pentateuch.

The International Organization for Septuagint and Cognate Studies (IOSCS) announced plans in 2005 to publish the SBL Commentary on the Septuagint (though no volumes have appeared at time of writing).

2.1.2 Aquila, Symmachus, Theodotion

Known primarily from the fragmentary sources of Origen's Hexapla, "the Three" represent Jewish Greek translations from the early Common Era (though there are some early traditions that Symmachus and even Theodotion were Ebionite Christians). Extensive Syro-Hexaplaric fragments and remnants of the Three exist in other languages (notably Armenian). Bibliographies, concordances, and introductions on the Three are also listed in works on the LXX above (see also *HJPAJC* 3.1:493–504).

Text: Field, Fridericus. *Origenis Hexaplorum quae supersunt.* 2 vols. Oxford: Clarendon, 1875. Available online at http://archive.org. Other fragments have surfaced since Field, thus see the bibliographies and introductions noted under LXX. Also note that Göttingen LXX volumes list Hexaplaric traditions in the bottom apparatus. An English translation of Field's own Latin prolegomena to this work has been produced by Gérard J. Norton (Paris: Gabalda, 2005). The "Hexapla Institute" has announced plans to publish a new critical edition of Hexapla fragments (see http://www.hexapla.org).

Concordance: Reider, Joseph and Nigel Turner. *An Index to Aquila.* VTSup 12. Leiden: Brill, 1966. Use in addition to the listing in Hatch and Redpath, Vol. 3 (see under LXX).

Commentary: Salvesen, Alison. *Symmachus in the Pentateuch.* JSS Monograph 15. Manchester: University of Manchester, 1991.

2.2 Targumim

Aramaic translations and paraphrases of the OT are known from as early as the Qumran community. The targumim appear to originate from liturgical use in the synagogue, when a *meturgeman* would compose an (occasionally paraphrastic or expansive) Aramaic rendering of the biblical text to be read in the service.

Such targumim can testify to how the biblical text was interpreted in Judaism. "Official" targumim on the Pentateuch (*Tg. Onqelos*) and the Prophets (*Tg. Jonathan*) ha been passed down from Babylonian rabbinic circles, while parallel traditions are also known from Palestine. There are additional targumic traditions for each of the non-Aramaic books of the Writings. Besides MSS and printed editions devoted to targumim, the official targumim are printed with the MT in Rabbinic Bibles alongside traditional rabbinic commentaries. Targumic texts also occur in Polyglot editions (e.g. those printed in Antwerp, Paris, and London [=Walton's]) in parallel with the MT and other translations. The issues of dating and transmission history of the various targumim are often quite complex.

2.2.1 General Bibliography *Bibliography:*

Grossfeld, Bernard. *A Bibliography of Targum Literature.* Vols. 1 and 2: Bibliographica

Judaica 3 and 8. New York: Ktav, 1972, 1977. Vol. 3: New

York: Sepher-Hermon, 1990.

Forestell, J. T. *Targumic Traditions and the New Testament: An Annotated Bibliography with a New Testament Index.* SBL Aramaic Studies 4. Chico, CA:

Scholars, 1979.

Nickels, Peter. *Targum and New Testament: A Bibliography together with a New Testament Index.* Scripta Pontificii Instituti Biblici 117. Rome: Pontifical Biblical

Institute, 1967. Updated in Forestell.

Ongoing listing of publications in the *Newsletter for Targumic and Cognate Studies*

(now with its own website, including some targum translations at http://targum.info). Note also the bibliographic articles by Díez Macho in Vols. 4 and 5 of *Neophyti 1* (listed below).

Critical Texts:

Sperber, Alexander. *The Bible in Aramaic: Based on Old Manuscripts and Printed*

Texts. 4 vols. in 5. Leiden: Brill, 1959–1973. Vol. 4b presents a series of helpful studies on the preceding volumes. Major critical text of *Targums Onqelos* and *Jonathan*; less reliable on the Writings.

Translations:

McNamara, Martin, gen. ed. *The Aramaic Bible.* 22 vols. Edinburgh: T & T

Clark, 1987–2007. Standard contemporary translation series, with typically good introductions and notes. *Also see*: Etheridge under Pentateuch. Some translations are also being made available online (see http://targum.info/targumic-texts). Eldon Clem is producing English translations for Accordance Bible Software of Targums Onkelos, Jonathan, Neofiti, and Pseudo-Jonathan; see http://www.accordancebible.com and note the review in *Aramaic Studies* 5 (2007) 151–58.

Concordances:

Searchable morphologically tagged Aramaic texts are currently available for Accordance, BibleWorks, and Logos software packages. These are based on texts from the Comprehensive Aramaic Lexicon Project (sometimes drawing on older editions, such as those by Lagarde).

Lexicons:

Cook, Edward M. *A Glossary of Targum Onkelos: According to Alexander Sperber's Edition.* Studies in the Aramaic Interpretation of Scripture. Leiden: Brill, 2008.

Dalman, Gustav. *Aramäisch-neuhebräisches Wörterbuch zu Targum, Talmud, und Midrasch.* Göttingen, 1938. Available online at http://archive.org.

Jastrow, Marcus. *A Dictionary of the Targumim, the Talmud Babli and Yerushalmi, and the Midrashic Literature.* 2 vols. New York: Pardes, 1950; singlevolume repr. New York: Judaica, 1971 and Peabody, MA: Hendrickson, 2005. Convenient resource for translating all targumic and early rabbinic literature. Available online at http://www.tyndalearchive.com/tabs/jastrow.

Levy, J. *Chaldäisches Wörterbuch über die Targumim und einen grossen Theil des rabbinischen Schriftthums.* 2 vols. Leipzig: Baumgärtner, 1867–1868; repr. Köln: Joseph Melzer, 1959. Available online at http://archive.org.

Sokoloff, Michael. *A Dictionary of Jewish Babylonian Aramaic of the Talmudic and Geonic Periods.* Dictionaries of Talmud, Midrash and Targum 3. Ramat-Gan, Israel: Bar Ilan University Press; Baltimore: Johns Hopkins, 2002. Sokoloff's dictionaries generally employ better informed lexicography than Jastrow.

Sokoloff, Michael. *A Dictionary of Jewish Palestinian Aramaic of the Byzantine Period.* 2d ed. Dictionaries of Talmud, Midrash and Targum 2; Ramat-Gan, Israel: Bar Ilan University Press; Baltimore: Johns Hopkins, 2002. Also

contains a marvelous set of indexes to the passages cited.
Also see: Comprehensive Aramaic Lexicon Project of Hebrew Union College
at http://cal1.cn.huc.edu. This website includes a searchable database of Aramaic lexical information and of Aramaic texts through the 13th century.
It also houses a bibliographic database, and lists "Addenda et Corrigenda" to the two Sokoloff dictionaries above.
Grammars:
Dalman, Gustaf. *Grammatik des Jüdisch-Palästinischen Aramäisch: Nach den Idiomen des Palästinischen Talmud des Onkelostargum und Prophetentargum und der Jerusalemischen Targume.* 2d ed. Leipzig: Hinrichs, 1905; repr. Darmstadt: Wissenschaftliche Buchgesellschaft, 1960. Available online at
http://archive.org.
Fassberg, Steven E. *A Grammar of the Palestinian Targum Fragments from the Cairo Genizah.* HSS 38. Atlanta: Scholars, 1991. Focuses primarily on phonology
and morphology.
Golomb, David M. *A Grammar of Targum Neofiti.* HSM 34. Chico, CA: Scholars,
1985. Attends primarily to morphology, but contains a final chapter reviewing matters of verbal and nominal syntax.
Kuty, Renaud J. *Studies in the Syntax of Targum Jonathan to Samuel.* Ancient Near Eastern Studies Supplements 30. Leuven: Peeters, 2010. Whereas other
studies focus on morphology, this highlights key syntactical matters.
Stevenson, William B. *Grammar of Palestinian Jewish Aramaic.* 2d ed. Oxford:
Clarendon, 1962. Beginning grammar (though without exercises) introducing
the language of both Palestinian and Babylonian post-biblical Jewish Aramaic. Includes syntactical notes missing in Dalman. Secondedition
reprint of 1924 with a new "Appendix on Numerals" by J. A. Emerton.
Some beginning grammars of Biblical Aramaic also touch on Targumic Aramaic
(and other works of rabbinic origin); e.g. F. E. Greenspahn, *An Introduction*
to Aramaic. 2d ed. Atlanta: SBL, 2003. Also see Y. Frank, *Grammar for Gemara* (below under Babylonian Talmud).
Introductions:

Bowker, John. *The Targums and Rabbinic Literature*. Cambridge: CUP, 1969. An introduction to the targumim in relation to other rabbinic literature. Also contains a translation of a substantial portion of *Tg. Ps.-J.* to Genesis.

Díez Macho, Alejandro. *El Targum: Introducción a las traducciones aramaicas de la Biblia.* Textos y Estudios 21. Madrid: Consejo Superior de Investigaciones Científicas, 1982. The classic introduction by the foremost member of the "Spanish school."

Flesher, Paul V. M., and Bruce Chilton. *The Targums: A Critical Introduction.* Studies in the Aramaic Interpretation of Scripture 12; Leiden: Brill, 2011; Waco, TX: Baylor University Press, 2011. Significant recent introduction that covers a wide array of academic topics.

Gleßmer, Uwe. *Einleitung in die Targume zum Pentateuch.* TSAJ 48. Tübingen: J. C. B. Mohr [Paul Siebeck], 1995.

Grelot, Pierre. *What Are the Targums? Selected Texts.* Trans. Salvator Attanasio; Old Testament Studies 7; Collegeville, MN: Liturgical, 1992. Selections of expansive targumic passages with introduction. Caution is required since Grelot combines different targumic traditions.

Le Déaut, Roger. *Introduction à la Littérature Targumique.* Rome: Institut Biblique Pontifical, 1966. "Premiere partie" and thus incomplete, but quite helpful. Also see his brief article in *CHJ* 2:563–90; and his more substantial treatment of "Targum" in L. Pirot and A. Robert, *Supplément au Dictionnaire de la Bible.* Paris: Letouzey, 2005, 13:1*–344*.

Levine, Etan. *The Aramaic Version of the Bible: Contents and Context.* BZAW 174. Berlin: de Gruyter, 1988. Addresses the targumim as a whole, focusing on targumic themes.

McNamara, Martin. *Targum and Testament Revisited: Aramaic Paraphrases of the Hebrew Bible.* 2d ed. Grand Rapids: Eerdmans, 2010. Also contains a helpful appendix that introduces all extant targums.

See also: the useful articles by P. S. Alexander in *Mikra* 217–53 and in *ABD* 6:320–331; also note *HJPAJC* 1:99–114; *CHJ* 2:563–590.

2.2.2 Targumim on the Pentateuch Divided into the following categories:
(1) Official Targum of Babylonia = Onqelos (text in Sperber above).
(2) "Palestinian Targumim" (editions noted below)

(a) Neofiti 1
(b) Pseudo-Jonathan
(c) Fragment Targum
(d) Cairo Genizah Fragments
(e) Toseftot
(f) Festival Collections
(g) Targumic Poems

For texts and bibliography on the last three categories see: Sperber, *Bible in Aramaic* 1:354–57 (above); *Mikra* 251; and Klein, *Genizah Manuscripts* Vol. 1: xxviii– xxxix (below).

Texts:

Diez Macho, Alexander, L. Diez Merino, E. Martinez Borobio, and Teresa Martinez Saiz, eds. *Biblia Polyglotta Matritensia IV: Targum Palaestinense in Pentateuchum.* 5 vols. Madrid: Consejo Superior de Investigaciones Científicas, 1977–88. Contains Palestinian Targumim in parallel columns (Neofiti, Pseudo-Jonathan, Fragment Targum, Cairo Genizah fragments) along with a Spanish translation of Pseudo-Jonathan. Very helpful.

Díez Macho, Alejandro, ed. *Neophyti 1: Targum Palestinense MS de la Biblioteca Vaticana.* 6 vols. Textos y Estudios 7–11 and 20; Madrid-Barcelona: Consejo Superior de Investigaciones Científicas, 1968–1979. Text of *Tg. Neof.* with facing Spanish translation and appended French and English translations. Each volume is prefaced with extensive introductory essays by Díez Macho. Volumes 2–5 also include verse-by-verse listings of (mostly rabbinic, but also pseudepigraphic and Christian) parallels to the interpretive elements in *Tg. Ps.-J.* and *Tg. Neof.* Volume 6 contains addenda, corrigenda, and indexes. A photocopy edition of the manuscript also exists (Jerusalem: Makor, 1970).

Ginsburger, M. *Pseudo-Jonathan (Thargum Jonathan ben Usiël zum Pentateuch). Nach der Londoner Handschrift (Brit. Mus. add. 27031).* Berlin: S. Calvary, 1903; repr. New York: Hildesheim, 1971. Editor's name can also be spelled Ginsberger in catalogs. There is another edition of this manuscript by D. Rieder (Jerusalem, 1974), reprinted with Modern Hebrew translation in 2 vols. in 1984–85. Also note the edition by Clarke (below under Concordances).

Klein, Michael L. *Genizah Manuscripts of Palestinian Targum to the Pentateuch.* 2 vols. Cincinnati: Hebrew Union College, 1986. Vol. 1 contains introduction, text, and translation of Genizah MSS of Pentateuchal targumim, also of festival collections, toseftot and targumic poems (additionally listing helpful bibliography for locating other toseftot, festival collections and targumic poems). Vol. 2 includes notes, glossary of vocabulary, and plates.

Klein, Michael L. *The Fragment-Targums of the Pentateuch: According to their Extant Sources.* 2 vols. AnBib 76. Rome: Biblical Institute Press, 1980. Vol. 1 introduction, text and indexes; Vol. 2 translation. Strongly preferred over Ginsburger's 1899 edition.

For Onqelos see Sperber (§2.2.1 above). Note also Masorah in Michael L. Klein, *The Masorah to Targum Onqelos: as preserved in MSS Vatican Ebreo 448, Rome Angelica Or. 7, Fragments from the Cairo Genizah and in Earlier Editions by A. Berliner and S. Landauer.* Targum Studies 1. Academic Studies in the History of Judaism; Binghamton, NY: Global Publications, SUNY Binghamton, 2000.

Translation:

Etheridge, J. W. *The Targums of Onkelos and Jonathan ben Uzziel on the Pentateuch with the Fragments of the Jerusalem Targum.* 1862; repr. New York: Ktav, 1968. Available online at http://targum.info/targumic-texts/pentateuchal-targumim and at http://archive.org. Also available for BibleWorks and Logos software. The McNamara *Aramaic Bible* series above is now generally preferred.

Le Déaut, Roger, with collaboration by Jacques Robert. *Targum du Pentateuque.* 5 vols. SC; Paris: Cerf, 1978–1981. French translation of Targum Neofiti and Targum Pseudo-Jonathan in parallel pages, with brief translational notes. The fifth volume serves as a topical index.

Also see: The *Aramaic Bible* series (above under 2.2.1 Targumim General Bibliography).

Concordances:

Brederek, Emil. *Konkordanz zum Targum Onkelos.* BZAW 9. Giessen: Alfred Töpelmann, 1906. Available online at http://archive.org.

Clarke, E. G., W. E. Aufrecht, J. C. Hurd, and F. Spitzer. *Targum Pseudo-Jonathan of the Pentateuch: Text and Concordance.* Hoboken: Ktav, 1984. Contains the same manuscript as Ginsberger and Rieder with KWIC

concordance; on the concordance see M. Bernstein's cautious review in *JQR* 79 (1988) 227–30.
Kassovsky,. 5 vols. in 1. Jerusalem: Kiriath Moshe, 1933–40. For Onqelos.
Kaufman, Stephen A., Michael Sokoloff, and with the assistance of Edward
M. Cook. *A Key-Word-in-Context Concordance to Targum Neofiti.* Publications
of the Comprehensive Aramaic Lexicon Project 2. Baltimore: John Hopkins University Press, 1993. Also presents English glosses of the Aramaic words.
Note also some rabbinic search software contain searchable targumic texts (see under Rabbinic Literature).
Commentaries:
Aberbach, Moses and Bernard Grossfeld. *Targum Onkelos to Genesis: A Critical
Analysis together with an English Translation of the Text.* New York: Ktav,
1982. Text of A. Berliner with English translation and comments (based on Sperber's edition).
Drazin, Israel. *Targum Onkelos to Exodus: An English Translation of the Text With Analysis and Commentary.* New York: Ktav, 1990. Text of A. Berliner with
English translation and comments (based on Sperber's edition). Drazin has produced similar commentaries for *Tg. Onq.* to Leviticus (1994), Numbers (1998), and Deuteronomy (1982). Drazin emphasizes the literal translational elements of the Targum rather than seeing it as a full rabbinic interpretation. Note the cautious reviews by Emerton in *VT* 43 (1993) 280–81 and by Levine in *CBQ* 57 (1995) 766–67.
Grossfeld, Bernard. *Targum Neofiti 1: An Exegetical Commentary to Genesis, Including Full Rabbinic Parallels.* New York: Sepher-Hermon, 2000. Includes
transcription of text and commentary with emphasis on rabbinic texts that parallel the Targum. 2.2.3 Targumim on the Prophets
Targum Jonathan forms the "official" targum to the Former and Latter Prophets (text in Sperber, *Bible in Aramaic*, Vols. 2 and 3). There are also Palestinian Toseftot (marginal comments of other targumic traditions alongside Targum Jonathan in the MSS). On the Toseftot: see pp. vi–xlii of De Lagarde, *Prophetae Chaldaice* (below); see also Sperber, *Bible in Aramaic*, descriptions on pp. ix–x of Vol. 2 and p. xi of Vol. 3; further bibliography in *Mikra* 252. Translation (with notes) in McNamara, *The Aramaic Bible* (see above).
Text:
De Lagarde, Paul. *Prophetae Chaldaice.* Leipzig: Teubner, 1872. Standard edition

before Sperber (on which see §2.2.1 above). Available online at http://archive.org.

Stenning, J. F. *The Targum of Isaiah.* Oxford: Clarendon, 1949. A pointed critical text of Targum Jonathan to Isaiah with translation; Palestinian Toseftot to the Targum on pp. 224–28.

Concordances:

Moor, Johannes C. de, et al., eds. *A Bilingual Concordance to the Targum of the Prophets.* 21 vols. Leiden: Brill, 1995–2005. A concordance of the individual books of *Tg. Jon.* to the Former and Latter Prophets. Also lists Hebrew equivalents to the Aramaic vocabulary (providing English glosses to both the Aramaic and Hebrew terms).

Van Zijl, J. B. *A Concordance to the Targum of Isaiah: Based on the Brit. Mus. Or. MS. 2211.* SBLAS 3. Missoula, MT: Scholars, 1979.

Commentaries:

Levine, Etan. *The Aramaic Version of Jonah.* New York: Sepher-Hermon, 1975. Introduction, text, translation, and commentary of *Tg. Jon.* to Jonah.

Smelik, Willem F. *The Targum of Judges.* OTS 36. Leiden: Brill, 1995. Extensive introduction and commentary.

Van Staalduine-Sulman, Eveline. *The Targum of Samuel.* Studies in the Aramaic Interpretation of Scripture 1. Leiden: Brill, 2002. Commentary, translation, and study.

2.2.4 Targumim on the Writings

No known rabbinic targumic traditions exist for Daniel or for Ezra-Nehemiah (note these books already employ Aramaic). The study of the targumim to the Writings necessitates caution since frequently several targumic recensions exist for any one OT book (for overview see *ABD* 6:320–331). Note that Targum Job is different than the Qumran Job Targum (=11QtgJob =11Q10; see DJD 23 and further bibliography below under "Dead Sea Scrolls"). Two targumic traditions to Esther are recognized (Targum Rishon and Targum Sheni = *Tg. Esth I and II*). A so-called "Third Targum to Esther" exists in the Antwerp Polyglot, but it is disputed whether this Third Targum is essentially a condensation of Targum Rishon, the predecessor of Rishon, or properly a targum at all.

General Texts:
Sperber, Alexander. *The Bible in Aramaic: Based on Old Manuscripts and Printed Texts.* Vol. 4a. Leiden: Brill, 1968. Contains *Tg. Chron* (MS Berlin 125) and *Tg. Ruth* as in the De Lagarde edition, and includes from Brit. Mus. Or. 2375: *Tg. Cant, Tg. Lam, Tg. Eccl, and Tg. Esth* (mixed text type of Esther, due to the manuscript used).
De Lagarde, Paul. *Hagiographa Chaldaice.* Leipzig: Teubner, 1873. Text of Targumim to the Writings, including those not in Sperber (Psalms, Job, Proverbs, and both Esther Rishon and Esther Sheni). Available online at http://books.google.com.
Individual Texts:
Díez Merino, Luis. *Targum de Salmos: Edición Príncipe del Ms. Villa-Amil n. 5 de Alfonso de Zamora.* Bibliotheca Hispana Biblica 6. Madrid: Consejo Superior de Investigaciones Científicas, 1982. Introduction, text, Latin translation (by Alfonso de Zamora) and studies on this manuscript of *Tg. Psalms.*
Stec, David M. *The Text of the Targum of Job: An Introduction and Critical Edition.* AGJU 20. Leiden: Brill, 1994. A fine edition.
Díez Merino, Luis. *Targum de Job: Edición Principe del Ms. Villa-Amil n° 5 de Alfonso de Zamora.* Bibliotheca Hispana Biblica 8. Madrid: Consejo Superior de Investigaciones Científicas, 1984.
Díez Merino, Luis. *Targum de Proverbios. Edición Principe del Ms. Villa-Amil n° 5 de Alfonso de Zamora.* Madrid: Consejo Superior de Investigaciones Científicas, 1984. The next major edition of *Tg. Proverbs* since De Lagarde, *Hagiographa Chaldaice* (above).
Levine, Etan. *The Aramaic Version of Ruth.* AnBib 58. Rome: Biblical Institute Press, 1973. Introduction, text, translation, and commentary.
Jerusalmi, Isaac. *The Song of Songs in the Targumic Tradition: Vocalized Aramaic Text with Facing English Translation and Ladino Versions.* Cincinnati: Ladino, 1993.
Alonso Fontela, Carlos. *El Targum al Cantar de los Cantares (Edición Critica).* Collección Tesis Doctorales. Madrid: Editorial de la Universidad Complutense de Madrid, 1987.

Melamed, R. H. *The Targum to Canticles according to Six Yemenite MSS.* PhiladelJEWISH phia: Dropsie College, 1921. Covers the Yemenite recension, which differs from the Western texts at points. Reprinted from a series of articles
in *JQR* n.s. 10–12 (1919–1921). Available online at http://archive.org.
Díez Merino, Luis. *Targum de Qohelet: Edición Principe del Ms. Villa-Amil n° 5 de Alfonso de Zamora.* Bibliotheca Hispana Biblica 13. Madrid: Consejo Superior
de Investigaciones Científicas, 1987. An important edition of a manuscript otherwise unavailable.
Levine, Etan. *The Aramaic Version of Qohelet.* New York: Sepher-Hermon,
1978. Photocopy of MS Urb. 1 with translation and "conceptual analysis."
Levy, A. *Das Targum zu Qohelet nach sudarabischen Handschriften herausgegeben.*
Breslau, 1905. Critical edition of *Tg. Eccl.*
Brady, Christian M. M. *The Rabbinic Targum of Lamentations: Vindicating God.*
Studies in the Aramaic Interpretation of Scripture 3. Leiden: Brill, 2003. Study of this targum that includes a transcription of Codex Urbinas Hebr. 1 and translation.
Heide, Albert van der. *The Yemenite Tradition of the Targum of Lamentations: Critical Text and Analysis of the Variant Readings.* Leiden: Brill, 1981. The
Yemenite tradition is significantly different from the Western text tradition.
Levine, Etan. *The Aramaic Version of Lamentations.* New York: Hermon, 1976.
Introduction, text, translation, and commentary.
Ego, Beate. *Targum Scheni zu Ester: Übersetzung, Kommentar und theologische
Deutung.* TSAJ 54. Tübingen: Mohr Siebeck, 1996.
Grossfeld, Bernard. *The Targum Sheni to the Book of Esther: A Critical Edition
based on MS. Sassoon 282 with Critical Apparatus.* New York: Sepher-Hermon, 1994. Includes a full-length concordance and a photocopy of this manuscript.
Grossfeld, Bernard. *The First Targum to Esther: According to the MS Paris Hebrew 110 of the Bibliotheque Nationale.* New York: Sepher-Hermon, 1983. Critical text, translation, and commentary with introduction to Targum
Rishon to Esther. Includes plates.
Le Déaut, R., and J. Robert. *Targum des Chroniques (Cod. Vat. Urb. Ebr. 1).* 2

vols. AnBib 51. Rome: Biblical Institute Press, 1971. Vol. 1 introduction and (French) translation; Vol. 2 text, indexes, and a glossary of vocabulary in Aramaic, French, and English.

Concordance:

Grossfeld, Bernard. *Concordance of the First Targum to the Book of Esther.* SBLAS 5. Chico, CA: Scholars, 1984. For the Second Targum (Targum Sheni) see the KWIC concordance in Grossfeld's edition noted above.

2.3 Other (Latin and Syriac)

Whereas the Vulgate is clearly Christian (translated by Jerome), the lineage of the Old Latin is more obscure. A frequent dependence on the LXX, and occasional portions that agree with Jewish tradition over the LXX, make it possible that the Old Latin contains some certifiable Jewish passages. The Peshi☐ta, though ultimately a Christian Bible, may originally have been allied with Jewish tradition, especially 252. when it agrees with the targumim. For sake of space, standard Latin and Syriac grammars and lexicons are not listed below. Other early translations that appear largely dependent on the Septuagint, such as Bohairic Coptic or Christian Palestinian Aramaic, are not represented below. For introductions see *Mikra* 255–97, 299–313; *ABD* 6:794–803.

Old Latin Texts: Vetus Latina: Die Reste der altlateinischen Bibel. Freiburg: Herder, 1951–. Critical edition currently covering Genesis, Canticles, Wisdom, Ecclesiasticus, and Isaiah from the OT and Apocrypha. Projected 26 volumes (with multiple parts).

Sabatier, Petri, ed. *Bibliorum Sacrorum Latinae Versiones Antiquae.* 3 vols. Rheims: Reginald Florentain, 1743–1749. Vulgate and Old Latin in parallel columns. Some volumes available on http://archive.org.

Peshi☐ta Bibliography:

Dirksen, P. B. *An Annotated Bibliography of the Peshita of the Old Testament.* Monographs of the Peshita Institute 5. Leiden: Brill, 1989.

Syriac Peshita Text:

Vetus Testamentum Syriace Iuxta Simplicem Syrorum Versionem [= *The Old Testament in Syriac According to the Peshita Version*]. Leiden: Brill, 1973–. In four parts, with multiple fascicles.

Peshita Translation:
Lamsa, George M. *The Holy Bible from Ancient Eastern Manuscripts: Containing the Old and New Testaments, translated from the Peshitta, the authorized Bible of the church of the East.* Philadelphia: Holman, 1957; repr. San Francisco: Harper & Row, 1985. Not fully reliable. Available online a http://www.aramaicpeshitta.com/OTtools/LamsaOT.htm.
Gorgias Press has inaugurated its Surath Ktobh series (overseen by George A. Kiraz, projected to be 30 volumes), featuring facing pages of the Peshiṭta (without textual apparatus) and a literal English translation.

Peshita Concordances:
Borbone, P. G. and K. D. Jenner, eds. *The Old Testament in Syriac According to the Peshitta Version: Part 5 Concordance.* Vetus Testamentum Syriace. Leiden: Brill, 1997–. Strothmann, Werner, Kurt Johannes, and Manfred Zumpe. *Konkordanz zur Syrischen Bibel: Die Propheten.* 4 vols. GOF Reihe 1, Syriaca 25. Wiesbaden: Otto Harrassowitz, 1984. They also produced a four volume 1986 concordance for *Der Pentateuch* (GOF Reihe 1, Syriaca 26).
Peshiṭta texts are increasingly coming available for Bible software (e.g. Accordance and BibleWorks).

Peshita Introduction:
Weitzman, M. P. *The Syriac Version of the Old Testament: An Introduction.* University of Cambridge Oriental Publications 56. Cambridge: CUP, 1999.
See also: Pp. 1057–59 in *EDEJ.*

3. Apocrypha
Various Christian OT manuscripts (Greek, Latin, Syriac, etc.) contain books not found in the Masoretic tradition. Translations may be found in some English Bibles (e.g. RSV, NRSV, NEB, REB) of the Greek (LXX) apocrypha as well as Latin "2 Esdras." Other translations may be found in the editions edited by Charles, by Charlesworth (for 4 Ezra), and by Kümmel listed under General Pseudepigrapha Bibliography below (cf. esp. Charlesworth, *OTP* 2:609–24 for apocryphal Psalms).
English "2 Esdras" is listed in the Vulgate as 4 Ezra and should not be confused with LXX 2 Esdras (which is the Greek version of OT Ezra and Nehemiah). Most modern scholars believe 4 Ezra is a compilation, often

designating (the probably Christian) chapters 1–2 and chapters 15–16 as 5 Ezra and 6 Ezra respectively. Thus the name "4 Ezra" in much modern scholarship has been reserved for Vulgate 4 Ezra 3–14.
The above listed LXX editions and concordances serve for the Greek Apocrypha. Greek fragments of 4 Ezra have been discovered (see Denis, *Fragmenta pseudepigraphorum* below under Pseudepigrapha). Latin versions of these books as well as the whole of 4 Ezra are also known in the Old Latin (see above) and Vulgate (for concordances to Latin 4 Ezra, see Denis or Lechner-Schmidt under General Pseudepigrapha Bibliography below). For Syriac editions, see the Peshita bibliography above. Many books of the Apocrypha are thought to stem from Semitic originals. Prior to the DSS, fragments in Hebrew were known of Ben Sira (= Sirach = Ecclesiasticus). Hebrew and Aramaic texts have been found in the DSS for Tobit (4Q196–200 in DJD XIX), Sirach (2Q18 in DJD III; 11QPsa [=11Q5] xxi–xxii in DJD IV; some Masada texts) and some of the apocryphal Psalms (11QPsa in DJD IV; for 4Q380–381 see Schuller, *Non-Canonical Psalms from Qumran* below under "Dead Sea Scrolls"); for a list see Peter W. Flint "Appendix II," in Flint & Vanderkam, eds., *The Dead Sea Scrolls After Fifty Years*, pp. 666–68 (see "Introductions" under Dead Sea Scrolls below).

Other Bibliography:
Reiterer, Friedrich Vinzenz, ed. *Bibliographie zu Ben Sira.* BZAW 266.
Berlin: de
Gruyter, 1998. Not well indexed or annotated.
See also: Bibelwissenschaft by Franz Böhmisch (http://www.animabit.de /bibel/sir.htm). *Other Texts (Ordered by apocryphal book):*
Beentjes, Pancratius C. *The Book of Ben Sira in Hebrew: A Text Edition of all Extant Hebrew Manuscripts and a Synopsis.* VTSup 68. Leiden: Brill, 1997. Paperback repr. Society of Biblical Literature (2006).
The Book of Ben Sira: Text, Concordance and an Analysis of the Vocabulary. The Historical Dictionary of the Hebrew Language.
Jerusalem: Academy of the
Hebrew Language and Shrine of the Book, 1973. Synoptic edition of Hebrew MSS with concordance.
Yadin, Yigael. *The Ben Sira Scroll from Masada.* Jerusalem: Israel
Exploration
Society, 1965. Repr. from *Eretz-Israel* vol. 8.
Schechter, S. and C. Taylor. *The Wisdom of Ben Sira: Portions of the Book of Ecclesiasticus from Hebrew Manuscripts in the Cairo Genizah Collection Presented to the University of Cambridge by the Editors.*
Cambridge: CUP, 1899.
Klijn, Albertus Frederik J. *Die Esra-Apokalypse (IV. Esra): Nach dem lateinischen*

Text unter Benutzung der anderen Versionen übersetzt. GCS. Berlin: de Gruyter, 1992.

Stone, Michael E. *The Armenian Version of IV Ezra.* University of Pennsylvania Armenian Texts and Studies. Missoula, MT: Scholars Press, 1979.

Sievers, Joseph. *Synopsis of the Greek Sources for the Hasmonean Period: 1–2 Maccabees and Josephus War 1 and Antiquities 12–14.* Rome: Editrice Pontificio Istituto Biblico, 2001. Useful for comparative and historical studies. Texts are only presented in Greek.

Weeks, S. D. E., S. J. Gathercole, L. T. Stuckenbruck. *The Book of Tobit: Texts from the Principal Ancient and Medieval Traditions. With Synopsis, Concordances, and Annotated Texts in Aramaic, Hebrew, Greek, Latin, and Syriac.* Fontes et subsidia ad Bibliam pertinentes 3. Berlin: de Gruyter, 2004.

Wagner, Christian J. *Polyglotte Tobit-Synopse: Griechisch, Lateinisch, Syrisch, Hebräisch, Aramäisch: mit einem Index zu den Tobit-Fragmenten vom Toten Meer.* Mitteilungen des Septuaginta-Unternehmens 28. Göttingen: Vandenhoeck & Ruprecht, 2003. Greek, Latin, and Syriac in parallel columns, with separate section on Hebrew and Aramaic fragments.

See also: Berger synopsis of 4 Ezra with 2 Baruch (below under Pseudepigrapha: 2 Baruch). *Other Concordances:*

Barthélemy, D. and O. Rickenbacher. *Konkordanz zum hebräischen Sirach mit syrisch-hebräischem Index.* Göttingen: Vandenhoeck & Ruprecht, 1973. Also see concordance in *The Book of Ben Sira* (above).

Muraoka, T. *A Greek-Hebrew/Aramaic Index to I Esdras.* SBLSCS 11. Chico, CA: Scholars Press, 1984.

Strothmann, Werner, ed. *Wörterverzeichnis der apokryphen-deuterokanonischen Schriften des Alten Testaments in der Peshitta.* Göttinger Orientforschungen Reihe 1, Syriaca 27. Wiesbaden: Otto Harrassowitz, 1988. Also provides a Latin gloss for each Syriac word.

Winter, Michael M. *A Concordance to the Peshi☐ta Version of Ben Sira.* Monographs of the Peshitta Institute 2. Leiden: Brill, 1976.

Lexicon:
For Greek see above under Septuagint and below under General Pseudepigrapha Bibliography. For Hebrew text of Ben Sira see Clines, ed., *Dictionary of Classical Hebrew* (below under Dead Sea Scrolls).

Introductions:
Brockington, L. H. *A Critical Introduction to the Apocrypha.* London: Gerald Duckworth, 1961.
DeSilva, David A. *Introducing the Apocrypha: Message, Context, and Significance.* Grand Rapids: Baker, 2002.
Harrington, Daniel J. *Invitation to the Apocrypha.* Grand Rapids: Eerdmans, 1999.
Kaiser, Otto. *The Old Testament Apocrypha: An Introduction.* Peabody, MA: Hendrickson, 2004. Translation of his 2000 German edition.
Longenecker, Bruce W. *2 Esdras.* Guides to the Apocrypha and Pseudepigrapha; Sheffield: Sheffield Academic Press, 1995. Other helpful introductions have also appeared in this series, including Bartlett on *1 Maccabees*, DeSilva on *4 Maccabees*, Coggins on *Sirach*, Grabbe on *Wisdom of Solomon*, Otzen on *Tobit and Judith*.
Metzger, Bruce M. *An Introduction to the Apocrypha.* Oxford: OUP, 1957.
Oesterley, W. O. E. *An Introduction to the Books of the Apocrypha.* New York: Macmillan, 1935.
Torrey, Charles Cutler. *The Apocryphal Literature: A Brief Introduction.* New Haven: Yale University Press, 1945. Also introduces many books of the Pseudepigrapha.
See also: Nickelsburg, *Jewish Literature*; *JWSTP*; *HJPAJC* Vol. 3; *CHJ* 2:409–503; *ABD* 1:292–94 and s.v. by book; *EDEJ* 143–62 and s.v. by book.

Commentaries:
Abel, P. F.-M. *Les Livres des Maccabées.* Études Bibliques. Paris: J. Gabalda, 1949.
Larcher, C. *Le Livre de la Sagesse ou La Sagesse de Salomon.* Études Bibliques n.s. 1; 3 vols. Paris: J. Gabalda, 1983–1985.
Scarpat, Giuseppe. *Libro della Sapienza: Testo, traduzione, introduzione e comment.* 3 vols. Biblica Testi e studi 1, 3, 6. Brescia: Paideia, 1989–1999.

Talshir, Zipora. *I Esdras: A Text Critical Commentary.* SBLSCS 50. Atlanta: Society of Biblical Literature, 2001.

Commentaries exist on each book in some biblical commentary series. In English note especially Septuagint Commentary Series (Brill), Commentaries on Early Jewish Literature series (de Gruyter), Anchor Bible series (Doubleday), Jewish Apocryphal Literature series from Dropsie University (Harper), and Stone on *Fourth Ezra* in the Hermeneia series (Fortress). Shorter but still helpful are the volumes in the Cambridge Bible Commentary series (CUP) and the OT Message series (Michael Glazier). Also see the UBS Handbook Series (United Bible Societies) for translation comments. In German note the Herders Theologischer Kommentar zum Alten Testament series (Herder), Das Alte Testament Deutsch: Apokryphen, Neuer Stuttgarter Kommentar Altes Testament (Katholisches Bibelwerk), and Die Neue Echter Bibel (Echter). Some one-volume commentaries also include the Apocrypha; e.g. *Eerdmans Commentary on the Bible* (Eerdmans, 2003).

4. Pseudepigrapha (Jewish)

The term "pseudepigrapha" properly refers to literature written under an assumed name (generally of some famous OT person). However, "the Pseudepigrapha" has become almost a catch-all category for intertestamental works which do not fit elsewhere. The translation volume edited by Charlesworth, while focusing on works of primarily Jewish origin, also includes some Christian works. Below are listed the most important pseudepigraphal works for the study of Judaism. Since some Christian pseudepigrapha may include original Jewish material, a few of these are also noted. For bibliography of other Christian pseudepigrapha and some lesser known works see Haelewyck, *Clavis Apocryphorum* (noted below).

Pseudo-Philo and named Jewish authors are listed later in this bibliography.

4.1 General Pseudepigrapha Bibliography

Bibliography:

Orlov, Andrei A. *Selected Studies in the Slavonic Pseudepigrapha.* SVTP 23. Leiden/ Boston: Brill, 2009. Note the "Selected Bibliography on the Transmission of the Jewish Pseudepigrapha in the Slavic Milieux" on pp. 201–434.

DiTommaso, Lorenzo. *A Bibliography of Pseudepigrapha Research 1850–1999.* JSPSup 39. Sheffield: Sheffield Academic Press, 2001. 1067 very helpful pages.

Lehnardt, Andreas. *Bibliographie zu den jüdischen Schriften aus hellenistisch-römischer Zeit. JSHRZ* VI/2. Gütersloh: Gütersloher Verlagshaus, 1999. Very useful.

Haelewyck, J.-C. *Clavis Apocryphorum Veteris Testamenti.* CChr. Turnhout:

Brepols, 1998. Valuable list of texts, translations, and concordances for each pseudepigraphal book.

Charlesworth, James H. *The Pseudepigrapha and Modern Research with a Supplement.*

New ed. SBLSCS. Chico, CA: Scholars, 1981. Dated, but also contains competent brief introductions.

See also: Arbeitshilfen für das Studium der Pseudepigraphen (http://www.unileipzig. de/~nt/asp/index.htm).

Texts (general):

Stone, Michael E. *Armenian Apocrypha Relating to Adam and Eve.* SVTP 14. Leiden:

Brill, 1996. Not all of this material is early. Also see W. Lowndes Lipscomb, *The Armenian Apocryphal Adam Literature.* University of Pennsylvania Armenian Texts and Studies 8. Scholars Press, 1990.

Stone, Michael E. *Armenian Apocrypha Relating to the Patriarchs and Prophets.*

Jerusalem: Israel Academy of Sciences and Humanities, 1982.

Denis, Albert-Marie. *Fragmenta pseudepigraphorum quae supersunt graeca.* PVTG 3.

Leiden: Brill, 1970. The standard edition of Greek fragments. Bound with Black's edition of Greek 1 Enoch.

See also: Online Critical Pseudepigrapha (http://ocp.tyndale.ca), which provides

introductions (with bibliography on modern editions of texts) and original language texts for many works.

Translations:

Charles, R. H., ed. *The Apocrypha and Pseudepigrapha of the Old Testament in English.* 2 vols. Oxford: Clarendon, 1913. Still quite useful, though supplanted

by Charlesworth and Sparks. Available online at http://archive.org or at http://www.ccel.org/c/charles/otpseudepig.

Charlesworth, James H., ed. *The Old Testament Pseudepigrapha.* 2 vols. New

York: Doubleday, 1983–1985; paperback repr. Peabody, MA: Hendrickson,

2009. The current most common English translation; includes helpful introductions and notes (see also Scripture Index listed below). Many contributions are excellent, but some have been critiqued for poor textual basis or for inadequacies in the notes and introductions; cf. the detailed reviews by S. P. Brock in *JJS* 35 (1984) 200–209 and *JJS* 38 (1987) 107–14. [=*OTP*] Kümmel, Werner Georg, et al., gen. eds. *Jüdische Schriften aus hellenistischrömischer Zeit.* Gütersloh: G. Mohn/Gütersloher Verlagshaus, 1973– 2005. A highly respected multi-volume German translation series with fine introductions and commentary. [= JSHRZ]

Lichtenberger, Hermann and Gerbern S. Oegema, gen. eds. *Jüdische Schriften aus hellenistisch-römischer Zeit Neue Folge.* Gütersloh: Gütersloher Verlagshaus, 2005–. Multi-volume continuation of *JSHRZ.* [=*JSHRZNF*]

Sparks, H. F. D., ed. *The Apocryphal Old Testament.* Oxford: Clarendon, 1984. A

useful one-volume edition with succinct introductions of a subset of works also found in Charlesworth's *OTP*; for comparison with *OTP* see review by G. W. E. Nickelsburg in *CBQ* 50 (1988) 288–91 and those by M. E. Stone and R. A. Kraft in *Religious Studies Review* 14 (1988) 111–17. [= AOT]

Further important translations appear in Spanish (Alejandro Díez Macho, et

al., eds., *Apocrifos del Antiguo Testamento.* 5 vols. Madrid: Ediciones Cristiandad,

1982–1987) and in Italian (Paulo Sacchi, et al., eds., *Apocrifi Dell'Antico Testamento.* 5 vols. Turin: Unione Tipografico-Editrice Torinese/

Brescia: Paideia, 1981–1997).

A new two-volume collection of lesser known pseudepigrapha is due out soon, published by Eerdmans and edited by Richard Bauckham and James R. Davila under the auspices of the More Old Testament Pseudepigrapha

Project (see http://www.st-andrews.ac.uk/divinity/rt moreoldtestamentpseudepigrapha).

Also see: Translations of varying qualities available online at http://sacredtexts.

com/chr/apo/index.htm and at http://www.piney.com/ ApocalypticIndex. html and at http://jewishchristianlit.com/Texts.

Concordances:

Bauer, Johannes B. *Clavis Apocryphorum supplementum: complectens voces versionis Germanicae Libri Henoch Slavici, Libri Jubilaeorum, Odarum Salomonis.* Grazer theologische Studien 4. Graz: Institut für Ökumenische Theologie und Patrologie an der Universität Graz, 1980. Not a concordance to the

original languages but to German translations. For his book-by-book concordance of Greek pseudepigrapha, see below under "Lexicon."

Denis, Albert-Marie. *Concordance grecque des Pseudépigraphes d'Ancien Testament:* Concordance, Corpus des textes, Indices. Louvain-la-Neuve: Institut Orientaliste, 1987. Very useful. Denis produced an earlier concordance of the Greek version of Baruch (Leuven: Peeters, 1970).

Denis, Albert-Marie. *Concordance latine des Pseudépigraphes d'Ancien Testament:* Concordance, Corpus des textes, Indices. Turnhout: Brepols, 1993. A fine work. Denis released an earlier concordance of the Latin version of Jubilees (Université catholique de Louvain, 1973; repr. Turnhout: Brepols, 2002).

Lechner-Schmidt, Wilfried. *Wortindex der lateinisch erhaltenen Pseudepigraphen zum Alten Testament.* TANZ 3. Tübingen: Francke, 1990. Also contains some texts.

See also: the *Thesaurus Linguae Graecae* database for searchable Greek texts, as well as tagged Greek modules available for Accordance, BibleWorks, and Logos software.

Scripture Index:

Delamarter, Steve. *A Scripure Index to Charlesworth's The Old Testament Pseudepigrapha.* London/New York: Sheffield Academic Press, 2002. Indexes all references to OT and NT books in the introductions, notes and margins of *OTP*; necessarily dependent on the work of the original translators (which varies "in terms of quantity and focus" from book to book).

Lexicon:

Wahl, Christian Abraham. *Clavis Librorum Veteris Testamenti Apocryphorum Philologica.* Leipzig: Johannes Ambrosius Barth, 1853; repr. Graz: Akademische Druck, 1972. Repr. contains Wahl's lexicon of the Greek Apocrypha and Pseudepigrapha, and J. B. Bauer's book-by-book concordance of the Greek Pseudepigrapha.

Introductions:

De Jonge, M., ed. *Outside the Old Testament.* Cambridge: CUP, 1985. Selected Jewish Pseudepigrapha excerpts with commentary.

Denis, Albert-Marie, et al. *Introduction à la littérature religieuse judéo-hellénistique.* 2 vols. Turnhout: Brepols, 2000. Also note his previous *Introduction aux Pseudépigraphes grecs d'Ancien Testament.* SVTP 1. Leiden: Brill, 1970.

Díez Macho, Alejandro. *Apocrifos del Antiguo Testamento.* Vol. 1: Introduccion General a Los Apocrifos del Antiguo Testamento. Madrid: Ediciones Cristiandad, 1984.

Turdeanu, Emile. *Apocryphes slaves et roumains de l'Ancien Testament.* SVTP 5. Leiden: Brill, 1981.
See also: Nickelsburg, *Jewish Literature*; Helyer, *Exploring Jewish Literature*; *JWSTP*; *HJPAJC* Vol. 3; *CHJ* 2:409–503; *EDEJ* 143–62 and s.v. by book. Older introduction by Torrey (see under Apocrypha). Individual introductions are appearing in the "Guides to the Apocrypha and Pseudepigrapha" series from Sheffield Academic Press (some are noted below).

4.2 Special Pseudepigrapha Bibliography (alphabetical by book)
This list contains the best-known books with likely Jewish lineage in collections of "Old Testament Pseudepigrapha." The principal languages of extant MSS for each book are noted below. Dates largely concur with those in Charlesworth *OTP*. If the texts available are clearly Christian (with an assumed Jewish substratum), this is indicated. Not included are some highly fragmented texts and those unlikely to be of Jewish provenance. Pseudo-Philo and other individual writers are found later in this bibliography. Consult also the General Pseudepigrapha Bibliography above (especially Lehnardt's *Bibliographie* and the introductions and translations in *OTP* and *JSHRZ*). More detailed bibliography of texts (including fragments and later versions) in Haelewyck, *Clavis Apocryphorum* and DiTommaso, *Bibliography*.

AHIQAR (Aramaic; 7th–6th cent. BC).
In the Elephantine papyri, with later recensions in many languages; thought to be related to the (Greek) Life of Aesop and so listed in Denis, *Fragmenta pseudepigraphorum* (see above).
Text and Translation:
Porten, Bezalel, and Ada Yardeni. *Textbook of Aramaic Documents from Ancient Egypt.* Vol. 3: Literature, Accounts, Lists. Winona Lake: Eisenbrauns, 1986–1993, 23–53.

Cowley, A. *Aramaic Papyri of the Fifth Century B.C.* Oxford: Clarendon, 1923,
204–48. Widely known edition with translation and extensive notes.
Available online at http://archive.org.
Conybeare, F. C., J. Rendel Harris, and Agnes Smith Lewis. *The Story of
A☐i☐ar
from the Syriac, Arabic, Armenian, Ethiopic, Greek and Slavonic Versions.*
London:
C. J. Clay & Sons, 1898. Extensive introduction with translations
of versions listed in the title plus texts of Greek (Life of Aesop), Armenian,
Syriac, and Arabic. Available online at http://archive.org.
Commentary:
Lindenberger, James M. *The Aramaic Proverbs of Ahiqar.* JHNES.
Baltimore:
Johns Hopkins University Press, 1983.
Grammar:
Muraoka, Takamitsu and Bezalel Porten. *A Grammar of Egyptian
Aramaic.* 2d
rev. ed. Leiden: Brill, 2003.
Concordance:
Porten, Bezalel and Jerome A. Lund. *Aramaic Documents from Egypt: A
Key-
Word-in-Context Concordance.* Winona Lake: Eisenbrauns, 2002.
APOCALYPSE OF ABRAHAM (Old Slavonic; 1st–2d cent. AD)

Text, Translation, and Commentary:
Rubinkiewicz, Ryszard. *L'Apocalypse d' Abraham en vieux slave:
Introduction, texte critique, traduction et commentaire.* Lublin: Société des
Lettres et des Sciences de l'Université Catholique de Lublin, 1987.
Apparently edited without
reference to the Philonenko edition.
Philonenko-Sayar, Belkis and Marc Philonenko. "L'Apocalypse
d'Abraham:
Introduction, texte slave, traduction et notes." *Sem* 31 (1981) 1–119.
APOCALYPSE OF ADAM (Coptic; 1st–4th cent. AD)
Found among Nag Hammadi gnostic texts, yet considered to be Jewish in
origin. Consult Nag Hammadi scholarship for further translations (e.g. J.
M.
Robinson, ed., *Nag Hammadi Library in English*) and concordances (e.g.
Folker
Siegert, *Nag-Hammadi-Register*). Another possible Jewish gnostic text is
Poimandres in the *Corpus Hermeticum* (see further *JWSTP* 443–81).
Text and Translation:

Parrott, Douglas M., ed. *Nag Hammadi Codices V,2–5 and VI with Papyrus Berolinensis 8502, 1 and 4.* NHS 11. Leiden: Brill, 1979, 151–95. Text edited
by G. W. MacRae.
Text, Translation, and Commentary:
Morard, Françoise. *L'Apocalypse d' Adam (NH V, 5).* Bibliothèque copte de
Nag Hammadi: Section textes 15. Québec: Les Presses de l'Université Laval, 1985.

APOCALYPSE OF ELIJAH (Coptic, Greek; 1st–4th cent. AD)
Christian text with likely Jewish substratum.
Text and Translation:
Pietersma, Albert, Susan Turner Comstock, and Harold W. Attridge. *The Apocalypse of Elijah based on P. Chester Beatty 2018.* SBLTT 19. Chico, CA,
Scholars, 1981. Coptic text and translation, includes appendix on Greek fragment. Also in Denis, *Fragmenta pseudepigraphorum* (above). See also material in *HJPAJC* 3.2:799–803.

APOCALYPSE OF MOSES (*see* Life of Adam and Eve)
APOCALYPSE OF SEDRACH (*see note below* under 4 Ezra)
APOCALYPSE OF ZEPHANIAH (Coptic and Greek fragments; 1st cent. BC–1st cent. AD) Christian with possible Jewish substratum.
Text and Discussion:
Steindorff, Georg. *Die Apokalypse des Elias, eine unbekannte Apokalypse und
Bruchstücke der Sophonias Apokalypse.* TU 17.3. Leipzig: Hinrichs, 1899. Available online at http://archive.org. Also see Denis, *Fragmenta pseudepigraphorum.*

APOCRYPHON OF EZEKIEL (Greek and Hebrew fragments; 1st cent. BC–1st cent. AD)
Probable Jewish work with possible Christian influence in extant fragments.
Text, Translation and Discussion:
Stone, Michael E., Benjamin G. Wright, and David Satran, eds. *The Apocryphal
Ezekiel.* SBLEJL 18. Atlanta: Society of Biblical Literature, 2000. Includes the five fragments previously published by Mueller plus other possible contenders. Also studies later Christian traditions about Ezekiel.
Mueller, James R. *The Five Fragments of the Apocryphon of Ezekiel: A Critical Study.*
Journal for the Study of the Pseudepigrapha Supplement Series 5. Sheffield:
Sheffield Academic Press, 1994. Also see Denis, *Fragmenta pseudepigraphorum.*

(PSEUDO-) ARISTEAS, [LETTER OF] (Greek; 2nd cent. BC, possibly later)
Critical Text, Translation, Notes, and Concordance:
Pelletier, André. *Lettre D'Aristée à Philocrate: Introduction, texte critique, traduction et notes, index complet des mots grecs.* SC 89. Paris: Cerf, 1962. Best current critical text. A text can also be found appended to Swete's *Introduction to the Old Testament in Greek. Critical Text:* Wendland, Paul. *Aristeae ad Philocratem Epistula cum Ceteris de Origine Versionis LXX Interpretum Testimoniis.* Leipzig: Teubner, 1900. Available online at http://archive.org.
Text and Notes:
Hadas, Moses. *Aristeas to Philocrates (Letter of Aristeas).* New York: Harper &
Brothers, 1951. Includes text, lengthy introduction, and brief notes.
Meecham, Henry G. *The Letter of Aristeas: A Linguistic Study with Special Reference to the Greek Bible.* Manchester: Manchester University Press, 1935. Notes focus on use of Greek language.
Online see http://www.voskrese.info/spl/miller-arist.pdf (Greek text and translation) and http://www.ccel.org/c/charles/otpseudepig/aristeas.htm (Charles, ed., translation).
Introduction:
See Jellicoe, *Septuagint and Modern Study* 29–58 (under Septuagint); Bartlett, *Jews in the Hellenistic World* 11–34 (under Josephus).
ASCENSION OF ISAIAH
(Ethiopic, Latin, Greek fragments, etc.; 2d cent. BC–4th cent. AD)
Christian with a probable Jewish section known as "Martyrdom of Isaiah" in
1:1–3:12 [omit 1:2b–6a] and 5:1b–14.
Texts:
Bettiolo, Paolo, et al. *Ascensio Isaiae: Textus.* CChr.SA 7. Turnhout: Brepols,
1995. Contains Ethiopic, Greek, Coptic, Latin, and Slavonic texts (with Italian translation). Earlier edition of Ethiopic and Latin texts by Dillmann (*Ascencio Isaiae: Aethiopice et Latine*, Leipzig: Brockhaus, 1877) available
free at http://books.google.com. Greek text also in Denis, *Fragmenta pseudepigraphorum.*
Translation and Commentary:
Charles, R. H. *The Ascension of Isaiah.* London: Adam & Charles Black, 1900.
Also includes Ethiopic, Latin, and Slavonic (transcribed) texts in parallel columns. Available online at http://archive.org.
Tisserant, Eugène. *Ascension d'Isaie.* Paris: Letouzey et Ané, 1909. Available

online at http://archive.org.

Introduction:
Knight, Jonathan. *The Ascension of Isaiah.* Sheffield: Sheffield Academic Press, 1995.
Commentary:
Norelli, Enrico. *Ascensio Isaiae: Commentarius.* CChr.SA 8. Turnhout: Brepols, 1995. In Italian. Assumption (Testament) of Moses (Latin; 1st cent. AD)
Text, Translation, and Commentary:
Tromp, Johannes. *The Assumption of Moses: A Critical Edition with Commentary.* SVTP 10. Leiden: Brill, 1993. Supplants R. H. Charles, *Assumption of Moses.* London: Black, 1897. Abraham Schalit also began a commentary on chapter one before his death which was later published as *Untersuchungen zur Assumptio Moses* (Leiden: Brill, 1989). 2 BARUCH (=Syriac Apocalypse of Baruch; also Greek fragments and Arabic version; 2nd cent. AD)
Text:
Gurtner, Daniel M. *Second Baruch: A Critical Edition of the Syriac Text With Greek and Latin Fragments, English Translation, Introduction, and Concordances.* Jewish and Christian Texts in Contexts and Related Studies 5. London: T & T Clark, 2009.
Leemhuis, F., A. F. J. Klijn, and G. J. H. Van Gelder. *The Arabic Text of the Apocalypse of Baruch: Edited and Translated with a Parallel Translation of the Syriac Text.* Leiden: Brill, 1986.
Dedering, S., ed. *Apocalypse of Baruch.* Vetus Testamentum Syriace IV, 3. Leiden: Brill, 1973. For the final *Epistle* the Leiden edition remains forthcoming, use M. Kmoskó, *Epistola Baruch filii Neriae,* in R. Graffin, *Patrologia Syriaca* 1,2 (Paris: Firmin-Didot, 1907) col. 1208–1237. For Greek fragments see Denis, *Fragmenta pseudepigraphorum* in general bibliography.
Translation and Commentary:
Bogaert, Pierre. *Apocalypse de Baruch: Introduction, traduction du syriaque et commentaire.* 2 vols. SC 144–45. Paris: Cerf, 1969.
Also see: Berger, Klaus, Gabriele Fassbeck, and Heiner Reinhard. *Synopse des Vierten Buches Esra und der Syrischen Baruch-Apokalypse.* TANZ 8. Tübingen:

Francke, 1992. Based on German translation.
3 BARUCH (= Greek Apocalypse of Baruch; Slavonic version in two recensions;
1st–3rd cent. AD) Christian with Jewish substratum.
Text:
Picard, J.-C. *Apocalypsis Baruchi Graece.* PVTG 2. Leiden: Brill, 1967.
Commentary:
Kulik, Alexander. *3 Baruch: Greek-Slavonic Apocalypse of Baruch.* CEJL. Berlin: de Gruyter, 2010. 4 BARUCH (*see* Paraleipomena Jeremiou)
1 ENOCH (Ethiopic Enoch; also in Greek, Aramaic fragments, and other versional fragments; 2d cent. BC–1st cent. AD)
Texts (and Translations):
Knibb, Michael A., in consultation with Edward Ullendorff. *The Ethiopic Book
of Enoch: A New Edition in the Light of the Aramaic Dead Sea Fragments.* 2
vols. Oxford: Clarendon, 1978. Vol. 1: Text and Apparatus; Vol. 2: Introduction,
Translation, and Commentary. Supplants previous editions
by R. H. Charles (1906) and A. Dillmann (1851).
Milik, J. T. and Matthew Black. *The Books of Enoch: Aramaic Fragments of Qumrân Cave 4.* Oxford: Clarendon, 1976. Texts, translations, plates, and extensive comments.
Black, M. *Apocalypsis Henochi Graece.* PVTG 3. Leiden: Brill, 1970. Edition of
Greek text; bound with Denis, *Fragmenta pseudepigraphorum.* For addenda
and corrigenda see Black and Vanderkam, *The Book of Enoch or I Enoch* (below).
Commentaries:
Black, Matthew, in consultation with James C. Vanderkam. *The Book of Enoch
or I Enoch: A New English Edition with Commentary and Textual Notes.* SVTP 7. Leiden: Brill, 1985. Extensive commentary, consciously revising Charles's 1912 commentary. With Otto Neugebauer on chaps. 72–82.
Charles, R. H. *The Book of Enoch or 1 Enoch.* Oxford: Clarendon, 1912. Translation with extensive commentary. The author prefers this (what amounts
to a 2d edition) over his earlier *The Book of Enoch* (1893). Available online
at http://archive.org.
Nickelsburg, George W. E. *1 Enoch 1: A Commentary on the Book of 1 Enoch,
Chapters 1–36; 81–108.* Hermeneia; Minneapolis: Fortress, 2001.

Nickelsburg, George W. E. and James C. Vanderkam. *1 Enoch 2: A Commentary on the Book of 1 Enoch, Chapters 37–82.* Hermeneia. Minneapolis: Fortress, 2012. Nickelsburg and Vanderkam have also produced *1 Enoch: A New Translation.* Philadelphia: Fortress, 2004.

Stuckenbruck, Loren T. *1 Enoch 91–108.* CEJL. Berlin: de Gruyter, 2007.

Tiller, Patrick A. *A Commentary on the Animal Apocalypse of I Enoch.* SBL Early Judaism and Its Literature 4. Atlanta: Scholars, 1993. Earlier important commentaries by A. Dillmann (Vogel, 1853) and François Martin (Letouzey, 1906). Short commentary article by Daniel C. Olson in J. D. G. Dunn, gen. ed., *Eerdmans Commentary to the Bible.* Grand Rapids: Eerdmans, 2003.

2 ENOCH (Slavonic Enoch, in two recensions; 1st cent. AD)

Text and Translation:

Vaillant, A. *Le Livre des secrets d'Hénoch.* Paris: Institut d'Etudes Slaves, 1952.

Translation and Commentary:

Morfill, W. R. and R. H. Charles. *The Book of the Secrets of Enoch.* Oxford: Clarendon, 1896.

Concordance to German Translation:

See above Bauer, *Clavis Apocryphorum Supplementum.*

3 ENOCH (Hebrew Enoch; 5th – 6th cent. AD): *See below* under Hekhalot literature.

4 EZRA (*see above* under Apocrypha)

Several Christian pseudepigraphic works also draw on Ezra as a central figure and may be indebted to Jewish sources (e.g. Greek Apocalypse of Ezra, Vision of Ezra, and Apocalypse of Sedrach); *see* Charlesworth *OTP* 1:561–613; text of some in Otto Wahl, ed. *Apocalypsis Esdrae—Apocalypsis Sedrach—Visio beati Esdrae.* PVTG 4. Leiden: Brill, 1977.

HISTORY OF JOSEPH (*see* Charlesworth, ed., *OTP* 2:467–75)

HISTORY OF THE RECHABITES (Greek, Syriac, and many versions; 1st–4th cent. AD) Substantially Christian, possible Jewish substratum.

Text and Translation:

Charlesworth, James H. *The History of the Rechabites. Volume I: The Greek Recension.* SBLTT 17. Chico, CA: Scholars, 1982. Critical Greek text; an edition of the Syriac text is still desired. Brief commentary by Chris H. Knights in *JSJ* 28 (1997) 413–36. **JANNES AND JAMBRES** (Greek and Latin fragments)

Text, Translation, and Commentary:
Pietersma, Albert. *The Apocryphon of Jannes and Jambres the Magicians.* Religions in the Graeco-Roman World 119. Leiden: Brill, 1994. Includes facsimile
plates. **JOSEPH AND ASENETH** (Greek and Latin versions in two recensions,
also Armenian, and other versions; 1st cent. BC–2d cent. AD)
Text and Translation:
Burchard, Christoph. *A Minor Edition of the Armenian Version of Joseph and Aseneth.*
Hebrew University Armenian Studies 10. Leuven: Peeters, 2010. Diplomatic text supplemented with 12 other important manuscripts.
Fink, Uta Barbara. *Joseph und Aseneth: Revision des griechischen Textes und Edition der zweiten lateinischen Übersetzung.* Fontes et subsidia ad Bibliam pertinentes 5. Berlin/New York: de Gruyter, 2008. Important revision of Burchard's provisional Greek text of the long recension (though without a
full textual apparatus), with a synoptic edition of Latin "L2" manuscripts. Includes study of manuscript stemma. See review in *BBR* 20 (2010) 110–12. Burchard, Christoph with Carsten Burfeind and Uta Barbara Fink. *Joseph und Aseneth: Kritisch Herausgegeben.* PVTG 5. Leiden/Boston: Brill, 2003. Critical edition focusing on the longer Greek recension (which Burchard believes is earlier than the short recension). While the apparatus is excellent,
the text itself remains the same as Burchard's "provisional" Greek text. Burchard himself translated this longer recension into English in Charlesworth, *OTP*. Philonenko, Marc.
Joseph et Aséneth: Introduction, texte critique, traduction et notes. SPB 13. Leiden: Brill, 1968. Standard edition of the shorter Greek reJEWISH
cension plus word index. ET of this shorter recension in H. F. D. Sparks, *Apocryphal Old Testament. Introduction*:
Humphrey, Edith M. *Joseph and Aseneth.* Guides to the Apocrypha and Pseudepigrapha 8. Sheffield: Sheffield Academic Press, 2000.
Other:
Burchard, Christoph. *Gesammelte Studien zu Joseph und Aseneth.* SVTP 13. Leiden:
Brill, 1996. Collection of significant articles on the text, importance, and state of study (including bibliography). Includes a reprint of Burchard's
Vorläufiger Text ("provisional text") of the long recension (pp.

161–209).

Reinmuth, Eckart, ed. *Joseph und Aseneth: Eingeleitet, ediert, übersetzt und mit interpretierenden Essays.* Scripta Antiquitatis Posterioris ad Ethicam Religionemque pertinentia 15. Tübingen: Mohr-Siebeck, 2009). Note also "The Aseneth Home Page" at http://markgoodacre.org/aseneth/index.htm.

JUBILEES (Hebrew fragments; Ethiopic Versions; Latin, Greek, and Syriac fragments; 2d cent. BC)

Hebrew Texts:
For extensive Qumran cave 4 fragments (4Q216–228) see DJD 13; other fragments in DJD 1, 3, and 7. Also cf. *RevQ* 12.4 [= 48] (1987) 529–36; *RevQ* 14.1 [= 53] (1989) 129–30. For possible Masada fragments see *Er-Isr* 20 (1989) 278–86.

Texts:
Vanderkam, James C., ed. *The Book of Jubilees: A Critical Text.* CSCO 510. Leuven: Peeters, 1989. A critical text of the Ethiopic, supplanting the older edition by R. H. Charles (Oxford, 1895); also with Greek, Syriac, Latin, and some Hebrew fragments (though not the bulk of 4Q216–228). Not all Greek and Syriac fragments are included (cf. Denis, *Fragmenta pseudepigraphorum* above).

Translation and Textual Notes:
Vanderkam, James C. *The Book of Jubilees.* CSCO 511. Leuven: Peeters, 1989.
Translates his critical text (including the fragments), with extensive notes on text and translation.

Translation and Commentary:
Charles, R. H. *The Book of Jubilees or The Little Genesis.* London: Adam & Charles Black, 1902. Available online at http://archive.org.

Concordance to German Translation:
See above Bauer, *Clavis Apocryphorum Supplementum.*

Introduction:
Vanderkam, James C. *The Book of Jubilees.* Guides to Apocrypha and Pseudepigrapha. Sheffield: Sheffield Academic Press, 2001.

LADDER OF JACOB (Slavonic)
Only known from Slavonic Christian excerpts, H. G. Lunt (in *OTP* 2:401–411) suggests a possible 1st-cent. date and potential Jewish Greek substratum. Cf. *HJPAJC* 3.2:805.

LIFE OF ADAM AND EVE

The subject of Adam and Eve appears in different manuscript traditions: Greek (= Apocalypse of Moses; also Armenian and other versions; 1st cent.
AD), Latin, two Slavonic recensions, the Armenian "Penitence of Adam," and
other recensions.

Textual Synopsis:
Anderson, Gary A., and Michael E. Stone, eds. *A Synopsis of the Books of Adam and Eve.* 2d rev. ed. SBL Early Judaism and Its Literature 5. Atlanta: Scholars, 1999. Armenian, Georgian, Greek, Latin, and Slavonic texts. Also see their website with translations (http://jefferson.village.virginia.edu/anderson, which links to http://www2.iath.virginia.edu/anderson).

Text:
Tromp, Johannes. *The Life of Adam and Eve in Greek: A Critical Edition.* PVTG 6. Leiden: Brill, 2005.

Stone, Michael E. *Texts and Concordances of the Armenian Adam Literature.* Volume 1. SBLEJL 12. Atlanta: Scholars Press, 1996. Volume 1 includes the
Penitence of Adam, the Book of Adam, and Genesis 1–4 in Armenian (with concordances to each and a non-critical text of each). Volume 2 has been published as *A Concordance of the Armenian Apocryphal Adam Books* (Leuven: Peeters, 2001). For a critical edition of the Armenian texts see above works by Stone and by Lipscomb under General Pseudepigrapha
Bibliography; also M. E. Stone, *The Penitence of Adam.* 2 vols. CSCO 429–430. Leuven: Peeters, 1981.

Text, Translation, and Commentary:
Dochhorn, Jan. *Die Apokalypse des Mose: Text, Übersetzung, Kommentar.* TSAJ 106. Tübingen: Mohr-Siebeck, 2005.
Bertrand, Daniel A. *La vie grecque d'Adam et Eve: Introduction, texte, traduction et commentaire.* Recherches intertestamentaires 1. Paris: Maisonneuve, 1987.

Introductions:
De Jonge, Marinus and Johannes Tromp. *The Life of Adam and Eve and Related Literature.* Guides to the Apocrypha and Pseudepigrapha 4. Sheffield: Sheffield Academic Press, 1997.
Stone, Michael E. *A History of the Literature of Adam and Eve.* SBL Early Judaism and Its Literature 3. Atlanta: Scholars, 1992.

LIVES OF THE PROPHETS (Greek, Latin, Syriac, Armenian, Ethiopic, and other versions; 1st cent. AD). Christian with Jewish substratum.
Text, Translation, and Commentary:
Schwemer, Anna Maria. *Studien zu den frühjüdischen Prophetenlegenden Vitae Prophetarum: Einleitung, Übersetzung und Kommentar.* 2 vols. TSAJ 49–50; Tübingen: Mohr-Siebeck, 1995–1996. Based on the Greek text, which is edited in a synoptic edition at the end of Vol. 2 (this edition has also been published separately as *Synopse zu den Vitae Prophetarum*). Previous edition by C. C. Torrey (SBLMS 1; Philadelphia: Scholars Press, 1946). For other versions see listing in Schwemer's Vol. 1, pp. 18–22 (cf. Haelewyck, *Clavis Apocryphorum* 167–73).
3–4 Maccabees (Greek, Syriac, and other versions)
3 Maccabees (1st cent. BC) is edited in the Göttingen LXX, and 4 Maccabees
(1st cent. AD) is found in Rahlfs's LXX; both appear in the LXX concordances;
translations in *OTP* 2:509–64. See also LXX bibliography above.
Introduction:
DeSilva, David A. *4 Maccabees.* Guides to the Apocrypha and Pseudepigrapha 7. Sheffield: Sheffield Academic Press, 1998.
Commentaries:
Commentaries can be found in the Jewish Apocryphal Literature series (Dropsie/Harper) by Hadas, and in the Septuagint Commentary Series (Brill) on 3 Maccabees (by N. Clayton Croy) and 4 Maccabees (by David A. deSilva).
MARTYRDOM OF ISAIAH (*see* Ascension of Isaiah)
(PSEUDO-) MENANDER (Syriac; 3d cent. AD)
Traditionally included with Jewish corpus, though actual provenance is unsure.
See discussion and translation in *OTP* 2:583–606; also *HJPAJC* 3.1:692–94.
ODES (*see* Septuagint)
ODES OF SOLOMON (Syriac, also portions in Greek and Coptic; 1st–2d cent. AD) Christian, though some propose a Jewish origin.
Texts, Translations, Concordance, and Bibliography:
Lattke, Michael. *Die Oden Salomos in ihrer Bedeutung für Neues Testament und Gnosis.* 4 vols. OBO 25. Fribourg Suisse: Editions Universitaires/Göttingen: Vandenhoeck & Ruprecht, 1979–1986. Band I contains texts (with a separate part Ia printing a Syriac facsimile with plates). Band II includes

a concordance of each language. Band III is an extensive annotated bibliography of studies on Odes (from 1799 to 1984). Band IV is a collection of articles by Lattke (note he extends his bibliography list to 1997 on pp. 233–51).

Text and Translation:
Charlesworth, James Hamilton. *The Odes of Solomon: The Syriac Texts.* SBLTT 13. Missoula, MT: Scholars Press, 1977. Corrected repr. of 1973 OUP edition. See also facsimile edition *Papyri and Leather Manuscripts of the Odes of Solomon* (Duke University, 1981). Charlesworth also released a translation under the title *The Earliest Christian Hymnbook* (Eugene, OR: Cascade, 2009). Also see the Rendell Harris items listed under the Psalms of Solomon. An older text with German translation by Walter Bauer. *Die Oden Salomos.* Berlin: de Gruyter, 1933.

Translation and Commentary:
Lattke, Michael. *Odes of Solomon.* Trans. Marianne Ehrhardt. Hermeneia. Minneapolis: Fortress, 2009. Translates his 3 volume German commentary originally in NTOA 41. Göttingen: Vandenhoeck & Ruprecht, 1999–2005. Lattke produced a German translation with shorter notes for Fontes Christiani. FC 19. Freiburg: Herder, 1995.
Pierre, Marie-Joseph, with the collaboration of Jean-Marie Martin. *Les Odes de Salomon.* Apocryphes 4. Turnhout: Brepols, 1994.

Concordance to German Translation:
See above Bauer, *Clavis Apocryphorum Supplementum.*

PARALEIPOMENA JEREMIOU (also called 4 Baruch; Greek in two recensions, Ethiopic and other versions; 1st–3d cent. AD)

Text, Translation and Commentary:
Herzer, Jens. *4 Baruch (Paraleipomena Jeremiou).* SBLWAW 22. Atlanta: Society of Biblical Literature, 2005. Fine critical text.
Riaud, Jean. *Les Paralipomènes du Prophète Jérémie: Présentation, texte original, traduction et commentaries.* Université Catholique de l'Ouest, 1994.

Text and Translation:
Kraft, Robert A. and Ann-Elizabeth Purintun. *Paraleipomena Jeremiou.* SBLTT 1. Missoula, MT: Society of Biblical Literature, 1972.

PRAYER OF JACOB and PRAYER OF JOSEPH (*see* Charlesworth, ed.,

OTP 2:699–723; cf. *HJPAJC* 3.2:798–99)
PRAYER OF MANASSEH (*see* Septuagint; also in Charlesworth, ed.,
OTP
2:625–37)
PSALMS OF SOLOMON (Greek and Syriac; 1st cent. BC)
Greek Text:
Wright, Robert B. *The Psalms of Solomon: A Critical Edition of the Greek Text.*
Jewish and Christian Texts in Contexts and Related Studies 1. London: T & T Clark, 2007. Wright also offers a CD-ROM with color images of extant Greek and Syriac manuscripts (see p. 224).
Gebhardt, Oscar von. *Die Psalmen Salomos.* TU 13/2. Leipzig: Hinrichs, 1895.
Earlier critical text of Greek that only collates 8 of the 12 available MSS. Available online at http://archive.org. A handy Greek text can be found in Rahlfs's LXX edition (based on Gebhardt).
Syriac Critical Text:
See above "Syriac Peshita Text" (Vol. IV, 6).
Greek and Syriac texts:
Trafton, Joseph L. *The Syriac Version of the Psalms of Solomon: A Critical Evaluation.*
SBLSCS 11. Atlanta: Scholars, 1985. Comes with a separate fascicle of facing Greek and Syriac texts (with apparatus). See review in *JSS* 32 (1987) 204–207.
Translation:
Also translated in the NETS LXX translation (see above under Septuagint and http://ccat.sas.upenn.edu/nets/edition/31-pssal-nets.pdf).
Commentaries:
Atkinson, Kenneth. *An Intertextual Study of the Psalms of Solomon.*
Studies in the
Bible and Early Christianity 49. Lewiston, NY: Edwin Mellen, 2001.
Includes
Greek text, translation, parallel passages in other Jewish literature (esp. OT and Apocrypha), and commentary.
Rendell Harris, J. and A. Mingana. *The Odes and Psalms of Solomon Re-edited.* 2
vols. Manchester: John Rylands University Library, 1916–1920. Also note Rendell Harris's earlier *The Odes and Psalms of Solomon: Now First Published from the Syriac Version.* Cambridge: CUP, 1909. Both are available
online at http://archive.org.
Ryle, Herbert Edward, and Montague Rhodes James. *Psalms of the Pharisees
Commonly Called The Psalms of Solomon.* Cambridge: CUP, 1891. Classic

edition with text, translation, introduction, and extensive notes. The Pharisaic identification is not accepted by all. Available at http://archive.org.

Viteau, J. *Les Psaumes de Salomon: Introduction, texte grec et traduction.* Paris:
Letouzey et Ané, 1911. With extensive notes. Available online at http://archive.org.

SENTENCES OF (PSEUDO-) PHOCYLIDES (Greek; 1st cent. BC–1st cent. AD) Wisdom poetry of Jewish origin, but with muted OT references and written under a pagan Greek pseudonym.

Text:
Young, D. *Theognis, Ps-Pythagoras, Ps-Phocylides, Chares, Anonymi Aulodia, fragmentum teleiambicum.* 2 vols.; Leipzig, 1961, 1971. Volume 2 includes the critical text of Ps.-Phocylides.

Text, Translation, and Commentary:
Horst, P. W. van der. *The Sentences of Pseudo-Phocylides: With Introduction and Commentary.* SVTP 4. Leiden: Brill, 1978. Also includes a concordance.
Wilson, Walter T. *The Sentences of Pseudo-Phocylides.* CEJL. Berlin: de Gruyter, 2005.

SIBYLLINE ORACLES (Greek with Latin fragments; 2d cent. BC–7th cent. AD) Large portions of Books 3 and 5 are considered Jewish; book 4 may have been ultimately redacted by a Jewish editor, and books 11–14 may have a later Jewish origin (this is disputed).

Greek Text:
Geffcken, Johannes. *Die Oracula Sibyllina.* GCS. Leipzig: Hinrichs, 1902. Available online at http://archive.org.

Introductions and Studies on Jewish Sections:
Buitenwerf, Rieuwerd. *Book III of the Sibylline Oracles and its Social Setting: with an Introduction, Translation, and Commentary.* SVTP 17. Leiden: Brill, 2003. Collins, John J. *The Sibylline Oracles of Egyptian Judaism.* SBLDS 13. Missoula, MT: Society of Biblical Literature, 1974.
Nikiprowetzky, Valentin. *La troisième Sibylle.* Ecole pratique des hautes Etudes Sorbonne; Etudes juives 9; Paris: Mouton, 1970. Includes text, translation, notes, and extensive introduction.
Parke, H. W. *Sibyls and Sibylline Prophecy in Classical Antiquity.* Ed. B. C. McGing. London/New York: Routledge, 1988.

See also: Bartlett, *Jews in the Hellenistic World* 35–55 (under Josephus); older

translation of Books 3–5 by H. N. Bate (SPCK, 1918).
TESTAMENT OF ABRAHAM (Greek, also Coptic and other versions; 1st–2nd cent. AD) Exists in both a long and short recension, with likely common ancestry.

Critical Text:
Roddy, Nicolae. *The Romanian Version of the Testament of Abraham: Text, Translation, and Cultural Context.* SBLEJL 19. Atlanta: SBL, 2001.
Schmidt, Francis. *Le Testament grec d'Abraham: Introduction, édition critique des deux recensions grecques, traduction.* TSAJ 11. Tübingen: Mohr-Siebeck, 1986.

Text and Translation:
Stone, Michael E. *The Testament of Abraham: The Greek Recensions.* SBLTT 2.
Missoula, MT: Society of Biblical Literature, 1972. Based on M. R. James's (1892) edition of Greek texts. An older translation by G. H. Box (London: SPCK, 1927) exists of both recensions along with Gaselee's translation of the Testaments of Isaac and Jacob.

Commentary:
Allison, Dale C. Jr. *Testament of Abraham.* CEJL. Berlin: de Gruyter, 2003.
Delcor, Mathias. *Le Testament d' Abraham: Introduction, Traduction du texte grec, et Commentaire de la recension grecque longue.* SVTP 2. Leiden: Brill, 1973.

Bibliography:
Nickelsburg, George W. E. Jr. "Review of the Literature." In *Studies on the Testament*
of Abraham, ed. George W. E. Nickelsburg Jr. SBLSCS 6. Missoula, MT: Scholars Press, 1976, 9–22. The same volume also contains translations of the Church Slavonic and Coptic versions.

TESTAMENT OF ADAM (Several recensions in Syriac, Greek, Armenian,
and other versions; 2d–5th cent. AD). Christian, with possible Jewish substratum.

Texts and Translations:
Robinson, Stephen Edward. *The Testament of Adam: An Examination of the Syriac*
and Greek Traditions. SBLDS 52. Chico, CA: Scholars, 1982. For Armenian
editions, see Stone volumes in General bibliography of Pseudepigrapha. See further Haelewyck, *Clavis Apocryphorum* 8–12.

TESTAMENT OF ISAAC and TESTAMENT OF JACOB (both Coptic, Arabic, Ethiopic; 2d–3d cent. AD). Christian, with some possible Jewish elements; see both Delcor and Box under *Testament of Abraham*, and

note *OTP* 1:903–18; *JTS* n.s. 8 (1957) 225–39.
TESTAMENT OF JOB (Greek, also Coptic and Slavonic; 1st cent. BC–1st cent. AD)
Bibliography:
Spittler, Russell P. "The Testament of Job: a history of research and interpretation." In *Studies on the Testament of Job*, ed. Michael A. Knibb and Pieter W. Van Der Horst. SNTSMS 66. Cambridge: CUP, 1989, 7–32. The
same volume also has an edition of the Coptic text.
Text:
Brock, S. P., ed. *Testamentum Iobi*. PVTG 2. Leiden: Brill, 1967.
Text and Translation:
Kraft, Robert A., et al., eds. *The Testament of Job: According to the SV Text.*
SBLTT 5. Missoula, MT: SBL, 1974.
TESTAMENT OF MOSES (*see* Assumption of Moses)
TESTAMENT OF SOLOMON (Greek; 1st–3d cent. AD)
Christian, with possible Jewish substratum.
Text:
McCown, Chester Charlton. *The Testament of Solomon.* Leipzig: Hinrichs, 1922.
Available online at http://archive.org. For translation and introduction see *OTP* 1:935–87.
Commentary:
Busch, Peter. *Das Testament Salomos: Die älteste christliche Dämonologie, kommentiert und in deutscher Erstübersetzung.* TU 153.
Berlin/New York: de Gruyter, 2006.
TESTAMENTS OF THE TWELVE PATRIARCHS (Aramaic and Hebrew fragments; two Greek recensions; Syriac, Armenian, and other versions; 2d cent. BC with later interpolations [disputed]). Christian, with Jewish substratum. Cf. with 1Q21 (in DJD 1), 3Q7 (in DJD 3), 4Q213–215 (in DJD 22); 4Q484, and 4Q537–541.
Bibliography:
Slingerland, H. Dixon. *The Testaments of the Twelve Patriarchs: A Critical History of*
Research. SBLMS 21. Missoula, MT: Scholars Press, 1977.
Text:
Stone, Michael E. *An Editio Minor of the Armenian Version of the Testaments of the Twelve Patriarchs.* Hebrew University Armenian Studies 11. Leuven:
Peeters, 2012.
Text (based on 11 selected extant MSS), translation and commentary.

De Jonge, M., et al. *The Testaments of the Twelve Patriarchs: A Critical Edition of the Greek Text.* PVTG I,2. Leiden: Brill, 1978. Updates Charles's 1908 edition
and De Jonge's own shorter Brill edition of a single Cambridge UL manuscript from 1964 (entitled *Testamenta XII Patriarcharum*). Includes word index and partial listing of Armenian variants (note bibliography on p. 193).

Stone, Michael E. *The Armenian Version of the Testament of Joseph: Introduction,
Critical Edition, and Translation.* SBLTT 6. Missoula, MT: Scholars Press,
1975.
Stone, Michael E. *The Testament of Levi: A First Study of the Armenian MSS of the
Testaments of the XII Patriarchs in the Convent of St. James, Jerusalem: with Text, Critical Apparatus, Notes and Translation.* Jerusalem: St. James, 1969.
Charles, Robert Henry. *The Greek Versions of the Testaments of the Twelve Patriarchs: Edited from nine MSS together with the Variants of the Armenian and Slavonic versions and some Hebrew Fragments.* Oxford: Clarendon, 1908; repr.
Darmstadt: Wissenschaftliche Buchgesellschaft, 1966. Available online at http://archive.org. Versional materials are unfortunately only in retroverted
Greek. Aramaic fragments from Cairo Genizah.
Commentary:
Charles, R. H. *The Testaments of the Twelve Patriarchs: Translated from the Editor's Greek Text and Edited, with Introduction, Notes, and Indices.* London: Adam & Charles Black, 1908. Available online at http://archive.org.
Hollander, H. W., and M. de Jonge. *The Testaments of the Twelve Patriarchs: A
Commentary.* SVTP 8. Leiden: Brill, 1985.
Introduction:
Kugler, Robert A. *The Testaments of the Twelve Patriarchs.* Guides to Apocrypha
and Pseudepigrapha. Sheffield: Sheffield Academic Press, 2001.
TREATISE OF SHEM (Syriac; 1st cent. BC [disputed])
Text and Translation:
Charlesworth, James H. "Die 'Schrift des Sem': Einführung, Text und Übersetzung," in *ANRW* II.20.2. Berlin: de Gruyter, 1987, 951–87.
END

www.ingramcontent.com/pod-product-compliance
Lightning Source LLC
Chambersburg PA
CBHW070722020526
44116CB00031B/1004